PRAISE

John Quincy Adams

"Traub's work is a reminder to Americans that politicians can be devoted to national issues, promote their principles, and still maintain their integrity."

—*Choice*

"Well-written and highly readable biography . . . highly accessible work."

—*Chronicles*

"Had I the resources, the one new book I'd give every delegate to the national political conventions that are meeting later this month is James Traub's masterful biography, *John Quincy Adams*."

—George Weigel, *First Things*

"[An] excellent biography. . . . [John Quincy Adams'] life is worth meditating on, and Traub's biography is an indispensable resource for doing so."

—*Washington Free Beacon*

"James Traub has admirably captured the man inside the public figure, giving us a view of a typical New England grandee, puritanical at his core, molded as a traditionalist republican with no love for pure democracy, convinced that governing was intended for the class born and bred for it."

—*The Arts Fuse*

"*John Quincy Adams* is a sharp portrait of the fascinating statesman who helped bring about the consolidation of the United States from fragile upstart into emerging major power. Traub's plentiful source material—Adams kept a journal throughout most of his life—reveals a complex man: a Puritan patrician, a genius diplomat, a villain to many and hero to a hopeful few, including the *Amistad* defendants. *John Quincy Adams* is a magnificent work."

—*Shelf Awareness for Readers,* **starred review**

"Traub is careful not to betray his own feelings or political beliefs in portraying the many struggles and contributions that marked Adams's life and work.

However, he does take care to help us understand the importance of John Quincy Adams in keeping the ship of state from being smashed on the rocks of nullification and other favorite campaigns of people who tried to tear apart the United States. Traub's attention to small, sometimes seemingly insignificant, details creates a vivid picture of Adams, his family, his colleagues and adversaries, and the society in which he lived and worked."

—Roanoke Times

"Traub concentrates on the ample cosmopolitan dimensions of John Quincy's life with a greater acuity than any of the recent books about the man. . . . Although Traub is very good at personalities, he's even better . . . in painting a picture of America on the world stage, groping for a sense of its own identity in a rapidly changing world. . . . This is a fine addition to the newly swelling ranks of JQA biographies, and one of the finest political lives to appear so far in 2016."

—Open Letters Monthly

"Traub thoroughly, even quite engagingly, follows Adams through the years during which he served in the diplomatic corps, building up the reputation as the new republic's best representative abroad."

—Booklist, **starred review**

"A meticulous study of the statesman's public service and private life. . . . Adams surfaces as an ambitious intellectual with deeply held convictions striving to hold his family together through illness, tragedy, and financial woes while relentlessly promoting a strong, active federal government as the young but rapidly expanding and diversifying nation grappled with geographic sectionalism and political partisanship. This rich . . . account emphasizes Adams's distinguished early career tenure as diplomat and secretary of state, the heated 1824 presidential election resulting in Adams defeating longtime personal and political foe Andrew Jackson, and his tireless effort to force the issue of slavery onto the Congressional floor as a post-presidential member of the House of Representatives."

—Library Journal

"An essential biography of a complex man. . . . Traub shows that without imperiling national unity, Adams's persistent, perspicacious opposition to slavery 'shattered the overweening confidence of the South' and confirmed his place in America's history."

—Publishers Weekly, **starred review**

"Traub depicts a fully fleshed character, an extraordinary man driven by his birthright principles, a voluminous diarist, scholar, poet, polymath, eccentric, and iconoclast. The author also offers a masterly portrait of Adams's wife, Louisa. An impassioned biography of 'a coherent and consistent thinker who adhered to his core political convictions across his decades of public service.'"

—*Kirkus Reviews*

"James Traub's new biography of John Quincy Adams is exceptionally strong. Adams was a complicated hero, a patrician visionary but also, as Traub puts it, a militant spirit, one of the most important diplomats in all of American history and, finally, slavery's greatest enemy in American politics."

—Sean Wilentz, author of *The Rise of American Democracy: Jefferson to Lincoln*

"By rights, John Quincy Adams should be one of America's most famous presidents. His life story is remarkable. The son of one of the nation's founding presidents, the only one to serve in an elected office after leaving the White House, and a man of vast intelligence and even greater political courage who died while debating in the House of Representatives. Yet he is an obscure figure in American history. James Traub has rectified this in a book worthy of its subject. Traub is a splendid storyteller and a perceptive guide to foreign policy. The result is an utterly compelling book."

—Fareed Zakaria, author of *The Post-American World*

"John Quincy Adams was a great statesman and a heroic crusader for freedom, whose finest hours, ironically, came both before and after his time as president. James Traub does us a service by bringing him to life again for a new generation. With a journalist's touch, Traub paints a vivid portrait of the man in all his complexity."

—Robert Kagan, author of *Of Paradise and Power*

"In lucid prose and with canny insight, James Traub illuminates the life and political career of John Quincy Adams. Driven by grim purpose and consistent values, Adams was hard to love but demanded respect as he matured into a champion of liberty for all. Traub admires Adams [and is] tinged with sadness for the absence of his type in our own times."

—Alan Taylor, author of *The Internal Enemy: Slavery and War in Virginia, 1772–1832*

"Certainly by modern standards, John Quincy Adams doesn't seem like presidential material: all high seriousness and rectitude, uncompromising to a fault, precisely not a guy with whom you want to sit down and have a beer. But James Traub's beautifully written, absolutely definitive biography is a surprising page-turner that made me admire this other President Adams as he finally deserves to be admired—and to wonder if the species of American civic virtue he embodied, always rare, always endangered, has not become extinct."

—Kurt Andersen, host of *Studio 360* and author of *True Believers*

"In the crowded pantheon of politically glamorous Adamses, John Quincy has long been overshadowed. Here he has finally been given his due. James Traub, one of America's most incisive journalists on foreign affairs, has crafted a moving biography of an unlikely hero—a tense, introspective man who had no gift for small talk and felt beleaguered by criticism from members of Congress as well as his own three sons. By capturing Adams's unflashy brilliance and do-the-right-thing convictions, Traub convinces us that our sixth president is as worthy of our affection and gratitude as any before or after him."

—Deborah Solomon, author of *American Mirror: The Life and Art of Norman Rockwell*

JOHN
QUINCY
ADAMS

JOHN QUINCY ADAMS

Militant Spirit

JAMES TRAUB

BASIC BOOKS

New York

Basic Books
Hachette Book Group
1290 Avenue of the Americas, New York, NY 10104
www.basicbooks.com

Printed in the United States of America
Originally published in hardcover and ebook by Basic Books in March 2016
First trade paperback edition: October 2017
Published by Basic Books, an imprint of Perseus Books, LLC,
a subsidiary of Hachette Book Group, Inc.

The Hachette Speakers Bureau provides a wide range of authors for speaking events. To find out more, go to www.hachettespeakersbureau.com or call (866) 376-6591.

The publisher is not responsible for websites (or their content) that are not owned by the publisher.

Print book interior design by Cynthia Young

The Library of Congress has cataloged the hardcover edition as follows:
Traub, James.
    John Quincy Adams : militant spirit / James Traub.
        pages cm
    Includes bibliographical references and index.
    ISBN 978-0-465-02827-6 (hardcover)—ISBN 978-0-465-09879-8 (e-book)
    1. Adams, John Quincy, 1767–1848. 2. Adams family. 3. Presidents—United States—Biography. 4. United States—History—1783–1865. 5. United States—Politics and government—1783–1865. 6. United States—Foreign relations—1783–1865. I. Adams, John Quincy, 1767–1848. II. Title.
E377.T73 2016
973.55092—dc23
[B]
2015030745

ISBNs: 978-0-465-02827-6 (hardcover); 978-0-465-09879-8 (ebook); 978-0-465-09383-0 (paperback)

LSC-C

10 9 8 7 6 5 4 3 2 1

To the memory of my father,
Marvin Traub

CONTENTS

PART III
TERRITORIAL EXPANSION

PART IV
INTERNAL IMPROVEMENT

INTRODUCTION

JOHN QUINCY ADAMS WAS A PLAIN MAN. VISITORS WHO TRAVELED to Quincy, Massachusetts, to speak to the old man, the former ambassador to the courts of London and St. Petersburg, secretary of state to James Monroe, and sixth president of the United States, were taken aback by the austerity of his furniture and the simplicity of his frock coat, which seemed always to carry a fine layer of dust, as if from the old volumes he had been scrutinizing only a moment before. Adams was plainspoken, for all his immense erudition. There was no guile in his manner and little irony. He was a faithful Christian who never missed Sunday service and often attended two.

Adams was also a hard man. He did not aim to please, and he largely succeeded. He drove away many of his old friends and offended most of his one-time allies. He frightened his children and exasperated his long-suffering wife, Louisa. He was that rare politician who is happiest alone. He knew this and perpetually rebuked himself for his bearish manner, but he did not really wish to be otherwise. He lived according to principles he considered self-evident. Others of his contemporaries did so as well, of course; what set Adams apart was that his principles were so inviolable that he eagerly sacrificed his self-interest to them. As president he accomplished very little of his ambitious agenda in part because he refused to do anything to reward his friends or punish his enemies. Such inflexibility is a dubious virtue for a politician.

It is, however, an estimable virtue for a man who needs to hold fast in the face of adversity. Though he never wore a uniform or saw battle, Adams was a figure of immense physical and moral courage. His bravery was a form of patriotism. So complete was his identification with the nation that came into being when he was a boy of nine that he did not flinch at either the prospect of death or—what may be harder for men of great ambition—the wreckage of his career, so long as he believed that service to the nation required it. When, starting in 1835, the "slavocracy," as Adams called the Southern representatives in Congress, sought to silence debate over slavery by banning petitions on the subject, no man save Adams was prepared to face their overwhelming power in the House. Adams received, and blithely ignored, innumerable assassination threats over his role. Twice the

Southern planters in Congress sought to bring down on him the grave punishment of censure; both times he left them furious and humiliated. Few things gave him more satisfaction.

John F. Kennedy devoted a chapter of *Profiles in Courage* to Adams. Kennedy characterized political courage as the willingness to stand up for the nation's best interests in the face of opposition from one's own party or even constituents. He could have chosen many incidents from Adams' career. The future president focused on the moment, in 1807, when Adams was serving in the Senate and his own Federalist Party rose as one to block the trade embargo that President Jefferson had imposed on Great Britain in response to its high-handed seizure of American ships and impressment of American sailors. The embargo threatened to wreck the economy of the Federalists' native New England. Adams was the only party member to support the policy, though he knew it would end his career as a Federalist—which it did. Kennedy cites Adams' defiant assertion that, "highly as I reverenced the authority of my constituents . . . I would have defended their interests against their inclinations, and incurred every possible addition to their resentment, to save them from the vassalage of their own delusions."

Thanks in part to his contempt for his own political prospects, in 1828 Adams was soundly defeated in his bid to be reelected president by Andrew Jackson, the populist hero. At that moment the essential meaning of Adams' career appeared to be fixed: he was an old-fashioned New England republican, a Puritan, an elitist, who had been left behind in America's new democratic age. And yet his unshakeable commitment to principle ultimately proved to be his salvation. In 1831 Adams agreed to stand for Congress, telling his friends that no office was too mean for one dedicated to public service—and admitting to himself that he could not live without the urgency of a life in politics. He had not expected to lead any crusades. But his hatred of slavery, his commitment to the right of petition, and his sheer vehemence placed him at the forefront of the burning issue of his day. And he succeeded: the prohibition on anti-slavery petitions was lifted in 1844, when Adams was seventy-seven. Finally, in his last years, Adams enjoyed what one newspaper editor called "the sober second thought of the people." Upon his death in 1848 at age eighty, Adams was mourned, and revered, as the last remaining link to the heroic generation of the founders.

ADAMS' GREATNESS RESIDES ABOVE ALL IN WHO HE WAS. AND YET HE was also extraordinary in what he did, what he said, and what he wrote.

Appointed minister to the Netherlands at the age of twenty-seven, Adams quickly became President Washington's most prized and trusted source of intelligence in Europe. Returning to the United States in 1801 after serving in Berlin as well, Adams was elected to the Senate, where he might have come to play a dominant role had his own party not dismissed him for the heresy of his support for Jefferson. He then served as America's first minister to Russia and a member of the delegation that signed the Treaty of Ghent, ending the War of 1812 on terms remarkably favorable to the United States. He returned in 1817 to become secretary of state. In that role Adams enunciated a new foreign policy for a restless but still peaceful nation, and wrenched from Spain not only Florida but also a line across the southwest all the way to the Pacific Ocean. He was elected president in 1825, serving one term in what was arguably the least successful stage of his career. He then became the only president, before or since, to serve afterwards in Congress. The apogee of his career came in 1841, when he persuaded a pro-slavery Supreme Court to free the African captives of the slave ship *Amistad*.

Adams was a coherent and consistent thinker who adhered to his core political convictions across decades of public service. He was deeply imbued with the belief that the United States was the greatest experiment in government the world had ever known—and that such an experiment was, by its very nature, endangered in a world of aggressive and autocratic states. As a young diplomat, he was supremely, even hyperbolically, alert to the threat to American independence posed by the struggle for global supremacy between Britain and France. Neutrality was his watchword, and his letters from Europe helped shape Washington's Farewell Address, which admonished Americans to stand apart from Europe's inveterate rivalries.

As America grew rapidly in size and strength, and the threat of foreign intervention receded, Adams worried that a self-aggrandizing nation would lose itself in imperial adventures. In his July 4 address in 1821 he famously said that America "goes not abroad in search of monsters to destroy," and he went on to warn that a militarized nation "might become the dictatress of the world; she would no longer be the ruler of her own spirit." Cold War "realists" like the diplomat-scholar George Kennan, who warned against a moralistic and militaristic foreign policy, acknowledged Adams as their intellectual fountainhead. Adams' persistent argument for husbanding US diplomatic and military power is his single most lasting contribution to the corpus of the nation's governing principles.

At the same time, Adams believed, as the founders had, that the United States was destined, by God as well as by its favorable geographic position, to spread across the continent and become the most powerful nation in the world. It is to Adams, more than anyone, including President Monroe himself, that we owe the Monroe Doctrine, which simultaneously asserted a doctrine of noninterference in European conflicts and a self-confident demand that the European powers cease their meddling in both North and South America. His overall diplomatic goal was to maintain peace abroad in order to enable expansion at home—a doctrine that China, the rising power of our own age, calls "peaceful rise."

By both temperament and philosophy, Adams was a conservative, as was his father, John Adams. Like the elder Adams, he feared the mob and viewed strong government as the bulwark against unruly passions. He shared Edmund Burke's horror at the wild convulsions of the French Revolution. The scholar Yuval Levin has divided Americans into followers of Burke and those of the revolutionary pamphleteer Thomas Paine. Adams lionized Burke and introduced himself to the reading public through a ferocious attack on Paine's *The Rights of Man*. Like many other New England Federalists, Adams would have described himself more as a republican—a believer in representative government—than as a democrat.

But a conservative of 1800 could be very much a liberal in our own terms. Adams believed not only in firm government but in active government. In his first address to Congress as president, in 1825, he declared that "the great object of the institution of civil government is the improvement of the condition of those who are parties to the social compact." This was heard, and intended, as a direct blow at the Jeffersonian faith in limited government, especially limited federal government. Along with his secretary of state, Henry Clay, Adams was a leading apostle of a policy that combined "internal improvements," which today we would call infrastructure, with protective tariffs, designed to promote domestic industry by restricting foreign competition. A united opposition as well as Adams' own political ineptitude doomed this ambitious vision. As with the abolition of slavery, Adams did not live to see his hopes realized, though his vision of activist government would reemerge a generation later as the agenda of the Whigs and of the early Republicans, above all Abraham Lincoln. Adams was thus the living link between a long-defunct Federalism and an emergent nationalism. He was, again to use terminology Adams himself would not have recognized, a progressive conservative.

Adams dedicated his life to preserving the union against both internal and external threats. His rhetorical assault on the slave forces in Congress, which deepened the divide between North and South, looks at first like a departure from his central path. In fact, it summed up the preoccupations of a lifetime. Adams had long understood slavery as a moral blot but not a political issue. The question did not really command his attention until the debate over the Missouri Compromise in 1820. Then he saw, as if by lightning flash, that the compromise between slave and free states that had kept the union whole was morally corrupt and politically unsustainable. As secretary of state, Adams stood apart from the debate. When he entered Congress a decade later and seized the role of chief tormenter of the slavocracy, he saw, far more clearly than the abolitionists did, that slavery could not be ended peacefully. He could not bring himself to call for abolition at the cost of civil war. Neither could he accept the endless perpetuation of slavery. Thus he was forced into the strange, lonely position of storming the barricades of slavery while refusing to support abolitionism. It was a spectacle that, characteristically, mingled heroism, isolation, and pathos.

Adams' moorings, both personal and intellectual, held him fast as his country changed unrecognizably. One historian has plausibly described Adams as the first American thinker to articulate a "comprehensive grand strategy" designed to further national interests at home and abroad.

IT WOULD BE GOOD TO SAY THAT ADAMS COULD RELAX HIS GRIM visage in the company of his loved ones. His father, though thin-skinned and vindictive, was an adoring husband and a loving, if very overbearing, father. Alas, the son was a model of consistency. His wife, Louisa Johnson, had grown up in fine style in London, a shy creature of the parlor with a gifted singing voice and a sharp eye for human vanity. Adams was quite smitten by her, but even during their courtship he worried that she was too frivolous, and too delicate, for the public life he envisioned—and he bluntly told her so. Louisa never escaped the fear that she had been judged and found wanting. Though all of Washington attended her parties during her husband's tenure as secretary of state, she was happiest in the company of friends and family, and she often withdrew to her bedroom with an unspecified nervous condition. Louisa viewed the White House as a vast prison cell and escaped whenever she could to the baths in upstate New York or to Quincy. John and Abigail Adams had been joined in mind and soul; John Quincy loved and admired Louisa, and yet at times he seemed to barely understand her.

They had four children. The only girl, Louisa, died at age one and carried away with her a great deal of her mother's vivacity. Only one of the boys, Charles Francis, lived to carry on the great Adams name. (The historian and memoirist Henry Adams was his son.) His father was hard on him and harder still on his older brothers, George and John, neither of them made from sturdy Adams stock. As young boys, they had to do without their parents, then abroad on diplomatic missions. Adams, the very model of a self-defeating parent, wrote George, the eldest, long letters on biblical exegesis. When they were together, Adams worried that Louisa would spoil them; Louisa feared that she hadn't been mother enough to them. Both would die young. John Quincy and Louisa would reconcile over their own shared suffering and over his devotion to her well-being.

ADAMS WAS A BRILLIANT MAN WHO SEEMED TO KNOW EVERYTHING about everything. Philip Hone, a diarist of the era, wrote that Adams "has probed deeply into the arcana of all the sciences, understands and can explain all subjects, from the solar system down to the construction of a tooth-pick. He has the Holy Scriptures at his fingertips, knows every line of Shakespeare, can recite Homer in the original Greek." Adams' output of written work was similarly prodigious—and eccentric. What other president wrote an epic poem set in medieval Ireland (*Dermot MacMorrogh*)? Or a treatise tracing the history of units of weight and measurement? Or a travelogue on Silesia? He was a polymath who distributed his gifts profusely but idiosyncratically.

Over the course of his life Adams produced one imperishable work of political literature—his journals. He started keeping a diary at age twelve, wrote intermittently for a few years, and then devoted himself virtually every day of his life to the recording of whatever he did, said, saw, thought, and felt—about fifteen thousand pages in all. No other president, and perhaps no other public figure in American history, kept a diary so vigilantly. Public men, after all, tend to care most about public forms of expression. For Adams, no form of expression was so precious as the writing he did for himself alone, often late at night by candlelight. His memoirs allowed him to commune with himself, to examine his own thoughts and feelings, to say to himself what he would not say to others. They are the record of a solitary man.

Adams' journal is as mutable a document as any lifelong record would be. As a young man, he wrote about the girls who caught his eye, though he was much tougher on their petty vanity than most young men would be. As a diplomat, he studied deeply the behavior of princes like Tsar Alexander of Russia, as well as the ludicrous fripperies of court etiquette. As secretary of state, he wrote about the great issues that divided the cabinet of President Monroe. As president, he gave a running account of his lost battles.

The journal allows us to know this guarded and taciturn man and to occupy his world. At times Adams suffered from debilitating bouts of depression; he writes of "a listlessness which without extinguishing the love of life, affects the mind with the Sentiment that life is nothing worth." Though notorious for his withering summations of all his leading contemporaries, Adams was no less brutal when he looked in the mirror: "I am a man of reserved, cold austere and forbidding manners; my political adversaries say a gloomy misanthropist, and my personal enemies, an unsocial savage." The agony he suffered over the death of baby Louisa and then George and John was terrible, but he hid it from everyone save his wife—and his journal. He hid, too, his moral romance—his giddy fantasy of throwing himself into the breach of a great cause. When he introduced a treaty to ban state-sponsored piracy—the kind of global code of conduct that would not emerge until the twentieth century—he wrote, "I feel that I could die for it, with joy." The same sense of glory in a great cause propelled him as he prepared for the *Amistad* case. Few men, if any, knew this Adams.

In his letters and political pamphlets, Adams sometimes reached the Augustan heights of a Burke or a Samuel Johnson. He was one of the most celebrated speakers of America's golden age of public speech. But the journal, which he told his son Charles Francis he wished to keep forever private, is Adams' great literary gift to posterity. Charles ultimately published twelve volumes of his father's diary; they cover barely 40 percent of the total.

WHY WRITE—OR READ—ABOUT THIS MAN, ARCHAIC EVEN IN HIS own time? Adams and his contemporaries studied history as a record of eternal truths and above all of moral truths, whether about the nature of justice, personal honor, or patriotism. With our own sense of history as a narrative of progress, if a very uneven one, we are more skeptical that the past can speak to us directly about our own experience, or even that moral truths are fixed. But writing about the past is almost never a purely antiquarian exercise; we can't help but see ourselves in our forebears. Writing about John Quincy Adams is a way of recovering something vital in American experience, all the more so because it has been obscured by time.

We are all Jacksonians—all democrats, very much including Republicans. Our leaders are proud to say that they are led by public opinion. Yet proclamations of faith in the wisdom of the American people are all too often a species of pandering. Politicians in thrall to special interests cloyingly remind us of their obligation to "listen to their constituents." Adams despised such evasion. Leadership, for him, meant indifference to party affiliation and, as John F. Kennedy observed, freedom from the preferences of his own voters. Adams' contemporaries shook their heads at his antique principles: a fellow legislator once told him that he seemed to regard political propositions with the purity of a Euclidean theorem, an observation Adams proudly recorded in his journal.

Adams, in short, represents a defunct evolutionary line in American political life. It is easier for us to recognize his faults than his virtues. But we need his virtues. We need to hear Adams' voice. So much of the joy of writing this book, for me, was listening to, and then evoking, that voice, scouringly truthful, unforgiving even of himself. To know Adams is not to love him. It is, however, to admire him greatly.

PART I

HE IS FORMED FOR A STATESMAN

CHAPTER I

The Flame Is Kindled

(1767–1778)

O N THE MORNING OF JUNE 17, 1775, JOHN QUINCY ADAMS walked with his mother, Abigail, to an orchard atop Penn's Hill, the highest point near their home in Braintree. The air was filled with the roar and crash of artillery, for at dawn British forces had begun their cannonade of Bunker Hill, which stood at the crown of a peninsula immediately north of Boston. Abigail and her four children had been cowering at home; her husband, John Adams, was three hundred miles away, at the second Continental Congress in Philadelphia. But so much turned on this long-awaited battle that Abigail felt she had to see it for herself. Perhaps she felt that her eldest son, then not quite eight years old, should see for himself the mortal consequences of the fight his father and his fellow colonists had undertaken, or perhaps she was simply very frightened and needed company. It was a clear, hot day, and even from ten miles away Johnny, as his parents called him, could see the flash of cannon fire from British ships in the harbor, the smoke from the colonists' muskets, and the great wall of flame as the wooden houses and churches of Charlestown, at the very tip of the peninsula, burned beneath a hail of British incendiary shells. The noise was deafening, and the panorama of destruction must have been even more terrifying to the boy than to his mother.

The battles of Lexington and Concord, two months earlier, had been skirmishes; Bunker Hill was the opening encounter of a war. The British lost almost five hundred men in desperate charges straight up the hill and along its flank, but the militias mustered from Boston and the small towns nearby had neither the men nor the ammunition to resist for long and ultimately fled back home over the narrow causeway of Charlestown. Word reached Braintree later that day that Joseph Warren, thirty-three years old, a fiery orator, a military leader, and an admired doctor, had died in the final charge. While others had fled, Warren had chosen to make a last stand amid the ruined fortifications. Warren was the Adams' family physician.

A moment so rich with elation, fear, reverence, and grief would have made a deep impression even on a boy far less precocious that John Quincy Adams. In a letter written seventy years later, he recalled that he had "witnessed the tears of my mother, and mingled them with my own, at the fall of Warren, a dear friend of my father, and a beloved Physic to me." Warren was a friend, but he was also a hero, a brave man who had died defending the cause of American liberty—the same cause, as his mother never failed to remind him, his own father had gone to Philadelphia, under the most trying circumstances, to advance. Every night during these months, his mother instructed him to repeat, along with the Lord's Prayer, an ode to martyred soldiers written by the British poet William Collins: "How sleep the brave who sink to rest / By all their country's wishes blest!" In the letter, Adams wrote out all twelve lines of the ode and observed to his correspondent that even after all those years he hadn't forgotten a word.

John Quincy Adams understood, as a very young boy, that his life belonged not merely to himself, but to his country and its cause. He would never forget that a life properly lived required commitment to principle, sacrifice, and suffering.

ABIGAIL ADAMS GAVE BIRTH TO A SON ON JULY 11, 1767. AT THE request of her mother, Elizabeth Smith, she and John named him after Elizabeth's own father, Colonel John Quincy, then very close to death. (Both the family name and the town were pronounced "Quin-zee.") The Quincys, who traced their roots in England back to the era of William the Conqueror, had arrived in the Massachusetts Bay Colony soon after its founding; they had owned the land on Mount Wollaston, the family compound, since 1635. They had given their name to the town in which they lived. Abigail was raised in the finest house for miles around. And the Quincys were as respectable as they were prosperous. Elizabeth married a minister, William Smith, who served for forty-five years as pastor to the nearby town of Weymouth. They had three daughters—Mary, Abigail, and Elizabeth—all of whom also married well. Only the one boy in the family proved to be a mortifying failure: William Jr. died a wastrel, leaving behind a wife and children whom John and Abigail would take into their household.

The Adamses were every bit as venerable as the Quincys, if less grand. The family had arrived in Massachusetts in 1632 and had served quietly as deacons and selectmen and sheriffs in and around Braintree ever since. John Adams' father, known as Deacon John, had married Susanna Boylston, from a family no less illustrious than the Quincys. Still, the Adamses had not attended college; Deacon John was a farmer and a shoemaker. But John Adams was immensely proud of his family—not of their social position but of their moral uprightness. In one of his bristlingly defensive moods, he wrote a friend that his family had lived in Braintree for 160 years, and during all that time "no bankruptcy was ever committed, no widow or orphan was ever defrauded, no redemptor intervened and no debt was contracted with England." For a man like Adams, a descendant of New England's Puritan founders, "standing" was not a social but a moral attribute. The Adamses, like the Quincys, had been upright figures since Englishmen had arrived on the continent. They were the aristocracy of the new world, and John Adams' extensive exposure to the aristocracy of the old world later on in life only deepened this conviction.

John Quincy Adams was born in a modest wood-frame cottage about a mile from the village of Braintree and two miles from the ocean. Next door was the house in which his father had grown up and his grandmother still lived. On its ground floor the Adams' house had four rooms wrapped around a steep staircase: a small, square parlor; a narrow kitchen running the length of the house in the rear; a dining room; and another front parlor, which John had turned into his law office. The staircase led to two bedrooms in the front of the house and two tiny rooms squeezed under the eaves in the rear—the house was steeply gabled. The upstairs would have been very crowded at night, since all four children lived there: Abigail, known as Nabby, born in 1765; John Quincy; Charles, born in 1770; and Thomas Boylston, born two years later.

Johnny and his brothers and sister grew up on a modest ten-acre farm. The Adamses kept chickens, sheep, and cows as well as horses for plowing; grew their own fruit and vegetables; and chopped down their own trees for firewood. The family's income came from John's law practice, but the farm supplied most of their needs; they were self-sufficient, as city folk were not.

John worked on the farm, and while Abigail had a servant, there was little the servant did that Abigail couldn't, and didn't, do herself.

Beyond the Adams property lay other small farms with their orchards and fields, their stables and sheds and cider mills. Braintree rolled toward the ocean in gentle hills, though at its southwestern edge a steep hill of granite served as the quarry for the region and furnished the stone from which many of the fine homes of Boston were built. The life of Braintree revolved around the church, Puritan until 1750 and Unitarian thereafter. The only other building in the village not devoted to farming was the store, from which Abigail could buy anything from a carton of pins to a glass of rum, as the sign in the window read. And yet the great city of Boston, with a population of perhaps fifteen thousand, lay only ten miles away down the coastal road. The people of Braintree were modest farmers, but they were not yokels.

No one among them had pressed more eagerly into the larger world than John Adams, a figure of great gifts, boundless energy, focused ambition. As a Harvard student, he identified the other bright young men, got to know them, read what they read. As a lawyer, he combined tireless preparation with passionate advocacy. Adams had a strict, Calvinist sense of morality and propriety. But as a young man he was scarcely the dour figure conjured up by the word "Puritan." He had, by his own admission, an "amorous disposition" and loved nothing more than spending an evening in the company of ladies. But he never committed an indiscretion, for which he thanked his own parents, whom, he said, "held every species of Libertinage in such contempt and Horror, and held up constantly to view such pictures of disgrace, of baseness and of ruin, that my natural temperament was always overawed by my principles and Sense of decorum." That was Adams—passion kept in check by principle, like the wooden staves of a barrel held together by copper hoops.

John Adams was voluble, buttonholing, argumentative, headlong. He could talk and write a blue streak. In one of his first letters to Abigail, in 1761, when they were pledged to one another but not yet married, the twenty-five-year-old attorney wrote, "I mount this moment for the noisy, dirty town of Boston, where parade, Pomp, Nonsense, Frippery, Folly, Foppery, Luxury, Politicks and the soul-Confounding wrangles of the law will give me the Higher Relish for Spirit, Taste and Sense at Weymouth, next Saturday." Adams had a dim view of his fellow man but did not yet suffer from the splenetic temper of his later years. He published a series of mock-rural letters, in country vernacular, under the name Humphrey Ploughjogger.

He wrote little sketches of the people he met at inns and in the courts for Abigail's amusement.

But Adams was also a politically conscious man, and in 1764, when the English began to impose a series of onerous taxes on the colonies, culminating in the Stamp Act, Adams responded by publishing a legal essay titled *A Dissertation on the Canon and the Feudal Law*. Soon afterwards, in the *Braintree Instructions*, he gave voice to the townspeople's decision to defy the Stamp Act as a violation of their rights as Englishmen not to be taxed without representation. Forty other towns, including Boston, adopted the instructions, thus catapulting the fiery young lawyer into the first ranks of patriotic activists. Adams soon found that he had to choose between opportunities to capitalize on his legal gifts and his patriotic convictions. And he never hesitated. In 1768, with his family growing, he was offered a lucrative post in the Court of Admiralty. He immediately refused, as he had refused such offers in the past, owing to "my Scruples about laying myself under any restraints, or Obligations of Gratitude to the Government for any of their favours." When he explained that he held opinions contrary to those of His Majesty's government, he was told that he would remain perfectly free to express those views. He still said no.

Politics inexorably drew Adams away from the quiet life of a prosperous lawyer. When a detachment of British soldiers in Boston fired on a mob of young men on March 5, 1770, killing three and wounding two—the riot that came to be known as the Boston Massacre—Adams agreed to defend Thomas Preston, the senior British officer. Abigail burst into tears when he told her that he would take the case—or so Adams wrote much later in his *Autobiography*—for he appeared to be bent on destroying the finest legal prospects in Massachusetts. Nevertheless, she agreed that he could not act otherwise. The right to counsel was precisely the kind of principle enshrined in England's unwritten constitution, which the colonists insisted must apply to themselves. Beyond that, the sacrifice of interest in the name of principle lay at the very core of the moral order John and Abigail held dear. Many of Adams' friends were bewildered by his decision but ultimately embraced it as an act of exalted patriotism. Thanks to Adams, Thomas Preston was acquitted; only two of the eight other soldiers were found guilty, and they on reduced charges.

In June 1774, Adams was appointed by the state legislature as one of the five Massachusetts delegates to the first Continental Congress. He would be away for much of the next three years, leaving Abigail to raise four children and run the family farm largely on her own.

Abigail and her sisters had been educated at home, as was the custom. "Female education," she wrote in her old age, "in the best families, went no further than writing and arithmetic, in some few and rare instances, music and dancing." The Reverend Smith had instilled an air of piety in the household that was, in turn, reinforced by Elizabeth Quincy Smith, a paragon of New England modesty and rectitude. But it was a bookish home as well, with a library that held the English classics as well as the Bible. When John's friend Richard Cranch began courting Mary, he appointed himself tutor to all three, reading Shakespeare, John Milton, and Alexander Pope with them. Abigail was a highly intelligent young woman who had more exposure to literature, and thus to serious thought, than was normal even for a well-born woman of New England.

Abigail was a tiny woman with dark, piercing eyes under fine, arched brows; one early portrait, admittedly by an amateur, makes her look quite lovely, though later ones painted by more talented artists are not quite so flattering. Even at fifteen, when she first met John, Abigail was forceful and intellectually self-assured in a way that Adams must have found remarkable, and thrilling, in the cloistered female world of small-town New England. Adams took her seriously, which she must have found flattering; he was a worldly and ambitious man with an exceptional mind and a playful spirit. The famous letters between them overflowed with love and desire from the very first. "I hereby order you to give him as many Kisses and as many hours of your company after 9 o'clock as he shall be pleased to demand," John wrote, pretending to be the "bearer" of a debt. Abigail, much younger and more prim, wrote back of "a tye more binding than Humanity and stronger than friendship, and by this chord I am not ashamed to say that I am bound." She began to sign her letters "Diana," the beautiful huntress of Greek myth, and John was delighted to address her so.

Within her own necessarily circumscribed sphere, Abigail proved to be an extremely competent and resourceful young woman. In her husband's absence she managed the family farm and made a small income on the side by selling whatever products he was able to send her, first from Philadelphia and later from Europe. Though confined to home and hearth for the first forty years of her life, Abigail had a far-reaching mind. She once wrote to a cousin that "I would have been a rover if of the other sex," but instead depended on men to indulge her curiosity. Very few women of her time succeeded in living a public life, and she was thrilled and fascinated by those who did. She carried on a long and intimate correspondence with Mercy Otis Warren, a historian and playwright and wife of James Warren, a

Massachusetts patriot, and with Catherine Macaulay, a British historian who championed the cause of the colonies. She envied them their intellectual freedom and their ability to advance the cause of liberty, as men did. Of Macaulay, she wrote to her cousin, "I have a curiosity to know her Education, and what first prompted her to engage in a study never before Exhibited to the publick by one of her own Sex and Country."

Abigail was, in fact, the intellectual equal of the women she most admired. She had committed a vast amount of English poetry to memory, and her letters brim with long citations from Milton, as well as from Pope and the other Augustans. She read a great deal of classical history, though in translation, for girls were not taught Latin or Greek. And she shared her husband's ardor for knowledge. Years later, when Abigail overcame her resistance to crossing the ocean in order to join her husband in London, where he had been appointed minister, she reported in a letter home that she had signed up for a series of lectures and attended talks, including experiments, on "Electricity, Magnetism Hydrostatics optics pneumatics. . . ." The experience, she wrote, "was like going into a Beautiful Country, which I never saw before, a Country which our American Females are not permitted to visit or inspect."

The first stirrings of revolution roused the same passion in Abigail as it did in John. In the days leading up to the Boston Tea Party, in December 1773, she wrote to Mercy Otis Warren, "The flame is kindled and like lightning it catches from soul to soul. Great will be the devastation if not timely quenched or allayed by some Lenient Measures." Like John, she was an early convert to the cause of independence: in February 1775 she wrote that she had concluded "that we cannot be happy without being free, that we cannot be free without being secure in our own property, that we cannot be secure in our own property if without our consent others may take it as of right." Abigail despised the British generals who had quartered themselves in the homes of her friends and dined off their crockery. And she revered George Washington. Abigail met General Washington when the Continental Army reached Boston in the summer of 1775. "You had prepared me to entertain a favourable opinion of him, but I thought the one half was not told me," she wrote John. She was reminded of a line from Dryden: "He's a temple sacred by birth, and built by hands divine."

Abigail did not shrink from the necessity of war. In early 1775, when many patriots still hoped for a peaceful settlement with England, she wrote to Mercy Otis Warren that "the Sword is now our only, yet dreadful alternative." And though she cowered before the awful bombardment of Bunker

Hill, she soon learned to accept, and even welcome, those thunders. In February 1776, with General Washington shelling the British on nearby Dorchester Heights, she walked up to Penn's Hill once again, listened to the cannonades, and reported to John, "The sound I think is one of the Grandest in nature, and is of the true Species of the Sublime." Whatever suffering might come, Abigail never doubted that the Lord would smite the British and protect the patriotic cause.

Few couples were more exquisitely matched than the Adamses: each was restless, brilliant, high-minded, eager for self-sacrifice. John was the more abrasive, Abigail the more sententious—which is only to say that the one was a man of his time, the other a woman of her time. They were, in fact, remarkably similar in temperament. By a strange twist of fate, John Quincy Adams would spend his childhood and youth in the company of either his mother or his father, but almost never both. His mother had sole charge of him from ages seven to eleven, his father from eleven to sixteen. The two so completely reinforced each other that it would not be easy to trace his character as an adult to one as opposed to the other. What is clear, in any case, is that both poured themselves into the raising of their eldest son and that he dutifully, indeed reverently, absorbed their lessons and their example. He became what they wished him to be.

Both John and Abigail regarded the upbringing of children as a sacred and solemn obligation. They did not embrace the French Enlightenment view of humans as inherently rational creatures and education as the encouragement of natural propensities. Though deeply steeped in that tradition, John and Abigail were heirs to a Puritan culture that saw human beings as fallen creatures who must be redeemed from sin through the most conscientious acts of cultivation. "Education has made a greater difference between man and man, than nature has made between man and brute," John wrote Abigail in 1775. "It should be your care, therefore, and mine to elevate the minds of our children and exalt their courage; to accelerate and animate their industry and activity; to excite in them a habitual contempt of meanness, abhorrence of injustice and inhumanity, and an ambition to excel in every capacity, faculty and virtue." Abigail and John would have recoiled at the idea that intellect could be taught in the absence of morality, for they believed that the goal of education was to produce both goodness and usefulness.

John was quite content to leave Nabby's education up to Abigail, but the boys had to be prepared to help forge a new world in which the colonists would prove themselves fully equal to the Englishmen who now treated them as subjects. The time had come, he wrote Abigail, when the boys were four, six, and nine, to "think of forming the Taste, and Judgment of your Children. . . . Have no mercy on an affected Phrase, any more than an affected Air, Gate, Dress or Manner." He suggested she instruct them to write descriptions—"of a Battle, a Storm, a siege, a Cloud"—as well as to declaim speeches on various topics. As a young man, John Adams had seen to his own education in the most laborious manner possible, copying sentences he wished to memorize, writing out the definition of every difficult word in Latin, carrying his quill pen and a tablet of paper everywhere he went in order to memorialize any new thought or observation or wise expression he happened upon. He had left nothing to chance, and now he would give the children the benefit of his own method.

John Adams had pronounced ideas about education, but they were not his alone. The men who were to found the United States understood that while a nation of masters and servants needed only to elevate the one and abase the other, a nation of free men needed to cultivate the gifts of all its citizens. "Every man in a republic is public property," as the physician and patriot Benjamin Rush put it. A monarch could compel acquiescence, but a free people could be governed only through consent. A republic would work only if citizens could be trained to overcome their natural selfishness, pettiness, and factionalism. The virtues that John Adams prized in himself were those that needed to be inculcated in the next generation—disinterestedness, a contempt for meanness, an abhorrence of injustice.

The civic virtues that John and Abigail wished to instill in their son rested on a foundation of Christian virtues. A child must learn—for it would not happen by itself—to seek the good and abhor the bad. In one of her letters to her husband, Abigail explained why she had decided not to send Johnny to Braintree's primary school. "I have always thought it of very great importance," she wrote to John, "that children should in the early part of life be unaccustomed to such examples as would tend to corrupt the purity of their words and actions that they may chill with horror at the sound of an oath, and blush with indignation at an obsene expression." The nursery itself had to be kept pure. In later years, when Nabby herself became a mother, Abigail recommended Isaac Watts' "Moral Songs for Children," an immensely popular Christian tract that, she wrote, taught "brotherly love, sisterly affection, and filial respect and reverence." Nursery rhymes like "Jack and Jill," Abigail sniffed, had "neither a rule of life, nor sentiment worth retaining."

In the absence of school, Abigail put John Thaxter, one of Adams' idle law clerks, to work as John Quincy's tutor. But as a woman who read widely, wrote with great force and pungency—if erratic spelling—and had large amounts of literature at her fingertips, Abigail was a teacher whom very few men could match. And she thought as deeply as her husband did about the forming of children's minds. In her very first letter to Mercy Otis Warren, written in July 1773 after a visit to Mrs. Warren's home at Plymouth, she recalled that she had told her new friend of a work on child rearing, *On the Management and Education of Children: A Series of Letters Written to a Niece*, by a British author—and a woman—Juliana Seymour. Abigail had been very much taken with Mercy's children, and she wanted to know if the program laid out by Mrs. Seymour "corresponds with the plan you have laid out for yourself." Abigail made her own preferences clear when she described education as "rearing the tender thought"—not instilling commandments but nurturing the immature mind. She ended her letter with lines of verse describing the parent who seeks to learn "What Bias Nature gave the mind." The teacher seeks not to uproot that bias but to shape it through careful cultivation—and through love. What delight, the poet observes,

> Each Boisterous passion to controul
> And early Humanize the Soul
> The noblest Notions to inspire,
> Her offspring conscious of her care
> Transported hang around her chair

Abigail spent long hours reading to her son as he sat at her feet before the hearth. But Abigail would never have thought that loving attention, from either mother or son, was enough. She expected Johnny to read aloud to her, so that she could critique him and help him along. She reported to her husband that she had gotten the seven-year-old boy to read to her every day from Charles Rollins' *Ancient History of the Egyptians, Carthaginians, Assyrians, Babylonians, Medes and Persians, Macedonians and Grecians*, a best seller published six years earlier that, one scholar points out, "seamlessly melded classical themes with Christian ends." It was, of course, written for adults. And she encouraged the boy to write. In his first letter to his father, October 13, 1774, the seven-year-old Johnny wrote, "Sir—I have been trying ever since you went away to lern to write you a Letter." He apologized for his meager effort—an exaggerated sense of his own insufficiency which a lifetime of achievements would barely make a dent in—and concluded, "I hope I grow to be a better boy and that you will have no occasion to be ashamed of me when you return."

On his own, Johnny read fairy tales and adventure stories and *The Arabian Nights*, slaying dragons and rescuing damsels in his imagination. At age ten, poking through a closet in his mother's bedroom, he found copies of the Shakespeare comedies. He fell under the magical spell of *The Tempest*. Half a century later, he recalled how quicksilver Ariel and monstrous Caliban "made for me a world of revels, and lapped me in Elysium." He also found an edition of *Paradise Lost*. This, he knew, was grown-up literature, and he was determined to read what his parents read. Perhaps going outside for safety, he smoked his father's pipe and read his parents' Milton—and felt sick at the one and frustrated to tears at the other. He gave up Milton until he was older, though he never stopped smoking.

John Adams began writing directly to his son in the spring of 1776. His first letter must have overawed the boy: "I hope that you will remember how many Losses, dangers, and Inconveniences, have been borne by your parents, and the inhabitants of Boston in general, for the sake of pursuing freedom for you and Yours." Johnny probably needed very little reminding about sacrifice: in the aftermath of the Boston Tea Party in 1773, the British had blockaded the port of Boston and placed the city under martial law. Even the most basic products were unavailable or impossibly expensive. Abigail, always self-sufficient, laid in her own stores of flax and wool in order to make the family clothes and linen herself. By the spring of 1775, the Adams family servants had either returned home or joined the militia, leaving Abigail to make the soap, nurse the sick, tend to the animals, and of course care for her children virtually on her own. The battle of Bunker Hill, that June, offered only the most vivid lesson in the sacrifices compelled by the pursuit of freedom.

As the children grew older, the father's instructional program, conveyed by post, became more sophisticated and demanding. John Adams always found time to write home with admonitions about the children's upbringing. They must learn French, he told Abigail, for "it will become a necessary accomplishment of an American Gentleman and Lady." He asked if Johnny was following news of the war in the newspapers and asked her to quiz him on his reading of history: "Which character he esteems and admires? Which he hates and abhors?" He sent Johnny a line in Latin and instructed him to go through it word by word with Thaxter so that he could construe it properly when his father came home. And he should read

Thucydides: "You will find it full of Instruction to the orator, the States-man, the general, as well as to the Historian and the Philosopher."

If there was a curricular core to the emerging education for citizenship, it was the study of ancient history—Cicero, Tacitus, Plutarch, Sallust, and of course Thucydides, the great historian of ancient Greece. "The classics" was not a subject, like geography or history, but rather a lens through which to examine and understand the life around you. Here one could learn of the rise and fall of empires and of republics as well, and learn that they often died not from the outside but from the inside—from corruption and sloth, just as despotic and grasping England had begun to do. Rome was every-thing—both the very type of overweening empire (like Great Britain) and the great antecedent to America. Roman vice was English vice, but Roman patriotism, the love of the republic, was the great model for America. The Adamses revered Cicero, the brilliant orator, senator, and sage who sacri-ficed himself for the good of Rome. They recoiled at the tyrant Caesar and admired the courage of Brutus, his assassin.

At times, in fact, you can almost hear the Adamses fashioning themselves after the Roman heroes they so admired. Abigail signed her letters to John "Portia," after Brutus' patient and long-suffering wife. To the Adamses and their contemporaries, the Romans were not simply emblems of individual virtue but paragons of citizenship. The colonists looked to republican Rome for lessons in patriotism, an attribute they exalted above almost all others. In a letter to Mercy Otis Warren, apparently written in January 1776, as John was leaving home yet again for the Continental Congress, Abigail wrote:

> Our Country is as it were a Secondary God, and the first and greatest parent. It is to be preferred to parents, to wives, children, Friends and all things the Gods only excepted. These are the considerations which prevail with me to consent to a most painfull Seperation. I have not known how to take my pen to write to you. I have been happy and unhappy. I have had many contending passions dividing my Heart, and no sooner did I find it at my own option whether my Friend should go or tarry and resign; than I found his honour and reputation much dearer to me, than my own present pleasure and happiness, and I could by no means consent to his resigning at present, as I was fully convinced he must suffer if he quitted.

The classics taught the revolutionary generation to repress "present pleasure" in favor of something "much dearer." But the classic world was, of course, pagan, and while the civic virtues eighteenth-century New England most admired were Roman ones, the moral order itself, which dictated a person's deepest obligations, was Christian. John and Abigail were far removed from the apocalyptic world of their Puritan ancestors, with its vision of mankind dangling over the fiery pit of perdition, but they were infused with a deep sense of sinfulness and a corresponding horror of wrongdoing. One can hear this both in Abigail's fear that public school might corrupt her son's moral purity and in the boy's apologies for his shortcomings. Abigail, especially, had grown up in a household infused with piety, and God was never far from her thoughts. She kept her son's mind perpetually focused on the narrow path he must tread and on the thorns that lay to either side. When he went off to Europe at age ten, she admonished him, "Adhere to those religious Sentiments and principals which were early instilled into your mind and remember that you are accountable to your Maker for all your words and actions."

The essential components, then, of John Quincy Adams' early education were a passion for knowledge and intellectual accomplishment, an abiding Christian faith, and an extraordinary awareness of the dramatic moment in history in which he was living. In the Adams household, the ancient, the divine, and the contemporary fused into a single reality and a single sense of calling.

By the time Johnny was seven, in 1774, "Pharaoh," as Abigail called the British overlords, had begun to visit his plagues on the people of Boston, which is to say that the British quartered themselves in the town, requisitioned homes, and restricted movement into and out of the town. The population began to flee, and the little house in Braintree filled with soldiers and friends and sometimes complete strangers who told tales of privation and flight. By early 1775, Abigail lived in fear. Should the British attack, John wrote, "fly to the woods with our Children." In the aftermath of the battles of Lexington and Concord, thousands of militiamen poured from the countryside into Boston and Cambridge. Johnny saw the soldiers and felt both the terror and the majesty. He watched his mother melt the family pewter to make bullets. And then came Bunker Hill, a catastrophe that at the same time felt like the lighting of a great fuse.

The Adamses were not simply playthings of history but makers of the national destiny. Abigail would read John's letters to the children as they gathered around the fireside. Those letters pulsed with an awareness of the magnitude of the events unfolding before him; he wrote of the "awe" he felt at the Congress' accomplishments. He wrote about General Washington and about Ben Franklin, strangely subdued but always pushing for the boldest measures. He sent them news of Thomas Paine's rousing pamphlet "Common Sense," which he thought overpraised. (Adams was convinced that the publication of his own letters calling for independence had done far more to influence public opinion than had Paine's broadside—a decidedly minority opinion.) It was John Adams, perhaps more than any other individual, who defined the American revolution. A British spy once said that Adams had a talent for "seeing large things largely" (though not, he added tartly, "correctly"). He was a self-dramatizing figure at a moment of supreme drama. And his exploits filled his son's mind and fired his imagination.

Johnny did not, of course, live in history. He was a boy growing up in the woods and fields of New England. During much of the year Braintree was blasted by the frigid winds sweeping in from the ocean, but in the summer it was heavenly. In summer, wrote John Quincy's grandson Henry Adams of his own boyhood seventy years later, a child "rolled in the grass, or waded in the brook, or swam in the salt ocean, or sailed in the bay, or fished for smelts in the creeks, or netted minnows in the salt-marshes, or took to the pine-woods or the granite quarries, or chased muskrats or hunted snapping-turtles in the swamps, or mushrooms or nuts on the autumn hills."

But Johnny knew that play was a luxury; he had a nagging conscience, and a sense of responsibility, at an early age. "My head is much too fickle, my thoughts are running after birds eggs play and trifles," he confessed to his father just shy of his tenth birthday. "I wish Sir you would give me some instructions with regard to my time & advise me how to proportion my studies & my play in writing & and I will keep them by me, & endeavour to follow them." Not just his parents' sober instructions but his own immediate experience were making him grow up prematurely. He was the oldest boy in the household, and Abigail depended on him, for example, to ride the seven miles to Boston to drop off and pick up the precious mail.

John Adams finally came home from his labors in late November 1777. He was prepared to resume his legal career, which he had dropped four years earlier, leaving his family to survive on dwindling savings. But it was not to be. General Washington had won a smashing victory over Burgoyne at Saratoga in September and October, and American prospects had begun to look less grim than they had a year before; but the British had a vast advantage over the Americans in men and materiel, and victory seemed impossible without foreign—that is, French—help.

The Continental Congress asked Adams to go to France to replace Silas Deane, who had been negotiating for assistance and for recognition of American sovereignty, along with Benjamin Franklin and Arthur Lee Jr.

Adams had no wish to leave home and certainly none to make an Atlantic crossing in the dead of winter. And he was less worried about being lost at sea than he was about being captured by the British, who, he was quite certain, would execute him as a traitor. But in December, when the Congress formally asked him to go, he agreed without hesitation, as was his habit. Abigail begged him not to go and then asked him to take her and the children. He refused. But when Johnny implored his father to let him come, Adams relented. And Abigail—Portia—agreed to a Roman sacrifice. She would surrender both husband and eldest son. She agreed that Johnny would profit from the experience. Abigail fretted that her boy would be trapped by the "snares and temptations" of the old world, but she acknowledged that "to exclude him from temptation is to exclude him from the World in which he is to live."

John Quincy Adams would spend much of the next seven years of his life far from the world of bloodshed and heroism in which he had been raised; he would gain a knowledge of statecraft, of literature and philosophy, of painting and theater, which would have been impossible at home. He could have become a dandy and a snob; he did, in fact, become a formidable and rather imperious young man. But the patriotism drilled into his soul from birth would prove to be ineradicable.

CHAPTER 2

His Thoughts Are Always Running
in a Serious Strain

(1778–1780)

I N ORDER TO AVOID DETECTION, JOHN ADAMS AND HIS SON SET out from Quincy in the dead of night. Adams knew that British spies were everywhere and would be watching the roads as well as the harbor. It was February 15, 1778. The Adams men walked in the moonlight to a spit of land called Moon Head, near Wollaston, the Quincy family seat. From then they would take a rowboat out to the *Boston*, the ship that would take them across the ocean. At Hoff's Neck, not far from their destination, the travelers were accosted by an old woman—a remote Adams relation—who screeched, like a Shakespearean witch, "The Heavens frown, the clouds roll, the hollow winds howl!" The ten-year-old boy may have been spooked, but he was in the company of his all-knowing father, who sneered at superstition and dire auguries. They cinched their greatcoats against the biting cold and climbed aboard the rowboat.

Neither John Adams nor his son had ever sailed the ocean; even John, who had represented ships' captains in court for years, had done virtually all his traveling by land. The mid-winter Atlantic crossing was thus an experience fraught with both mystery and peril. The *Boston*, a 504-ton frigate, was a fine ship with an experienced captain, Samuel Tucker. After setting off in a snowstorm, the ship put in at the port in Marblehead, about twenty miles to the north. There friends of the captain and crew came aboard and told hair-raising tales of the cruel treatment meted out to captives taken by British men o'war. John Adams grew increasingly impatient and nervous. On the eighteenth, the *Boston* took advantage of fair winds and sailed north. On the twentieth, it was chased by a British ship, rousing Adams' fear of capture. He urged Tucker to fight with everything he had; the alternative was too horrible to contemplate. The *Boston* put all its guns out; every man waited for battle. And then, with the English warship steadily gaining, a tremendous storm hit.

Lashed by violent winds, the waves rose up mountainously and fell away in a terrifying abyss. The ship rolled and pitched like a cork, the cargo smashing against the hold, the mates falling and cursing. The sealed door to the powder room flew open, threatening to annihilate the ship with an explosion before it could be sent to the bottom by the flood. The noise from the wind, from the screaming of the ropes, from the straining of the timbers, which seemed about to crack into a thousand pieces, was so deafening that a man couldn't hear a word shouted into his ear. A lightning bolt hit the mast, which splintered with a tremendous crack. For three days the storm raged on. Adams and his son braced themselves against the bed of their stateroom to keep from splitting their skulls. And Johnny proved to his father that he was no ordinary boy. "Fully sensible of the Danger," his father wrote, "he was constantly endeavouring to bear up under it with a manly courage and patience, very attentive to me, and his thoughts always running in a serious Strain."

This was the first time that the boy had been alone with his father for a protracted period. More than that, it was perhaps the first time that he had ever seen his father, rather than simply heard about him, as a figure of authority among other men. Here was a new form of education for a boy at a very suggestible age. John Adams had spent the previous two years watching over the Continental Army, consuming vast amounts of military history and doctrine, serving on congressional committees and proposing reforms, growing impatient at failures of nerve and of command. He watched the routines of the *Boston* with the same acute and censorious attention to detail. As soon as the storm subsided, he made a list in his journal of everything wrong with the ship and its crew: the space between decks was too narrow and stifling; the deck held too many guns, making navigation slow and unsteady; the ship was filthy, the crew swore too much, and the meals arrived irregularly. Adams gave broad hints to the captain and found to his satisfaction that the decks were soon washed, swept, and aired. He was a man who wanted and expected responsibility.

Father and son shared a cabin and must have spent countless hours in conversation. John Adams was a man of bottomless curiosity who wanted to understand everything. He wondered about the Gulf Stream, which bore the ship forward and carried storms along its track. "What is the course of it?" he asked himself. "From what Point and to what Point does it flow? How broad is it? . . ." What were the fish that swam in the ship's wake? And he yearned to know about the world to which he had been sent. What was the state of Europe's armies, navies, and finance? How many ships did it have, with how many guns? What were the British plans? Adams never hesitated to talk to his son about the most grown-up subjects; Johnny listened and watched while his father's restless mind turned over every riddle and mystery.

Most of the time, Adams was too seasick and too wet to focus on much of anything. Johnny, however, seemed delighted with the voyage. The elder Adams had brought a French grammar book with him, and he asked Nicholas Noel, a French doctor returning home, to teach his son the language. Johnny proved to be an eager student and made quick progress. Very much his father's son, he pestered the captain to tell him the name of every sail and to explain how the compass worked. In mid-March, the *Boston* chased and seized the *Martha*, a British merchant ship with cargo said to be insured by Lloyd's for 70,000 pounds—a thrilling moment for everyone. But the victory came with a cost: One of the *Boston*'s guns exploded; Barron, the sailor manning the gun, had to have his leg amputated. John Adams held Barron in his arms during the operation. Barron died two weeks later; his body was placed in a casket laden with shot. Everyone, Johnny included, stood solemnly on deck while Barron's body was committed to the ocean with a prayer.

On March 28, six weeks after leaving, John Adams spied the Ile de Re, an island off the French coast, and then the great round towers that guarded the harbor of La Rochelle. A pilot arrived to guide the *Boston* to the port of Bordeaux. As they cruised down the Gironde, the river tapered, and on either bank they could see farmers and cattle. In Bordeaux, they were invited aboard a merchant ship for a splendid meal. The Adams took a chaise through Poitiers, Amboise, Tours, and Orleans. They reached Paris on April 8. John was once again pleased to see that his son seemed not the least worse for wear from the five-hundred-mile trip.

Several days later, they visited Benjamin Franklin at his home in Passy, at a chateau known as the Hotel de Valentinois. Silas Deane, whom Adams had come to replace, had just vacated the courtyard pavilion known as the

Basse Cour, and Franklin invited the Adamses to lodge there. The newcomers could scarcely have done better: at that time, Passy was a charming village close to the Bois de Boulogne and a few miles from the center of Paris; the chateau itself sat on eighteen acres, which ran downhill to the Seine. (The house occupied a site near the current rue Singer.) The gardens surrounding their cottage were filled with acacia, linden, and chestnut trees. Here was nature tamed and beautified: not the hillocky, swampy farm in Braintree, with its chickens and cows, but the kind of delightfully arranged pastoral fashioned with an effortless elegance by a society devoted to artifice and rationality. Both father and son were thoroughly delighted.

Within a week, John Adams had installed Johnny in the private boarding academy of Monsieur Le Coeur, where Franklin had placed his grandson, Benjamin Bache (later the publisher of the *Aurora*, a notoriously anti-Adams newspaper). Monsieur Le Coeur taught dancing, fencing, music, and drawing, as well as French and Latin. His father was soon mortified to discover that his son "learned more French in a day than I could learn in a Week with all my Books." (He did, however, say the same of his servant.) Within a month, Johnny was writing plausible letters in French. He described the austere routine in a letter to his mother: rise at six, study until eight thirty, breakfast and "play," study from nine to twelve, dinner and play until two, study until four thirty, play until five, study until seven, supper, study, bed. He also showed her a new strain of seriousness. By now, he wrote—it was April 20—she would have heard of the treaty with France, "which I believe will rouse the hearts of the Americans exceedingly and also the desire of the English to make peace with us and of the Commissioners dispatched from England for that Purpose."

Sometimes Johnny was allowed to join his father for excursions. He wrote to his cousin Billy Cranch that he had joined Dr. Franklin and his son, William Temple Franklin, and "other Gentlemen and Ladies" at a dinner at a chateau in Montmartre. He wrote to cousin Lucy Cranch that he had gone to the *Comédie Italienne*, where he had seen a succession of plays, among them *Nymphs of Diana*. "All the actresses," he wrote, "had on white silk gowns with part of them dragging behind on the ground with a case of quivers at their backs." Johnny loved the theater the way other boys love the circus. He wrote to Nabby that of all the amusements in Paris his favorite was "the Spectacles," popular shows with song and dance. "Pappa won't let me go to them as often as I wish," he lamented. He enjoyed the opera and the *Comédie*, but, he added breathlessly, "the language the wit the passions the sentiment the oratory the poetry the manners the morals are at the

French comedy." He would become a lifelong connoisseur of the theater, in many languages.

Johnny took his cues from his father, and John Adams had been seduced by the French. Days after reaching Paris, he wrote to Abigail, "stern and haughty Republican as I am, I cannot help loving these People, for their earnest Desire, and their assiduity to please." Adams was no killjoy. He found much about France beautiful and charming. The women were beguiling—all the more so because they made intelligent conversation. (He may have added this for Abigail's benefit.) Johnny understood that he was allowed to be delighted. But he was not to surrender to this glorious fleshpot. His father *was* a stern and haughty republican; though his fondness for the French people never slackened, he began to find the opulence sickening. He yearned for the simple pleasures of home. And so, Johnny claimed, did he. In June, still a month shy of eleven years old, he wrote to his mother that he would "much rather be among the rugged rocks of my own native town than in the gay city of Paris." He must have liked the sound of this noble sentiment, since he repeated it in a letter to brother Charles, and added, with startling sententiousness for a boy his age, "Your business & mine are upon the Same foundation to qualify ourselves to be useful members of Society & to get a living in the world."

Johnny absorbed from his father not a mixed but a mingled message: Europe was wonderful, but virtue lay elsewhere. From Abigail, however, the message was more severe. At times Abigail could be sportive, even whimsical, but her fear of the snares of the old world and the heedlessness of youth—of young men, above all—darkened her already somber tone. "Improve your understanding," she wrote in her first letter to Johnny, but bear in mind that learning "will be of little value and small Estimation, unless Virtue, Honor, Truth and integrity are added to them." Let yourself be guided by religious sentiments and the precepts of your father, she went on, "for dear as you are to me, I had much rather you should have found your Grave in the ocean you have crossed, or any untimely death crop you in your infant years, rather than see you an immoral profligate or a Graceless child." This sentiment, shocking to our own ears, might have been stinging even to his.

John Adams was enormously proud of his son—of his French fluency, his intellectual growth, his gift for impressing adults—and he often said so to Abigail. "Your son is the joy of my heart," he wrote. But Abigail seemed to worry that praise would go to the boy's head. She reminded Johnny—unremittingly, it must have seemed to him—of the responsibilities he bore. If Providence had preserved him from death at sea, she wrote, then he must treat such mercy as a debt to be discharged: "in the first place to your Great Preserver, in the next to Society in general, in particular to your country, your parents and yourself."

Warming to this theme, Abigail described precisely what he owed to each. She counseled him to practice self-scrutiny. By this Abigail did not mean, as a modern would, that he should sound the depths of his being in order to know what lies there, but rather that he should purge the "mist," as she put it, which "Self love and partiality" cast before his eyes. "Whoever will candidly examine themselves," she wrote, "will find some degree of passion, peevishness or obstinacy in their Natural tempers."

This was Enlightenment psychology: to know yourself was to learn to master the passions that threatened to eclipse reason. John Adams had mastered his "amorous nature" by recalling the stern precepts of his own parents. Abigail may have felt that Johnny was similarly constituted. "You my dear son are formed with a constitution feelingly alive," she wrote, "your passions are strong and impetuous, yet with pleasure I have observed a frankness and generosity accompany your efforts to govern and subdue them." Perhaps she felt that she needed to instill in her son the same contempt and horror of "libertinage" that Deacon John had imbued in her husband. Abigail promised to further expand on the subject of self-knowledge in subsequent letters.

Johnny had largely internalized his parents' admonitions. He wrote faithfully to his relatives; when he was home from school, he and his father sat around a table at the Basse Cour, each with his own ink and quill pen. His letters grew longer and more grave. He wrote to Charles and Tom listing all the French grammar books he was reading, including "one so rational, ingenious and curious that the book is as entertaining as a romance tho the subject is dry." He began to grow into the finely balanced and rather elliptical prose style he was to master as an adult. In September 1778, two months past his eleventh birthday, he wrote to his mother about the consequences of keeping a journal, as his father had asked him to do: "Altho I shall have the mortification a few years hence, to read a great deal of my Childish nonsense, yet I shall have the Pleasure, & advantage, of Remarking the several steps, by which I shall have advanced in taste, judgement, & knowledge." (Another year would pass before he would take his father's advice.) A week later, he wrote to his two little brothers at home a very long letter setting out a suggested reading list of works in French.

John Adams, meanwhile, was feeling idle and increasingly frustrated. The delegates had completed a treaty with France before Adams arrived, and the French seemed to be in no hurry to extend loans or any other form of assistance to the Americans. A month after arriving in Paris, Adams had written to the Continental Congress suggesting that they needed not three representatives but one. He probably hoped that the Congress would leave him there and order Franklin and Arthur Lee Jr. home. But in February 1779 Adams received word that the revolutionary government had decided instead to leave Franklin in Paris and order himself and Lee back home. He was more than ready to leave—save that he had finally learned to speak French quite comfortably, if not nearly as well as his son, and was feeling more and more at home.

By this time, Johnny was out of school, and his father had very little to do. They took long walks together in the Bois de Boulogne. Adams took his son with him on his social calls. He kept him at his studies. John Adams had always believed in the pedagogic value of brute force labor. Now he gave Johnny French verbs to conjugate and instructed him to list every person in every tense, so that the boy might fill two sheets of paper on a single verb. He was laying down the habits of a lifetime.

On June 17, the two set sail for Boston aboard a French frigate, the *Sensible*. Johnny, who had been tutored in French on the *Boston*, returned the favor by teaching English to France's new ambassador to the United States, Anne-César, the Chevalier de la Luzerne, and his secretary, François de Barbé-Marbois. His father found them one day in his stateroom, Johnny flanked by the chevalier and his secretary, the chevalier reading from Blackstone, Johnny "correcting the pronunciation of every Word and Syllable and Letter." The boy, exclaimed the chevalier, "was the master of his own language like a professor." The two, Adams wrote in his diary, "are in raptures with my son."

Six weeks later, Johnny was perched once again on the rugged rocks of Braintree. He planned on studying until he could be admitted to Harvard. (At that time, before the advent of widespread secondary schooling, Harvard and other colleges admitted students as young as fourteen.) The war with England had reached a stalemate, and John Adams' services were still very much in demand. The town of Braintree named him as a delegate to the state constitutional convention, and Adams spent the next several months single-handedly drafting the Massachusetts constitution. This literary and legal masterpiece helped secure Adams' reputation. The spirit of the great English liberal thinkers, above all John Locke, breathes through the work: The "body-politic . . . is a social compact, by which the whole people covenants with each citizen, and each citizen with the whole people, that all shall be governed by certain laws for the common good." (Adams described his own work as "Locke, Sidney, Rousseau and de Mably reduced to practice.") Here was the new American credo in a nutshell: the people covenant with one another, not with the king or clergy.

In October, Adams received word that Congress had appointed him to return to France to negotiate a peace treaty with Great Britain, though at that time peace was scarcely in the offing. Once again, though it must have broken Abigail's heart, he immediately consented. Barbé-Marbois had written to Adams specifically suggesting he take Johnny, the precocious language instructor, with him. Adams wrote back to say that his son "had already learned to esteem and respect the French Nation," but that the time had come for him to begin his education at home. And then, fatefully, he changed his mind. Adams decided to bring not only his eldest son but the nine-year-old Charles, along with John Thaxter, their tutor, and a private secretary, Francis Dana. On November 14, they returned to Europe on the *Sensible*. John Quincy would not return to America until he was almost eighteen.

This time the boy brought with him a new piece of equipment: a diary. John Adams had kept a diary since youth and had urged his son to keep a journal of "the events that happen to me, and of objects that I see, and of Characters that I converse with from day to day." Later on, Adams would buy five-hundred-page hard-bound volumes, but now he brought with him a small sheaf of papers bound by a string. (The string may have been looped through the pages later on.) On the front the twelve-year-old boy hopefully wrote, "JOURNAL BY ME."

The ship sprang a leak after only four days at sea, and ten days later the hole had grown so large that the passengers had to take turns manning a pump. In his journal, Johnny wrote of his own trip to the hold. After he was whacked in the skull by a beam, he drew the profile of a head with curvy lines, then a bird and stars.

The *Sensible* limped into Ferrol, on the very northwest corner of Spain, almost a thousand miles from Paris, the first four hundred of which would take the Adams party on the rough, mountainous track along Spain's northern coast. In twenty years of very hard traveling, John Adams wrote, "I never experienced any Thing like this journey." But, he wrote, both Johnny and Charles had endured the five-week trip without complaint. Once in Paris, the Adams entourage took an elegant suite of rooms at the Hotel de Valois in the rue de Richelieu. The boys were soon enrolled at a school in

Passy. Monsieur Pechigny's academy was much as Monsieur Le Coeur's but more rigorous: Johnny was learning Greek roots and grammar as well as Latin, geometry, and writing. His father thought the time had come to drop frivolous pursuits and wrote to Monsieur Pechigny asking that the boys be excused from fencing and dancing. Johnny was no longer a boy of ten, after all. Adams wrote to his son to tell him to pay special attention to Latin and Greek, and let math and geography, as well as writing and drawing, fall by the wayside. And by the way, he added, improve your penmanship: "Can't you keep a steadier hand?"

The family's time in Paris turned out to be brief. John Adams had again found himself with nothing to do, since the British were not yet prepared to treat with the Americans. He decided to remove himself to Amsterdam, where he understood that pro-American feeling ran high and loans to the cash-starved revolutionary cause might thus be available. Adams enrolled the boys in the Latin School on the Singel, Amsterdam's innermost canal. Since he didn't speak Dutch, Johnny was placed in a class with younger children, which made him miserable. For perhaps the only time in his life, he misbehaved; the school's rector wrote a letter to John Adams complaining of the "disobedience and impertinence of your eldest son," who was "doing his best to corrupt his amiable brother." John Adams promptly withdrew his children. A young American doctor, Benjamin Waterhouse, suggested that Adams send the boys to Leyden, a university town where he had just completed his medical training.

Leyden was a sacred city in America's mythos, for the Puritans who founded the Plymouth colony had left from there, having first fled from England to the more tolerant Dutch city. It was a medieval town of steeply gabled houses lining broad canals spanned by bridges. On one side of the Rapenburg Canal stood the great buildings that held the classrooms of the University of Leyden; the Rapenburg was Leyden's finest street, lined on both sides of the canal with tall trees. Johnny and Charles lived with Dr. Waterhouse on a narrow, curving street known as Langebrug, across the canal from the university. Their house lay just behind the great brick mass of the Pieterskirk, the church at which the Pilgrims had worshiped.

As soon as the canals froze, the whole city took to its skates, and in December Johnny wrote to his father asking for skates as well as breeches and boots for riding. It was, he pointed out, Christmas vacation. John Adams could be indulgent toward his eldest son, whom he had come to regard as something of a prodigy, but he would not relax the grip of instruction: you can have skates, he responded, so long as you "confine yourself to proper hours, and to strict Moderation." And he admonished the boy that skating was not simply "Velocity or Agility," but required mastery of the same principles involved with dancing and riding.

Waterhouse secured a tutor—admirably versed in the classics, Thaxter reported to John Adams—to spend two hours a day teaching the boys Latin and Greek. Johnny kept at his own studies of the Old Testament in Greek. He attended public lectures in jurisprudence and natural philosophy at the university, at that time perhaps the foremost such institution in Europe. Thanks to his father, he had gotten to know Jean de Luzac, a highly regarded classical scholar and later the university rector. He was living in an increasingly adult intellectual world. He had the scholarly Thaxter for company, as well as Waterhouse, later one of America's most prominent physicians.

Johnny heard regularly from both his parents. His father wrote to say that the boy must begin reading the Roman historians and moralists—Sallust, Tacitus, Livy, and, of course, Cicero, the model of models. Another letter proposed Demosthenes, and still another, the English poets. Abigail admonished her son to comport himself as a gentleman: "I hope, my dear boy, that the universal neatness and Cleanliness, of the people where you reside, will cure you of all your slovenly tricks." Now Abigail was writing to Charles as well, and the difference in her tone is striking. She gently chided her middle son not to let all the fuss people made over him go to his head. Charles was younger and more delicate, but also not so obviously a prodigy as Johnny.

A modern reader, scrutinizing these letters to a teenage boy living far from home, searches in vain for expressions of love or words of gentle support—from one of them, at least. And it would not be correct to say that parents of that time were unable or unwilling to open themselves emotionally to their children in that way; Elizabeth Smith Shaw, for example, was much warmer in her letters than was her older sister Abigail. John Quincy Adams might have had a much happier life, and perhaps even been a better husband and father, had one of his parents offered him unconditional love and approval. But that wasn't their way: both John and Abigail felt they could do their son no greater favor than holding him to the highest possible standards. John Quincy Adams, for better or worse, would have been the first to agree.

CHAPTER 3

As Promising and Manly a Youth as Is in the World

(1781–1785)

FOR THE FIRST THIRTEEN YEARS OF HIS LIFE, JOHN QUINCY Adams had been educated in the most direct and explicit way possible: first his mother and then his father had, in effect, opened up his head and filled it with fixed principles, stern admonitions, heroic characters, great ambitions. He had faithfully absorbed every syllable. And then, at what was still a very tender age, he was thrown into the world, and he began to profit from his own experience and observations. This premature self-reliance may account for the extraordinary certainty and assurance that would mark his later life.

In June 1781, John Adams' secretary, Francis Dana, learned that he had been appointed minister to St. Petersburg, with the goal of enlisting Russia in the American cause. Dana spoke little French, the universal language of diplomacy, and when the young man he had approached to serve as his secretary backed out, dreading the prospect of a sojourn in Siberia, Dana and John Adams agreed that Johnny would make the perfect aide.

John Quincy Adams was not yet thirteen years old. Yet he had crossed the ocean twice with perfect equanimity, mastered French, studied at Europe's greatest university, and learned to write with admirable fluency in two languages. He was a boy, but a remarkably steady and self-possessed one. His happy idyll in Leyden thus came to an abrupt end. He and Dana traveled eastward across Germany, from Cologne to Bonn to Frankfurt to Leipzig to Berlin, and then on through Poland and Latvia. Johnny made note in his diary of the quality of the roads, the soil, and the crops, just as his father would have wanted him to do. He seemed to take this epic journey very much in stride. He and Dana reached St. Petersburg on August 27, at the beginning of the Russian autumn. They took lodgings in the Hotel de Paris, an inn whose only luxury was its name.

The tsarina, Catherine, who had famously sheltered Voltaire and Diderot, was thought to be "liberal" and thus at least potentially sympathetic to the revolutionary cause. In fact, Catherine abhorred republicanism and had no intention of disturbing her relations with Great Britain by according recognition to an American minister. Though Dana, to his great credit, tried every way he could to gain access to Catherine's court, he might as well have tried to knock down the walls of the Hermitage Palace with his hands. His mission was doomed.

Johnny was at first both impressed and intrigued by his new home. He wrote to Thaxter that St. Petersburg was far superior to Paris, both for the breadth of its streets and the elegance of its private buildings. He hoped to find a tutor to continue his studies, but as Dana wrote to John Adams, "Here there are neither schools, instructors, nor books." The young man would have to educate himself. From the evidence of his letters and diaries, young Adams passed much of his fourteenth year sitting inside reading. He plowed through Hume's six-volume *History of England*, tolling off the pages of each—503, 515, 472. . . . Then he read Macaulay's three-volume history of England. He translated Cicero. He read Adam Smith. He tried to teach himself German. His father wrote, asking for details, as always: What are the houses built of? How high are they? What paintings does Russia have? And his son dutifully wrote back: brick and plaster, two to four stories . . . He wrote to Thaxter in French explaining the ingenious system by which Russians kept their houses warm.

John Quincy was a diplomat in embryo. He paid close attention to Russia's political order and described it in detail to his mother. "The Sovereign," he wrote, "is Absolute, in all the extent of the word. . . . And the nobility have the same power over the people, that the Sovereign has over them. The Nation is wholly composed of Nobles and Serfs, or in other words, of Masters and Slaves." The system, he wrote, is disadvantageous even to the sovereign, for the nobles continually rebel against absolute power. And even serfs who had grown immensely rich, he pointed out, were prepared to pay vast sums to obtain their liberty, for slavery is contemptible even when softened by wealth. This was, of course, republican orthodoxy, and Abigail wrote back with a disquisition upon tyranny, showing how the Assyrians gave way to the Persians, the Persians to the Greeks, the Greeks to the Romans. (She must have been rereading Charles Rollins.) "Yet even this mistress of the world, as she is proudly stiled, in her turn, defaced her glory, tarnished her victories, and became a prey to luxury, ambition, faction, pride, Revenge and avarice."

That first winter, the temperature fluctuated between 20 and 30 degrees below zero, and a flu epidemic kept the city coughing. Nevertheless, Dana wrote to Adams to say that his son was in "high health." Dana had undertaken to serve in loco parentis and reported that his young charge was busy translating Cicero's *Orations*. "Do you think 'tis time for him to read history," he asked, "and which shou'd you prefer?" Should he compose in French? Dana was loathe to part with his secretary and companion, but he wrote to Adams in May 1782, suggesting that the boy return to Leyden to resume his studies. Adams himself wished nothing more. He wrote to his son to report that Thaxter was going back to America, leaving him alone. John Quincy then wrote to his tutor saying he wished he could go with him, "*car je suis tout à fait* homesick." He was, after all, barely a teenager. By the fall of 1782, he could find nothing to record in his diary save the weather and the name of his dinner companion—always an adult, since he seemed to know no one of his own age. He was bored out of his mind.

John Quincy left St. Petersburg on October 30, arriving in Stockholm three weeks later. He had a delightful time in the Swedish capital, staying out at masked balls until six in the morning, playing cards, dining with diplomatic friends of his father's, paying court to attractive women. He had grown so accustomed to speaking French that he was now writing his diary in French. Though his father was urging him to come to Holland, the young man took a leisurely trip southward through Denmark and Germany. Perhaps he was hugely relieved to have escaped from his confinement in Russia. Beyond that, for the first time he was tasting the joys of adult life—with no nagging parents nearby. This was precisely what Abigail feared. But John Quincy was made of stern stuff; he made it through the courts of northern Europe without committing an indiscretion.

John Quincy reached the Hague in April 1783, but his father was then in Paris. The boy remained in Holland, studying with a new tutor, Charles William Frederick Dumas, a family friend. His father sent a volley of letters, with the usual admonitions: improve your handwriting, keep up your journal, work on your Latin and Greek, write to your family, never be too wise to ask a question. Abigail wrote complaining that her son appeared to have forgotten about her existence: "Has the cold northern region frozen up that Quick and Lively imagination which used to give such pleasure to your Friends?" (This when she thought he was still in Russia.) The fact is that he didn't write her very often, perhaps because he didn't care for the lessons in comportment; on the other hand, he wrote much less frequently to Nabby, whom he adored. Life in the great capitals of Europe was a lot busier than it was on the farm in Braintree, and between one thing and another he didn't find much time to write. But Abigail's needling finally hit home, and John Quincy wrote back to say, "I must beg your pardon for having scratch'd out of your letter the words *to be forgotten by my son*, for I could not bear to think that such an idea should ever have entered the mind of my ever honoured mamma." He was genuinely horrified at the accusation; never, throughout his life, would John Quincy Adams speak of either of his parents with anything save love and devotion.

In the fall of 1782, John Adams had joined John Jay and Benjamin Franklin in Paris to negotiate the termination of the war with Great Britain. At the end of November they had reached an agreement that doubled the size of the infant nation, guaranteed navigation on the Mississippi and fishing rights on the Grand Bank of Newfoundland, and, above all, contained the stipulation that launched America into the world: "His Britannic Majesty acknowledges the said United States . . . to be free, sovereign, and independent states." In the United States, the Treaty of Paris was deemed a tremendous victory. John Quincy Adams, who was himself to become America's leading diplomat, always held out the treaty as a standard to judge himself by—just as his father's career would be the standard by which he judged his own.

John Adams remained in Paris in the ensuing months in order to sign the final version of the agreement. He rejoined his son in the Hague in July 1783 and returned with him to Paris the following month. John Quincy was now his father's secretary and confidante. John wrote to Abigail to report, "He is grown a man in understanding and in stature as well"—though, at five foot seven, he was no taller than his father, who might have considered that quite tall enough. John Quincy had arrived just in time, for in September his father fell ill with a fever, and John Thaxter, who had been his constant companion, finally left for America. Adams' doctor advised him to move out of the city for his health.

In September, father and son removed to a grand if somewhat decayed villa in Auteuil, at the opposite end of the Bois de Boulogne from Passy, their former neighborhood. Very much the man about town, John Quincy frequented the theater, visited art collections, dined with the leading diplomats in Paris, and held long talks with the learned *abbés* he had met through his father. He also found his first true chum. John Quincy may have been a rare bird, but in Peter Jay Munro he found one of the same feather. Munro, also sixteen, was in Paris serving as the private secretary to his uncle, John Jay, a leading revolutionary and now, like John Adams, one of the tiny cadre of America's infant diplomatic service. Jay had been part of the negotiating team on the Treaty of Paris. He and Peter, his ward, lived at Franklin's home in Passy, where the Adamses had been before them. Peter Jay Munro was quite possibly the only other young man in the world whose experience of life so closely approximated John Quincy's. The two learned and worldly diplomatic aides often met at Franklin's home. They read Samuel Johnson's *Life of Pope* together. They got into scrapes, to which they referred only obliquely. "I beg you would let me know," John Quincy wrote from London, "whether your uncle or aunt know any thing about a certain foolish affair that happened once between you and me. I have my reasons for asking—tho' I hope they don't for it was a business of which we ought both to be ashamed."

The Paris idyll ended when John Adams' doctor suggested a trip to England to restore his health. In October the two traveled to Calais and boarded a ship for Dover. Neither father nor son had seen London before, though of course each had spent their lives reading about it and hearing about it. They received a private visit to Buckingham Palace; the Boston painter John Singleton Copley, who had moved to London, arranged for them to visit the House of Lords to hear King George speak at the opening of Parliament. Like any other first-time tourist, they visited the British Museum, the Tower of London, Windsor Castle, the Eton School, and the factory that made the famous Wedgwood ceramics and plate ware. Of course they went to the theater.

John Quincy had promised to give a running account to his friend Munro, whom he sometimes jocularly addressed as "Dear Moron." Soon after arriving he wrote to declare that he had just seen "that *wonderful, wonderful, wonder of wonders*, Mrs. Siddons," the brightest star of the London stage. "She out Garrick's Garrick, Sir, cent per cent." John Quincy was half-joking; he added parenthetically that while he was in England he would talk like the English. He used the letters to try out a new rakish persona that would have appalled his mother. "I go pretty often to the Plays here," he wrote, "because, if there was no other enticement, than this, you are sure to find a number of fine Women there, it would be enough for me, for a long time; every evening I went, I was in Love, with a new Object."

John Quincy was also harkening to a poetic muse that would preoccupy him, and sometimes vex him, for the rest of his life. Embarrassed about his authorship, he sent verses to Munro with the mock pretense that he had read them in a newspaper or heard them on the stage. He wrote barroom ditties and satires in the manner of Alexander Pope and even a bit of doggerel on the hot air balloon, a recent invention. But in a few of the poems, he dropped the cool pose of the flâneur and wrote about his heart, or, rather, his desire. One began:

> Oh love, thou tyrant of the breast,
> Thou hast deprived me of my rest,
> Oh thou hast changed me quite,
> I lay me down upon my bed
> Chloë comes straight into my head
> And keeps me 'wake all night.

John Quincy dropped hints about his crushes, almost certainly unrequited: "Alas! Alas! I have left her. Heaven knows when I shall see her again."

John Quincy adored London, telling Munro that it was "as much superior to Paris, in beauty and convenience, as the Sun to the Moon"—wider boulevards, sidewalks, splendid shops. But years of patriotic education had inoculated him against the bug that turned so many American visitors to London or Paris into permanent expatriates. He wrote to his cousin Elizabeth Cranch to say, perhaps hyperbolically, that he could think of no worse punishment than "to be condemned to pass my life in Europe." He wrote to a friend that "my country has over me an attractive power which I do not understand." Of course it wasn't so hard to understand, since he was traveling across England with the most ardent of patriots and receiving letters from his equally zealous mother. In one, Abigail congratulated him on the fine delineations of Russia he had made in his own letters and added, "Let your observations, and comparisons produce in your mind, an abhorrence of Dominion, and Power, the Parent of Slavery ignorance and barbarism." Behold the empires that lie in ruins.

John Adams' health was still fragile, and in December he and his son visited the resort of Bath, where his doctor had suggested he go as a restorative. While there, the elder Adams received a message from home reporting that the expenses of war had exhausted the loans he had secured in Amsterdam; America could no longer pay its bills. Adams would have to return to Holland. He was in no condition for an ice-bound passage northward, and he felt there was little chance of success. Nevertheless, as he wrote in his journal, "no man knows what he can bear until he tries," a sentiment that might have been translated into Latin in order to decorate the family coat of arms.

On January 5, father and son put out to sea in a violent squall. Blown off course, they finally made landfall on the desolate strand of a peninsula at the southern edge of Holland. The sole inhabitant they encountered informed the party that they had landed four to six miles from the nearest town, with no conveyance available for the trip. Sick, miserable, and frozen to the core, John Adams prepared himself to die. But his son bore him up, as he had on their first Atlantic crossing. "He was in fine spirits," John Adams wrote in a reminiscence many years later; "his gaiety, activity, and attention to me encreased as difficulties multiplied." The father had come to depend on the son, even as John Quincy continued to look to his father for knowledge and guidance.

The Adamses remained in Holland throughout the first half of 1784. In June, John Quincy returned to London on his own. Following his father's instructions, he attended Parliament in order to hear the great orators of the day. This, too, was part of the republican education his father continued to map out for him. John Quincy sat through an interminable eleven-hour debate over the recent election in Westminster. But he offered his father characters of each of the heroes of the House of Lords, noting of Charles James Fox that "his ideas are all striking, but they flow in upon him, in such numbers that he cannot communicate them without difficulty." Taking up the theme of public leadership, his father wrote back, "Whenever a great able and Upright man appears, there will be ever a Swarm of little, corrupt, weak or wicked ones, who will find among the people Such Numbers like themselves, as to form a body capable of obstructing, diverting and interrupting him." The older Adams got, the more he would brood over this theme; his years as president would provide the final proof that the common herd of mankind envied and even despised great men. This conviction made him sympathetic, if not to aristocracy itself, then to the rule of a natural aristocracy of the best men. His son imbibed this dim regard for the wisdom of the common people, though he was never quite as dyspeptic as his father on the subject.

The correspondence between the two Adamses had become increasingly an exchange of equals. But the older man was still very much the lawgiver. He instructed his son to continue with his translations into French of Suetonius' *Lives of the Twelve Caesars*, a 462-page project he would complete that summer. He asked him to return to Holland so that they could learn Dutch together. And he offered his usual steady stream of advice: "Don't fatigue yourself in traveling. Keep your mind easy and your body cool, your spirits cheerful and your humour gay." Few men, he reminded him, had suffered as many vexations as he, and he had done his best to hew to his own maxims, though not always successfully. He was, at the same time, immensely proud of his son. He described John Quincy to Abigail as "the greatest traveller of his age, and without partiality, I think as promising and manly a youth as is in the world."

John Quincy rejoined his father in the Hague at the end of June. But soon he found himself hurrying back to England. For the last year, John Adams had been imploring Abigail to join him. The prospect of an ocean voyage terrified her, and much though she missed he husband, Abigail had grown quite accustomed to her vicarious roving through the instrument of books and menfolk. But she finally consented to come and to bring Nabby with her. On July 30, 1784, in a London hotel, John Quincy was reunited with his mother and sister after an absence of four years. All three of them must have shed many tears. Abigail and Nabby were much taken with John Quincy's manliness and gravity. He had become, after all, a rather formidable young man. And he was handsome, with dark, shining eyes, a delicate mouth, and his mother's narrow, finely tipped nose.

Within weeks John Adams was summoned to Paris to negotiate treaties with France. The family arrived in mid-August and moved back to the villa in Auteuil. Whatever London's superior virtues, it was Paris where John Quincy felt most at home. Paris had formed his taste and his manners. He haunted the Palais Royal, which the Duc de Chartres, cousin to Louis XVI, had begun to turn into a center of leisure and pleasure—a kind of proto-Times Square. "This place offers a vast fund of entertainment to the observor," Adams wrote in his journal. "It is the most frequented walk in Paris at every hour of the day, and of the night too, you will never fail of finding company here, and it is very curious to see the different dresses and appearance of the people you find there." He marveled at the Raphaels, Rembrandts, and Rubenses in the Duc's gallery. (The Louvre, across the way, would not open for another eight years.) He indulged his love of theater both at the Comédie Française and the Théâtre des Variétés, a hastily improvised stage that specialized in knockabout farce. He was shocked that Racine and Corneille showed to empty houses, while "low buffoonery" packed the stalls. He ogled the dresses in the shop of Mademoiselle Bertin, the queen's milliner. Here was a petticoat that cost a thousand guineas. Naval heroes' reputations last months, he mused with the polished cynicism of a Paris courtier; Mademoiselle Bertin's is imperishable. The French Revolution was only four years away, but King Louis XVI sat securely on his throne. Paris was a world of glittering trifles John Quincy deplored and loved to deplore. He was a precocious moralist.

The great friend of this period of his life was Thomas Jefferson. The author of the Declaration of Independence had been sent to Paris to succeed Benjamin Franklin. Jefferson had suffered the shattering loss of his wife, Martha, as well as two of his children, and had come to Paris with his daughter, Patsy. He happily allowed himself to be adopted by the bustling, cheerful, embracing Adams family. He paid elaborate, if always proper, court to Abigail; worked daily with John; and became a mentor to young John Quincy, who hero-worshiped him. Jefferson had taken a modest house with a garden among the grand *hotels de ville* in the Cul-de-Sac Taitbout, just off the Chaussée D'Antin in the fashionable heart of Paris. John Quincy dined there almost every night, often in the company of luminaries like the Marquis de Lafayette or the naval hero John Paul Jones. In his diary he wrote of Jefferson "whom I love to be with because he is a man of very extensive learning and pleasing manners." Young Adams was already so well connected that he could arrange to introduce Jefferson and the marquis to his friend Benjamin West, the celebrated portraitist.

When he wasn't amusing himself, John Quincy was working as his father's secretary. The two began each morning with a long walk through the Bois before settling down to business with Jefferson and Franklin. At night, when the young man was home, they worked together, with the father helping the son prepare for Harvard. The elder Adams had contemplated enrolling his son at Oxford but had dropped the idea when he had learned that matriculants had to subscribe to the Thirty-Nine Articles of the Church of England. The very first article, "Of Faith in the Holy Trinity," violated Adams' own Unitarian convictions.

It was, therefore, admission to Harvard for which John Adams set out to prepare his son. They read Greek and Latin together. They worked their way through algebra, plane geometry, decimal fractions, and even, the older man proudly reported in a letter to Benjamin Waterhouse, differential calculus, which he barely recalled from his own college days. Ordinary folk might sit by the fireside making goodly conversation; for the Adamses, supreme contentment required books and abstruse talk. Abigail evoked the scene in a letter to a friend: "The table is covered with mathematical instruments, and you hear nothing 'til nine o'clock but of theorem and problems bissecting and dissecting tangents and sequents."

John Adams, though as intellectually gifted as any of the leading figures of a remarkably gifted generation, was quite dazzled by his son's intellect—not that he would risk turning his head by telling him so. "If you were to examine him in English and French poetry," he told Waterhouse, "I know not where you would find anybody his superior." He had translated vast passages from Virgil, Tacitus, Horace, Tully. Peter Jay Munro had written to him repeating the commonplace opinion that Virgil's *Aeneid* was much the superior work to Milton's *Paradise Lost*, and John Quincy used a series of letters to argue him into the ground on the subject. Rather than simply excerpt passages and insist upon their excellence, which might only have demonstrated his partiality, he cited a staggering array of English authorities on the merits of Milton's poem—Addison, Dryden, Hume, the poet Thomson, and even Samuel Johnson, notorious for having written of *Paradise Lost* that "no man would have wished it longer." And he sagely added a bit of advice—"never to decide a thing in your own mind upon hearsay alone but to examine things yourself and judge for yourself."

These, then, were the forces that shaped the life of this brilliant young cosmopolite. John Quincy Adams knew Europe and Europeans as few other Americans did, and perhaps none of his generation. He knew art, literature, theater, politics. He could comfortably converse with the most learned of men. He had sampled the pleasures—most of them—of European life. But he had also been trained from earliest childhood to believe that life was not about pleasure but about service and that it was the special destiny of an Adams to serve not just God, and not just the family, but the republic his father had helped usher into being. He had one foot in the European world that had nurtured him and another in the New England world to which he was returning. He wrote an epigram from Voltaire on the cover of his diary for 1785: "*La molesse est douce, mais la suite est cruelle*"—ease is delightful, but the consequence is cruel. The young man who swooned over Mrs. Siddons and traded jaded quips about dressmakers might well have become a dandy, but Adams' foundations had been laid so solidly that no amount of frivolity could unsettle them.

For all that, he heaved a sigh of relief when he learned in April that his father was to be appointed minister to London, because of course he would have to stay. To return to America, to train for the law, would mean long years and donkey labor before he had distinguished himself. A new strain of self-reflection permeated his diary. Starting on his new life, he wrote, was "a prospect somewhat discouraging for a youth of my ambition; for I have ambition, though I hope its object is laudable." On the other hand, what laudable ambitions could he satisfy in London or Paris? He could not give way to *molese*. In the very same diary entry he wrote, "I am determined that so long as I am able to get my own living in an honourable manner, I will depend on no one." Better to die than to live as a dependent. So he must return home, he must go to Harvard, he must study law, as his father wished. John Quincy Adams would not question the stars; he always accepted, perhaps all too readily, the tyranny of "must." In mid-May he boarded a carriage for the Breton seaport of L'Orient, "with such feelings as no one that has not been separated from persons so dear can conceive." Two weeks later, accompanying seven hunting dogs he was to deliver to George Washington as a gift from the Marquis de Lafayette, he set sail for New York.

CHAPTER 4

You Are Admitted, Adams

(1785–1788)

BETWEEN THE AGES OF TWELVE AND SEVENTEEN, JOHN QUINCY Adams had lived the life of a prince in a fairy tale. Now the romance had come to an end, and he had been deposited back home to live with his own people and to find his level among them. He was excited and frightened by the prospect in equal measure. He had brought with him from Europe a rather lofty idea of himself and his standing, but his self-image would take a battering in the new world of his peers. Adams would be a less self-confident man at twenty-two than he had been when he arrived in New York at eighteen.

The America to which Adams returned in the summer of 1785 was, of course, an independent nation; New York was the seat of its government. And the young man belonged to one of the first families of the new nation. On his second morning in town he breakfasted with Richard Henry Lee, the president of the Confederation Congress. Lee insisted that Adams stay at his home while the young man was in New York. He met with the Massachusetts delegation to Congress and dined with the Virginia delegation. John Adams had had to bull his way into the realm of public affairs by sheer force of talent and ambition; his son was welcomed there as by right. He would struggle against a status he felt he had not earned.

Adams had crossed the Atlantic with Jacques Le Ray de Chaumont, the son of his former host at the Hotel Valentinois in Passy, who was going to visit a family farm near Albany. Chaumont suggested they travel northward by horse rather than stage or ship. Adams thought this would be a fine way "to form some opinion of the country, and to make some acquaintance which may be of use hereafter." He bought a horse, and the two young men set off for New England, speaking French. He was struck, as so many Europeans were, by the American character. Even fifty miles from New York he noticed "bluntness, and an assurance" he hadn't found in the more aristocratic capital city. He was appalled by the provincialism of townsfolk who knew nothing of the world ten miles away, and was shocked to find a woman of low standing—a woman whose like no gentleman in Holland would consent to be seen with—in "the best Company in the city." Young Adams was a parvenu in his own country.

John Quincy reached Boston on August 25 and then proceeded on to Braintree. Whatever doubts he still felt about the decision to leave Europe, he was overwhelmed with emotion at his return home after an absence of six years. He went first to the home of the Cranches: Abigail's sister Mary; her husband, Richard; and their two daughters, Lucy and Betsy. They stared at one another, so overcome that at first none of them was able to speak. He stopped off at his parents' home, now deserted. He couldn't bear to stay or even to describe his feelings in his journal. Yet life had warped him out of the provincial orbit of Braintree. The Cranches were mightily impressed, and slightly terrified, by the world traveller in their midst. Mary wrote to Abigail to say, "he enters into characters with a penetration that astonishes me. If I had anything in my disposition that I wish'd to hide, I would not be acquainted with him. He is formed for a Statesman." She could, she said, get nothing done when John Quincy was in the room, since she stared and stared, seeing first his mother, then his father, in his countenance.

The time had come for John Quincy to arrange his future. He rode back to Cambridge to meet with President Joseph Willard of Harvard and secure his enrollment. He had always been considered an exceptionally erudite young man, as indeed he was, but President Willard, a stickler's stickler, found his Greek rather scanty—as in fact it was—and suggested he find a tutor and return in March to be examined for admission in the spring semester. From Harvard's point of view, Adams was not ahead of his peers, as he had supposed, but behind them. This was a stinging blow to an ego that, until then, had received a good deal of gratification. It appeared that his merits were not quite so self-evident in America as they had been in Europe. The young scholar was sent to study under his other uncle, the

Reverend John Shaw, in Haverhill. He traveled there, about forty miles to the north, the following week.

The Haverhill of 1785 was a much livelier place than Braintree, then little more than a crossroads with outlying farms. Haverhill was the county seat and commercial capital of Essex County, near the current border with New Hampshire. Situated on the Merrimack River, Haverhill was a mill town and manufacturing center, with a prosperous class of merchants who could afford to keep the Reverend Shaw in a fine parsonage house. At "Assembly" every two weeks the citizens would gather for talk and dancing, and young people could socialize at parties held at a rotating series of homes.

Before he left England, John Quincy had struck a bargain with Nabby that each would send the other letters with their doings, as well as their innermost thoughts. Whether because Nabby had no interest in his bookish flights or because he was quickening to life in his new setting, John Quincy wrote with little of the sententiousness that had given his missives from Europe such precocious gravity. He told his sister whom he had dined with, whom he had met, who was rumored to have a fancy for whom, who was getting married. Mostly he wrote about girls. Haverhill was filled with alluring young women. The boys and girls would go dancing and sleigh-riding—for now winter had arrived—and shyly show their poems to one another. Peggy White asked the young swain to write something in her "Poetry Book," and he quickly produced a quatrain invoking the Muse "to sing your praises as the Poets use."

At the same time, Adams really did buckle down. Until now, his haphazard studies had been left largely to his own taste and that of his tutors. But the habits his father had drilled into him had made hard work second nature, while his mother's perpetual evangelizing on the virtues of self-mastery had made the young man proof against distraction—as least as proof as a young man could be.

The Shaws were delighted to have the young scholar board with them. Elizabeth raved about his modesty, his perfect manners, his genius, and his uncanny resemblance to his father. Elizabeth was not only a deeply reflective but also a very gentle soul, and she came to find her supremely worldly nephew rather intimidating: he appeared to harbor a dim view of almost everything and everyone. In a letter to Nabby, Elizabeth declared that John Quincy was "exceedingly severe upon the foibles of Mankind," and particularly upon those he felt were "degrading, and debasing themselves beneath the Rank, which the God of Nature assigned them, in the Scale of Being."

Apparently the young man still had more of the European courtier in him than the American republican.

In a later letter to Abigail, as he was leaving for Harvard, Elizabeth sounded a note of grief at his departure, but added that the young man "was rather peculiar in some of his opinions, and a little too decisive, and tenacious of them." This may have been a reference to an argument that broke out when he insisted to the Reverend Shaw, with an undergraduate's scorn for pious convention, that "Self was the ultimate motive of all actions, good, bad, or indifferent." Adams admitted in his diary that his vehemence "has made persons suppose that I was obstinate and dogmatickal." He vowed to "think more upon the subject." Over the years, he would think about this a great deal without becoming a jot less vehement.

There was more than a little bit of intellectual vanity in this insistence on arguing his elders into submission. And Adams had a temper: He could be cool and correct in his manners but passionate in dispute. His father was thought obstinate and pedantic, and in this, as in so much else, he was his father's son. The young man had a lofty opinion not so much of himself as of the standards, moral and intellectual, to which people should be held, and he found much of the world wanting. And unlike his father, he was especially harsh on the female sex, whom he found, in general, silly and vain. Nabby felt that she had to rebuke him from London: "A Gentleman, who is very severe against the ladies, is also upon every principle very impolitick. His Character is soon established, for a Morose severe ill-natured fellow." And she reminded him that young women were not to blame for their haphazard education. Adams knew that, but he couldn't help comparing the educated and worldly young women he knew in Europe to the chatterboxes he met in Haverhill. A more playful man might have been more tolerant of frivolity, but Adams wasn't very playful at heart. "Most of our damsels are like portraits in crayon," he wrote in his diary, "which at a distance look well, but if you approach near them, are vile daubings."

ON MARCH 15, 1786, JOHN QUINCY ADAMS SUBMITTED TO AN examination by President Willard and the rest of the Harvard faculty—four tutors, three professors, and the librarian. Adams was asked to construe three stanzas from Horace and a passage from the *Iliad*, then quizzed on the works of Locke, on Euclid, and on geography. President Willard asked him to translate several English sentences into Latin. The president then disappeared for fifteen minutes, returned and said, "You are admitted, Adams." This was Adams' first exposure to the bizarre rules the humorless Willard had imposed on the college. Undergraduates could be addressed only by their surname; the use of "Mister," much less a given name, was a punishable infraction. So was walking in the yard with a hat, save in inclement weather. President Willard did agree to waive the young man's tuition in recognition of his father's public service (and perhaps also his scant income as a diplomat).

The Harvard of 1786 was not a terribly impressive place, at least compared to a great university like the one Adams had attended at Leyden. The only important scholar, John Winthrop, a professor of natural philosophy whom John Adams had greatly admired, had retired in 1779. The school was otherwise much as it had been in the elder Adams' day, or indeed in 1720. Two buildings, Harvard Hall and Massachusetts Hall, fronted on the street. (The wall that now separates the campus from the town had not yet been built.) Two other buildings, Holden Chapel and Hollis Hall, sat farther back in the yard, which otherwise consisted of scattered trees and several rickety outbuildings. Each of the four classes had forty to fifty students. Undergraduates wore a uniform of blue-gray coat, waistcoat, and breeches. (Trousers of olive, black, or nankeen—a pale yellowish cloth—were also permitted.) Sophomores wore buttons on their cuffs, and freshmen did not. Students' daily life was largely regulated by the tutors, most of them recent graduates of the college who had imbibed the spirit of contempt for the undergraduate from their own tutors. These martinets, as one historian later put it, "regarded the undergraduates as inmates in a reformatory."

And yet within a few weeks Adams knew that he had been right to leave Europe for Harvard. The Cranches had helped him move a few sticks of furniture from Braintree to Cambridge; cousin Lucy had taken him shopping for a few additional items. Adams liked his roommate and their digs on the third floor of Hollis; he liked his classes, and he loved the fellowship of his classmates. The one thing this privileged young man had never had was peers. He was good at befriending strangers; he had been doing it for most of his life. Within a few weeks he was able to write to his father that he had gotten to know every one of his classmates and complained that the separation among the four classes was so rigid that he had found it almost impossible to meet students above or below him. (His father wrote back in his typical vein of arduous self-improvement: "Find out who are the best scholars and drop in upon them frankly. Observe what books lie upon their tables.") He joined social clubs, including the A.B. Club, where he read essays, and Phi Beta Kappa, which at the time had an elaborate initiation rite and a secret handshake. Later he would join the Greek Club, the Music Sodality, and the Society, which held dances. He taught himself to play the flute.

No one in Adams' class, and possibly no one in his generation, had been exposed to the great world of Europe as he had been. He had mingled with royalty, great thinkers, and beautiful women; he spoke perfect French. And his father was one of the nation's most renowned figures. But Harvard didn't care. Adams was not rich, and he did not carry a great name, like Hancock. He was very smart and very well-read, but so were several of his classmates. He was not a leader of his class; when it came time to elect a president and vice president, he was not chosen (though, to be fair, he was a newcomer). That was fine with him; he was seeking fellowship, not social distinction. He was a young man of average height, indifferent in his dress and grooming, sometimes overbearing in argument but otherwise even-tempered, serious in his conversation but alive to foibles and absurdities, a good listener who held his tongue more than was normal for a young man with a deep fund of conversation. He was happy just to be accepted as part of the group.

Adams spent his free time doing what students do—sitting around and talking. He deeply admired several of his classmates, liked most, and despised a few. He set himself the task of producing character sketches of them—all forty-six, produced in alphabetical order over a period of months, listing the birth date and home of each. Few of them escaped unscathed from Adams' harsh judgment. Of James Sever, whose family, like Adams', would later give its name to a Harvard building, he wrote, "His genius is very good, but he is devoid of all moral principles."

Despite President Willard's elaborate body of rules, the undergraduates embarked on regular rampages. The sophomore class was notoriously rowdy. A few days after Adams had settled in, a group of them got drunk and smashed the tutors' windows. Harrison Gray Otis, a contemporary and long-time friend of Adams and of the Adams family, was then a senior and describes being constantly fined for disorderly behavior, including playing ball and drinking on the Sabbath. Adams was no prude, and he enjoyed the bottle as much as his friends did, but his ingrained respect for rules kept him to the straight and narrow. The only thing he appears ever to have been fined for was oversleeping and arriving late for six A.M. prayers. He was, on the other hand, exceptionally slovenly, even for a college student. At the end of his first semester, his aunts, uncles, and cousins paid him and Charles, then a freshman, a visit in their rooms. While Charles was quite neat, John Quincy was covered with "*learned dirt*," as his cousin Betsy Cranch put it. They removed his filthy gown in favor of a clean one, and, Betsy reported to Abigail, "I took my Scissors and put his Nails into a decent form."

The bulk of the day was taken up with public lectures and classes led by tutors, known as "recitations." Then as now, students often did their homework secretly during lectures while the professor droned on. Adams attended lectures in Greek, in divinity, in Locke—his metaphysics rather than his politics—and in experimental philosophy. He was especially fascinated by this last class, which focused on optics, astronomy, and physics. Harvard had a modest assemblage of scientific instruments in the Philosophy Cabinet upstairs in Harvard Hall—along with collections of stuffed birds and preserved fish—and at times Mr. Williams, the professor of experimental philosophy, permitted his students to look through a microscope, or a camera obscura, causing a stampede of excitement.

The academic feature Adams most enjoyed was debate, known as forensics. The debates were often held in Holden Chapel, which could accommodate the whole undergraduate body of 160. It was the ideal training ground for a future legislator and public orator. If Adams took a part, he would copy his entire argument into his journal—the closest thing we have to his college papers. He took himself too seriously to relish arguing against his own convictions and was always relieved when he was assigned the side that coincided with his views. He was gratified to be given the affirmative on the question, "Whether the immortality of the human soul be probable from natural Reason."

Adams' argument is lucid and occasionally ingenious, if recognizably undergraduate. "Man," he said, possesses a body as animals do and is thus susceptible to bodily ills, as animals are. Only his reason distinguishes him from the beasts. "It is therefore natural to conclude," he asserted, "that the factor which we alone possess . . . is totally independent of the body. And if so, I know of no reason to suppose that it began with the body, or that it will end with it." Adams had the intellectual honesty to pose a serious counter to his own claim. If, he posited, we suppose that reason is not an intrinsic human attribute but rather extends in an infinite gradation from Newton to insects, must we not grant an immortal soul to the beasts? It was, he conceded, hard to "distinguish aright."

After a delightful spring semester, Adams returned to Braintree to spend the summer reading and tramping around the farm.

BY THE TIME JOHN QUINCY ADAMS HAD RETURNED HOME, THE common enemy that had united the colonies was long gone, and divisions of class and geography among Americans had begun, inevitably, to surface. The late summer and fall of 1786 proved to be a period of turmoil and social disorder, above all in New England. A serious recession led to both rising unemployment and a credit squeeze. Merchants who could no longer pay off their debts called in loans they had made, setting off a cascade of credit demands that ended with farmers who had financed purchases through debt. With commodity prices depressed, many farmers found themselves insolvent; creditors took them to court. Some farmers were thrown off their land; others were jailed. Farmers and artisans began to petition state legislatures to loosen credit by issuing paper money. Most states refused, and protestors, especially in Massachusetts, thronged around courthouses to prevent cases from going forward.

In late August, 1,500 farmers blocked the Court of Common Pleas in Northampton, and then moved on to Worcester, Taunton, Concord, and Great Barrington. In several cases, militia conscripts refused a direct order from Governor Nathaniel Bowdoin to disperse the protestors. The populist insurgency, know as Shays' Rebellion, seemed to threaten the legitimacy of government itself, and turned even the most fiery revolutionaries into defenders of the established order. Samuel Adams, hero of the Boston Tea Party, helped sponsor the Riot Act, which authorized the suspension of habeas corpus.

Harvard knew very well where it stood in a battle between merchants and farmers with pitchforks. Harrison Gray Otis recruited a light infantry from among his friends to be put at the disposal of the governor. John Quincy Adams had no fortune to protect and no intention of joining a militia, but in this, the first serious political conflict of his adult life, he immediately arrayed himself with the forces of duly constituted order. He had no sympathy for the protestors' complaints. "Citizens," he wrote in his journal, "must look to themselves, their idleness, their dissipation and extravagance, for their grievances."

To Adams, the Shaysites were not a democratic force but an insurrectionary one; unchecked, the protest would lead to anarchy and civil war. Order must be protected from popular passion. In a forensic over the question of equality, he took the view that the laws could offer no protection if every citizen felt free to change them. Government must be entrusted to those who understood best how to govern—a sentiment difficult to square with the American faith that all are created equal. "In arguing against equality," he acknowledged, "I am combating against the sentiments of perhaps a large majority of the inhabitants of this Commonwealth." But nature itself had created inequality among men, and it was not for anyone to seek to make it otherwise.

This conservatism, which feared the mob more than those who ruled them, was very much the Adams family credo. When the news of Shays' Rebellion reached London, in November, Abigail wrote to say that "a popular Tyranny never fails to be followed by the arbitrary government of a Single person." She reported that her husband was working on a new treatise on "the different forms of government, both ancient and modern." This was to become *A Defense of the Constitutions of Government of the United States of America*, a massive tract that constituted Adams' chief contribution to the debate over the organization of government in the new nation. Adams argued, then and later, that a republic could not preserve people's liberties without a strong executive, independent from the legislature. "The people," he wrote, "can be as tyrannical as any king." In fact, he told Abigail, he would be perfectly happy to establish a constitutional monarchy, so long as it was constrained by the legislature and the judiciary. John Adams viewed the utopian optimism about the American people that resounded through the works of Thomas Paine—and Thomas Jefferson—as dangerous fantasy. Shays' Rebellion turned what had been an abstract question of political philosophy into an urgent matter on which men took sides. And John Quincy Adams, an acorn from the family oak, could scarcely have differed from his father on this great question.

The rebellion burned through New England in the last months of 1786. The rioters organized into regiments, hoping to overthrow the state government. In late November, rumors spread through Harvard that 1,500 Shaysites had gathered four miles from Cambridge, prepared to march on the town. For months, Adams wrote, no one spoke of anything else: the American experiment in self-government seemed to be in danger of collapsing from within. In January the Shaysites launched an attack on the Springfield armory, only to be repulsed by cannon fire and grapeshot. Several weeks later, Governor Bowdoin was authorized to declare martial law and to wipe out the rebels. By June, the first domestic insurgency in American history had been crushed. And John Quincy Adams had come down forcefully on the side of the state's right to enforce its authority—its legitimate authority—in the face of a popular uprising.

Adams had never been happier than he was at Harvard. He was no longer a hybrid creature, half-European, half-American. And he was staying in one place. For the first time, he had been able to make dear friends. He had been reunited with his brothers, Tom and Charles, and took very much to heart his parents' admonitions that he watch over them. He sought to prepare Tom for Harvard with the same sentiments he had heard from his own father: "I could wish you to be upon good terms with all your classmates, but intimate with few, endeavour to have no Enemies, and you can have but few real friends." Never permit popularity to overcome the dictates of your conscience, study six hours a day, and, all in all, ensure that "both your moral and your Literary character be set as an example for your own classmates, and the succeeding classes to imitate." At age nineteen, this moralistic and unironic language came quite naturally to Adams.

As the spring semester wound to a close, and graduation loomed, Adams was assailed by fears about his future and gloom about his coming departure. "It is not without many melancholy reflections that I bid a last adieu to the walls of Harvard," he wrote in his journal. "I have never once regretted but I have frequently rejoiced that I left Europe to pass a twelvemonth here." Harvard, he wrote, "has been productive of good effects, particularly in reducing my opinion of myself." He had entered Harvard as the Adams family prodigy and emerged as just another bright young man hoping to make his way in the world. He understood that life would not be easy. That, in fact, was what worried him and haunted his last days at school. He didn't want to study law, but how else could he earn a living? There was no family business to enter and certainly no family fortune to batten upon. And his father had decreed that the Adams boys would be lawyers.

What, then, was next? Both the Reverend Shaw and Cotton Tufts, the family lawyer, suggested Adams read law under Theophilus Parsons, a scholarly attorney in the town of Newburyport who had served with John Adams in the convention that wrote the Massachusetts state constitution in 1780. In late June, it was agreed that Adams would spend the next two years of his life studying for the law with Parsons. It felt to the young man like a prison sentence. On July 11, his twenty-first birthday, he wrote, in a tone of self-flagellation that would become increasingly common, "I am good for nothing. Three long years I have yet to study in order to qualify for business, and then!—oh, and then, how many years am I to plod along mechanically, if I should live, before I shall really get into the world?" For Adams, as for so many recent graduates before and since, leaving college felt like being expelled from Eden.

The Harvard commencement of the day was an elaborate public ritual in which students were expected to demonstrate their mastery through performance, including orations in Latin, Greek, Hebrew, and English; forensics; and syllogisms, an exercise assigned to the academic also-rans. Adams' graduating class had spent months deliberating on the all-important parceling out of these assignments. Adams had graduated second in the class; as one of the intellectual stars he was assigned to deliver an English oration. His topic would be "the necessity of public faith to the well-being of a community." This was a distinction, and a performance, that mattered a great deal to him.

Commencement was held July 18. A procession formed up at eleven A.M. at the door of Harvard Hall. First came last year's graduating class, then President Willard, then the Harvard Corporation, the Governor, and the Overseers, which then meant the Commonwealth legislature. The participants proceeded to the Cambridge meetinghouse, where they were met by a company of light horse. It was in Adams' nature to overprepare; he had spent long hours honing his oration. His theme was the stark contrast between the "austere republican virtues" of the revolutionary generation and the "selfish and contracted principles" now in ascendancy. The fear of being corrupted by luxury—as, it was believed, England had been—was a common New England theme of the day. This was also the way older men talked about the younger generation, and young though he was, Adams was very much inclined to cry, "*o tempora, o mores.*"

Adams called for moral regeneration—"a rekindling of the patriotic spark." He expressed sublime hopes for the nation's future. This young man who had been raised on the heroic siege at Bunker Hill and the epic debate at the Continental Congress expressed a poignant sense of living in the aftermath of greatness. "Nature," he told his classmates, "has not formed you, it is true, to tread the rugged path of an active life. But yours is the nobler influence of the mind. . . . When the warrior returns from the field of battle with the laurel in his hand, 'tis yours to twine it round his head." This sounds very much like what today we would call "greatest generation syndrome." For Adams, it was intensely personal. How could he ever live up to the glory of his own father, or of the likes of George Washington? Only through the nobler influence of the mind.

Adams worried that he would be outshone by his friend Nathaniel Freeman, who was delivering the other English oration. The family consensus—for of course the Shaws and the Cranches came to commencement and threw him a party afterwards—was that while Freeman was the more elegant and had the more musical voice, Adams had more of pith. Both his aunts were struck by how vividly, and transparently, Adams' emotions expressed themselves on his face—a sign not of artfulness but of intensity of feeling. His address was deemed important enough to be reprinted in a leading Philadelphia newspaper. He was, he conceded, "complimented and flattered on every side." It was a last burst of ego gratification before years of legal drudgery.

CHAPTER 5

Friend of the People

(1788–1794)

T HE NEWBURYPORT TO WHICH JOHN QUINCY ADAMS TRANS-
planted himself in early September of 1788 was a city of five thousand or so, a thriving port and manufacturing center located on the
south bank of the Merrimack a few miles from the ocean. The city sloped
steeply downward from the High Street to the river, where a great commercial
armada of fishing smacks and whaling ships lay at anchor. Schooners from the
world's great port cities disgorged fine textiles and wine and gunpowder as well
as sugar and molasses from the West Indies. The broad avenues running down
from the High Street were lined with the fine homes, of brick as well as wood-
frame, owned by the town's shipbuilders and merchants. Newburyport was a
provincial town but a busy and prosperous one, with a multitude of contract
and other work for lawyers like Theophilus Parsons.

In his first months in town, John Quincy Adams barely had time to
look up from the deadening mass of legal texts he was obliged to master—
William Blackstone's four-volume *Commentaries* surveying English law, Sir
Edward Coke's *Institutes of the Laws of England*, Sir Michael Foster's *Crown
Law*, and the like. Fortunately for Adams, Theophilus Parsons was an unusually erudite attorney, a serious dabbler in botany, chemistry, astronomy,
and mathematics, as well as a master of the classics. He assigned his charges
works of history and ethics in order to ward off the "universal skepticism"
that comes of "defending indiscriminately the good and the bad."

Most days, Adams would arrive at Parsons' law office at nine, chat with his fellow law clerks, read until lunch time, and then read again until dark. At times this wearying round would be interrupted when Parsons would call the clerks together to discuss a case then in the courts. Parson was "himself a law library," Adams wrote, with a genius for legal disputation. Adams' happiest moments came when the clerks, some of them former Harvard classmates, sat up at night talking about history, poetry, religion, and politics. For a moment, he could imagine he was back at Hollis Hall. But then Blackstone would beckon once again.

Throughout this period, for reasons mysterious to himself, Adams was sinking into a very dark depression. He first recorded this affliction in December 1787, the very same night when he had stayed up with his friends talking about life. "I felt a depression of spirits to which I have hitherto been entirely a stranger," he wrote. He lay awake for hours and then suffered from strange and troubling dreams. The experience may not, in fact, have been entirely novel, for several months later he would write to Billy Cranch that the feeling was "similar to what affected me about two years since." Adams felt overcome with despair about his future; he saw nothing before him but an awful nullity. He filled his diary with his most abject thoughts and feelings. "If I continue this trifling away my time, I shall become an object of charity, if not of pity." "Indolency I fear will be my ruin." "I have no fortune to expect from any part, and the profession is so much crowded, that I have no prospect of securing myself by it for several years after I begin."

Though John Adams, too, had suffered from what he called "the blue devils," he had never been paralyzed as his son now was. A self-made man, John Adams had been the agent of his own success and the author of his own ambition. The situation with his son was almost the opposite. John Quincy had known since the earliest childhood that he had a destiny to fulfill. It was not for him to choose a path through life. And since he had been given everything he needed to succeed, failure would be unforgiveable. Worse still, should he fall short, he would be failing not himself, but his parents, his nation, his Christian obligations. Is it any wonder that, with youth and college behind him, and the future for which he had long been prepared before him, he gave way to despair? On the contrary: the wonder is that he didn't buckle altogether beneath the weight of expectations. His brothers would do so, as would, in turn, his own sons. Unlike them, John Quincy was able to summon the will to become the person his parents had told him that he must be.

John and Abigail Adams had returned home after their years in England in June 1788. John Quincy had joyfully ridden to see them at their new house, known after its former owners as "the Vassall-Borland place," about a mile and a half from the ancestral farm. He helped his parents unpack and then rode back to Newburyport. He returned home again in early September in order to deliver an address before the Phi Beta Kappa Society at Harvard, an early sign that he was being singled out for special distinction. These orations attracted the leading political and intellectual figures of the day. Governor John Hancock attended Adams' talk, as did John and Abigail. His topic: the prospects before "a youth about to enter the scenes of active life."

Adams never referred to his own prospects, but the address was transparently personal. The young man contemplating career shuttles between a "fantastic dream" of fame and glory and a nightmare of mediocrity. At times he will feel that the obstacles he faces are so intractable that he will be "almost ready to settle into a state of fallen despondency." The prudent young man will therefore "circumscribe" his wishes "within rational bounds," selecting one of the "intermediate stations" of law, medicine, trade, or ministry in which he can be useful to his fellow man. Perhaps Adams was rationalizing his growing fear that he would never achieve his father's greatness. In his commencement address, after all, he had said that it was not for his generation to earn the laurels of heroism.

Yet there was, Adams went on, one exception to the middling destiny: "the walks of Literature & Science," which offer the possibility of great achievement in the service of humane ends. Here, too, lay the opportunity for the rising generation to demonstrate its patriotism, for America's modest attainments in these arts had led many mocking Europeans to "assign us a station among the inferior animals of creation." How often the young Adams must have seethed at that condescension. But for an American of Adams' day, scholarship was not a profession but an avocation. What's more, Adams concluded, in an "infant country" such as the United States, men must enter the "active professions." The life of the mind could serve only as a "secondary object"—a hobby. So it would remain for the rest of Adams' life.

Adams returned to Newburyport, but his depression immediately rendered him unable to work or sleep. Desperate to recover his health, he went not to Braintree, but to Aunt Elizabeth Shaw in Haverhill. Elizabeth knew how this would look, and she wrote to Abigail to say that John Quincy hadn't gone to Braintree only because "it was too far—& if he can get what he wants, (a little kind attention) nearer, it would not be worth his while." But she added that the young man hadn't been well since he left Braintree and asked, perhaps only half-jokingly, what Abigail had done to him. Elizabeth knew no more how to cure depression than her sister did—she gave him valerian tea and quinine—but Adams rallied. He overcame his insomnia and began to feel calmer. Elizabeth reported, "He thinks he is half Curred because he has got somebody to care for him."

Perhaps Adams did go to Haverhill because it was closer. But he may have needed a place where he didn't have to be John Quincy Adams, future leader of the Republic. Elizabeth Shaw doted on all of the Adams boys and admired John Quincy almost without reservation. When he had first arrived on her doorstep, in September 1785, Elizabeth had barely been able to contain her joy. In his looks, and even in his gestures, she said in a letter to Abigail, the boy reminded her of his father, before he "had assumed the Austerity, and dignity of the Statesman, and the Republican." (Others noticed that he laid his head against his shoulder and closed one eye just as his father did.) John Quincy could talk to Aunt Elizabeth about anything—even about the girls he liked, a topic that came with solemn assurances that his experience of womanhood in Europe had taught him to curb his passions. Elizabeth believed that her talented nephew had worried himself sick. She wrote Abigail that he was "so avaritious in coveting the best Gifts" that he had injured his health through study. Lucy Cranch, John Quincy's cousin, made the same observation in her own letter to Abigail: "He is determined to be *great* in *every particular*." The ambition his parents had instilled in him was eating him up.

Adams returned to Newburyport in the fall of 1788 but found that he was no better. In mid-October, he wrote in his diary that "I think I am on a way to recover this evening"—and then he stopped writing anything at all. His journal, which he had kept with very few breaks from the age of twelve, does not pick up again for almost a year, though he did scribble one-line lists of his daily activities in an almanac. He wrote few letters. Perhaps he could find nothing to record that did not make him feel worse. He spent the first several months of this period back in Braintree. Only by late March, six months after he had first been felled by his disorder, did he feel that his health was sufficiently restored for him to return to his studies. Over time Adams' most debilitating symptoms of depression would subside, while the self-accusation, the expectation of bad endings, would prove almost impervious to contrary experience. He would, after all, succeed greatly. But John Quincy Adams was not fashioned to be happy.

NEWBURYPORT WAS, IN FACT, AN EXCELLENT PLACE FOR THE HIGH-strung Adams to spend his first years after college—small enough to offer him an enfolding community, big enough and wealthy enough to offer the social life he craved. In the spring of 1789, his spirits having lifted, Adams would amble up and down the High Street, where he and his fellow clerks were sure to meet the unmarried young ladies of town. Sometimes Adams would bring his flute, the better to serenade impressionable women. There were the usual dances and card games, and sleigh rides in the winter. Adams began writing little sketches of his favorites, though usually in the censorious mode that had drawn a rebuke from Nabby: "Miss Dublois is not wholly destitute of that vanity which is naturally a companion of beauty. She puckers her mouth a little, and contracts her eyelid a little, to look very pretty, and is not wholly unsuccessful."

Adams began to fasten his attentions on one young lady in particular. The previous summer he had met the Frazier sisters and written, in his usual jeering style, "As they are handsome, I had rather look at them for five minutes, then be with them for five hours." But the flippancy dropped away when he returned to Newburyport and fell very much in love with Mary Frazier, who was then fifteen. Mary was the daughter of Moses Frazier, a respected selectman in town; her cousin, Nathaniel, was one of Adams' pals.

Moses Frazier was one of the wealthiest men in Newburyport; his fine three-story frame house, with its distinctive squared-off roof, lay on Green Street, a block or two up from the river. Adams spent many of his evenings between the spring of 1789 and the early summer of 1790 in the Fraziers' front parlor. He wrote only the most cryptic entries in his diary, and he appears to have destroyed many of the letters he wrote about Mary. He put a hash mark on top of a letter written in April 1790 to Billy Cranch, explaining in a note that any letter so marked should be burned or hidden away. He wrote of feelings "which I submit to merely from the total impossibility to help myself." His legal training was almost finished, and he wrote to Cranch that he had to leave Newburyport as soon as possible. "Three more months," he wrote, "may be fatal," for Mary was "acquiring graces and virtue in addition to incomparable beauty." (No pictures of Mary survive or perhaps were ever made.) It was not only the smitten Adams who thought so. After hearing an account of Mary from brother Charles, Nabby wrote to say, "You may worship without Idolatry—for he asserts that there is nothing so like perfect, in Human Shape appeared since the World began." Nabby also wrote to suggest that he first settle in the world and move in a wider social circle—"if it is not too late to advise."

Was it too late? Adams didn't know. A man was expected to wait until he could support his future wife. John Adams had begun seriously courting

Abigail when he was about twenty-seven, a fully practicing lawyer with property inherited from his father, who had recently died. But John Quincy Adams was in love. In a poem dedicated to "Clara" and composed in the alexandrine couplets he had learned from Pope, he wrote, "The partial gods, presiding at her birth / Gave Clara beauty, and yet gave her worth." The flimsy curtain of fiction parted to reveal the author as the swain himself:

> On thee thy ardent lover's fate depends,
> From thee the evil or the boon descends;
> Thy choice alone can make my anxious breast
> Supremely wretched, or supremely blest

Adams knew that he would soon be admitted to the bar, and then would leave Newburyport for Boston, where he would take up his law practice—or try to. What was he to do about Mary Frazier? In June, he recorded "a walk in the grove with Miss Frazier"—a rare moment when they could be alone together. In early July, he spent almost every evening at the Frazier household. On July 15, he was admitted to the bar. He rode into Boston to arrange his office, in a house his father owned on Hanover Street. He returned one last time to Newburyport and then moved to Boston. Whatever correspondence passed between him and Mary has not survived. But Adams' feelings were so raw that he opened himself up to his friend James Bridges in a way that he almost never did, writing that "all my hopes of future happiness in this life center on that girl." This was far too grave a matter for his usual juvenile sarcasm.

Abigail apparently began to catch on that her son was in imminent danger of surrendering to love. In August she wrote, "I will give you one piece of advise, never form connexions until you see a prospect of supporting a family." A few weeks later John Quincy wrote back to promise that he would never do so. In October, Elizabeth Shaw wrote to her sister to say that she had heard from some of the Newburyport girls that "a certain Lady is highly favoured." Abigail had heard enough. She wrote to John Quincy that she was "sorry" to hear of these rumors, for they would do harm to the reputation of the young lady in question since his own prospects "are not such as can warrant you in entering into any entanglement." She asked for reassurances that he would break off the relationship. The following week, Adams wrote in his journal, and then sharply underlined, "Letter from my mother." And he wrote back to say that the relationship was over and the lady in question forty miles away.

Abigail's words sound very cold to the modern ear. They *were* cold. But we should remember that a marriage in eighteenth-century New England was very much the business of the parents as well as of the prospective partners. It was understood that the union of two individuals united two families as well and reflected credit or discredit on those families. Mary came from a fine family; that wasn't the issue. The problem was money. Had John Adams been a wealthy merchant, like the fathers of so many of the boys with whom John Quincy had attended Harvard, he could have afforded to support his son until the young man had begun earning his own living. But he wasn't, and he couldn't. In September, the vice president wrote to his son to say bluntly he could not augment his allowance, since "you have Brothers and a Sister who are equally entitled." And if he couldn't support Mary, he couldn't marry her—not respectably, in any case. Money woes would continue to haunt the Adamses for long years to come, humiliating some family members, terrifying others, and at times exacting a dreadful emotional cost.

John Quincy tried hard to solve what seemed to be an intractable problem. In October 1790, the Fraziers came to Medford, a town near Boston. Adams often rode back and forth from Boston. He asked Mary to consider herself betrothed but to put off marriage until he had put his affairs on a solid footing. Mary must have considered this a fool's bargain; she insisted on a public proposal. And Adams declined. Abigail's decisive letter appears to have arrived after, not before, this exchange and thus can not be considered the direct cause. Adams could not bring himself to defy social expectations and his parents' wishes. Such a thing was not impossible: five years later his brother Charles would marry Sally Smith, the younger sister of Nabby's husband, Colonel William Smith, against his parents' express command. But John Quincy Adams could not violate what he understood to be his duty. He and Mary swore to one another, with touching naïveté, that they would marry no one unworthy of the other.

This was a dark time for Adams. He had endured a "depression of spirits," which today we would probably call a breakdown. He had suffered terribly over his love for Mary Frazier. And as a novice lawyer he felt like a total failure, just as he had feared he would. As he earned little or no money, he depended on handouts from his father, which utterly mortified him. Vice President Adams wrote from New York to say that he was happy to pay the subsidy—and then reminded his son that he was not a rich man and had other children to support as well. The younger Adams lost his first case and had found himself almost deprived of the power of speech when he had to address the court. Charles wrote to buck him up: "Do you know a man of great knowledge who has not succeeded at the bar?" But his older brother saw only the dark side.

Adams was also, or so his diary obliquely implies, tormented by unsatisfied desire. He and his friends often walked in the mall on Boston Common, which had recently been planted with trees and paved with gravel. But in the late summer of 1792 he began taking himself in a different direction, possibly westward along Beacon Street to the lower-class neighborhood known as Mount Whoredom, Boston's red-light district. Prostitution had become increasingly common in Boston during the second half of the eighteenth century, and in the area near the wharves women openly offered sex.

Adams filled his diary with barely veiled references to his exploits: "Mall. I got fortunately home." "As before—idleness instigates to everything bad." "Oh! Shame, Where is thy blush! Late home." "Evening at my office. Foolish adventure afterwards. Discretion prevailed." Adams was horrified by his own behavior: he used the word "fortunate" to mean "nothing happened." But sometimes he made a "lamentable mistake"—whatever that meant. He arranged to meet a woman at night at the steps of the venerable Brattle Street Church, where he was very well known. He waited, and she did not come. Then he waited again the next night, with what must have been agonizingly mixed feelings. Again he "escaped unhurt." This pattern of adventuring in the demi-monde would continue until he left Boston in 1794.

Adams could not shake Mary from his mind. In June 1792, he wrote in his journal, "Miss Jones—long conversation with her upon an interesting subject. M.F. If I forget thee, may my right hand forget its cunning." He did not forget her. In a diary entry written when he was an old man of seventy, he recalled that "four years of wretchedness" followed his break with Mary. "Nor was the wound in my bosom healed till the Atlantic Ocean flowed between us."

ADAMS WOULD NEVER BE CRUSHED BY ANY OF HIS PRIVATE TRIB-ulations, great though they were, for his mind always turned away from the personal to the great issues of public affairs. His years of legal apprenticeship occurred in the midst of a new epoch for the American republic. The Articles of Confederation, which had been adopted once the revolution had been won in 1781, had been found to be hopelessly inadequate to the job of governing a nation. The Articles had granted virtually all powers to the thirteen states, leaving them unable to adopt any coherent domestic or foreign policy. The nation's leading men had gathered in Philadelphia to adopt a national constitution. That document, in turn, had been submitted to the states for ratification. People across the country began to debate the great questions of the division of power between the state and national government, and among the envisioned institutions of the latter.

The Massachusetts convention convened in Boston in January 1788. Theophilus Parsons was a delegate and a staunch Federalist, as the pro-Constitution faction called itself. So was John Adams, for the Constitution contained the strong executive he had argued for, as well as an upper house of the legislative branch—the Senate—which would, like the House of Lords, operate as a check on the more rash and populist lower chamber. John Quincy Adams, for all his father's influence and his years spent in the courts of Europe, worried that a powerful national government would infringe on the rights of the people. At Harvard, he had always taken the republican side of the debate over the proposed constitution against his aristocratic classmates. Adams was not a democrat: he had little faith in the wisdom of majorities, and he still abhorred the mob. But he feared the rise of an English-style hereditary ruling class. "No branch will represent the people," he wrote to Billy Cranch. Both houses of Congress, he thought, would represent the interests of the rich. This principled insistence on the distinction between the interests of the whole people and those of one's own faction prefigured Adams' break with the Federalists twenty years later.

But Adams was too practical to cling to an abstraction. A visit to the convention in February persuaded him that the opponents of the constitution, known as the anti-Federalists, objected to any central authority, which he considered a far graver danger. He was, he decided, a Federalist. He could hardly have remained otherwise, for by the end of that year the new Electoral College was to choose his Federalist father as the vice president under President George Washington. If there was any man whom Adams revered as much as his father, it was General Washington.

Adams had been too preoccupied with his legal studies to visit the new government. But in late January 1791, Adams traveled to Philadelphia, the temporary capitol, while the new city of Washington was being built. Both Thomas and Charles were there as well—the first time the Adams sons had been under the same roof with both of their parents since they were small boys. Once again Adams found himself treated as a member of

America's ruling aristocracy. He visited President Washington, watched debates in Congress, and attended a splendid assembly of the nation's leaders on the president's birthday, February 22. He heard about the growing split between the Federalists and the Jeffersonian faction, soon to be known as Republicans, and heard his father complain bitterly about the rise of faction and his grossly unfair treatment, as he saw it, at the hands of his adversaries.

The young man was still deeply disconsolate. Abigail fretted to her sister Mary that John Quincy "appears to have lost much of his sprightlyness and vivacity." At times he moaned that he would have been better off as a farmer or a merchant. Adams returned to Boston in the spring. Back in the life he had chosen for himself, or rather that had been chosen for him, he felt irresolute and faintly disgusted with himself. He picked up his journal and put it down again. He wrote admiringly of a friend who had had the honesty to recognize that he would never succeed as he had hoped—but then added the thought that a man needs "perseverance and fortitude."

Adams was torn between aspiration and resignation. "My heart is not conscious of an unworthy ambition," he wrote another day. "But it is conscious, and the consideration is at once painful and humiliating, that the ambition is constant, and unceasing"—while his efforts were "feeble, indolent," etc. He had thought of undertaking "some literary performance," but his legal work got in the way. And he could not pursue a "public career" without seeming to exploit his father's position, a thought that filled him with loathing. What then? He made a resolution: he would, like his friend, adjust his expectations to his prospects, and seek "at least a respectable reputation." He would depend not on genius, but on perseverance. First Harvard and then his own languishing career had cured him, he felt, of the delusion of his own genius.

The problem was that Adams was trying very hard to do what he did not want to do; he was at odds with his own gifts. What he cared about were those debates he had heard in Congress and, before that, at the constitutional convention. Adams wanted to join those debates, but he needed an opening. Then he found one. In early 1791, Thomas Paine had published *The Rights of Man*, a ringing defense of the French Revolution intended as a rebuttal of Edmund Burke's *Reflections on the Revolution in France*. Paine's work first appeared in London, but Thomas Jefferson had passed it on to a printer in Philadelphia with a note that the pamphlet would refute "the political heresies which have sprung up among us." That was read as, and almost certainly intended as, a shot at John Adams, whom Jefferson and the other anti-Federalists viewed as a monarchist bent on curbing the unruly force of democracy. Adams had recently published his own Burkean meditations on the revolution in a series of essays titled *Discourses on Davila.*

The prospect of defending his father and, no less important, the principles of Federalism proved strong enough to overcome Adams' sense of constraint. In June, he began publishing in the *Colombian Centinel*, a Federalist newspaper in Boston, a series of weekly letters attacking Paine. He used the pen name Publicola—"friend of the people." Paine had sought to vindicate not only the French Revolution but the "inherent, indefeasible right" of a people "to abolish any form of government it finds inconvenient." Thomas Jefferson had asserted that right in the Declaration of Independence, but he had stipulated that a government must be "destructive" of basic human goods rather than merely "inconvenient" in order to justify a revolution. And Jefferson was only thinking of the rights of the colonists against King George. Paine called for a "general Revolution" against all aristocratic forms of government, including England's. He scoffed at the English constitution, in whose name John Adams and others had once demanded their rights as Englishmen. And he justified the worst of mob violence, which arises, he wrote, "as an unavoidable consequence, out of the ill construction of all old Governments in Europe."

These were shocking sentiments, and the fact that Jefferson had chosen to associate himself with so radical a program provoked a fear that the growing horrors of the French Revolution, including the tumbrels and the guillotine, could cross the ocean. The tension between individual rights—the sovereignty of each citizen—and the powers of institutions like the legislature and the presidency, to which citizens had delegated some portion of their sovereignty, had run through the debates over the federal constitution. In 1788, James Madison wrote to Jefferson, "America has less to fear from a powerful government; It is much more to be dreaded that the few will necessarily be sacrificed to the many." Jefferson, of course, thought otherwise; he had come to be seen as the head of one faction, and John Adams as the other.

John Quincy Adams had inherited his father's horror of the mob, to which had been added the experience of years spent in the courts of Europe. In Shays Rebellion he had seen an insurrection against legitimately constituted authority, and he had recoiled. Paine's call for general revolution struck him as a form of madness. In the first of his ten Publicola letters, Adams ridiculed the idea that "that which a whole nation chuses to do, it has the right to do." It may have the *power* to do what it wishes but not the right, for the people have delegated some of their rights to their representatives. Republics do not need violent revolutions in order to reform themselves precisely because they have representative institutions that can do so. In his fourth letter, Adams observed that the colonists had rebelled against England only after suffering sixteen years of oppression from a contemptuous power located three thousand miles away. Did the very fact of living under a monarchy mean that the English people themselves were similarly afflicted? He defended the English constitution and assailed the savagery of the new French government. And of Paine's claim that the mob could become a force for liberty, he wrote, "They are altogether incapable of forming a rational judgment either upon the principles or the motives of their own conduct."

It was a brilliant performance: tightly argued, elegantly composed, and dripping with scorn. The essays were reprinted in London, Glasgow, and Dublin; they provoked a response in France. It was universally agreed that the author was John Adams; a Philadelphia magazine even claimed to have uncovered secret communications between Adams and Edmund Burke. Jefferson himself was certain of Adams' authorship, as was Madison. When the latter finally learned the truth, he claimed not to be surprised, writing, "There is more of method also in the arguments, and much less of clumsiness and heaviness in the style, than characterize his [John Adams'] writings"—a backhanded compliment to the son. The Publicola essays marked Adams as a powerful warrior in the Federalist camp.

Adams also began to emerge, very hesitantly, as a public speaker. His father had urged him to attend town meetings in Boston, appending a list of fourteen things he could learn there, including "the machines, Arts and Channels by which Intelligence and Reports are circulated throughout the town." He had dutifully begun doing so and then found himself called on to participate. He argued in favor of a petition to separately incorporate North Braintree as the town of Quincy, and the motion was carried. Henceforth, the Adamses would hail from Quincy. He was asked to speak in favor of police reform, but his nerves failed him in front of the crowd—"700 men who looked as if they had been collected from all the Jails on the Continent," he wrote to Tom. The Boston town meeting was a pure democracy: measures carried by majority consent of those gathered. The spectacle, Adams wrote, in a vein his father would have understood very well, confirmed his "abhorrence and contempt of simple democracy as a Government."

Boston was subject to fits of puritanical moralizing, and when, in late 1792, an ordinance was passed prohibiting theatergoing, Adams stood in opposition. He loved the theater, and he recoiled at any attempt to impose private morality on the public. He even defended actors who had mounted a play in defiance of the law, arguing in a published essay that this species of civil disobedience was justifiable when legislation violated individual rights. Apparently a little bit of Tom Paine was tolerable in a just cause. Nevertheless, the town council refused to change the law. Adams later wrote to his father that he ought to keep away from politics, since "my sentiments in general are as unpopular as my conduct relative to the town police or to the theatricals." He added, in a touch that must have gladdened his father's heart, "I have no predilection for unpopularity as such, but I hold it much preferable to the popularity of a day, which perishes with the transient topic upon which it is grounded."

But Adams was drawn to controversy, on large topics as well as small. In April 1793, Edmond-Charles Genêt, a minister sent by the French revolutionary government, arrived in Charleston, South Carolina, and set about recruiting American volunteers to help in France's wars against England and Spain. Genêt received a hero's welcome. Many Americans saw the French Revolution as Paine did—as the next step in the progress of the republican principles enunciated in the Declaration of Independence. "Democratic societies" sprang up around the country; enthusiastic supporters solemnly planted the Tree of Liberty symbolizing the French cause. The butchery of the Terror had not yet occurred, and American enthusiasts of the French Revolution dismissed the violence against real and imagined defenders of the old order (including the execution of the king) as minor excesses. Thomas Jefferson wrote, with Tom Paine's nonchalance in the face of mayhem, that "the random violence and careening course of the French Revolution were, part of a lamentable but passing chapter in a larger story of triumphant global revolution."

Genêt was acting in open defiance of American policy, for President Washington had declared American neutrality in France's wars. Genêt nevertheless outfitted privateers to attack British ships, manned them with American sailors, and began seizing the cargo of captured merchant vessels. Washington, outraged, revoked Genêt's accreditation and nullified Genêt's appointment of an equally obstreperous vice consul. Genêt then raised the stakes yet further by insisting that the Constitution gave the president no such rights over ambassadors and took his case to the American public, sending a volley of letters to newspapers and state bodies.

Everything about the affair was bound to outrage John Quincy Adams. The French Revolution was the defining ideological event of his youth. Men took sides, and Adams' own scorn for the revolutionary cause had only hardened as the most fanatical faction of the Jacobins gained power in mid-1793. Genêt had insulted President Washington and trifled with the Constitution. And his sympathizers were drawn from the ranks of the Republicans, an increasingly coherent force of opposition both to Washington and to his own father. Adams sprang to the attack in letters to the *Colombian Centinel*, written under the name Marcellus in late April 1793. He warned of the danger of being drawn into Europe's wars. "It is our duty," he wrote, "to remain, the peaceable and silent, though sorrowful spectators of the sanguinary scene." The imagery of Americans as "spectators" of European affairs, if emotionally engaged ones, would recur in Adams' writings in years to come. The United States had national interests that had to supersede sympathy with any and all foreign causes.

Adams wrote additional letters in November and December, after Genêt's worst provocations. His sails filled with patriotic fury. The Constitution, he pointed out, specifically arrogated to the president the power to treat with diplomats and to Congress the right to regulate foreign affairs. This "petulant stripling"—Genêt was four years Adams' senior—had thus insulted both America's beloved founder and its government. The annals of diplomacy furnished no comparable instance of audacity or impudence. Was Genêt a minister or an insurrectionary? Plainly he hoped to turn one faction of the people against another and ultimately to conquer America for France by dividing it. But it was just as certain that Genêt would fail, for, as Adams wrote in a splendid peroration, "perish the American, whose prostituted heart could forsake the genuine purity of our national worship, and offer at a foreign shrine the tribute of his slavish adoration!"

This time Adams' writing had an effect far beyond what he could have imagined. The citizens of Boston invited him to give the July 4 oration. President Washington soon learned the identity of the author who had so stoutly defended him, his powers, and the Constitution itself. Washington also shared Adams' convictions about the dangers of extranational loyalties, a subject that was to become the great theme of his Farewell Address. Adams was an authority on international law with a deep knowledge of Europe and European affairs. He was the son of the vice president. He was, in short, precisely the kind of young man whom the president would like to have in his government.

A job became available when Washington appointed his minister in Holland as the new representative to Spain. On May 29, 1794, the president nominated John Quincy Adams to be minister to the Hague. His father, acutely aware of John Quincy's sensitivities, wrote that the nomination was "the result of the President's own observations and reflections," and not his own influence. This appears to have been true, but the nomination was also the realization of the great hopes both Adamses held for their eldest son and the life for which they had so assiduously trained him. He had become the man they had hoped for. "I have often thought he was more prudent at 27 than his father was at 58," John wrote to Abigail that spring.

Adams was shocked at the offer—and not happily so. In his journal he wrote, "I had laid down as principle, that I would never solicit for any public office whatever." People would say that he had been singled out not for his talent but for his family name. The fact that this might not actually be true scarcely mattered; reputation depended not only on what a man did but on what he was seen to have done. At the same time, he knew very well that he could not refuse a request from the president. And the offer must have piqued his own ambition, which until that moment had been scantily nourished. He hesitated for several weeks before traveling to Philadelphia to be briefed by Secretary of State Edmund Randolph. His background reading included six folio volumes of his father's diplomatic correspondence from Europe, which he regarded as a precious storehouse of wisdom. While in Philadelphia he dined with Joseph Fauchet, Genêt's successor, who sought to persuade him that England was seeking to forge a European alliance that would menace not only France but the United States. Adams was noncommittal but reflected that, as a growing commercial power, the United States would willy-nilly become England's great rival and thus need the support of France. This was also his first experience of the perpetual campaign by each of the two great powers to enlist the United States against the other.

In July, Adams wrote an anguished letter to his father. He was, he felt, taking a post of "nominal respectability and real insignificance" thanks to which he would be "elevated to a public station much beyond my own wishes and expectations." And this artificial elevation would lead in turn to an equal, and humiliating, descent when he returned from his assignment to find his peers far ahead of him in the practice of law. He was mortified by the prospect of leaving friends and family. All of this, which his father might well have seen as ingratitude and even unmanly whining, was prelude to a request: he sought a prior understanding that if he were no longer needed after three years, he could return home. His father made no such commitment.

On September 17, Adams sailed for Europe on the *Alfred*. He was accompanied by his brother Tom, whom he had persuaded to join him as diplomatic secretary. His thoughts were melancholy. His friend Nathaniel Frazier, Mary's cousin, and Daniel Sargent, later Mary's husband, had gone with him as far as the Boston lighthouse. He looked back at their boat until he could see it no longer. "When it got out of sight," he wrote, "I did not, but could have, turned my eyes and wept."

CHAPTER 6

I Shall Be Much Mistaken
If He Is Not Soon Found at the Head of
the Diplomatique Corps

(1794–1795)

W HEN THE *ALFRED*, A SHIP SO LEAKY HE DESCRIBED IT AS
an "eggshell," made landfall in England on October 14, 1794,
Adams' life as a professional and public man, the life for which
his parents had long prepared him, finally began. It's telling that he resumed keeping his journal the day he boarded the ship: he recorded the
changes of weather, the fish and the birds he had seen, the endless games of
cards, the tedium, the "self-conceit" of a captain whose "intellectual and
convivial powers were below the level of mediocrity." Perhaps Adams remembered that he had first begun keeping a journal when he boarded a
ship for France at age twelve. But his return to Europe after an absence of
twelve years offered, not boyish adventure, but a sense of new beginnings,
of setting out on life's path. Over the next seven years—before he returned
home—his life would intersect with history. His penetrating diplomatic
correspondence would make him America's most important observer of
European affairs at a time when the great powers threatened the new nation's very existence. And his sense of America's place in the world would
help shape the foreign policy of both President George Washington and
President John Adams.

Adams' return to European soil did not begin auspiciously. He had been entrusted with secret documents for John Jay, then negotiating a treaty with England. Just as his carriage reached London Bridge, Adams heard a thump and saw, to his unspeakable horror, that the trunk containing the documents was gone. It had been lashed to another carriage traveling in front, and now it was nowhere to be seen. Both vehicles stopped, and Tom, scrambling around in the darkness, found that the trunk had lodged, intact, beneath their own carriage. The brothers concluded that the straps had been cut—perhaps, Adams thought, by English spies. His mind reeled in horror. What if the documents had found their way to the British negotiating team? And what if his enemies back home then learned of his ruinous carelessness? "What a field for the aspersions of malice!" Far better to have perished beneath the waves. He was so distraught that he drove straight to Jay's home to deliver the papers, though it was the middle of the night. Always inclined to doubt his own capacities, Adams was reminded of his inexperience before he even took up his post.

Adams reached the Hague, the seat of Dutch government, on October 31. This was, of course, another capital he knew intimately, both from his father's time and from his own period studying nearby, in Leyden. He rented an apartment on the Hofstraat, immediately behind the great stone hulk of the Binnenhof, the seat of Dutch government. Adams would pass much of his time in the Hague there and in the homes of his fellow ministers, most of which would have been located in the same quarter. He took long walks along the city's canals, across its parks, and into the woods beyond. The Hague was neat, orderly, and attractive, like all Dutch cities, but it was not a great commercial capital, like Amsterdam, or an intellectual center, like Leyden. Adams was not terribly impressed with its booksellers or its theaters. His social life revolved around the diplomatic community, and he became close friends with the ministers of Prussia and Portugal, as well as with the French officials who held the country in a tight grip.

Adams had arrived in Holland at a climactic, and ruinous, moment in Dutch history. American patriots had once harbored a strong sense of kinship for the United Provinces, as the country was called, for over the last century the provinces had functioned as a republic under the loose control of an executive known as the *stadtholder*. Both John and Abigail had urged their son to read the history of Holland in order to understand how republics evolved and survived. But the Dutch had long since lost the capacity to defend themselves and had come to rely on the support of England and the Hapsburgs. The French revolutionary army had attacked the Low

Countries in 1792 and again in 1794; Austria could not, and England would not, come to the provinces' defense. The great Dutch cities were surrendering to France literally as Adams arrived. In May 1795, the provinces signed the ruinous Treaty of the Hague, agreeing to pay France 100 million guilders as well as an enormous loan and to pay for the upkeep of a French army of twenty-five thousand troops.

Adams found himself living in the midst of a national pantomime. France was in many ways a traditional expansionist power, but it rationalized its behavior in explicitly revolutionary terms. Two years earlier, the National Assembly had declared that "it will grant fraternity and assistance to all people who wish to recover their liberty" and had instructed the nation's generals to act accordingly. The French, that is, invaded neighboring countries in an early version of the doctrine we now call "democracy promotion." France renamed Holland the "Batavian Republic," and both the French rulers and the Dutch subjects agreed to pretend that it was just such an entity. Adams was not fooled. In his diary he jotted down a quote from Laurence Sterne: "Disguise thyself as thou wilt, Slavery! Still thou art a bitter draught." He happened to be in Amsterdam in mid-January when the capital city capitulated—to a force of twenty-five to thirty French hussars. By that evening, patriotic orange had largely disappeared from the city, replaced by the French flag and the tricolor cockade. Adams took himself to the theater, as he often did, and found himself watching a ballet featuring the Tree of Liberty. Everyone stood and applauded. He was, he felt, in an occupied city.

For Adams, a fervent believer in the cause of republicanism, the scene was invested with a terrible pathos. In Holland he saw a people who had lost the will to defend themselves. "A state of lifeless imbecility characterizes this people," he wrote to his father. The Dutch had fallen prey to faction, a destiny that both father and son feared for their own nation. Each faction had yoked itself to a foreign benefactor. Adams learned in a history of Holland that after William II, the Prince of Orange, had married Mary, the daughter of James II of England, in 1641, the royal party had allied itself with England; the opposition had sought the aid of France. The disease of dependence had seeped into the national bloodstream like a poison: over time the Dutch had allowed their once formidable navy to rot in order to demonstrate themselves incapable of harm. And now the patently moderate Dutch had even begun to catch the French contagion of radicalism. Patriotic clubs arose in every Dutch city, each vying with the other for revolutionary fervor. The Rotterdam club marched on the city council demanding the arrest of members of the old regime, who surrendered rather than face mob violence. Adams thus saw for himself the madness of the populist passion that Thomas Paine and the Jacobin sympathizers back home had celebrated. He felt anew America's great good fortune in being able to stand apart from Europe's violence and turmoil. And he recognized that liberty would mean nothing without the force required to repel predators.

Adams' father had always advised him to speak less and listen more; the son was better suited by temperament to follow this counsel than was the father. Adams continued writing "Characters," but now his subject was not his fellow undergraduates but the political and military leaders of the Batavian Republic. He wrote with the ripening insight of a man of the world. Of France's great generals, like Charles-François Dumouriez and the Comte de Custine, Adams wrote, "Each of them too hastily concluded themselves to be the pivot upon which the affairs of the world were to turn, and neither had the talent to disguise or conceal the opinion." By contrast, General Jean-Charles Pichegru, who had risen through the ranks to become commander of French troops in Holland and one of France's most brilliant soldiers, "has learnt wisdom from the example of their fate, and covers himself with a mantle of humility." Like many another eighteenth-century moral critic, Adams saw vanity everywhere he looked. He noted that Mr. Scholten, a senior Dutch government official, "values himself much upon his frankness and sincerity; upon his disregard of ceremony, and contempt of the little complaisances usual in Society." At bottom, though, Scholten was "jealous, suspicious, timid, vain and above all selfish."

Adams filled his journal with minute descriptions of exchanges with his diplomatic colleagues, often including long verbatim passages of table talk. Only rarely did he engage in the painful self-reflections common in his earlier years. His absorption in his work may have helped cure his self-absorption. Or perhaps he had come to feel that those tortured passages belonged to his youth; now he was a professional and a public servant. What he heard and saw mattered more than what he felt. He came to think of his journal (which he now kept in a five-hundred-page hardbound volume) as a fragment of the historical record. He recorded an endless story he had heard about Silas Deane, the highly controversial American minister to France whom John Adams had been appointed to replace in 1778, explaining that it was "a testimony from the first hand of a circumstance which will be doubtless noticed in the General History of America."

Still, Adams could never leave off his exhortations to himself, nor hold himself to a standard lower than the one he applied to others. On the front page of a new volume of his journal, begun in March 1795, he wrote out in

Greek a line from *The Odyssey*: "Be thou also bold, / And merit praise from ages to come." Beneath that he wrote out a very different sentiment from Francis Bacon: "Be it rather your ambition to acquit yourself in your proper station, than to rise above it." And underneath that he penned seven Latin mottoes, including "Know thyself," from Solon, and "Measure is best," from Cleobulus. He appears not to have been conscious of the contradiction between blazing ambition and humble resignation—attributes that in him lived uneasily alongside one another. In his heart, as he had once written, he was not conscious of an "unworthy" ambition, yet he recognized that his ambition was "constant."

Adams could not complain of his treatment in Holland. The new French masters accorded him the elaborate respect due to the representative of the American republic, and a perfectly Francophone one at that. The Dutch submissiveness to their new masters contributed to an overall air of peace and harmony. Since Adams had little business to transact, he spent much of his day reading the paper, taking walks, and enjoying endless palaver with the aristocratic gentlemen who served as ministers from Europe's courts. He was especially fond of Baron de Bielefeld, the Prussian minister, and the baron's son, who served as Russia's chargé d'affaires. "We talked much of the rights of man," Adams recorded in his journal after a conversation with the latter, "the origin and foundation of human society, and the proper principles of government." During the fifteen years he would spend as a diplomat, Adams would never tire of the intellectual curiosity and sense of play that he found among these gentlemen of leisure. These bookish hours were the reward he enjoyed for enduring the cold formality of court dinners, a frequent sense of powerlessness, and embarrassment about his inability to reciprocate for the lavish entertainments he received.

Adams spent much of his day writing letters. Tom served as his secretary, a task that mostly involved making copies of the minister's correspondence. Unlike his older brothers, Tom had never been to Europe before, and his own social ambit was limited by the fact that he spoke no Dutch and scant French, and spent the first year or so of his time in Holland becoming fluent in the latter. Tom was not quite twenty-two when he arrived in Europe for the first time, and he deferred without apparent qualms to his gifted and formidable older brother. He had never rebelled against family rules, as Charles had in marrying Sally Smith. He was wry, genteel, amiable, undemanding.

Adams was to write some of the most brilliant dispatches in the history of American diplomacy. His initial flights, sent to Secretary of State Edmund Randolph, provided vivid detail of the dismantling of the Dutch republic, of the internal squabbles that beset the "patriotic party" opposing French control, of the growing reach of the new "revolutionary" States-General. They were extremely formal in tone, yet infused with Adams' distinctive combination of rhetorical balance and polemical fire, which gave the color of supreme reason even to the most extreme conclusion. Adams observed that the Dutch republic had been "irretrievably ruined," and then tolled off the evidence in rolling periods of Augustan prose:

> With a commerce stagnated, with manufactures scarcely extant, with public payments suspended, with a country which has just suffered the invasion of an enemy, and the most destructive protection of an ally, subjected at once to ravages of war and the ruin of inundations . . . with a dominant party discordant among themselves and a national character timid, irresolute, averse to sacrifices and considering property as the most precious of all human blessings, the most sanguine Patriot can discover in the future destiny of this country nothing but subjection, aggravated by the recollection of its former glories, and wretchedness, embittered by the memory of its former opulence.

When Adams wrote to his father, by contrast, he went on at much greater length—the letters sometimes ran to three thousand words or more—and with a very different texture: rambling and speculative, intensely political as well as philosophical, sardonic, and utterly incisive. In these letters, rather than in the formal works of political philosophy his father had produced, Adams began to articulate a coherent worldview. He had always braced himself for the worst; he was, if anything, inclined too much toward pessimism. This habit of mind made Adams an astringently realistic figure. He had the quality, very rare in a man as young as he was, of never confusing what he wished to be true with what he believed to be true. And as he was disinclined to believe that the world would be governed by his own wishes, so he was unimpressed with the fine ideals professed by statesmen. States, he believed, acted out of hardheaded calculation of interest.

Surveying the entire continent from his perch in the Hague, the young minister wrote his father that "the prophecy of Rousseau, that the ancient monarchies of Europe cannot last much longer, becomes more and more infallible. . . . From the moment the great mass of the nations in Europe were taught to inquire, why is this or that man possessed of such or such an enjoyment at our expense, and of which we are deprived, the signal was given of a civil war in the social arrangement of Europe, which cannot finish but with the total ruin of their feudal constitutions." His prediction was, of course, several generations premature, though he certainly was right about the direction of history. But while any ardent enthusiast of the French Revolution might have seen the sweep of events as Adams did, he went on to write that "the arts, the sciences and the civilization of Europe" would probably perish along with the feudal constitutions. He understood, that is, that injustice would provoke revolution, but he abhorred the chaos and the democratic leveling he saw in France, and which he supposed would be the universal pattern of anti-monarchic uprisings.

But Adams was not being paid to prognosticate remote events. The United States maintained a rigorous posture of neutrality toward all states; the great question for American statesmen in the mid-1790s was how America could cling to its principled position amid French ambitions and the alignments and realignments forming among European nations to check those ambitions. In 1793, the revolutionary leader Danton had declared that France would expand to its "natural boundaries"—the Pyrenees, the Alps, the Rhine. The French had often used such grandiose language, but the revolution had produced a fresh burst of nationalism. That same year the National Assembly had voted a *levée en masse*—universal conscription, which allowed the French to muster a massive army of eight hundred thousand. A French army had marched into the Low Countries in late 1792, and England had responded by declaring war several months later. By the middle of 1795 France had expelled Austria from Belgium and Holland, and pushed eastward to the left bank of the Rhine. Even as the French Revolution erupted in a series of aftershocks, with Danton swallowed by the Terror in 1793, and Robespierre and the notorious Committee of Public Safety drowned in the ocean of blood they had themselves unleashed the following year, the French army continued on its path of conquest.

The clash of French and English ambitions, and the combination of French supremacy on land and English domination of the seas, would keep Europe locked in war for the next two decades. Neither of the great powers could dominate Europe by itself, so both continually sought to build coalitions against the other, with the result that European politics between 1792 and 1815 was a vast canvas of alignments and treaties and proclamations of neutrality forever being erased and reconstituted, with loyalties fixed by perpetually recalibrated national interests. France and England could exhaust one another but not decisively defeat one another. And as one historian has written, "both parties entered the war without a concept of peace"—without, that is, a settlement the other could live with.

The United States wished only to stand apart from the bloody whims of Europe's kings and revolutionists, but it did not have that luxury. Both the French and the English economies depended heavily on trade with the United States. Both, therefore, feared an American alliance with the other, and each tried to undermine American relations with the rival power. England, with its vastly superior navy, sought to block French trade with the United States and with the French colony at Santo Domingo; France depended more on its political influence in the United States. Americans continued to resent high-handed English treatment and harbored a reservoir of good will toward France, which had come to its rescue during the American Revolution and had then fomented a revolution of its own. This, in turn, accounted for the friendly reception Adams had received when he had arrived in Holland. But throughout this period the United States and Great Britain had been negotiating a treaty to finally settle claims outstanding from the Revolutionary War; that was why Adams had been carrying documents to John Jay.

In November 1794, the two sides signed Jay's Treaty, which called for the withdrawal of British troops remaining at prerevolutionary forts and referred other disputes to arbitration. The United States, in exchange, agreed to sacrifice the principle that neutral ships had the right to carry noncontraband goods in time of war. The United States and France had enshrined "the freedom of the seas," as it was known, in their own treaty of 1778. In effect, the United States was permitting England to block shipments to France, but not the other way around. The treaty also made possible the full restoration of trade relations and diplomatic amity between the countries—a disaster for France. The French were outraged when they received news of the treaty in early 1795.

In a letter to his father in May 1795, Adams reflected on the relationship between France's fortunes on the Continent and its designs on America. After describing the subjection of Holland, he suggested that "the policy of the French government at present is to make *use* of the United States, as they are now making use of these Provinces . . . as a passive weapon in her hands against her most formidable enemy." The wars of the last few years, though successful, had left France exhausted and eager to sign an advantageous peace with its enemies—Austria, Russia, and England. In order to do so, France needed to enlist the remaining states on its own behalf. France feared that Jay's Treaty would move the United States from neutrality to the English side of the board. Since the treaty had not yet been formally ratified by either side, France still had a chance to drive a wedge between them.

What subterfuges would it deploy? And if the treaty were ratified despite its best efforts, would France turn from friend to enemy, as the pro-French faction in Congress claimed?

At this point in the correspondence, Adams paused to explain to his father that in his letters to Secretary of State Randolph he had "scarcely hinted" at the ideas he was about to express. They were, after all, his own "speculations." Adams predicted that if the United States ratified Jay's Treaty, "perhaps a coolness on the part of France will again be discernible, but from which no ill consequences whatever are to be dreaded." The reasons, he suggested, were that France depended on American goods, France always responded to "the degree of firmness or of acquiescence discovered on our part," and "our friendship and neutrality must be more agreeable and advantageous to them than a state of variance."

In short, French interests dictated acceptance, no matter the rhetoric that might accompany it. But the treaty was very unpopular at home, in part because of the agreement to sacrifice freedom of the seas. If the Senate failed to ratify, "the French will exert themselves for the purpose of hurrying us into a war" against Great Britain. France, that is, would see a chink in the American commitment to neutrality and seek to exploit it. In such a contest, he suggested, the partisans of France at home and abroad "will promise wonders from their co-operation . . . and the final result of the whole matter will be, that all this tender sympathy, this amiable fraternity, this lovely coalescence of liberty, will leave us the advantage of being sacrificed to their interests, or of purchasing their protection upon the most humiliating and burdensome conditions." Edmond-Charles Genêt had given the United States all the experience it should need of this species of diplomatic perfidy.

Adams was not generously disposed toward either France or England, but also not antipathetic to either. This made him far more reliable than James Monroe, America's minister to France, who was considered so partial to the French that he would later be recalled from his post. Thomas Pinckney, the minister to England, was then in Spain negotiating a treaty of amity. The country's only other diplomats resided in Spain and Portugal. Adams thus served as one of the few reliable sources of information about Europe, and by far the most penetrating. A Federalist senator, Uriah Tracy of Connecticut, described Adams as "unquestionably the most intelligent, and at the same time most industrious man, we have ever employed in a diplomatic capacity."

John Adams was in the habit of showing his son's correspondence to President Washington. The president, who had been resisting domestic pressure from Jefferson and others to forge a closer alliance with France and who remembered John Quincy Adams as the brilliant young polemicist who had come to his defense during the dispute with Genêt, found much to like in the correspondence. Young Adams had provided strong justification for his own policy. And he said so to John Adams. In late June 1795, a very proud Vice President Adams wrote to his son, "I have no language to express to you the pleasure I have received from the satisfaction you have given to the President and the Secretary of State, as well as from the clear, comprehensive and masterly accounts in your letters to me of the public affairs of nations in Europe." That summer, the president, perhaps aware of the three-year promise John Quincy had tried to extract from his father, wrote to the senior Adams, "Mr. J Q Adams Your Son must not think of retiring from the walk he is now in. His prospects if he continues in it are fair and I shall be much mistaken if in as short a period as can be expected, he is not found at the head of the Diplomatique Corps." He singled out the May 22 letter, which, he noted, "discloses much important information and political foresight." Both parents wrote to their son to convey this presidential imprimatur.

At the time Adams was writing, most Americans were far more worried about England, their traditional enemy, than they were about France, their great ally from the Revolutionary War. In order to block trade with France, English warships were intercepting American shipping; in order to replenish a navy racked by desertion, the English were impressing the far-better-paid American sailors into service. War with England seemed far more likely than war with France. Many Americans relished the prospect. But Adams wrote to his father to say that his countrymen vastly underestimated British naval strength as well as financial power. And he wrote to his friend Daniel Sargent to say that even justified outrage was no grounds for a war that would be bound to prove ruinous: "If *resentment* were a good or a safe foundation for policy measures, few Americans perhaps would be disposed to go farther than I should. But of all the guides that a nation can follow, passion is the most treacherous, and prudence the most faithful." Years abroad had cured Adams of the American habit of thinking about the world in romantic terms and habituated him to the blunt European language of *raison d'état*.

It was France whose power and ambition was growing in the middle of the 1790s, and it was France whose designs triggered Adams' fears for his fragile republic. With the twenty-six-year-old Napoleon Bonaparte taking command of the Army of the Alps in late 1795, the French soon overran much of Italy, forcing Austria to retreat there as it had in the north. Adams saw that France's goal was to block all trade between the Continent and England; if France could win the United States to its side as well, it might starve the English into submission. He was deeply disturbed by the news that the House of Representatives had refused to appropriate funds to pay off private prewar debts to England, as Jay's Treaty stipulated, for the British would then refuse to abandon their Western forts, in which case France would put into place its scheme of manipulating American public opinion into ending neutrality. He knew how this sounded, and he told his father that he ought not think that "my imagination is apt to raise phantoms and then tremble before them." Adams was a Cassandra: like the mythological figure, his dire warnings often proved accurate.

One of Adams' great themes was that professions of neutrality meant nothing to France. The French were trying to provoke European neutrals like Sweden into a war that would ultimately help France build a coalition against England. Napoleon was snatching up allegedly neutral Italian states like Tuscany. The danger France posed to the United States was less outright aggression than political and ideological subversion. He wrote to his father, but not to Thomas Pickering, who had replaced Edmund Randolph as secretary of state, about French designs on American politics. He viewed both Thomas Paine and James Monroe as French agents seeking to weaken the cause of American neutrality. He reacted with alarm to the news that George Washington would not stand for a third term. The French, he feared, would fill the vacuum with their own partisans. At one point he even wrote his father that France was hatching a plot to remove George Washington and put in his place a Directory such as now ruled France itself.

Adams was actually more measured than the most fanatically anti-French Federalists back home, and in calmer moods he could reassure friends that Thomas Jefferson, should he become president, could be trusted to stand up for American interests. But he still feared the influence of the Jacobin faction, which he viewed as a virtual fifth column. President Washington had recalled Monroe in the summer of 1796, but in December the Directory had refused to receive Monroe's replacement, Charles Pinckney, a Federalist. Adams stormed over this indignity, and over Monroe's flattering farewell speech to the Directory. The Directory, he explained to his father, had fallen into the hands of a virulently anti-American bloc. He wished that someone back home would sound the alarm, as he had done with Genêt. Adams knew very well that his father was showing his letters to Washington, and perhaps he hoped that this one would galvanize the president to action.

Adams worried deeply about Washington's decision to step down, even though doing so made room for his own father to succeed him as president. He believed that only Washington had the standing to trump both domestic factions and preserve neutrality. He wrote to his brother Charles to say that America's political dependence on France, and commercial dependence on England, endangered its freedom: "Every hour of neutrality now has a tendency to extricate us from both these shameful dependencies." America was dependent because it was still a weak state compared to England and France, with a much smaller population and economy and no standing army or navy. But the balance of power was shifting in America's favor. The new nation needed nothing but time to achieve the magnificent destiny made possible by its remote position, its size, and its fertility. If Washington's "system of administration now prevails," he wrote to a friend, "ten more years will place the United States among the most powerful and opulent nations on earth." And if not? The United States would turn into Europe—"a parcel of petty tribes at perpetual war with one another," with each tribe enjoying the hypocritical support of Europe's rival powers—just as he had written in the May 22 letter to his father.

In the course of dozens of letters to the State Department, to his father, and to influential friends, Adams had articulated the essential Federalist worldview. In so doing, he had furnished hard evidence for the general proposition that America should not, under any provocation or temptation, surrender its commitment to neutrality. These views were to find their most famous expression in President Washington's Farewell Address, a written text published in September 1796. Washington warned of "permanent, inveterate antipathies against particular nations, and passionate attachments for others." And he added, "If we remain one people under an efficient government, the period is not far off when . . . we may take such an attitude as will cause the neutrality we may at any time resolve upon to be scrupulously respected." The speech was largely written by Alexander Hamilton, the secretary of the treasury, who was himself a leading exponent of the doctrine of neutrality. Many others, including John Adams himself, fully shared those convictions. But all of these men had read John Quincy Adams' diplomatic correspondence, whose ideas had mingled with their own. As a witness to events abroad that all of them followed closely and anxiously, Adams was able to provide firsthand evidence of the perilous consequences of forsaking neutrality. Young though he was, Adams played a crucial role in the forging of the first generation of American foreign policy.

CHAPTER 7

A Young Lady of Fine Parts
and Accomplishments

(1795–1797)

D URING HIS TIME IN HOLLAND, ADAMS SAID LITTLE ABOUT his feelings in either his letters or his journals. But in a letter to Abigail in late 1795 he asked plaintively, "Can a widowed heart, an heart which at the monition of parental solicitude and tenderness, has offered up at the shrine of worldly prudence the painful sacrifice of an ardent affection . . . can such a heart readily submit to the controul of other bonds?" Could he, that is, ever love again? Adams had finally put that ardent affection behind him, he said, but the intensity of his suffering "was never known but to myself." It was a terrible accusation to have flung at his mother, though couched in the form—a form Adams himself would have consciously accepted—of filial obedience and "worldly prudence."

Abigail must have felt the sting, for she wrote back to say that she understood his pain at the decision, which had been "your father's wish"—a case of selective amnesia on her part. Perhaps, she said, Providence had intervened, for the public service he had provided the nation had required him to be single. But she assured him that his power to love could be rekindled. And she added, in a wan and perhaps desperate effort at reassurance, that Mary would surely remain single as long as he did and might still be available, if less beautiful, when he returned.

At the time Adams wrote the letter he was in Rotterdam, waiting to leave for London. In mid-October he had received a note from Secretary of State Pickering ordering him to England to oversee the formal ratification of Jay's Treaty. Jay had gone home, Thomas Pinckney was away, and a senior American diplomat was necessary to solemnize the event. Adams left Tom behind in the Hague to represent the United States. He then spent three incredibly frustrating weeks waiting for a ship to be able to sail from Rotterdam. Worse still, he had forgotten to bring a good novel.

Adams' restiveness may have eaten away at his always frail self-esteem, for he responded to his father's letter about the president's high esteem for his abilities by declaring that "undeserved estimation is still more dangerous than flattery." He felt burdened, he went on, by *the magnitude of the trust, and my own imcompetency*" (emphasis in the original). He was, he said, perfectly content with his insipid post at the Hague, which was "adequate to my talents" and left him free time to pursue his studies. He wished no further advancement. The young man who spotted vanity everywhere had so fortified himself against this folly that he responded to praise with a paroxysm of self-abasement. But this was no mere show: Adams' fear of failure was far more vivid than his hopes of success. He was the same young man who had imagined a lynch mob gathering at news that the state papers he carried for John Jay had fallen into the enemy's hands.

By the time Adams reached London, the treaty had been signed. He had no real business, but since Pinckney was still en route from Spain he remained in London as the senior American diplomat present. He was bewildered by the treatment he received from officials in the Foreign Office—not because it was harsh, but because it struck him as unduly solicitous. Lord Grenville, the foreign minister, insisting on addressing him as "Minister Plenipotentiary," when he was only the resident minister in Holland. (Grenville had perhaps understandably used the title borne by John Jay, treating Adams as Jay's stand-in.) Pinckney was America's minister in England, but Grenville's secretary, Hammond, insisted that the English would much prefer Adams himself, son of the vice president and former minister. Flattery, of course, put Adams on his mettle. "If I stay here any time," he growled in his journal, "he will learn to be not quite so fond, nor yet quite so impertinent." He even wrote to Grenville insisting that he be addressed by his proper, more modest title. No doubt the British were trying, in their own way, to gain Adams' loyalty and thus counteract French influence in America. Hammond also insisted that George Washington was about to be impeached over his support for Jay's Treaty.

Adams' intemperate reaction may have perplexed his hosts and limited his own diplomatic effectiveness.

Soon after the New Year of 1796, Adams began visiting the home of Joshua Johnson, a wealthy expatriate merchant who served as American consul in London. The Johnson household, in Coopers Row, facing the Tower of London, had been a social hub for Americans when John Adams was minister; Adams had picked up his mail there. By this time, Pinckney had returned to London, and Adams had very little to do save amuse himself. Soon he was spending every evening at the Johnson parlor, chatting with the three eldest daughters, Nancy, Louisa, and Caroline (there were seven in all and one son), and listening to them sing and play airs on the harp. Apparently Abigail had known his heart better than he himself had.

Adams was a good catch for one of the Johnson girls, who had been forbidden to consort with Englishmen. He was a handsome young man with delicate features, dark eyes, and the high brow thought to bespeak intelligence. His expression had not yet taken on the grim fixity of later years. He was urbane and impossibly learned, the son of the vice president of the United States and a revered founder of the republic, and he appeared to have a fine career before him. At the same time, he was not wealthy, and he was too formidable, too correct, too solemn to be charming. He dressed badly, as befits a man who was vain of his lack of vanity. He was prone to bouts of silence. He was possibly the kind of man whom parents like more than daughters do. Indeed, Adams' manner was so correct, and so oblique, that no one could be sure which girl he thought he was courting. The Johnson family assumed that it was Nancy, the eldest. Actually, Adams had taken a shine to Louisa, who was just shy of her twenty-first birthday when they met.

The Johnsons, though not from Boston, were the right kind of family. Joshua came from old Maryland stock; his brother had served as governor of the state and later as a justice of the Supreme Court. A merchant, he had moved to London in 1771 and earned his fortune in the trans-Atlantic trade. There he met Catherine Newth, a pretty, gregarious, working-class girl of perhaps fifteen. Louisa later wrote that her mother and grandmother were "not of maids the strictest," while her mother's father had a character "very indifferent." In fact, Louisa was illegitimate: church records show that her parents did not marry until she was ten. There is no evidence that Louisa knew that, though her sometimes imperious insistence on the respectability and gentility of her family may have been exacerbated by her anxiety about her mother's origins.

During the Revolutionary War the family moved to Nantes; Louisa had grown up speaking French. She had attended Catholic school, where she absorbed a lifelong fondness for Catholic ritual. She was a sickly child, prone to bouts of melancholy, easily bored by routine, proud, and a bit headstrong. Once the family returned to London after the colonies gained their independence, Louisa had lived an insular life, her every want attended to by adoring parents and a bevy of liveried, bewigged servants. Her father doted on her, and she on him; he would not go to sleep until she sang him a song.

Louisa had been raised to be a fine, if useless, ornament; she was dark-eyed, pale, delicate, and petite. She rarely left home. She had sat quietly while her parents entertained American diplomats like Thomas Pinckney and John Jay; she herself knew next to nothing about the great world of politics and diplomacy. She read a great deal, and not just the pulp novels of the day; unlike Adams, she had fallen in love with *Paradise Lost* at a young age. Louisa had briefly had a beau who worked in her father's office, but he had returned to the United States. She did not think of herself as the family beauty. She had grown accustomed to watching the social action rather than participating in it, and she had developed a habit of keen observation and a gift for mild satire, in the English fashion. It had not at first crossed Louisa's mind that the latest visitor was planting himself in the parlor on her account. For that very reason, she wrote later, she was able to be far more relaxed with this slightly terrifying young man than she would otherwise have been.

Adams' diary had become terse and cryptic again by this time, perhaps because the tenor of his life was now private rather than public. In late January the Johnsons threw a ball for Louisa's twenty-first birthday, and he stayed until three in the morning. "Very agreeable evening," he wrote. A week later he recorded "a partial explanation with one of the ladies"—presumably, Louisa—"which gave some satisfaction." Two weeks later he was "displeased with several trifling incidents" and displeased with himself for "suffering such things to possess an influence over me." And he still couldn't bring himself to propose. He obviously found Louisa very attractive and perfectly marriageable, but he was not impelled by headlong passion, as he had been with Mary Frazier. Perhaps Adams really did have a widowed heart: he had erected a shrine to Mary that Louisa was powerless to topple.

By the end of January Adams was telling himself that "some end must be put to the present state of things." But still he hesitated. In mid-March he noted a "partial conversation with Louisa." At the end of the month he wrote to his mother hinting that he was thinking of marriage. The Johnson family must have been prepared to exercise a great deal of patience with so reputable a suitor, but by mid-April they had become so exasperated that Mrs. Johnson "demanded an explanation." Adams finally professed his wish to marry Louisa, though it was scarcely the done thing to plight one's troth to a young lady's mother. Adams was so flustered, or so unsure of his own intentions, that his diplomatic skills had deserted him. Three days later he proposed to Louisa, and she accepted.

What was all the hemming and hawing about? Adams may have doubted his own feelings. He might have worried that a hothouse plant like Louisa would not flourish in Yankee New England, or that the Johnson family's lack of demonstrated patriotic loyalty would sit ill with his parents. Perhaps he had grown comfortable with his bachelorhood. What he certainly talked about, though, was money. Adams was convinced that he could not support a family on the $4,500 salary he received as minister. Mr. Johnson was rich, but that could not figure in the calculations of so fiercely independent a figure as Adams. The young envoy assumed that he would be going home to resume his legal career in a year or so—that was the bargain he had tried to strike with his father—and he wanted Louisa to wait until then. He would return to Holland; she would stay in London. He had made much the same request of Mary Frazier, and she had refused. Louisa and her parents reluctantly accepted. And then life went on as before.

The certainty of marriage did not mellow Adams' character. He had begun to dress better in response to Louisa's chaffing on the subject, but when she complimented him on his clothes, he sternly informed her that the woman he married must not interfere in his dress. In that case, said Louisa, dropping his arm and crossing the room to her mother, you are free to find someone more compliant. Adams may have been shocked to see that this self-contained young woman had not only a mind, but a will, of her own. He quickly apologized, but Louisa did not forget. Many years later, she wrote, in her own journal, "Thus it was with me there was a sense of unnecessary harshness and severity of character presented to my view which often led me to fear something I knew not what, and cast a damp upon my natural spirits which I never overcame."

ADAMS WAS BACK IN THE HAGUE BY THE BEGINNING OF JUNE 1796. After the social whirl in London, life in Holland was rather slow but, he noted in his journal, "infinitely better suited to my taste." Nearing thirty,

Adams was evolving a new and rather bearish view of himself. "I was not formed to shine in company," he wrote, "nor to be delighted with it." As a young man he had, in fact, shone in company and probably enjoyed it more than he would admit to himself; now, with marriage and family life looming, he seemed to have wished that younger man away or perhaps forgotten that he had ever existed. The new Adams would be diligent, disciplined, scholarly; he would wake earlier and write more. He noted his daily schedule: rise at six; read "books of instruction" until nine; breakfast; read the papers and translate Dutch state papers until eleven or twelve; dress, write letters, and attend to other business until two or three; walk until three thirty; dine until five; read "works of amusement" until eight or nine; walk again; light supper, cigar, and bed by eleven. Adams would keep these monthly accounts of his daily schedule for much of the rest of his life—a spur to self-improvement and a reminder of discarded resolutions.

Adams was operating in a remarkable number of languages, though he scarcely considered it remarkable himself. He and Baron de Bielefeld were learning Italian together, reading Torquato Tasso's *Gerusalemme Deliverato*. He was teaching himself Dutch, which he found "very similar to English," though "the differences are wholly to its disadvantage." He was studying and translating the Latin historians. And he was reading Adam Smith's *Wealth of Nations*, which he found fascinating and deeply persuasive, as well as French literature and history. He was, all in all, modestly pleased with himself.

Adams had written his first letter to Louisa almost the moment he reached land in Holland, telling her how he gazed longingly at the miniature of her she had given him and describing for her the image in his mind's eye to which he continually recurred: "I see you sitting on the Sopha with the table before you, working at a Vandyke, and Caroline at the other end with her silken net-work pinn'd before her, while Nancy calls the very soul of harmony from the forte-piano." Apparently he missed not only Louisa herself but the delight of being ensconced in a room full of women all of whom treated him as a young prince. This and the many letters Adams would write Louisa over the next year contain only the most restrained hints of physical passion. Adams was obviously no stranger to desire, but his profound distrust of passion, his commitment to reason and to principle, leached out the strongest emotions before he gave them expression—perhaps before he even consciously experienced them. His father's letters to Abigail when the two were engaged, by contrast, were headlong and ardent and fairly blazing with desire. The life force that burned in John Adams had been banked in his son.

Louisa finally wrote back almost a month later. She was plainly intimidated by her supremely articulate swain and only wrote because he had implored her to do so. And she lacked his self-control. "Oh Philosophy," she cried out, "where art thou now without thy aid my present sensations will carry me beyond myself and far exceed the limits of my Paper." She ended the letter after only a paragraph.

By this time Portugal's ambassador in Philadelphia, no doubt privy to the diplomatic gossip in London and the Hague, had told the Adamses that their son had formed an attachment, though they seem not yet to have identified the object of his affections. John Adams wrote to say that while he wished the event had occurred at home, "you are now of an Age to judge for yourself." Abigail, on the other hand, passed up the opportunity to demonstrate unconditional acceptance, writing, "I would hope for the Love I bear My Country, that the Syren, is at least *half Blood*." She even had the temerity to ask of "Maria," the name she used for Mary Frazier, "has she no claims?" Her son wrote back to say curtly, "She has none, but to my fervent and cordial good wishes for her welfare."

Adams was hoping to end his time in Holland as soon as possible, return to his law practice in Boston, and marry Louisa. Or maybe he would buy some property and settle in the South, a prospect he broached with his brothers. But he never followed up his plantation fantasy, and he appears to have done nothing to prepare to return to his law practice, probably because he dreaded the prospect of doing so. Then, in early August 1796, he learned that President Washington had appointed him minister to Portugal. The message from the secretary of state instructed him to remain in his post for several months longer. That forced a question: Would he come to London, marry Louisa, and bring her with him to Portugal? Or would he continue to insist that she wait until they could both return to America, he knew not when?

Adams did not trust Louisa to master the etiquette of a diplomatic wife, which worried him a great deal; worse still, he appeared to have no sense of how she would feel to learn how little he trusted her. "For your own happiness," he wrote her, "endeavour to acquire the faculty not merely of acquiescence, in unavoidable inconveniences, but even of a cheerful conformity to things which must be endured, and above all establish as an invariable rule for your conversation, to express no general or national reflections." In other words, no opinions. And, he added, she would have to "suppress some of the little attachments to splendor that lurk at your breast." That drew a riposte: Louisa said that she had no idea why he "erroneously supposed me dazzled with what you stile rank." Adams asked for a truce on explanations between them. His parents had never needed such a truce, for they had been raised in the same world and understood one another intuitively.

The truce, in any case, lasted only until November, when Adams wrote to say that he would probably have to go directly to Lisbon. The consolation, he helpfully observed, was that "it will not expose us to form habits of attachment to the empty baubles of a life connected with Courts." He was still convinced that Louisa pined for empty baubles, perhaps because she had always had them. The following week he added, "You are still at a period of life when reflection is not a welcome guest . . . and Pleasure announces herself as the principal or sole object of pursuit." Adams had surely been abetted by a letter from his father, who cautioned that "a young lady of fine Parts and Accomplishments, educated to drawing dance and Music . . . will be in danger of involving you in Expences far beyond your Appointments."

Louisa must have wondered what, exactly, her fiancé saw in her. She wrote back to say that she was devastated to learn that they would remain apart for an indefinite period. She admitted that she was a stranger to suffering and disappointment, and begged his indulgence for her weakness. Louisa understood that a display of stoicism—Philosophy, as Adams called it—would raise her in his esteem far more than weepy complaint, and so she wrote back to implore him not to consider resigning his new post on her account. Then she added "a feeble ray of Hope": since her father would soon be sending a ship to Holland, she and her father could pay a visit.

Adams immediately concluded that Louisa had concocted a ruse in order to marry him in Holland. He wrote to Joshua Johnson saying that a marriage at this point in his life would be "an act of folly." And he then wrote a strikingly cold letter to Louisa, pointing out that "you will be sensible what an appearance in the eyes of the world, your coming here would have; an appearance consistent neither with your dignity, nor my delicacy." This very nearly provoked a rupture between the two. Louisa wrote back to say that his letter "astonished and mortified me so much, that I can scarcely believe you recollected to whom you were writing." She had, she said, proposed the expedient of visiting Holland only because the "cruel disappointment" of learning that he would not marry her in London had made her ill, and she thought that "if I could but see you for a few days, I should acquire fortitude and resignation to ensure our lengthened separation." She was, she added tartly, "much surprized at the frequent repetition of the words suspicion and distrust in your last and several of your former letters."

John Quincy Adams comes out of this exchange very badly, and especially to the modern ear. He seems to be hurling missiles at his defenseless fiancé from the massive fortifications of his principles. He is intent not only on asserting his perfect rectitude but on securing his dominion over his wife-to-be. Louisa puts up a brave defense but is overwhelmed, for Adams' willingness to jeopardize their relationship in the name of propriety gives him the upper hand. The situation was, however, slightly more complex. First of all, Adams was right about Louisa's intentions, her angry protestations notwithstanding. Many years later she admitted in her journal that her suffering had become so terrible that her father had invented the pretext of the trip to Holland in order to corner Adams into a marriage. And Adams was probably also right that such a connivance would have provoked the kind of malicious gossip that, at that time, could have dogged the couple in future years and offered to the Adamses' many political opponents a cudgel with which to belabor them. Nevertheless, Louisa was deeply afflicted by what felt to her like abandonment, and her pain would color their marriage in its own way. Another man might have felt compelled to find a way to alleviate his beloved's suffering; Adams counseled Philosophy.

The letters between the two continued in this vein until the middle of 1797. At times Adams writes to Louisa from dizzying heights of condescension: "You imagine that I receive with anger the information that you pay little attention to the Harp, and cannot yet play a single song—By no means—I hear it with great indifference: it is indeed as you say a charming, but it is also a trivial accomplishment." At other moments his hard heart melts, and he writes as a swain, admitting that when he doesn't receive a letter from Louisa, he walks the three miles to the seashore and gazes out over the horizon to where the coast of England lies. Louisa, for her part, bows before Adams' masterly reserve: "I shall soon, by my unremitting attention, and solicitude, for your welfare, convince you that your Louisa's heart is entirely devoted to you." But she was not altogether daunted and sometimes held up a mirror to his foibles, whether his excessive concern for dignity or his withdrawal into solitude and books or his penchant for dwelling on "the dark side of things." Self-critical as he was, Adams could not accept even this loving, rallying form of advice and replied that such displays of "spirit" forced him to choose between an equally spirited rejoinder and "acquiescence and obsequiousness, painful to him who makes and unworthy of her who receives the sacrifice." In short, he could criticize her, but she could not criticize him.

In February, John Adams had narrowly squeaked past his great rival, Thomas Jefferson, to become the second president of the United States. He appointed William Vans Murray, a Federalist and staunch loyalist, to succeed his son as minister to Holland. While John Quincy Adams waited for his replacement to arrive, and thus for permission to depart, he went back and forth on the question of whether he would come to London to marry Louisa and bring her to Lisbon. In the meanwhile, Joshua Johnson solved the problem of transportation by arranging to have one of his schooners carry the couple from London to Lisbon. Whether Adams felt that this removed a practical obstacle or rather that such an extravagant courtesy left him no other option, he now wrote to Louisa to say that he would come to London. On June 29, he and Tom went to the port of Maasluis, next to Rotterdam, to await a boat.

And then Murray, who had already arrived, sent Adams a note with shocking news. President Adams had changed his son's assignment: he would be going not to Lisbon as he had imagined, but to Berlin as American minister to Prussia. Only a few weeks before, Adams had written to his mother to say that he would accept the ministry in Lisbon because it had been decided by President Washington, but "you may rest assured that I never shall hold a public office under the nomination of my father." Adams objected to nepotism as a violation of republican principles, but at a much more visceral level he could not bear the idea that others would think he had gained a position through his father's influence rather than his own merit. This amounted almost to a mania with him, and he had written Abigail about it a number of times. President Adams had showed one of the letters to Washington, who had responded just as Adams probably imagined he would: "The sentiments do honor to the head and the heart of the writer, and if my wishes should be of any avail, they should go to you in a *strong hope* that you would not withhold merited promotion from Mr. Jn. Adams because he is your son." That, of course, was good enough for the father.

The son, however, was flummoxed. He had finally accepted the idea that he would begin his new life as a family man in Lisbon. He had secured lodging there; boxed up and sent his beloved collection of books; spent $2,500 on furnishings, which he was unlikely ever to recover; and agreed to Joshua Johnson's offer of free passage. And now, instead, he was to go to distant Berlin, where he knew no one—and at his father's behest. He had arrived in London July 12, and there received his official commission from the president as well as instructions from the secretary of state. He wrote to his father to say that the appointment was "totally contrary to every expectation and every wish I had formed." Nevertheless, he had agreed to accept the post for two reasons: because his father had asked him to, and because "the new destination will be so much more inconvenient and troublesome to myself, than that to which I had already been appointed." No one, that is, could accuse his father of giving him a plum.

Once in London, Adams had what one can only hope and imagine was a joyous reunion with Louisa, who had been in agonies as he wavered about their fate. Her trousseau had been laid out for months. Now he informed her that they would not, in fact, be going to Lisbon but to Berlin, though to her the one was no less strange than the other. Louisa wanted to get married right away, as did her father. The previous September, Joshua had written to Adams with what the latter must have found very alarming news: he had to leave for the United States no later than the following spring if he was to rescue his fortune. He offered no details, but one of the reasons he had been eager for Adams to make up his mind was so that he and Catherine could leave for America, with or without Louisa. But now Adams had new preparations to make, and he began to fret over how he could afford to stay in London longer than he had planned. Joshua gallantly, if perhaps a bit desperately, offered to let Adams move from Osborne's Hotel to the family home once he had married.

John Quincy Adams and Louisa Catherine Johnson were married, at long last, on July 26 at the Johnson church, known as All Hallows Barking. According to the marriage certificate, the witnesses consisted of Mr. and Mrs. Johnson, Tom, and two of Adams' friends, Joseph Hall and James Brooks. In his journal, Adams drily notes these bare facts, adding, "We were married before 11. in the morning: and immediately after, went out to see Tilney House; one of the splendid Country seats for which this Country is distinguished." Adams was no longer in the habit of confiding unbridled feelings to his journal. But with his good friend William Vans Murray he was less restrained. "You see I have really joined the honorable fraternity, into which I was when I left you, a candidate for admission," he wrote a week after the wedding. "I am just now too happy to be good for anything as a correspondent, and hope my friends will excuse the shortness of my letters."

THE NEW MINISTER TO PRUSSIA COULD NOT LEAVE UNTIL HE received instructions from the State Department, so John Quincy and

Louisa spent the ten weeks after their wedding in London. Adams had taken up Joshua's offer to move into the family home on Coopers Row. He and Louisa had scarcely ever been alone with one another before, much less shared a bedroom. Adams, as was his wont, drew a veil across whatever delight he experienced, though he did note in his diary one morning that he had arisen late from "an inevitable cause." Adams passed his days reading Milton; browsing the booksellers'; meeting with Rufus King, the American minister in London; and writing to the secretary of state, his father, and his friends. He spent the evenings at a dizzying succession of postwedding fetes with the Johnsons. On September 8, he and Louisa had a farewell dinner with the Johnsons, which concluded with a "distressing scene." Joshua Johnson was being hounded by creditors and could stay in England no longer. He insisted that all would be well so long as he could return home, for he had property in Georgia that would redeem his fortune. It is unlikely that Adams believed him. At four thirty the next morning the Johnsons slipped out of London for Margate and a waiting ship. Louisa, who had never been without her parents, was devastated. Her parents' departure was, she later wrote, "the most wretched moment of my life."

And then things got worse. On October 7, Adams received a letter from a Frederick Delius, postmarked Bremen. Joshua Johnson, said Delius, "went off largely indebted to me" after having "promised me most faithfully to come to a settlement before he leaves the Country." Delius said that Johnson had duped others as well and that his credit was "worse then notting." Delius asked Adams to pay off Johnson's debt to him, which amounted to 500 pounds, and added a threat to expose his father-in-law's peculations. In his journal, Adams wrote, "Find the affairs of Mr. J. more and more adverse. This trial is a strong one. More so indeed than I expected. And I expected it would be strong." Adams wrote back to Delius saying that even if his claims were true, "I am not the person to judge between you," and then added sternly, "But when you threaten *me* with a publication against *him* you cannot expect that I should receive the threat other than with defiance."

Adams was the son of the man whose greatest boast was that for 160 years no one bearing his name had committed the smallest infraction against public morality. He conducted himself so as never to give his enemies, or his father's, even the tiniest opportunity of just reproach. And now he was the son-in-law of a bankrupt who had fled his creditors. For Adams, this was immeasurably worse than the loss of a future legacy. He wrote to Joshua Johnson to say that the allegations had called into question "something more than merely your credit" and urged him to settle his debts immediately. For Louisa, though, the pain was yet deeper. Her father, whom she worshiped, now stood accused—in her husband's mind as well as the world's—as a scoundrel. She trembled with every knock on the door, lest a new creditor appear and add terror to shame. Worse still, she had urged Adams to marry quickly, and now it looked as if she wanted to hurry him to the altar before he learned the awful truth. Adams may never have said as much, but he probably did a poor job of hiding his shock and humiliation. "It was strict and rigid justice and I had nothing to complain of," Louisa wrote in her journal.

Louisa did not commit her memories to paper until many years after this terrible incident, when she decided to record the story of her life for her grandchildren. Her chief motivation was not to clear her own name but her father's, and in this late-life memoir she writes again and again of his guilelessness and generosity. But the journal is laced with a bitter self-abasement; one installment is titled "The Adventures of a Nobody." She writes that from the moment of the Delius letter, "all confidence was destroyed for ever in me and mine," and describes her father's downfall as "a phantom that has unceasingly followed me through every stage of life."

Louisa would suffer more than her share of calamities in the years to come, and she may, in retrospect, have been hyperbolically attributing all the suffering to this one mishap. But the discovery that she had brought nothing to the marriage—nothing, that is, save herself—made her feel unworthy of her brilliant husband, who, she imagined, could have made a far more advantageous match. Adams loved Louisa, and there is no evidence that he regretted the match he had made, but neither did he have warmth enough, or perhaps understanding enough, to melt her fears. Adams did not, after all, expect happiness from life. Louisa had, but life had taught her otherwise. Between them, over the years, there would be respect and compassion and sometimes love—but never the sense of perfect trust and mutuality that allows couples to surmount whatever problems life puts in their way.

CHAPTER 8

President Adams' Political Telescope

(1797–1801)

ONE OF THE PECULIARITIES OF JOHN QUINCY ADAMS' DIPLO-
matic career is that he rarely served in a hot spot. Holland, of
course, had been a backwater, though Adams insisted that he
wished and deserved nothing more. Years later he would serve in Russia,
but only in the period before the tsar formed the Holy Alliance, which
posed a challenge to the republics of the New World. He was appointed
minister to England, but only after the War of 1812 had come to an end.
The only time he would work inside the crucible of war and peace was
when he helped end that war by serving on the delegation that signed the
Treaty of Ghent. Adams was a great diplomat not because his personal in-
terventions abroad proved so momentous, nor because he had a gift for
winkling secrets from foreign ministries, but because his mind was so fine.
He saw further than other men did. His three and a half years in Berlin
would be as calm as a zephyr, but Adams would provide insight that helped
keep America from fighting what might have been a ruinous war.

On October 19 Adams left London with Louisa, Tom, and their two
servants, Whitcomb and Epps. Louisa fell ill as soon as she boarded the
ship; she had a frail constitution. The party endured violent gales on the
passage to the mouth of the Elbe, and soon enough everyone was ill. "Almost sick myself," noted Adams, a veteran of a great many storms at sea.
They made land at Hamburg and then took a laborious coach ride along

sandy paths to Berlin, which they reached November 7. With no accommodations of their own, the party put up at the Hotel de Russie near the Unter Ten Linden, the city's Champs Elysée. They knew no one, and none of them spoke German. Louisa was miserable. Still deeply wounded and fearful that she was unworthy of her partner, she was also pregnant. (Louisa was always to suffer terribly through her pregnancies.) She had no one to care for her save her seventeen-year-old servant, Epps, and she recoiled from the commonness of the hotel and what she considered the crude manners of the innkeepers and the other guests. The Russie was one of the city's finest establishments, but Louisa had very little experience of hotels. Tom was sick as well, adding to the air of chaos and helplessness.

After four days, Adams found an English doctor who proved to be both kindly and professional. But Louisa's condition only grew worse. Within a week, it became clear that she would lose the child. On November 17, Adams wrote in his journal, "A dreadful night again, passed in continual expectation, and with the torture of disappointment prolonged which yet continues." He counseled submission to the divine will but added, "The mind at least submits, however the heart will rebel." Louisa miscarried two days later. Sickness would often bring Louisa to the edge of death, and Adams, who always expected the worst, would be prostrated with anxiety and often prove to be more of a burden to her than a source of support.

When Adams left Louisa's bedside, he began to see to his professional responsibilities. Berlin was a great city of 150,000, busier and grander and more formal than the Hague. It was the capital of Prussia, which had become one of Europe's most powerful states under the rule of Frederick the Great, the famed "philosopher-king" and friend of Voltaire. Frederick had vastly increased Prussia's territory by conquering much of the region to the east. And he had used the empire's growing wealth to turn Berlin into a modern metropolis, with broad, perfectly straight tree-lined avenues, parks, and gardens. The central boulevard, the Unter Ten Linden, was lined with neoclassical palaces. Under his rather dissolute successor, Frederick Wilhelm II, Prussia had relaxed its martial rigor, and Berlin had gained a reputation as a city of gaiety and dissipation.

Adams happened to have arrived at the moment when this king, the least of the Fredericks, was dying. He passed away in mid-November, and his son and successor, Frederick Wilhelm III, waiving diplomatic protocol, agreed to see Adams and accept his diplomatic credentials almost immediately after ascending the throne. This new Frederick Wilhelm was only twenty-seven—three years younger than Adams; Luise, his beautiful and much-admired queen, was twenty-two, the same age as Louisa. He made a good first impression on Adams, who wrote to William Vans Murray: "His disposition is martial. His manners and personal appearance remarkable for great simplicity, his habits industrious and active." In fact, the new king, though far more correct in outward manner than his father, inherited his philandering ways, as well as his general aversion to bloodshed.

Adams had worried about arriving in a new place where he knew no one, but as America's first minister to the Prussian court, not to mention the son of the president of the United States, he enjoyed a very warm welcome. The social demands on a minister in Berlin were immensely greater than those in the relaxed setting of the Hague. The city had a dizzyingly complicated nobility, for each small German state had its own petty prince, its landgrave or margrave. Moreover, Adams had to be presented, seriatim, in a stultifyingly redundant parade, to the chief members of the royal family. Adams found the rigmarole time-consuming and tedious. Of one ball, he wrote: "stiffness, coldness, formality, politeness, labored affability, studied attention."

Meanwhile, he and Louisa had gone looking for a place to live. Adams was now making $9,000, double his previous salary, but scarcely enough to pay for his lodgings, furnishings, dress, and the other expenses attendant upon a ministerial position. Everything they looked at was either unaffordable or appalling, but neither could they afford to stay in the Hotel de Russie. Finally they took an apartment beneath the Brandenburg Gate, a fashionable spot at the edge of the Unter Ten Linden. Louisa, however, could hear soldiers drill all day long, a form of background music she didn't particularly enjoy. Several months later they moved to a more central address on Friedrichstrasse, where many of Adams' fellow diplomats lived. The lodgings themselves, however, were very spare, as Adams had warned. The study, Louisa recalled, included a "list carpet," made from cast-off strips of material, "pine wood bookshelves, a mahogany writing desk, a second hand Sopha and a few Chairs." Her own bedroom had no carpet on the floor. They could not afford a fire in winter, Louisa recalled, or German lessons for her.

Indeed, Adams didn't seem to know quite what to do with a ministerial wife. Louisa stayed home while her husband made the rounds. Nobody came to call. Finally, one of the court ladies explained to her that she could not receive visitors until she had been presented to the queen, who was perplexed by the delay and had been heard to wonder if the American minister was, in fact, married. Adams had somehow overlooked this element of protocol.

Pauline, Countess Von Neale, a minor court figure as maid of honor to the King's cousin, kindly took Louisa in hand, arranged the presentation, dressed her properly, and prepared her with an explanation of the elaborate protocol. Louisa was petrified. By the time Pauline, who herself was only eighteen, had deposited her at the queen's private apartments, Louisa was so overcome with fear that her body trembled from head to foot, and she stood rooted to the spot. "The Queen," she wrote, "perceiving my great embarrassment and pitying my situation waived all ettiquette and came forward to speak to me kindly telling me how much she had been interested for my situation which she had heard of very fully from my physician." Louisa was smitten and would ever afterwards regard the Prussian queen as a goddess and a paragon. Her Majesty asked her to dine that evening with the ladies of the court. Once again Louisa had to overcome her sense of mortification. But she survived and went home that night to regale her husband and brother-in-law with the astonishing things she had seen. And so Louisa's life as a diplomatic wife began.

Louisa slowly began to emerge from the chrysalis in which she had passed her entire life. She befriended an English family and then other expatriates—usually titled—as well as diplomats and ladies in the queen's circle. She mastered the court gossip, even as she recoiled at its meanness of spirit. She danced with the king, with the celebrated Beau Brummel, and with Lord Elgin, of the Parthenon marbles, whom she described as "a remarkably handsome roué." She learned to survive by herself at parties, for her bored husband would sometimes leave her to make it home on her own. She could barely have survived without Tom, a good dancer who accompanied her almost everywhere. He was easy and undemanding company, and full of attention to his sister-in-law, whom he liked very much. Soon after the wedding, he had written to his mother to say that Louisa was "a most lovely woman, and in my opinion worthy in every respect" of her new husband—an endorsement that Tom knew Louisa very much needed. The feeling was mutual. Louisa spoke of Tom as a brother figure who had "soothed me in my afflictions" and "corrected gently my utter want of self-confidence."

Louisa became a fixture on the social scene. During carnival, a period that consumed much of January and February, she attended masked balls, which astonished her by their magnificent display. She was the only foreigner invited to the Ridotto, at which the queen and one of the royal princes and their retainers reenacted the marriage of Queen Mary of England and Philip of Spain, the Holy Roman Emperor, in 1554. The court minutely scrutinized paintings of the period for clues on dress and deportment. Louisa herself spent six weeks on her costume, with her husband grousing about the expense. "The Queen," she recalled, "was covered with Diamonds; wearing all the Crown Jewels superbly set; and her *own*, which were magnificent! On her head she wore the Royal Crown, and her rich Robes of State, with the broad ermine, were supported by Youths brilliantly dressed as Pages; with her eldest Son, and the eldest Son of the Princess of Orange walking a little behind her, holding the large tassels attached to her robes."

It was a shimmering world of fancies invented for the very rich and very idle. Both the Adamses were fascinated and appalled by it, but to different degrees. A world of rank and aristocracy was natural to Louisa, and the high artifice of Prussian court life was more a source of wonder to her than of disgust. The court ladies, including the queen, urged the very pale Louisa to wear rouge, as they did. Adams bridled at this violation of the principles of republican simplicity. One evening Louisa applied her makeup and before coming downstairs asked Adams to snuff the light. This imposture failed, and he forced her to wash her face. She tried yet again. This time, she recalled, she "walked boldly forward to meet Mr. Adams—As soon as he saw me, he requested me to wash it off, which I with some temper refused; upon which he ran down and jumped into the Carriage, and left me planté là! even to myself appearing like a *fool* crying with vexation." Perhaps, though he would never have let on, Adams was vexed about and a little jealous of his wife's rapid conquest of the hearts of gentlemen, rakes, and even a king.

PRESIDENT ADAMS HAD HAD GOOD REASON TO ASSIGN HIS SON TO Berlin rather than to Lisbon. In mid-1797 Napoleon had just completed his triumphal march through Italy, decisively defeating Austrian as well as local forces and imposing on Austria the Treaty of Leoben, by which France gained formal title to Belgium as well. With Prussia neutralized by its own treaty with France, the coalition that had formed to defeat France and reverse the revolution had fallen apart. France seemed prepared for further conquests, while England would do whatever it could to counter French ambitions. The elder Adams wrote to his son that he needed to have a "political telescope" trained on Prussia, Austria, and Russia, as well as Sweden and Denmark, the neutral states of the north. "In short," he concluded, "what is to be the future system of Europe, and how We can best preserve friendship with them all, and be most Useful to them all, are Speculations and Inquiries worthy of your head and heart." It was the president's good fortune that America's most gifted diplomat was his son, and he made it clear that he expected to receive regular intelligence from him separate from what the minister wrote in his official capacity to Secretary of State Pickering. John Quincy Adams thus served as the president's back channel on European affairs.

The young minister viewed France as a revolutionary power bent on dominating the world—something like the way diplomats of a later generation would see the Soviet Union. Napoleon had christened the conquered Italian states "republics," with gaudy names like the Cisalpine Republic, though in fact they functioned as satellite states of France, just as the Batavian Republic had after 1794. "They are tearing up the very roots of Italy in the name of liberty and equality," Adams reported to his father; "they are edging an insurrection in Spain, and are carrying on the proselytism of atheism and democracy with more vigour than ever throughout Europe." Adams believed that England, then in the midst of a financial crisis, would experience its own revolution before long, though whether monarchical or democratic, he wasn't sure. Here, as sometimes happened with Adams, he erred on the side of pessimism.

Adams had feared since the time of Genêt that France would turn its unholy engines on America. In his view, James Monroe and other Republican partisans had persuaded the French that the United States was divided between pro-French and pro-British factions, and thus that adroit propaganda could sway Americans to one side or the other. He believed that France had a secret plan to foment an uprising that would pit the south and west against the Eastern Seaboard states, and he viewed French partisans like Thomas Paine and Benjamin Bache, Franklin's grandson and publisher of the scabrously Republican *Aurora*, as a fifth column in this conspiracy. He was convinced, that is, that the America experiment was far more imperiled than most Americans understood.

Startling though this sounds to us today, most leading Federalists, including Adams' friend William Vans Murray and Secretary Pickering, shared this view. The Directory really did hope to purchase Louisiana from Spain and thus gain a very sizeable foothold in North America. At the time, nothing came of these ambitions, but the truculence of French revolutionary diplomacy gave Americans good reason to fear France's intentions. Starting in late 1796, French privateers had begun to seize American merchant ships and auction off their cargoes with increasing frequency, while American ships had been embargoed in the port of Bordeaux. In early 1797, the Directory refused to receive Charles Pinckney, Monroe's replacement as minister, and drove him from France.

President Adams agreed with his son and others that France could be dissuaded only by a show of resolve. On May 16, 1797, he convened a special session of Congress to warn that France was seeking to separate the American people from their own government, and to admonish France that Americans were not a "degraded people" to be treated with such contempt. A great believer in the security of warships, which he called "wooden walls," Adams called for an active effort to build up a navy to counter French depredations. But he also insisted that diplomacy could avert hostilities; he appointed two additional envoys to join Pinckney in Paris. This was the opening American move of what would come to be known as the "quasi-war" with France—a war that didn't happen but easily could have.

During this trying period—the great crisis of his presidency—John Adams often turned to his son for counsel. "Is France to establish a universal Domination over the whole Globe," he asked in July 1797, "by Land and by Sea?" His son wrote back to say that Europe was, indeed, on the brink of dissolution before France. Edmund Burke, the great defender of the old European order, had just died, and this in turn had put Adams in mind of Cicero, who had braved the rabble commanded by Caesar and been put to death by Mark Antony as a result. In Adams' mind, it was *always* time to take a stand, and now he felt that America was directly, urgently threatened by the forces of insurrection. On September 4, Napoleon had helped lead the so-called coup of Fructidor, which replaced more moderate members of the Directory with committed revolutionaries deeply hostile to John Adams and to the American government. John Quincy Adams warned his father that "all the preparation possible to meet such conduct on their part *must be made.*"

This very long letter, written September 19, includes a majestic assault upon absolutism of which Burke himself might well have been proud:

The French Revolution was commenced in the name of the People, in their name all its horrors have been palliated and excused, in their name the Guillotine has mowed its thousands and the grapeshot have swept off their tens of thousands. . . . For them, for their unlimited and unalienable sovereignty have these deeds without a name which make an humane mind ready to deny its own nature and shrink from the name of Man, been almost justified, always palliated, as the unpleasant but necessary means for the attainment of a glorious end.

It would, of course, be left to the twentieth century to plumb the full horror of the principle that revolutionary ends justify savage means, but in the supposed doctrine of the "sovereignty of the people," Adams identified what he considered the core of absolutism. In his own understanding of limited democracy, citizens freely chose to surrender a portion of their sovereignty to representative institutions. Only under the most extraordinary circumstances, as he had written in his critique of Paine, do they seek to reclaim their rights through direct action. The doctrine of revolutionary France, by contrast, stipulated that sovereignty resides, and remains, in "the whole mass of the citizens" and thus may be exercised at any moment to destroy those institutions—as Paine himself had argued.

Adams' friends back home considered his letters a bulwark against Jacobinism. Abigail arranged for the publication of some of his letters to her and to his father, usually without telling her son in advance. When Adams complained of misprints, Abigail turned to William Cranch, her nephew and the dear friend of her son, to see to the publication of excerpts, which she marked out with commas on the page. In other cases, she suggested that he choose "such passages as you conceive will tend to enlighten our Country men with respect to the views and intrigues of France." By this means, Adams remained an active figure in the heated debates back home over French conduct, as well as a target for the poisoned shafts of Benjamin Bache and his ilk.

Adams was an advocate for diplomatic as well as military preparedness. In the Farewell Address, President Washington had counseled that the United States have as little to do with Europe as possible consistent with maintaining good trade relations. For many Americans, this meant isolation. In a letter to his father in January 1798, Adams observed that France and Great Britain, and their respective partisans in America, had been eager to reinforce that view so as to remove the United States as an obstacle to their ambitions. In fact, he wrote, "the experience of the last six years has abundantly shewn how impossible it is to keep us disconnected with the affairs of Europe while we have such essential mercantile connections with the great maritime States, and the numerous injuries we have suffered alternately from both parties amply prove how essential it is to our interests to have other friends than either."

The mood in Europe grew steadily darker. In early November 1797, Murray, who heard the news from France long before Adams could, wrote to say that the Directory had rejected the three-man commission the president had sent. Adams and Murray agreed that the time had come to prepare for war. Their anxiety only increased when Murray learned, in January 1798, that France had issued a decree stating that any ship carrying cargo from England or its colonies would be deemed hostile; in addition, no ship that had entered an English port would be permitted to enter a French one. France's goal was to bring England to its knees by choking off imports, and it was prepared to wreck the American economy in order to do so. Adams told Murray that France had left the United States with no real choice: we "must either bow down, as others have, or engraft a *military spirit* upon our national character and become a *warlike people.*" There may have been more of resentment than of prudence in this proposal; Adams was not always equal to the counsels of dispassion. He even proposed to Secretary Pickering that the United States sign a pact of armed neutrality with Prussia and others—a proposal Pickering scotched on the grounds that it would inflame England as much as France.

Adams was a vehement man, but he rarely allowed his passions to conquer his sober judgment for long. Once this outburst of temper had subsided, he urged his father to adopt a policy of restraint. When Murray wrote to propose a coalition against France with England and neutral states like Prussia and Sweden—which didn't sound much different from what Adams had proposed to Pickering—Adams cautioned him against it. He would not abandon neutrality, and he believed that the American people would accept a war only if France started one. He was prepared to continue working for a change in French policy.

Then came the shocking news of the so-called XYZ affair. Agents of the French foreign minister, Charles-Maurice de Talleyrand, had demanded a bribe of 200,000 livres—a stupefying $250,000—from President Adams' diplomatic team. The revelation of this outrage, in April 1798, provoked an explosion of popular emotion the likes of which America had never before seen. Town councils, merchant societies, and local militias drew up resolutions demanding a declaration of war. Congress approved funds for an expanded army and navy, suspended commerce with France and French possessions, and authorized the capture of French privateers. It was within this atmosphere of war hysteria that Congress passed—and President Adams readily signed—the notorious Alien and Sedition Acts. Some French diplomats left before they could be expelled. Harvard canceled the annual French oration in its commencement exercise.

Talleyrand's contempt for diplomatic norms—or rather, for American diplomatic norms—confirmed everything John Quincy Adams believed about France, where revolutionary ideology masked the same gross cynicism that had obtained under the despised Bourbon monarchy. He was so furious about the XYZ affair that he wrote a letter to his mother full of minute details of the treachery, fraud, and avarice that lay behind it. And yet in June, Adams wrote to Pickering to say that, despite a furious and thoroughly disingenuous response by Talleyrand to the XYZ allegations, the Directory had "declared their desire to live at peace with the Americans," and thus that he had some "feeble hope that a war may be avoided."

The Directory had been shocked by the bellicose American response to the scandal. In July, soon after he received word of the popular fury, Talleyrand sent a private envoy, Louis-André Pichon, to William Vans Murray with the message that France sought a reconciliation. The following month, Pichon showed Murray a conciliatory letter Talleyrand had written to Elbridge Gerry, the one American envoy who had remained behind in Paris to continue negotiating. The letter renounced the demand for a loan, made no mention of the bribe, and promised to end the attacks on American shipping in the French West Indies. Murray, who deferred to Adams as his diplomatic and intellectual senior even though he was six years older, wrote to him immediately with the latest news. In order to maintain secrecy, Murray had decided to tell only Adams and the president about Talleyrand's clandestine diplomacy, though he did write to Pickering of the change in mood. On September 25, Adams wrote to his father to report "a great and important change" in France's conduct toward the United States. The insolence and contempt of a year earlier had given way to moderation. The moral was perfectly clear to Adams: "In proportion as our spirit of resistance has become manifest, theirs of oppression and extortion has shrunk back." Events had vindicated Adams' faith in what today we would call "diplomacy backed by force." Two weeks later, he wrote to Pickering to suggest that Murray be nominated as the new envoy to France.

Throughout the spring and summer of 1798, the Congress had passed, and President Adams had signed, one war measure after another. The president was expected almost daily to issue a declaration of war; Secretary of State Pickering insisted that France had left the United States no other choice. But in June, John Marshall, one of the diplomats Adams had sent to France, returned to the United States and reported the softening of the French position. The president learned of Talleyrand's approach to Gerry and Pichon's to Murray. Above all, he had read his son's dispatches. The leading historian of the period concludes that John Quincy Adams' private letters had persuaded President Adams that the Directory did not, as he had assumed, want war. (The president also learned that in August England had wiped out much of the French navy at Aboukir.) In a solemn address to Congress on December 7, 1798, the president declined to seek a declaration of war but also insisted that France must make the first move by sending a minister of its own.

In mid-January 1799, Tom Adams, who had finally persuaded his brother to let him return home, reached Philadelphia and gave his father letters from both Murray and John Quincy confirming the French wish to avoid hostilities. That very day, the president told Secretary Pickering to prepare for new negotiations. And on February 18, Adams reversed course and announced that he had nominated Murray as minister to France, thus outraging the Federalist war hawks and delighting the pro-French Jefferson and the Republicans. It was an act of political courage by the president, one he recognized at the time might cost him the presidency by dividing his own party.

Minister Adams continued to play an active role in diplomacy with France, conveying regular guidance to his friend Murray. Congress had insisted on sending two other emissaries, who reached France in early 1800. A new treaty with France was signed October 1, formally putting a peaceful end to the quasi-war. Adams watched in fascination as Napoleon recovered from the fiasco in Egypt, secured his control over France itself by naming himself first consul after the coup of Brumaire in late 1799, crushed the forces of Austria at Marengo, and smashed the second coalition that had formed against him. At first Adams had loathed Napoleon as a blood-soaked Caesar, but he concluded, with the intellectual detachment so characteristic of him, that his temperament had evolved with his victories. To his mother he wrote that France was better off under Napoleon than it had been under the Directory and that Napoleon had put an end to their "plundering and barbarous decrees" against neutrals.

THROUGHOUT THIS PERIOD, ADAMS WORRIED CONSTANTLY ABOUT money. He knew that public service would virtually pauperize him, as it had his father, and so depended on prudent investments to provide a cushion for his return. He had entrusted most of his funds to his brother Charles, who had not yet been admitted to the bar and who was living in New York with no fixed profession. But Charles seemed strangely apathetic. In the summer of 1797, a few weeks after marrying Louisa, John Quincy tartly asked his younger brother what, if anything, he had done with the $2,000 he had asked him to invest, and suggested he write with fewer personal details and more business matters. Adams' sense of urgency only increased after he learned that his father-in-law would be a charge on him, not a support to him. He asked Charles to find him a house in Boston that could serve as a rental property; he was prepared to spend $5,000 and then to send another $800 to $1,000 for further investments. But he heard nothing.

Charles had been a winning boy in a way that his older brother had never been. His parents doted on him, and he exchanged long letters with his father full of news and intellectual speculation. One of his missives began, "The Samaeens were a Sect of philosophers of India," and went on to compare this Buddhist sect to the Hindu Brahmins. John Adams enjoyed the correspondence enormously and sent along his own speculations on political philosophy and science. But Charles had been a scapegrace at Harvard, accused of joining a group of boys who had run naked through the Yard. There was something scattershot about Charles, both in his reading and in his drifting life. In fact, he was something much worse than that, though no one seems to have known until it was too late. Charles was a faithless husband and an alcoholic who had frittered away John Quincy's money in bad investments—thus the silence—and squandered his own funds as well, leaving his wife, Sally, and their two sons almost destitute. "I renounce him," a bitter John Adams wrote when he learned the truth from Sally in the fall of 1800.

On November 30, Charles died. He had been, in Abigail's more charitable estimate, "no man's enemy but his own." John Quincy grieved when he heard the news, but he had already transferred his remaining funds to Tom, by now back in Boston. And in his fear for his future, he was remarkably stern with his far more level-headed brother, writing to say that he insisted on "regular, formal accounts of my property," observing that he would put no store by promises rather than legal documents, and warning that "you will never think yourself entitled to betray my confidence because I am your brother, or to ruin me, because I cannot take the law of you." Tom had demons of his own, but they would not reveal themselves for many years. He proved to be a responsible steward of his brother's funds and a very reliable accountant. He put up with his brother's lectures with perfect equanimity and perhaps secret amusement.

Adams had grown heartily sick of the parties, balls, and vapid protocol that made up so much of court life. He had set projects for himself. He was learning German and had become deeply impressed with the cascade of books produced by the German publishing industry. He began reading the poetry of Christopher Martin Wieland, who wrote epics exploring

Germany's misty and medieval folk culture. Adams set himself the task of translating Wieland's *Oberon*, which he considered the best of them (though he was dismayed to learn that an English translation already existed). He also worked on a translation of Juvenal's *Satires*—translation was the way Adams taught himself languages and improved his skill in those he knew. At night he would read to Louisa from Chaucer or Alexander Pope's *Iliad*.

These years were a time of great physical suffering for Louisa. She had endured another miscarriage only three months after her first one. This one was equally agonizing for Louisa and terrifying for her husband, who sat by his wife's bedside night after night, wringing his hands helplessly while an equally helpless doctor, who spoke neither English nor French, attended. In the summer of 1798, Louisa was standing by a window at a diplomatic supper and, happening to glance outside, saw a child crushed to death by a cart. She fainted and, when she miscarried yet again several days later, blamed the loss on her shock. At another ball in December 1799, Louisa's friend Mrs. O'Farrill tripped on the carpet, fell, and broke her ankle. Louisa, standing a few feet away, fainted, and Adams and two other men placed her in the carriage to return home. For the next four hours, Adams wrote in his journal, she experienced "a continual succession of fainting fits and cramps amounting almost to convulsions." Several weeks later she suffered another set of seizures. On January 9, Louisa had her fourth miscarriage. "I can only pray to God, that there may never again be the possibility of another like event," Adams wrote. "A better hope, it were folly to indulge."

During the summers Adams took Louisa to the German countryside in the hopes of improving her health. In the summer of 1800 they traveled across the rugged eastern frontier known as Silesia (today's southwestern Poland and northern Czech Republic). The province had very little to offer in regard to paintings or cathedrals, but every town had its own industry and artisans, and Adams made a thorough study of the region's economy. In the first town he came to, Grunberg, just east of Frankfurt, six to seven hundred looms produced wool. Adams noticed that each of these small-scale operations carried out the entire process of manufacture—spinning, dying, weaving, pressing, and so on. Adams was attracted by a preindustrial economic logic. In one of a series of long letters he sent to Tom, in lieu of keeping a diary, he wrote:

It is possible, for I cannot dispute the principles of Adam Smith, respecting the *division of labor*, that by the separation of all these single operations, the same quantity of industry, might produce a greater quantity of work'd materials, but it is very doubtful whether it would produce a competent subsistence to so many individuals. . . . The single workman, is thus placed altogether in the dependance of the great capitalist, and must of course become his drudge. Thus hundreds of laborious men will be compelled to groan and sweat under a weary life, for the sake of adding thousands more to the thousands of one merchant.

Adams was fascinated by the pottery works, glassworks, and vitriol works he saw in the towns he passed through, and he described them at great length. He was endlessly curious about how things worked, including things that didn't turn a profit. In Bunzlau he visited a carpenter who had built a machine representing the Passion of Christ. It was so wondrous that it left Louisa in tears. But like his father, Adams was always on the lookout for practices Americans could adopt or benefits America could reap. He noted that Bohemian glass was so much cheaper than it was in England that it could be profitably exported to America despite the far greater transportation cost. One of the goals of the trip, he wrote, was to see whether America could lessen its dependence on English manufactures.

Soon, however, he passed beyond the realms of commerce into a semilegendary landscape. The minister climbed to four thousand feet in order to see a glacier. He rose at two A.M. to surmount the highest peak in the region, the Riesenkoppe, or Giant's Head. From there he gazed in wonder across all of Silesia, Bohemia, and Saxony. For all his crotchets and complaints, Adams was, at thirty-three, still young, healthy, and enthusiastic. Louisa, however, began to fade; it became clear that she was pregnant once again. They cut short the trip and drove to Dresden and thence to Berlin. By this time, Tom had decided to have the so-called Silesian Letters published in the *Portfolio*, a new periodical he was associated with. Adams, as always, scoffed at the vanity production—and then, having written thirty letters during his travels, wrote another twenty-four on the demography, geography, borders, languages, politics, history, ecclesiastical governance, educational system, universities, arts, and culture of Silesia. It was a slightly stupefying performance, and it demonstrated that Adams would have made a very good historian, if a much more literal-minded one than his grandson Henry.

Louisa was still, miraculously, carrying the baby when the time came for her confinement in early 1801. The king ordered both ends of the Adams' street sealed off, lest any sudden noise disturb her rest. The queen sent messengers daily to ask after Louisa's health. She fell ill in January, recovered, and took a turn for the worse in March. But she survived and on April 12 gave birth to a son. Adams decreed that his name would be George, after George Washington, who had died more than a year before. With his typical hyperbolic regard for discretion and propriety, Adams informed his family by writing a long letter to Abigail about European and American affairs, and then noting, at the very end, "The day before yesterday, at half-past three o'clock afternoon, my dear Louisa gave me a Son."

ADAMS HIMSELF HAD VERY LITTLE WORK TO DO. IN JULY 1799, HE had concluded a maritime treaty with Prussia to supersede one signed in 1785. He had been instructed to reach a treaty agreement with Sweden, another neutral, but that never came off. He thought increasingly about returning home. But what was he to do there? As he wrote to his mother in the summer of 1800, he might want to stand for office in the state legislature or even Congress, but Charles had ruined his fortune. The thought of returning to the practice of law was abhorrent to him. Perhaps he would stay abroad if his father were reelected. He could wait until "party bitterness and rancor" had subsided, which perhaps was a roundabout way of saying "until my prospects improve." Abigail gave him no comfort on that score; she wanted her eldest son home. "It is too long to be parted from those who have but a short leise of Life remaining to them, and to whom you are very dear," she wrote.

And then life determined Adams' course. Thomas Jefferson defeated his father in a bitterly fought and very close contest. That John Adams had, in effect, sacrificed the presidency in order to avoid a needless war with France would quickly become unquestioned Adams family wisdom, though Jefferson was more popular than Adams, drawing on votes not only in the South but also the West, the most rapidly growing part of the country. President Adams then terminated his son's appointment in order to avoid the embarrassment of having Jefferson do so.

On July 17, Louisa, George, and John Quincy left the port of Hamburg on the *America*, sailed into a dense fog, and came very near to running aground. The metaphor seemed all too apt. Though now America's leading diplomat at the tender age of thirty-four, a husband, and a father, Adams was returning home with absolutely no idea of his future.

PART II

WAR AND PEACE

CHAPTER 9

I Feel Strong Temptations to Plunge into Political Controversy

(1801–1803)

THE JOHN QUINCY ADAMS WHO ARRIVED IN PHILADELPHIA with his wife and infant son on September 4, 1801, was a man with a brilliant reputation and no obvious prospects. He could not make a living as a diplomat, since America had no professional diplomatic or foreign service. He was a lawyer by training, but he had not been a very effective one when he had last practiced. He had begged his father to limit his diplomatic service to three years so that he wouldn't fall too far behind his peers, but first President Washington and then President Adams had found him too valuable to permit a return to private life. Surely, with patience, he could reestablish his practice in Boston. But Adams wasn't patient. He was restless and ambitious, like his father. John Adams had discovered his calling in politics; John Quincy had inherited that calling. He was a man born to and for controversy. In the years to come, Adams would discover that the solution to his life lay in politics. He had a gift not for avoiding the storms of partisanship, but for weathering them.

Adams' first thought when he disembarked the *America* was of home and family. He wanted to leave for Quincy right away. But Louisa, who was desperately worried about her father, felt as great a sense of urgency about seeing her own family in Maryland. Philadelphia was much closer to

Fredericksburg than it was to Quincy; Adams could have accompanied Louisa home and then left for Massachusetts. Moreover, his wife had never been to the United States and had not been parted from him since they had married. The ocean voyage had left her ill and quite weak. She had a baby to care for. Simple decency would have dictated that Adams escort her home before continuing northward. But he could not see Louisa's needs as equal to his own. He peremptorily decreed that they would go their separate ways; he told Louisa that he would retrieve her and George before the winter. He saw them into a coach heading south, while he went to New York and then Boston.

Adams reached Quincy on September 21. He was, he recorded, filled with "inexpressible delight" at the joyous reunion with his parents, as well as with aunts and uncles and cousins. His return marked a moment of ingathering for the widely dispersed Adams clan. The elder Adamses had taken in Charles' widow, Sally, and her two daughters as well as Louisa Smith, the twenty-eight-year-old unmarried daughter of Abigail's ne'er-do-well brother William, who had died in 1787. Nabby and her three children had come for the summer as well, so Adamses were crammed into the fine new home John and Abigail had purchased years before but rarely occupied, as well as the two old houses on the farm. Perhaps the only discordant note came from John Adams' reaction to his son's decision to name his firstborn after the father of his country rather than his own father. Abigail had even imaginatively rechristened the boy John George in a letter to her son. To Tom she wrote, "I am sure your brother had not any intention of wounding the feelings of his father, but he has done it—had he called him Joshua"—after Louisa's father—"he would not have taken it amiss." John Adams was not an easy man; in his eyes nothing, including reverence for the nation's founder, superseded filial obligation.

Adams spent the next few weeks seeing old friends. He had dinner in Boston with the members of the Saturday Club, which he had frequented before leaving for Europe; they included Daniel Sargent, Nathaniel Frazier, Harrison Gray Otis, and some of his former law clerks from Newburyport. Adams began to make arrangements to resume his life as a Boston lawyer. He spent $6,000 to buy a house at 13 Hanover Square in Boston from Isaac Smith, one of his mother's relations. He bought shares in the company building a canal to connect Boston Harbor to the Merrimack River to the north.

Louisa had returned to a far more melancholy household. Soon after reaching home, she had written to her husband begging him to come as soon as possible. She wrote again two weeks later. Her father, she wrote, is "very, very much broke." But Adams stuck to his schedule. He boarded a coach for Washington in mid-October. Adams made good time through Rhode Island and Connecticut. But yellow fever, which plagued the Eastern Seaboard cities in the summer months, was raging in New York City, and Adams had to circumvent New York by taking a ferry to Elizabeth in New Jersey. He reached the Johnson household in Washington October 21.

Whatever hopes Adams had entertained about his father-in-law's ability to restore his former status were now dashed. President Adams had found a sinecure for Johnson as postmaster for the District of Columbia, but President Jefferson had removed him in the course of a wholesale purge of Federalist officeholders. Now Johnson asked his son-in-law to look over his finances. "He has been unfortunate in his trusts," Adams concluded, "and considered as a prey by every man with whom he has dealt. I am strongly apprehensive of the issue of his principal causes now depending." The proud former consul and merchant was practically destitute.

With Johnson in tow, Adams paid calls on President Jefferson, as well as James Madison, the secretary of state; Albert Gallatin, the secretary of the treasury, and the secretaries of war and the navy—that is, the entire cabinet. He had known most of these men before, but his standing with them was very much changed: he was no longer a promising young man and the son of John Adams, but America's most polished diplomat. He took the elder Johnsons and Louisa to dinner at the president's, along with Madison and his wife, Dolly. He then brought them on a courtesy visit to George Washington's widow, Martha, at Mount Vernon. He did so, of course, after he had learned the truth of his father-in-law's finances; perhaps he hoped that someone would take pity on the ruined merchant and offer him another sinecure. Or perhaps he felt that honor required him to overcome his sense of mortification and introduce Mr. Johnson to America's leading figures.

The time had come to head back to Quincy. On November 1, Adams and Louisa, along with Joshua and Catherine Johnson and three of Louisa's sisters, took the stagecoach to Frederick, Maryland, the Johnson family seat. Joshua grew more and more ill on the way. It was plain that he would not live long. Louisa, who had lived for the first twenty years of her life like a happily caged songbird, had learned a great deal about suffering in recent years. Now she was to suffer the worst blow of all. As Louisa prepared to leave Frederickstown on November 11, Catherine advised her not to tell her father she was going, for the shock could have shattered him; it would have shattered her as well. She would never see him again.

Stagecoach travel at the time was extremely unpleasant for those not accustomed to it. The post roads, more like cleared paths in the woods, were deeply rutted. The pace averaged about four miles a hour. Of course there were no lights along the way, and the lanterns hanging from the coachman's seat barely pierced the surrounding gloom. The coach could be jammed full of as many as twelve people, who would be jostled into one another as the coach jounced over rocks and holes. Nothing save leather flaps on either side kept out the dust and the wind or the rain and snow. As the Adams party headed north, the weather grew ever colder; at New Jersey they crossed the Hudson in an open boat, with a freezing rain lashing down. It was November 24 by the time the Adams party reached Boston—two awful weeks from the time they had left Frederickstown. Louisa arrived half-frozen, exhausted, ill, reeling from the grief of parting with her father—and terrified of the prospect of finally meeting her supremely formidable in-laws, with their strange New England ways.

With her own family decimated, Louisa was, she knew, meeting the family into which she was to be inducted. She knew that her husband regarded his parents with reverence and also that he was not the kind of man to spare her from whatever judgments they might form of her. Even when healthy, Louisa was small, slim, and pale, happiest in a cozy parlor rather than in a kitchen, much less in the out of doors. She felt feeble and insignificant next to these oaken New Englanders. And she was meeting them not in an urban setting, where she might at least feel comfortable, but in the ancient, rustic village of Quincy. Louisa recorded her first impressions decades later with a horror that had lost nothing with the passage of time. "Had I stepped into Noah's Ark I do not think I could have been more utterly astonished—Dr. Tufts! Deacon French! Mr. Cranch! Old Uncle Peter! And Captain Beale!!! It was lucky for me that I was so much depressed, and so ill, or else I should certinly have given mortal Offence."

The Adams clan treated Louisa as if she were a hothouse plant in danger of expiring in the hardy atmosphere of country life. "I had," she recalled, "a separate dish set by me of which no one was to partake, and every delicate preserve was brought out to treat me in the kindest manner." The fuss and solicitude only made Louisa withdraw yet further into herself, and she became, she wrote, "cold and reserved." Louisa's idea of running a household consisted of telling the servants what to do, and she felt ashamed before Abigail, a woman more than twenty years her senior who woke before dawn every morning to skim the milk and who seemed equal to all of life's vicissitudes.

And Louisa was quite right about the way she was seen. Abigail wrote to Tom that her new daughter-in-law was "so slender and her frame is so delicate that I have many fears she will be of short duration." As for her son, she wrote, "The constant state of anxiety which has harassed his mind upon her account has added a weight of years to his brow, which time alone could not have affected in double the Space." Abigail, that is, blamed Louisa for her son's loss of vitality. This may have been unfair: Adams worried about everything and not just his wife's health. Louisa did, however, have one staunch supporter in the family: John Adams took an immediate liking to his pretty, refined, and acutely observant daughter-in-law, and forever after would treat her kindly and look forward to her amusing letters.

The Adamses settled into their new life as a prominent young couple in Boston. The city still lagged far behind Philadelphia, America's foremost city, which had proper drainage and lighting and well-paved thoroughfares. Henry Adams compared the Boston of 1800 to an old English market town, writing, "The footways or sidewalks were paved, like the crooked and narrow streets, with round cobblestones, and were divided from the carriageway only by posts and a gutter. The streets were almost unlighted at night, save for a few oil-lamps rendering the darkness more visible and the rough pavement rougher."

Nevertheless, Boston was in the midst of transforming itself from a provincial town to a mercantile capital. Boston's population had sunk to six thousand during the British occupation in the 1770s. In less than a quarter of a century that number had quadrupled, to twenty-five thousand. Developers began buying up the city's swamps and pasture lands. In 1795, the painter John Singleton Copley sold much of Beacon Hill to a group of speculators led by Harrison Gray Otis. The group flattened the hill, at the top of which a lighthouse—a beacon—had long stood, and used the landfill to extend the city out into Boston Harbor. Filling out, the city lost both its hilly topography and its peculiar outline, which resembled a hermit crab with a long, narrow tail at Roxbury connecting it to the mainland. The space within its confines became urbanized. In the winter of 1801, Adams went skating on the old mill pond at the eastern tip of the city; by 1803 the pond had been filled with earth from Beacon Hill.

The staid, brick-fronted Boston we know today was rising across the city's finer precincts, very much including Beacon Hill. Otis and his team commissioned the architect Charles Bulfinch to build a London-style arc of connected town houses called Tontine Crescent on Franklin Street. Bulfinch built a fine new home for Otis in 1796 and then two others, in and around Beacon Hill, a decade later. In 1795 the town bought a plot of land on a rise above the Boston Commons from the heirs of John Hancock, and it commissioned Bulfinch to build a new statehouse there. Once completed three years later, this splendid, gold-domed building, and its surrounding neighborhood of Beacon Hill, became the center of the city's commercial life, displacing the ancient district around Faneuil Hall.

Adams, characteristically, clung to the old Boston; his home and office lay in the area around Faneuil Hall, in what is today North Boston, rather than in the fashionable district rising near the Commons. Still, Adams hopped on the investment carousel, though perhaps more out of fear for his future than out of hope for great wealth, which he never sought to amass. In January 1802, he added to his inventory of real estate by purchasing a home at 13 Franklin Place for $6,500 and then used it as a rental property. He bought stock in the Middlesex Canal project and another scheme to build a bridge over the Neponset River, which separated Boston from Quincy to the south. He owned bank stock as well, though he sold $3,600 worth to furnish the house on Hanover Square. An 1802 list of his property valued the total at $43,702.54. It would have been more, had Charles not frittered away somewhere between $6,000 and $10,000 of his assets. This was a remarkable sum for someone who had been barely surviving on a government salary, testifying to Adams' astute and conscientious management of his funds.

Adams was doing quite well, but his peer group, as he had feared, was outdistancing him. Harrison Gray Otis had grown rich on his real estate investments. The Boston bar teemed with gifted and eloquent men like Otis and Josiah Quincy, both the same age as Adams, and older figures like Fisher Ames and Theophilus Parsons, Adams' own law teacher, who had moved from Newburyport. He was far behind where he would have been had he stayed home. Adams haunted the Court of Common Pleas and the Supreme Court and did what he could to dig up work, but breaking into the first ranks of Boston lawyers would be a long struggle. And Adams, who had grown accustomed to the dignity and deference accorded to a minister in a great European capital, had no appetite for that grim fight.

His ambitions lay elsewhere. In late February 1802, Adams admitted to himself that "I feel strong temptation and have great provocation to plunge into political controversy. But I hope to preserve myself from it. . . . A politician in this country must be the man of a party. I would fain be the man of my whole country." Adams would have heard a tirade against the rampant spirit of party every time he went back to Quincy, which he did most weekends. His father was filled with prophetic wrath against Alexander Hamilton, a Federalist who had broken with President Adams and urged party members to support South Carolina congressman Thomas Pinckney instead of Adams in the election of 1800. The elder Adams was writing his *Autobiography*, in which he planned to expose all those who had crossed him.

Still, politics, and above all controversy, was the Adams family business. The only way to have a career in politics was to rise through a party, and the Adamses were Federalists, even if apostate Federalists. In March 1802, the younger Adams agreed to stand for the state senate, and two months later he won election in a town meeting. He wrote to Tom with some embarrassment: "Thus you see what has become of my resolutions to renounce the career of politics." At one of the first sessions of the senate he attended, Adams proposed to form a bipartisan group "by way of conciliatory procedure." The suggestion was spurned—an introduction to political reality.

For all his alleged reluctance, Adams immediately began looking for the next rung up the ladder. That fall, he began receiving feelers from the Federalists to stand for Congress. The party had trouble recruiting talented men from around Boston; most preferred to make money than to make laws, and in any case they insisted on doing the first before chancing the second. Otis had stepped down from Congress in 1800 in order to cultivate his law practice and his business interests, as he had promised his wife he would. Josiah Quincy, a Braintree neighbor and distant relation of Adams, was slated to run against the Republican incumbent, William Eustis, but backed out. Adams agreed to stand. He carried Boston but lost in the outlying districts; the final tally was Eustis 1,899, Adams 1,840. It had rained heavily that morning, and Adams' friends blamed his loss on the weather. "This is one of a thousand proofs," he sourly reflected, "how large a portion of federalism is a mere fair-weather principle, too weak to overcome a shower of rain."

Adams attended to his work as a state legislator: paying down the state debt, debating legislation to prohibit horse racing, chartering banks and insurance companies. This last function made state legislators a crucial target for the new class of entrepreneurs and served as a potential source of wealth for the lawmakers themselves. In early 1803, Adams was quietly approached by Otis for help with a project. Otis was developing a bank, and he understood that Adams might well cast the deciding vote on the application for a charter. Otis worried that Adams would oppose the charter. He explained that "all the respectable men" of the town had joined him as investors. Adams answered that he opposed only the bank's plan to reserve some shares for the legislators themselves, which he plainly regarded as a corrupt bargain. That was not the answer the investors wanted to hear. A few days later James Lloyd, another of the investors, repeated the request, and Adams explained again that he favored a "general subscription" of shares. These men were Adams' friends; he and Louisa spent many of their evenings with them. Nevertheless, Adams had made perfectly plain that his principles were not available for rent or purchase.

Adams' life had now settled into a pattern. During the day he worked at the senate or went to his State Street office, where he studied law and met with the occasional client. He had been appointed a commissioner of bankruptcy, a post that offered a new source of income. He spent most evenings at home with Louisa and George. He often read to Louisa and her younger sister Kitty, who had come up to Boston with her mother in 1802 and remained behind as a companion: the *Dunciad*, *Paradise Lost*, essays of Locke. He was, characteristically, preparing for the obligations of fatherhood by reading Plutarch on the education of children. Once a week, Adams joined a group of gentleman scientists to perform experiments. One evening Josiah Quincy delivered a lecture on electricity. "We broke two of our Leyden jars by charging them too highly," Adams wrote. He was suffering from pain in his shoulder, and he allowed his friends to administer a few electric shocks in the hopes of speeding his recovery—an early version of the electric stimulation now used by physical therapists. Other sessions involved inquiries into chemistry and algebra.

Louisa's first months in Boston were not very happy ones. She remained convinced that Abigail viewed her as "a maudlin hysterical fine Lady." She also thought that Nabby had wanted John Quincy to marry Caroline, Louisa's more worldly older sister. To make matters worse, on the passage from Berlin, her husband had told her of his former love for Mary Frazier, and of course this had only convinced Louisa of her unworthiness. When she met Mary, which she appears to have done twice, she found that her husband's former belle was "*all* that she had been described." And then in April 1802, she received word that her father had died, a bankrupt held in contempt by the world. Louisa could not think of his demise without a sense of shame and of anger at a world that had subjected her father to such unmerited humiliation.

But Louisa was not quite as frail as she appeared, either to the Adamses or to herself. She was a woman of uncommon intelligence who would later dabble in writing poetry, drama, and fiction. She was emotional and expressive, where her husband was rational and withdrawn. She needed friends, and she had a gift for making them. The entire Boston elite called on her: "The Amory's, the Codman's, the Russells, The Sheaffes, the Sergeants, the Cushing's, The Paynes, the Sullivans, the Babcocks, the Gores, the Hubbards, the Tudors, the Quincy's," and so on, as she listed them in her journal. Louisa went to parties and gave some of her own in the house on Hanover Square. She felt very close to Otis and his wife, Sally, whose home was the center of genteel society in Boston and who carried themselves with an effortless grace she could only wistfully admire. "They were both," she wrote, "so calculated to shine by the ease of their manners, their distinguished minds, and their liberal hospitality, it was impossible to know them without feeling their claim to admiration and acknowledging it." And she became pregnant once again. On July 4, 1803—an auspicious date—she gave birth to another boy. And this time the boy was named John. She had produced two heirs to the Adams family name.

The young couple spent their week in Boston and their weekends in Quincy. Adams was a prodigious walker, as his father had been, and sometimes he would walk from Boston to Quincy and time himself—two and a half hours, at a speed of sixteen minutes a mile (meaning that the trip was nine and a half miles). Once in the countryside he would go hunting or fishing, or walk the property with his father. John had dubbed the eighty-acre farm that came with the Vassall-Borland house Peacefields and had since added more adjacent property, so that his total holdings came to six hundred acres. Abigail had never been altogether satisfied with the house, which she found low and small, and in 1800, while her husband was in Washington, she had added a wing that virtually doubled its size. This long, three-story clapboard house had fine parlors with furniture and porcelain Adams had acquired in Europe, a broad staircase leading to spacious bedrooms, and a separate kitchen to keep the smoke and heat away from the living quarters. A French visitor in 1788 had marveled that the former American diplomat lived in a home no second-rate Paris lawyer would accept as a country place; now Adams had a home suitable to his status as America's only living ex-president.

Peacefields was John Adams' shelter from the political—and personal—battles that had defined his life for the past four decades. Abigail thought she had never seen him so tranquil. She, herself, though at times quite ill, delighted in the fruit trees in her garden—pear and apple, plum and peach. The Adamses were not dilettantes; the farm had served as their source of support their whole lives together. And then this beloved shelter and family retreat was threatened with destruction. On April 1, 1803, John Quincy received a letter from London stating that Bird, Savage and Bird, the London bank that held his parents' assets, had failed. John Adams had patriotically purchased about $16,000 worth of matured American bonds during the revolution, and John Quincy had transferred the funds from Holland to the British firm, which offered a higher rate of interest and a greater sense of security. Bird Savage served as the bank for the US Treasury in England.

John Quincy's sensible investment had backfired. Checks written on his father's account were immediately returned with demand for payment. John Quincy hurried home to deliver the disastrous news to his parents. "They felt it severely, but bore it with proper firmness and composure," he wrote in his journal. Indeed, stoicism in the face of loss was deeply etched in the family ethos. "If I cannot keep a carriage, I will ride in a chaise," Abigail wrote defiantly to Tom. "If we cannot pay our labourers upon our Farms, we will let them to the halves, and live upon a part."

But the farm itself was at risk, for it was the only substantial remaining asset the elder Adamses owned. The Adams' friends in London, including Rufus King, the minister to England, wrote promising to cover outstanding debts—but they would have to be repaid. Only John Quincy was in a position to do so. "I feel myself in a great degree answerable for this calamity," he wrote, "and of course bound to share largely in the loss." Adams was prepared to empty his own purse to save his parents. He tried to sell his insurance—and his father's—but couldn't find a buyer. He tried to sell back his own home, but Isaac Smith refused. He did sell the house in Franklin Street for $7,175—a 10 percent profit after one year.

John Quincy now thought of a more drastic solution. He asked his father's brother, Peter, to appraise the value of the farm. Peter came back with a figure of $16,803 for the land as well as four houses and three barns. And John Quincy agreed to give his parents $12,813 for 250 acres, the barns, and all the houses save his parents'. His parents would have the use of the entire property for the rest of their lives, and it would revert to him upon their death. Thus John Quincy Adams became the owner of the family farm and his parents' savior—at the cost of virtually his entire fortune. As a struggling lawyer and state legislator, he had reason to fear that he would not be able to climb out of the hole he was digging for many years, but he never hesitated. In his own mind he was only repaying them for a lifetime of nurture and instruction. Given the almost disabling sensitivity he felt about the advantages conferred on him by his father's exalted station in life, he may also have taken some deep satisfaction at the reversal of the family order. His parents now depended on him and would forever after.

ADAMS TURNED THIRTY-FIVE IN 1802. AS A LAWYER, AND AS AN investor, he remained far behind his peers. But as a political thinker he was already fully evolved. He had developed an identifiable worldview, one compounded of Puritan morality and Federalist conservatism, but steeped in a study of history as well as in personal experience of the great conflicts between monarchy and republicanism in Europe. In late 1802, Adams was invited to give the annual oration celebrating the Pilgrims' landing at Plymouth Rock. He spoke of Leyden, his former home, from which the Pilgrims had set out for the New World. The other settlers in America had come with many motives, including the hope of gain. Only the Pilgrims, he said, had obeyed a command of conscience. They remind us, he told his listeners, of the fundamental fact upon which all social life must rest: "Man was not made for himself alone." The social compact binds the person to his country; the Christian obligation of "universal charity" links the individual to other human beings. Even before they reached New England, the Pilgrims had drawn up a compact by which they hoped to build a community founded on faith and truth—and, Adams noted, love of the very country that had driven them out. Patriotism, like conscience, was "a sacred bond."

The political life the Pilgrims had established in Massachusetts was based on eternal truths. And yet the form it took was adapted to real human nature. Adams observed that the Plymouth Compact had envisioned the collective ownership of property but that the settlers had tried the experiment and then wisely abandoned it. Forbidding the private ownership of property "discourages all energy, by destroying its rewards." Adams rebuked Jean-Jacques Rousseau for his naïveté: "To form principles of government upon too advantageous an estimate of the human character is an error of inexperience." The French Revolution had furnished abundant evidence of this mistake. Adams was continuing the argument he had begun with his Publicola letters, defending the Burkean wisdom drawn from tradition and lived experience as against the a priori principles Rousseau and Thomas Paine had derived from an alleged state of nature.

The limit on Adams' political fortunes turned out to be a short-lived one. In late 1802, Jonathan Mason, one of Massachusetts' US senators, decided not to run for reelection. The leading candidate to replace him was Timothy Pickering, the fiery secretary of state John Adams had dismissed for insubordination in 1800. Pickering, in turn, had joined Hamilton's scheme to unseat the president. Pickering was the leader of the hard-line, pro-British faction known as the Essex Junto. His history made him controversial, and the state party agreed that if he weren't chosen after two ballots, they would look elsewhere.

Adams was the obvious alternative, though the bitter feelings between his family and the hard-liners posed a problem as well. Party officials were also considering Fisher Ames, a former congressman, a golden-tongued attorney, and a member of the Junto. Adams deferred to Ames, as he had to Josiah Quincy, but Ames, too, had no wish to run. Adams had no fortune to protect; all his wishes centered on politics. He agreed to stand, and when, on February 3, 1803, Pickering's candidacy failed, the younger man was chosen to become a US senator. Several weeks later, the state's other senator, Dwight Foster, resigned, and Pickering was chosen to fill out the remainder of his term, thus becoming Massachusetts' junior senator, a status he found galling. The man of no party and the hard-core partisan would make for very fractious colleagues in Washington.

CHAPTER 10

Curse on the Stripling,
How He Apes His Sire

(1803–1804)

NO ONE WHO VISITED WASHINGTON IN THE FIRST YEARS OF
the nineteenth century could avoid remarking on the shocking
gap between the magnificence of the city's conception, meant to
accommodate the government of an emerging world power, and the pitiful
condition of the city itself. When Albert Gallatin, a Swiss national familiar
with Europe's great cities, came to Washington to serve as President
Jefferson's secretary of the treasury, he wrote to his wife Hannah, "Around
the Capitol are seven or eight boarding-houses, one tailor, one shoemaker,
one printer, a washing-woman, a grocery shop, a pamphlets and stationery
shop, a small dry-goods store and an oyster-house. This makes the whole of
the Federal City connected with the Capitol."

The Capitol, like the city itself, was projected for magnificence but remained in a very humble state. Only the north wing, intended for the Senate, had been built when President Adams and the legislature moved from
Philadelphia in 1800. The Senate met on the ground floor in a semicircular
columned space with six tall windows at the rear and fireplaces on either
side. At first the House of Representatives met in the Library of Congress
on the second floor, but in 1801 it moved into a hastily built elliptical structure erected on the foundations of the south wing and known as "the oven,"

owing both to its shape and the stuffy, overheated interior. This was the jerry-built complex in which Adams and his colleagues worked. The Congress had never appropriated enough money for upkeep, and the roof leaked so badly that lawmakers were forced to adjourn for three days in the fall of 1803 while masons repaired the damage. Since this happened to fall during horse-racing season, most congressmen were happy to knock off work. Several months later, the Senate passed a resolution, never carried into effect, to stop work on the Capitol, move the legislature to the president's house, and buy the president a new home.

The Senate had a gallery upstairs, but visitors, when there were any, often milled around among the senators. Vice President Aaron Burr took exception to this practice, and one morning in late 1803 he ordered the floor cleared of everyone save members of the House. This sparked a lively debate, with several senators insisting that "ladies" should be allowed to stay, "since their presence gave an animation to debate, that is not only pleasing but necessary," according to a contemporary account. Three others, including Adams, demurred, insisting that "their admission introduced noise & confusion into the debate—that several senators frequently left their places—& that debates were protracted to arrest the attention of the ladies." Adams was, as we would say today, a work horse, not a show horse. The work horses carried the day.

The president's house lay a mile and a half from the seat of the legislature, across a swamp, with virtually nothing between them. The entire city of Washington had 109 permanent structures in 1800, though quite a few derelict ones, as well as empty warehouses and collapsed bridges; the private developers who had been expected to build the place up had failed to invest, while the government had appropriated funds for very little beyond the construction of the president's house, the Capitol, and the Treasury. The Congress would not pay to begin grading the streets until 1807. Most legislators did not bring their families with them and lived in one of the boarding houses near the Capitol. Louisa was fortunate to have her sister and her mother's family with her. But having grown up in London and lived for four years in Berlin, Louisa was as shocked as Gallatin. In her memoirs she recalled, "The City not being laid out; the Streets not graduated; the bridges consisting of mere loose planks; and huge stumps of trees recently cut down intercepting every path; and the roads intersected by deep ravines continually enlarged by rain."

Jeffersonian Washington was a shabby, dusty, and rather solitary place. But in part for this very reason the city had an air of intimacy unimaginable in a European capital. Neither the president nor the legislators had a staff, and almost all the employees of the federal government lived elsewhere, working as postmasters, revenue collectors, or soldiers. Only a few countries had sent ministers. There were few journalists to look over anyone's shoulder and few servants to bar the door to visitors. President Jefferson's convictions about democracy dictated an informal style of governing as much as a blueprint for government itself. Soon after taking office, Jefferson decided that as a matter of policy he would abolish the idea of fixed appointments and would make himself available to callers at any hour of the day. The president practiced dishabille as a matter of principle. He was in the habit of greeting visitors to his home in faded corduroys and down-at-the-heel slippers. The new British minister, Anthony Merry, a figure of frosty propriety, arrived for his formal presentation to the president kitted out in diplomatic finery; the president wore a tattered bathrobe. Another of Jefferson's democratic decrees was that he would not observe orders of precedence between diplomats and government servants, or for that matter among diplomats. Merry was shocked to be seated "pell-mell"—a favorite expression of Jefferson's—among the dinner guests.

Adams was able to bring his wife and son with him to Washington only because he stayed at the fine Georgetown home of Walter Hellen, a prosperous tobacco merchant who had married Louisa's older sister Nancy. (The other Johnson sisters, Caroline, Kitty, and Adelaide, remained unmarried.) The Hellens' brick-fronted home was in the 2600 block of K Street, at least as Pierre Charles L'Enfant had laid out the still-hypothetical nation's capital. Every day Adams walked the two and a half dusty or muddy miles from home to the Capitol, a solitary journey through a largely barren landscape. At times he trudged through snowstorms. And yet his journal records absolutely nothing of his personal habits or of his social life. He wrote almost exclusively of the battles raging in the leaky, half-finished Capitol—struggles that to him echoed with vast import, even if to others they seemed to amount to little more than partisan haggling for advantage. The remainder of Adams' day, by his own account, consisted of reading books he had borrowed from the Senate library, writing letters, and dining with the family. He pleaded two cases before the Supreme Court.

The Adamses did, in fact, attend a regular circuit of card parties and balls and dinners, as Louisa informed Abigail that winter. The lack of other forms of entertainment may have made the tiny community of lawmakers, government officials, and diplomats socialize all the more enthusiastically. Because they lived in a fine house of their own—or at least of their in-laws—the Adams often entertained at home. And of course they were frequent guests at the White House.

The Adamses were among the president's most regular visitors. He would have them over for a small dinner, where brilliant company could be expected. "The entertainment was handsome," Louisa recalled. "French servants in livery, a French Butler, a French cuisine, and a buffet full of choice Wine and Plate." But the fire was barely lit on a freezing day, and the whole assembly huddled together after dinner, their teeth chattering.

John Quincy Adams had never stopped enjoying Jefferson's company. As a young man in Paris, he had hero-worshipped this tall, elegant, impossibly erudite and clever gentleman, who had in turn doted on him like a favored nephew. Jefferson had the charm of the not-Adams, for he was self-indulgent and pleasure-loving and at times irresponsible; he couldn't seem to recall his own transgressions, but neither did he hold a grudge, which the Adams men could do for decades on end. Both John and Abigail Adams felt betrayed by Jefferson; the lively correspondence among them had ceased once Jefferson became president. All attempts at brokering a rapprochement had failed.

Senator Adams shared his parents' view of Jefferson's perfidy; still, Thomas Jefferson was the president, and John Quincy was not going to refuse his invitations. And he was still Thomas Jefferson—extravagant, improbable, wonderfully digressive. Adams delighted in his conversation, though now he had enough perspective to mock his excesses as well. "Mr. Jefferson tells large stories," he wrote after his first dinner. "You can never be an hour in this man's company without something of the marvellous." He returned from another evening to write, "Speaking of the cold he said he had seen Fahrenheit's thermometer *in Paris*, at 20 degrees below 0, and that, not for a single day, but that for six weeks together it stood *thereabouts*. Never once in the whole time, said he, so high as 0, 'which is *fifty degrees* below the freezing point.' He knows better than all this; but he loves to excite wonder."

You never knew what you would hear at a White House dinner; but you would never be bored, at least if you had a range of interests like Adams'. One night the president talked about wine, one of his great obsessions, and then about Epicureanism. "The President said that the Epicurean philosophy came nearest to the truth, in his opinion, of any of the antient systems of philosophy. But that it had been misunderstood and misrepresented." Adams himself, of course, was more Stoic than Epicurean. Senator Samuel Mitchell of New York spoke at great length. "Dr. Mitchill's conversation was very various, of chemistry, of Geography, and of natural philosophy, of oils, grasses, beasts, birds, petrifactions and incrustations, Pike and Humboldt, Lewis and Barlow; and a long train of et cetera." Jefferson turned the conversation to agriculture, saying that Madison knew more of the subject "than any other man of science." All in all, said Adams, it had been a delightful evening.

Adams was also one of the very few men in the Senate who could not reliably be counted to vote with one party or the other. Almost alone among the Federalists, he did not despise the Republicans. Throughout New England, the last, shrinking redoubt of Federalism, Jefferson was viewed as a monster, a bogeyman to frighten children. The clergy denounced him as a licentious atheist, the Anglophiles as a slave to France, the chauvinists of Massachusetts and Connecticut as a Southern loyalist prepared to divide the nation in half. (The fact that Jefferson was a slave owner barely entered into the picture.) Theophilus Parsons Jr., the son of Adams' gifted law tutor, recalled that he never saw a Jeffersonian, "to know him," until he was ten, and then was shocked to find one at the family dinner table, speaking just like a respectable citizen.

The firebrands of the Essex Junto spoke of republicanism the way fervent Cold Warriors would speak of Communism in the depths of the 1950s. In an 1801 oration, Timothy Dwight, the president of Yale and one of America's leading men of letters, said, "The great object of Jacobinism . . . is to destroy every trace of civilization in the world, and to force mankind back into the savage state. . . . The ties of marriage with all its felicities are severed and destroyed; our wives and daughters are thrown into the stews; and children are cast out into the world from the breast and forgotten." Timothy Pickering, who bunked at a Federalist-only boarding house, insisted that Jefferson was prepared to abrogate the Constitution and declare himself president for life, like Napoleon crowning himself emperor.

The Federalists had dwindled to a mere remnant in a few short years and could count on only eight of the thirty-two votes in the Senate. They had begun as America's national party—the party that saw the Constitution as the defining document of a federal state rather than a mere "confederation" of autonomous states—and had over time become the narrow domain of an old elite of New England and Mid-Atlantic merchants. The Federalists were, increasingly, a party of nostalgia; their dominant mood was cantankerous opposition, whether to John Adams or Thomas Jefferson. And in the fall of 1803, just as John Quincy Adams was arriving in Washington, the Federalist ire at Jefferson was kindled into flame by the astonishing windfall known as the Louisiana Purchase.

Jefferson's acquisition of the Louisiana Territory was a lucky break of cosmic proportions. Napoleon had regained Louisiana from Spain through the secret Treaty of Ildefonso in 1800. He planned to land troops at New Orleans and move up the Mississippi, gaining control over the Gulf of Mexico and pushing America's border back to the east, perhaps as far as the Alleghenies. This was precisely the threat Adams and others had warned about during the quasi-war. But Napoleon's ambitions for the New World collapsed when a forty-thousand-strong army he sent to quell the slave revolt of Toussaint L'Ouverture in its West Indian colony of Santo Domingo, soon to be known as Haiti, was all but wiped out by yellow fever and then finished off by the insurgents.

While the battle for Santo Domingo was still raging, Jefferson had sent James Monroe to Europe in the hopes of purchasing West Florida from Spain and New Orleans from France. By the time Monroe arrived, Napoleon had abandoned the entire scheme of conquest and, in one of his lightning-fast shifts, had determined to sell the entire territory to the Americans in order to replenish his coffers and turn his armies toward Austria, a far more familiar foe. After much frantic dickering, the United States bought 828,000 square miles of territory, effectively doubling its size, for $15 million, or 3 cents an acre. At that moment, America began to become the continental nation Jefferson, Adams, and, indeed, most of the Founding Fathers had always imagined it would be—though only after a far greater lapse of time. For the previous decade, American foreign policy had focused on preventing European rivalries from spilling over to the United States. Now foreign policy would also become a matter of incorporating territory to the west and south, sometimes violently, and dealing with the consequences of new land and new people.

The Republicans saw the Louisiana Purchase as a colossal political triumph; slaveholding states hoped to legalize slavery in the new states that would join the Union, thus decisively tipping the balance of power in their favor. The Federalists saw it as a catastrophe. The union they had joined had consisted of thirteen states, most of them coastal and mercantile. Now the country was expanding to include vast inland territory, which would not share their interests or outlook. The Boston nobs viewed the West with undisguised horror. "Should this precious treaty go into operation," cried the celebrated lawyer Fisher Ames, "I doubt not thick-skinned beasts will crowd Congress Hall," not to mention "Buffaloes from the head of the Missouri and Alligators from the Red River."

The Federalists grounded their opposition to the Louisiana Purchase on the Constitution, which had, they pointed out, no provision for the incorporation and government of new territories. Indeed, some of them claimed that the Constitution applied only to the territory existing at the time of its adoption and that the founders did not foresee any further expansion of the nation. The United States could have colonies but could not, as the treaty foresaw it would, absorb foreign lands into its own territory with the ultimate goal of incorporating them as states. The Federalists chose to overlook the fact that with the Northwest Ordinance of 1787 the United States had claimed a vast tract of territory from Great Britain—and then admitted the territorial governments as American states.

Adams agreed with neither side. On November 9, barely a week after he had reached Washington, he made his position clear in the Senate: "I am in favor of the treaty," he said, "although it is made in direct violation of the Constitution." Adams favored the purchase because he believed that it was America's destiny to expand across the continent and surpass even the greatest nations of Europe. Though he accepted the Federalist claim that the Constitution did not foresee the assimilation of new territory, he felt the problem could be circumvented.

But Adams foresaw an entirely different dilemma, and in this he was remarkably foresighted. The legislation putting the treaty into effect would establish the equivalent of a colonial government in the new territory, in which federal officials and judges would govern the acquired peoples prior to statehood. Some Republicans explicitly accepted the prospect of colonial rule, but Adams insisted that it would be monstrous for the United States to impose taxation without representation, as the British had done to them. He suggested that the Senate appoint a committee to amend the Constitution so that it would conform to the terms of the treaty. The idea went nowhere. Then he proposed a resolution explicitly stating that the Senate lacked the power to impose taxes on the people of Louisiana and, still later, a constitutional amendment that would "extend to the said inhabitants all the rights, privileges and immunities which are enjoyed by native citizens of the United States under the Constitution." The efforts were quixotic.

Adams' views seemed perverse to his highly partisan colleagues. He favored the Louisiana Purchase but found that it violated the Constitution; he deplored slavery but would not vote to prohibit it there because "as connected with Commerse it has important uses," and in any case Congress had no right to legislate for the territory without its consent. He may have made his position more complicated than he needed to, and yet he approached the Louisiana Purchase as a matter of principle rather than politics. He wrote to Tom that he was shocked at his colleagues' complete indifference to the welfare of the people whose territory they had just annexed. The final bill authorizing the Louisiana Purchase came up for vote February 18. Adams was alone in arguing against it. "All power in a republican government is derived from the people," he reminded his colleagues, some of whom may have felt that they needed no reminding. "The people of that country have given no power or authority for us to legislate for them. The people of the United States could give us none, because they had none themselves. The treaty has given us none, for they were not parties to it—it was made without their knowledge." The legislation passed easily.

History would ultimately judge Adams wrong on the Constitution, for America would continue to annex adjacent territory, but right on the treatment of the people thus incorporated. A century later, Secretary of State Elihu Root would conclude that the United States had an obligation to extend to the people of the Philippines, which it had annexed as a colony, the fundamental rights contained in the Constitution. A commission appointed by President William McKinley argued that "it will be safe and desirable . . . to extend to the Filipinos larger liberties of self-government than Jefferson approved of for the inhabitants of Louisiana."

Within months of arriving in the US Senate, Adams had become its most iconoclastic member. He would not barter votes or join coalitions or make small sacrifices of principle in order to win larger victories—that is, he would not legislate. He sometimes carried principle to the point of eccentricity. Though the "Barbary pirates" were seizing American ships and imprisoning American sailors in North Africa, he registered the sole opposing vote on a resolution to declare war on Morocco, on the grounds that it was too precipitate. Adams began to worry that he was making a fool of himself. He spent a long night in painful self-examination. "Of the errors, impudences, and follies which reflection discovers in my own conduct," he wrote, "I do not correct myself by the discovery. Pride, and self-conceit and presumption lie so deep in my natural character that when their deformity betrays them, they run through all the changes of Proteus, to disguise themselves to my own heart."

Adams had good reason to worry; even his friends and party allies found him unreasonable. William Plumer, a senator from New Hampshire who often voted with Adams and considered him a good friend, wrote in his notes on Senate proceedings, "He is a man of much information—but too formal—his manners are too stiff & unyielding—he is too tenacious of his opinions." For all of his self-doubt, Adams felt that his faith in the Constitution, and in principles of justice and the law, demanded that he pursue his course, no matter how futile. The Federalists who had sent Adams to Washington began to regret the choice. "Curse on the stripling, how he apes his sire," wrote Theodore Lyman Jr., an old Bostonian, to Thomas Pickering.

At the same time, Adams was perfectly prepared to join the Federalist minority when he felt that the Republican majority was seeking to aggrandize itself. Republican radicals in the House initiated a series of impeachment trials against Federalist judges, which Adams viewed as a transparent attempt to abridge the independence of the judiciary and purge the government of Federalist officeholders. Their first target was John Pickering, a federal district judge in New Hampshire and an alcoholic who had earlier been judged insane. Adams agreed that he was unfit for the bench but was outraged that the supreme engine of impeachment proceedings, which had never before been used against a judge, would be turned on one plainly innocent of "high crimes and misdemeanors." The real issue, he believed, was the constitutional balance of powers, and he raged—in his journal more than on the floor—at the Republicans' unwillingness to hear testimony from the accused, at the collusion of House and Senate Republicans, at the nonchalance with which the charges against Pickering had been framed. Was it enough for Pickering to be found "guilty" of the acts alleged, no matter how trivial? If so, as he wrote in his journal, "insanity, sickness, any trivial error of conduct in a judge, must be construed into misdemenours, punishable by *impeachment*." Once again, Adams was plainly in the right: the impeachment process was wholly untried, and it would soon be rectified along lines he suggested. But he was, again, far ahead of his time. On March 17, 1804, Pickering was found guilty on a party-line vote, 21 to 7.

ON APRIL 2, THE FIVE-MONTH LEGISLATIVE TERM HAVING ENDED, Adams went home. And he went home alone. This was the product of the kind of misunderstanding that he and Louisa often seemed to have. Adams had concluded that he could not afford to maintain two households and suggested that Louisa and the children spend the year at Quincy. Very few congressmen, after all, had brought their families to Washington. Louisa apparently surprised him by saying that, in that case, she would stay in Washington with her own family. Adams had not considered that Louisa might not look forward to a long winter under the same small roof as Abigail. He wrote her to point out that keeping her and the children in Washington would be more costly than keeping them in Quincy—though of course he accepted her choice. Louisa could not let this pass. She wrote back, "My life ever has been and ever must remain a life of painful obligation. Cease then to talk of expence on my account." Send me the money for the trip, she said, and I will come, so long as I can bring one of my sisters with me. Adams didn't take her up on the suggestion.

Adams returned to his own family, which now included Tom, who had moved back home from Philadelphia after conclusively proving to himself that he was unfit for the law. He edited the *Portfolio*, a high-minded Federalist publication full of literary criticism, essays, and translations, some of them, like the Silesian letters, from his brother's pen. John Quincy planted one hundred fruit trees, tramped across the property with his father, and went "gunning" for birds with Tom. But Adams had no gift for relaxation, even on his summer vacation. He set himself tasks: in order to make him a more effective representative of the people of Massachusetts, he reviewed the complete chronological annals of the laws of the United States. He compared Pope and Cowper's translations of the *Iliad* and the *Odyssey* to one another and to the Greek original, scrutinizing the notes and studying maps for geographical accuracy.

Adams had an extremely fine feel for poetry and a gift for literary exegesis. After he had finally finished with Homer, he wrote, "One remark I made in comparing the Translations with the original is that Pope in his departures from it almost always generalizes ideas which there are special. It gives a moral and sententious turn to the work, which does not belong to it. I have noted many such passages." This is a remarkably self-aware observation from a man who himself lived very much with Pope's Augustan ether, which sought to reconstitute the messy world in coherent moral terms. Adams also made the striking observation that Homer had his heroes participate in Olympic games only days after a major battle. Didn't any of them, he wondered, need time to recover from their wounds?

At times Adams wrote to Louisa in a romantic spirit; he sent her a quatrain from one of John Donne's love sonnets. When more time than usual passed between letters, he wrote that he was terrified that she had fallen ill—as she, by coincidence, had just written to him. The misunderstandings that separated John Quincy and Louisa would never cease to cause pain and confusion and even anger, and yet they were deeply, irrevocably bound to one another.

In early August, Adams heard the shocking news that Mary Frazier had died of consumption at the age of thirty, leaving an infant behind. When Louisa sent him a consolatory note, he wrote back stiffly to say that he "lamented her loss as I should have done that of any other young woman the wife of my friend." Adams sincerely believed that his moral sensibilities trumped even his most ardent desires. Perhaps, though, he was more troubled in the depths of his soul than he let on. Many years later, as an old man of seventy-one, he took a walk in the Mount Auburn Cemetery in Cambridge on a Sunday in November. There, by chance, he saw a headstone with the name "Maria Osborne Sargent"—the daughter of Daniel Sargent and Mary Frazier. She had died young, as her mother had. And his mind immediately reeled back to Mary—"to me the most beautiful and the most beloved of her sex." The ancient, long-suppressed feelings welled up inside him, and this old man, long married, cried out in the privacy of his journal, "Dearly!—how dearly did the sacrifice of her cost me, voluntary as it was. . . . Four years of exquisite wretchedness followed this separation." And then, finally, he had formed "other and more propitious ties."

CHAPTER 11

The Boylston Professor of
Rhetoric and Oratory

(1804–1807)

DEMOGRAPHICALLY AND GEOGRAPHICALLY, THE AMERICA OF 1800 was very much the America of the Revolution: a coastal nation, hemmed in by "western" mountain ranges like the Alleghenies, with only a few thousand miles of rutted post road linking cities and states to one another. As the historian Henry Adams, John Quincy's grandson, wrote, "The same bad roads and difficult rivers, connecting the same small towns, stretched into the same forests in 1800 as when the armies of Braddock and Amherst"—in the time of the French and Indian War—"pierced the northern and western wilderness, except that those roads extended a few miles farther from the seacoast."

But America *was* changing economically, politically, and psychologically. The West had already begun to exert its magnetic force; visitors from Europe were astonished at the geographic mobility of Americans, picking up from the cities and moving into the hinterland. A new class of entrepreneurs harnessed steam power and water power, while merchants grew rich trading with the new colonies on the West Coast. And new habits made new men, who valued risk and self-reliance. Americans were becoming less European and more American.

Thomas Jefferson was the tribune of this emerging nation. Jefferson once wrote, "The revolution of 1800"—the change, that is, brought about by his election—"was as real a revolution in the principles of our government as the revolution of 1776 was in its form." Many historians accept that this was so. Although we tend to think that it was Andrew Jackson who ushered in the democratic transformation of America, the process really began with the election of Jefferson. As much an aristocrat in his own way as John Adams, Jefferson nevertheless put an end to rule by a New England elite that had deeply identified with England and with aristocratic principles of government. Jefferson's simple clothing and offhand manner in the White House, so different from his predecessor's more pompous style, offered a new image of a defiantly homespun America. He ruled in the name of the ordinary American, sweeping the Federalists out of government and replacing them with citizens of humbler background. His election ushered in a new era of citizen participation in government that ordinary Americans, and especially the new Americans of the West, found deeply appealing.

By securing the unfathomably large territory of Louisiana, Jefferson cemented the support he already enjoyed in the South and the West and indeed across the country. In the election of 1804, Jefferson and the Republicans won a smashing victory, taking 162 of 176 electoral votes, 27 of 34 Senate seats, 116 of 141 House seats. Jefferson won Massachusetts and Connecticut, the opposition heartland. The Federalist Party was finished as a national rival to the Republicans. Indeed, it had been finished for some while. By the time of the 1802 by-election, Henry Adams remarked, "Federalism was already an old-fashioned thing; a subject of ridicule to people who had no faith in forms; a halfway house between the European past and the American future."

The New England old guard viewed themselves as the repository of American values and virtues; they could not accept the unfamiliar America they saw taking shape before them. In a kind of decorous dress rehearsal for the bitter arguments over territorial expansion that would soon divide the country and help usher in the Civil War, senior Federalists began calling for a New England secession. Timothy Pickering declared, "The people of the East can not reconcile their habits, views and interests with those of the South and the West. The latter are beginning to rule with a rod of iron." Fisher Ames said flatly, "Our country is too big for union." Even William Plumer, a moderate who shared Adams' views of the Louisiana Purchase, favored disunion. "We feel that we are Virginia slaves now," he wrote to a correspondent, "and that we are to be delivered over to Kentucky and the other Western states, when our Virginia masters are tired of us."

John Quincy Adams felt as primordially attached to New England as any of these men despite his long years in Europe. He shared their fear of eclipse. In the late summer and early fall of 1804, with the national election approaching, he wrote a series of broadsides meant to discredit the "Virginia faction," as he called it, of the Massachusetts state legislature, as well as the national Republican Party. Writing under the pen name Publius Valerius, he warned of "the singular phenomenon" of a party "who build all their hopes of success upon the basis of unlimited devotion to a system, the first feature of which is annihilation of New England's weight and influence in the Union." Among other proofs of this sulfurous claim Adams cited was the opposition by Massachusetts Republicans to an effort, which Adams himself had strongly supported, to put an end to the so-called three-fifths compromise enshrined in the Constitution, which had inflated the political power of the slave-owning states by counting each slave as three-fifths of a citizen for the purpose of apportioning seats in Congress.

Adams also, intriguingly, cited the Louisiana Purchase, which of course he had supported. The new states formed from the territory, he noted, would be "thrown into the scale of southern and western influence." Adams went on to assert that "in the relative situation of the United States, New England and the maritime states have been constantly declining in power and consequence; they must continue to decline in proportion as the growth of the southern and western parts shall be more rapid than theirs." But, Adams added, this change, "being founded in nature . . . cannot be resisted"—a recognition that set him apart from Federalist zealots like Pickering. Adams accepted the painful reality that he lived in a contracting sphere. As he would be a man of no party, so he would be a man of no region. He considered regional chauvinism an even greater threat to the union than was partisanship. Adams' colleagues understood that he was not to be approached on the question of separation, though he was still party to the rumors and the whispered conversations by the Senate fireside.

Adams did not refer to the secession plot either in his journal or in his letters of the time, but in 1828, when he was serving as president, he publicly alleged that plans for secession had been formed in late 1803, "immediately after, and as a consequence of, the acquisition of Louisiana." The conspirators, Adams said, were led by "a distinguished citizen of Connecticut" and had chosen a "military leader." The old men who had once hatched this plot angrily denied the claim, and indeed some of the most prominent

Federalists had told Pickering that they would never join his plot. But William Plumer publicly admitted that a group of Federalists had planned to "establish a separate government in New England," perhaps including Pennsylvania as well.

In an open letter to Adams, Plumer wrote that Uriah Tracey, a senator from Connecticut, informed him in early 1804 that Alexander Hamilton had agreed to meet with the secessionists in Boston that fall. The meeting never happened because on July 11, 1804, Aaron Burr killed Hamilton in a duel. There is no reason to believe that Hamilton would have approved a plan for secession. Burr himself was probably the "military leader" of whom Adams was thinking, for Pickering and others had approached him, as well as Hamilton, about joining their ranks. Though then serving as Jefferson's vice president, Burr, a supreme opportunist and protean figure, knew that he was to be dropped in the 1804 election and was prepared to serve as the cat's-paw of the secessionists. Hamilton, according to virtually all evidence, was not; one of the provocations for the duel was that Hamilton had denounced Burr as a "Catiline"—a traitor. Burr went on to prove Hamilton right, for in 1805 he embarked on a tour of the West apparently designed to raise an insurrection against the government. He was arrested and tried for treason (and acquitted).

The United States in 1804 still felt improbable. The states had been separate colonies for generations before they had bound themselves together in a federation a quarter of a century earlier. The Constitution had been in force for fifteen years. Travel between north and south was almost unheard of. Thomas Jefferson never stirred more than a few miles north of Washington, nor did John Adams ever venture below it. A citizen of Massachusetts might feel more at home in England than in Virginia or certainly than in Kentucky. The forces that drove these men apart were strong, and the habit of accepting adverse political outcomes—even of believing in legitimate difference of opinion—was very new. The power of Virginia would only grow over the ensuing years, and New England's leaders would seriously contemplate separation again in 1810 and yet again in 1814. The doctrine of secession was born not in South Carolina, but in Massachusetts and Connecticut. Adams would resist Northern threats to the union as fiercely as he later would the threat from the South.

ADAMS' SELF-ASSIGNED ROLE AS MINORITY OF THE MINORITY WAS wearing on him. John and Abigail almost seemed to regret the paces they had put him through as a boy. In late 1804, John wrote from the farm, "Virtuous and studious from your youth, beyond any other Instance I know, I have great confidence in your success in the Service of your Country, however dark your prospects may be at present." A few months later, John wrote again to try to rally his son's spirits: "For fifteen years, i.e. from the year 1760 to 1775 I was in the Valley, the dark Valley of Grief, Gloom and disappointment; Unalterably devoted to Principles whose Advocates were for a great portion of that time a Smaller Minority than yours is now."

I would never seek to compare my tribulations to yours, the ever-dutiful son responded. But, he added, "you had a great consolation—the honor and profit which you never failed to derive from your profession." That consolation, said the younger Adams, he would never enjoy. His father, in turn, rejoined that John Quincy had all the gifts required to be a great lawyer, if only he cared to use them. "But you are too much disposed to gloom and despondency." That was so, though hearing it wouldn't make him otherwise.

The elder Adamses were still adjusting themselves to the difference between the energetic young man who had left Boston in 1794 and the altogether more solemn, even joyless husband, father, and officeholder he had become. Abigail tried to make light of the change she saw in him, though it plainly worried her. She said that she had smiled when she read a letter to his father in which he admitted to a certain "stiffness of temper." She thought that might be an encouraging sign of self-awareness. In fact, she wrote to him, he had "contracted a reserve and a coldness of address which was not natural to you."

A few years earlier, Abigail had blamed her son's solemnity on the cares Louisa had heaped on him; having already exhausted that explanation, she now attributed his manner to the fact that "your having resided abroad during such critical periods as you witnessed both in Holland and England, you were obliged in your public capacity to be constantly upon your guard, that nothing improper escaped you either in words or looks." She was suggesting that John Quincy had increasingly come to wear his diplomatic mask as his own face—a piercing insight. Or perhaps, she added, he had grown too accustomed to the company of books rather than of men and women. "I am anxious," she wrote, "that you should have what Lord Chatham calls, Benevolence in trifles"—that he should smile on his friends, that he should not take everything so seriously. "I know it to be in the Heart; to the outward Man only it is wanting." Yet Adams' exterior had become so impenetrable that only those closest to him, and not always they, knew what was in his heart.

Abigail was receiving intelligence about her son's habits in Washington from her friend Elizabeth Susan Quincy, Josiah Quincy's wife. She was hardly surprised to learn that he was paying too little attention to his health and his appearance. In late 1805 and early 1806, Abigail sent a volley of letters to Washington that were arguably more suitable to a fourteen-year-old boy than a US senator and former minister to Prussia. She warned John Quincy against taking walks on an empty stomach. Soon afterwards, she wrote again to say, "Your dijestion is defective, your food does not nourish you, you do not derive spirits or strength from it. I would recommend to you to eat a hard Bisquit, and 3 figs daily, between meals, Make the experiment, add a Glass of wine, and tell me after one month if you do not feel the benifit of it." A few months later she had a new complaint: "Now I hope you never appear in Senate with a Beard two days old, or otherways make, what is called a shabby appearence. Seriously I think a mans usefulness depends much upon his personal appearence." Adams took no more note of this advice than he had of his mother's suggestion that he show benevolence in trifles. He was a man of settled habits, and he recoiled before almost any counsel that did not originate with himself.

AT THE END OF THE 1805 CONGRESSIONAL SESSION, ADAMS LEFT for Quincy, as he always did; this time, however, Louisa came with him. Perhaps she felt that she had won the battle over residence but had lost the war. Life in Quincy, under the eyes of her mother-in-law, turned out to be very much the mixed blessing Louisa had feared. She and her husband and the two boys now lived on their own in one of the family homes at the foot of Penn's Hill. There was never a shortage of reminders that Louisa was no Adams. She was mortified to discover that she could not get the hang of milking a cow. She and her sister Kitty, whom she had brought with her, were expected to do the cooking and the household chores, like all Adams women, but tottered around in a state of clumsy confusion. By this time Tom, who had seemed to be on the edge of inveterate bachelorhood, had married Nancy Harrow, a Haverhill girl he had courted for years, and moved in with his parents. Abigail and Nancy understood one another, and got along with one another, as Abigail and Louisa never managed to do.

Louisa and John Quincy could not settle on a system of living that satisfied them both. When they were preparing to return to Washington that fall, Adams announced to his wife that their children would be staying behind—baby John to live with his grandparents, George to stay down the road with the Cranches, his great aunt and uncle. This was the way things had been done in the Adams household, though very much not, of course, in the Johnson household. Louisa was devastated to be deprived of her boys and repented of her decision to leave Washington. She found the situation so intolerable that the following year she gave in altogether, moving up to Quincy and staying there.

Adams himself seemed rather lost in Quincy. On May 29, 1805, he wrote, "I was again quite unwell all this afternoon. I find it yet impossible to reverse the doom of idleness and mental imbecility to which I have been condemned." And then, a few weeks later, came a bolt of good news that offered the possibility of a different and far less vexatious life: Josiah Quincy called to say that the Harvard Corporation had chosen Adams to serve as Boylston Professor of Rhetoric and Oratory. Nicholas Boylston, a relation on his mother's side, had left a bequest thirty years earlier to establish such a position, but sufficient funds had accumulated only in recent years. The donor's nephew, Ward Nicholas Boylston, had insisted that his good friend John Quincy Adams should get the post.

A year earlier, Quincy had approached Adams with the news that Harvard was thinking about choosing him to succeed President Willard, who had just died. Other friends with important Harvard connections had urged him to make himself available. Grumbling that he was not formally qualified, he had spurned the offer. But Adams loved Harvard, and he was eager to perform great works of scholarship. Not only had he studied the classic works on the subject, as many educated men had, but he had heard the great masters in Congress, in Parliament, and in the pulpit. He had tried—and failed, he would have said—to form himself into a great orator. The subject mattered deeply to him. Beyond all that, the professorship would give a purpose to his vast but aimless reading.

In early August, Adams sent an unusual letter to Samuel Dexter, chairman of the Committee of the Harvard Corporation and the Board of Overseers. Rather than simply accept the offer, Adams pointed out that he already had a job that would keep him away from Cambridge half the year. He proposed that rather than give one lecture a week for forty weeks, he give two per week for twenty weeks. And since, as any professor knows, he would have to do a great deal of preparatory work before teaching a new course, he proposed to give only twenty lectures each of the first two years. Also, he hoped that students could give their declamations on the same day he taught, so he could accomplish all his work in a single day.

Most remarkably, Adams asked to be excused from a religious test to be required of the holder of the chair. "With the most perfect deference and respect for the legislature of the college," Adams wrote, "I must question their authority to require my subscription to a creed not recognized by the Constitution or the laws of the state." Perhaps Adams was thinking of his father, who had chosen not to enroll him in Oxford in order to avoid a formal subscription to the Trinitarian creed. Harvard, on the other hand, wasn't asking Adams to profess any beliefs he did not in fact hold. He objected on principle to making a formal declaration of his faith, especially on behalf of a position for which religious principles were plainly irrelevant. He concluded the letter by expressing the wish that the Corporation "altogether discard every consideration of personal accommodation to me." Dexter and his colleagues may have choked on the disingenuousness of this last sentiment.

Harvard tried, within reason, to satisfy Adams' extraordinary demands. The pledge of religious faith was waived. The Corporation proposed to use a substitute to carry out whatever duties Adams proved unable to satisfy. Adams wrote back at length to explain how such a stipulation would be inconsistent "with the manifest intention of the Boylston foundation itself." In short, no. Coming from someone else, such relentless pettifogging would have amounted to egotism. In Adams' case, it is probably best to take his objections at face value. He would not bend on anything he considered a matter of principle, no matter what the possible cost to his own happiness. And with Adams, practically everything was a matter of principle. Harvard capitulated.

And now Adams' summers had a purpose beyond gunning and rambling and writing letters and comparing translations of Homer. He memorized Greek roots every morning at dawn and then read the New Testament in Greek. He read Aristotle, Plato, and Ovid. Above all, he read Cicero on oration—Cicero, whose elegantly balanced measures offered the image not only of perfect oratory but of perfected thought, of measure itself. Rhetoric, in Adams' day, meant classical rhetoric—the study of the means by which the classic authors deployed the arts of persuasion. Oratory was spoken rhetoric. Here Adams undertook a study of his contemporaries—above all, those in the pulpit. He wondered, for example, why a Reverend Flint, though quite eloquent, seemed to repel his congregants. "His defect," Adams concluded, "is mere monotony, from two causes. 1. The want of proper inflexions in the voice, and 2. a pronunciation given to almost every syllable the same *quantity* of time. He must have formed this habit, by too much anxiety to speak *distinctly*." He noticed that another preacher, Mr. Richardson, dropped the *r* after a vowel in longer words, "as Tabenacle, Constenation, Govenor, Propety."

Adams often belabored himself for his deficiencies as an orator. He believed that he suffered from an incurable problem: "slowness of comprehension." It is unlikely that anyone who ever met Adams agreed with this diagnosis, but he could find no other source for his shortcomings. "Sometimes," he wrote, "from inability to find the words to finish a thought commenced, I begin a sentence with propriety, and end it with nonsense." But Adams always believed that effort, especially heroically disciplined effort, could be brought to bear on every defect. He hoped that "by continual exertions, application and self-censure part of the ill-effects of these infirmities may be remedied." Adams' conscientious study of oratory was designed both to improve his understanding of the art and to remedy his flaws as a public speaker. The plan must have worked, for he would become, over time, one of the most celebrated orators of America's greatest age of oratory.

THE INTERVAL OF INTERNATIONAL PEACE THAT COINCIDED WITH Thomas Jefferson's first term began to fray in 1805, when English seizures of American ships became intolerable. The British navy had responded to a problem for which Americans did not feel responsible—ill-paid and ill-treated British sailors deserting in order to sign up with American captains—by boarding American ships in order to seize suspected British turncoats and "impressing" American sailors while they were at it. The numbers of Americans taken at sea was always tiny compared to the number of Englishmen who deserted for American ships, but Americans were outraged at the high-handedness of British captains who lurked off the American coast and boarded American ships. And as hostilities with France resumed, England began to crack down on American shipping. In 1805 the British Admiralty further outraged American merchants by placing onerous restrictions on the long-standing trade between the French West Indies and Europe. By the end of the year, with the public aroused against a foreign nation as it had not been since the XYZ affair, a naval war with England was looking increasingly possible. In January 1806, James Madison, Jefferson's secretary of state, published an essay, which he had placed on the seat of every legislator, arguing that Britain had violated American neutrality and international law.

Adams was not only immune to Federalist Anglophilia but, unlike many of the wealthy merchants now serving in Congress, had no personal economic ties to the Atlantic trade; nor, for that matter, did many of his yeomen constituents. Adams shared the Jefferson administration's view that the United States must show England that it was not to be trifled with. In February 1806, Senate leaders introduced a series of resolutions condemning the new British ruling on trade, calling on the president to demand the restoration of American goods and the return of sailors, and proposing "nonimportation" of British goods—a one-way embargo. A committee was drawn up to consider the measures, and Adams was then appointed to a three-man subcommittee tasked with finding language that could gain wide acceptance. Adams himself was asked to do the drafting.

Ever since Adams had staked out his lonely position on the Louisiana Purchase, the Republicans had come to see him as an important asset. When Adams had stopped in Philadelphia the previous November on his way to Washington, his friend Dr. Benjamin Rush had told him that Jefferson and Madison held him in high esteem and were thinking of him for a diplomatic mission. In his usual way, Adams had waved off the suggestion as an improbability, while taking care to convey that he "would not refuse it merely because the nomination should come from" the Republican president. This was not a coded message that he wished to switch parties so much as an expression of Adams' belief that he must stand outside of any party.

Adams began to see himself as something other than a principled loner. He had never, he acknowledged to himself, "taken the lead." But he felt that the nation needed him to do so. It was crucial for Congress to present a united front to the former colonial master, which still harbored ambitions of restoring its dominion. He fretted that he lacked the gift of geniality, which he saw in some of his other colleagues. That wasn't all. "I feel," he wrote, " a distressing consciousness of my own weakness of capacity, together with a profound and anxious wish for more powerful means. I lament the want of *genius*, for I want a mighty Agent for the service of my country." In fact it wasn't genius Adams lacked but the gift of leadership, and yet he needed to find a way to lead. "I see that the advancement or declension of my influence will depend on my conduct throughout this affair more than on any other single subject. But the occasion calls for every exertion of my faculties to serve the public."

But how could he conciliate men divided by party spirit? Adams was disgusted by the pusillanimity of his fellow Federalists, unwilling to adopt any serious measure to check Britain and fully prepared to excuse British depredations. Even Uriah Tracy, "with his all talents, which are very great, and all his virtues, which are many, cannot divest himself of party feelings," he wrote. The Federalists were prepared to vote for the measures condemning English trade restrictions and demanding the restoration of American goods, but not for nonimportation, which would wreck the transatlantic trade on which New England's economy depended.

Over a weekend, Adams sequestered himself with books of maritime law and produced a new version of the three bills. When the committee convened on Monday, the Federalists objected to Adams' harsh language; among other things, he had accused the British of committing "wanton" violations. Adams, forgetting all his fine resolutions, rejoined "with warmth" that "wanton" was a perfectly apt characterization of those violations. He could control neither his temper nor his intellectual vanity, as he admitted to himself in his journal that night. He did, however, agree to excise the epithets. Ultimately, the committee, and then the full Senate, adopted all three resolutions, though the Senate accepted President Jefferson's request that nonimportation be delayed until November, in the hopes that a resolution could be found in the meantime. Such was the public mood that Adams' Federalist colleagues voted in favor of condemning England and demanding restoration, yet he was the only member of the party to vote for nonimportation. It was a fateful choice that would lead before long to the end of his career as a Federalist politician.

ADAMS HAD NOW BECOME THE CHIEF FOCUS OF THE FAMILY'S attention and hopes—and its chief source of support. His father had retired to Peacefields, his brother Charles had died, Tom had no income of his own, and Nabby's husband, William Stephens Smith, had turned out to be a shiftless charmer with a flair for ruinous schemes. In the spring of 1806, Smith, deeply in debt, had been jailed for joining a plot to overthrow Spanish rule in Venezuela. Though soon released, Smith was stripped of the job as surveyor of the Port of New York that John Quincy Adams had arranged for him. Senator Adams was now the sole family breadwinner.

Adams was formally installed as the Boylston Professor of Rhetoric—the title exists to this day—on June 12, 1806. At the time Harvard had only about half a dozen professors, so Adams was adding materially to the stock, and the prestige, of the faculty. The ceremony was terribly solemn, and Adams was sufficiently flattered that he recorded it in his journal in great detail: "From the philosophy chamber"—in Massachusetts Hall—"we went in procession to the meeting-house" beyond the campus. "The president began by an introductory prayer. Next followed an Anthem. Then an Address by the President in Latin. Mr. Ware read the regulations of the Professorship. I read and subscribed the declaration, and delivered it to the Governor as Chairman of the Overseers." He then gave a speech—"it was well received; but the company was very small."

In that speech Adams introduced the main themes that would animate his course of lectures. Adams knew very well that for many of his students "rhetoric" described a set of hurdles and obstacles and obscure regulations designed to limit the torrent of writing and speech to an orderly stream. Adams intended to rescue this ancient art from its modern slumber. In Adams' richly stocked mind, now fortified with months of study, rhetoric and oratory constituted a point of convergence of the classical, the Christian, and the republican—the three orienting points of his life. Had not God given Aaron to the tongue-tied Moses in order to speak his law to the Israelites? For the ancients, of course, "the talent of public speaking was the key to the highest dignities." That was no longer true, not because eloquence was a form of decoration with which moderns could dispense, but because moderns, unlike the citizens of Rome and Athens, no longer governed themselves through the kinds of "deliberative assembles" in which the gifted orator could shape the destiny of a nation. Since America was the one nation in which a vestige of those republics survived, it needed eloquent men as no other, lesser nation did. Men of the cloth, of course, still swayed their congregation through oratory; so did men of the bar.

Adams closed with a peroration meant to demonstrate the power and urgency of the art and science he planned to delineate. "Sons of Harvard!" he cried. "It cannot be necessary to urge upon You the importance of the art, concerning which I am speaking. Is it the purpose of your future life to minister in the temples of Almighty God"? Or "to defend the persons, the property, and the fame of your fellow citizens from the open assaults of violence, and the secret encroachments of fraud?" Or are you one "whose bosom burns with the fires of honorable ambition; who aspires to immortalize his name by the extent and importance of his services to his country"? If so, he concluded to his modest audience, "let him catch from the relics of ancient oratory those unresisted powers, which mould the mind of man to the will of the speaker, and yield the guidance of a nation to the dominion of the voice."

In his ensuing lectures, Adams offered crisp definitions of his subject, observing that oratory was the art, and rhetoric, the science, of "speaking well." Laboriously he cleared the ground of accumulated misconceptions about this art and science—that they were frivolous or pedantic or even, as Socrates had alleged, pernicious to the life of a republic. The opposite was true: "Eloquence is the child of liberty." Adams traced the history of rhetoric and oratory. He spoke of Demosthenes and of Cicero, the greatest orator of all, who dedicated his powers and his life to Rome's republic at the moment it was sinking into tyranny. He sketched out a scheme of classification, including the oratory of the assembly, the courtroom, and the pulpit, and described the methods peculiar to each.

Adams' lectures were popular. One of his students, Edward Everett, who would become governor of Massachusetts and president of Harvard, later said that visitors—what we would now call auditors—typically filled the classroom. The lectures would provide one of the absorbing preoccupations of Adams' life for the next three years; even while sitting at his desk in the Senate he would ponder and write and revise while the endless speechifying faded into a dim background hum.

During this summer Adams was bunking in Cambridge with his old friend Benjamin Waterhouse. Louisa had stayed in Washington once again, this time because she was pregnant, and had long since learned that her only chance to carry a pregnancy to term was to immobilize herself. The bitterness of the previous summer had subsided or perhaps sunk into the deep deposit of unexpressed feelings between them. A lonely Adams wrote Louisa letters full of affection. "I send you *les plus tendre baisers de l'Amour*,"—the sweetest kisses of love—he wrote in one. In another he sent her a lyrical description of a solar eclipse he had just witnessed. Then, in late June, Louisa wrote with devastating news—the child, a boy, had been stillborn. Calling on the stoicism that was second nature to him, Adams passed through the ensuing day without betraying his feelings and then went back to his room "and there yielded to the weakness, which I had so long struggled to conceal and restrain." That is, he wept. But he was also overwhelmed with gratitude that his wife had survived the misfortune. Louisa's letter, he wrote, "affected me deeply by its tenderness, its resignation, and its fortitude."

John Quincy and Louisa were often separated during the latter years of Adams' tenure in Washington, either because she was in Washington during the summer or because she remained in Quincy with the children over the winter when he returned to the capital. (She had gone north with the children after her miscarriage.) Louisa would send news of George's health, to which her husband would react with alarm, forcing her to reassure him that a cough was not a mortal blow. Once he wrote a letter to little George in French, for he worried that George's French might not be up to snuff. After Adams left Quincy for Washington in November 1806, and Louisa stayed behind with the children, they wrote to one another every few days. He had promised George a rocking horse if he kept up with his French, and he wrote sternly to say, "No French—no horse." Little brother John decided that *he* would win the horse and walked around reciting a little poem in French he had memorized. On New Year's Day 1807, Adams wrote to Louisa to say, in his formal but deeply heartfelt way, "To offer you, the kindest wishes of the season, my best friend, is almost unnecessary; my happiness, and felicity, in this world, is so interwoven with yours, that I fondly believe, the one cannot be sensible of a joy, or a pain, which is not sincerely participated by the other."

It was not easy for Adams to express himself as people ordinarily did. In late 1806, Nancy Hellen's two-year-old son died, and Louisa wrote to implore her husband to offer Nancy simple words of consolation. He responded defensively. "For your sake and for that of your Sisters I have often wished that I had been that man of elegant and accomplished manners, who can recommend himself to the regard of others, by *little attentions.*" This transparently condescending gibe stung Louisa, and she responded with a mixture of fondness and mockery that no one else could muster in the face of Adams' massive solemnity. "I was a little surprized at your appearing *so angry* at the observations made in my letter," she wrote back. "I merely meant to insinuate that by now and then addressing *her* particularly in conversation, and leading her to partake of it, she would feel herself highly flatter'd. This my testy friend was all I required, and you must really think me mad, if you supposed that by *little attentions*, I could possibly think of *Chesterfieldian graces*. Any one really possessing them, would laugh at the Idea."

In fact, Adams knew that he was in the wrong, even if it was not quite in his nature to admit it. He sat down to write something to Nancy, for this was his way. He later admitted to Louisa that the lines "were instigated by your remarks; and with a view to shew some of that attention which I am sensible is too often neglected by me." His condolence took the form of a poem of seventy-odd lines:

> Oh! Nancy! be that solace thine:
> Let Hope her healing charm impart;
> And soothe, with melodies divine,

The Anguish of a *Mother's* Heart.
Oh! think, the darlings of thy love,
Divested of this earthly clod,
Amid unnumber'd Saints above,
Bask in the bosom of their God.

Adams' verses were suffused with deep feeling, not with Chesterfieldian graces. He was so accustomed to holding his feelings in check that he needed the artifice, the high convention, of poetry in order to express emotions that would otherwise have felt unseemly. Louisa wrote back as soon as she had received a copy:

How shall I express my gratitude, my thanks, my admiration, of your very beautiful lines, my best beloved friend you have more than answer'd my every wish and evidently proved how little trouble it costs you to gain the hearts of all those you wish to please. . . . My tears flow every time I peruse them and my heart is filled with sensations utterly impossible to express, but your heart will understand what I cannot describe.

Adams' reticence was extreme even for his time and place, and at times it frustrated the people closest to him. Louisa knew his heart as no one else did and understood that he felt far more than he would permit himself to say—which perhaps explains why she continued to admire him, and perhaps also to love him, despite his harshness and occasional cruelty. He had always written poems to her and about her; a kind of alter-ego Adams peeked through his rhymes. That Adams was as likely to be playful as mournful. He was, in fact, in a poeticizing mood during that winter of 1806–1807. Loneliness may have awakened his muse—as well as his desire. After returning from a party where he had ogled what passed for a scantily clad young woman, he sent Louisa a piece of doggerel "To Miss _____ in Full *Un*-Dress at a Ball." After recounting how in the Garden of Eden nakedness had been a sign of innocence but had since become a mark of the jade, he proceeded to his subject:

Dear Sally! let thy heart be kind—
Discover *all* thy charms—
Fling the *last* fig-leaf to the wind,
And snatch me to thy arms!

Louisa said that she had been startled by his "saucy" lines, but she did not, apparently, worry over her husband's wandering eye. And soon he paid her a rich tribute of her own. Louisa's birthday fell on February 12, and that day he set out to compose a birthday gift of verse. He would, he decided, chronicle his day, from dawn until he snuffed out his bedside candle; it took him four days to complete all fourteen of his eight-line stanzas. The last of them read:

> Thus, in succession, pass my days,
> While time with flagging Pinion flies,
> And still the promis'd hour delays,
> When *thou* shalt once more charm my eyes
> *Louisa*! thus remote from thee
> Still Something to each joy is wanting;
> While *thy* affection can, to me
> Make the most dreary Scene enchanting.

CHAPTER 12

If We Must Perish, Let It Be in
Defense of Our Rights

(1807–1809)

BY 1807 AMERICA STOOD AT THE LIP OF A FUNNEL DOWN which it would slide, slowly but inexorably, toward war with England. The preparations for war would heighten the divide between those Americans who identified with Britain and benefited from its trade and those who did not. The Federalists would increasingly become a minority faction clinging to America's old colonial master and to the nation's past, and Adams would be forced to choose between Federalist and Republican, and indeed between New England and the nation. The process that began with Louisiana—or perhaps with his first days in the Massachusetts State Senate—would end with the debate over policy toward England. Adams would, of course, choose exile and ostracism.

The first months of the new legislative session were calm; Adams often whiled away the time in the midst of boring speeches by writing letters or planning the next year's lectures on rhetoric. Only toward the end of the term did something consequential occur: news reached Washington that James Monroe, the minister in England, had won agreement on a treaty designed to end the rising hostilities. Jefferson and Madison had instructed Monroe to demand an end to impressment and a restoration of the trading rights of neutral powers. But by this time Britain and France were embroiled in an escalating trade war, with Napoleon seeking to starve Britain into submission by blockading all the European ports over which France exercised control, and the far stronger British navy seeking to choke off commerce from France's (and Spain's) West Indian colonies. George Canning, the British foreign minister, refused to end impressment and insisted on maintaining England's right to retaliate against neutrals unless they had broken relations with France. Monroe, exceeding his instructions, had signed a pact that preserved those British prerogatives. Jefferson and Madison rejected the agreement as an unwarranted and unnecessary show of deference to a superior power and refused to even submit it to the Senate. The United States and England were drifting toward war, though both the president and his secretary of state were eager to find some way out of the impasse.

Then the British perpetrated an atrocity that aroused the nation to patriotic fury. On June 22, the captain of the HMS *Leopard*, a British warship patrolling the waters just a few miles off the Virginia coast, demanded the right to board the USS *Chesapeake*, a naval vessel, in order to search for British seamen on board. When the American captain refused, the *Leopard* opened fire, killing three and wounding eighteen. The *Chesapeake* had been caught unawares, and the captain, who had himself been wounded, ran down its flag. Officers from the *Leopard* boarded and seized four seamen, of whom only one was a true deserter (and was forthwith hanged from the yardarm).

News of this humiliation raced up and down the Eastern Seaboard; the *Chesapeake's* unfortunate captain was court-martialed. Mobs destroyed whatever British property they could find; towns passed resolutions ending all commerce with England. In Boston, however, the Federalists refused to convene a town meeting. Any confrontation with England would prove disastrous for the merchants whose wealth had fueled the development of Boston and whose interests the Federalists steadily protected. Moreover, the Essex Junto so feared and despised Napoleonic France—and the allegedly pro-French President Jefferson—that some were prepared to rationalize incidents like the attack on the *Chesapeake*, to John Quincy Adams' disgust.

The state's Republicans, by contrast, were eager to convene and called a meeting for July 10. Adams, already a renegade Federalist, attended—a coup for his party's rivals. He was asked to serve on a seven-man committee that drew up a resolution condemning the naval assault and vowing to support "with our lives and fortunes" whatever measures might be required to defend national honor. The following day, Adams recorded that a friend had told him, "*I should have my head taken off*, for apostasy, by the federalists." He began hearing rumors that he had switched parties. The grain of truth behind the story was that his position within his own party was rapidly becoming untenable.

THAT SUMMER ADAMS WAS SETTLING INTO HIS NEW LIFE AS HARVARD professor. He delivered his lectures every week and spent some time trying to referee a confrontation at the college, where President Samuel Webber had demanded that students sign a confession admitting to disciplinary infractions, on pain of expulsion. The students dared him to expel them instead. Asked to intervene, Adams advised the students to comply; most didn't and simply abandoned Cambridge for home, leaving Adams' classes half-empty. Nevertheless, Adams devoted himself heart and soul to his lectures, which he described in his journal as "the labors of Sisyphus." He was no longer rooming with Waterhouse; he had purchased a new home at the corner of Nassau Street and Frog Lane, later Boylston Street, though he complained that it both smoked and leaked.

The great event of the summer was the birth on August 18 of a third boy, Charles Francis. Louisa's labor was agonizing, and Adams, never calm at such moments, feared that he would lose either his wife or his child. Both recovered rapidly, though two weeks later Adams recorded that Louisa was in such intense pain that she could not sleep without laudanum, the opiate applied to all excruciating ailments of the day. Charles Francis and George were ill as well. Adams himself had a severe cold and sore throat, which he treated with "rasped spermaceti" and loaf-sugar. Everyone recovered, if slowly.

In mid-October, Adams and Louisa headed down to Washington with Charles Francis, for President Jefferson had asked Congress to convene three weeks early in order to confront the crisis with England. (George and John once against stayed back with their grandparents.) Adams' own situation in the Senate had changed radically, and he scarcely knew what to make of it. Of his closest friends in his own party, William Plumer had retired, and Uriah Tracy had died. The remaining Federalists largely spurned him. In his journal Adams noted, "I have met with at least as much opposition from my party friends as from their adversaries, I believe more." The Republicans, on the other hand, embraced him, for who could better promote their cause than a New Englander known for his uncompromising commitment to truth? Adams was made chairman of the committee considering a bill to exclude British warships from American ports—the "aggression bill," it was derisively called in New England—and another to consider whether to expel Ohio senator John Smith, a Federalist who had for a time aided Burr's conspiracy. At the end of the year he wrote, in a state of perplexity, "My general consideration among my fellow-citizens, though not marked by any new public testimonial in the course of the year, has been to my observation apparently rising."

Adams gazed over the horizon and saw the outlines of a coming war. He was, it's true, an alarmist temperamentally disposed to see calamity encroaching from all sides. There may have been as well a part of him that sought war, as a test of whether he had the inner steel of his father and his father's generation. "May I meet it as becomes a Man!," he abjured himself. Yet Adams was torn. Jefferson was following a policy of procrastination, hoping that the problem would eventually sort itself out without hostilities. Adams fretted that both the pacific president and his docile Congress were simply unwilling to grasp the nettle of conflict. "I observe among the members," he wrote, "great embarrassment, alarm, anxiety, and confusion of mind. But no preparation for any measure of vigour." At the same time, his constituents were suffering; the nonimportation law was wreaking havoc with the shipping industry. Adams could not keep telling them to endure privation for the good of the country. The historian Samuel Eliot Morison, writing in 1913, called Jefferson's embargo "the greatest failure of any political experiment ever tried in the United States." Morison notes that the political effects of the embargo were almost as calamitous as the economic ones, for it threw the Federalist Party back into the arms of the Essex Junto, thus deepening Adams' isolation in the party. When Josiah Quincy asked Adams to present to the Senate a petition from eight hundred Boston citizens seeking modification of the rules, he agreed. Adams favored repeal but would not deny President Jefferson the negotiating leverage the law provided.

Adams' greatest fears were realized in mid-December, when word arrived of an astonishingly onerous British Order in Council requiring all American shipping to pass through a British port and pay a British license. The rule seemed to have less to do with Britain's contest with France than with its desire to undercut the competitive advantage of the American fleet and place the United States in a state of complete dependence on England. Had Jefferson been looking for a casus belli, he might well have found it here. But he wasn't. Like John Adams, he was prepared to go to the very edge of war but was deeply reluctant to fire the first shot, or even to provoke it. Instead the president whipped through Congress a bill placing an embargo on all British maritime commerce. Adams was, once again, the only Federalist to support the measure.

Meanwhile, Adams was working night and day, weekends and even Christmas, on the question of whether to expel Smith. Many Federalists viewed the Burr conspiracy as a Republican fabrication and thus saw Adams' role as yet another act of betrayal. Senators James Bayard of Delaware and James Hillhouse of Connecticut (who had succeeded Tracy) delivered stinging attacks on the floor; Adams fumed and bit his tongue. He was enduring withering criticism in the press for his role on the "aggression bill" and for his vote on the embargo. He knew that New England merchants would circumvent the embargo, but he saw it as the only alternative to war. In a long letter to his father on December 27, he agonized over the embargo and over Smith. His position, he said, was "singular"—though rejected by his own party, "I have no communication with the Administration, but that which my place in the Senate of course implies." He had intended to be a man of no party; now his wish had been granted him in the worst possible way. He didn't—couldn't—regret his choice, but it had brought him a terrible isolation.

If there was anyone who could understand his predicament, it was his own father. John Adams wrote to say, with a brutal form of sympathy, "You are supported by no Party. You have too honest a heart, too independent a Mind and too brilliant Talents, to be sincerely and confidentially trusted by any Man who is under the Dominion of Party Maxims or Party Feelings: and where is there another Man who is not? You may depend upon it then that your fate is decided." He would be an honorable outcast, like his father.

John Quincy often turned to his father in these trying times. The elder Adams, who had nothing left to dispense but advice, was only too happy to oblige. He often prefaced his letters by saying that he knew all too well the press of business, that of course his son should feel quite free to ignore the meanderings of an old gentleman with time on his hands, and so forth. Then he would launch into the subject at hand. The "too honest a heart" letter went on for about three thousand words, which is to say that it must have taken much of the day to write. Senator Adams had asked for help on the question of international law as it bore on impressment, and the ex-president cited Roman and French law, British common law, the difference between British and American doctrines of naturalization, and on and on. He also pointed out that the United States would never have found itself in such a predicament in the first place had Jefferson adhered to the principles of vigorously enforced neutrality, which he, Adams, had devised. And so forth. The elder Adams couldn't help himself: he not only sympathized with his son but wished he were standing and fighting alongside him. As he wrote the following week, "I, who perhaps ought to be indifferent to all Things in this World, and certainly should conscientiously resign all Men, Measures and Events to Providence, must acknowledge myself to be not less anxious about public affairs, than in my Youth or middle Age. I know not but I am as solicitous about your responsibility as I was formerly for my own."

John Quincy was torn not simply between party and country but between the dangers of war and of disunion. He had seen a letter from the British governor-general of Nova Scotia to leading Federalists alleging, absurdly, that the French were conspiring with President Jefferson to start a war to gain control of British colonies in North America. Adams believed that the British were seeking to lure the Federalists into collaborating with them, and he feared that if tensions grew higher they might well succeed. The secessionist murmurings of 1803–1804 might well become a reality. Whatever faith Adams previously entertained in his own party had all but evaporated.

This may explain why Adams then took a step that was extraordinary even by his own standards of stubborn nonpartisanship. On January 23, 1808, Republican legislators convened a party caucus to nominate a candidate to succeed Jefferson. Adams was invited to attend and agreed to do so. He later explained weakly to Tom that he hadn't known that no other Federalists would go. Senator Stephen Bradley of Vermont, who organized the meeting, had said that all save "inveterate opponents" would be invited. In fact the meeting had been called to advance the candidacy of James Madison over the more radical James Monroe. Adams had been invited in an unsubtle effort at recruitment. He even received a vote for vice president.

And yet Adams spoke as if he did not believe that he had broken from his party or advanced his position in the rival party. When, the following week, Senator William Branch Giles of Virginia spoke elliptically to him about the possible advantages of crossing party lines, Adams asked the Republican whether he thought trading parties for personal benefit "was a sound course of proceeding on moral and political principle." Giles, apparently little daunted, responded that while Jefferson would never offer a position to an ex-Federalist, Madison might feel otherwise. Adams rejoined that whatever support he might give to any party "shall be governed solely by public considerations." And Giles, perhaps amused rather than offended by this zeal for purity, conceded that "he believed I considered every public measure as I should a proposition in Euclid, abstracted from any party considerations."

For once, Adams' behavior had flabbergasted even his loved ones. Abigail, of all people, wrote to say that attending the caucus was "inconsistent both with your principles, and your judgment." Adams had never been so judged by his own family, and he wrote in his journal that the letter from his mother, as well as another from his father, "contain a test for my firmness, for my prudence, and for my filial reverence." (His father would take his side in subsequent correspondence.) In Washington, Josiah Quincy took him aside to say, as a friend, that Adams' principles "were too pure for those with whom I was acting, *and they would not thank me for them.*" Adams of course protested that he sought no thanks. He told Quincy that a division in the country over the question of war with England would end "either in a *Civil War* or in a dissolution of the Union with the Atlantic states in subserviency to Great-Britain." And to avert such an end he was prepared "to sacrifice everything I have in life, and even life itself."

The Federalists did not view Great Britain as their enemy; they viewed the Republicans as their enemy. John Adams had conciliated the Republicans a decade earlier; now his son had defected to their side. Adams received anonymous letters denouncing his conduct. The embargo was destroying the economy of New England with no sign that it was squeezing Great Britain to make concessions. Citizens were staging a spontaneous revolt: juries refused to convict merchants accused of violating trade restrictions. Adams worried that the embargo he had favored would provoke the civil dissension he feared. He introduced a resolution to replace it by the arming of merchant ships, as many New Englanders preferred. It was rejected. Adams was placed in the acutely uncomfortable position of defending a policy that was politically toxic *and* had very little chance of succeeding. But he defended it anyway.

Now the Essex Junto went on the attack. On February 16, Timothy Pickering, Adams' inveterate foe in the Senate, sent a letter to Governor Daniel Sullivan of Massachusetts, later published as a pamphlet, accusing Adams of doing Jefferson's bidding and Jefferson in turn of doing the bidding of Napoleon. "By false policy, or by inordinate fears," Pickering wrote, "our country may be betrayed and subjugated to France as surely as by corruption." Pickering had apparently swallowed the allegations made in the secret letter from the British governor-general. His letter was reprinted in the Federalist press all over the country. Several leading Republicans approached Adams and asked him to publicly refute the rumor of secret designs with France. Adams sought a private meeting with the president. On March 15, Jefferson reassured him that no such deal existed, and he also reiterated his view that war with England could be and should be avoided. Adams took the president at his word.

Now fully certain of his ground, Adams set out to clear his name. He decided to publish his response to Pickering in the form of an open letter to Harrison Gray Otis, an old friend and a leading member of the Junto. This was a common means of joining one side of a public controversy. The decision, he noted in his journal, "will be to me of the first importance. It will not be without importance to the Nation. It was taken from a strong sense of duty. That it will increase the difficulties and dangers of my situation I am fully aware. That it will bring upon me the fury of all my former enemies and a host of new ones, I perceive." This was, for once, no exaggeration. On March 31 Adams sent the letter to William Smith Shaw, asking him to send copies to his father, to Otis, and to Governor Sullivan, and to see to its publication.

Adams' response to Pickering ran to about ten thousand words, densely argued and mostly temperate. He began on the solid ground of federal authority. Pickering had called on the "commercial states" to refuse to enforce the embargo—that is, to defy the authority of the federal government. If New England can nullify a federal statute, Adams observed, so could the Southern states. How, then, would the Union stand? Here he anticipated by a generation the argument over states' rights and "nullification," which would lead to the creation of the Confederacy. The peril, even then, was scarcely hypothetical, since Adams knew that only a few years earlier Pickering and other leading members of the Essex Junto plotted to secede from the Union.

States, Adams went on, must act not out of partial interests, but for the good of the country. He acknowledged that the embargo was hurting the region, and he reminded readers that he had sought unsuccessfully to bring it to an end. But it was too early to say that it had failed. And what was the alternative? Would the United States simply accept British terms? The Order in Council would restore the era of the tea tax and the Stamp Act. Adams sought to explain British politics: the liberals had come to accept American independence, but the Tories, now in power, hoped to restore America to a state of subjection. Those like Pickering who insisted that the United States had no quarrel with British policies offered, in effect, "unconditional surrender to the pretensions of our antagonist." And such a cringing policy was bound to fail: "Submission never yet set boundaries to encroachment." Perhaps war could not be avoided. "If we must perish," Adams ringingly concluded, "let it be in defense of our RIGHTS."

This was a battle Adams could not win; his father even wrote to say that his arguments would never sway those being harmed by the embargo.

Printers in Massachusetts published five thousand copies of the letter, and then five thousand more, but Boston printers, in league with the Junto, refused to print the letter at all. The embargo, which had largely idled the merchant fleet and devastated the regional economy, was wildly unpopular. By this time armed mobs in some Massachusetts ports were preventing federal customs officials from enforcing the measure. Federalist journals tore into Senator Adams. The *Hampshire Gazette* called him "a party scavenger." In the *Salem Gazette*, Adams was one of "Bonaparte's Senators." The *Greenfield Gazette* went yet further: Adams was a traitor "associating with the assassins of his father's character." His family despaired over the onslaught, though Adams did not regret a syllable of what he had written. Many years later, when the pamphlet was republished, he added a note describing the whole episode as "one of the transactions of my public life to which my memory recurs with the most gratifying recollections."

The Tenth Congress ended in a manner that drove a few more nails in Adams' coffin. On April 7, the Senate convened as a judicial body to consider the expulsion of Senator Smith, a man whom Adams did not despise but whom he nevertheless considered unworthy of holding his seat. It fell to Adams to serve as chief prosecutor, and he held the floor for four hours. The movement to expel fell one vote short of the two-thirds required, an outcome Adams felt "sufficiently reprobated" the offender without depriving him of his seat. But Adams' role further inflamed his party members against him. The week following, Adams once again called for a lifting of the embargo, substituting in its stead suspension of trade with England, France, Spain, and Holland and restoring commerce with the colonies. This, too, was rejected.

On April 23, just before the Senate was to adjourn, Adams was approached by Senator Nicholas Gilman, a New Hampshire Republican, saying that "it was the wish of several gentlemen with whom he had conversed to *bring me forward*, in some active and distinguished station." Apparently Adams relished the euphemism. All he needed to do, said Gilman, was to write something clarifying that he did not favor "monarchical government," since some Republicans, identifying him with his father, feared that he did. Adams recoiled before all mandatory oaths. He would not, he said, "speak ten words, nor write two lines to be President of the United States"—nor, to clear up any possible confusion, "to be anything subordinate to that."

Adams returned to Boston. For the first time in his life, he did not feel welcome in his own hometown. He went to a dinner at Harvard, a pleasant affair, he wrote, until a Dr. Osgood from Medford "attacked me in a rude and indecent manner on the subject of my letter to Mr. Otis." His old friend

Judge Davis thought he was wrong; indeed, all but one or two of his friends thought so. Theophilus Parsons, his law teacher, mentor, and friend, now a judge and a leader of the Junto, told him that the British had every right to seize American merchant ships. "He also thinks the people of this country corrupted, already in a state of voluntary subjugation to France, and ready to join an army of Bonaparte if he should send one here, to subdue themselves. The only protection of our liberty, he thinks, is the British Navy." Many of Adams' great friends seemed to him to despise their own country—and to scorn him for defending what they deemed indefensible. Adams felt so beleaguered that he could scarcely concentrate on the lectures he was preparing.

In a genuine blow, Harrison Gray Otis broke off relations and pointedly ignored Adams at social events. Louisa felt closer to the Otises than to anyone else in Boston; the break was terribly painful for her. The friendship between the families had begun forty years earlier with Otis' uncle and Adams' father. It would resume, but never as before. The temperate Otis would characterize the entire line of Adams men as "a peculiar species of our race exhibiting a combination of talent & good moral character, with passions and prejudices calculated to defeat their own objects & embarrass their friends." Adams, in turn, would call Otis "an adder in my path."

Pickering's immediate goal in disseminating his pamphlet had been to poison the incoming state legislature against the senior senator from Massachusetts, and in this he succeeded. At the end of May, legislators voted 248–213—closer than one might have expected—to appoint James Lloyd Jr. to succeed Adams, even though Adams' term ran to 1809. The legislature also instructed its federal representatives to vote to overturn the embargo. This was an extraordinary rebuke—in effect, a recall. John Adams had managed to keep the loyalty of his party until he was president; his son had worsted him, at least in this regard. Rather than waiting for the guillotine to fall, Adams responded to the vote with a terse letter of resignation. He was already back home in Boston; now he would stay.

Adams spent the second half of 1808 delivering his lectures and corresponding with Massachusetts Republicans in Congress like Orchard Cook and Ezekiel Bacon, as well as other leading Republican figures. To William Branch Giles he wrote, "I have felt on this occasion a little of the spirit of martyrdom; knowing that my governing motives have been pure, disinterested and patriotic, I can consider every calumny cast upon me, as the tribute of profligate passions to honest principle." In a later letter he told Giles that he could not find a single Federalist willing to stand with him in public, whatever they would say to him in private. (He would later publish these letters as evidence of the Federalist secession plot.) But Adams had long since recognized that the embargo wasn't working. He favored replacing it with "non-intercourse" with France and England, though others, including his father, felt certain that New England merchants would undermine and evade the one as they had the other.

Whatever Adams' intentions were, his flinty integrity had made him a valuable political commodity. In the first weeks of the fall of 1808, leading Republicans visited him at home to ask him to run for Congress. Adams was hardly averse to returning to Washington, including as a Republican, but he would have had to stand against his friend Josiah Quincy, a moderate who had not distanced himself from Adams as others had. He declined. He thought seriously of running for governor of Massachusetts but ultimately chose not to. There were so many rumors of secret deals Adams had reached with the Republicans in exchange for his support on the embargo that he may have felt that anything he did under a Republican banner would be taken as proof of an unseemly bargain. Nevertheless, in retirement he was shaping the debate over the response to British depredations. On New Year's Day 1809, Republican Senator Orchard Cook wrote to say, "Your Letters do much good, are treated with *very great respect indeed*—I think you have now more influence than when here—not mere opinion in which you deal very sparingly but the excellent Arguments & reasons you give for every conclusion." Cook implored Adams to keep writing with advice.

Adams for once had time to spend with his family. He had been vowing for years to bolster George's French, though he found that he lacked both the patience and the perseverance for the job. He worried constantly over the children's spills and sneezes. When George banged his head on a stone step, Adams was, he admitted, "unhinged" by his fears and prayed for fortitude. In December, all three children fell ill, and Adams drove Louisa crazy with his desperate anxiety. His fears were so inordinate that they both wound up laughing. They often disagreed about how to raise the boys. Adams bridled when Louisa sent George to dancing school. All civilized people, as Louisa understood it, learned to dance; Adams himself had learned to dance in France and Holland, though he had been a bit older. Adams groused that it was foolishness. In this case, Louisa won.

In late January 1809, Adams left for Washington to argue a case before the Supreme Court. By this time New England was, as Adams feared, up in arms over the embargo. Judge Davis had agreed to hear an argument that the embargo violated the state constitution. Adams wrote to Louisa from New York to say that everywhere he went he was asked whether the court would nullify the statute, whether the New England states would secede, whether it was true that ships were massing in the harbors to break the embargo. On February 1, the Massachusetts legislature passed a resolution calling on states to meet to consider forming a New England confederation. Adams' inveterate fear that the pull of foreign loyalties would tear apart the Union was proving to be not at all hyperbolic. Talk of noncompliance with the embargo was everywhere.

Adams spent his first few weeks in Washington attending the Supreme Court and feverishly preparing for his argument in *Fletcher v. Peck*, a case which had grown out of a dispute over sales of a massive tract of land that would later become the states of Mississippi and Alabama. He argued the case March 2 and left certain that the judges had been averse to his view and that his presentation had been "dull and tedious almost beyond endurance."

The embargo gave way before the Union did. In Washington, Southern congressmen, who had remained staunch supporters of the embargo, began to waver. On March 1, 1809, in the final days of the Jefferson administration, Congress repealed the embargo by enacting instead the Non-Intercourse Act, setting restrictions on trade to British and French ports and lifting all other embargoes—precisely the course Adams had proposed. He was hardly alone, but it may be that Orchard Cook was right in saying that his influence had become greater once he had been forced out of office. In fact, Madison was no more eager for war than Jefferson had been; like Jefferson, he hoped that the problem would solve itself over time.

On March 6, President Madison, who had just taken office, asked Adams to visit him at his home on Capitol Hill. (Jefferson hadn't yet moved out of the president's house.) Madison informed Adams that in literally half an hour he would be submitting his name to the Senate as minister to Russia. The "pressure of business," he said, had prevented him from discussing his plans until now. President Madison explained that while he had no specific negotiations in view, Tsar Alexander was eager to establish diplomatic relations with the United States. In recent years the Russian army had played a key role in blocking Napoleon's advance to the east, but otherwise had remained a neutral between the two great combatants. The other neutrals, like Sweden, were far too weak to resist concerted pressure from either France or England. Russian support, both commercial and diplomatic, could enable the United States to remain independent of the two great powers. Russia was the most powerful nation in the world with whom the United States had not yet established diplomatic relations. It was an assignment very much befitting America's most seasoned and brilliant diplomat, but it was also extremely onerous owing to Russia's remoteness and its dismal climate. When Adams asked how long the assignment would be, Madison said that the duration was indefinite "and might last three or four years." The president needed an answer right away. Adams said that he "could see no sufficient reason for refusing the nomination."

On March 8, however, the Senate voted against sending a minister to Russia, on the grounds that no such mission was necessary. Adams hadn't yet plucked up the courage to tell Louisa, or his parents, of a new stage in his life that would horrify all of them. Now he wrote to Louisa to say that he imagined she would be pleased to hear that a diplomatic mission he had been offered had been rejected. He said he, too, was relieved. He then returned to Boston. Adams spent the spring and early summer practicing the law in his desultory way, reading, and seeing to George's education, as his parents had seen to his. Every morning before eight he and George took turns reading to each other four chapters of the Bible, and then father and son talked about the meaning of the passages. He showed George the countries of the world on a map. He took George and John to a performance of *Hamlet*.

The private life Adams assured everyone that he craved seemed to be unfolding before him. Then, on July 4, he attended an Independence Day celebration that began at the statehouse and proceeded to the Old South Church. While he was there, his cousin William Smith Shaw brought him papers that included an official notification from the secretary of state that after another vote in the Senate he had been confirmed as minister to the court of St. Petersburg. Adams informed the thunderstruck Louisa that they would soon leave for Russia; in addition, he had decided that they would bring the baby with them but leave George and John with the Cranches. Louisa had consented to live without the boys for a few months at a time, but even then very unhappily. Now her husband was not asking but informing her that she would have to do without them for years on end—no one knew how long. Louisa was crushed. "O it was too hard!" she would write later. "Not a soul entered into my feelings and all laughed to scorn my suffering at crying out that it was all affectation—Every preparation was made without the slightest consultation with me." That, of course, was the Adams way. Abigail had watched her husband and son sail away to Europe not once but twice, and she had stifled her tears. An Adams understood that one lived not for oneself but for the nation. All Louisa wanted was to live as others did, among their friends and loved ones. The first great wound of Louisa's life had been her father's public disgrace. The second would be the abandonment of her boys. And there would be others, worse still.

Adams didn't have to go, of course; the nation scarcely needed this mission as it had his father's to France thirty years before. He used his journal, as he often did, to review his own thought process. "My personal motives for staying home are of the strongest kind," he wrote; "the age of my parents, and the infancy of my children both urge to the same result. My connection to the College, is another strong tie which I break with great reluctance; and by refusing the Office I should promote my personal popularity more than by accepting it"—by rebutting the presumption of a quid pro quo over his support for the Republicans. Louisa's feelings evidently did not figure in his calculations; she did not matter in the way that his parents and children—his blood relations—did.

On the other hand, he wrote, he had "the duty of a citizen to obey the call of his country," the opportunity to leave behind "the most virulent and unrelenting Persecution," the "vague hope" of actually doing some good, and the wish to justify President Madison's confidence in him. He addressed God directly, as he often did at moments of supreme importance, humbly asking for his blessings and praying for "the entire extrication of my Country from her difficulties and dangers, and for myself the continued consciousness of purity in my motives, and so far as it has been or may be deserved, the approbation of my Countrymen." He did not, however, ask God for guidance. That he found within himself.

Adams spent his last few weeks packing up thousands of books for storage, paying a last round of visits, trying to rent out part of his home, resigning his board memberships. Every well-born and underemployed young man in Boston seemed eager to accompany him as private secretary. Adams agreed that he would take Nabby's son, William Steuben Smith, who had found little to do in New York City and whose father was hopelessly incapable of supporting his own family. He decided as well that Louisa's younger sister Kitty should come along to keep Louisa company, though Russia was hardly the place for a single young woman concerned about her marriage prospects. Abigail and Aunt Cranch came to Boston for a last visit. Louisa went with them back to Quincy for a heart-rending farewell with her two older boys. Adams secured passage on the *Horace* for the traveling party, which also included Martha Godfrey, Louisa's maid, and Nelson—his last name doesn't appear in extant documents—Adams' black manservant. On August 5, the day of his departure, Adams composed a devotional poem imploring Providence to steady his soul so that he might do good to mankind.

CHAPTER 13

A Bull-Dog Among Spaniels

(1809–1812)

T HE LAST TIME ADAMS HAD SAILED FOR EUROPE HE HAD
been a novice of twenty-seven, easily flustered and very worried
about the impression he would make. Now, fifteen years later, he
was a husband and father of three, a former US senator, and an influential
thinker and legislator. He had already experienced tumult; as he boarded
the *Horace*, he seemed to be leaving in his wake the wreckage of his political
career. Adams felt the separation from his parents as he never had before;
perhaps he would never see them again. And he had left his boys to grow
up without their parents. He was a man with many cares, and already, at
forty-two, the thin line of his mouth and the sharp set of his jaw conveyed
a settled air of solemn watchfulness. In his journal he scrupulously described each stage of the trip to the wharf in Charlestown, listed the names
of each of the passengers on the *Horace*, noted the salute from other ships
as they sailed out of the harbor. He felt the weight of the moment.

Adams felt the peril as well. He was sailing into the middle of a maritime war between France and England, each with its own allies. Both sides
tried to prevent neutrals like the United States from trading with the other.
In mid-September, off the coast of Norway, a Danish warship demanded
that the *Horace* put into the harbor of Christiansand. The Danes enforced
the French blockade of Northern Europe. The *Horace*'s Captain Bickford
refused; the Danish officer ordered his men, standing by in a rowboat, to

board the American vessel, and Bickford instructed his sailors to resist. "We had in half a minute a dozen or fifteen men with pikes, axes and swords on the quarter-deck," Adams wrote to Tom, "and the men from the boat pressing forward to her forecastle to attempt boarding us." The Danes blinked first, and the *Horace* survived what would have been a very bloody clash.

But that was only the beginning. A week later, after rounding the northern tip of Denmark, the *Horace* was boarded by officers from a British man-o'-war. The British were enforcing their own blockade against Copenhagen to the south. Nor could an American ship be permitted to pass without a search for fugitive English sailors. The British captain demanded to see the crew's papers and strode up and down—with infuriating arrogance, Adams thought—inspecting every last sailor to make sure that each man matched his description. The *Horace* was allowed to pass only when Adams insisted on seeing the admiral of the fleet and explaining his diplomatic mission.

The ship sailed southward until it reached the narrow channel between Sweden and Denmark. And then a tremendous North Atlantic storm blew up, snapping the *Horace*'s foremast in half, though Captain Bickford quickly rigged up a new one. For ten days the storm raged, and the ship remained stuck off the eastern coast of Sweden as if fastened to the bottom. To the left, on the Danish side, was the island of Elsinore, where Shakespeare had set *Hamlet*, which Adams regarded as the greatest of all works of the human hand. From somewhere he produced a set of watercolors and in his journal made a sketch of Elsinore castle and another of a harbor with sailing ships.

It was now mid-October. Captain Bickford, who had made the voyage eleven times before, dreaded the winter passage through the Baltic and the Gulf of Finland and "absolutely despaired of reaching his destined port this winter," Adams wrote his brother. The Danish pilot they had taken on board, who had made the trip thirty-six times, was yet more certain that the *Horace* would be trapped in ice before reaching the Russian port of Cronstadt. And there would be no place along the way to put in.

These deeply experienced sailors were telling Adams that they all risked death if they continued onward. Captain Bickford proposed that they retrace their path to Kiel, in northern Germany, from where Adams could, if he wished, make a 1,500-mile overland passage to St. Petersburg. Or, more likely, they could pass the winter there. Everyone on board favored turning around, but Adams alone refused. He could not accept the prospect of arriving months late, even though no urgent business awaited him. Still, though he was happy to risk his own life, he had to think of his family. He finally agreed to go to Kiel but insisted that they double back if the wind changed over the next few days.

The wind promptly changed, and Captain Bickford resumed the forward journey. But the winds reversed themselves again the following day. Bickford wanted to turn around once again, but Adams refused. Bickford angrily told Adams that he alone would bear the consequences for whatever mishap they suffered. Adams promptly accepted. The winds stayed adverse for an agonizing thirty-six hours. And then they blew fair once again and stayed that way. The *Horace* reached Cronstadt on October 22; by the next day, the Adams party had docked at a quay on the Neva River just opposite the famous equestrian statue of Peter the Great in St. Isaac's Square. Adams felt that he had narrowly averted disaster—but not the disaster of being locked in ice. He later wrote to Tom, "I cannot but reproach myself for this momentary compliance, as it indicated a flexibility, which ought not belong to me." This would be the first of many instances in which Adams demonstrated a cool nonchalance in the face of mortal danger. This was not the acquired courage of a man who had overcome the natural fear of death in battle but a kind of principled insistence on placing one's own life beneath that of the republic—the courage of a Cicero or a Cato, the classical exemplars of Adams' era. That, certainly, is how Adams would have described the matter to himself. However, the "compliance" with which Adams taxed himself was, in fact, his very meager consideration for the lives of his wife and children, as well as those of the captain and crew. He felt that the duty imposed upon him obliged him to endanger as well all those who happened to be accompanying him.

The Adams party was lodged at the Hotel de Londres overlooking the river on the Nevsky Prospect. This establishment was a good deal more rudimentary even than the Hotel de Russie in Berlin. Louisa later recalled that her room was "a stone hole entered by Stone passages and so full of rats that they would drag the braid [bread] from the table by my bedside which I kept for the Child." But apartments in the city were ruinously expensive and scarcely affordable on Adams' salary of $9,000, the same figure he had received in Berlin a decade earlier. Worse yet, diplomats were expected to be kitted out in an elaborate uniform—even republicans like Adams. On his first day in town he was taken to the tailor, the milliner, the wigmaker, the shoemaker, and so on. A few days later, Louisa wrote to Abigail asking her to send cotton cambric, muslin for cravats, fine cotton stockings, and other articles for her husband's wardrobe. She asked little for herself or the baby.

Adams found that life in St. Petersburg was like life in Berlin but on an immensely grander and more opulent scale. He was invited to dancing parties, balls, masquerades, luncheons, outings. Everyone gambled at cards and dice. The French ambassador, the Duc de Caulaincourt, entertained on a colossal scale; his budget, Adams learned, ran to a million rubles a year. A lunch "*sans ceremonie*" at his palace began at three thirty, proceeded through a theatrical performance by French actresses, dancing, a light dinner, sleight-of-hand tricks, and more dancing. Adams got home after one in the morning. At the *bal masqué d'enfants* (children's masked ball) held soon thereafter, Charles Francis, at not quite two and a half years of age, made his debut in St. Petersburg society dressed as an Indian.

As in Berlin, Adams was fortunate to represent his country at a court ruled by an energetic young prince. Alexander had ascended to the throne in 1801, when conspirators had murdered his father, Paul, a paranoid and unstable figure who had threatened to drag the empire down with him. By the time Adams arrived in St. Petersburg, Alexander was thirty-one, amiable and gracious, a liberal and a reformer by the standards of the Romanovs. He was a tall, handsome man with blue eyes and fair skin. Adams had been formally presented to the emperor within days of his arrival—an auspicious sign, he thought. Alexander had taken him by the arm and asked him, in French, about his family, his voyage, the principal cities of America. Adams had been very impressed. He wrote to Tom of Alexander's "spirit of benevolence and humanity."

At forty-two, Adams was closer in age to Alexander than were the other members of the diplomatic corps. And only one other minister was accompanied by his wife. Alexander and Empress Elizabeth felt a sense of kinship with the young American family, as had Frederick Wilhelm and Luise. Louisa had been terrified to be presented to the beautiful Elizabeth—a contemporary and thoroughly smitten English traveler described her elegant figure as "lilylike"—but the empress had done her best to put the overwhelmed young woman at her ease. Alexander and Elizabeth had lost two children before the age of two, the last one only eighteen months before the Adamses arrived, a shattering event for the tsarina. They were much taken with Charles Francis. Louisa reported to Abigail that the imperial majesties had played with the toddler for an hour, both speaking English to him, though the boy was actually more comfortable in French and German. "His Majesty told Mr. A he was a most charming Child."

Adams was fortunate to have a charming and socially adroit wife in Louisa, and an adorable child in Charles Francis, for the minister himself had already taken on the aspect of a graven idol. "He sat in the frivolous assemblies of St. Petersburg like a bull-dog among spaniels," as a British visitor put it, "and many were the times that I drew monosyllables and grim smiles from him and tried in vain to mitigate his venom." Adams' hostility toward the British, especially at this period, probably accounts for this menacing description, but it is true that he often turned what this official called his "vinegar aspect" on the world. He could not, like Caulaincourt, seduce through charm.

AT THIS TIME, RUSSIA PLAYED A KEY ROLE IN NAPOLEON'S FAR-flung constellation of alliances. Starting in 1805, Napoleon had won a string of victories that had made him master of much of Europe and given him the upper hand in his perpetual bid to isolate Great Britain and bring his great rival to its knees. He had defeated the Austrians at Austerlitz and the Prussians at Jena, marching into Berlin in 1806. The following year he took on and defeated the tsar's forces at Eylau and Friedland, and he forced Alexander to sue for peace at the conference of Tilsit in July. There the tsar had signed a treaty of alliance with his fellow emperor and had agreed to join the so-called Continental System, a series of embargos that kept English goods, whether carried by English ships or neutrals like the United States, out of the ports of Europe. Napoleon had invaded Portugal and Spain in the hopes of sealing off the Continent to English trade.

Adams' central task was persuading Alexander and his advisors to make an exception from the Continental System for American ships. Russia had not formally blockaded American vessels, but on one pretext or another merchant ships that made it as far as the Russian ports of Cronstadt or Archangel had typically not been permitted to unload their cargoes of sugar and coffee, cotton and indigo. But Adams found that he had an even more pressing problem to address: on his passage through Denmark he had learned that Danish privateers had impounded as many as fifty American ships with cargo valued at no less than $5 million. The goods, in most cases, were destined for Russia. Soon after his arrival, Adams had spoken to the Danish minister, who had said that he was powerless to help because Denmark had little choice but to do France's bidding. He then approached Alexander's foreign minister, Count Nikolai Rumiantsev, pointing out that the Continental System—like Jefferson's ill-fated embargo—had done little to damage England or turn English public opinion against war and was mostly doing harm to neutrals like the United States.

Rumiantsev, the most pro-French figure at court, demurred. But Adams pressed on. Could he ask the tsar to intercede with Denmark, a small nation that could scarcely afford to vex Russia? Rumiantsev, despite his own disapproval, agreed to transmit the message, and several days later he returned to say that, to his great surprise, Alexander had ordered him to inform the Danes that the emperor would like to see American claims processed quickly and American ships released. The foreign minister added that Alexander had been eager to demonstrate his partiality to America. Two months later, in February 1810, Rumiantsev related to Adams a conversation he had just held with the Danish minister, who said that his country, wishing to oblige the tsar, had agreed to expedite the American claims. This was a remarkable diplomatic victory to have won in so short a time.

Exactly how much credit Adams—or Louisa or Charles Francis—deserves for this change of heart is impossible to say. Rumiantsev often told the American minister how very well disposed the emperor was to him, but flattery was second nature for so accomplished a courtier. And Caulaincourt, whose job was to entertain his way into the heart of the Russian court, recognized that he was not making as much headway as his unique social position would seem to imply. He wrote to Napoleon to say that "beneath all his natural benevolence, honesty, and loyalty, beneath all his exalted ideas and principles, there is a strong element of royal dissimulation born of an obstinacy which nothing can conquer." Alexander did not trust Napoleon and bristled as France engulfed Poland, whose aristocracy was deeply tied to his own. And Russian merchants were clamoring over the loss of trade that had come with the French alliance.

In that first winter of 1809–1810, Adams discovered that St. Petersburg was a place of marvels. The city turned perfectly white, and the Neva itself, frozen as solid as marble, seemed to disappear into the flat vista. The gaily painted rooftops turned white, as did the men's long beards. The low-wheeled *droschkas* (carriages with leather aprons projecting from either side) gave way to sleds, which shot down the broad avenues at astonishing speeds; the vehicles of the nobility were borne along by splendid horses with the gait of greyhounds, one in harness and the other, loosely bound, prancing and curvetting in perfect synchrony. Caulaincourt held a magnificent party at his country villa. A giant hill had been fashioned from snow and ice; elegant women in fur-lined riding regalia scooted down the slope on sleds whose runners fit into grooves carved in the ice. Adams, of course, stayed inside and talked to Baron Blome, the Danish minister. This rustic fantasia concluded with a cotillion danced by men and women who had exchanged clothes with one another. Louisa, who was both mildly scandal-ized and ashamed of her humble wardrobe, declined.

Louisa was not pleased with her new life, and not being an Adams, she lacked the high tone of self-sacrifice that was second nature to her husband and his family. She wrote desperate-sounding letters to Abigail about the exorbitant costs and the dreadful habits of their social circle. The women of the nobility, she wrote soon after arriving, "are cold and haughtily repulsive in their manners but there is at the same time a degree of freedom and un-restraint which is utterly impossible to describe[.] Everything like wit or superior sense is entirely exploded and nothing but sentiment of the most languishing and susceptible kind can be tolerated." Even compared to Ber-lin, St. Petersburg society was indolent, frivolous, and wildly extravagant. A gentlemen was expected to run up immense debts and as often as not repu-diate them. Adams, of course, would do no such thing: instead, the family scrimped and saved and lived like church mice amid the stupefying luxury of the court. Adams wrote home to describe his epic struggle against debt.

Abigail had never wanted her son to leave; she wrote to Louisa's mother, Catherine, to say that she had consented only because she felt he needed to escape the obloquy and the loss even of dear friends that he had suffered after the debate over the embargo. In August 1810, Abigail took matters in hand in a way that very few mothers would or could have done: she wrote to President Madison to inform him that "the outfit and sallery allowed by Congress" to a minister was so grossly inadequate to her son's expenses in Russia that "inevitable ruin must be the consequences to himself and fam-ily." She asked the president to bring Adams home.

Two weeks later, Madison wrote back to say that since he had no wish to bankrupt her son, the minister could return home with no damage to his reputation. The president may have imagined that Adams had been too embarrassed to speak on his own behalf and so had asked his mother to do so for him, since he then wrote directly to Adams describing the exchange with Abigail and saying that he would send a blank commission permitting him to sign over the powers to someone of his own choosing. It is true, the president reflected, that the emperor could not fail to take such an abrupt departure as a personal affront. Of course Adams would sooner have gone to the bottom on the *Horace* than leave his post on such conditions.

Adams had a gift for adapting to his circumstances without ever sacri-ficing an ounce of his essential nature. The St. Petersburg winter drove ev-eryone inside—but not the American minister. Even in the dead of winter, when the temperature often fell to 25 below zero, Adams donned his bearskin coat, his fur hat, and his thick mittens and trudged out into the blinding whiteness along the Neva Prospect and the river, alone save for the occasional hunched-over figures zipping by in sleds—and the emperor. Alexander liked to travel around the city with only his carriage driver for company, often stopping to talk to his subjects, and he kept up this habit even in the winter. The conversation between tsar and minister was usually banal, but always warm; Adams had suffered an inflammation of the eyes—a chronic condition—and the emperor asked with what seemed to Adams a genuine show of concern if he had yet recovered. Alexander often practiced his English on the American minister.

Alexander was a man in whom both piety and license were equally pronounced. His many romantic affairs were public knowledge, and before long he had fixed his eye on Kitty, a flirtatious young woman who already had acquired a sizeable collection of beaux in St. Petersburg. He paid Kitty such attention that she and Louisa stopped taking their usual walk for fear of provoking gossip. When they resumed, the emperor happened upon them again and said, looking straight at Kitty, that they must not omit their daily stroll. In May 1810, when Caulaincourt gave a ball in honor of Napoleon's marriage to Marie Louise of Austria, Kitty was explicitly invited even though she had not been presented at court—normally a serious breach of etiquette. At the ball, Alexander asked Louisa to dance a Polonaise, a kind of syncopated stroll, and then asked where her sister was. "I'll get her," said a shocked Louisa. "No, I will," said the emperor. Soon the two were dancing, and Louisa was horrified to see that her unschooled sister was behaving as if the tsar of all the Russians was a prize catch, laughing out loud and prattling about who knows what. Dinner was delayed twenty-five minutes while the emperor enjoyed his flirtation. An actual affair between the two, which Alexander evidently had in mind, would have been a scandal of colossal proportions, and while it was impossible for the Adamses to keep Kitty at home, or stop the emperor from holding private chats with her, they kept a careful watch over her. The relationship developed no further.

Like most of his colleagues, Adams had a great deal of time on his hands and began to develop eccentric hobbies of his own. He became fascinated, and then obsessed, by the variation among the weights and measures of various nations. The actual height or weight or volume denoted by terms of measurement had not yet been fixed, so that it was not possible to compare measurements in different countries with perfect certainty. This fact did not seem to bother most men, but it consumed Adams. After intense study of reference works and exacting calculations, he was able to determine that a Russian pound corresponded to 6,316.596 grains English troy weight. One day Adams wrote in his journal that he had become absorbed by the proportions between the French *pied du roi* and the English foot. Before he knew it, hours of the day were gone. "Any occupation to which a spur of inclinations impels me," he lamented, "operates as a sort of compulsion upon me, and leaves me no longer master of my own time."

The elder Adams had a metaphysical bent; his son was, at bottom, a systematizer. The younger Adams had always loved to count and measure things, such as how long it took him to walk from Cambridge to Quincy. But over time, this wish to impose intellectual clarity and arithmetic order upon the fuzzy world became a more marked element of his mental life.

ADAMS WAS NOW AMERICA'S MOST SENIOR, AND MOST HIGHLY regarded, diplomat. Throughout 1810 he wrote extensive letters to Secretary of State Robert Smith examining Russia's fluctuating sympathies toward France, England, and the United States. In April, he predicted that Russia's need for English trade ensured that it would eventually break with Napoleon's Continental System. But in the ensuing months he watched, with all of Europe, as Napoleon went from victory to victory, first fully absorbing Holland, then conquering northern Belgium, then Westphalia, Hanover, Hamburg, Lubeck, Norway, and a region of northern Germany known as Swedish Pomerania. Could Russia really afford to defy the French diktat? The Danes, acting on French orders, were still seizing many American vessels bound for the Baltic. American ships landing at Archangel were still being detained with one pretext or another. Rumiantsev offered unconvincing explanations. Perhaps, Adams wrote, Caulaincourt was circumventing Rumiantsev and going directly to the tsar—a suspicion he was willing to commit to correspondence only in cypher, for he knew that his letters might be opened by Russian, French, or English officials.

Adams spent much of his time preaching to Rumiantsev about the futility of the Continental System; he knew that the Russian minister repeated much of what he said to Caulaincourt, whom he believed to be sympathetic to the American cause. He often buttonholed Caulaincourt himself. It was hard to know if he was making any headway, since expressions of sympathy were the cheapest currency of the court. Leverett Harris, the American consul who had been established in St. Petersburg before Adams arrived, reported that Alexander was said to have told his foreign minister, "The Emperor Napoleon may do as he pleases. I will not quarrel with the Americans." Rumiantsev himself had plainly become more pro-American and less pro-French as he had watched the emperor's own sympathies shift. Convinced that he had worn out his welcome, Caulaincourt asked in the late spring of 1810 to be recalled to Paris. In October, the count told Adams that Alexander's feelings about the United States "were as strong and fixed as they ever had been; and he might even say stronger. Our attachment to the United States, says he, I assure you is *obstinate; More obstinate than you are aware of.*"

Rumiantsev apparently knew something he could not tell the American minister. Tsar Alexander had been provoked by Napoleon's continual push to the east and the north. He had, as Adams had predicted, come under pressure from merchants damaged by the embargo. And he had not wanted to sacrifice relations with America to Napoleon's insatiable war aims. On December 31, 1810, the emperor issued a ukase lifting all restrictions on exports from Russia and on imports coming by sea, while at the same time imposing a heavy tariff on goods arriving overland, most of which came from France. Alexander thus broke decisively with the Continental System. This was a tremendous diplomatic triumph for the United States, since most cargo carried to Russia by ship came in American vessels, whether the cargo was American or English. Napoleon, who had forged a crucial alliance with Alexander at Tilsit only three years earlier, would soon conclude that he had to invade Russia in order to preserve his domination of Europe.

BY THE MIDDLE OF 1810, THE ADAMS FAMILY HAD BECOME SETTLED in St. Petersburg, if not quite comfortably so. They had taken over a house left by a departing ambassador, paying $1,500 a year. Adams found that it was impossible to live a respectable life in the capital city without a retinue that struck him as wildly extravagant and unnecessary. He described his household in his journal: "We have a Maitre d'Hotel, or Steward. A Cook who has under him two Scullions, Moozhiks, A Swiss or Porter, Two footmen, A Moozhik to make the fires, A Coachman and Postillion, and Thomas the Black man, to be my valet de chambre, Martha Godfrey the maid we brought with us from America, A femme de chambre of Mrs. Adams, who is the wife of the Steward, A House-Maid and a Laundry maid. The Swiss, the Cook, and one of the footmen are married; and their wives all live in the house. The Steward has two Children, and the washerwoman a daughter; all of whom are also kept in the house." Virtually all of the servants considered petty thievery a privilege of their position, and Adams was forever double-checking the wine cellar.

Despite his desperate efforts at household economy, Adams considered himself comfortably established, and he very much enjoyed the marks of respect he received from the emperor. He was deeply engaged in the never-ending struggle to remove obstacles from American trade in Russia. He did not know that Abigail's efforts to have him returned home—the consequence of his earlier complaints—had finally born fruit. On February 26, 1811, Secretary Monroe sent Adams a letter that referenced the correspondence between Abigail and President Madison and announced that the president had nominated him to fill a vacant seat on the Supreme Court.

The news had already shot around Quincy, producing a flood of letters from delighted family members. Abigail described the appointment as "a call of Providence" and the post of Justice as higher even than that of "First Majestrate." She assured him that the job had not been solicited by his friends and glossed over the fact that it had already been refused by Madison's first choice, while the Senate had rejected the second. "I will," she wrote, "take it for granted that after mature reflection you will resign yourself to the call of your Country." She took it so for granted, in fact, that she told George and John that their parents would soon be coming home and wrote separately to Louisa with congratulations. John Adams wrote to say that, astonishingly, the Senate had immediately and unanimously confirmed the nomination, and that "both parties vie with each other in expressions of Satisfaction." The elder Adams acknowledged that his son had said before that he had no wish to be a judge, but reminded him of the joys of family and fatherhood that awaited him. Hoping, apparently, to foreclose any possible path of escape for his very prickly son, he added, "Such is the Popularity of the appointment that your Refusal of it, will create a National Disgust and Resentment. It will be imputed to Pride, Oddity, Fastidiosity and an unbridled unbounded Ambition."

Adams did not receive official notice of the appointment until early July, but by April he had read about it in the English newspapers. And in early June, after a period of reflection, he wrote a letter to the president declining. Adams had often said, and plainly believed, that a man in public service must be prepared to heed his country's call, whatever it was. That was the trump card he had played with Louisa when she had begged him not to accept the post he now occupied. But when the nation's call collided with his own wishes—as it had not in the case of his ministerial position—he could make the kind of exceptions to which he would never admit. He wrote to Tom to say, "I am also, and always shall be, too much of a political partisan for a judge." Adams viewed a Supreme Court judgeship as a gloriously upholstered prison cell with a lifetime sentence. Of course he could not say as much to Madison. To the president he noted, with elaborate circumlocution, that Louisa was pregnant and so could not travel. She had suffered yet another miscarriage a few months earlier, and there could certainly be no question of an arduous ocean passage with an infant. But that was also a useful pretext.

To his father Adams admitted that nothing had ever satisfied him more than the news of his unanimous confirmation, which he could now enjoy in the retirement to private life he said he had in mind. Is that, in fact, what he had in mind? John Adams' allusion to "unbounded Ambition" had been meant to alert his son to the widespread assumption that only a man aiming for the presidency would turn down a lifetime appointment to the Supreme Court. The possibility that he would set tongues wagging would scarcely deter the stubborn diplomat. There is no evidence that Adams seriously entertained that hope this early in his life, but he had been raised from childhood to make himself fit for the nation's highest honors, a euphemism no one had to define.

John Adams was too logical a man to maintain the argument, but he knew that the withdrawal of which John Quincy wrote was as contrary to his temperament as cool impartiality. "Shall you retire, and devote your Life to Science, Litterature and publish your Studies from Time to Time?," he wrote. "Your Nature cannot bear it. Your dearest Friend can not endure it. And what is harder to resist than your Wife's Nature, your Country will not Suffer it. This Nation will not cease to irritate and torment you, both with Flattery and Reproach till they force you out, that they may have the pleasure of insulting and abusing you." This, too, was the shared Adams ethos.

Adams' decision was devastating to his parents, perhaps to his children, and certainly to Louisa. She had grasped at every scrap of hope that they might all return to the familiar world of Quincy, and above all to George and John. And she had just suffered a serious blow. In May 1811 a letter had arrived from Walter Hellen announcing the terrible news that Nancy, his wife and Louisa's older sister, had died in childbirth, leaving him a frail widower with three young children. Both Louisa and Kitty were deeply stricken, Louisa so much so that the doctor had to administer two doses of laudanum despite the fact that she was then at the end of her second term of pregnancy. It seemed likely that she would lose the baby, as she had so many others, but she didn't.

A new summer had arrived, always a shockingly swift transition from the hyperborean winter. St. Petersburg became an entirely new city as the snow and ice receded. The city took on distinct form once again, as the broad, straight boulevards, the winding Neva, and the massive granite palaces emerged from their shaggy blanket of snow. The gilded spires and domes of the churches and the gaily painted roofs of the mansions of the nobility shone in the brilliant sun. Sleds gave way to *droschkas*. The ice on the Neva finally broke, marking the official end to the city's punishing winter. This boon was celebrated by an ancient ritual: the governor of the province offered the emperor a glass of river water, and the emperor rewarded him with a hundred ducats. The river filled with gondola-like boats, and the peasants sang ancient folk tunes as they paddled along.

The Adams' landlord had forced them out of the home they were renting on the grounds that it had been requisitioned by the court, but they had turned this misfortune to good account by renting a house on Apothecary's Island, a tiny spot of land in the middle of the Neva then (and still) used for summer homes and entertainment. Their cottage was adjacent to the magnificent gardens of Baron Stroganoff, through which they could wander. Charles Francis had a little world of his own to roam. Adams himself was thoroughly delighted with his quiet perch. "From my Cabinet windows," he wrote, "I see all the boats passing up and down the river, and am as quiet and undisturbed, as if it were an hermitage a hundred miles from the City."

Adams' natural state was fretfulness, but that summer he felt useful, busy, hopeful, and almost contented. On July 26 he wrote a passage in his diary that was more than usually reflective, as well as candid:

I have this day been married fourteen years, during which I have to bless God, for the enjoyment of a portion of felicity resulting from this relation in Society, greater than falls to the generality of mankind, and far beyond any thing that I have been conscious of deserving. Its greatest alloy has arisen from the delicacy of my wife's Constitution, the ill health which has afflicted her much of the time, and the misfortunes she has suffered from it. Our Union has not been without its trials; nor invariably without dissensions between us. There are many differences of Sentiment, of tastes and of opinions in regard to domestic economy, and to the education of children between us. There are natural frailties of temper in both of us; both being quick, and irascible, and mine being sometimes harsh. But she has always been a faithful and affectionate wife, and a careful, tender, indulgent and watchful mother to our children, all of whom she nursed herself.

Adams knew himself; he knew that he was a difficult man, and he felt grateful that he had found so admirable a partner. His sense of unworthiness was altogether sincere. And yet he could not, or would not, curb his temper, or modify his views of "domestic economy," or ward off in advance the "dissensions" between himself and Louisa. He would never be easy, whether as a husband, a father, or a friend.

In mid-August, after twelve hours of severe labor, Louisa was delivered of a baby girl—the first after three boys. Her husband insisted on naming the child Louisa. The mother was at first gravely ill, as she had been after her previous births, but in two weeks she was able to take a walk around the island and to delight in the new baby. Even the stern father was besotted with his daughter. In November, he wrote to his mother to say, "We are daily seeking for resemblances in her countenance, and associate her in fancy with all our dearest friends—She has the eyes of one; the nose of another, the mouth of a third and the forehead of a fourth, but her chin is absolutely and exclusively her own."

Adams had begun to think more and more about his children's education. On this, as on many other subjects, Adams' views were instinctively retrograde. He found much to agree with in "Discourse on the Education of Children and Youth," by the early-eighteenth-century churchman Isaac Watts, who railed against "fashionable education" and came down on the side of "severity" and "rigour." Louisa favored gentle persuasion over harsh instruction. But by now experience had cured Adams of his tendency to approach such a subject theoretically. He wrote to Tom that he had once thought of writing a treatise on education, like Locke or Rousseau, "but when George was born I very soon found that a child is not itself a piece of clay to be made according to the fancy of every potter; and secondly, that the clay, such as it was, was not committed exclusively to me, to be molded by my taste alone."

Adams had rediscovered this wisdom with Charles Francis, who was reading quite well, in French, before his fourth birthday. "He comes to me of his own accord," Adams wrote in his journal, "but it is for his apple or pear, or sugar plums, without which I cannot prevail upon him to read. . . . The sight of a boat, a noise in any other part of the house, a fly lighting upon the table, everything that can catch his eye or his ear diverts him from his book." Adams sadly, and perhaps hyperbolically, accused himself of the same distractedness—"the greatest, perhaps the only Cause, which has bound the voyage of my life in the shallows."

Adams received glowing reports about George from his mother and from Aunt Cranch, who raved about his "capacious mind," his "quickness of apprehension," his attentiveness, his love of history. George was an insatiable reader, like his father. Adams nevertheless tried to direct George's education from afar. He wrote to Tom to say that he must pay attention to George's French but also to his drawing, fencing, shooting. He must have sport, but "nothing delicate or effeminate." He should be inured to labor and fatigue. Tom and their father should subject George to a monthly examination on his studies, one that would test not simply his memory but his understanding. But all education, at bottom, was moral education, and he wrote to George with exactly the sort of warnings he used to receive from his own parents: "I hope to always hear that among your companions, the best boys are your best friends, and I trust you will always be ashamed to let any one of them learn faster or by his good conduct make himself more beloved than you."

ADAMS CONTINUED TRACKING THE STORM SIGNALS OF WAR WITH a practiced doomsayer's sense of fatality. He wrote to Secretary Monroe that Napoleon, deeply confident of his military superiority, would attack Russia no later than the summer of 1812. He warned friends and family of the folly of entering war with England. He recoiled when he heard talk of defending America's "rights," much though he believed that England had trampled on those rights. As he wrote to Abigail, "In the present condition of the world, and it is much to be doubted whether it will ever be otherwise, that right is not worth a straw, which a Nation has, without force to defend it." To his father, the great enthusiast of "wooden walls," he wrote that the United States could build a navy just fast enough to provoke Britain but not to seriously contest its control of the seas. He counseled patience; France and England would destroy one another before either could turn on the United States. A grain shortage in England had made the country dependent on trade with America.

The forces of France and Russia advanced toward one another like two terrible juggernauts. On a walk in mid-March, Adams encountered the emperor, who said grimly, "War is coming." Adams asked, "Are all hopes vanished of still preserving the peace?" And Alexander responded, "My will is yet to prevent it, but we expect to be attacked." On April 21, Rumiantsev told him that the emperor had left to review the troops gathered at the Prussian border. "The forces which were assembled on the frontier, were immense," according to the count. "On both sides. There was in history, scarcely anything like it. It was like Romance. What it would come to he knew not." On June 28, word reached St. Petersburg that the French had crossed into Russian territory at the Niemen River, at Kovno. Alexander vowed to fight until the last French soldier had been expelled from Russia. Napoleon's terrible romance had begun.

Adams had been right about war between France and Russia but premature about war between the United States and England. The British had reacted to President Madison's decision to reimpose nonimportation in early 1811 by stepping up their attacks on US shipping. The hated impressment of American sailors continued apace. The actual number of abducted navvies remained modest, but the practice made for an ideal casus belli. Officials in Washington were more confident of American abilities than Adams was, and they felt that in Napoleon they had a trump card. Buoyed by reports like those from Adams, Madison was convinced that Napoleon would conquer Russia and then turn what appeared to be his irresistible force on England, and thus that the latter would be in no mood for a draining war across the Atlantic. Canada looked ripe for the plucking.

In fact, this was a gross miscalculation. The British worried less about Napoleon than Madison imagined. And London made a symmetrical misjudgment of its own: the government was convinced that the Americans had neither the stomach nor the wherewithal for a fight, which is why the Royal Navy continued to harass American shipping. At the same time, the British did not want war, and on June 16, 1812, His Majesty's government revoked the Orders in Council authorizing the seizing of cargo destined for France and its allies. This should have made war unnecessary, and in an era of instantaneous communication, it would have. But two weeks earlier Madison, under pressure from war hawks who hoped to further expand American territory, had asked for a declaration of war. On June 18, ten days before Napoleon began his dreadful campaign in Russia, Congress complied. America would fight the British for the second time in thirty-five years.

ADAMS HAD BEEN CHEERFUL FROM THE TIME OF LOUISA'S BIRTH and the move to Apothecary Island. By the fall of 1811, though, the family had had to move back to a house on the mainland, at Voznesenskoi and Little Officers' Street. Adams sighed for the days of garden walks. That spring, he and Louisa received a letter from Abigail with an almost unimaginable skein of bad tidings: Aunt and Uncle Cranch, whom Adams loved and with whom his sons had spent precious years, died within hours of each other; Louisa's mother, Catherine Nuth Johnson, had died; and so had John Buchanan, who was married to Louisa's sister Caroline. And as if these were not heavy enough blows, Adams' sister, Nabby, had been diagnosed with breast cancer, and one of her breasts had been removed. Scarcely had they digested this mass of misfortune when they received a letter from Tom saying that his daughter, his first child, had died of whooping cough at eight months.

Both of the Adamses were prostrated by the news. Nevertheless, they had their own small children to dote on. Adams and Charles Francis took walks together almost every day, and the father spent hours listening to his four-year-old son read La Fontaine's *Fables* in the original and teaching him to read English. Little Louisa had begun saying "Momma" and "Poppa." On August 20, Adams made a brief notation in his journal: "Louisa very sick with dysentery." She was slightly more than one year old. Louisa recovered, and then the symptoms returned, more violently. Dr. Galloway, the family physician, was out of town. At eleven at night Adams sent a carriage for another physician, Dr. Simpson, who sent back word that he would come in the morning. Adams then went to the man's home himself and rousted him from bed. Galloway returned and suggested that fresh air might help. The Adamses removed to a village seven miles from the city, but Louisa grew weaker and weaker. On September 8, the little girl was having convulsions; the family rushed back to St. Petersburg. The doctors thought that her fever might be connected to teething, and they sent for a surgeon to lance her gums; but in fact her baby teeth were not ready to appear.

The next few days were almost unendurable. Sometimes Louisa seemed to rally, and desperate hope washed over the family. Then she relapsed into shaking and high fever, and she shrieked with pain. Adams found himself wishing that her agony, which no medicine seemed able to palliate, much less cure, could come to an end. His wife, tormented, sat unmoving by her daughter's cradle for days; when she finally dropped with exhaustion, Kitty took over and kept vigil for forty-eight hours straight. Adams, hopelessly distraught, went from one to the other. The doctors tried every kind of quack remedy—blisters, warm baths, laudanum, digitalis. Simpson shaved the little girl's head to apply a blister to her skull. Finally, mercifully, at 1:25 on the morning of September 15, Louisa Catherine Adams died—"as lovely an infant as ever breathed the air of Heaven," Adams wrote.

Adams did not "murmur at the dispensations of Divine Providence," as he put it. But the consolations typically offered to assuage grief—she had been spared earthly trial and so forth—had no force. "She was precisely at the age," he wrote, "when the first dawn of intelligence begins to reward the Parents pains and benefits. When every gesture was a charm, every look delight; every imperfect but improving accent, at once rapture and promise. To all this we have been called to bid adieu: And in renouncing all those expectations of exquisite enjoyment of which we had fondly looked forward to the prospect, we are stung by the memory of what we already enjoyed in her beaming intelligence and angelic temper."

Louisa's grief was immeasurably greater; it amounted almost to madness. She blamed herself for the child's death—she had weaned her too early, she thought—and her mind could conjure nothing but her daughter's image. "My heart is buried in my Louisa's grave," she wrote in her own journal, "and my greatest longing is to be laid beside her even the desire of seeing my beloved Boys gives way to this cherished hope." She meant this quite literally. Months later, she found herself beset with terror when a member of the expatriate American community fell gravely ill; she feared that Mr. Cabot would "usurp the space next to Louisa." Her wits would not fully return until a year after her daughter's death.

CHAPTER 14

Restoring the Peace of the World

(1812–1814)

URING THE SUMMER AND FALL OF 1812 THE FATE OF EUROPE hung in the balance. When Emperor Alexander left St. Petersburg for Vilna in April, John Quincy Adams understood very well that immense forces were about to clash at the continent's eastern frontier. Alexander's generals were men whose names we know today from Tolstoy: Prince Volkonsky; Prince Bagration, who was to be mortally wounded at Borodino; and Marshall Kutuzov, the old man who would trust Russia's fate to the ravages of time and winter. Adams knew them all at court. He followed the news from the front with the full knowledge that St. Petersburg was Napoleon's bull's-eye, and he might well have to flee with his family and the rest of the court. By July, the emperor had retreated to Russia before Napoleon's advancing forces; Bagration had given way at Minsk. On September 23—only a week after baby Louisa's death—the French had taken Moscow. The ancient city was being put to the torch. The diplomatic corps in St. Petersburg began to dissolve since France and its allies were no longer welcome at court. Both Count Lauriston, who had replaced Caulaincourt, and the minister from Holland came to Adams and asked him to store their diplomatic archives. Monsieur de Laval, who collected Renaissance paintings, left St. Petersburg with an enormous landscape by Claude Lorrain strapped to his carriage.

Yet Napoleon's terrible misjudgment very soon revealed itself, for the vast Russian army hemmed him in at Moscow and began to cut his forces to bits. With little shelter and less forage, his men began to starve and freeze. On October 27, the cannons in St. Petersburg fired to signal the retaking of Moscow; the event was celebrated with a Te Deum at the magnificent Kazan Cathedral. In December, Napoleon made a solitary dash for Europe along a frozen path littered with thousands of corpses of French and allied soldiers and their horses.

Adams' great source of worry during this period was the American war with England, which had broken out at almost the same time as France's war with Russia. In October 1812, on the same day he learned that Moscow had been retaken, Adams received a diplomatic dispatch informing him that General William Hull, who had been sent north to invade Canada, instead had surrendered Fort Detroit, with its men and munitions, to a combination of British and Indian forces. "The honor of my country!" Adams fumed in his journal. "Oh! God! Suffer it not to go unredeemed." Adams exchanged letters with his parents expressing disgust at the pusillanimity of American land forces, as well as occasional reverence for the country's extraordinary naval leaders. He feared national humiliation as much as military catastrophe. This was a war Adams believed ought never have been waged, but he had concluded that, as Europe was addicted to warfare, the United States would have to learn the arts of war to defend itself. "Occasional War is one of the rigorous instruments in the hands of Providence to give tone to the character of Nations," he wrote to Tom. He also wrote to suggest that naval officers rouse their men's flagging spirits by reminding them that America was fighting to end impressment—a proposal that would have seemed presumptuous in a letter to Monroe, but that he may have hoped his brother would circulate.

Adams had an important ally in St. Petersburg. The emperor wished both sides to stop fighting one another. So long as Napoleon lived, Russia needed England to concentrate all its power on defeating him, rather than skirmishing with the United States. Alexander also viewed the United States as a valuable ally and authorized Rumiantsev to tell Adams that no matter what alliances Russia contracted, "he would assent to nothing which could interrupt or impair his relations of friendship with the United States," as Adams wrote in a letter to Monroe. Adams' greatest achievement in Russia—and it was a very consequential one—was preserving and increasing the deep warmth the otherwise autocratic Alexander felt for the young republic across the ocean. In September 1812, Rumiantsev approached Adams to say that the emperor wished to serve as a mediator between England and the United States. Adams promptly conveyed the offer to Washington.

(Rumiantsev had also spoken to the English minister and had written to Russia's minister in the United States.)

The American war effort was going badly, and Napoleon, fleeing for his life, was in no position to distract England, as American officials had hoped, so Madison eagerly grasped at the Russian offer of mediation. In April 1813, he appointed Federalist senator James A. Bayard of Delaware and Albert Gallatin, the treasury secretary and probably the most able man in government, to sail to Russia to join Adams in negotiations. Adams had been hoping to finally go home and had even asked Monroe to let him return. Unbeknownst to him, Abigail had sent another entreaty to the president to bring her son back. But now he had to lead the team of negotiators. Monroe wrote to say that, in case of peace, the president wished him to serve as minister to Great Britain, adding that Madison had especially wished him to convey that he "has derived much useful information from your correspondence."

AS THE PANIC OVER NAPOLEON'S ADVANCE SUBSIDED, ADAMS FOUND himself becalmed in a semideserted capital. Louisa was prostrated with grief at her daughter's death, and Adams was plunged into a deep melancholy. He finally lost his temper with his consul, Levett Harris, whom he knew very well was taking bribes to provide American papers to the captains of British ships. And he confronted Kitty and his secretary, William Stephen Smith, who had been having a not-very-secret affair. The idea of scandal in his own household was, of course, anathema to the upright diplomat. "I had a long and very serious conversation with Mr. Smith," Adams wrote in his journal in January 1813, "who finally avowed a disposition to do right." Three days later he noted that he had carried Smith's proposal to Kitty, and she had accepted. The two would marry at the end of February.

Adams spent more and more time with Charles Francis, who was outgrowing the nursery. Louisa was too distracted with grief even to attend to her little boy. Father and son took long walks together, went on sleigh rides, and gawked at the exotic sights of the winter carnival. And Adams lavished his pedagogical ambitions on his youngest child. By the spring of 1812, he was spending at least three hours a day with his son, who, several months shy of his fifth birthday, was reading French, German, and English. By the end of that year, Charles was reading from the *Book of Common Prayer*. Adams found it very difficult to listen in silence to his son's flawed, multilingual English pronunciation and to endure his perpetual distraction.

"The most painful struggle," he wrote, "is to suppress the anger, which the perverseness of indocility occasions."

At the end of 1812, Adams wrote that "religious sentiments become from day to day more habitual to my mind"—a consequence perhaps of his suffering over his child's death. He had become an increasingly serious student of religious literature, reading deeply in the sermons of Jean-Baptiste Massillon, a divine who had preached the funeral oration of King Louis XIV and was much admired in later years by Christian skeptics like Voltaire and Jean le Rond d'Alembert. He was also closely studying the works of John Tillotson, dean of Canterbury Cathedral in the last third of the seventeenth century and a leading voice of religious tolerance. The year before, he had begun writing an extraordinary series of letters to George about the Bible. They were pitched far above the understanding of even a very bright and bookish ten-year-old. Adams understood this; he expected George to read the letters with the help of Tom and others, and to refer to them later in life. Perhaps he was thinking of the letters, deeply soaked in Scripture, which his own mother had once sent him, but these long and carefully argued texts felt much more like essays composed by a man who has pondered a subject deeply and feels the need to put his thoughts in order.

In the fall of 1811, Adams wrote a sort of introductory letter in which he explained to George that the Bible needs to be examined in different contexts—as revelation, as the early history of the world, as the history of one people, as the source of the particular system of morality and belief Christians profess. He then tackled each of these topics in a subsequent text. In his second letter he took up the idea of revelation. Beginning not with Scripture but with what he would have called natural reason—an intellectual appeal very far from the homespun world of Abigail's letters—he asserted that "it is so obvious to every reasonable being that he did not make himself, and that the world which he sees could as little make itself, that the moment we begin to exercise the power of reflection, it seems impossible to escape the conviction that there is a Creator." This was a principle with which few in the pre-Darwinian world would have disagreed. And then Adams proceeded through the doctrine of the immortal soul, of an all-powerful but immaterial God, of God's righteousness and superintendence of the universe.

The ensuing letters, continuing through 1813, were equally learned, grave, thorough—and strikingly nondogmatic. Adams regarded the Bible not as infallible text but as a human narrative inspired by revelation—the greatest of all works of literature. He knew all the debates and did not wish to be distracted by them from the central message. He told George that it was unknowable, and unnecessary to know, whether Jesus was "a manifestation of almighty God" or simply his only son. He explained why the ethical system of Scripture was superior to that of the classical world Adams otherwise admired so deeply: in the solicitude Jesus expresses toward the widow, the orphan, the deaf and the blind, and his own enemies, "we see a tenderness to the infirmities of human nature, a purity, a sublimity of virtues which never entered I say not into the codes of the Antient legislators but into the imaginations of their profoundest and most exalted Philosophers." The great moral revelation of the gospel was: "You must love one another." Adams did not say so here, but the doctrine of the brotherhood of man was the source of his conviction that democracy was founded on Scripture and thus that the Declaration of Independence was a realization in political form of the Gospels.

No record survives of George's response to this masterpiece of exegesis. But the letters tell us a great deal about his father. Adams was a passionate scholar and a relentless intellectualizer who believed that deep study illuminated every subject, whether the jumble of weights and measures or the mysteries of Christian faith. He was a man of science, and it would have been contrary to his nature to believe that the dictates of reason and of faith contravened one another. His rationalism, in turn, made him skeptical about narrow or doctrinal religious claims and predisposed him to tolerance. (This was the same man who had refused to sign an oath of religious belief at Harvard.) Yet he comfortably accepted what a deist like Jefferson might not: that revelation marked a point beyond which reason could not go. Adams was a New England Puritan raised in the spirit of Enlightenment reason.

The period after the death of baby Louisa was a time of drift and despair for both Adamses. In his journal Adams complained of "a lassitude which has almost, but not quite yet suspended all my Industry. . . . An oppression at the heart which without being positive pain is more distressing than pain itself." The minister had begun locking himself in his study. "Mr A is even more buried in study than when he left America," Louisa wrote to her mother-in-law, "and has acquired so great a disrelish for society, that even his small family circle appears at times to become irksome to him. His health is very indifferent, and the melancholy prospect, of public affairs all over the World, preys upon his spirits."

Louisa suffered yet another miscarriage in early 1813; she was so gravely ill, and so despondent, that Adams worried for her life. She began to stir as winter finally ebbed. She resumed her diary on April 4, though she wrote that she was torn between the wish to leave Russia and the horror of abandoning the spot where her daughter was buried. That same day she wrote to Abigail. Louisa usually dispensed with commas, but here the lack of punctuation lent her letter a breathlessness that seemed to border on hysteria: "my heart is almost broken my health is gone and my peace of mind is I fear for ever destroy'd." She could not, she said, bring herself to write to her boys, and she asked her mother-in-law to assure them of her love lest she never see them again. Louisa admitted that she was desperate to leave St. Petersburg, "but Mr. A wont hear of it, and I am condemned to wear out my existence, in this horrid place, without a friend, or a single human being who can participate in my feelings."

That summer, the Adams family suffered a terrible tragedy: on August 14, 1813, Nabby died of breast cancer. She died at home, with great dignity and little complaint despite unbearable pain. She had known very little serenity since marrying William Smith but had never complained of him either. Within the family Nabby was regarded as an angel, and her death was far more devastating to Abigail than Charles' had been. It was, in fact, the worst thing that had ever happened to Abigail, and her letters, even many months later, are shot through with pain. After receiving one of Louisa's doleful letters, she wrote back to say, "I was grieved to find how deeply you had been wounded." But, she added, with an unmistakable air of reproof, even though Nabby's death was a yet greater loss, she still reminded herself of her blessings. And then, having made her point, she offered gentle little sketches of Louisa's boys: John the fiery one, called "Hotspur" by his friends, and George the quiet scholar who went to his books when school was over. Adamses did not indulge in despair. Creatures of oak, they bent with the years and withered, but they did not break.

BY THE TIME SECRETARY GALLATIN AND SENATOR BAYARD REACHED St. Petersburg in July 1813, Adams had learned that Lord Liverpool, who had become the British prime minister a year earlier, had rejected the emperor's offer of mediation. The English had, however, offered to speak directly to the American team. For the Americans, the war was a question of national survival, but for Great Britain it was a distraction from the great contest for Europe provoked by Napoleon. And Napoleon kept rising from the ashes like a demigod. By the fall of 1813 his generals were facing five hundred thousand men. He suffered a series of devastating defeats in

Austria, raised yet another army, gained several improbable victories, and finally provoked England into joining the coalition led by Alexander. On March 31, 1814, the allied forces, led by the tsar himself, entered Paris at the old Saint-Martin gate and marched down the rue Royale. The quarter century of European convulsion that had begun with the French Revolution had largely, though not quite, come to an end.

In January 1814, Bayard and Gallatin left for England in the hopes of pursuing negotiations. Adams, still minister to St. Petersburg, remained behind, though he no longer had anything to do. He wrote his father to say that Napoleon's demise meant that the British navy would no longer need to impress sailors in order to fight him, thus ending the one remaining outstanding cause for war with America. Since Great Britain would never agree to end the practice, the United States could make peace by remaining silent on impressment. This turned out to be a remarkably prescient observation.

Adams was at last rescued by events. In late 1813, after American forces had blunted a number of British attacks, Lord Castlereagh, the foreign minister, offered to open negotiations for peace. Madison immediately accepted and nominated Adams, Bayard, and Speaker of the House Henry Clay to serve as the American team. He later added Gallatin and Jonathan Russell, the minister to Sweden. Adams received the news on March 20; he was instructed to join the negotiations in Gothenburg, Sweden. He wrote no more of lassitude. On April 28, the same day he learned that Napoleon had abdicated, Adams boarded a coach headed for Estonia, leaving Louisa and Charles Francis behind. From there he sailed for Sweden.

When the minister reached Stockholm at the end of May, he learned that the English had switched the venue to Ghent, the capital of Belgium; it looked very much as if they were stalling in the hope of gaining more military victories. Adams felt quite sure that he was wasting his time, but he pushed onward. On June 22 he reached the Hague, a city he had known as a boy of thirteen, a romantically minded young man of seventeen, and a novice diplomat of twenty-seven. Now, not quite forty-seven, balding, and increasingly portly, he felt old to himself—and to most people who met him—but deep, strong feelings still flickered inside him like a fire in an underground mine. Now, in the Hague, they burned through that thick crust he had built over his soul. In his journal he wrote:

> It was here that the social Passion first disclosed itself with all its impetuosity in my breast. It was here, that ten years later, I made my entrance on the political Theatre as a public man. It is not in my

command of language to express what I felt on passing through the Yard of the House in the wood, and thence through the town, along the road between the Canal and Ruswick to Delft. It was a confusion of Recollections so various, so melancholy, so delicious, so painful, a mixture so heterogeneous and yet altogether so sweet, that if I had been alone I am sure I should have melted into tears.

Adams reached Ghent three days later. Bayard and Clay had already arrived; Gallatin was soon to come. Rarely, if ever, has the United States been represented at negotiations by so distinguished a group of men. Gallatin had been born in republican Switzerland to a wealthy and refined Swiss family. In 1780, at age nineteen, he had left Geneva to join the American Revolution. He had been elected to the Pennsylvania state legislature and then the US Senate and House, before Thomas Jefferson had asked him to serve as secretary of the treasury. A financial and administrative wizard, Gallatin had overseen a system of taxation and revenue that had helped Jefferson leave a sizeable surplus behind. He had become President Madison's most trusted confidante, and the president had appointed him to the peace negotiations with the understanding that he would remain in his post. Gallatin, who was six years Adams' senior, had deeply impressed the younger man during their time together in St. Petersburg. That spring Adams had written to Abigail, "I had several opportunities of observing his quickness of understanding, his sagacity and penetration, and his soundness of judgment."

As House Speaker, Henry Clay was one of the most powerful men in Washington; indeed, by making himself the master of Congress, Clay transformed that job into something like what it is today. Clay was every inch a self-made man. Though raised in a backwoods town in Virginia and schooled in a log-cabin schoolhouse with a dirt floor, Clay showed such precocious gifts that at fourteen he was apprenticed to study law to George Wythe, one of the most learned members of the Virginia bar. At age twenty he had moved out to frontier Kentucky and quickly made a name for himself as a crackerjack lawyer—fast on his feet, witty, charming, theatrical. Tall and lanky, blonde and blue-eyed, Clay had something of the cultivated backwoods charm Abe Lincoln would later ride to the presidency. He could play the fiddle, curse, and drink as well as any man. A prodigiously gifted politician, Clay had become Speaker at age thirty-five and quickly made himself leader of the war hawks, relentlessly pushing a reluctant President Madison into war. He was moralistic, imperious, utterly self-assured.

Madison had appointed him to reassure the hawks that Adams, the former federalist, and Gallatin, the European, would not surrender America's interests to England, and to balance the interests of the East with those of the West, which looked to Clay as its most forceful advocate. It was all but inevitable that he and Adams, a very different man with very different views, would clash at Ghent. The two would find their fates entangled, and their ambitions coming into conflict, throughout the next generation.

In mid-July, the delegation moved out of their hotel and into an elegant neoclassical villa, the Hotel Alcantara, on the rue des Champs. They found a man to supply food and wine, though Adams, suspicious as always, demanded the right to buy their own wine as well for a corkage fee of one franc per bottle. Adams was a man of settled habits, not at all accustomed to adjusting his daily routine to suit others. He often ate by himself and took long solitary walks to the gates of the city and beyond, since no one else would come with him. The others would dine later, smoke cigars and drink their bad wine, and eventually go out to coffee houses and then come back for cards and billiards. Clay had the room next to Adams, and at times Adams would find himself waking just as Clay was going to sleep. The two men quickly began to get on each other's nerves. In mid-July, James Gallatin, Albert Gallatin's seventeen-year-old son and secretary, wrote in his diary, "Mr. Adams in a very bad temper. Mr. Clay annoys him. Father pours oil on the troubled water." James made several such notations.

There was very little to do at first, because the English had not gotten around to appointing their own negotiators. They were obviously in no hurry to reach an agreement. Over the summer, the war cabinet had dispatched additional forces across the Atlantic in the hopes of taking the major cities of the Eastern Seaboard and threatening American territory to the west. By the end of the year, the British hoped, the Americans would be suing for peace. The British negotiators finally reached Ghent in mid-August.

Lord Golbourn, the leader of the British team, promptly laid down the British terms: no relaxation of impressment, as-yet-unspecified territory to be yielded up, and the establishment of a buffer zone to protect England's Indian allies from American aggression. This last was an entirely new claim. The British were insisting that the tribes be given control over an area equal to the entire extent of the United States. In addition, England would put an end to the right of New England fishermen to catch and dry fish on the Grand Banks of Newfoundland—a right John Adams had fought for and won in the Treaty of Paris, which ended the Revolutionary War. To this utterly unacceptable, and in fact grossly insulting, set of terms the British quickly added another: that the United States demilitarize the Great Lakes by removing its fortifications and ships, though the British would remain free to patrol the waters from their own bases.

These were the kind of extortionate terms a victor expects to impose on the vanquished. But the British had won nothing. The American ministers, each of them patriots and strong nationalists, believed that the British were suffering from an unearned sense of superiority. Their adversaries apparently had not reconciled themselves to the fact that the United States was a nation among nations and not a refractory ex-colony. To yield ground in the face of these peremptory demands would be to jeopardize the independence for which their fathers had fought and for which their own generation was fighting still. (The War of 1812 was often described in the United States as "the second war of independence.") The American experiment was still less than forty years old. Adams and his colleagues were acutely conscious that the experiment itself was now at stake. They would stand firm, come what may.

In fact, neither side was prepared to compromise in order to bring the fighting to an end, and neither trusted the other. The Americans believed that the British were playing for time, waiting for the war to turn decisively their way. On the other hand, Lord Golbourn wrote to the Earl of Bathurst in London that the Americans were plainly negotiating in bad faith, "with the sole view of deriving from the negotiations some means of reconciling the people of America to the continuance of war." Golbourn told Adams in a private conversation that the British needed the buffer zone to prevent the United States from attacking Canada. Adams replied indignantly that the United States had no such designs, though the truth was that the Madison administration had always viewed Canada as potential war booty.

Adams was especially incensed by the British insistence on granting Indians permanent territorial rights. "To condemn vast regions of territory to perpetual barrenness and solitude," Adams shot back, "that a few hundred savages might find wild beasts to hunt upon it, was a species of game law that a nation descended from Britons would never endure. And was impossible. It was opposing a feather to a torrent." Adams was actually comparing the relationship between America's settlers and its indigenous population to that between British gentry and poachers on their land. This was ingenious, preposterous, and grotesque—though Clay, Bayard, and Gallatin would have said no less. In any case, Adams never doubted that Providence intended the European settlers of America to spread across, and dominate, the continent—a principle that would later be called Manifest Destiny.

A negotiation Adams had been certain would collapse after a few weeks now began to stretch into months. He still expected the English to walk away from the talks at any minute, releasing him to return to St. Petersburg; he advised an increasingly impatient Louisa to wait. By September, a pattern had set in: the British would present a set of demands, the Americans would produce an extensive response reiterating their position, and the British team would then send the American document to London. The English negotiators, Adams sneered, were little more than a "Post Office." Indeed, the Americans were both more adroit and more independent than their British interlocutors. Adams was deeply impressed with his colleagues. In a letter to Louisa, he confided, "They are certainly not mean men who have been opposed to us; but for extent and copiousness of information, for sagacity and shrewdness of comprehension, for vivacity of intellect, and fertility of resource, there is certainly not among them a man equal to Mr Gallatin—I doubt whether there is among them a man of the powers of the Chevalier." (Bayard was known as "the Chevalier.")

Adams was selling himself short on information and intellect, but perhaps not on temperament. He reported ruefully to Louisa that his colleagues had shredded a draft of a letter he had written to Secretary Monroe, while keeping far more of an alternate version written by Gallatin. The reason? "He is always perfectly cool, and I, in the judgment of my colleagues, am often more than temperately warm." He couldn't help himself—the English tone was "wormwood," and his fury crept into his prose. He envied the Chevalier's hard-earned self-mastery and his equanimity, his gift for derailing arguments with a well-timed joke, but at moments of high dudgeon, Adams could not swallow his righteous anger. It was ironic, to say the least, that this great diplomat was the least diplomatic of the group. And it was striking that this New England Federalist was the most unremittingly hostile of the group toward their English counterparts. He was, after all, the same John Quincy Adams who had been raised on the glories, and the horrors, of Bunker Hill.

Adams' draft notes resounded with phrases about "the moral and religious duty of the American Nation to cultivate their territory." This heroic vocabulary, second nature to the Adamses, did not sit well with his more pragmatic colleagues. At one point Adams admitted, "the terms God, and Providence and Heaven, Mr. Clay thought were canting, and Russell laughed at them." Adams wrote more than anyone else, save Gallatin, and encountered more opposition, in a fashion which he found humiliating. "Almost every thing written by any of the rest is rejected or agreed to with very little criticism verbal or substantial," he noted. "But every line that I write passes a gauntlet of objections by every one of my Colleagues, which finally issues for the most part in the rejection of it all."

Over time, both sides began to shed their nonnegotiable positions. President Madison had authorized his negotiating team to abandon the demand to end impressment. The British eliminated the giant buffer zone, but insisted instead on *uti posseditis*—the current state of possession, which would make permanent the English conquests in New York, Vermont, New Hampshire, and Maine, and possibly in the South as well. The Americans held fast on all territorial issues; they would accept only the status quo ante bellum—the prewar boundaries. The gap between the two sides was closing, but so slowly and grudgingly that it was reasonable to think they would never reach agreement.

The American suspicion that London was playing for time, counting on the superior numbers and professionalism of their troops, was fully justified. In the first days of October, Adams and his colleagues received the ghastly intelligence of the burning of Washington. This was, or at least felt like, the greatest national catastrophe since the early setbacks of the Revolutionary War. British troops were now poised to march north to Baltimore and beyond. Even the ever-optimistic Clay began to despair of American prospects. On October 21, Liverpool wrote to Castlereagh to predict that President Madison would soon be forced to sue for peace. "His government must be a weak one, and feeling that it has not the confidence of a great part of the nation, will perhaps be ready to make peace for the purpose of getting out of its difficulties." The British used Alexander Baring, the Americans' British banker, as a back channel to Albert Gallatin, whom they viewed, rightly, as the member of the team most open to compromise. Baring wrote sympathetic letters to Gallatin reminding him how very precarious was America's financial position.

Adams was, as always, terribly vulnerable to reports of misfortune. He wrote a friend to say that the British troops dispatched over the summer were so numerous and talented that "they *must* in the first instance make powerful impressions and achieve brilliant successes." The war would drag on for years; he worried that a peace-loving people would lose the will to fight. His fears precisely matched British hopes. "Never, since the national existence of my Country," he wrote to Louisa, "has it been in a situation of so much peril, and with prospects so terrible before it—No resource, but our own energies, no reliance, but upon ourselves and upon Heaven."

Louisa, marooned in remote St. Petersburg, poring over accounts of British atrocities from her husband and her mother-in-law, swelled with outrage; she sounded more and more like an Adams. "I could almost wish I were a man in these times," she wrote to her husband, as Abigail had written forty years earlier to John, "for I feel that sort of ardour and enthusiasm in the cause which I think in a man would produce great things." When she learned that in Massachusetts, preachers were inveighing against the war—Abigail had stopped attending church in protest—and legislators were once again plotting secession, Louisa burst out in a very uncharacteristic manner, "I blush to think that my Sons are brought up in that hot Bed of Treason and Cowardice which makes one ashamed of owning it for ones Country."

Louisa was growing yet more unhappy in St. Petersburg. She had lost her most important source of companionship in late July, when Kitty and her husband and baby daughter had sailed to Europe. In October, she wrote her husband that she had moved into a small apartment to save money but feared nevertheless that he would blame her for extravagance. She had arranged to buy wood for the winter, but the seller had backed out when he had gotten a better price, and she had been forced to pay more—though still less than was usually charged. "If from want of judgement or habit of management I have injured my Children's property," she wrote, "I must submit to *their* reproaches as I have for many years submitted to yours." In fact, she sounded more angry than apologetic. If he didn't want her to waste money, she added, he shouldn't leave her alone in a foreign country. As the winter drew on, her hopes of being soon reunited with her husband dimmed. "I am so sick and weary of it I would willingly run all the risks attached to the Voyage in the present state of things than undergo it much longer," she wrote.

The tides of war turned back and forth in the fall of 1814. Adams' fears and British hopes about the American will to fight were, in fact, completely misplaced. Americans were enraged at the desecration of the nation's capital—and at Madison for letting it happen—and more determined than ever to fight on. In short order, American forces turned back the British at Lake Champlain, Plattsburgh, and Fort Erie. Lord Liverpool began to wonder if time was, in fact, on his side. Still, he hoped to improve his negotiating position and wrote to the Duke of Wellington in Paris proposing that he lead a naval campaign against the American upstarts. In a famous note, Wellington responded that while he would do so if ordered, the failure of

British forces to take and hold American territory gave London no right to demand *uti posseditis*, or indeed "to demand any concession of territory from America." This letter, written November 9, effectively put an end to British pretensions.

Meanwhile, the Americans at Ghent continued to fight among themselves. The British had offered to retain American fishing rights on the Grand Banks in exchange for the reciprocal privilege of freedom of navigation for British ships on the Mississippi. This was an ingenious means of turning Adams and Clay against one another. For Adams, the fishing rights were sacrosanct, both because New England depended on them and because his father had won them. Clay viewed American control of the Mississippi as no less indispensable to the people of the South and the West. And he was convinced that the British would use their presence in the West to keep stirring up the Indians against the settlers. Throughout October and November, as the American team drew up a draft treaty of their own, Adams and Clay fought over the language. And Gallatin, with his tact and patience and droll wit, served as referee.

Then the situation on the battlefield began to swing further in the Americans' favor. In late November, both sides learned that the American army had repulsed the British attack on Baltimore. Britain's leaders began to conclude that the game was not worth the candle. Peace at home could no longer be taken for granted: France was in turmoil, for the Bourbons, whom England had put back on the throne, were deeply unpopular. Years of war had left the Exchequer in a shambles; a new property tax had provoked widespread anger. Liverpool concluded that he had little choice but to take Wellington's advice. On November 25, the British team presented a new draft treaty that dropped all previous demands while also rejecting the American terms.

Clay, the poker player, had always thought the British were bluffing. Adams, the deep pessimist, had never believed they would settle. And he still didn't believe it. Adams wrote to Louisa to say that he had seen through the British "game of duplicity," which involved offering to settle "rags and tatters of contention" while holding out on points they knew the United States could not accept. He and Clay continued to argue over whether either fishing rights or navigation on the Mississippi could be bargained away. Gallatin, like Adams, did not view the Mississippi issue as inviolable. Clay had a volcanic temper; and as his control over the debate slipped away, so did his composure. In mid-December he told his colleagues that he was prepared to fight three more years rather than concede navigation rights.

Gallatin and Bayard tried to calm him down. But Clay, Adams wrote in his journal, "walked to and fro across the chamber repeating five or six times, 'I will never sign a treaty upon the Status Quo Ante Bellum, with the Indian Article, so help me God.'"

On December 22, the British team proposed to cut the Gordian knot: all remaining points, including both fishing rights and the Mississippi, would be put off for settlement at a later date. Clay wanted to hold out for an explicit renunciation of navigation rights, but now he was isolated. The following day, after a marathon thirty-hour session, the two sides agreed to terms. The war thus ended precisely where it had begun. This was a peace that only a diplomat could love, but it was nevertheless a tremendous victory for the Americans. The British had hoped for, and expected, so much more. And they could have gotten it had the American team not waited until the military campaign swung in their favor, or had Gallatin prevailed on his colleagues to take a softer line—which he did not seek to do—or had either Adams or Clay walked out of the talks. The United States that would have emerged from Ghent, in that case, would have been a weaker, more vulnerable, and more divided country.

The two sides signed a draft treaty on Christmas Day 1814. Adams wrote to Louisa to say that though he still had doubts about the document, "I consider the day on which I signed it the happiest of my life; because it was the day on which I had my share in restoring the peace of the world." He asked her to come to him right away, though of course it was the dead of winter. And he wrote to his mother to say that if President Madison did, as was rumored, ask him to serve as minister to Great Britain, she should send George and John to London.

The American negotiators parted on bad terms—or rather, the two chief protagonists did. Adams insisted that, as the lead negotiator, he should have custody of their papers. Clay said that the papers belonged to the State Department. The two men bickered. With Adams absent, the others took a vote and agreed to give the papers to Clay, who would turn them over to State. Adams was furious. Clay tried to calm the waters by saying that he "did not want to part in enmity." This only made Adams stiffen into a mask of propriety, insisting that personal feelings didn't enter into the question. Adams then wrote an intemperate letter to all three accusing them of misrepresenting their position on the stewardship of the documents. At another meeting January 6, Clay flew into a rage. "You *dare* not, you *cannot*, you *shall* not, insinuate that there has been a cabal of three members against you," he shouted at Adams; "no person shall impute any thing of that kind to me with impunity." He appears to have been an inch away from challenging Adams to a duel. In the end, they agreed that Adams would take the papers, while the books and other effects would go to an agent in London.

THE WAR OF 1812 HAS LARGELY DISAPPEARED FROM AMERICAN historical memory. Neither side won; no great principles were settled. And yet the Treaty of Ghent marked the end of the first, and very fragile, stage of American political history. First England, then France, and then England once again had seemed poised to crush the infant republic with its vastly superior military might. At the same time, both powers played on American sympathies to advance their cause. The English had exploited the Anglophilia of the New England Federalists, while France had played on the Jeffersonian admiration for the Revolution. American politics had become precisely what George Washington had feared: a contest between partisans of foreign powers. The great statesmen—Washington and Adams, Jefferson and Madison—had tried to rise above this bitter debate, ideological as well as sectional. And some of them had paid a very bitter price. John Adams had ended his political career despised as a turncoat by many in his own party. His son had been so battered by abuse from the Essex Junto that he had been only too happy to leave for Russia.

And now, finally, it was over, and the nationalists had won. The bitterenders of the Junto met at Hartford in December 1814 with the hopes of finally realizing their dream of separation. But the delegates to the Hartford Convention refused to call for secession, and the subsequent news of Andrew Jackson's great victory at New Orleans in January 1815, and then of the Treaty of Ghent, made even the more modest demands of the separatists sound ludicrous. The treaty was universally embraced by a nation sick of war and happy to escape without humiliating concessions. America was at last free to pursue the destiny its most farsighted and ambitious leaders, very much including John Quincy Adams, had foreseen. No longer burdened by the fear of foreign invasion, America would become a continental nation with a size and a power to rival Europe's great powers and ultimately Europe itself.

CHAPTER 15

A Card of Invitation to a Dress Party
at the Prince Regent's

(1815–1817)

ADAMS' FINAL WEEKS IN GHENT WERE THOROUGHLY DELIGHT-ful. The citizens had taken to the republican cause and from the outset treated the Americans as honored guests, inviting them to judge art contests, visit courtrooms, attend dinners and balls. Local musicians had asked for a patriotic tune; after Gallatin's black servant, Peter, whistled "Hail Columbia!," this proto-anthem was heard all over town. (Francis Scott Key was just then penning his ode to the "rockets' red glare.") Adams was feeling quite pleased with himself. On January 3, 1815, he wrote to Louisa in a tone of sheer ebullience: "A happy New-Year! And many, many happy years to my beloved wife, and to my beloved son Charles, and his far distant brothers!" After Marianne Meulemeester, the twelve-year-old daughter of a dear friend in Ghent, played the harp and sang couplets in praise of the American mission, Adams, perhaps still in his state of rapture, spent the day devising a response that teetered on the edge of the inappropriate:

> Fair maid of Ghent! Were mine the days,
> Of beauty and of Youth;
> And mine the Bard's ecstatic lays,
> Inspired by Love and Truth,

> *My* harp, of all that Poets dream
> The sweetest song should chuse;
> Thy virgins charms should be my theme,
> And thou shouldst be my Muse.

There was a great deal more in that strain. One can only say that he must have been extremely moved. Adams left reluctantly for Brussels and then, a week later, for Paris.

Adams and Louisa wrote each other regularly throughout this period, usually twice in a week. Louisa reported that the impossibly precocious Charles Francis, now seven and a half, had picked up Racine's tragedy *Britannicus* and was asking her if she didn't find it very beautiful. Charles Francis wrote a letter of his own to his father: "Mrs. Betancourt has taken away my Gun and has given me another, a smaller and a lighter Gun; but I hope to learn to handle my Gun in such a way as to be able to defend both my Country and the ladies in case of need." He was well on his way to becoming John Quincy Adams in miniature.

Louisa had lived in St. Petersburg longer than she had any other place since she had married, but she had never felt drawn to the city or learned its language, and she had suffered the greatest tragedy of her life there. She no longer wanted to be buried in Russia; she longed to leave. In early January she wrote that the New Year's holiday was oppressing her: "I feel so isolated among all the gay folks & it makes me feel our separation more keenly than ever." On January 20 Louisa received her husband's letter telling her to come to Paris immediately. She began frantically to sell what belongings she could, to ship some things and pack others, and to prepare for the arduous journey. She hoped to leave no later than mid-February.

Adams reached Paris in early February. The last time he had been there he had been a romantic young man, and barely familiar sensations now flooded back, as they had when he had seen the Hague once again. "There is," he wrote in his journal, "a moral incapacity for industry and application, a *mollesse*"—that Voltairean word for softness he had written at the head of his diary in his last months in Europe before setting off for Harvard—"against which I am as ill-guarded as I was at the age of twenty." He went to see Molière's *Le Misanthrope* and looked on in delight as his neighbors in the pit repeated every line from memory and critiqued each gesture and intonation. He took lodgings in the Hôtel du Nord in the rue de Richelieu and walked down the street to inspect the Hôtel Valois, where he had stayed with his father more than thirty years before. It was a melancholy reunion: the old apartment, he reported to Abigail, was much dilapidated. He visited old friends. The Marquis de Lafayette came to Paris from his country seat expressly to thank him for having looked after his son-in-law, Victor de Tracy, who had been imprisoned in Russia during the Napoleonic invasion.

On March 12, Adams recorded an astonishing rumor he had heard: Napoleon was at Lyons with an army of twelve thousand. A year earlier, Napoleon's generals, hopelessly outnumbered by an alliance of all Europe, had finally turned against the emperor and forced him to abdicate. Napoleon had accepted exile on the tiny Mediterranean island of Elba. His brilliant and bloody twenty-year campaign of conquest had finally reached what Adams and so many others viewed as its foreordained end. But it hadn't—not quite. Napoleon escaped from Elba on February 26, arriving at Golfe-Juan with barely a thousand men. The troops sent to capture him instead had flocked to his side. He and his men began the five-hundred-mile march northward to Paris. On March 19, Adams wrote to Abigail to say that Napoleon was believed to be only six days from the capital. "The Government," he reported, "has been collecting a force upon which they could depend which will meet him before he can arrive here, and the first actual resistance he meets will I think determine his fate." For once Adams erred on the side of optimism; perhaps he could not bring himself to believe that this man who had littered Europe with corpses still enjoyed the favor of his own people.

He wasn't the only one, of course, to underestimate Napoleon's appeal. Louis XVIII sent Marshall Ney, who had forced the emperor to abdicate, to deliver the final blow, and Ney, too, defected. On March 20, Adams watched in wonder as the king and his court fled northward. The following day, Napoleon's advance guard marched to the royal palace in the Tuileries. The crowds lined the streets to shout "*Vive l'empereur!*" Adams wrote to his father that "the walls of all the public places were covered with the proclamations of Napoleon . . . pasted over the proclamations scarcely dry of Louis 18 declaring Napoleon Buonaparte a traitor and rebel." A huge bonfire in the middle of the Palais Royal consumed all the books and pamphlets denouncing Napoleon—no doubt kindled, Adams drily noted, by the same people who had printed them in the first place. It was much the same scene he had witnessed twenty years earlier when the good republicans of Holland had woken up one fine morning as French revolutionaries in tricorne hats. Personal experience had taught Adams to distrust fine professions of faith; few men had the courage of their convictions when they were put to the test.

Adams also began to wonder what had become of Louisa. Napoleon's march had led to a mass exodus. Adams worried that she might have been unable to find a post horse to bring her to Paris. Was she stuck somewhere?

In fact, Louisa had endured an ordeal that her husband could barely have imagined. She had left St. Petersburg on February 12 with Charles Francis, a French nurse named Babet, a personal servant, and Baptiste, a former Napoleonic soldier who would serve as her guard. She carried Russian, French, and German passports, letters of credit, and gold and silver sewn into a hidden pocket. She and her son traveled in a fine covered carriage known as a *berline*, whose delicately sprung wheels would be replaced by runners until, further south, the snow gave way to frozen earth and mud. The servants would bring up the rear in a *kibitka*, a rough Russia sled with a bonnet-like covering.

Louisa had just turned forty. Her hair had begun to gray, and she was no longer as slender, or as vain, as she had been. The days when she had argued over rouge were long behind her. Louisa had been through a great deal; she remained physically frail, but she was no longer the hothouse plant she had once been. She had lived by herself in St. Petersburg since Adams had left almost a year earlier. Nevertheless, she was very much a woman of her time: she had never traveled by herself for any great length before and certainly not over much of the expanse of Europe, in the dead of winter, with a small child, in countries whose languages she did not speak and in the company of people she did not know. What was second nature to her husband must have been terrifying to her.

Louisa's journey across war-torn Europe reads at times like the harrowing tale of a wandering damsel from the pages of the *Faerie Queen*. Outside Mitau, a provincial city in Latvia, she found herself beset by danger in a dark wood. The postilion admitted to her that he was utterly lost. Should they turn back? Louisa ordered him to continue. They traveled on by the wan light of a slim moon. "We were," Louisa wrote, "jolted over hills, through swamps, and holes, and into valleys, into which no Carriage had surely ever passed before, and my whole heart was filled with unspeakable terrors for the safety of my Child." Baptiste rode off to look for help, leaving Louisa and the terrified servants trembling. At last Baptiste returned with a gallant Russian officer, who proceeded to escort them to the safety of his home.

As they continued to ride westward from Berlin, Louisa began to pass through the remnants of war. In Leipzig, she found herself crossing a vast field pitted with bones and the shreds of boots and clothing—the reminders of an appalling battle between Napoleon and an allied force in October 1813 in which perhaps a hundred thousand men had died. Worse still, she began hearing rumors of the return of Napoleon. At Frankfurt, both Baptiste and her servant, terrified of being impressed into Napoleon's army, refused to proceed, nor would any able-bodied men agree to take their place. Louisa and Charles Francis and Babet proceeded westward, toward they knew not what, in the company of Dupin, a fourteen-year-old boy.

At Baden, they found wagonloads of troops rushing past them to the border. At the eastern bank of the Marne, Louisa found herself among a crowd of coarse women—camp followers of the imperial guards. She had caught up with the rear of a military detachment. The women cried, "Tear them out of the Carriage; they are Russians, take them out and kill them." At that moment, soldiers seized the horses of Louisa's carriage and trained their guns on the postilions. Babet went pale with fear. At that moment, a group of officers rode up, and Louisa explained—in her perfect French—that she was the wife of an American minister. Now the soldiers were shouting, "*Vive les Americains!*" Louisa, on advice from the commanding officer, shouted back, "*Vive Napoleon!*," and waved her handkerchief. Charles Francis sat upright in the carriage in a state of utter terror—"like a marble statue." Babet, the maid, was close to nervous collapse. The French officer strongly advised Louisa to assume an air of complete calm. By this time, she had had a good deal of experience feigning confidence. She waved and smiled and brought off the imposture with aplomb. The officer escorted her to an inn, where the landlady, after much conversation, agreed to take them in so long as they sat in a darkened room behind a locked door.

Dupin informed his mistress that a rumor was abroad that Louisa was the sister of Napoleon—a rumor he had artfully encouraged by shrugging and looking cryptic whenever asked. And so, at last, Louisa proceeded, unhindered, into Paris through the Saint-Martin gate and down the rue de Richelieu to the Hôtel du Nord. And there, at eleven at night on March 23, she found her husband. Whatever either of them felt at that moment, neither wrote a word about it.

Louisa did not keep a contemporary record of her trip but pieced it together from memory many years later, in 1836. That forty-day, two-thousand-mile odyssey through the wreckage of post-Napoleonic Europe had made her a different person; she had confronted dangers on her own for the first time and had taken responsibility for her own life and the lives of others who depended on her. There was barely a trace of the "maudlin hysterical fine Lady" whom she supposed that the Adamses had once taken her for. She had, above all, surprised herself. In her "Narrative of a Journey from Russia to France," she wrote in her usual tone of self-abnegation that "it may perhaps at some future date serve to recall the memory of one, *who was*—and show that many undertakings which appear very difficult and arduous to my Sex, are by no means so trying as imagination forever depicts them." Louisa *was*—a painfully modest claim that poignantly summed up her struggle to preserve her own individuality, her distinctive self, amid a life she never would have chosen and perhaps could not fully accept.

ON APRIL 5, ADAMS RECEIVED NOTICE FROM PRESIDENT MADISON that he had been appointed as the minister to England. (His father had served as minister before him; his son, Charles Francis, would hold the job during the Civil War.) That put an end, though not an immediate one, to his delightful holiday in Paris. On May 16, he and Louisa took a carriage for Le Havre and from there boarded a ship to London. Abigail and John had learned of the appointment in early March and had immediately resolved to send George and John to their father, as they had promised to do. Both grandparents were devastated; for well over five years they had cared for the boys as their own. John Adams put his grandsons on board ship in the company of an old friend, Samuel G. Perkins, a colleague on the Harvard Board of Trustees. Adams, age eighty, felt very much *in loco parentis*. When his grandsons had been at sea for a little over two weeks, he wrote them with the kind of advice he had sent to his own son decades earlier: "Remember your youth and inexperience, your total Ignorance of the great World, be always modest, ingenious, teachable, never assuming or forward, treat all People with respect; preserve the Character of youthful Americans, let nothing unbecoming ever escape your lips or your Behaviour. You have Characters to Support, Reputations to acquire; I may Say, you have the Character of your Country, at least of its Childhood and youth to Support." And always carry a notebook, a pen, and ink.

On May 25, John Quincy and Louisa arrived at their hotel in Cavendish Square, and found George and John already there. Louisa fainted— twice. George had recently turned fourteen and at five feet five and three-quarter inches—John Quincy's exacting measurements—he was barely an inch shorter than his father. He was a diffident boy, bookish and quiet. John was small for an eleven-year-old—four foot five—and impetuous. Neither was remotely as disciplined as their iron-willed father or for that matter as their little brother; they had, after all, grown up with their aunts and uncles and grandparents. John Quincy put the two younger boys in a boarding school and began to prepare George for entrance to Harvard. He had George read to him from the Bible in French while he himself followed along in Latin; then they would switch, and John Quincy would read from the French. He put George to work translating Gibbons' journals into French, which must have been extremely slow and unpleasant-going, given George's very imperfect command of the language.

Peppery old John Adams wrote from Quincy with dire warnings about his son's new post, as if it were once again 1783 and the fate of the nation hung on diplomacy. "My son! You are now in the most difficult and dangerous situation that you ever was in. You will be courted by Dissenters by Republicans, by Courtiers. Reserve! Reserve! Of which I know not whether your nature is capable, will be indispensable." The old warhorse had been roused by the whiff of grapeshot. "I shall write to you incessantly," he said. And he did, generally in the same melodramatic key. But it was unnecessary: the son had vastly deeper stores of reserve than his rash father ever had. In any case the new minister would have a more tumultuous relationship with his own colleagues than he would with his British counterparts. When it came time to sign the final version of the Treaty of Ghent, Adams insisted that the United States and Great Britain alternately affix their names first at every point in the treaty, so that neither could claim precedence over the other. Clay and Gallatin, pragmatists both, were mystified at Adams' vehemence about what appeared to be a strictly symbolic issue. Adams viewed this formal equality as a matter of national honor. He prevailed, and ever after the United States and Great Britain signed their treaties according to this principle of alternation.

Adams was much busier than he had been during the endless winters of St. Petersburg, when he had indulged his mania for weights and measures. He had his family about him, a vast weight of correspondence, an active social life, and regular sessions with the foreign minister, Viscount Castlereagh, and the Earl of Bathhurst, the secretary of war and the colonies. He and Bathhurst tried to reach a solution to the problem of fishing and drying the catch on the Grand Banks. In the end, the issue was transferred to Washington.

With Castlereagh, Adams had a vast agenda to discuss, and the two met regularly. Along with Prince Metternich, Castlereagh was the great diplomat of the age. He was an Olympian figure—"cold, but not entirely repulsive," as Adams put it in his diary. Unlike with Count Rumiantsev, Adams had a relationship with Castlereagh that was strictly professional, but both men were professionally dispassionate and deeply versed in the arts of diplomacy, and they worked without friction. On January 22, 1816, Adams sent the viscount a long letter dilating on the issues they needed to discuss. Two days later, they met for four hours at Castlereagh's home. In order both to ensure that he did not neglect to raise an agenda item and to recollect them all afterwards—for he did not take notes or bring a secretary with him—Adams mentally assigned each subject a heading, the first beginning with *A* and the last with *J*. In his journal he was able to recreate the conversation, and thus preserve it for himself, in extremely fine detail.

Adams spoke to the foreign minister about, among other things, impressment, the return home of destitute American sailors, concerns that the British were instigating the tribes in Canada, alleged British intrigues in the South, and the obligation of Great Britain to repatriate stolen property—that is, slaves who had been sold in the West Indies. Adams wrote elsewhere that "a living, sentient being, and still more, a human being, was to be regarded in a different light, from the inanimate matter, of which other private property might consist." But in this instance the British regarded the slaves as chattel, and Adams raised no objection to treating them as such. (The issue remained unresolved.) Adams proposed joint demilitarization of the Great Lakes. Castlereagh agreed. The following year, the two sides would sign a treaty formalizing the agreement—"the first instance of reciprocal naval disarmament in the history of international relations," according to the diplomatic historian Samuel Flagg Bemis.

But actual diplomacy took up only a small fraction of Adams' time. He found that he was inundated by Americans bearing introductions from friends and relatives back home. And a steady stream of "projectors" found their way to his doorstep. Only thirty-five years had passed since James Watt had begun to build his new steam engine, helping to inaugurate the Industrial Revolution. The great age of invention was now under way, and its capital was London. Inventors appeared to be united in the belief that America would welcome a man with an improvement in hand and make him rich. These men applied to the American minister for advice, for introductions, and for money.

Adams had been fascinated by scientific discovery ever since he and his friends in Boston had performed experiments with Leyden jars a decade earlier; he listened with more attention than might be expected from a minister with a busy schedule. There was the gentleman who had invented the "seaman's friend"—a life jacket, made from cork, which for some reason the British Admiralty had declined to buy; Captain Johnson, an alleged friend of Robert Fulton, who had perfected a torpedo system to use with Fulton's steamship that would send the Barbary pirates to the bottom; the author, apparently a "lunatic," who had dropped off a book on Chinese astronomy; and the geniuses who had perfected eight inventions, including "a new method for bleaching Cotton Canvas and all vegetable substance." Two gentlemen Adams viewed as harmless frauds, Studley and Service, spoke to him "unintelligibly" of their innumerable inventions, including gaslights and "iron pavements." When they returned several weeks later with an expanded list, Adams drily observed to them that "the Iron Pavement was omitted."

Most of these projectors were chemists, but some were mechanics. A Dr. Busby detained Adams for an hour with his explanation of "a machine or Carriage to travel or transport merchandize by land, with a velocity equal to one hundred miles an hour." It was to be used on "the iron railways now used in this Country." (Steam engines already operated on tracks in quarries but would not be used to move public passengers until 1825.) "He is," Adams wrote in his journal, "one of the numerous class of inventors who are mad with regard to their main objects and sober in all calculations of detail."

Adams soon feared that he would be overwhelmed by distractions. In late July 1815, he and Louisa and the boys moved out of London to Little Ealing, a rustic seat eight miles west of Hyde Park. There, by a delightful irony, they moved into Little Boston House, a fine home located on the property of the Jacobean Boston Manor. Little Boston was a rarefied version of his home at Quincy. "The house we have taken," he wrote in his journal, "is not large but neat and elegant and fitted up with all that minute attention to comfort which is so characteristic of English domestic life. We have a coach house and stable, fruit and kitchen garden." The garden, "though small," Adams wrote, "is laid out with taste and elegance, with forest-trees, fruit-trees, shrubs, Plants, herbs, kitchen vegetables, and flowers in profusion. It is a little paradise, vocal with the harmony of every feathered songster of the Spring."

Adams kept a small office on Craven Street, between the Strand and the St. James Embankment on the Thames. Nabby's younger son, John Adams Smith, was now serving as Adams' secretary and performed his duties with far greater professionalism than had his older brother, the rakish William Stephens Smith. Adams was thus able to spend much of his time in Little Ealing, taking the charming walk into London when necessary. He got to know his neighbors. Dr. Nicholas, the headmaster of the Great Ealing School, which John and Charles Francis attended, lived only about a mile away and often invited the Adamses to elegant dinners with the local gentry. Ellen, the eldest Nicholas daughter, played the harp and sang charmingly, as Louisa Johnson had once done.

Adams was about as serene as he would ever be, but by this point in his life he was often suffering from some form of physical affliction—rheumatism in his hands or an intense sensitivity in his eyes, a problem he shared with his father. He teared up all the time, which would have been embarrassing for any public man but was all the more so for one who tried to turn a stoic and impersonal face to the world. In late 1815, Adams feared he would go blind. The pain was so overwhelming that he could not sleep and could not bear even wan light. His eyes swelled and discharged a fluid that made his lids stick together. Adams' doctor applied six leeches to his eyes, and the bleeding briefly reduced the swelling. But the pain returned, to the point where Adams became almost delirious. "It seemed to me," he wrote, "as if four hooks, were tearing that side of my face into four quarters." Finally, after about a week, the swelling, and the agony, subsided. He could read again—but he couldn't write, for he had bought a pistol to show the boys how to shoot, and the report had injured his hand. For several weeks he had to dictate his journal to Louisa.

BY THE TIME THEY HAD BEEN IN LONDON FOR A YEAR, THE AMERICAN minister and his wife, for all that they professed to prefer the comforts of home, had become fixtures on the social scene. One day in the summer of 1816 Adams recorded the blizzard of invitations that had landed on his doorstep: "Before leaving home I had received a Card of invitation from Lord Castlereagh to dinner, next Friday the 12th. instant, and a Card for Mr. and Mrs. Adams, of Mr. Penn at Home this Evening. At the Office I found a Card of invitation, from the Lord Chamberlain to Mr. and Mrs. Adams, to a Dress Party, a Ball, at the Prince Regent's, on Friday next, to have the honour of meeting the Queen. A Card to Mr. and Mrs. Adams, of the Marchioness Dowager of Lansdowne, at Home, Sunday, the 7th. to meet the Duke and Duchess of Cumberland, and a Card to the American Ambassador, of the Countess of Jersey at Home, on Monday the 8th."

Adams generally socialized in an aristocratic rather than mercantile setting. But he also got to know the more boisterous arrivistes of the City. He was taken up by the lord mayor of London, Matthew Wood, a druggist from Exeter. (Then and now, the lord mayor has little real power, and the post generally goes to a wealthy man of business who can afford to entertain liberally.) Wood held dinners at the drop of a hat: to celebrate Easter, to felicitate the Duke of Wellington, to bring together the Worshipful Company of Fishmongers, of which he was a member. Wood must have taken a shine to the American minister, for Adams was usually the only foreign minister at these events and sometimes the only government official, domestic or foreign.

Wood was in the habit of drinking from a great gilded cup, delivering a suitably orotund toast, passing it to his wife to do the same, and so on down the company. Adams in turn would deliver an elaborate toast to England. He became a student of the toast. Whether at the lord mayor's or some other celebratory function, Adams, once he sussed out that a toast was expected, would revolve his thoughts in his head while the conversation bubbled around him—indeed, while talking—though somehow he was still able to recall the conversation in great detail the following day. At a dinner for the Society of Friends of Foreigners in Distress, Adams, after apologizing that he was very much at a loss for words, launched into a long and lavish address that rose to a thunderous peroration: "Gentlemen, the sublime language of your immortal Poet, who asked a Kingdom for a Stage, Princes to act, and Monarchs to behold the swelling Scene, is not large enough for the purposes of your Institution. Your Theatre, is not a single kingdom, but the whole habitable globe." And so on. The former Boylston Professor of Rhetoric and Oratory had found a delightful outlet for his gifts.

The Adamses remained at Little Boston House, and very happily so. Adams had begun to relax his iron grip on the children's education. Abigail, knowing him all too well, wrote to warn against "overplying the constitution of our children with studying," and he wrote back to say, "The great and constant of them all, including George, is to escape from study, and to this effort I have given up all opposition as vain." Adams took long walks with the boys and read up on astronomy, his new passion. He reread his journals back to 1809 with the hope of producing an index, for he often consulted the journals when trying to recall a meeting or a conversation from the past. He visited his good friend Benjamin West, then almost eighty, who was reworking the monumental painting *Death on a Pale Horse*. He went to see a cricket match on the splendid lawn of another friend, Mr. Copland.

Adams, who seemed to move from one obsession to another, now caught the poetry bug, which held him in thrall during the autumn and early winter of 1816. He worked up an ode to fortitude in the manner of Gray, which he felt slightly less mortified by than he had by the romantic material he had written before. He began writing an epistle in the style of Pope. He lay awake at night making rhymes, and he wrote verses in his head while in the carriage to London. What would he do with it? He would dedicate it to his mother. Sometimes he felt ashamed of his labors, but he couldn't commit them to the fire: "I argue to my own heart that my great purpose is to give pleasure to my Parents; especially to my Mother." Within two weeks, the epistle had grown to five or six hundred lines. He took time out to write verses for Ellen Nicholas' birthday, which she had specially requested. When they were finished, he dispatched John to the Nicholas household to deliver them in person. Finally, at the end of December, he concluded that the epistle was too bad to be sent to Quincy; no record remains of the work.

Adams was, quintessentially, a man of prose; he was too analytical, too dogged, too literal-minded to write with anything like genius in an expressive and emotional vein. He was more suited to delineating the social structure of Silesia, or the chronology of the Old Testament, or the relationship of the verst to the mile. And yet he loved poetry. And he did not simply love to read and recite poetry, as so many educated men of his day did, but to write it. He wrote romantic poetry to girls just young enough that he could not be accused of playing the swain. The artifice of poetry allowed him to express ardent feelings he otherwise kept firmly tamped down. For Adams, an unplayful man, poetry offered a form of play—an outlet, we would say today. He could express feelings he didn't actually have but might dream of having, as well as those he did. And the fact that he wasn't so very good at it reassured him; poetry was, after all, a hobby. But at times he wished it were more. "Could I have chosen my own Genius and Condition," he confided to his journal, "I should have made myself a great Poet. As it is, I have wasted much of my life in writing verses; spell-bound in the circle of mediocrity." The journal, too, of course, was a place where he could admit his deepest feelings to himself.

THROUGHOUT THIS PERIOD, ADAMS WAS MEETING REGULARLY with Castlereagh and sending frequent dispatches to Secretary Monroe. The secretary authorized Adams to open discussions with London on a new commercial treaty, but in the summer of 1816, Castlereagh informed the American minister that His Majesty's government had no interest in the idea, and no intention of opening up American trade with the British colonies of the West Indies. Europe remained becalmed, but underneath the glassy surface, Adams felt the ongoing struggle between monarchy and republicanism, which he understood as a fundamental current of history and which he had been speaking of in diplomatic dispatches since the middle of the 1790s. The great event of the day was the insurrection in Spain. Adams reported that while the British public, like the American public, sided with the republicans, the British government would continue to support King Ferdinand. He predicted—very prematurely—that the deeply unpopular Bourbons would not be able to hold onto power and speculated that France might be carved up like Poland.

In the spring of 1816, Monroe had beaten his only rival for the Republican nomination, Secretary of War William Crawford, and since the Federalists had disappeared as a national party, he was all but assured the presidency. By November, Adams had begun hearing rumors that Monroe would appoint him secretary of state. According to stories being circulated by both friends and opponents of Adams, Monroe was considering either Gallatin or Clay for the post as well, and Clay had responded by loudly arguing that Adams was unsuitable for the post. But Monroe viewed Clay as a serious potential rival in 1820 and was not about to give him the traditional stepping-stone post of secretary of state. In fact, Monroe would later write to Jefferson that he could not appoint another Southerner to the post without appearing to confirm fears of a Virginia dynasty, which would turn Northern Republicans against him. He needed a man of the North, as well as one not known for overweening ambition. On March 6, he wrote to Adams to tell him of the appointment. Adams did not have a particularly high regard for Monroe, who had failed in diplomatic assignments in Paris and London, but for reasons both of patriotism and of personal ambition, it would have been unthinkable to say no.

As Adams began to contemplate this new and immensely consequential stage of his career, he returned with increasing frequency to the great principle of Union he had inherited from his father, which had animated him throughout his career. He designed a family coat of arms, as his father once had: an American eagle bearing a lyre, surrounded by the thirteen stars. Horace had explained that Orpheus had used his lyre to civilize the savage men of his time and make them submit to law and religion. "The moral application of the emblem," Adams wrote in his journal, "is, that the same power of harmony which originally produced the institutions of civil government to regulate the Association of individual men, now presides in the federal association of the American States. . . . The Lesson of the emblem is Union."

Adams wrote to his father to say that he no longer felt like much of a Massachusetts man. "My system of politics more and more inclines to strengthen the Union and its government." New England factionalism had reduced the Federalist Party to a disgruntled rump of secessionists. The true American principle, the doctrine of self-government, was threatened by the growth of absolutism in Europe. "The Royalists everywhere detest and despise us as Republicans," he wrote. Tsar Alexander had formed a Holy Alliance—an alliance of monarchs—with Prussia and Austria. Spain was seeking to crush republican movements in its South American colonies, while France and Britain were coming to the aid of Spain against its own citizen insurgency. "How long it will be possible for us to preserve peace with Europe it is impossible to foresee." The great responsibility of the secretary of state would be to defend republicanism from autocracy while resisting the provocation to war.

Adams spent his last months in London going to plays with the boys, attending debates at the House of Commons, and enjoying dinner parties with his friends. On April 28 he took a last walk around the garden, thanked the gardener and his son, and closed the gate behind him. "I have seldom, perhaps never in the course of my life," Adams wrote, "resided more comfortably than at the house which we now quit, and which I shall probably never see again." He had had his boys around him, and he and they and Louisa had enjoyed health and contentment; the strife that was sure to await him in Washington was still an ocean away. He was popular, sought-after, admired; he had little to regret. Adams' soul had perhaps never been so much at rest and never would be again.

The family moved into the ministerial office on Craven Street, and Adams began to prepare his departure. His final meetings with Castlereagh made it plain that the United States and Great Britain now stood on a far more solid and more equal footing than they had when he had arrived two years earlier. His Majesty, said the viscount, was deeply satisfied with the current state of affairs between the two nations. The United States and Spain were then arguing over the ownership of Florida, which Washington claimed had been included in the Louisiana Purchase but Spain disputed. Castlereagh asked if the United States would welcome an offer by Great Britain to use its good offices to mediate the dispute. Adams politely demurred.

The only rough patch came when Adams formally took his leave of the prince regent. It was customary throughout Europe for sovereigns to lavish

gifts on departing ministers, a form of thanks not very much distinguish-
able from a bribe. Adams was told to expect five hundred pounds. Adams
considered the practice absurd, as well as corrupt, and was mildly shocked
to hear that some of his predecessors as American minister had accepted the
douceur. In any case, the Constitution explicitly forbade the exchange of
such gifts. Adams explained to the courtier in charge of such matters that,
"for American ministers to be receiving gifts from foreign Princes, whose
diplomatic agents in America never receive any thing in return, would exhibit them rather as beggars receiving alms, from opulent Princes than as
the Independent Representatives of a high minded and virtuous Republic."
Castlereagh said that the opinion did him credit.

In early May, Adams dined with Jeremy Bentham, the great English
political philosopher, polymath, and eccentric, an atheist and radical reformer whose lasting contribution to the world is the principle known as
utilitarianism. Bentham had been eager to meet Adams because he had
been led to believe that they were distantly related. This turned out not to
be the case, but it may have only been a pretext to arrange a meeting. Bentham was an inexhaustible talker, and the two men quickly found that they
had a great deal to talk about. Bentham was sixty-nine but perfectly spry,
and he and Adams often walked together for three hours after breakfast,
usually around Hyde Park and Kensington. These two men, both impossibly learned and full of certainties, the one a freethinker and the other a
faithful if undoctrinaire Christian, found a match in one another, waving
their walking sticks and arguing their way across London.

Bentham was a great admirer of American democracy and of the principle of social equality. He had just written a tract, *The Catechism of Reform*,
which had become a cause célèbre and was debated in the House of Commons before anyone had even had a chance to read it. Adams was no more
a friend of revolution than he had been when he railed against Thomas
Paine, and on one of their long walks he asked Bentham how he could reconcile his call for social leveling with the British constitution, with its balance between the monarchic, aristocratic, and democratic estates. Bentham
rejoined that the crown and the aristocracy had so overborne the popular
power vested in the Commons that "the Liberties of the Country were utterly gone." Why, Bentham asked, should Englishmen not enjoy the same
liberties as Americans? Adams rounded on the old sage: "I considered him
as having conceded that reform with democratic ascendancy would lead to
the abolition of the Crown and the Peerage. But these institutions were too
powerful and too deeply rooted to perish without a struggle; and what

would be the consequences of that?" Civil war, Bentham acknowledged. Bentham, a genuine radical, could accept the consequences of his principles. Adams, a Burkean conservative, could not.

Bentham was also a shameless self-promoter, and in early June he sent Adams a box containing twenty-five copies of most of his works, to be distributed to the governor of every American state and a few other important figures. Bentham had high hopes for the cause of reform in the New World, but his efforts do not appear to have sparked a utilitarian cult across the Atlantic. On June 10, Adams left London with Louisa and the boys. He recorded, as always, the exact distance and cost, to the farthing, of the trip from London to Southampton. On June 15, the family boarded the *Washington*. Adams was right in his premonition that he would never again see Little Boston. He was only a month shy of fifty years old and still had thirty more years to live, but he would never again cross the Atlantic.

PART III

TERRITORIAL EXPANSION

CHAPTER 16

A Line Straight to the Pacific Ocean

(1817–1819)

T HE JOHN QUINCY ADAMS WHO DISEMBARKED IN NEW YORK in the summer of 1817, with his wife and three boys and four servants, was no longer thought of as the son of the second president; he was the designee to serve as secretary of state, the traditional steppingstone to the presidency, and thus the second greatest man in the land. His station was now equal to the immense gravity with which he had always held himself. Adams was portly, with pink cheeks and receding hair; the sharp lines of his face had gone soft, but his dark eyes still pierced the world around him. Adams spoke little but appeared to know everything. His father had cautioned him to be watchful and reserved; he had, if anything, learned the lesson all too well. In Washington, as in London and Moscow and Ghent, he would succeed—when he succeeded—by sheer force of argument rather than by the gentler arts of persuasion.

Adams had returned to a nation at peace: the United States was no longer menaced by foreign invasion. The questions that faced President Monroe and his secretary of state had less to do with protecting the country than with increasing American influence and expanding American territory. America was what we would call today a "rising power"—indeed, the world's preeminent rising power. And it was hemmed in by territory controlled by England, by Russia, and above all by Spain, which was very much a declining power. This state of affairs could not, and would not, last. In any case,

Spanish colonial control of South America was coming to an abrupt end. The so-called United Provinces of La Plata—today's Argentina—had defeated Spanish troops, declared independence, and sent an emissary to Washington to agitate for recognition. Republics had arisen in Chile, Venezuela, and Colombia. The world Adams confronted was thus ripe with opportunity for a confident and expansionist United States, though also beset with dangers for a nation inclined to overestimate its powers. He would spend the next seven years enhancing American territory and prestige while warning against what he considered to be reckless adventures.

Adams had been away from the United States, and his family, for eight years. More than anything, he wanted to see his elderly parents. The Adamses spent only a few days in New York City, took steamships up the coast, and then went straight from Providence to Peacefields. There they were reunited with John and Abigail, both miraculously not just alive but hale, as well as with Tom, his wife, and their five children. As soon as the news of Adams' arrival spread, the grandees of Boston began making a pilgrimage to the elegant three-story family home. Harvard president Kirkland invited him to commencement. Boston insisted on having a grand dinner of its own, at the Exchange Coffee House; apparently the Federalist apostate had been forgiven the transgressions of 1808. Adams was delighted at the improvements made to the town since he had last seen it, though saddened to see that old Beacon Hill had been flattened to make way for development.

After so many years away from home, Adams certainly could have tarried in Quincy and Boston. But his hyperactive conscience would not let him do so. He enrolled John and Charles at the Town Grammar School in Boston and put them up with his old friends the Welshes. George was to be tutored for admission to Harvard as a sophomore, but dysentery and typhoid were prevalent in Cambridge, and at the last minute Adams agreed that George could come to Washington. On September 9, the family left for the Capital.

Adams had been making the trip up and down the Eastern Seaboard for more than thirty years. As a young man he had bounced over rutted roads, waited for shifting winds to permit a packet ship to leave port, swung wide to avoid cities afflicted with yellow fever. No longer: the era of the steamship had fully arrived. Adams, always fascinated by machinery and technological progress, was agog. There were organized lines of steamers that left at scheduled times—no need to buy tickets in advance. The trip from New York to Boston had taken an astonishing forty hours: he had boarded the *Connecticut* in New York Harbor and stepped off in New Haven, and then immediately transferred to the *Fulton* to New London, where stage coaches stood waiting to whisk passengers to Providence or Boston. Now the family made the same trip in reverse and then took another steamer and stagecoach to Trenton, where they stayed in an inn operated by the steamship company. Then they boarded yet another ship to Philadelphia, where they mingled with passengers from all over the country as well as old friends from Europe. The last steamer, which chugged down the Chesapeake Bay, had an awning to protect passengers from the sun. The new generation of steamships had separate cabins for women, in which men were not admitted; both the refreshments and the accommodations were of the quality of a fine inn. On the way down the Chesapeake Adams sat in comfort reading a biography of Fulton; when he arrived in Baltimore, he wrote, "We finish here for the present our Steam-Boat Navigation, which for the purpose of travel has surpassed my highest expectations."

Adams took the oath of office September 22 and was introduced to the five clerks who constituted the professional staff of the State Department. Adams appointed one of them, Daniel Brent, as his chief clerk and translator. The department's budget amounted to $19,410, though the government spent another $103,000 to maintain its ministers and consular officials abroad. Adams himself had to accept a severe pay cut, for the secretary's salary was fixed at $3,500. (It would be raised to $6,000 in 1819.) The old department headquarters had been burned down in the war, along with the president's house, and had been rebuilt immediately to the west of it. Adams would share the building with the War and Navy Departments. State occupied five rooms on the second floor and four more in the attic. Adams had a new desk and bookcase. For a man whose idea of a foreign ministry was Lord Castlereagh's vast establishment, or Count Rumiantsev's, this was a very humble homecoming. But neither in his letters nor in his journals did Adams murmur a word of protest.

The department's work had piled up in the six months since Monroe had left to become president, appointing an interim figure in his stead. Letters and dispatches were sitting around unopened. Newspapers came in from all over the country, only to be thrown out at the end of the day, read or not. The clerks often left town on private business. Adams, a devoted systematizer, began cleaning the Augean stables. He established a filing system for diplomatic correspondence, consular correspondence, and material from foreign ministries. He had the newspapers kept and filed so that he could compile his own record of relevant articles. He pondered a new system of instructions for ministers embarking on missions. Which elements should be uniform, he wondered, and which particular to the mission? He assigned specific responsibilities to each of the clerks. Adams was the first professionalizer of the State Department, just as he had sought to professionalize the diplomatic service while abroad. The effort was costly: within days of arriving Adams was suffering from symptoms of overwork. He woke up in the middle of the night with a toothache. He tried to rise at four or five, but found that he was sleepy all day. Instead he woke at five or six, worked until ten, breakfasted, walked the mile and a quarter to the office (a twenty-two-minute trip, he noted), worked until three or so, and then went to see the president.

Adams never met a burden he wasn't prepared to shoulder, but in this case he had very little choice. President Madison had proposed that the United States establish a Home Office, after the British fashion, but the Congress had refused. The president could scarcely take up the slack, for he had no staff of his own. Much of the routine work of government had thus come to land in the State Department. State was responsible for publishing laws, conducting the census, keeping a registry of federal officials, affixing the great seal to presidential commissions. The secretary sat on the board of the sinking fund that administered the federal debt. Congress had assigned to the department the responsibility to publish the records of the Constitutional Convention of 1787 and a report on weights and measures—the great obsession of Adams' years in Russia. All these obligations fell on Adams and his handful of clerks.

When President Monroe and his cabinet members returned from their summer vacations and began meeting at the White House in late October, they faced an urgent decision about the US role in the ongoing struggle between Spain and its South American possessions. The European powers supported Spain's colonial pretensions; King Ferdinand VII of Spain held out hopes that France or Great Britain might dispatch a force to reclaim the renegade provinces. The United States had not yet recognized any of the self-proclaimed republics. American foreign policy had never deviated from the strict neutrality first declared by President Washington. This was Europe's affair, even if in America's backyard. At the same time, the South American rebels consciously emulated the language of the American patriots, and many Americans viewed them as brothers-in-arms, as they had the French revolutionaries of 1789. How could the United States remain neutral between the despotism of monarchical Europe and the citizens of the self-proclaimed republics? Newspapers across the country set up a clamor for recognition.

At the first cabinet meeting Adams attended, on October 30, President Monroe distributed a series of questions about policy toward Spain. The first question was: "Has the executive power to acknowledge the independence of the new states whose independence is not recognized by the parents country and between which parties war exists?" Adams did not doubt that the executive had that power but was not prepared to abandon neutrality, which he saw as the great bulwark of American strength, simply to gratify the wishes of the South American patriots or their American supporters. And he had no illusions about America's relative power: he feared that recognition might provoke European monarchs into sending an expeditionary force to crush New World republicanism or even to declare war against the United States. He complained in a letter to his father that, "as at the early stages of the French revolution, we have ardent spirits who are for rushing into the conflict, without looking at the consequences."

Adams viewed the contest more dispassionately than did many Americans: Spain, he wrote, had been thoroughly brutal, but so had the insurgents, who "present to us the prospect of very troublesome and dangerous associates, and still more fearful allies." Adams' paramount goal was to strengthen America; siding with the Spanish colonies would be morally satisfying but strategically reckless. Adams thoroughly approved of an expedient the president had adopted earlier that year of sending a fact-finding commission to South America. The commissioners still hadn't left, and the president seemed to be in no hurry to send them.

Monroe's next question was: What should be done about Amelia Island? This was a dot of Spanish-owned land off the Georgia-Florida coast that a group of South American revolutionaries had seized and used as a base to launch privateering missions against Spanish shipping. Spain controlled the Floridas, a region that stretched along the Gulf of Mexico all the way to New Orleans. The United States had been seeking to buy the territory since the early part of the century; the privateers might make life miserable enough for the Spanish garrison to help persuade the king that Florida was more trouble than it was worth. Perhaps, then, these rogues should be regarded as patriots. Adams found his colleagues "backward upon giving their opinions." He was not: piracy was piracy, no matter the cause. He advised the president to evict the "marauding parties" immediately. Monroe agreed and dispatched a land and naval force that occupied the island on December 23.

Spain quite naturally expected the United States to turn over Amelia once the pirates had been ejected. That was Monroe's inclination as well. At a cabinet meeting on January 6, 1818, William Crawford, secretary of the treasury, argued for returning the territory, as did William Wirt, the attorney general, and Secretary of the Navy Benjamin Crowninshield. Crawford said that Spain might view continued American occupation as a casus belli. Adams, who had already conceived a low opinion of the treasury secretary, sneered at the idea. He and John Calhoun, the secretary of war, argued for keeping Amelia. Adams was already engaged in border negotiations with the Spanish minister, and he wanted to make it perfectly clear that America had the stronger hand and would play it. On January 9 Adams met privately with Monroe to press his case. He succeeded: on the twelfth, Monroe announced that the United States would hold on to Amelia "for the present." The following week, Monroe had second thoughts when he heard a rumor that the Spanish governor of Cuba would retaliate for the decision by seizing all America ships in the harbor. Adams was disgusted with the president's "alarm"; the secretary of state was not a man to flinch in the face of danger. Fixity of purpose was his watchword. The rumor, in any case, proved false.

It was Spain's misfortune to be perched at the turbulent edges of the expanding American republic. Frontiersmen from Kentucky and Tennessee were moving not only to the west but to the south, toward Georgia, Mississippi, and Louisiana—territory the United States had bought in the Louisiana Purchase but Spain still regarded as its own. Settlers pressed up against the northern border of Florida, a refuge both for runaway slaves and for Indians displaced from their homes; conflict between the white and nonwhite populations was inevitable. In late 1817, American troops evicted Seminoles from a village north of the border, burning down their encampment and killing several villagers. The Seminoles counterattacked, murdering forty members of a supply convoy, including women and children, along the Apalachicola River, which separated east from west Florida. The blood-curdling details of the raid were given a great deal of play in the American press—far more, of course, than were those of the American assault. The federal government was bound to respond.

Days after news of the raid reached Washington, Secretary Calhoun wrote to General Andrew Jackson ordering him to assemble a militia to drive the Seminoles south of the border. Jackson had routed the Indians of Georgia in the Creek War of 1812–1813 and then had won millions of acres of land for the United States through a series of treaties with defeated or thoroughly intimidated tribes. Calhoun authorized Jackson to pursue the Seminoles into Spanish territory but to refrain from attacking any Spanish fortification, since the president had no wish to antagonize Spain while the United States was seeking to win Florida through negotiations. Jackson had scant regard for any authority save his own, and in any case, as President Monroe and Calhoun would have known very well, was committed to territorial expansion south of the current border. Indeed, even before receiving instructions from Calhoun, Jackson had written to the president promising that on a quiet signal from an unofficial source "that the possession of the Floridas would be desirable for the United States," he would see that it was done "in sixty days." Monroe later claimed that he had never seen the letter and would never have countenanced its rash proposal. Perhaps he hadn't, or he may have wanted what would nowadays be called "deniability."

Jackson destroyed unresisting Seminole villages in Florida and seized the Spanish garrison in the east. He captured two British citizens whom he accused of conspiring with the Seminoles, subjected them to a summary court-martial, saw to their conviction, and executed them. The general then promptly turned west, where no threat to American settlers existed, and took Pensacola, the capital of the Spanish empire in Florida. Jackson expelled the Spanish authorities and placed West Florida under American jurisdiction—thus attaining by force the goal Monroe had been seeking through diplomacy. It had taken him about ninety days, rather than sixty.

Jackson had fought a personal, unprovoked war against a European power on America's border. He had violated express instructions from both the president and the secretary of war in order to bring about an outcome that the president almost surely welcomed by means that he could not be seen to accept. The dashing general was on his way to becoming America's Napoleon, a dangerous figure but also an adored war hero—the first since George Washington himself. Monroe now found himself in the kind of quandary he could not abide. He was loathe to rebuke this supremely tempestuous figure but also unwilling to permit him to openly flout executive authority. The president convened his cabinet officers on July 15 to discuss what action he should take against Jackson; they would meet almost every day for the next week.

This was a foreign as well as a domestic crisis: both the Spanish and the French ambassador had written to Adams demanding that the United States repudiate Jackson and restore Spanish territory. Adams reported the messages to the president, adding mockingly that "there was something tragical in the manner of both these gentlemen." Adams had, in fact, sided unhesitatingly with Jackson, and he had assumed that the president would be of like mind. After all, he noted, "we could not suffer our women and children on the frontiers to be butchered by savages, out of complaisance to the jurisdiction which the King of Spain's officers avowed themselves unable to maintain against these same savages."

But at the cabinet meeting, Adams discovered that he was wrong. The president believed that Jackson needed to be reprimanded. Calhoun wanted to see him court-martialed. Even Crawford, who had shared Jackson's own bloodlust a few months earlier, favored some form of punishment. Adams was, in fact, alone. In his journals, where he kept an extensive record of the debate, he wrote that Jackson's actions were justified by "the necessity of the case, and by the misconduct of the Spanish commanding officers," by which he meant their unwillingness to stop the Seminoles themselves. (In fact, the Spaniards were too weak to stop either the Seminoles or the Americans.) Jackson, he insisted, had recognized that the border had become indefensible and thus had had no choice but to seize Spanish territory.

At first, Adams won no converts to his side, but he succeeded in forcing the debate to another day. He continued to defend Jackson and to advance the hardheaded view that the public would support him and the taking of Pensacola, while the European powers, including Spain, would resign themselves to a fait accompli. Adams recognized that he was on logically shaky ground in characterizing Jackson's aggression as necessary to the defense of America sovereignty. "But if the question was dubious," he wrote in his journal, "it was better to err on the side of vigour than on the side of weakness"—a telling sentiment. Better to err defending a heroic officer than the rights of America's enemies, and better to err on the side of executive power than to apologize for its exercise.

Monroe concluded that the United States had to return Pensacola and reprimand Jackson, if lightly. This was still a far milder response, and far less satisfying to Spain and its European allies, than Monroe and Calhoun had intended before Adams had weighed in. Adams drafted a letter to Don Luis de Onis, the Spanish minister, acquiescing to the demand for the return of Pensacola but including, in his usual stubborn way, his own justification for Jackson's conduct. His colleagues struck that out; Adams would spend a lifetime having his texts softened by cooler heads. Monroe wrote a painstakingly mollifying letter to Jackson, asserting that in "transcending the limit prescribed" by his orders "you acted on your own responsibility," but also suggesting that his belligerent letter to the president had been written "under the press of fatigue and infirmity." If America is to have war with Spain, the president noted, it must do so on secure constitutional grounds, not as the aggressor—a point one might have thought Adams himself would have taken to heart. Monroe was more cautious than his secretary of state, but he was not weak-willed or indecisive, as Adams sometimes thought him to be.

Adams had many reasons for unconditionally backing Jackson's Florida campaign. He had been horrified by reports of Seminole atrocities, which included grisly tales of Indians seizing children by the ankles and dashing out their brains against the sides of boats. At this point in his life, it would not have occurred to Adams that the Seminoles had the right to defend their own territory against the ceaseless depredations of US settlers and soldiers; he regarded them more as part of the order of nature than as individuals endowed with rights. He admired Jackson's martial vigor, and he recoiled at much of the criticism of the campaign, which he regarded— rightly, in some cases—as partisan. He shared Jackson's view of America as an inexorable force destined to spread across the continent, and, like Jackson, he was inclined to favor any course that enhanced American power. Adams himself was engaged at this very moment in his own diplomatic effort to win a vast expanse of territory from Spain. Jackson's campaign of brutal intimidation only tipped the balance further between the rising and the declining power. It is striking that so self-consciously moral and Christian a figure as Adams was prepared to excuse bellicose behavior in the name of national self-aggrandizement. For Adams, American destiny had a moral force of its own.

The United States had been negotiating with Spain over continental territory since the Pinckney Treaty of 1795 had given Americans the right to navigate the Mississippi and had defined the borders of Florida. The negotiations had been stalled by Spain's insistence that the Louisiana Purchase had been illegitimate and that in any case it had not included western Florida, which Spain had not granted to France. Monroe himself had served as minister to Spain and had tried and failed to win Florida as well as the territory west to the Rio Bravo in eastern Texas. Under Madison, however, the United States had annexed portions of West Florida to its Mississippi and Louisiana territories. And by the time Monroe became president, Spain had become increasingly unable to support its colonies and was prepared to sacrifice Florida in the hopes of saving Mexico and the Southwest, including Texas.

Adams was fortunate to have in Don Luis de Onis, the Spanish minister, a diplomatic foil fully as experienced as himself, determined to maximize Spain's position but fully aware of its weakness. Onis had served the Spanish government in various capacities since 1780 and had been appointed minister to the United States in 1809. Adams' assessment of him may be taken as a backhanded tribute to a worthy adversary:

> Cold calculating, wily, always commanding his own temper; proud because he is a Spaniard, but supple and cunning, accommodating the tones of his pretensions precisely to the degree of endurance of his opponent; bold and overbearing to the utmost extent at which it is tolerated; careless of what he asserts, or how grossly it is proved to be unfounded, his morality appears to be that of the Jesuits, as exposed by Pascal.

That was too harsh a judgment; Onis was a passionate monarchist and reactionary, but also a supple diplomat perpetually probing for the limits of the possible. The two men began a series of meetings on January 10. Each restated largely familiar claims on the Louisiana Territory. Adams demanded the sale of the Floridas; Onis temporized. Adams noted ominously that if Onis didn't negotiate the sale soon, he wouldn't have them to give away—a not-at-all subtle reference to General Jackson and his troops. The Spanish minister responded with a note angrily observing that Adams had asked Spain "to cede provinces and territories of the highest worth without proposing an equivalent or compensation." But Onis was backpedaling all the while. He acknowledged that Spain was prepared to surrender Florida—a major concession. And he sent a messenger to Spain seeking instructions.

After an exchange of letters with his foreign minister, Onis resumed the discussion in the summer of 1818. He visited Adams in his State Department office, where the secretary pulled from the shelf a copy of *The Map of the United States and Contiguous British and Spanish Possessions*. Onis now offered to acknowledge US ownership of territory along the Gulf of Mexico up to 100 miles west of the Mississippi. Adams demanded an additional 150 miles (between what is now Houston and San Antonio). The Spanish minister asked the secretary of state what the United States wished beyond that. According to a letter Onis wrote to his foreign minister, Don Jose Pizarro, Adams suggested drawing a line north to the Missouri River, "thence straight to the Pacific Ocean." This appears to have been the first time any American diplomat proposed extending American sovereignty from ocean to ocean. Onis was shaken by the magnitude of the American claims. "Here are their views, clear enough," he wrote to Pizarro. If Spain couldn't win the support of the major European powers, as seemed increasingly clear, Onis concluded, it should make "the best settlement possible, seeing that things certainly won't be better for a long time."

Adams' project of extending American power to the farthest reaches of the continent required testy diplomacy with Great Britain as well as with Spain. In the course of the War of 1812 the United States had abandoned, and the British seized, a trading outpost on the Columbia River. Both Adams and President Monroe were determined to reassert sovereignty over this toehold on the Pacific. In his first weeks in office, acting on Monroe's instructions, Adams ordered a warship, the USS *Ontario*, to sail around South America and back up the distant coast in order to raise the flag over this lonely outpost. When Sir Charles Bagot, the British ambassador, heard the news, he hastened to the State Department to say that he had been deeply disturbed to learn that the United States was dispatching a ship "for the purpose of disturbing the British settlement" in the northwest. Not at all, Adams said blandly; the *Ontario* had been sent to reclaim American property. "It would hardly be worth the while of Great Britain," Adams added, in the same measured tone, "to have any differences with the United States on account of the occupation of any part of so remote a territory." Sir Charles immediately submitted a complaint to London, but Lord Castlereagh, who had no wish to quarrel with the United States over what was, in fact, a remote piece of territory, instructed his forces to let the Americans hoist their flag.

WITHIN WEEKS OF ARRIVING IN WASHINGTON, THE ADAMSES HAD rented a house at the corner of C and Four and a Half Street, northwest of the Capitol. The White House was no longer the hub of Washington's social life, for President Monroe's wife, Elizabeth, was often unwell, and Monroe was averse to entertaining without her. What's more, reversing Jefferson's republican informality, the president announced that he would receive foreign diplomats only at specified times. Adams himself had little interest in entertaining, but Louisa was a polished hostess, attentive to her guests and reveling in good conversation. She saw as well that she could best advance her husband's career by opening their home to Washington's leading citizens. The Adamses held regular dinners for twenty or so guests, most of them drawn from the diplomatic community, the Supreme Court, Congress, and the cabinet. Later Louisa would hold fortnightly "sociables" or "teas"—evening events with drinks and dancing to which she typically invited up to a hundred people.

Had her husband any gift at all for small talk or bonhomie, he might have quickly improved on his bearish reputation and made friends who could prove useful to him. But in this regard, he was incurable. Adams recorded the following strange observation in his journal: "I went out this Evening in search of conversation," he recorded, "an art of which I never had an adequate idea. Long as I have lived in the world I never have thought of conversation as a school, in which something was to be learned. I never knew how to make, to controul or to change it. I am by Nature a silent animal, and my dear mother's constant lesson in childhood, that children in company should be seen and not heard confirmed me irrevocably in what I now deem a bad habit."

Adams was in fact one of the celebrated talkers of the age. The diarist Philip Hone recalled a breakfast at Adams' home in which the latter expatiated for an hour "on the subject of *dancing girls*; from those who danced before the ark and the daughter of Jairus [a reference to one of Jesus' miracles] . . . through the fascinating exhibition of the odalisques of the harem down to the present times of Fanny Ellsler and Taliogni [celebrated ballerinas]." Disquisition is not, of course, the same thing as conversation, which depends on mutually pleasurable exchange. Conversation with Jeremy Bentham was worthwhile, but the same could not be said for the drawing room. If Adams wasn't actually learning something, he felt that he was wasting his time. "I am scarcely ever satisfied with myself, after going into company, and always have the impression that my time at home is more usefully spent." One imagines Adams sitting silently at one of Louisa's dinners, all too obviously revolving his own thoughts in his own mind while the prattle twirled around him—just as he had in the court of St. Petersburg. Louisa admitted that her husband's "habits of study have unquestionably given a sort of coldness to his manners which to those who do not seek his acquaintance and only see him in public make him seem severe and repellent."

Adams spent a good deal of his time worrying about his sons, who he feared would disappoint him. John, the willful, ungovernable "Hotspur" of years past, wrote his father a series of letters complaining of harsh treatment from his uncle Tom, who apparently was forcing the boy's nose to the grindstone. Adams responded with almost shocking brutality: "You boast of your studying hard, and pray for whose benefit do you study? Is it for mine, or for your uncle's? Or are you so much of a baby that you must be taxed to spell your letters by sugar plums? Or are you such an independent gentleman that you can brook no control, and must have everything you ask for? If so, I desire you not to write for anything to me." George, who had returned to Cambridge to continue his studies, fared little better. George's tutor had written to Adams with a discouraging report on the boy's progress, and Adams wrote to his eldest son accusing him of "a propensity to skulk from real study." Rather than prepare an essay for the Bowdoin Prize, Adams advised George to write a dissertation on the adage "Mind your business."

In his own mind, Adams was raising his boys with the same unforgiving rigor with which he himself had been brought up. He did not wish, and perhaps could not wish, that his parents had treated him any other way. He expected his sons to excel just as it had been expected of him. He was not given pause by the fact that the parental techniques had self-evidently failed with Charles and had scarcely spurred Tom to high achievement. And Adams brought to the task of child rearing a grim and humorless determination that made him a harsher taskmaster than even his own parents had been. Louisa preferred to raise the boys with honey rather than vinegar, but, she reflected, "he ruled his children, and I quietly acquiesced to his right of controul."

Adams could not relax. If he wasn't meeting with the cabinet or writing diplomatic dispatches, he was working on his study of weights and measures, keeping up his journal, writing letters. But he had never endured a Washington summer, and by June, when the temperature hit 94 degrees, he was coming unstrung. He could barely sleep even with the doors and windows thrown wide open. One night he lay awake with what he thought was prickly heat but found that his body was covered with "tiny spiders" that tickled "like a thousand feathers passing over your body." By the end of August he was ready to take a vacation in Quincy.

ADAMS SPENT MUCH OF SEPTEMBER SITTING IN HIS FATHER'S LIBRARY in Quincy and picking up whatever book he had a mind to read. He received daily dispatches from the State Department. Every few days he sat for Gilbert Stuart, who had asked to paint his portrait. And he subjected the boys to private exams, George in Algebra and Plato, John and Charles in Greek and Latin. He was not particularly impressed, though he acknowledged to himself that his worrying over them was inveterate. "None of them will probably ever answer to my hopes," he wrote sourly. "May none of them ever realize my fears!"

Adams returned to Washington in mid-October. Soon he began receiving worrying letters about his mother's health from his old friends Harriet

Welsh and Benjamin Waterhouse. It was all too clear that Abigail was dying. By November 1 he was quite certain that she was dead. His anguish mounting, Adams took to his journal to record his private feelings. "My mother was an Angel upon Earth," he wrote. "Yet she has been to me more than a Mother. She has been a Spirit from above watching over me for good, and contributing by my mere consciousness of her existence, to the comfort of my life. That consciousness is gone; and without her the world feels to me like a solitude."

Perhaps, had Adams been a more modern man, his love for his mother might have been tinged with resentment for her exacting standards and her ceaseless and sometimes killjoy moralizing, which as a young man had chilled his soul and left him grave and gray. But Adams could not imagine blaming his mother or his father for defects of which he was all too aware. He blamed himself only. On November 2, he received a letter from John saying that Abigail had died October 28. He immediately left his office and would not return for several days. He did not receive visitors and went on a solitary two-hour walk, thinking of his mother's unremitting goodness, worrying about how his father would survive the blow. Indeed, as he was writing to his father November 2 to convey his grief and his condolence, his father was writing to him.

DON LUIS DE ONIS HAD BEEN MAKING HEADWAY DURING THE summer and fall of 1818; the circle of reactionary aristocrats around King Ferdinand VII had begun to accept the reality of their situation, which explains the instructions sent to Onis to make the best deal possible while retaining Texas and the Southwest. Nevertheless, Onis continued to insist on a line just west of the Mississippi. President Monroe, running out of patience, directed Adams to bring the negotiations to a conclusion or break them off—an ultimatum the secretary was delighted to convey. Adams wrote to Onis with the administration's final offer. The secretary of state was prepared to sacrifice Texas, which he knew that Onis had been charged to preserve, in order to push America's boundary westwards and win the line to the Pacific, which would run along the forty-first parallel to a spot just below the border with Oregon. The "line" was quite literally just that, since Great Britain owned the territory to the north and Spain that to the south. It was less an acquisition than a placeholder, a statement of future purposes. The line, by itself, scarcely seemed worth the cession of Texas, and both men would be blamed by Westerners for giving up this vast property. But Monroe feared that the addition of Texas, where slavery would be sure to spread, as it already had elsewhere in the Southwest, could outrage Northerners and thus destabilize the union. He was perfectly content to postpone the problem, and Adams apparently agreed.

Onis was not yet ready to yield, and he rejected Adams' offer. At that point the secretary of state did something very much in character: he sent diplomatic instructions to George Erving, the American minister in Spain, which were intended to be made public and serve notice on Spain and its European allies that the United States was not prepared to budge. The letter included a highly colored narration of the Seminole War, which began, Adams claimed, when a force of "runaway negroes," "savage Indians," pirates, and traitors waged "an exterminating war" across the Florida border. Adams vigorously defended every action of General Jackson, including the execution of the two British agents. The real blame, Adams concluded, fell on Spain, which lacked the force to prevent these "banditti" from violating American sovereignty. Spain must thus decide either to fortify Florida—which of course it could not do—or surrender to the United States "a province of which she retains nothing but the nominal possession."

Adams was not trying to win the argument on the merits—or maybe, since he couldn't help himself in such matters, he was—but rather to demonstrate a national resolve it would be foolhardy to resist. His ten-thousand-word essay was considered a polemical tour de force. Jefferson wrote to Monroe that the letter, as well as another Adams had written to Onis making much the same case, "are the most important and are among the ablest compositions I have ever seen," and suggested they be translated into French and sent to all American ministers and consular officials to be presented at capitals. Indeed, Lord Castlereagh was so impressed by the force of Adams' argument, or perhaps by the unyielding American position, that he conceded that the two British citizens Jackson had court-martialed had deserved their fate. He chose to let the issue subside—a startling decision that virtually ratified America's forceful seizure of Spanish territory.

Florida was just about to drop from the Spanish colonial tree like an overripe peach. But Onis continued to resist, and now a new question arose, for in July the president's commission had returned from its fact-finding mission to Latin America. Adams was vexed to find that one member favored granting independence to all the new republics, while another considered all of them save the United Provinces hopelessly unprepared for self-rule. Adams viewed recognition as a practical matter rather than an avowal of republican kinship. At the moment, he thought, it would do more harm than good, but he was not averse to using recognition as a bargaining chip with Onis. As the boundary negotiations drew to a close in the last days of 1818, Adams informed the French minister, Baron Hyde de Neuville, who had been serving as an intermediary with Onis, that the United States planned to recognize Buenos Aires. In fact the administration had no such plans; Adams was probably hoping to panic Onis into acquiescence, for he knew very well that Onis would be blamed for such a calamitous outcome. Here, as elsewhere, one is struck by Adams' complacent willingness to use means both ruthless and wily in pursuit of ends whose rightness he never doubted.

On January 3, 1819, Onis received new instructions ordering him to settle the dispute on American terms if need be. That very day, while Adams was walking up Pennsylvania Avenue to the office, Hyde rushed over, asked him to climb into his carriage, and then laid out for the secretary of state the new Spanish offer. Adams had a deal, Hyde said, if he would move the proposed line to the Pacific northwards from 41 to 43 degrees latitude and promise that the United States would not recognize the breakaway republics. Hyde was a charming and obliging statesman of whom both Adams and Louisa were very fond. Nevertheless, Adams was curt. The second term, he said, was of course out of the question. As for the first, "if Mr. Onis was not prepared to agree to our ultimatum, I hoped he would intreat him not to write me a word about it, for I could not express the disgust with which I was forced to carry on a correspondence with him, upon subjects which it was ascertained that we could not adjust."

When Onis made further concessions on a westward boundary, Monroe felt that the time had come for the United States to pocket its winnings. Adams disagreed; he felt sure that he could squeeze Onis harder and get still more. He won the backing of the cabinet. Onis and Adams continued to pore over maps. Back and forth they went, day after day in the first three weeks of February 1819, with the great continental expanse of North America at stake. Onis agreed to cede everything above the forty-first parallel. He was trying to win some face-saving concessions—not for his own professional pride but rather, as he told Adams, because Ferdinand's counselors "were always setting up the honor and dignity of Spain, the glory of the Monarchy, and talking as in the time of Charles the Fifth." They had to feel that "the interest and honour of Spain" had been preserved. Would America accept boundaries in the middle of the rivers rather than on the banks? No. Would America grant Spain a right of navigation? No. Adams was merciless. On February 16, Hyde came to Adams' office to say that Onis had accepted everything.

On the eighteenth, Onis came with a copy of the treaty stipulating borders in the middle of the rivers. A cabinet meeting the next day authorized Adams to refuse the terms. Adams called on Hyde to explain that the president was prepared to inform Congress that the negotiations had failed; he would not stop legislators from unilaterally annexing the Floridas. Hyde pleaded with Adams to desist; Onis might have to break off the negotiations himself rather than accept a treaty his own compatriots would deem extortionate. That, Adams said, is up to him. The following day, Onis assayed a few last quibbles, Adams gave no quarter, and Onis agreed to sign the treaty as it was. On the twenty-second, he and Onis signed copies of the Transcontinental Treaty, as it came to be called, in Spanish and English.

Adams never gave Onis credit for the treaty. He was much more generous with Hyde. "He is a man of singularly compounded character," Adams wrote. "A mixture of ultra-royalism and republican liberality. Frank, candid, honourable, generous, benevolent, humane, devoted to and adoring his Country." Adams gave Hyde great credit for bringing Onis around. He would later write to Richard Rush, the US minister in London, that no foreign diplomat in American history had rendered "a service so transcendently important to this country."

Adams had yielded Texas, which he had never expected to gain, and in exchange won Florida—the great prize—and gained unimpeded title to all the land ceded by the French in 1803. The line to the Pacific was a coup none of Adams' predecessors had had the boldness to seek, much less win. The Louisiana Purchase had been a windfall; the Transcontinental Treaty, by contrast, was a diplomatic coup Adams had won by a combination of patience, guile, mastery of detail, and an unyielding commitment to American national interest. That night Adams came home late from a dinner and confessed in his journal that he had experienced "perhaps the most important day of my life." He continued: "The acquisition of the Florida's has long been an object of earnest desire in this Country. The acknowledgment of a definite line of boundary to the South Sea"—the Pacific—"forms a great Epoch in our History. The first proposal of it in this Negotiation was my own; and I trust it is now secured beyond the reach of revocation."

CHAPTER 17

The Bargain Between Freedom and
Slavery Is Morally and Politically Vicious

(1819–1820)

ADAMS HAD BECOME SECRETARY OF STATE AT A MOMENT
when Americans could afford to be less preoccupied with Europe,
and more focused on domestic well-being, than they ever had been
before. The eight years of James Monroe's presidency constituted an interval
of relief from the partisan strife between Republican and Federalist and then,
later, between Republican and Democrat. In June 1817, soon after taking office, Monroe traveled up the Atlantic seaboard to New England—the first of
the Virginia presidents since George Washington to make such a trip. The
president came with a healing message for the Federalists who had opposed
his candidacy and, more importantly, the War of 1812. "Discord does not
belong to our system," he proclaimed in Boston, and Boston responded in
kind. "We are now all republicans," emphatically declared Henry Lee, a local
merchant, "even the Essex Junto." It was a local newspaperman who coined
the term "era of good feelings" to describe Monroe's warm welcome.

Even Adams, a man inclined to see conflict and treachery lurking beneath the dulcet tones of peace, was impressed by the new spirit. In October 1817, days after he had arrived in Washington, he wrote of Monroe's
tour to his nephew John Adams Smith, noting that "party spirit has indeed
subsided throughout the union to a degree that I should have thought

scarcely possible." No doubt the United States would become tangled again before long in Europe's inveterate conflicts, but "in the mean time the general prosperity of our country, and the contentment which pervades every part of it, are delightful to the patriotic feelings of an American, and most especially of an American arriving from Europe." What neither Adams nor any of the leading men in Washington could foresee was that the issue of slavery, artfully avoided by the framers of the constitution, would begin to vex the mood of national satisfaction.

America's Founding Fathers had been united in the belief that political parties were inimical to republican government, on the grounds that they served as vehicles for selfish or sectional interests as opposed to national and collective ones. Party spirit had nevertheless arisen in the struggle between Federalists and Republicans, but once the Federalists shrank into insignificance, the nation had returned to one-party, or in effect no-party, rule. The great divisive issue of activist versus limited government had also lost something of its salience, for the ruling Virginia Republicans had grown increasingly comfortable with the Federalist vision. Madison had agreed to charter the Second Bank of the United States, argued for federally financed "internal improvements," built up the peacetime navy, and signed a tariff bill protecting Northern manufactures. Monroe had also preserved the Madisonian consensus. In 1820 he would run uncontested for reelection; had one New England elector not selected John Quincy Adams on his ballot, Monroe would have been elected unanimously.

And yet the absence of party temporarily prevented recognition of rising internal conflict. As the nation rapidly expanded and diversified, the Founding Fathers' ideal of a single patriotic national interest became increasingly untenable. Sectional interests had long pitted the manufacturers and traders of New England against the agriculturists of the South. But now the nation's center of gravity was shifting as settlers poured into the west. Between 1810 and 1820 the number of Americans living beyond the Appalachians doubled from one to two million. Between 1816 and 1821, five new Western states were admitted to the union—Indiana, Mississippi, Illinois, Alabama, and Missouri. (Maine was also admitted in 1820.) The absence of organized parties meant that interests gathered around individuals and thus that the inevitable clash of interest and ideology would be intensely, and often brutally, personal. It was not, of course, in John Quincy Adams' nature to minimize conflict. The seven years he would spend in President Monroe's cabinet would be a period of fierce rivalry, rising suspicion, and, finally, open political warfare.

At the White House, Adams found that he was moving in a world more portentous, more personal, and more intensely dramatic than any he had known before. After one cabinet meeting, he wrote, "These Cabinet Councils open upon me a new Scene and new views of the political world. Here is a play of Passions, Opinions and characters different in many respects from those in which I have been accustomed heretofore to move." Adams got on well with Attorney General William Wirt, a big, shambling figure, warm and bookish, who had no ambitions beyond his current job and was inclined, so far as Adams could tell, to give way to Monroe on almost everything.

On the other hand, Adams took an instant dislike to the treasury secretary, William H. Crawford, a Georgian who had served as minister to France and secretary of war under Madison before running against Monroe in 1816. Crawford was a big, fleshy, pink-cheeked man, a natural politician who took little interest in the large intellectual questions that preoccupied the secretary of state. A man of action, Crawford had killed a rival in a duel. Adams found him petty-minded, self-aggrandizing, interested only in politics rather than policy. On the other hand, no less an authority than Albert Gallatin, his much-admired colleague in Ghent, wrote that Crawford "united to a powerful mind a most correct judgment and an inflexible integrity."

The one figure Adams accepted as an intellectual equal was the youngest of them, John Calhoun, the thirty-five-year-old secretary of war. After Calhoun had the good sense to agree with Adams on the disposition of Amelia Island, the latter wrote, "Calhoun thinks for himself, independently of all the rest, with sound judgment, quick discrimination and keen observation. He supports his opinions too with powerful eloquence." Calhoun had been raised in South Carolina, studied law at Yale, and won a seat in Congress at age twenty-eight. He had been, along with Henry Clay, one of the leading war hawks in the House. Calhoun was a deeply serious man who did not smoke or play cards and drank little; his dark and deep-set eyes were often described as "blazing" or "burning," for he seemed to barely restrain intense passions. George Waterston, a Washington observer of the day, compared Calhoun to Burke or William Pitt the Younger. "On all subjects," he wrote, "whether abstract or ordinary, whether political or moral, he thinks with a rapidity that no difficulties can resist, and with a novelty that never fails to delight." Calhoun would later become the intellectual fountainhead of the states' rights movement that would justify secession. But at this time he was, like Adams, a proponent of a strong central government and a strong executive. On many, though hardly all, questions they agreed.

Monroe himself was even more a throwback, or remnant, than was his secretary of state. The president was the last, and the least, of the great Tidewater aristocracy to serve as chief executive. He was tall and thin and dressed in the archaic republican fashion—knee breeches rather than trousers, long hose, buckled shoes. He often wore a dark beaver hat and on solemn occasions donned his old uniform from the Continental Army. Monroe came from a humbler background than Jefferson and Madison, received a less thorough education, climbed the ladder of success more arduously. He had not been chosen as a delegate to the Constitutional Convention, a failure that rankled. He had served as a diplomat but not a very successful one: George Washington had recalled him from Paris for excessively pro-French sympathies, and Jefferson had ignored the treaty he had signed with Great Britain in 1807. He later served as Madison's secretary of state and, briefly, war; though some blamed him for the reverses the United States suffered during the War of 1812, he never lost the support of either Jefferson or Madison.

Monroe was an extraordinarily good man, but he was not a brilliant man. His mind was "neither rapid nor rich," wrote William Wirt, and thus he moved slowly and warily in the face of new information. Monroe made few important decisions without consulting Madison and Jefferson; the latter, especially, felt free to offer his advice on almost everything, though always with disclaimers about his remoteness from men and events, and so forth. The president laid out all issues before his cabinet and was prepared to wait patiently for consensus to form among them. This habit did not sit well with his decisive secretary of state. In his journal he noted, "There is slowness, want of decision and a Spirit of procrastination in the President which perhaps arises more from his situation than his personal character."

Monroe would not have chosen Adams as his secretary of state had he not felt that politics compelled him to do so. He had first encountered Adams as the author of the Publicola essays, which he considered an apologia for monarchy and an overt endorsement for reactionary Great Britain over revolutionary France. The two would never become close friends, but they worked well as a team. Jefferson remarked that they were well suited to one another: "Adams has a pointed pen; Monroe has judgment enough for both and firmness to have *his* judgment controul." Monroe found that he could rely on Adams' nonpartisan judgment and deep knowledge of foreign affairs, as well as his gift for foreseeing even remote consequences of present actions. The president made it clear to Adams that he could visit him privately at any time, and on his way to the State Department Adams often stopped at the White House, as many Washingtonians had come to call the president's house after the damaged walls had been replastered and painted white.

The structure, in fact, was still being rebuilt when Monroe was inaugurated, and painters and carpenters would be hard at work for years to come. Chunks of masonry lay in the dirt at the sides of the structure. The north and south porticos still lay open to the sky. At the same time, the Francophile first family had imported masses of Louis XVI furnishings for the downstairs public rooms of the White House—mahogany escritoires with gilded brass finish, bronze clocks, silver and fine porcelain, chandeliers and candelabra. The White House had begun—just barely—to look like the dwelling of the nation's chief magistrate. Adams would typically walk upstairs to meet with Monroe in the less pretentious Treaty Room, which the president had furnished like a library or study.

Monroe had assembled a cabinet of highly capable but also exceptionally ambitious men; they were divided less by ideology than by personal rivalry. Crawford resented Calhoun, who had backed Monroe in the 1816 election, and saw Adams as a rival, whether for 1820 or 1824. The proud and solemn Calhoun detested Crawford even more deeply than Adams did; both viewed him as a secret ally of the Speaker of the House, Henry Clay, who had made himself the administration's sworn enemy. Adams was convinced that Crawford and Clay would stop at nothing, including harm to America's interests, in order to secure Adams' own defeat. Crawford, Calhoun, and Adams would clash constantly, and sometimes violently, over the course of Monroe's two terms, and it is a testimony to the president's patience and modesty that he was able to preserve a modicum of harmony in the cabinet until almost the very end.

Clay, meanwhile, had been waiting for the opportunity to turn his oratorical guns on the administration. He had been furious when Monroe had offered State to his rival Adams, and he had refused to consider the second-tier slot of secretary of war. Beginning in the spring of 1818, he lambasted the administration's cautious policies toward the Spanish republics, which Adams himself had done much to shape. Working with Manuel Aguirre, the minister from the United Provinces of La Plata, which had declared its independence from Spain two years earlier, Clay demanded recognition of the new nation, though doing so would have required overturning the Neutrality Act.

Clay was what we could call today a foreign policy idealist, demanding that America act abroad according to its values at home, rather than according to a strict calculus of its interests. He had the bully pulpit of the Speakership and a gift for swelling oratory. On the floor of the House Clay majestically evoked a new world, an American world, in which the southern republics hoped to form an alliance with their elder brother to the north. "At the present moment," he cried, "the patriots of the South are fighting for liberty and independence—for precisely what we fought for. . . . The moral influence of such a recognition, on the patriots of the south, will be irresistable." The longer Clay talked, the more impassioned he became on behalf of America's brethren to the south, famed for their "great quickness, genius, and particular aptitude for the exact sciences." Who could deny that such men were fitted for self-government? That, pronounced Clay, was "the doctrine of thrones."

Clay had opposed the taking of Amelia Island as an impediment to Spanish revolutionaries, and he had opposed Andrew Jackson's campaign in Florida, discovering in himself a regard for the rights of Indians that flabbergasted even some of his allies. Clay used his iron control over the House to call for the Monroe administration to furnish documents on the decision over Amelia and the question of recognition, and he impaneled hearings on the subjects that ran for four days. When it became clear that he lacked the votes to demand recognition, Clay attached to the administration bill establishing the South American commission a rider authorizing funds for a minister to Argentina. He was roundly defeated.

Adams' friends began to warn him that Clay and Crawford were scheming to destroy his reputation and political prospects, and urged him to fight back, if not in the same way. Alexander H. Everett, a Boston lawyer and diplomat who had served as Adams' secretary in St. Petersburg and now looked to him as a mentor as well as a source of employment, often came to dinner at the Adams home. One evening in March 1818 he asked Adams what he was planning to do to advance his own future candidacy. "I told him I should do absolutely nothing," Adams rejoined. "He said that as others would not be so scrupulous, I should not stand upon equal footing with them. I told him that was not my fault." This would set the pattern for Adams' interactions with even his most zealous boosters in the years to come.

The growing power of the West and of Clay, its great advocate, lent a new political dimension to President Monroe's calculations. In April, the president called Adams to his office to look for suitable candidates for foreign postings. He needed to satisfy every region—if possible, every state.

Ever since he had denied the State Department to Clay, Monroe admitted, he had been trying to mollify the West through appointments. Indeed, Adams himself privately complained of "backstairs influences" on the president's appointment decisions, which he would learn of only after the fact. Adams spied the hands of Clay and Crawford everywhere. Their allied newspapers—the *Kentucky Reporter* and the *Richmond Enquirer*, respectively—criticized the administration's conduct in Florida and toward the South America republics. Adams worried that Monroe was giving way under the pressure. He fretted constantly about the president's spine.

And then, with the Florida campaign, Andrew Jackson muddied the picture yet further. Even if Jackson harbored no political ambitions of his own, he was a rival for the sympathies of the West and thus a possible impediment to Clay's presidential ambitions. And, like many other leading figures of the time, Clay viewed Jackson as a genuinely dangerous man, a Caesar in waiting. As Congress convened in November 1818, the long knives came out for Jackson. After Adams received a visit from one of the general's enemies, he reflected, "This Government is indeed assuming daily more and more a character of Cabal, and preparation not for the next Presidential election but for the one after that is working and counterworking."

At the end of the year, Clay called for a full-dress congressional investigation of Jackson's seizure of Pensacola. The hearings, which began in early January 1819, lasted almost a month—the longest debate on a single subject the House had ever staged. With the galleries jam-packed, Clay delivered a stinging, sardonic, wildly hyperbolic assault on the hero of New Orleans, accusing him of insubordination against civil authority and against the Constitution itself. Jackson's friends waited their turn and then launched a counterattack. And when the dust had settled, the general had been cleared on every count. Clay's immense self-confidence often made him rash; now his direct assault had strengthened Jackson and made him suddenly plausible as presidential timber.

The fates of Clay, Jackson, and Adams would remain entangled for the next generation. Jackson now conceived an abiding hatred for Clay and a deep sense of gratitude toward Adams. To a friend of the secretary he wrote, with mangled syntax, "I think him a man of the first-rate mind of any in America as a civilian or scholar, and I have never doubted of his attachment to our republican Government." The two men had almost nothing in common as a matter of temperament, and over time each would come to regard the other with the deepest suspicion. But for the moment, Jackson served as the military wing of Adams' statecraft, which gave them a strong interest in defending one another. And Adams, who took a dim view of most of his contemporaries, felt something like veneration for Jackson.

Adams had viewed himself as the secondary target of the Florida inquiry. Clay's allies blamed Adams for defending Jackson's behavior in the letter to George Erving, which had gained wide circulation. Adams waited, in vain, for his friends to rally, as Jackson's had. "There is not in either house of Congress an individual member who would open his lips to defend me, or move a finger to defeat any combination to injure me," he fumed. Adams often gloried in his principled solitude, but this Federalist-turned-Republican had few natural allies on either side. And he lacked the social gifts that are usually second nature to a politician.

When he wasn't working, Adams wanted to be alone in his study. He treasured the little time he had to work on the papers of the 1787 federal Constitutional Convention, which seemed hopelessly snarled, or the report on weights and measures, or a solitary effort to bring the books of the State Department up to date. (Adams had taught himself double-entry bookkeeping, which he also deployed in order to make sense of his own finances.) Sometimes he daydreamed of a life of study. After meeting a man who had invented a means of efficiently converting steam to power, he thought how very fine it would be to devote one's life to the study and classification of metals or perhaps to write a history of inventors and their characters. Ought not the secretary of state devote himself to improving the Patent Office? Yes, but there was no time, and it was all he could do to keep up with the press of business.

Once again Adams was unable to leave for Quincy until late August. The family house was teeming with Adamses, but he felt the chill—the desolation—of his mother's absence. His father had reached the venerable age of eighty-four with his mind intact, but he now moved slowly and felt that he was coming unstrung. It could not be long, Adams thought, before he lost his father as well. After a few days, he moved to Boston, where he rented a fine house that had once belonged to John Hancock. He and Louisa and the boys took fishing expeditions to Dorchester and Nahant, coming back with baskets full of cod and haddock and perch. His anger at John seemed to have cooled. And he recognized that George, who had always loved literature as much as he had, was in fact "a student of great assiduity."

In the midst of this brief period of recuperation, Adams received a terrible shock: his brother Tom vanished from the family house. The kind and gently ironical young man who had accompanied his imperious older brother to Holland and Prussia, taken care of Louisa, and kept up her flagging spirits had returned home and never gained a firm footing. He had washed out first as a lawyer and then as a publisher. He had married late in life and produced six children, and he and they had become a collective burden on the family. They lived with John and Abigail in Quincy. Tom felt humiliated by his failure; he had begun drinking heavily and quarreling with his wife, Nancy, and his children. John Adams had lost all patience with him. And now Tom had fled in disgrace, no one knew where. Adams hurried to see Josiah Quincy, a lawyer and former congressman (and later president of Harvard) who served, along with Adams himself, as coexecutor of John Adams' estate. Quincy said flatly that Tom's return home would kill the old man. It was up to John Quincy Adams to prevent that, presumably by supporting Tom and his family.

Adams canceled his stay in Boston and returned to Quincy. Nancy begged him for help—she and her children had been abandoned to destitution. Adams felt that the poor woman had been driven almost out of her mind with fear about her future. With his mother dead and his father enfeebled, the whole weight of the Adams family was settling on John Quincy's shoulders. He felt himself tottering, and he walked to his mother's grave to commune with her spirit and ask for guidance. Perhaps Abigail interceded, for the following evening, Louisa reported that Tom had returned but was too unwell to speak until the following morning. Perhaps he was sleeping off a bender; Adams would have veiled such a squalid truth even from his own diary.

The next day, Adams promised Tom that he would take care of his family if Tom would reconcile with their father. When Tom quickly agreed, Adams unfolded the plan he had devised. In order to make restitution to their father, he would purchase the deed to Wollaston, the Quincy ancestral home, for $1,000 a year, just as he had purchased much of the estate years earlier when his father's investments had been vaporized in the fall of Bird, Savage and Bird. He then agreed with Tom to take the mortgage of a house in Medford Abigail had given to him, in exchange for a regular allowance for the family. The prodigal son returned to the family, and his father accepted him. The dutiful son was left with a towering pile of obligations and debts.

Tom's slow downward spiral, and his ultimate humiliation, offers a pointed reminder of how very hard it was to be an Adams. The family lacked the wealth that served as a safety net for the less lucky or gifted or driven members of other prominent families. At the same time, a merely ordinary disposition, much less a tender one, could not survive the pressure of family expectations. John Quincy had been forged in the fires and emerged whole and hard; neither Charles nor Tom had proved so fortunate. John Quincy Adams had put his own children through the same thresher, and that generation, too, would see a terrible winnowing.

FOR THE FIRST FEW YEARS OF THE MONROE ADMINISTRATION, THE great issues that had roiled the newspapers and the Congress had concerned America's relations with the European powers who had established themselves on the continent: Spain, England, and even Russia, which had built a colony on the northwest coast. But America's expansion produced internal contradictions that finally became too acute to be ignored, for the incorporation of each new state from annexed territory forced the dreaded question of slavery. Would the new state be slave or free? Kentucky had been admitted as a slave state in 1791, and then Tennessee. Much of the opposition to the Louisiana Purchase came from Federalists who feared that it would tip the balance forever between the free and slave states. The Northwest Ordinance of 1797 stipulated that states hewn from the Northwest Territory would be free; that covered Ohio and later Indiana. But Mississippi, Louisiana, and Alabama were all admitted as slave states.

In 1820, Missouri applied for admission to the Union as a slave state. At that point, half the twenty-two states were slave, and half free. Missouri would upset that balance. Much of the territory also lay above the northernmost point where slavery had been permitted up until that time. The Missouri application thus forced the questions of what kind of nation America would be and whether the uneasy compromise with which the Union itself had been forged would be permitted, or even could be permitted, to continue. The debate over the terms on which Missouri would be admitted to the Union brought out in bold relief the irreconcilable conflict that would tear the country in half forty years later. No one doubted that the question at issue was a momentous one. On January 21 Louisa went to the House of Representatives to hear the celebrated South Carolina orator Charles Pinckney speak on the subject. The gallery was thronged with ladies. Many in the audience, she was later told, had their eyes fixed on her in the hopes of discerning the views of her husband.

What were his views? Until that time, Adams had held two contradictory ideas in his mind—that slavery was an unmitigated evil and that the wishes of slave owners ought to be accommodated in the name of more pressing matters. The two principles appeared to exist in separate compartments of his mind. He did not doubt, for example, that England should be forced to make restitution for the slaves British officers had spirited away during the war of 1812; they were property, after all. In 1818, Castlereagh had sought to enlist maritime nations in a series of pacts to outlaw the international slave trade. The British foreign minister proposed that ship captains be permitted to board the ships of other signatories if they suspected slaves were being transported and then to seize the slaves and place them before a sort of international tribunal. So far as Adams was concerned, this was impressment by another name. In November, he had instructed Richard Rush and Albert Gallatin, ministers to England and France, to remind the British foreign minister that the United States had outlawed the slave trade in 1807, to point out that such mixed tribunals had no force under the US Constitution, and to explain that impressment was so repugnant to the American people that no such treaty could ever win confirmation in the Senate. Adams later told John Hay, President Monroe's son-in-law, that "the right to board vessels in peace time is more destructive of human liberty than slavery"—a sentiment that even at the time would have sounded to an enemy of slavery like gross sophistry.

Adams' constitutional view, as he freely told legislators who came to him for advice, was that Congress did not have the power to prohibit a territory in which slavery was already practiced from entering the Union as a slave state. He was prepared to live with a proposed compromise that would permit Missouri to enter as a slave state but would prohibit slavery north of 36° 30' latitude (the southern border of Missouri). And yet Adams despised slavery and the hypocrisy that surrounded it. A few months after the letter to his ministers, Adams was approached by the Committee of the American Colonization Society to help purchase African territory that free blacks could colonize. Adams refused, for he believed that the society's goal was not to assist free blacks but to rid America of them. (He also abhorred colonies.) He wrote bluntly that "the mass of coloured people who may be removed to Africa, by the Colonization Society, will suffer more and enjoy less than they would if they should remain in their actual Condition in the United States."

The debate over Missouri forced Adams for the first time to acknowledge slavery as a calamitous evil that could not simply be placed in balance with other wrongs. Listening to the great Southern orators dominate the debate over Missouri, he was seized with a romantic wish to step forward and smite them with his words:

If but one man could arise with a Genius capable of comprehending, a heart capable of supporting and an utterance capable of communicating those eternal truths that belong to this question, to lay bare in all its nakedness that outrage upon the goodness of God, human Slavery, now is the time, and this is the occasion upon which such a man would perform the duties of an Angel upon Earth.

John Quincy Adams would eventually become that man, but at this moment he was still dreaming of some other champion, not himself. He was, after all, the secretary of state, not a private citizen or a member of Congress.

The debate over the admission of Missouri forced slavery out of the shadows. Southerners who until now had simply insisted that slavery was part of their distinctive way of life now felt called upon it to defend it as a positive good. Nathaniel Macon, a senator from North Carolina, spoke of the supposedly deep sentimental bond between master and servant. Others found biblical justification for the practice. Southerners invoked the principle of "states' rights" to proclaim slavery off-limits to federal intervention. The crisis over Missouri drew together the disparate slave states and showed them their common cause. Because the issue ultimately would be papered over, the Monroe presidency continued to feel like an interval of consensus and has continued to be seen that way in the national imagination, but in fact it was an era when men began to feel that their interests clashed irreconcilably. The era of good feelings was also the seedbed of conflict.

Adams privately raged that all the best speakers lay on the Southern side of the question. He felt outnumbered. The president and all the most important cabinet members save Adams—that is, Crawford, Calhoun, and Wirt—were all Southern slaveholders. This had not been a particularly salient fact; now, suddenly, it was. On March 3, Monroe called a cabinet meeting to work out the administration's position on the admission of Missouri. All agreed that the Constitution gave the federal government the power to prohibit slavery in a territory. The state emerging from such a territory would thus enter the Union as free. But Crawford maintained that the legislature of that state could later vote to adopt slavery. Adams, who may have been looking for the opportunity to state the full measure of his views, jumped down Crawford's throat:

I said, that whatever a State Legislature might do in point of fact, they could not by any rightful exercise of power establish Slavery. The

Declaration of Independence, not only asserts the natural equality of all men, and their unalienable right to Liberty; but that the only just powers of government are derived from the consent of the governed. A power for one part of the people to make Slaves of the other can never be derived from the consent, and is therefore not a just power.

Crawford accused Adams of holding the abolitionist view that slavery violated natural human rights. Adams answered that this was precisely his view. "I did not want to make a public display of it, where it might excite irritation, but if called upon officially for it, I should not withhold it." Adams had stepped forward, before his colleagues, though not before the public, as many other opponents of slavery had.

As they left the White House, Adams and Calhoun fell into conversation. Calhoun may have been the one advocate of slavery whose intellectual integrity Adams would not think to question. The two had begun speaking of slavery the week before; now they resumed the discussion. Calhoun remarked that Adams' principles were "just and noble," but "in the Southern country, whenever they were mentioned, they were always understood as applying only to white men." Calhoun continued in this vein as they walked down Pennsylvania Avenue. That evening, or perhaps the next morning, Adams mused on the fact that a man as gifted as Calhoun could sincerely hold such repellent and, to Adams at least, self-evidently false convictions. There was a larger truth in all this, one that had not presented itself to Adams until now. Transcribing his train of thought as it came to him, Adams wrote that the practice of slavery "taints the very sources of moral principle. . . . It perverts human reason, and reduces men endowed with logical powers to maintain that Slavery is sanctioned by the Christian religion. . . . The impression produced upon my mind by the progress of this discussion is that the bargain between Freedom and Slavery contained in the Constitution of the United States is morally and politically vicious."

He had said it. Adams had long comforted himself with the fact that slavery, whatever its evils, had been enshrined in the Constitution, which he revered as the secular equivalent of Holy Writ. But now he saw that he had no right to that comfort. The constitutional bargain was morally intolerable. Henry Clay had brokered a deal in which Maine would be admitted as a free state at the same time as Missouri came in as a slave state; henceforth Clay would be known as the Great Compromiser. Adams began to wonder if this jerry-built solution was a futile effort to postpone the inevitable. With the intellectual honesty that was second nature to him, Adams followed the thought where it led him. Perhaps the era of compromise should have ended with Missouri, producing instead "a new Union of thirteen or fourteen States, unpolluted with Slavery, with a great and glorious object to effect: namely that of rallying to their Standard, the other states, by the universal emancipation of their Slaves."

This was an astonishing conclusion for a man who had been raised from the earliest moments of consciousness to regard Union as the supreme good, who had devoted his career as a diplomat and a politician to defending the integrity of the United States against foreign and domestic threats. Adams was a Burkean conservative who feared and abhorred revolutionary upheaval. Yet he had reasoned himself into a position that was too honest to reason himself out of. And perhaps he had also glimpsed in the abolition of slavery the great cause that he, who had been born too late to fight and had once accepted that his generation should resign itself to placing the laurel on the heads of those who had come before, could embrace with the will to heroism and self-sacrifice that had always lain so deep in his soul.

Adams could not get this gorgeous nightmare vision out of his head. In November 1820, the Missouri question rose again when the state legislature voted to ban free men of color from the state. The measure outraged Adams; he saw it as a provocation not only to the free states but to the very cause of human freedom. On November 29, Henry Baldwin, a member of Congress from Pennsylvania, paid Adams a visit at home, and when he asked about the new measure, all the thoughts, the feelings, and the immense premonitions brewing inside Adams came boiling out in a great torrent. And now, for the first time, Adams seemed to actually feel the injustice of slavery—and more remarkably, of racism—from the point of view of its victims. Speaking of the new clause of the Missouri constitution, he wrote in his diary:

> If acquiesced in, it would change the terms of the federal compact. Change its terms by robbing thousands of Citizens of their rights. And what Citizens—the poor the unfortunate—the helpless. Already cursed by the mere colour of their skin—already doomed by their complection to drudge in the lowest offices of Society, excluded by their colour from all the refined enjoyments of life, accessible to others, excluded from the benefits of a liberal education; from the bed, from the table, and from all the social comforts of domestic life, this barbarous Article deprives them of the little remnant of right yet left them—their rights as citizens and as men. Weak and defenceless as they are, so much the

more sacred is the obligation of the Legislatures of the States to which they belong to defend their lawful rights. And I would defend them should the dissolution of the Union be the consequence. For it would not be the defence, it would be the violation of their rights to which all the consequences would be imputable; and if the dissolution of the Union must come, let it come from no other cause but this. If Slavery be the destined Sword in the hand of the destroying angel, which is to sever the ties of this Union, the same sword will cut in sunder the bonds of Slavery itself. A dissolution of the Union for the cause of Slavery would be followed by a servile war in the Slave-holding States, combined with a War between the two severed portions of the Union. It seems to me that its result must be the extirpation of Slavery from this whole Continent, and calamitous and desolating as this course of Events in its progress must be, so glorious would be its final issue that as God shall judge me I dare not say that it is not to be desired.

It would be fifteen years before Adams would return to this elemental tragedy, to the worm of corruption in the American foundation. Thereafter, it would guide his life to the very end.

CHAPTER 18

She Goes Not Abroad in Search of
Monsters to Destroy

(1820–1822)

I N THE FALL OF 1819, JOHN QUINCY ADAMS GOT A NEW OFFICE. The year before, Congress had authorized funds for the construction of two new government buildings flanking the White House. Both were 157 feet long, built of brick, with two stories and an attic with dormer windows. The neoclassical façade of the Northeast Executive Building, where the State Department was lodged, featured a portico with six columns leading down to a broad staircase. The department occupied eleven of the fifteen rooms on the second floor and six more in the attic. Adams had an office in the southeast corner of the building. Down the hall, looking out over the portico, was a fine library three times the size of the other offices. Adams and his staff were far more comfortably housed than they had been in the cramped quarters on Seventeenth Street, which they had shared with the Departments of War and the Navy. At the same time, the State Department still consisted of six clerks and two messengers, which made it a modest institution compared to the foreign ministry of any of the major European states.

Such a scale of operations, though vexing to Adams, was properly proportioned to the nation's ambitions. The diplomacy of Europe was a diplomacy of war and the defense against war; this had been the reality of

European life for centuries. The United States was protected from the other great world powers by an ocean; England and Spain, the colonial powers that hemmed in the United States to the north, the west, and the south, posed no threat. The goal of American statesmen from the time of Washington was to maintain peaceable relations with Europe while expanding America's borders at home in order to accommodate a growing and restless population. It was the formula for national greatness. And over the course of his tenure as secretary of state, through policy and public speech, Adams would chart a path of aggressive expansion at home and cautious restraint abroad. He and Monroe were broadly in agreement. Nevertheless, Adams had to fight on both fronts. In the end, American foreign policy came to look very much like Adams' own worldview.

Adams believed that he had resolved America's greatest outstanding territorial dispute to the singular advantage of his own country. But his celebration had been premature. Onis had returned to Madrid with the signed treaty and discovered, just as he had feared, that the king's counselors in the Cortes Generale (the parliament) could find nothing in the treaty to preserve Spain's sacred honor. They advised the king not to sign, and Ferdinand, despite having pledged his "faith and word" to ratify the treaty, gave in to his counselors. Instead, he dispatched a new minister to replace Onis and to seek "clarifications"—that is, revisions—in the text. Monroe must have felt that he should have reined in his remorseless secretary of state when he had the chance.

As Monroe worked with the cabinet on drafts of his annual message in the last months of 1819, Adams tried to calibrate the exact amount of pressure that would make Spain capitulate without producing a backlash. First he suggested that the United States occupy Florida as the "assertion of a right, unjustly withheld," but do so with as little show of force as possible. Then, when he learned that Ferdinand did, in fact, plan to approve the treaty, he suggested that Monroe say that the United States had every right to seize Florida but for the moment would forebear to do so. He strongly advised the president against recognizing the Spanish republics, which would provoke Spain's conservative allies. In his annual message, Monroe adopted each of these proposals. The president had important reasons of his own for proceeding slowly. He saw that the prospect of a new frontier had released a rapacious and apparently illimitable appetite among his own people. "So seducing is the passion for extending our teritory," he wrote to Albert Gallatin, "that if compelled to take our own redress it is quite uncertain within what limit it will be confined."

Adams counseled patience because he understood that time would be on the side of the rising power and against the declining one. Spain's position would simply grow untenable. Events vindicated his expectations: a liberal convulsion in Spain led to the reconstitution of the Cortes. The new body approved the existing treaty in September 1820, and King Ferdinand signed it the following month. President Monroe nominated Andrew Jackson to serve as the first governor of Florida, and Spain was forever banished from the American Southeast.

LOUISA HAD STOPPED KEEPING A DIARY IN EARLY 1819, BEFORE HER tumultuous journey from St. Petersburg to Paris; it's not clear why. She began again in January 1819. Since her entries form the basis of letters to John Adams, Louisa's motive may have been to inform and amuse her aged father-in-law, the one member of the family whose love for her she never had reason to question. Louisa, in turn, revered and adored the old man. Twenty years later she would write in her diary, "Among all the great characters whom it has been my lot to meet in the devious paths of a long and mingled life, I have never met a man with a mind of such varied powers, such accute discrimination, and which I may use the expression was intrinsically sound. . . . The young listened to him with delight, the old with veneration."

Louisa had almost nothing to say of the affairs of the day but instead wrote about the parties she went to and the people she met, knowing that the old man had always enjoyed gossip and liked to stay au courant. One day she told Adams the details of a duel between cousins—Virginian officers, of course—who blasted away at one another from ten feet; one was killed and the other gravely wounded. When Andrew Jackson came to Washington to defend himself from Henry Clay's allegations, Louisa wryly described the bewilderment of locals who had expected to meet a savage and instead discovered a perfect gentleman.

Louisa once reflected that she was very much the same woman who had married at age twenty-one, though perhaps less timid than she had been then—"the same romantic enthusiastic foolish animal unfit for real life as I was then and as conscious of all my defects which as I rise become more striking." She took great delight in balls and parties and witty repartee. With her father-in-law she felt free to describe the whirl of life in the most breezy and self-mocking terms. "I assure you," she wrote in February 1819, "that Genl Jackson and the Spanish Treaty can not compare in interest to the Bagot ball and the unfortunate launch"—a reference to the controversial decision by the British ambassador to play "God Save the King"—"and you could scarcely believe that the two former were of vital importance to the Country and Nation at large."

Louisa was an eighteenth-century woman with a gift for the great eighteenth-century game of satire, though she did not dip her pen in quite as much acid as her husband did. Of the president's extremely unpopular daughter, Eliza Hay, she wrote, "This woman is made up of so many great and little qualities, is so full of agreeables and disagreeables, so accomplished and so ill bred, has so much sense and so little judgment, she is so proud, and so mean, I scarcely ever met such a compound." Louisa's insight into Henry Clay was penetrating but notably sympathetic: "If you watch his character," she wrote, "you almost immediately discover that his heart is generous and good, and that his first impulse is almost always benevolent and liberal. But a neglected education, vicious habits and bad company, united to overweening ambition, have made him blush to act the better part." As Clay became her husband's great rival, however, Louisa's sympathies flagged. The following year, she wrote of Clay, "He is always domineering and arrogant and usurps by his dictatorial manner the greater proportion of the discourse which he generaly contrives to make offensive to someone or other."

But Louisa also suffered greatly, both mentally and physically. Adams described one night when his wife woke in agony and he dosed her with twenty-five drops of laudanum—a very large amount. He then called for the doctor, who administered still more of the opiate before Louisa's pain subsided. She remained in bed for the ensuing four days. Her miscarriages, of course, were terrible. She suffered crippling outbreaks of erysipelas, a disorder known as Saint Anthony's fire, which turned the skin red and so swollen that at times her eyes would almost disappear. The disease was both extremely painful and humiliating, and Louisa would retire to her room until the swelling and the sensitivity subsided.

Women of Louisa's day—especially delicate, high-strung, well-born women—were so widely diagnosed with nervous disorders of one kind or another that it is impossible to say when Louisa was sick and when she was overcome by her emotions. She could be gay, as her husband could not, but her inner spirit often flickered, as his did not. She was prone to bouts of despair. During the long spells in her bedchamber Louisa sometimes fell into a sort of delirium, with day passing insensibly into night. Then she would feel that she was about to die, and it was not beyond her to welcome the prospect. The thought of infant Louisa was never far from her mind.

"Since God in his wisdom took my daughtre on whom I madly doated I have never found a thing which could fill the void in my heart," she wrote in the midst of one of her worst moments. She thanked God for taking her infant away so early, for had she died after reaching childhood, "madness or suicide must have been the result for me." And then she would rally, and rise from her bed, and rejoin the world.

In June 1820, the Adamses bought a large brownstone at 224 F Street in Washington, between Thirteenth and Fourteenth Street. (The address would now be 1333-5.) John Quincy spent the next several months supervising extensive renovations and of course quarreling with his contractor. He had the workers build what was almost a second house in the rear of the original structure, so that when finished the house had four large square drawing rooms measuring twenty-eight feet as well as more than half a dozen bedrooms. Louisa started throwing parties even before the construction was finished. Her fortnightly teas became so popular that she tried to restrict the crowd by decreeing that henceforward no dancing would be permitted, but Washington society came and insisted on dancing. Washington now had a little bit of the dazzle the Adamses had known in foreign capitals. When Congress was in session, balls and fine dinners were held almost every night. The most magnificent house in Washington had been empty since its owner, Commodore Stephen Decatur, the great naval hero of the War of 1812, had been killed in a foolish duel in March 1820. But now Baron Hyde de Neuville had purchased the three-story mansion on Lafayette Square and threw splendid parties there.

For a time, the Adams house was filled with music and dancing and even giggling and flirting. The three orphaned children of Louisa's sister Nancy Hellen—Mary, Thomas, and Johnson—had come to live with them. So had another of Louisa's relatives, Fanny Johnson. At various times they also took in the four children of Adams' brother Tom as well as Abigail Adams Smith, Nabby's eldest child. John Quincy Adams supported all of them without a murmur of protest. In January 1821, all three Adams boys were home as well. Mary took violin lessons, while George and Charles played the flute. A dancing master came for as much as three hours a day to teach all the young folk. Often they had their friends over for dancing parties.

Romance—and therefore trouble—was bound to bloom among them. Mary was a shameless flirt, plump and pretty, and the boys, one after the other, fell hard for her. Charles described her as "one of the most capricious women ever formed by a capricious race." She and George became engaged in 1823, when Mary was sixteen. Charles, who was Mary's age, admitted years later that he had "too deeply loved the woman," which almost certainly means that they were lovers. Mary would ultimately throw over both boys for John Adams II, who unlike the other two remained steadily in Washington and thus could stake a more permanent claim to Mary's affections. The two would marry in the White House.

Adams feared that his sons, and especially the two older ones, were idle and frivolous. In September 1821, while up in Cambridge, he asked to look at the Harvard class register. He was shocked to find that George, who had just graduated, stood thirtieth in the class, while John was forty-fifth, close to the bottom. As if that weren't bad enough, the next day he learned that George had given $35 to a complete stranger, who of course had made off with it. At George's age, Adams had traveled all over Europe by himself and taken care of his father in dangerous straits. He shouted at George, and the frail boy was so upset that Adams inwardly reproached himself. He lay awake all the next night worrying about his feckless children. "The blast of mediocrity," he gloomily reflected, "is the lightest of evils, which such characters portend." The greatest of evils, which he knew all too well from his own brother Charles, was self-destruction, with the accompanying shame to a great family.

Adams' own life had become immensely complicated by the extracurricular burdens peculiar to his job. Throughout 1820 and 1821, he was preparing the annals of the Constitutional Convention, the reports on weights and measures, the decennial census, the biennial register of federal employees, and—an entirely new congressional demand—a digest of commercial law, including the duties, tariffs, and other commercial regulation of all the nations with which the United States traded. It seemed unimaginable that one man—even with six clerks and two messengers—could accomplish all this while at the same time attending to the nation's diplomacy and foreign affairs. The 1787 records alone made him feel like Laocoon wrestling with his serpents. George Washington had deposited his own copy of the records with the State Department, but Adams found large gaps that had to be plugged with whatever documents he could find elsewhere, including from the few signers still living. The sheer chaos drove him to distraction.

Adams had come to view himself as a dray horse, long broken to the harness. "The operations of my mind are slow," he wrote; "my mind is sluggish, and my powers of extemporaneous speaking very inefficient. But I have much capacity for and love of labour." He set himself the task of making an index of his journals from 1795 to 1809 and then felt thoroughly disgusted at what seemed to him the pedestrian cast of his mind. The work, he reflected, "contains scarcely ever, either observation of reflection—incident or character—grave remark, or sally of humour." Surely, he concluded, the great mass of material "will never be fit for exposure to any eye but my own." Adams had something harsh to say about almost everyone, but the person he was most consistently unfair to was himself. His journals survive today not only as a precious resource for historians but as one of the great works of American political literature.

The same can not be said of Adams' report on weights and measures, of which he felt far more proud. The diary was labor; weights and measures were an addiction. Adams was pleased to discover that Washington had its very own keeper of weights and measures, a Mr. Leonard, who had a complete set of brass and copper weights from the half ounce to the twenty-eight-pound weight, as well as dry measures like the half bushel and peck, and liquid ones like the gill. Adams noted that the half bushel should contain 1089.353162 solid (i.e., cubic) inches, "which is a gill more than a half bushel Winchester measure." As he headed into the last lap in the summer of 1820, Adams was writing three pages a day of the report while still conducting elaborate research comparing French, English, and American units of measure, as well as the mathematical calculations required to measure the volume of liquids. He wondered what tiny object of uniform size might serve as a universal basis of measurement. Perhaps a grain of wheat? No: "the weight of the kernels differ from 30 to 50 to a penny-weight Troy." He explained his system at great length to the new British minister, Stratford Canning. Canning professed himself bewildered but took notes and promised to convey Adams' views to the Foreign Office. When Adams finally sent the massive report to the publisher in January 1821, Louisa wrote, with an almost audible sigh of relief, "Thank God we hear no more of Weights and Measures."

"The Report of the Secretary of State Upon Weights and Measures" is without doubt one of the strangest documents ever to be issued by that office. Most of its 135 pages—followed by appendices of equal length—consist of the kind of abstruse calculations Adams had made in his journals. Adams traced the evolution of weights and measures from the Hebrews and the Greeks; he dilated at impressive length on the evolution of standards of measurement in medieval and Renaissance England. "By the English system of weights and measures before the statute of 1496," he explained, "the London quarter of a ton was the one measure, to which the bushel for corn, the gallon, deduced by a measure, for ale, and the gallon, deduced by weight, for wine, were all referred." He wrote of the confounding diversity of national measurements and of the intrinsically diverse nature of measurement itself, founded on such infinite variables as human dimension.

But a theme shines through: "stimulated by the passion for uniformity," Adams wrote, "the philosophers and legislators of Britain" had striven to organize the mass of vague and primitive inherited terms—the cubit and the span, the bushel and the peck—into a self-consistent system. They had been defeated by popular resistance. But the French Revolution had succeeded where British liberalism had failed. In 1795 the Directory had decreed the adoption of the "republican measures" of the metric system—an instrument "for all people for all times," in the words of the Marquis de Condorcet, the great encyclopedist. Adams wrote that June 22, 1799, the day when French scientists had deposited the official meter and kilogram standard with the keeper of the public archives, marked "an epocha in the history of man."

The "universal uniformity" that was the object of thinkers and legislators on both sides of the Atlantic, Adams asserted, "is obtainable *only* by the adoption of the new French system of metrology." Straining his rhetoric to the very highest pitch, Adams stupendously declared that "if the Spirit of Evil is, before final consummation of things, to be cast down from his dominion over men," then "one language of weights and measures will be spoken from the equator to the poles." Such rapture before the altar of the Enlightenment puts Adams in the camp of Jefferson, who thirty years earlier had advanced a "Plan for Establishing Uniformity in the Coinage, Weights, and Measures of the United States." Adams was also a relentless improver who wished to bring order to all profuse and chaotic domains, including the State Department's filing system.

And yet . . . it wouldn't work. Adams saw that ordinary French people refused to divide time into tens or even to abandon traditional measurements, which made more sense to them than the new ones did. "Nature," he noted, "has no partiality for the number ten." And though "it is mortifying to the philanthropist, who yearns for the improvement of the condition of man," human activity proceeds from nature, not from abstract ideals. There was, in the end, far more of the conservative skeptic in Adams than of Jefferson or Condorcet. And so, after long years of "Alpine" labor, Adams concluded that "no innovation upon the existing weights and measures should be adopted." Instead the United States should officially state what those measures were and commission "positive standards" in brass or copper to fix the exact quantities.

The report on weights and measures had no discernible effect on US policy. Few people could have read it; even the ever-loyal John Adams confessed that he couldn't get through it all. The work, which Adams considered his greatest contribution to the literature of government, survives today as a monument to intellectual passion and obscure scholarship.

ON MARCH 9, 1821, HENRY CLAY PAID A RARE VISIT TO ADAMS AT his office. Clay had managed to largely exhaust his family fortune; he had temporarily retired from Congress in order to earn his way back to prosperity. Clay always had an eye out for the main chance; he had secured the position of the Bank of the United States general counsel for Kentucky and Ohio. The visit was no mere courtesy; Clay had been pressing for months for payment for his role in helping to negotiate a commercial treaty with Great Britain in 1815, immediately after the Treaty of Ghent. Neediness, Adams thought, had made Clay unusually forbearing toward him. The Kentuckian said that he wanted the money right away, but Adams could not oblige him. Adams turned the conversation to Clay's views on South America. He thought that Clay was naïve about the prospects of the republics, and said so:

> So far as they were contending for Independence I wished well to their cause; but I had seen and yet see no prospect that they would establish free or liberal Institutions of Government. They are not likely to promote the Spirit either of Freedom or of Order by their example. They have not the first Elements of good or free Government. Arbitrary power, Military and Ecclesiastical was stamped upon their education, upon their habits, and upon all their Institutions.

Adams agreed that the analogy Clay drew between the American and the Spanish colonies was perfectly just insofar as both had a right to rebel against a distant and oppressive master and to govern themselves. But he thought this had no bearing at all on the capacity of the South Americans to govern themselves democratically, as the Americans had done. For Adams, Clay's views smacked of a dangerous unreality, a commitment to principle in the absence of history, politics, national habit, and character. Like Burke, Adams reasoned from what men did, not from what one wished they did or imagined they might have done in an ideal setting. A foreign policy based on a priori assumptions about the world rather than a rigorous understanding of men and nations was bound to overreach and lead to grief.

Clay returned to Kentucky in the spring of 1821 and continued his attacks on the Monroe administration and on Adams. He called for America to support the South American patriots "by all means short of war." And then he made the remarkable suggestion that the United States join with the new republics in "a sort of counterpoise to the Holy Alliance." The alliance was a pact Tsar Alexander had signed with the kings of Prussia and Austria to defend the principle of absolute monarchy against the rising tide of republicanism. Clay was proposing a Republican Alliance, which would, presumably, commit the United States to the defense of independent South America—quite possibly from the forces of the Holy Alliance.

Adams was eager to answer Clay, as well as all the others he felt had been carping at the Monroe administration and at him personally. The British press had recently been filled with articles jeering at America's second-class status in the arts and sciences. And for all his own inveterate hostility to England, Adams himself was regularly attacked as an English lapdog and closet monarchist—just like his father, or so the claim went. As secretary of state, however, he felt that he could not personally respond to public criticism, much less from a potential political rival. Then the perfect opportunity presented itself when he was asked to deliver the annual July 4 oration in Washington, at the Capitol, a ritual event every diplomat, senior government official, and journalist in Washington felt obliged to attend.

In order to satisfy his own conscience as to the proprieties, Adams hit on the rather bizarre expedient of delivering the address in his Harvard gown. He would be speaking as a private citizen—or at least he could claim that he was. Independence Day addresses tended to be formulaic: the speaker spoke reverently of the Declaration of Independence, paid tribute to the sacrifices of the founders, predicted a glorious future for this mighty stripling of a nation. As an aspiring public figure of twenty-five, Adams had delivered in Boston precisely such a talk, replete with the purple prose considered obligatory for the occasion: "Seventeen times has the sun, in the progress of his annual revolutions, diffused his prolific radiance over the plains of Independent America." The address had received no more attention than it deserved. But this time Adams would use the address as a pretext to deliver a major statement of personal philosophy as well as a high-minded demonstration of his suitability to serve as America's next president.

Adams began with what appeared to be a gratuitous attack on England—red meat for his American audience. King George III, he said, had done everything in his power to trample the spirit of liberty that had arisen among the colonists, above all through the "public robbery" of taxation without representation. He compared the revolution to the story of David and Goliath. Adams insisted that he was speaking of years long past and sought "to rekindle no angry passion from its embers." But that wasn't what his listeners heard. Pierre de Poletica, the Russian minister, who had stayed away from a premonition of the speech's likely contents, described it to his foreign minister as "from one end to another . . . a violent diatribe against England." This was so widely remarked on that in the ensuing weeks Adams weakly explained to his correspondents that he could hardly have described England's behavior toward the Colonies in any other fashion.

Adams then moved on to a topic that may never before have been broached in an Independence Day oration. Standing before Congress in his Harvard robes, Adams observed, "How absurd and impracticable is that form of polity in which the dispenser of justice is in one quarter of the globe, and to whom justice is to be dispensed is in another." Colonialism, that is, was intrinsically unsustainable. Adams went on to explain why this was so. Each individual is bound to his country by a "chain of sympathy" arising from his domestic life, his community, and his friendships, but also from "the instinctive and mysterious connection between man and physical nature," so that all our emotions and memories are linked with "the spot of our nativity." This being so, no self-respecting individual will accept the legitimacy of a remote sovereign; nor could such a sovereign begin to understand the people over whom he ruled. Adams mentioned neither Spain nor South America, but no one could mistake his meaning. He was aligning himself with Clay and the other champions of the South American cause, though with none of their romanticism about the kinship between the United States and the republicans of the South.

In the typical July 4 oration, the speaker read the Declaration of Independence and then appended some remarks of his own. Everything Adams had said up to this point constituted a kind of preface, for only now did he read the Declaration. And then, in a Shakespearean apostrophe, he summoned Jefferson's great work as "a beacon on the summit of the mountain, to which all the inhabitants of the earth may turn their eyes for a genial and saving light, till time shall be lost in eternity, and this globe itself dissolve, nor leave a wreck behind." The British press, he observed, had recently taken to running articles on the theme, "What has America done for mankind?" Adams provided the answer to this impertinent question: it had "proclaimed to mankind the inextinguishable rights of human nature, and the only lawful foundations of government," which was of course popular sovereignty. The Declaration had thus "demolished at a stroke the lawfulness of all governments founded upon conquest." *All* governments—the Declaration was a universal doctrine that had completed the evolution of human disenthrallment, begun with the Magna Carta and left only "partially" achieved in England. That was what America had done for mankind.

And now, in his peroration, Adams turned—figuratively—to face Henry Clay and all the others thumping the tub for intervention on behalf of those same principles Adams had just delineated. America, he observed, "has abstained from interference in the concerns of others, even when the conflict has been for principles to which she clings, as to the last vital drop that visits the heart. . . . She goes not abroad in search of monsters to destroy. She is the well-wisher to the freedom and independence of all. She is the champion and vindicator only of her own." Should she involve herself in foreign wars and intrigue, Adams warned, "the fundamental maxims of her policy would insensibly change from liberty to force. . . . She might become the dictatress of the world; she would no longer be the ruler of her own spirit."

Adams was, in effect, reclaiming patriotism from the passionate advocates of the South American cause. By placing his call for a policy of noninterference at the very end of a long speech celebrating America's commitment to liberty and human rights, he was rebutting the claim that America could only fulfill its destiny by promoting liberty abroad as it had established it at home. Adams did not disagree with Clay and others about the universal applicability of the principles on which America had been founded. But he cared far more about the effect of American policy on Americans than on the people of Colombia or Mexico, and he believed that America would only harm itself by actively promoting republican principles abroad. Clay had bid America form a Holy Alliance of its own to advance republicanism; Adams believed that in the very act of doing so America would become a different kind of country—more like one of the states that made up the Alliance itself. Adams had laid out a program whose supreme goal was to preserve American values and extend American power.

Clay had a better feel for the American people than Adams did, and his idealistic views almost certainly had more political appeal than did Adams' austere doctrine of restraint. Americans felt a deep sympathy for republican insurgents abroad, whether in South America or in Greece. Americans resonated then, as they do now, to appeals to rally to the cause of freedom. Perhaps this is why Adams had gone to such lengths to make his call for prudence feel like the fulfillment, rather than the denial, of the deepest American ideals. But he believed that a true statesman was obliged to ignore, even to defy, public opinion, as he had so many times in the past.

These were the most famous words John Quincy Adams ever spoke. George Kennan, the diplomat-scholar who shaped the Cold War policy known as "containment," was fond of citing Adams' dictum about foreign monsters in the face of calls for American intervention. Advocates of foreign policy "realism," who call for a policy based on America's national security interests rather than its moral principles, often point to this passage as a kind of founding text. They acknowledge that Americans prefer leaders like Woodrow Wilson or John Kennedy or Ronald Reagan who summon them to great global commitments; "realism" is too chastened a doctrine— perhaps too selfish a doctrine—for a nation of idealists. Adams is the fountainhead of realism not only because he distinguished so sharply between American interests and universal goods, but because he expressed such deep skepticism about America's capacity to do good abroad. Those who now caution against "humanitarian intervention" or regime change or even democracy promotion have good reason to cite his words. He was, after all, the same man who had warned in his address at Plymouth against founding government upon "too advantageous an estimate of the human character."

All true; and yet Adams does not quite belong in their company. Today's realists often remind us that America has no monopoly on truth, that all nations claim to be exceptional, that we are all too prone to hubris. It is thus not only prudent but seemly that we keep our values to ourselves, however much we cherish them, and focus instead on the play of interests that bind states and pit them against one another. Adams would have considered this view a travesty: not for a moment did he doubt the moral superiority of America and of its republican system. The intellectual core of his Independence Day address was not the words we remember today, which came at the very end, but rather—as he insisted later to one of his correspondents—the crucial distinction he made between freedom as a donation or grant from a sovereign and freedom as an act of mutual acknowledgment among equals. This was America's great gift to mankind—a gift the American well-wisher hoped to see spread across the globe. Adams closed his address by invoking the "Spirit" of the Declaration. If it could come down to us from its "habitation in the skies," Adams cried, it would "address each one of us, here assembled, Britannia ruler of the waves, and every individual among the sceptred lords of humankind; his words would be, 'Go thou and do likewise!'"

WHEN ADAMS RETURNED TO WASHINGTON IN THE EARLY FALL OF 1821, he was confronted with a familiar problem: Andrew Jackson. President

Monroe had appointed Jackson as governor of Florida despite the latter's record of ignoring instructions from Washington and demolishing every obstacle in his path. Jackson had immediately begun doing what he seemed almost genetically programmed to do—take control. He gave orders to the military commander (though he himself no longer held military rank), threw one of the remaining Spanish officials in jail, and then defied a writ of habeas corpus issued by the territory's chief judge. Jackson thus managed in short order to precipitate a constitutional crisis that the Monroe cabinet had to resolve. What is instructive about those deliberations, given the enmity that later grew up between the sixth and seventh presidents, is that Adams sprang to Jackson's defense, as he had four years earlier. Monroe ultimately decided to relieve Jackson of his position but at the same time to publicly thank him for his service in the most laudatory possible terms. Adams heartily approved. "Gen. Jackson has rendered such services to this nation," he wrote in his journal, "that it was impossible for me to contemplate his character or conduct without veneration."

The issue of South America resolved itself as well. By early 1822, the United States no longer had to worry about Spanish reaction to American recognition of the republics. Mutinying troops had seized power from the autocratic King Ferdinand VII, establishing a republican government while he remained formally on the throne. In March the president sent a message to Congress recognizing the United Provinces, Colombia, Chile, and Mexico. Monroe appointed ministers, and in the spring of 1823 Adams wrote instructions to them. Adams always viewed the writing of diplomatic instructions as the most important aspect of his job, and these documents are rich with political insight, detailed historical background, curious digression. Adams' letter to Richard C. Anderson, the minister to Colombia, opened with a passionate denunciation of Spanish colonial practices, which Monroe struck out, as he did also a passage in which Adams explained that the South American revolutions bore no comparison to those of the United States, since "there was no spirit of freedom pervading any portion of that population, no common principle of reason to form an union of mind." Unlike many of his colleagues, Adams made a sharp distinction in his mind between a people's right to self-government and their capacity to govern themselves democratically. In this respect, too, he was a "realist" long before the term gained currency.

The documents also show that Adams was as preoccupied with economic as with political diplomacy. The vision of national greatness he entertained depended on promoting free trade among nations, for with its merchant fleet, raw materials, and nascent manufacturing capacity, America was bound to be a great exporting nation. Adams had sought to lower tariffs with both England and France. He reminded Anderson that the United States had always cherished the principle of perfect reciprocity between nations, but he added that "a still more expansive liberality" allowed the foreigner to trade on the exact same footing as the citizen. "It is the nature of commerce, when unobstructed by the interference of authority," Adams added in the spirit of instruction, "to find its own channels and to make its own way. Let us not undertake to regulate that which will best regulate itself."

The attack on Great Britain with which Adams had begun his July 4 oration was hardly out of character; he was quick to see signs of British bullying and to show that the United States would not be cowed even by the world's greatest power. The new British minister, Stratford Canning, a gifted diplomat a full generation younger than the secretary of state, came often to speak with Adams and sought to cultivate a special relationship with him. The two men had much to agree on: Great Britain had refused to join the Holy Alliance and sympathized with republican aspirations in South America and in Europe. Canning came with a brief to get the Americans to sign up for the treaty abolishing the slave trade, a profoundly liberal project no other great power would have thought to originate. But every time Canning brought the subject up—which he did constantly— Adams dismissively swatted it away.

In January 1821, Canning came to Adams in a state of great agitation: a congressmen had just spoken of plans for a new settlement on the Columbia River, which Canning claimed would violate the 1818 treaty between the United States and England. Rather than simply tell the minister that congressmen didn't make policy, Adams delivered a long, and no doubt condescending, lecture on the terms of the treaty. Canning, his deference wearing very thin, cried out, or so Adams recorded, "I am treated like a schoolboy!" The bulldog seemed intent on putting the spaniel in his place.

Canning returned the following day, and the argument resumed. Adams recapitulated it in his diary. He asked Canning if England had a claim to the mouth of the Columbia, and Canning, his temper growing, said, "Do you not *know* that we have a claim?

"I do not *know* what you claim," Adams shot back, "nor what you do not claim. You claim India—you claim Africa—you claim—

"Perhaps a piece of the Moon," Canning said irritably.

"No," Adams said. "I have not heard that you claim exclusively any part of the Moon; but there is not a spot on *this* habitable globe, that I could affirm you do not claim."

When Canning asked sarcastically if the United States also claimed the territory to the north, Adams said it did not. "There the boundary is marked, and we have no disposition to encroach upon it. Keep what is your's, but leave the rest of this Continent to us." This last was a gibe made in the heat of the moment but summed up very well Adams' own views: the continent belonged to America save for the increasingly marginal bits where it accepted the claims of European powers.

Adams and Canning would fight over the next two years, neither making much headway with the other. Adams set down in his journal his final judgment of the British minister: "He is of all the foreign Ministers with whom I have had occasion to treat, the man who has most severely tried my temper. . . . He has however a great respect for his word; and there is nothing false about him. . . . As a diplomatic man his great want is suppleness, and his great virtue is sincerity." It is not hard to imagine a fellow diplomat summing up Adams in similar terms. In fact, Canning's view of Adams was equally mixed: "more commanding than attractive in personal appearance, much above par in general ability, but having the air of a scholar rather than a statesman, a very uneven temper, a disposition at times well-meaning, a manner somewhat too often domineering, and an ambition causing unsteadiness in his political career."

CHAPTER 19

If He Wishes for Peace with Me,
He Must Hold Out the White Flag

(1822–1823)

JOHN QUINCY ADAMS CAME FROM A TRADITION IN WHICH ONE "stood for" rather than "ran for" office. To actively seek an elective office was to demonstrate your unfitness for it. It was widely assumed that Adams wanted to be president, just as it was widely assumed that William Crawford and Henry Clay and John C. Calhoun wanted to be president. But Adams never said so, either to the public or even to his close friends. Would-be supporters began to approach Adams about his plans even before Monroe won reelection in 1820, and he gave them all the same answer: "The principle of my life had never been to ask the suffrage of my country, and never to shrink from its call." He would, that is, *accept* a call to the highest office in the land, just as he had done with more modest offices. This doctrine was admirably suited to the era of George Washington and, in fact, to the person of George Washington.

Adams did, of course, want to be president, but only on his own terms. Perhaps he wished, like Cicero, to be chosen by popular acclaim. But the vinegary secretary of state was hardly the man to be hurrahed to the presidency. His two immediate predecessors had become president, but Adams could no longer count on that effortless path to the highest office; his rivals for the job would fight for it, whether he would or not. Adams stirred less enthusiasm than some of those rivals and was less prepared to campaign for the job than were some of the others. In a more democratic era, Adams would have had little chance to become president. Luckily for him, he came along at the last moment when an unpopular man who refused to court public opinion could still win the highest office.

Adams silently watched the other presumed candidates for 1824 steal a march on him. In 1819 Monroe had asked Calhoun to accompany him on a tour through the South and West, where they were met by cheering throngs. The following year Calhoun took a northward swing through Albany, Saratoga, and Boston. Crawford steadily attacked Calhoun over the alleged mismanagement of the War Department, and Adams over the negotiations with Spain. Adams wrote bitterly that "Crawford has been a worm preying upon the vitals of the Administration within its own body." Clay was steadily recruiting allies, and editors, to his side.

Newspapers had long propagandized for political candidates. But in recent years they had vastly increased in number and reach. The second decade of the nineteenth century witnessed the rise of the American small-town paper. Almost every new town cleared from forest and swamp was bound to have not just a bank and a dry-goods store but a printer, and that gentleman, after making a living turning out handbills, would soon be publishing a newspaper as well. The United States had four hundred papers in 1810 and double that number by 1825. Great Britain, with twice the population, had half as many newspapers. Improved postal routes spread these local products across the country, so that a concerned citizen could find out what people were thinking and doing all over America. John Quincy Adams read thirty to forty newspapers a day—a remarkable fraction of the total, since most papers were then weeklies. By this time newspaper editorials had largely replaced the open letter or pamphlet as the chief instrument for influencing public opinion. The journals of the day were "outrageously partisan," as one historian of the medium notes, and played a central role in organizing the factions into which the country was becoming divided. Politicians and editors learned that they could not get along, and need not get along, without each other.

Long before there was a recognizable campaign to succeed Monroe, there was a growing skirmish in the press. One of Adams' own clerks, John B. Colvin, published the *Washington Gazette*, which had started carrying fawning articles about the secretary of state as early as 1819. Adams told Colvin that while he was pleased to see the administration's initiatives enjoying favor, he would rather not be the object of praise. Adams feared that today's sycophant would be tomorrow's enemy, and in fact by 1821 Colvin was regularly attacking him in print and supporting the ambitions of William Crawford. At the same time, Adams carried on a running battle with newspapers that habitually abused him in the service of rival candidates, especially the inveterately anti-Federalist *Aurora* of Philadelphia—the paper started by his old schoolmate Benjamin Franklin Bache.

Adams was not entirely averse to buttering up editors. He sent a copy of his July 4 address to Robert Walsh Jr., an essayist who had founded America's first quarterly, the *American Review of History and Politics*. Walsh had probably first come to Adams' attention with an article attacking the same anti-American pieces in the British press that Adams had targeted in the address. Walsh had just founded the *National Gazette* of Philadelphia. Much more a polemicist than a political hack, Walsh was not averse to criticizing Adams, who nevertheless—or perhaps for that very reason—saw in him a man worthy of his attentions. They would correspond often and meet regularly in the coming years.

In 1817, Congress had passed a law requiring at least two newspapers in every state and territory to publish federal laws. The newspapers would be paid for the space, and at first the job of assigning this lucrative privilege was given (like almost everything else) to the State Department. Adams may have used this power as a means of currying favor with preferred editors, though he was more apt to record the embitterment of those he had passed over. In any case, his attitude toward the exploitation of the new medium was of a piece with his views of politicking in general. When Joseph Hopkinson, a Philadelphia congressman and staunch Adamsite, made one of the many futile efforts to induce the secretary of state to actively campaign, Adams told him, "I will have no stipendiary editors of newspapers to extol my talents and services." Hopkinson, who must have known what was coming, responded that it was precisely these archaic virtues that made Adams so attractive a candidate in his eyes but added that perhaps Adams might, as a small gesture, refrain from openly attacking Federalists on his next trip to Boston.

Adams' rivals were not so scrupulous. The *Richmond Enquirer*, voice of the Jeffersonians, was widely understood to play a crucial role in Crawford's campaign; Crawford also had loyal papers in Boston, New York, Philadelphia, and Portland, Maine. The *Argus of Western America*, a feisty broadsheet of outsize influence based in the frontier town of Frankfort, Kentucky, served as a Clay organ, as did papers in Cincinnati and elsewhere in the West. In the summer of 1822, John Calhoun spoke to Adams about his high-minded plan of starting a politically independent paper in Washington. Adams laughed; any such endeavor, he said, "would be beset on all sides by slander, obloquy and probably assassination." Perhaps, in any case, Calhoun was trying to throw dust in Adams' eyes: he had begun canvassing for president the previous December, and in September, a few months after this conversation, the *Washington Republican* would begin publication as a Calhoun paper. Soon the *Franklin Gazette* of Philadelphia would be running an adulatory nine-part profile on Calhoun.

The most politically gifted of the men vying to succeed Monroe was Henry Clay. Unlike Adams, Clay had built up a vast network of contacts during his years in Washington and was writing to friends in states across the country asking for their estimates of his standing. Clay calculated that with a three- or even four-cornered contest, no one was likely to win a majority of electoral votes, which would, according to the Constitution, lead to a choice by the House of Representatives among the top three finishers. Clay had good reason to feel that he would win any such contest: he simply needed to ensure that no one won an outright majority and that he himself made it into the final three. Clay may have believed that even if he couldn't keep Adams out of the House contest, he could play on popular fears in order to weaken him in a three-man battle with himself and Crawford.

Adams considered Clay a schemer—he viewed all his rivals as schemers—but he never doubted the Kentuckian's gifts. He was, Adams wrote, "an eloquent man with very popular manners, and great political management. He is like almost all the eminent man of this Country only half-educated. His school has been the world, and in that he is proficient." In fact Clay had deeper and more genuine political convictions than Adams would credit him with. In Congress and out, he talked up a plan he had labeled, with typical ingenuity, "the American system." In foreign affairs, Clay argued for a policy focused on the Americas rather than on Europe—a Holy Alliance of American democracies. "It is in our power," he said in a speech in the House in 1820, "to create a system of which we shall be the centre, and in which all South America will act with us. . . . We should be the centre of a system which would constitute the rallying point of human freedom against all the despotism of the Old World." Clay was perhaps the first American politician to recognize the political power of a romantic, and not merely nationalistic, foreign policy.

But the American system was preeminently a forward-looking vision for the United States. Clay argued that America had permitted itself to be an economic handmaiden to Europe. Instead, the United States should keep out cheap English manufactures through a system of duties and thus protect the infant industries of the Northwest as well as New England. He had shepherded a tariff bill through Congress in 1816 and then made an unsuccessful effort to raise duties in 1820. Clay also argued that the federal government should seek to knit the country together through public works programs, which at the time were known as "internal improvements." Roads and canals would help the manufacturers and farmers of the interior to bring their products to the major population centers of the coast and thus make such goods more competitive with foreign articles. Adams held virtually identical views of domestic policy, but he had never propounded them as clearly, or tied them as neatly, as Clay had.

But Clay *was* a schemer. In early 1822 he appears to have carried out an audacious plan to blacken Adams' reputation. For reasons that seemed obscure at the time, a congressman, John Floyd, had called on President Monroe to turn over to the House a complete record of the correspondence from the Treaty of Ghent. Clay appears to have inspired the request; he was probably hoping to rake up the old controversy between him and Adams over whether the British should have been permitted to keep the right to navigate the Mississippi in exchange for preserving the right of New Englanders to fish off Newfoundland. In fact, the other commissioners had sided with Adams, and in any case the proposed deal had fallen through. But now it could be made to appear that Adams had been guided by his family's pro-British sentiments—a false claim—and had been prepared to help his native New England at the expense of the West, which was at least arguably true.

In the course of gathering the material, Adams came across an unpublished letter from Jonathan Russell, a junior member of the delegation at Ghent, objecting to the proposed swap and suggesting that he would detail his concerns in a later letter to then Secretary of State Monroe. Russell had gone back to his position as interim minister to Sweden but had not been asked to serve as permanent ambassador—a failure he may have blamed on Adams. He had returned to the United States and won election to the Senate from Massachusetts. He joined Floyd in calling for the fullest possible production of documents. Adams asked Russell if he would mind including the letter. Russell said that he would not; indeed, he would like to include the later letter as well. This was nowhere to be found in the State Department archives, so he offered to furnish a duplicate from a copy he said that his daughter had made. On April 22, Russell dropped off the duplicate at the State Department.

What Adams read was shocking. After reciting claims and counterclaims with which Adams was perfectly familiar, Russell accused his fellow commissioners of deliberately ignoring instructions not to barter away the Mississippi for the fisheries. In fact, Secretary of State Monroe had issued such instructions in 1813 but then countermanded them in 1814—as Russell would have known perfectly well when writing the letter. From this fact, and other small discrepancies, Adams realized that the "duplicate" was a fake—a forgery designed to do terrible damage to his reputation and play right into the hands of Clay, the champion of the West. Adams concluded that Clay was the master puppeteer of the drama. He was far from alone in that assumption. Senator Daniel Barton of Missouri, no friend to Adams, described the Russell letter as "one of the artifices of Clay to render Adams unpopular & advance his own pretensions to the Presidency."

Provoking John Quincy Adams to righteous wrath was a poor idea. Adams immediately winkled the original of the letter out of President Monroe, confirming that, unlike the "duplicate," it made no allegations of bad faith. By going painstakingly over every jot and tittle, Adams found in all 172 variations between the two letters. Monroe, who had no wish to be coated with flying mud, asked Adams to keep the letter private, in exchange for which he would state that he had approved the transaction at Ghent. Russell, now realizing that his plot had miscarried, raced to the White House to tell the president that in fact there was no reason to release the letter; Adams found him there. Now the positions were reversed: Adams' good name depended on the release of the letter and the alleged duplicate. Monroe hated the idea; after a heated exchange, the president said that he would convey the letters only if Congress asked him to do so. Congress would soon adjourn, and the whole affair would be dropped. Adams now engaged in a subterfuge: he asked a friend in Congress to call for the letters. On May 7, Congress passed a resolution seeking the documents.

That very day—it must have been a happy one—Adams rode with the president to the House in order to deliver the letters and his report on the discrepancies. The report provoked the kind of newspaper donnybrook he professed to deplore. Russell had gotten his "duplicate" letter published in the *National Intelligencer*, which printed congressional debates and enjoyed a semiofficial status. Adams persuaded his friend Walsh to print both letters, along with yet another version Russell had supplied. Walsh added a commentary noting that Adams had been utterly vindicated. Now the anti-Adams press swung into action: the *Aurora*, the *Franklin Gazette*, and the *Richmond Enquirer* ran articles supporting Russell's allegations. Adams himself refuted Russell's claims in two letters to the *National Intelligencer*.

Louisa, up in Quincy, wrote almost daily to entertain her husband with news and gossip, as once she had done for her father-in-law. She implored him to have done with Russell; so did other friends. He had, after all, reduced the man to smoking rubble. It was a brutally hot summer, and Washington was almost empty. Adams must have yearned to go north to join his family. But he would not—not while Russell refused to admit guilt. "If he wishes for peace with me," Adams wrote a friend, "he must hold out the white flag." Adams committed all his thoughts on the subject to a pamphlet—in fact, a book—that he self-published in September under the title *The Duplicate Letters, the Fisheries and the Mississippi*.

Clay himself did not surface until November, when he wrote a letter to the *National Intelligencer* disavowing any connection to the "unhappy controversy." Clay noted, as if in passing, that "he thinks there are some errors (no doubt unintentional) both as to matters of fact and matters of opinion" in Adams' account. Clay should never have given the Adams beehive even a modest shake. Adams promptly wrote in to say that since Clay's enumeration of those errors "may chance to be postponed until both of us shall have been summoned to account for all our errors before a higher tribunal than that of our country," he wished to stipulate that in fact his own assertions would "be found to abide unshaken the test of human scrutiny of talents and of time." In the months to come, Clay would insist to correspondents that he had done nothing to instigate Russell, but few believed him.

Adams had fought a newspaper war and won hands down—not by calling on a "stipendiary editor" or conferring official favors but by deploying the gift for inspired polemic that had served him well since the era of Publicola. He had vindicated his honor and at the same time greatly raised his standing in the court of public opinion. He had utterly silenced his critics and dismayed Henry Clay. Adams received letters of support and congratulation from all over the country. He learned of one of the most unexpected tributes from Robert Walsh, who wrote to say that at a dinner he had heard the venerable Timothy Pickering—he of the Essex Junto—declare, "I regard Mr. Russell as a man fairly *done over*. Mr. Adams will be exalted in the estimation of New England by his Remarks, and ought to be exalted in any part of the world."

The Russell episode looks in retrospect like a smashing political victory, but if Adams thought of it that way, he never said so. For him, the stakes were far higher than office. To Louisa he described the fight with Russell as "an affair of more than life or death"—an affair, that is, of honor. In one of her letters to her husband, Louisa suggested that he come join her in

Philadelphia, which would permit him to do some campaigning as well. Adams refused. "There will be candidates enough for the Presidency without me, and if my delicacy is not suited to the times, there are candidates enough who have no such delicacy."

Was Adams lying to himself—or to Louisa and his friends and supporters? In our own time we take it for granted that people are propelled by their hungers, very much including those who won't confess to them. It is a staple of modern scholarship on Adams that he pursued higher office with as much ardor as his rivals, even if he deployed different methods. Ernest May, one of the great scholars of nineteenth-century American history, has subtly teased out the political calculations embedded in Adams' foreign policy views. Yet there is little if any evidence that Adams thought this way and a good deal of evidence that he didn't. This was the same man who had gotten himself recalled as a senator by taking positions directly at odds with the interests of his constituents.

Adams was not less ambitious than other men, but he had learned from childhood to force his appetites through the narrow straits of principle. Republicanism, for Adams, meant self-abnegation. He had never, as he said in his letter to Louisa, sought partisan allies in Congress, or in the press, or in state legislatures. Should he start now? Should he, who had not taken a day off in the blazing Washington summer, take a vacation from his job in order to campaign in Philadelphia? Tell my friends there, he said, "that I am going by another road and to another temple." Adams would fight only the fights he considered worthy, and he would do so, as always, by himself. On his fifty-fifth birthday, July 11, he was stuck in sultry and empty Washington. He must have been feeling very alone, for he wrote that, while he was beset by enemies, "I have my own errors to dread more than the power of my adversary. A single false step will ruin me. I need advise very much, and I have no one to advise me." Or rather, he would not listen to those who wished to advise him, and even he found it difficult to live always by his own counsel.

Adams' friends would not leave off goading him into action. In early 1823, Joseph Hopkinson, the Pennsylvania legislator, wrote in near despair to Louisa that she must persuade her husband to stop blocking every effort by his friends to advance his candidacy. Hopkinson accused Adams of adopting the policy of the wavering Macbeth when he says, "If chance will have me king, why chance will crown me / Without my stir." When Louisa showed the letter to her husband, a combination of literary playfulness and a deep sense of resolution moved him to respond with a letter he titled

"The Macbeth Policy." Had Macbeth only adhered to such a policy, Adams observed, "no tragedy." In any case, Adams went on, in a democracy what matters is the choice of voters, not the will of would-be leaders. He then imagined Hopkinson responding that the choice was, in fact, being made by "politicians and newspapers," whom the candidate needed to cultivate. "Here we come to the point," Adams wrote, throwing off the mask of irony. "He who asks or accepts the offer of friendly service contracts the obligation of meeting it with a suitable return. . . . If he asks or accept the aid of one, he must ask or accept multitudes." The only choice is to ask or accept nothing. The first alternative is "vitally and essentially corrupt." The latter is "the only principle to which no exception can be taken." Here was true republicanism, as John Quincy Adams understood it.

Adams would, of course, become president, and he would do so by finally throwing off the Macbeth Policy. He would relax his iron principles in order to be president, and that compromise would come to haunt him.

JOHN QUINCY ADAMS HAD A STREAK OF ICONOCLASM, OF INDIFFERENCE to received wisdom or to appearance, which was so pronounced that it often took the form of eccentricity. He was notorious for his neglect of dress; Adams would have been mystified that Stratford Canning's assessment of him would have begun with a reference to his looks. He still wrote poetry—he even amused himself trying to copy the versification of Byron, whom staid men like Canning considered utterly corrupt. Adams took up hobbies to the point of mania. He had begun swimming during the torrid summer of 1817. By 1823 he had become perhaps the most dedicated swimmer in the nation's capital. At dawn, Adams and his servant, Antoine, would walk an hour to the Potomac. Adams would strip off his clothes to reveal his pale flesh and slightly tubby form, place a pair of goggles on his balding skull, and then jump in. At the beginning of June, he and Antoine swam for thirty-five minutes. Two weeks later, they were up to an hour, then an hour and a quarter. Swimming, he decided, should be taught in school.

One day, as an experiment, Adams swam in his pants and stockings. That, too, he thought, should be taught in school. A few weeks later, he found himself fighting against a strong tide. He made a mental note: add that to the curriculum. The very next day he got trapped again far from the shore in a powerful tide and was barely able to fight his way back to the rock where he had left his clothes. By August he was swimming for almost two hours; faithful Antoine paddled behind in a canoe, which Adams would enter at points where the river grass rose too high. The two men never saw another soul, much less another boat. If anything went amiss, there would be no prospect of help. "It sometimes occures to me," Adams wrote sagely, "that this exercise and amusement as I am now indulging in is with the constant risk of life. Perhaps that is the reason, why so few persons ever learn to swim."

Adams left for Quincy in late August 1823. He sent a note to President Kirkland saying that he would be unable to attend commencement. Kirkland would not have had to wonder why—in May, John Adams II had been the ringleader of a group of seniors who had rioted over the arrest of one of their numbers. Kirkland had reacted by kicking the secretary of state's son out of Harvard. Adams had written to ask if John could receive his diploma nonetheless. The answer was no. This was a dreadful blow for both father and son, who had actually been improving his performance until then. Fortunately, Charles, who in his freshman year had written to his mother and brother George—but not his father—that he had fallen into "depraved habits" and was thinking of dropping out of school, had now found his footing and begun moving up in the class standing. Only Charles, it would turn out, had the inner oak of an Adams.

But Harvard was still very much in Adams' blood. He had written to other prominent alumni with the hope of raising funds to build an observatory at the college and endow a chair in astronomy. This had been one of Adams' enthusiasms ever since he had first stared through a telescope in the Philosophy Chamber of Harvard Hall. President Kirkland agreed to use a $20,000 bequest he had received for the purpose, at least as soon as the donor's widow died. Adams gave $1,000 of his own and began to contemplate where the telescope would best be placed, far from the lights of town.

His father was now bowed down with years, though mentally alert. Adams had asked Gilbert Stuart to make one last portrait of the old patriot—a painting that shows the eighty-eight-year-old ex-president with a still-appraising glance and an unyielding set to his mouth, and hangs today in the Boston Museum of Fine Arts. Adams paid a visit with his father to the Thaxters, old family friends. (John Thaxter had served as tutor to six-year-old Johnny.) The visit brought back ancient memories, and Adams spent the evening alone, lost in his reflections. Soon, very soon, he would be the family patriarch. Perhaps it was this thought that set him browsing for the first time through the old family records in the Braintree church. He traced the lineage back to his great-great-great-grandfather Henry, one of

Braintree's original settlers. He found records of his mother's family, the Quincys, including the grant of Mt. Wollaston to Edmund Quincy in 1633.

In his July 4 address Adams had spoken of the mystical ties that bind people to their native soil. For him this was no mere abstraction. His ancestors had roamed across the rough ground of Braintree since white people had first arrived on those shores, and they roamed there still. In their vigorous and irreproachable uprightness, still adamantine in the last years of life, and their flinty independence and self-sufficiency, the Adamses partook of the New England earth. And John Quincy Adams, who had traveled across the world, was happiest among the rugged rocks of his native town, as he had written from Europe at age ten. America was changing fast, but the Adamses, for better and for worse, were rooted to the spot. That sharp, thin line in the Adams mouth was the mark of fixity.

CHAPTER 20

The Most Important Paper That Ever
Went from My Hands

(1822–1823)

WHAT KIND OF NATION WAS AMERICA TO BE? VIRTUALLY all Americans believed that their country was different in nature from the nations of Europe, for it had been founded on principle, not conquest. How was a principled power to behave in an unprincipled world? The United States would not seek colonies, as European powers did. Would it permit them to survive on its own continent? Would it seek to evict them? America's great and successful experiment with republicanism had inspired brave men to fight for their freedom elsewhere in the world. What would Americans say when they asked for help? "Go thou and do likewise!," John Quincy Adams had proclaimed at the end of his July 4 oration—go, that is, and seize power from tyrants. Adams would confine America to the role of spectator of this great drama. But prudent circumspection was not very much in the American grain. Henry Clay and many other leading figures believed that the United States could and should play a transformative role in the world.

These great questions had remained latent during the decades when America's weakness had dictated a policy of defensive isolation behind its ocean barrier. But that fledgling era had drawn to an end; new powers required a new vision. In his July 4 oration and elsewhere, Adams had shown Americans the path he believed they needed to take. No other public figure of his generation had offered so cogent and deeply considered an answer to the question of America's role in the world. In the ensuing years, Adams would continue to argue inside the Monroe administration for his brand of assertive realism. And he would succeed: the supreme formulation of early-nineteenth-century American foreign policy known as the Monroe Doctrine would overwhelmingly bear Adams' stamp.

By the middle of 1822, the struggle between Spain and the South American colonies was largely over. One prize, however, remained in Spain's shaky grasp: Cuba. The small island just off the Florida coast was a source of great wealth both for Spain and for the United States: fifty American ships arrived every month at Havana harbor and returned home with coffee, sugar, and molasses. None of the South American republics could compare to Cuba as a trading partner. And with Florida now taken, the incorporation of Cuba seemed inevitable as well as deeply desirable. In the late summer of that year, President Monroe received word that a secret agent who had come from Cuba, a Mr. Sanchez, was seeking to provoke a revolt against Spain in order to gain acceptance as a new American state. In a cabinet meeting September 27, Secretary of War Calhoun said that he was all for it; he knew from correspondence, he added, that former president Jefferson was too. The British profited just as richly from the Cuba trade, and assimilating the island, Calhoun pointed out, would prevent Great Britain from doing so; it would also preclude the dreadful possibility of another "Negro revolt," like Haiti's. Jefferson had even said that the United States should be prepared to go to war with England over Cuba.

Adams wanted Cuba every bit as much as Calhoun or Jefferson did, but everything about the proposed intervention aroused his ingrained skepticism. First, he said, it wasn't clear whether the executive or legislature even had the constitutional authority to do what Sanchez proposed. Second, Spain would be outraged, as would its allies in the Holy Alliance. Third, in any war with Great Britain in the West Indies, the United States was bound to lose. Adams advised that Monroe say nothing—neither encourage the revolutionaries nor advise them to stick with Spain. Adams believed that Cuba would come to the United States in the fullness of time. In the meanwhile, why jeopardize the lucrative trade as well as relations with Spain and Great Britain? Monroe, who apparently remained silent on the question, decided in Adams' favor, as he so often did. The issue arose yet again the following March, with the same battle lines and the same outcome. The United States, for all its republican sympathies, acquiesced to Spanish colonial control.

Cuba had never sparked the public imagination, since most white Americans no more wanted to see a "Negro revolt" than Calhoun did. The great romantic cause of the day was Greece, which had rebelled against the Ottoman mantle in 1821. English intellectuals, including the poets Shelley and Byron, had rallied to the side of the Greek republicans. America, too, was inflamed; newspaper editorials and patriotic societies called for private help, and often an open avowal of support, for the Greek cause. Albert Gallatin, the minister to France and far from a republican hothead, wrote Adams to advocate not only recognition of Greece but the dispatch of naval forces to the Mediterranean. Adams had also received a letter from the self-styled "Envoy of the Provisional Government of Greece" asking for American recognition and aid.

In Greece the United States faced for the first time a public demand for intervention abroad. President Monroe, a Jeffersonian idealist who had championed the French Revolution, had planned to endorse the Greek cause in his 1822 message to Congress; Adams had succeeded in watering down the language to a vague expression of sympathy. In August 1823, Monroe raised the subject in the cabinet. Crawford and Calhoun supported Gallatin's suggestion; no one opposed it, save Adams. "Calhoun descanted upon his great enthusiasm for the cause of the Greeks," Adams noted caustically; "he was for taking no heed of Turkey whatever." Adams replied that he "thought not quite so lightly of a war with Turkey." And Calhoun had no practical plan for aiding the Greek patriots. "I have not much esteem for the enthusiasm which evaporates in words," Adams wrote. The discussion came to naught, just as Adams had hoped. It had foundered on practicalities, but for Adams the deep issue was whether the goal of American foreign policy was to shape a better world or to advance American interests. "Enthusiasm"—public passion—dictated the first; the lonelier counsels of prudence, the latter.

A very different, and perhaps more serious, problem was presented by Russia, a continental power with its own rising ambitions. Since the early eighteenth century Russia had claimed territory across the Bering Strait in Alaska and Canada, and in September 1821, Tsar Alexander had renewed the privileges and the exclusive trading rights of the so-called Russian-American Trading Company, extending its territorial limits from the fifty-fifth to the fifty-first parallel (the latitude of Calgary, 160 miles north of the current border between the United States and Canada). At the same time, and even more provocatively from the American point of view, he banned all foreign ships from 100 miles of the claimed coastline. This claim plainly conflicted with the British-American treaty of 1818, which established joint control over the Northwest from the forty-second parallel to a point that had not been established. Both London and Washington forcibly rejected the claim. And the tsar may have had second thoughts, for Henry Middleton, the American minister in Russia, wrote to Adams in late 1822 to say that Alexander had dispatched a new minister, Baron de Tuyll, to the United States in order to resolve the issue.

By the summer of 1823, the two nations had agreed to continue negotiations in Russia. Adams maintained that the United States should not accept the validity of any Russian possessions on the continent save for a few islands, but none of his colleagues were prepared to go as far. Monroe instead ordered Adams to instruct Middleton to accept Russian's claims above the fifty-fifth parallel but not below. Adams was clearly writing through gritted teeth. When the very genial and gracious Baron de Tuyll came to Adams' office in July to ask about the instructions to Middleton—it was his job to be in the know, as he pointed out—Adams said that the United States "should contest the right of Russia, to *any* territorial Establishment on this Continent; and that we should assume distinctly the principle that the American Continents are no longer subjects for *any* new European Colonial Establishments."

The instructions to Middleton had conceded Russia's right to territory, and thus to a colony, on the American continent. But Adams spoke to de Tuyll as if he had won the argument in the cabinet. Adams had been working out his principle of noncolonization at least since the time of the Independence Day message. In instructions to Richard Rush written in July 1823, he wrote that the American continent, "occupied by civilized independent nations," would henceforward "be accessible to Europeans and to each other on that footing alone, and the Pacific Ocean in every part of it will remain open to navigation of all nations, in like manner with the Atlantic." Adams objected to colonization in principle, but he was stipulating as a matter of doctrine that no new colonies would be allowed in the Americas—"Keep what is yours, but leave the rest of this Continent to us," as he had said to Canning. Adams had not deviated in the slightest from the principles he had enunciated in the opening months of his tenure as secretary of state: restraint in the face of Europe's internal affairs, resolution and even high-handed assertiveness on territory at home.

The most disquieting event of this period was the growing aggressiveness of the Holy Alliance. At the Tropau Conference of 1820, the signatories had bound themselves "to bring back the guilty state"—guilty, that is, of republican government—"in the bosom of the Great Alliance," by means of arms if need be. They made good on their vow the following year, when Austrian armies put down republican movements in Naples and the Piedmont. At the Conference of Verona in October 1822, Alexander had offered to send an army of 150,000 men into Europe to continue this providential work and above all to restore King Ferdinand to the Spanish throne. Instead King Louis XVIII of France agreed to rescue his fellow Bourbon, and in the spring of 1823 a French army routed the republicans.

The Spanish royalists still hungered to regain control over South America and had some hope that France might help. François, Vicomte de Chateaubriand, the great essayist and memoirist and, at that time, foreign minister, persuaded the French council of state to adopt his plan to install Bourbon princes on the throne of the new South American nations, possibly with the help of French arms. It was never an entirely serious proposition and in any case was meant to be contingent on reforms adopted by Ferdinand to make his own rule less onerous—reforms the feckless and brutal monarch was never going to adopt. But France's plans did worry the Monroe administration, as well as Great Britain, which was not about to sacrifice its commercial relations with South America to fall victim to reactionary French dreams.

It's impossible to be certain just how worried Adams or Monroe was about French or Allied plans in South America. Adams' journal has served as an indispensable guide for historians of this period, and Adams left off journalizing from January 11 to June 2, 1823. It seems, however, that what preoccupied Adams in the summer and fall of 1823 was not the prospect of a fight, whether for American or South American soil, but rather a clash of systems—of republicanism and royalism, of the rule of the citizen versus absolute power. The tsar, the Bourbons, and Prince Metternich viewed the American system as an infectious virus to be contained (though Alexander, to be fair, continued to have a soft spot for the United States). Adams was quite certain that the American system was the wave of the future, but for that very reason he knew that America had stirred up a violent and possibly dangerous reaction. He and the president and the other chief members of the administration knew that Great Britain, with its constitutional traditions and liberal sympathies, was trying to straddle both sides; they needed England to stand apart from Continental Europe but not necessarily to stand with the United States as an actual ally, for neutrality remained a core American principle. If the United States was to draw clear lines between systems, it would have to do so without clumsily alienating powerful states whose ambitions it still feared.

ADAMS RETURNED TO WASHINGTON FROM HIS GENEALOGICAL researches in Quincy in the middle of October. Fortunately for posterity, he resumed writing full diary entries on November 7, when Monroe convened the first of a series of almost nonstop cabinet meetings that would lead to the drafting of the Monroe Doctrine. The first order of business was to respond to a startling offer from George Canning, Stratford's brother and England's bold and brilliant new foreign secretary. That summer, Canning had asked Richard Rush, the American minister in London, to issue a joint statement with Great Britain opposing French ambitions to invade South America and restore colonial control. Rush prudently asked Canning if his government had decided to recognize the new nations, as the United States, alone so far, had done. Canning conceded that it had not. In a subsequent conversation, Canning asked Rush to sign a statement declaring that Spain could not expect to recover the former colonies and that the United States and England would not permit them to be "transferred to any other power" and "aim not at the possession of any portion of them ourselves." A less cautious diplomat might have jumped at the offer. However, Canning continued to leave recognition of the republics to "time and circumstances." One again, Rush demurred. His letter to Adams describing the negotiations had arrived two days before the cabinet meeting.

The Monroe administration had another important document to consider as well: on October 16 Baron de Tuyll had delivered to Adams a formal note stating unequivocally that the tsar would not receive any ambassador from the South American republics and thus would not acknowledge their legitimacy. This sounded very much like a shot across the bow from the Holy Alliance, perhaps even a token of its willingness to retake the colonies by force. Of course this increased the attractiveness of Canning's offer.

The cabinet meeting of November 7, and the meetings that followed, revolved around these two missives. What we know about them today comes largely from Adams' contemporaneous record, which means that inevitably we see the debates through his eyes. Calhoun, Adams wrote, immediately embraced Canning's suggestion; Adams did not. He was not prepared to forego the possibility that Cuba could choose to voluntarily accede to the United States. He considered the proposal unnecessary as well as unseemly. He couldn't tolerate the implicit show of deference to Great Britain. Why not, he asked, respond to both letters with a single statement? "It would be more candid as well as more dignified," he said, "to avow our principles explicitly to Russia and France, than to come in as a Cock-boat in the wake of the British man of War."

The convergence of events inspired a thought in Adams, and he expressed it to Monroe after the cabinet meeting broke up. The response to Tuyll and to Rush, as well as the instructions to be sent to Middleton in Russia for territorial negotiations, "must all," he suggested, "be part of a combined system of policy and adapted to each other." Monroe had been considering doing just that; both he and Jefferson had written in the past of the need for a coherent doctrine of American interests. Clay, of course, had articulated his "American system." The idea was in the air: America needed a new public statement of principle to supersede the Farewell Address.

Over the following week, Adams worked up a draft of remarks to be made to Tuyll, which the president read and edited. On November 12, Monroe came to Adams' office to ask for notes for his annual message to Congress, which he had begun preparing. Monroe had been alarmed to learn that the French army had taken Cadiz, the last bastion of the Spanish republicans. This had redoubled his fears over the Alliance's designs on South America and thus made Canning's proposal yet more appealing. He had sent Rush's letter to Jefferson and Madison and received unequivocal responses from them. Jefferson wrote that "the question presented by your letter is the most momentous which has ever been offered to my contemplation since that of Independence."

Beneath this typical Jeffersonian hyperbole was the recognition that the British offer constituted the kind of "entangling alliance" both he and George Washington had warned against. If anything, Jefferson went on, the interests that separated the new world from the old had grown yet more distinct as Europe had largely surrendered to despotism. Nevertheless, he wrote, the United States had more to fear from Great Britain, the world's great naval and trading power, than from any other nation, and with that country on its side the United States really could bid defiance to the world. The former president added, in an expression either Adams or Clay could have written themselves, that the United States must insist on an "American system" that excluded "all foreign powers" from "our land."

The cabinet convened again at 1 pm on the fifteenth. Adams found that the president had been ginned up to a state of high anxiety over the fall of Cadiz by Calhoun, who had been "perfectly Moon-struck" by the report and was already envisioning an army of the Holy Alliance crossing the ocean to reconquer the former colonies. Once again Adams tried to bring the collective temperature down with a reminder that, having successfully won their independence, the colonies were scarcely as helpless as some might think. Calhoun strongly favored giving at least a qualified assent to Canning's proposal; Monroe appeared to be taking his side, though the president, as was so often the case, hovered between competing views.

On the seventeenth Adams received another visit from Baron de Tuyll, who had several official documents from his foreign minister he needed to read to the secretary of state. In one of them, the tsar celebrated the Alliance's success in restoring King Ferdinand to the Spanish throne and putting down republicanism in Naples and elsewhere. Alexander reaffirmed his policy of "guaranteeing the tranquility of all the states of which the civilized world is composed." Adams had no trouble decoding the message and immediately asked the baron if Russia was supporting Spain's continued sovereignty over the colonies. It did, said the Russian minister. Adams interpreted the tsar's proclamation as an "'Io Triomphe' over the fallen cause of revolution, with sturdy promises to keep it down."

The following day Adams brought the dispatches from Tuyll to the White House. Calhoun was there, more certain than ever that the Alliance posed a mortal threat and the United States needed to ally with England in case of attack. Adams remained just as certain that it need do no such thing. The president still couldn't make up his mind. The cabinet met once again on the twenty-first without reaching a conclusion. Adams now told the others of the tsar's aggressive policy. The secretary suggested that the administration respond with a verbal declaration of its own. The message, he said, should assert the principles "upon which our own Government is founded; and while disclaiming all intention of attempting to propagate them by force and all interference with the political affairs of Europe, to declare our expectation and hope that the European powers will equally abstain from the attempt to spread their principles in the American Hemispheres or to subjugate by force any part of these Continents to their will." Even as he was helping Monroe draft his address to Congress, Adams was seeking to formulate a statement of principles that would respond all at once to England, France, and Russia. He wanted policy to proceed from principle, and those principles, of course, should be his. Monroe endorsed the idea.

The president then read a rough version of his message to Congress. Adams found that Monroe was largely hewing to the notes he had prepared—until he came to the French invasion of Spain, which he proposed to sharply rebuke. He also affirmed America's support for Greek independence and proposed sending a minister there. Calhoun agreed on both counts. Adams differed, embarking on a lengthy monologue in which he warned his colleagues that such a message would be heard abroad as "a summons to arms . . . against all Europe; and for objects of policy exclusively European." The secretary said that he would not be surprised if Spain, France, and even Russia would respond by breaking off diplomatic relations with the United States. Adams may well have been exaggerating for effect; he was plainly trying to craft a statement by the president that would bluntly avow America's ambitions on its own continent while forswearing any abroad, just as he wished to do in his own statement to Tuyll.

The argument continued to rage. Monroe and Calhoun insisted that French aggression against Spain was of a sort unprecedented in recent history and could not go unmentioned. Monroe pulled out what he must have felt was a trump card: a letter from George W. Erving, the minister to Spain, warning that the Alliance would support Spain, by arms if necessary, in the campaign to retake the former colonies. Adams did not blink: Erving, he said, knew no more than the rest of them did and was simply airing his prejudices. Finally, the president said that he would draw up two different messages and submit them to the cabinet. (These drafts, alas, seem to have disappeared.)

Adams was leaving nothing to chance. The following day he pressed his case with Monroe in private, openly addressing the president's own legacy and thus perhaps appealing to his vanity. The era now concluding, he said—the Era of Good Feelings—would be "looked back to as the golden age of this Republic"; it must end in peace, as it began. Adams repeated his formula: no interference by Europe in South America in exchange for no interference by the United States in exclusively European affairs. The president, he said, could mention Greece and Spain, but not in a way which the Alliance would deem hostile. And he shrewdly offered the president a secure exit: let Congress declare its adherence to the Greek cause. Foreign governments could shrug off such a resolution, as they could not do with a statement from the executive. That course would also still the endless clamor from Henry Clay. Two days later, Monroe read Adams the proposed passages from his message on all the sensitive subjects. "I was highly gratified, at the change," Adams wrote, "and only hope the President will adhere to his present views."

The cabinet convened again on the twenty-fifth, and Adams explained his proposed statement to Tuyll. Calhoun objected, and suggested that

Adams just read Tuyll the relevant paragraph from the president's address. Adams would have none of it; in the face of explicit anti-republicanism America must plead its cause "before the world of Mankind." In any case, he said, he knew Alexander well enough to predict that his good will toward America would survive any such declaration. The following day the president sent Adams an edited version of the verbal note with the entire paragraph enunciating general principles struck out. Usually Adams placidly accepted the president's cautionary editorial handiwork even when he disagreed with the substance. In this case, he could not, and he went to Monroe to say that the whole response to Tuyll rested on the foundation of republicanism and thus on the difference between the American and European systems. Adams apologized for his stubbornness by saying that he considered the note "the most important paper that ever went from my hands." Monroe, who could hardly have been surprised by this show of obstinacy, asked Adams for his original draft.

At three o'clock on the twenty-seventh, when the baron came by appointment to his office, Adams still hadn't received an answer from Monroe. A messenger from the White House arrived with a note from the president saying that while he still found the paragraph unduly harsh, he did not want to stand in Adams' way. The secretary, duly mollified, delivered the verbal note without the offending passage. Adams told Tuyll that the United States accepted the right of states to establish and modify their own governments as they wish, whether in monarchical or republican form. Washington had recognized the South American states not as an act of republican or anti-colonial sympathy but as the simple acknowledgment of their independence from Spain. The United States continued to observe neutrality among nations and had no intention to meddle in the affairs of Europe. It trusted other states would observe like principles. In the recent Russian declaration, Adams blandly asserted, "the President wishes to perceive sentiments, the application of which is limited . . . to the affairs of Europe." Leave the rest to us. Even without his grandiose statement of principles, Adams had largely codified his own principles as fundamental US policy.

In his address to Congress, Monroe adopted Adams' positions on all the questions on which the two had differed or where Adams held more decisive views. In the course of the *tour d'horizon* of foreign relations with which the document began, Monroe noted that the United States had asserted a new principle in its boundary negotiations with Russia: "that the American continents, by the free and independent condition which they have assumed and maintain, are henceforth not to be considered as subjects for future colonization by any European powers." Monroe then turned to the domestic state of affairs. After that, rather than concluding the address, he turned back to foreign relations in order to explicitly delineate the new "system" he and his cabinet had been brewing.

Monroe began by speaking of Greece in just the manner Adams had advised, asserting that the cause of its independence "is the object of our most ardent wishes" without making any commitment to help bring that about. Similarly, the president lamented the overthrow of republican governments in Spain and Portugal without mentioning France or the Alliance. "Of events in that quarter of the globe," he went on in a phrase that echoed Adams' July 4 speech, "we have always been anxious and interested spectators." Monroe then made the distinction between Europe and South America that Adams had adduced in his note to Tuyll and that Monroe, Jefferson, and others had long considered essential: "In the wars of the European powers in matters relating to themselves we have never take any part, nor does it comport with our policy to do so. . . . With the movements in this hemisphere we are of necessity more immediately connected."

The president then proceeded to the heart of the doctrine he and his colleagues had decided to state before the world. "The political system of the allied powers is essentially different in this respect from that of America. . . . We owe it therefore to candor and to the amicable relations existing between the United States and those powers to declare that we should consider any attempt on their part to extend their system to any portion of this hemisphere as dangerous to our peace and safety." Monroe was not simply asserting the United States' special protective relationship with other nations in its hemisphere; he was stating that in the clash of world systems, the new world was inviolably committed to republicanism, and the United States would not permit that commitment to be jeopardized. The Holy Alliance had flung down an ideological gauntlet; the United States had picked it up. The United States would express its views about the Alliance's absolutist project in Europe but remain only a "spectator"; in the Americas, however, it would insist on its own republican project. It was an extraordinarily brash declaration for a young nation with little navy, no army, a modest population, and a still infant economy.

The United States was now prepared to defend not only itself but "America"—that is, the Americas—from foreign interference. Monroe went on to say that while the United States would respect existing colonies in the hemisphere, it had recognized the independence of the South American republics; therefore, "we could not view any interposition for the purpose of oppressing them, or controlling in any other manner their destiny, by any European power in any light other than the manifestation of an unfriendly disposition towards the United States." The last debate the cabinet had held over the address had been over this very question: Should the United States commit to enforcing its prohibition with arms? William Wirt had taken the negative, on the grounds that the American people had no appetite for war to defend remote nations. Adams had argued otherwise, though he said that any such resolution should come from Congress. Monroe had come to the very edge of declaring intervention a casus belli but had not used the words.

WHO DESERVES CREDIT FOR THE MONROE DOCTRINE? ADAMS' biographers tend to give much of the credit to Adams, while Monroe's give it to Monroe. Dexter Perkins, a leading historian of the period, has argued that it was Monroe who decided to include the South American question in his annual message and wrote the actual words, while Adams played the lesser role of the president's "effective counselor and co-worker." But the doctrine's power, he concludes, "lies in the fact that it expressed what many men, great and humble, had thought, were thinking then, and were to think in the future." Monroe, that is, formalized a growing national consensus, as Washington had before him.

And yet that consensus operated only at a high level of generality. The noncolonization principle had not been in general circulation; that was Adams' handiwork. The idea of the reciprocal bargain—no interference in Europe in exchange for none in South America—was not Adams' alone, but it was one he had advanced for years. Jefferson, Monroe, and many others had envisioned a global clash of republicanism and absolutism, and the president would have spoken of it even without his secretary of state's contribution.

What Adams may have contributed most of all to the Monroe Doctrine was its astringency. Left to his own devices, Monroe would have offered a more idealistic vision of the American role as a force for the global advancement of republicanism. Adams blunted that with his dogged insistence that American policy serve American interests. Monroe's view, or Calhoun's—or, for that matter, Clay's—would have been more thoroughly in the American grain, more gratifying to the American self-image. Adams stirred his brand of vinegar into the mix.

Like Washington's Farewell Address, Monroe's message to Congress was not intended to alter existing American policy. It was, rather, a statement to the American people, and to others abroad, about America's understanding of its place in the world. It marked an end to the fundamental defensiveness of Washington's message. Most obviously, Monroe had asserted that the United States now had a "sphere of interest" that included all of South America. But Monroe also gave a new political meaning to that interest, which henceforward would include the protection and propagation of the great experiment in republican government that had begun on American shores half a century earlier. The Monroe Doctrine offered a warning to the world about the growing ambitions of a rapidly rising power wrapped around an ideological conviction about the sanctity of its system. This distinctive combination of raw assertion of power with a missionary sense of global purpose was to become the animating spirit of American foreign policy—to the world's eternal fascination and, often, dismay.

The Monroe Doctrine turned out to be more the end of something than the beginning. The era in which a president's annual message consisted largely of foreign affairs was drawing to a close. The business of building a state equal to the size and energy of the new nation would supplant the preoccupation with Europe, and then the threat of national disunion would supplant that. Monroe was arguably the last foreign policy president until William McKinley or perhaps even Woodrow Wilson. The issues at the heart of the Monroe Doctrine would come fully back into play only at the very end of the nineteenth century, when the United States itself became a colonial force as well as an increasingly intrusive presence in South America.

When that debate resumed, it was not Adams' balance and self-restraint that galvanized American public opinion but the muscular idealism of Clay and Calhoun. McKinley would justify colonialism in the Philippines as an exercise in moral and political uplift rather than national interest. Wilson would persuade Americans to fight a war in Europe in order to make the world safe for democracy. The Adams voice was too skeptical to appeal to an increasingly self-confident and self-righteous people. Henry Kissinger once wrote that the American people will not accept a "realist" president. But Adams' warning against reckless adventures abroad has always had important adherents. It may offer more to the American people today than it ever has before.

CHAPTER 21

Who Can Hold a Fire in His Hand by Thinking on the Frosty Caucasus?

(1823–1824)

T HE AMERICA OF 1824 WAS RECOGNIZABLY A REPUBLIC, IN THE
sense that ultimate sovereignty lay with the people, but much less
so a democracy, in which the people engage directly in the political
process. Of the twenty-four states, six, including New York, the biggest of
them, left the choice of president to the legislature, which chose the state's
presidential electors. In the others, legislators set the terms of the statewide
or district-by-district ballot that determined the outcome. While most
states had eliminated property qualifications for the franchise, only adult
white males, who constituted about 18 percent of the population, were eli-
gible to vote. (A few states gave the franchise to free blacks.) Fewer than
350,000 Americans, out of a population of 11 million, would vote in the
election of 1824.

A presidential race was not a popularity contest, as it soon would become; a candidate succeeded by appealing to other professional politicians
as much as to ordinary citizens. And the appeal itself remained oblique to
the point of coyness. A presidential candidate of 1824 could no more afford
to be seen openly campaigning than a candidate for the papacy can today.
Instead, candidates had proxies and campaign managers, politely known as
"friends." These gentlemen planted articles in the newspapers advancing

their man and undermining rivals, and they engaged in a ceaseless circuit of private talks with legislators and local power brokers. Candidates largely sat in one place and received reports from their friends, in person or by letter. Public addresses, either by candidates or their surrogates, were rare. If there were deals to be made, it was the friends who made them, allowing the aspirant himself to stand loftily above the fray. And as the fortunes of their candidate waxed and waned, these proxies would quietly approach one another proposing to combine forces, with one serving as the designated vice presidential candidate of another. But precisely because the race was so fluid, these offers almost always came to naught.

And yet even as the candidates comported themselves in public according to a code of ethics inherited from the Founding Fathers, the nation's real political culture had changed radically. Looking back no further than 1812, which was the last time there had been a serious contest for the presidency, the number of states had increased from eighteen to twenty-four; the population of the country had almost doubled, to about eleven million; and the West, where five of the six new states were located, had gained vastly in power. The 1812 contest had pitted a Republican incumbent, James Madison, against a Federalist, DeWitt Clinton; now there would be neither an incumbent nor a party nor even an obvious favorite, since Monroe chose not to indicate one. The 1824 election would thus be a strange hybrid: structurally, or organizationally, it bore the marks of an old-fashioned contest among political elites, but the traditional institutions were now subject to influences from new men and new places. And the collapse of the party system had created a vacuum that would be filled by representatives of regional or economic or cultural interests, all in search of a suitable candidate. For all these reasons, the election of 1824 was the most confused and wide-open national political contest America had ever seen.

As of the fall of 1823, men in the know considered Adams, Henry Clay, and William Crawford the front-runners. Each were seasoned officeholders; each represented a different region of the country. John C. Calhoun, then forty-two, was thought too young and untested for the highest office. (None of the first five presidents had been less than fifty-seven when taking office.) Indeed, Adams explained to a Calhoun supporter that the South Carolinian would be unable to recruit a cabinet, since "not a single instance had occurred of a person older than the President of the United States accepting Office as Head of Department under him."

Andrew Jackson was the wild card of the race. He had set his candidacy in motion in the summer of 1822 with his Delphic directive, "Let the people do as seemth good unto them." That was all it took for Jackson fever to begin to spread across the West. People all over the country knew the legend of Andrew Jackson: he had killed a man in a duel after being shot in the chest, fought alongside Davey Crockett to decimate a force of Red Stick warriors from the Creek tribe, won millions of acres for settlers in treaties imposed on Indian tribes, and annihilated the British force at New Orleans while losing only thirteen men. Newspapers wrote lavish profiles; supporters compared him to "the immortal Washington." Jackson made an even more elaborate show of indifference to his political destiny than Adams had. He told visitors that he cared for nothing more than the sweet peace of the Hermitage, his Tennessee plantation. To a correspondent from New York who suggested that the state would go for either an Adams-Jackson or a Jackson-Adams ticket, he wrote, as if holding an unpleasant article by his fingertips, "On the subject brought to my consideration by your letter, I have forborne to seek, for the reason of its delicacy."

Jackson was the first candidate to "run against Washington." He had the military's man scorn for the pettiness and haggling of political life, to which he joined an unflagging faith in his own honor. In his letters, which he expected to be reprinted in the press, Jackson harped ceaselessly on the theme that "intrigue, management and corruption" had undermined the nation's fabric. "Nothing but the virtue of the people," he wrote, could block the aspirations of Washington's Machiavellis, "and to them and them alone, I look for a proper stand." To one of his circle of military boosters, he wrote, "It is now a contest between a few demagogues and the people." This was both Jackson's view of the world and his campaign strategy. His backers promoted the idea that since Jackson had been a soldier rather than a politician, he could not be held responsible for political corruption, and since he had never traveled to Europe, he had no taint of Old World moral depravity. Jackson sometimes wrote as if he were, himself, the incarnation of "the people" and its wishes. This, too, may have been a form of demagoguery, but it was a new, democratic form, deeply appealing to the millions of men who disdained the old ways of the long-settled parts of the country.

And yet for all his show of indifference, Jackson was not about to let his campaign be dictated by subordinates. From the safe harbor of the Hermitage he directed his political fortunes with great care. Jackson's friends, most of them military officers, kept him up-to-date on the status of the other candidates. Jackson, in turn, sent them flattering letters about himself and suggested newspapers in which they should be placed. He authorized John Eaton, his chief aide and counselor, to place a series of anonymous letters extolling his achievements in the *Columbian Centinel*, a widely circulated newspaper. Eaton also saw to the publication and republication of a campaign biography. To a confidante Jackson tallied the states falling into his column, or so he believed—South Carolina, Alabama, Mississippi . . .

In the fall of 1823 Jackson agreed, somewhat uneasily, to let the Tennessee state legislature choose him to fill a vacant Senate seat. (He had served briefly in the House and Senate in 1796–1797.) Going to Washington could undermine his own implicit narrative, but it would put him before the public eye and help him lay to rest his image as a bloodthirsty Indian fighter. In early December 1823, the tall, hawk-faced general with the great shock of gray hair arrived in the nation's capital. He was much in demand socially and spent his first few weeks attending balls at night and reconciling with old rivals during the day. When unprovoked, Jackson was a gracious figure, easy in his sense of command, charming with the ladies. He made an excellent impression. "I am told," he wrote drily to a military comrade, "the opinion of those whose minds were prepared to see me with a tomahawk in one hand and a scalping knife in the other has greatly changed."

A few days after Jackson's arrival, Adams invited him to dinner and there secured his agreement to grace a grand ball at the Adams household celebrating the ninth anniversary of the victory at New Orleans. The great debate over Monroe's message to Congress was behind him, and Adams was surely thinking about the election to come—though he had done nothing yet to actively seek office. Jackson was obviously his rival. Adams may have been trying to identify himself in the public mind with the great war hero, but the fact is that his admiration for Jackson remained undimmed. Several months later, a friend would ask him whom he thought his supporters would choose were he to be knocked from the race. "Jackson," said Adams. Wouldn't that help Jackson gain the presidency? Yes, said Adams. "But what then? My friends would vote him on correct principles. His fitness for the place."

Louisa sent out five hundred invitations for the ball. She took the doors off the main rooms of the F Street townhouse and had pillars installed in the lower rooms to support the expected weight. She put John and Charles and the Hellens and all the other relations to work preparing the rooms; they hung chandeliers and placed laurel wreaths along the walls with roses in the center twined around a glowing lamp. Excited newspapermen described the scene: carriages choking the streets all around the Adams house from seven in the evening; as many as a thousand guests streaming through the front doors; tables laden with "pies, pastries, sweetmeats, game, candied fruits and fresh Florida oranges"—a gesture, perhaps, to another of General Jackson's celebrated campaigns. The great man himself arrived at nine; Louisa took him around and made introductions; the general toasted his hostess and promptly left. The party went on until one thirty and was deemed the great event of the social season. Adams and Louisa must have been immensely pleased, though they might have felt differently had they taken the full measure of Jackson's political potency.

Adams began, very tentatively, to express his views on national questions, chiefly in response to the many letters he received from newspaper editors. Joseph Pleasants of the Richmond *Constitutional Whig*, a rare defector from that state's Crawford consensus, wrote to say that he had read an account of Adam's strong endorsement of the federal right to foster internal improvement. If the report was false, Pleasants wrote, Adams should repudiate it. If true, perhaps Adams could write something that would help the editor "break the course of their effect on public opinion." In fact, like Clay, Adams was a well-known advocate of internal improvements. The Southern radicals whom Joseph Pleasants hoped to placate argued that the federal government had no right to authorize and pay for the building of roads, bridges, and canals. Adams wrote back to confirm his belief in the federal role. He added, no doubt for the benefit of the readers of Richmond, that he was doing nothing more than following President Monroe's own policy, for which "his countrymen will *rise up and call him blessed.*" This was disingenuous, since Monroe approved modest expenditures for internal improvements while holding to the Jeffersonian view that the Constitution prohibited a federal role. Adams added breezily that if Pleasants had now changed his mind about his candidacy, he should feel free to publish the letter "for your justification."

The tariff was an equally vexed question. Adams believed devoutly in the merits of unfettered trade, but he faced the same dilemma that politicians do today: manufacturing regions demanded protection from foreign imports. In the Western states, Pennsylvania, and inland portions of New York, the tariff was at least as powerful an issue as were internal improvements. But the agricultural states of the South, and to some extent the commercial states of New England, feared that high duties would result in reciprocal forms of protection against American products. Unlike Clay, the champion of tariff protection, Adams took a careful middle position, writing to Robert Walsh, his favorite editor, that he favored a "cautious" tariff. (Jackson described the kind of tariff he favored as "judicious.") But while he made an effort to place his views on internal improvements in prominent newspapers, he was more circumspect on the tariff.

Slavery was the most dangerous issue of all, and Adams chose not to respond to any of the letters he received on the subject. The reasonable inference is that Adams felt that he had more to lose than to gain by airing his deeply felt views on the subject. That is, though he would not misrepresent his views, he might withhold them. Despite his professions of political nonchalance, he was prepared to be prudent.

In the first months of 1824 the political odds favored William Crawford. Over the summer Crawford had suffered a debilitating stroke, but he was protected from the consequences by the prohibition against public appearances by candidates. The Georgian was widely expected to carry the South, thanks in part to a tacit endorsement from Jefferson. Owing to an alliance he had forged with Martin Van Buren, the shrewd Albany kingmaker, he seemed to have New York sewn up as well. But Crawford and Van Buren made a serious miscalculation. In previous elections the Republican Party had determined its candidate by holding a caucus among party members in Congress. Adams had attended the 1808 caucus, which chose Madison. Crawford had challenged Monroe in 1816 and lost. Now he insisted that the party choose its candidate by caucus once again.

But 1824 was not 1816: the era when men were prepared to let a small group of federal politicians gather in a room and choose the president had passed. Moreover, Crawford now had four rivals, not one, and they and their friends would never permit him to win an early knockout. Newspaper editors allied with other candidates railed against the caucus as a betrayal of democracy. In response to a canvass in late January, 181 members of the House and Senate vowed not to attend, while only 67 said they would. As the caucus approached, Crawford's rivals made it clear that they would not go. When one of Crawford's friends had the temerity to approach Adams suggesting that he attend the caucus as the treasury secretary's choice for vice president, he turned the man away with "an epithet . . . which I will not commit to paper." When the caucus was held on February 24, only 68 of the 309 senators and representatives voted. Crawford won 64 of the votes, but he had hurt himself far more than he had helped.

The next to fall was Calhoun, who had pinned his hopes on Pennsylvania, the second largest state, which he hoped would embrace his nationalist outlook. But when a state convention was held in Harrisburg on March 8, Jackson won 124 of the 125 votes; Calhoun was named as vice president on 88 ballots. Henceforward he could aspire no higher than the second slot.

Clay was exultant at Calhoun's failure. And when Crawford suffered another stroke, in May, Clay wrote exultantly to a confidante that the Georgian would soon die. The stroke had left Crawford nearly blind and had so impaired his circulation that he walked around with thick layers of cloth wrapped around his freezing feet. But Crawford, a huge, robust man, would recover once again.

Clay was the one candidate who could be said to be "running" for president. He had a platform, and he gave long, impassioned speeches on his favorite topics—the tariff, internal improvements, the South American patriots. But he knew very well that policy, by itself, would not carry the day. He needed his friends. One ally, Josiah Johnson, wrote to Clay that a local paper, the *Patriot*, could "be had in New York for some money." He was going there, he reported, "to accomplish this object." Soon thereafter, Johnson wrote back to report: "Secured the Patriot and returnd this morning." Clay was too careful a man to respond to this subterfuge, but neither did he warn Johnson off.

Adams, meanwhile, was, if not running, then at least unmistakably standing. His front door was spinning with friends, would-be friends, and friends of his rivals: he recorded at the end of March that he had received 235 visitors that month, or 8 a day, taking up at least four hours. They all endlessly turned over possible tickets. Crawford had approached Adams— or rather, friends had approached friends—to ask Adams to serve as his vice president. Jackson had approached Calhoun. The secretary of war was madly plotting: "Calhoun's game," Adams recorded in his journal, "is now to unite Jackson's supporters and mine upon *him* for Vice-President. Look out for breakers!" Adams looked on this "game" as proof that Calhoun was just another self-aggrandizing politician; from this time forward, encomia to Calhoun disappear from Adams' journals.

Some of Adams' friends had approached friends of Jackson to propose an Adams-Jackson alliance, with Calhoun as secretary of state or treasury (assuming that a President Adams sacked Crawford, the incumbent). In early April, Adams asked William Plumer Jr., the son and successor of the former New Hampshire senator, to approach Representative John W. Taylor of New York and Senator Horatio Seymour of Vermont, and together sound out Jackson's friends on the question. But a week later Adams told Taylor that Jackson's star was rising so rapidly that Taylor should hold off and "let the thing take its course."

Adams increasingly found that he needed to offer reassurances not only about his views, which was second nature to him, but about his willingness to find a place for men whose support he needed, which was precisely what his "Macbeth Policy" had sworn him not to do. He did not, he told visitors, favor Calhoun for vice president, but he could easily see him in his cabinet. What of DeWitt Clinton, the former governor of New York and a pivotal figure in that state? Adams reminded Representative Taylor that he had been sounded out on the subject before and had said that he could imagine Clinton in his cabinet, though he had forbidden his friends to convey such tidings to Clinton himself, and in any case he was "not disposed to sell the skin before the animal was taken." He authorized Taylor to tell Clinton's friend, a "Mr. Moore" of New York, that Adams had "more than once named him to the President, for nomination to important missions abroad." Indeed, he could say of Clinton that "there was no mission for which I did not consider him qualified." And when Moore himself paid a visit several weeks later and asked after his "sentiments with regard to Mr. Clinton," Adams allowed that while "there had been some things in his public career I had not approved," he "entertained a high opinion of his talents, his services, and his public spirit."

Adams was prepared to threaten as well as propitiate. On May 1, Joseph Reed, a Massachusetts Federalist, paid a visit. Reed said that many Federalists planned to support Crawford—no friend to their cause—out of a fear that Adams entertained such bitter feelings against them that he would appoint none of them to office. Adams rejoined that he found it ironic that the chief obstacle to his election was that Americans outside of New England viewed him as too much the Federalist, while New Englanders considered him too lukewarm in their behalf. Adams said, as he always did, that he would not be a "sectional" president. But he added pointedly that the opposition of the Federalists might actually strengthen his prospects; should he be elected, the Federalists "must be aware how much the difficulty would be increased of favoring them with appointments without disgusting those of the opposing party claiming the merit of friendly support against them."

Adams was divided against himself, as men like Clay and Crawford were not. He played the game of politics because he wanted to be president far more than he could ever admit to himself. He wanted it, but he did not want to want it. His internal struggle was robbing him of the sense of self-mastery he always sought but rarely found. In early May, he confided his inmost feelings to his journal, the one place where he felt safe:

Were it possible to look with philosophical indifference to the event, that is the temper of mind for which I should aspire; but

"Who can hold a fire in his hand
By thinking on the frosty Caucasus?"

To so suffer without feeling is not in human nature; and when I consider that to me alone, of all the candidates before the nation, failure of success would be equivalent to a vote of censure by the nation upon my past service, I cannot dissemble to myself that I have more at stake upon the result than any other individual in the Union.

Was this even true? Crawford, who had run for president once before, could certainly say the same. But Adams felt it to be so. His parents had raised him to believe not that he could be the nation's chief magistrate but that he *should* be—that he would otherwise be a failure. He had once counseled "philosophy" to Louisa. But philosophy could not cool off the red-hot coals of ambition.

ADAMS WAS STILL SECRETARY OF STATE, THOUGH AT TIMES HE despaired of getting back to his work. In early 1824, he was still conducting negotiations, personally or through his ministers, with England, Russia, and France (this last on commercial duties). Stratford Canning had never stopped pressing Adams to join with England in stamping out the horror of the slave trade, and Adams had never stopped citing America's resolute resistance to search and seizure on the high seas. But abolitionist sentiment was growing in the United States; in early 1823 the House had overwhelmingly passed a resolution calling on the president to negotiate a treaty "for the effectual abolition of the African slave trade, and its ultimate denunciation, as piracy, under the law of nations, by the consent of the civilized world." Suddenly the Monroe administration was standing in opposition not to America's old colonial master but to progressive American opinion. Adams may also have recognized that the political benefit of standing up to the British was trumped by the benefit of joining the campaign against the slave trade.

Adams ingeniously took a hint from the word "piracy." He reasoned that states had long insisted on the right to search and seize pirate ships. If slavery was understood as a form of piracy, then boarding on the high seas need no longer carry the taint of impressment. Adams wrote out a draft of such a treaty and submitted it to the cabinet, where it promptly ran into objections from William Crawford, who may well have seen it as the thin edge of an abolitionist wedge. Adams and Monroe did a great deal of redrafting and finally came up with a document that all agreed to send to London. Further negotiations ultimately led to a treaty, signed on March 13, 1824, which largely incorporated Adams' own language. The pact stipulated that both sides would agree to brand their citizens who engaged in the slave trade as pirates and that each would grant a reciprocal right of boarding. The captured ship was to be returned to its host nation for trial, thus correcting a feature of the original English proposal to which Adams had objected, and no crew member was to be taken—that is, impressed. Here was a tremendous diplomatic victory Adams had not at first sought or arguably deserved, as well as a signal advance in international and maritime law. In addition, the treaty would remove one of the chief remaining obstacles to harmonious relations with Great Britain.

In early May a copy of the convention, and of a law passed in Parliament declaring slavery to be piracy, reached Washington—and caused an uproar. It was a matter both of policy and of politics, though mostly the latter, one suspects. Editorialists accused Adams and Monroe of conceding the right of search, which had so long been resisted as a fundamental issue of sovereignty. And the slaveholding faction in the Senate, and above all the Crawfordites, cried down the measure. Crawford had no intention of supplying his chief rival with a political triumph. Adams later wrote to his Massachusetts friend and confidante Timothy Fuller that Crawford had turned on him when he had spurned the Georgian's advances to serve as his running mate, and then Crawford's captive press—that was how Adams thought of it—had rounded on him as well.

The Slavery Convention was the first missile. When it came to a vote, the Senate passed the treaty but struck out Article I, which allowed for the right of seizure off the American as well as the African coast. This allowed the Crawfordites to claim that they had accepted the treaty while preserving American sovereignty. But since from the British point of view the United States had just effectively exempted itself from the terms of the treaty, George Canning deemed the new version unacceptable. Adams' work, over the better part of two years, had come to naught.

Adams also continued with his effort to secure America's toehold on the Pacific Coast. He had to settle existing territorial claims with both England and Russia. In the summer of 1823, he had written to Richard Rush and Henry Middleton, his ministers in London and St. Petersburg, suggesting a coordinated effort. Rush would secure from England American control of the coast up to 51 degrees of latitude, in what is now southern Canada, while Middleton would grant Russia's claim to the territory north of the fifty-fifth parallel but not the demand Tuyll had conveyed for exclusive Russian control of the seas and trading rights. He was happy to grant England sovereignty over the space in between; what mattered was that US merchant ships and fur traders be allowed to operate unhindered. Adams was no more willing to surrender American commercial rights on the Pacific than he or his father had on the Grand Banks of the North Atlantic coast.

In the event, Adams did not have to fight that hard. The tsar was still well disposed to the United States and was prepared to override the interests of the Russia-America Company in order to settle the border question and preserve ownership of the portion of the continent closest to the Russian landmass. Russia's foreign minister, Count Nesselrode, promptly agreed to Adams' terms. He insisted only that the boundary line be marked slightly below 55 degrees. The United States would have undisputed access to the seas beyond Russian territory as well as the right to trade in unclaimed areas to the north. The convention was signed in April 1824 and easily passed the Senate. Adams' great project of making America a continental nation had advanced another step forward.

Negotiations with Great Britain proved rockier. George Canning had failed in his bid to bring the United States into an alliance on behalf of the South American republics and then watched as the Senate put impossible conditions on the piracy treaty, which had been the single most important issue his cousin Stratford had pursued in the United States. He may not have been in a compromising mood. Canning was vexed to find that the United States wished to claim territory north of Oregon, which Great Britain had explored and considered very much its own, and he was astonished that Adams had tried to finesse negotiations with Russia by asking England to agree that it would claim no land north of 55 degrees—a question to be adjudicated between the British and the Russians, after all. This may have been too clever by half on Adams' part. In early 1825 England and Russia concluded a treaty that settled the boundary between themselves. At this point, neither the United States nor England felt an overwhelming need to rewrite their earlier agreement to treat the Oregon Territory as shared and unclaimed space over the course of a decade.

AS THE SUMMER OF 1824 APPROACHED, THE ELECTION REMAINED wide open. Since no candidate enjoyed broad enough appeal to win an outright majority, the race would go to the House. With Calhoun eliminated, four men were now competing to finish in the top three. One candidate or another had already locked down most of the states with the most electoral votes, including Pennsylvania, Virginia, and Massachusetts (Jackson, Crawford, Adams). The great remaining prize was New York, where the election was left up to the state legislature. But this undemocratic and archaic method of choosing a president had provoked many of the same feelings that Crawford's national caucus had. And Crawford was once again the beneficiary of this closed system. Since there was no earthly reason that New Yorkers would vote for a Southern slaveholder and an avowed enemy of an active federal government, Crawford would have no chance in a public ballot. But inside Albany, Martin Van Buren could see to the outcome.

Statewide elections the previous November had brought to Albany many new legislators who favored direct elections. Thurlow Weed, a young state legislator and rival of Van Buren for the role of state kingpin, had thrown his support to Adams. Weed had never met the secretary of state and had little discernible interest in his views, but he saw Adams as a plausible rival to Crawford. Though a lad of twenty-seven, Weed was rapidly becoming Van Buren's equal as a political engineer. In the spring, with pressure mounting on Governor Joseph C. Yates to convene a special session of the legislature to consider a change in electoral law, Weed told Yates that he had overheard a man in a barroom saying that the governor didn't have the guts to stand up to Van Buren. Yates leapt to his feet in outrage, or so Weed delightedly recorded in an autobiography written decades later.

Yates called for the special session, which was to convene in July. A popular ballot would doom Crawford's hopes, though no one could be sure which of the other three it would most help. When the legislature convened, the state assembly, full of newcomers committed to reform, clamored for a vote. But Van Buren still controlled the state senate, and the senate voted to adjourn. On August 8 the legislature adjourned without taking action. Van Buren had won, and Weed had lost. But it was only the first round of a long and brutal prizefight.

Adams traveled up to Boston in the first days of September. His father had now reached the age of ninety. "His sight is so dim that he can neither write nor read," Adams found. Mentally, however, this remarkable old man was unimpaired. "His memory yet remains strong, his judgment is sound, and his interest in conversation considerable." John Adams continued to dictate letters, especially to his grandchildren. The two men rode around the neighborhood, visiting the modest houses, across the street from one another, in which each had been born, a setting that evoked for both of them an eighteenth-century world purer and more noble than the one in which they now lived. General Henry Dearborn, an important political ally, came out from Boston to announce that the secretary of state was to be honored at a great dinner at Faneuil Hall. Adams politely declined, on the grounds that such an event would look like electioneering—which of course was the whole idea.

At the end of September, Adams left Boston for Philadelphia in order to meet up with General Lafayette, the great French hero of the American Revolution and a friend of Adams for almost forty years. Lafayette was making a farewell tour of the nation he had done so much to help bring into being. Adams stayed by Lafayette's side as he took in the local sights and attended festivities in his honor, and traveled with this revered figure through Maryland and Delaware on their way to the nation's capital. Adams did not think that he was campaigning, but his close association with Lafayette served to remind voters of Adams' own patriotic lineage, his unique status as a son of the founding fathers. Adams reached Washington in mid-October. The twenty-four states of the Union were poised to begin choosing a president.

CHAPTER 22

I Tread on Coals

(1824–1825)

THE MOST IMPORTANT JOBS JOHN QUINCY ADAMS HAD EVER held were ones to which he had been appointed by a president—minister to the Netherlands, Prussia, Russia, and England; chief negotiator at Ghent; secretary of state. Of course he had sought electoral positions, but he had not shown much of a gift for attracting voters. He had lost his very first contest, for state assemblyman, and had been recalled as a US senator by a state legislature outraged at his stubborn independence. He did not like appealing to voters, did not believe he should have to, and was not good at it. And now he was living with the consequences. As a son of the Founding Fathers, a diplomat who had brought a successful conclusion to the War of 1812, a secretary of state who had negotiated treaties that had immensely expanded American territory, and a supremely seasoned figure with a firm grasp on every issue that faced the nation, Adams should have enjoyed a powerful claim on the presidency. But as the states began voting, by their own system and according to their own calendar, Adams could say nothing more than that he and Andrew Jackson would make it into the final round in the House.

The New York legislature convened in Albany on November 2. Everyone understood that the senate would choose Crawford, but the assembly was up for grabs. If the lower house chose a different candidate, both would have to convene for a joint selection—a kind of miniature version of the chaos lurking ahead in the House of Representatives. Thurlow Weed had been crisscrossing the state keeping tabs on his assembly colleagues on Adams' behalf. By the time the assembly convened, Weed knew exactly how many supporters each candidate could count on. He had, he believed, sniffed out a plot by his archrival, Van Buren, to bribe Adams supporters to cross over to Crawford. He had grown suspicious of one Adamsite, followed him to New York City, concluded that he was a traitor to the cause, and had him threatened with exposure.

Weed was a cheerful rapscallion. He had grown up on a small farm in upstate New York, begun supporting himself at age eight, joined the army as a teenager during the War of 1812, and then started working as a newspaper apprentice. He had his own newspaper by the time he was twenty-one. He ran for the state assembly in 1823 and won. New York state politics was already intensely factionalized and both nurtured and attracted a new kind of man—"the placatory professional politician," as the historian Richard Hofstadter put it, "whose leadership comes in large part out of his taste for political association, his liking for people, and his sportsman-like ability to experience political conflict without taking it as grounds for political rancor." That was Van Buren, and Thurlow Weed, to a fare-thee-well. Weed was everything John Quincy Adams was not and could not abide. But Adams depended on this upstart's ingenious machinations.

Crawford quickly won a majority in the state senate, but the assembly was divided among Crawford, Clay, and Adams supporters. Every night the Crawfordites adjourned for a secret meeting. Since they couldn't win in the lower house, they could resolve the issue only by switching their votes to one of the other candidates and then prevailing in joint session. "The air was full of rumor of bargains, plots and counterplots," a Crawford man recalled decades later. Van Buren finally decided that it was safer to go with Adams, and on November 13, eleven days into the balloting process, the Crawford men swung to him.

One of those counterplots, meanwhile, was hatching in the calculating mind of Thurlow Weed. Van Buren had promised to produce a ticket with a number of Clay's supporters, so that New York would divide its electoral vote between the two. But Clay's boosters were convinced that the Crawfordites in the assembly had gone with Adams. On Saturday night, the fourteenth, Weed brought Adams and Clay supporters together to propose an audacious move: rather than let the legislature fight over the two competing tickets, he would secretly print up a single joint ticket with thirty

Adams electors and six men formally committed to Crawford but known to be Clay supporters. He promised the Clay faction that they would emerge with seven of New York's votes, then thought to be enough to put Clay into the final three in the House.

The next morning, Weed locked himself in the empty office of a local pro-Adams paper, the *Daily Advertiser*, and printed up the joint ballot. The following day, the list was deposited in the ballot box instead of the expected all-Adams ticket, so that when Lieutenant Governor Erastus Root reached in, he pulled out the document and spluttered in amazement, "Split ticket!"

"Treason by God!," cried a Crawfordite. Pandemonium reigned. Senators tried to adjourn the meeting. In any vote, they knew, the more numerous assembly members would outvote them. Colonel James Tallmadge, an Adams man, rose and "in a stentorian voice" demanded in the name of the American people that a vote go forward. The Adams slate won 78 of the 157 votes. Since two electors submitted blank ballots, and one voted for Jackson, who wasn't competing in the state, Adams had won a bare majority of the 154 valid votes cast. But Root, a Van Buren ally, insisted on treating the three as having voted against Adams and refused to certify the choice.

Now pandemonium broke out once again. All afternoon men shouted, gestured, and milled about on the floor. Root finally stalked out of the chamber, taking much of the senate with him. But the Adams-Clay combination could no longer be put off. Both houses reconvened the following day, and after a series of votes, Adams emerged with twenty-five of New York's electors, Clay with seven, and Crawford with four. Adams had bested Crawford—or rather, Thurlow Weed had bested Martin van Buren. Adams was receiving news of the proceedings daily from three or four lieutenants; none of them so much as mentioned Weed's backstairs dealings. Adams did not have to know the truth of what had been done in his name.

State results had already begun arriving in Washington. Andrew Jackson proved to be the only candidate with true national appeal. He won all of Pennsylvania's electoral votes, as the Harrisburg convention had long since indicated, as well as those of New Jersey. And he surged as Clay faded in the West and Crawford in the South. Crawford won only in Georgia, Virginia, and Delaware. Clay carried only the three western states of Kentucky, Missouri, and Ohio. And Adams reaped the consequences of his stubborn refusal to mount a campaign. Only in New York, Massachusetts, and New Hampshire had a sizeable network of allies gone to work for him; elsewhere his prospects were largely left up to chance. And so Adams had won nowhere outside New England, though he had picked up votes throughout the country.

The last state to report in was Louisiana. Clay was counting on winning some or all of the state's votes. But in another split ticket, Jackson won three votes, and Adams two. Meanwhile, four of the apparent Clay voters in New York had switched back to Crawford. "You promised us seven votes!," the Kentuckian's supporters shouted at New York's conniving boy wonder, Thurlow Weed. But that was conditioned on your winning Louisiana, Weed rejoined. Perhaps it was, and perhaps it wasn't. "By a strict and literal construction of the understanding," Weed later wrote, he had played fair—though "the subject gave me much annoyance and solicitude."

In those states where citizens voted for president, Jackson had taken 153,544; Adams 108,740; Clay 47,136; Crawford 46,618. But it was the electoral votes that counted, and here the final tally read: Jackson 99, Adams 84, Crawford 41, Clay 37. The four defected New York votes had cost Clay his chance at the presidency. Clay was a supremely political animal, but in a letter to his friend Francis Brooke he admitted that he couldn't make head or tails of the New York vote. Now only Jackson, Adams, and Crawford, a broken man, survived. The vote in the House was scheduled for February 9.

Adams could have taken the position that the nation had spoken, that voters had chosen Jackson, that his candidacy had remained alive only by virtue of a constitutional technicality. That is, he could have withdrawn. Jackson's friends put it out that this would be the correct thing for Adams to do. There is no sign that this idea crossed his mind. Adams would not have acknowledged that anything in the Constitution could be deemed a technicality. And in any case, he had admitted to himself that not even the frosty Caucasus could cool off the fire of his ambition. Already he had allowed himself to offer the kind of veiled reassurances that once would have struck him as low political bargaining; now he would shred the fine tissue of his conscience.

The Constitution stipulated the formula whereby the House would determine the president: each state had one vote, to be determined by a vote taken among the congressmen from that state. Balloting would continue until one man won thirteen or more of the twenty-four states. What this meant was that little Rhode Island mattered as much as giant New York. Every congressman would have a hand in determining the next president.

On December 9, a full week before the final results were in, Adams began fielding a flood of visitors from the Congress, both at home and in the office. And he did something he had not done before: he went around to the rooming houses where almost all members of Congress stayed during the session. That is, he paid court. And he recorded the substance of his conversations in his diary. He spoke to friends of DeWitt Clinton, who intimated that he might wish to join an Adams administration; Adams repeated his feelings of high esteem for the former governor. He spoke to William Plumer Jr. about Daniel Webster, the great Federalist. Webster had earlier justified his preference for Clay on the grounds that Adams would never appoint a Federalist—though he, Webster, had no personal wish for a post. In fact, Plumer disclosed, Webster was "panting for London," which Adams said he might well be able to gratify, if not just yet. Adams had a long talk with Robert P. Letcher, a Kentucky congressman who was close to Clay and shared lodgings with him. Then Clay himself joined the conversation.

Once the results from Louisiana arrived, Clay was thrust into the role of kingmaker. On December 15, Edward Wyer, a former diplomat whom Adams used on sensitive missions and who was obviously in his confidence, came by to say that "he had it from good authority that Mr. Clay was much disposed to support me, if at the same time he could be useful to himself." Wyer returned the next day and repeated his story, refusing to disclose his source. On the seventeenth, Representative Letcher paid another call. Letcher spent a good deal of time beating around the bush, pretending to be interested in the census of 1820, before homing in on local politics. He explained that Kentuckians preferred Jackson to Adams, as Adams knew perfectly well. A faction of them were at odds with Clay himself; they were scarcely bound to one another by ties of loyalty. Clay wished to "stand with his friends"; his friends wished to stand with him. Then he got to the point: What were Adams' sentiments toward Clay? Letcher was obviously Wyer's source: he had reached out, friend to friend.

Adams said that he "harbored no hostility towards Clay," even though he believed Clay to have goaded Jonathan Russell to action. Letcher, who must have been prepared for this sally, said that Clay's letter claiming that Adams had misstated the facts from the negotiations at Ghent "was written in a moment of excitement." Clay "had spoken respectfully" of Adams, and so forth. Adams understood that Letcher was telling him that if he could reassure Clay's friends that their man would have "a prominent share in the administration," they would be prepared to disregard the instructions they received from Kentucky and vote for Adams. Letcher "made no definite propositions," and Adams himself responded "in general terms." Their work was begun but not concluded.

James Barbour, a senator and former governor from Virginia, came by. Barbour had no doubt that electors in his state would prefer Adams to Jackson once it became clear that Crawford had no chance. He sounded Adams out on the contentious issues of internal improvements and the tariff. Adams disposed of the first with no difficulty. He was for it, and that was that. On the tariff, he tried to walk a very fine line. His policy, he explained, with delicate if uncharacteristic spin, was *conciliation* rather than *collision*. If the current tariff needed to be changed at all, it was by reduction—a view very different from that of Clay, who with great effort had pushed increased duties through Congress during the previous session. Adams argued that revenue was sufficient, and manufacturers had quite enough protection; if commercial and agricultural interests favored a relaxation of duties, then Adams was prepared to do just that. Barbour could scarcely have expected to bring his colleagues more positive tidings.

Martin Van Buren wrote asking for a consulship in South America for a Mr. Winne. Adams paid a visit and said that if Mr. Winne could choose a port where he wished to reside, he would recommend him to the president. He was later able to inform Van Buren that Winne would in fact be nominated. Letcher kept coming by with hints and advice. Adams knew that he was straying very far indeed from the Macbeth Policy. "*Incendo super ignes*," he wrote to himself—"I tread on coals."

Clay, who had a taste for irony that his rivals conspicuously lacked, was enjoying his new role as unmarried beauty. He wrote a letter to a confidante describing how friends of each of the three remaining aspirants had beaten a path to his doorstep to proclaim that he, Henry Clay, had always been the candidate's second choice for the presidency and then implore him to throw his support to their man. The truth was, Clay went on, that Crawford was too sick for the rigors of the job, and as between "the two evils" remaining, Jackson would "give the military spirit a stimulus and confidence which could lead to the most pernicious results," whereas Adams would leave America's institutions as he had found them.

Jackson did pay a visit to Clay's rooming house, as Adams did, and Clay, who had been out, returned the favor—but he never dispatched an emissary to Jackson as he had to Adams. So much venom had passed between Clay and Jackson that even the all-forgetting waters of Lethe in which politicians routinely bathe could not put things right between them. And strictly as a matter of calculation, a President Adams might only last one term, while a President Jackson might prove impossible to dislodge. Clay would support Adams, but not without exacting a price.

At a New Year's Day dinner for Lafayette at the White House, Clay sidled up to Adams and whispered that he would like to have a "free & confidential visit" with him. On Sunday morning, January 9, Clay sent a note asking if he could pay the visit at six that evening. Adams consented. The text that morning at church came from Ecclesiastes: "I said, I will be wise; but it was far from me." Adams might well have taken that rueful lesson to heart. Clay came by as appointed. In the course of "a long conversation explanatory of the past and prospective of the future," Clay spoke of the advances he had spurned over the previous weeks, and explained, with his usual wry turn, that he had waited to "give a decent time for his own funeral solemnities as a candidate." And, he added with splendid disingenuousness, he had needed to reassure his friends that they should vote according to their own consciences. But the time had come for him to choose. "He wished me," Adams recorded, "as far as I might think proper, to satisfy him with regard to some principles of great public importance, but without any personal considerations for himself." That, apparently, had been left to Letcher. As for the contest in the House, "he had no hesitation in saying that his preference would be for me."

What did Adams mean by "prospective of the future"? What were those "principles of great public importance"? Did the two men discuss private matters as well? We don't know, because Adams chose to draw a veil over the particulars—or perhaps he never found the time to delineate them. (He left a blank space at the end of the passage, as if he had planned to write more.) Clay later wrote in a letter to an ally that, though Adams had made no promises, he concluded from the interview that he could have whatever job he wanted. That may well have been true.

Adams might have installed Clay in his cabinet under any circumstances. He admired Clay's judgment, if not his personal morals; he was one of the ablest men in the nation. But Adams understood that reassuring Clay and his followers would put Kentucky in his column, and probably Ohio and Missouri as well. Adams had not received a single popular vote in Kentucky—not one. Jackson was immensely popular there, and the state plainly would have gone for him had Clay not been a favorite son. Adams would never have to know how Clay would exert his influence, but he would know that the consequence was that the will of the people would be overborne. That was a grave violation of his own republican principles. Adams would have said that no price was worth paying for the sacrifice of principle, but there is no sign that he believed at the time that he had done any such thing. He was thinking about the goal, not the means. And the ambitious man must be prepared to tread on burning coals.

Four days after Adams' meeting with Clay, the Kentucky state legislature passed a resolution overwhelmingly pledging support for Jackson. Of course, the actual vote belonged to the state's congressional caucus, whose members were fully aware of the understanding between Adams and Clay. Senator R. M. Johnson of Kentucky confided to Adams that the delegation would vote for him, 7 to 5. Johnson was off by 1: on January 24, the delegation announced for Adams, 8–4. Clay had delivered his state, as Van Buren once planned to deliver his for Crawford. Senator Thomas Benton of Missouri, a confirmed Jacksonite, later wrote in his memoirs that while he had not been offended at the news of Adams' pact with Clay, since Clay had told him in mid-December that he would support the secretary of state, the gross violation of the will of the people of Kentucky was a crime.

But Kentucky was hardly going to put Adams over the top. Adams had spent a lifetime training himself to expect the worst, and he was still all but certain that he would lose. He heard that Jackson and Crawford had reconciled. The South and the West would join against him. The day after Kentucky swung into his column, Adams wrote in his journal that while the expectation he would win had gained "almost universal" currency, "I have little doubt that will be decisive the other way." In fact, Jackson and his allies *had* been courting the Crawford forces. Mrs. Jackson had agreed to accept a visit from Mrs. Crawford, which observers considered highly significant. If Jackson held on to his states and took Crawford's, it was all over. Adams wasn't even sure that he would keep New York.

Word of the agreement between Adams and Clay had leaked out even before the vote of Kentucky's congressional caucus confirmed that something was afoot between the two men; the Jackson forces did their best to make hay from the stealthy and most un-Adams-like transaction. In Illinois, the ballot would be cast by the sole representative, Daniel P. Cook, who was retiring. Two Jackson men, Samuel Ingham of Philadelphia and George McDuffie of South Carolina, cornered Cook in a hotel room. Adams and Clay had reached a devil's bargain, they said. Cook had a chance to defeat their designs: other western states would not migrate to Adams if Cook held fast. When Cook still resisted, they threatened that he would be ruined when the West rose as one against an Adams administration. Cook, a Clay man who had shifted to Adams, bravely rejoined that his own sense of duty would compel him to stand against that vast movement should it arise.

By now, news of the "corrupt bargain" between Adams and Clay had gone public. It was an astonishing last-minute bonus for Jackson, for the story reinforced the central theme of his campaign. On January 28, the *Columbian Observer* of Philadelphia printed an anonymous letter claiming that Adams had offered to make Clay secretary of state in exchange for his influence—which was more or less true—and that Clay's friends had then made the same offer to friends of Jackson, who had refused to "descend to such mean barter and sale"—which was not true. "It was," the author alleged, "one of the most disgraceful transactions that ever covered with infamy the Republican ranks." The plain implication was that John Quincy Adams was scarcely the man the public thought it knew. On February 4, the *National Intelligencer* reprinted the letter, now identified as coming from an unnamed Pennsylvania congressman. "It is now ascertained for a certainty," the editors wrote, that the alleged deal had been made.

On January 29, the day after the story broke, Henry Clay paid Adams another visit. Clay was utterly unbowed. That day he had written to a friend, "The knaves cannot comprehend how a man can be honest." The election was eleven days away; the outcome, despite Clay's machinations, was impossible to predict. Now certain of his own position, Clay put aside his sidelong, insinuating manner. "He spoke to me with the utmost freedom of men and things," Adams wrote, "intimated doubts and prepossessions concerning individual friends of mine, to all which I listened with due consideration." Adams may have understood for the first time what an invaluable ally he had in Clay, who shared many of his views but was also a far more shrewd judge of men than he was.

Adams held long conversations with President Monroe, who was preparing to nominate candidates for vacant ministerial posts. Adams begged him to make the decisions himself and do so before the election; should Adams win, he could not be seen as handing out plums in exchange for support, even through the instrument of the current president. He even memorialized the conversation in a letter to the president, presumably to be furnished later as evidence of his own innocence—another sign that Adams felt he had done nothing untoward with Clay. Monroe, however, was not prepared to make the nominations and so didn't.

Daniel Webster paid a visit on February 3. He had been skeptical of Adams, the Federalist turncoat, though Adams' effort at persuasion seem to have helped; he had written to a friend, "I think a *little* better of the kindness of his feelings toward us, than I have done." As recently as mid-January he had still been wondering what to do with his vote should Adams fail to carry a majority on the first ballot, but by now he felt more confident that Adams had thirteen states in his column. That morning, however, he had received a letter from a Maryland Federalist, Henry R. Warfield, asking if it were true that Adams would ban their ilk from office. Warfield confessed that he was the deciding vote in Maryland, which had gone for Jackson but might switch to Adams. And Maryland could be the deciding vote in the Union. What should he do? Webster now read to Adams a letter he intended to send reassuring Warfield on this score. Adams thanked him, though he felt compelled to add that Jackson or Crawford would doubtless pursue the same policy. Webster then sent the note to Warfield, adding in a postscript that he had read the letter to Adams and gotten his approval.

In the days before the scheduled vote, half the states seemed to be in flux—New York, Virginia, Maryland, Connecticut. Adams' life was a whirlwind, though he did find time to take in Richard Brinsley Sheridan's *School for Scandal*—"Cooper as Charles Surface, Mr. and Mrs. Barnes as Sir Peter and Lady Teazle." He attended a cabinet meeting at which he found that Crawford was so disabled that he could neither read nor write. Louisa's regular Tuesday party on the night of the eighth was more crowded than ever— at least four hundred people, and many congressmen. It is unlikely that John Quincy Adams, always a troubled sleeper, got much sleep that night.

Political enthusiasts began pouring into the nation's capital. The runoff was expected to be political theatre of the highest order. Expert opinion held that no candidate would win on the first ballot; this was likely to be a two-day or perhaps even three-day affair, the likes of which had never been seen before. By Wednesday, February 9, the day of the vote, not a bed was to be had in the city's lodgings. It was a cold and snowy day, and the session would not begin until noon, but spectators began lining up outside the House doors early that morning. Both chambers convened in the House. The electoral votes were formally unsealed, and the results announced: John Calhoun had been elected vice president with 182 votes, while Jackson, Adams, and Crawford would contest for the presidency. The senators now returned to their own chamber, while members of the House seated themselves according to the order in which the states would be polled— north to south down the Eastern Seaboard, then south back up to north in the interior. Each state had its own ballot box, with its own teller to confirm the result.

That morning, old Stephen Van Rensselaer, a member of the New York delegation and a patroon of ancient vintage, had been struggling mightily with his conscience. He had been pledged to Adams, but he preferred Crawford. Van Rensselaer realized that he might well represent the tying vote—a terrifying thought for this genteel soul. As he reached the Capitol, shifting back and forth inside his own not particularly forceful mind, the patroon was waylaid by Henry Clay, who bade him pass a few moments in the Speaker's chambers. There they were joined by Webster. The two made it clear that a vote for Crawford was a vote for Jackson, and a vote for Jackson was a vote for mad populism and social tumult—a calamity for a man of property like him.

By the time Van Rensselaer had staggered away from Webster and Clay, he had plunged into a state of miserable confusion. Louis McLane, a Delaware congressman and Crawfordite, found the old gentleman "in tears literally." Van Buren received a message from one of his managers, William S. Archer of Virginia, that he was needed urgently on the floor to speak to Van Rensselaer. The Sage of Kinderhook hurried down and found Van Rensselaer, who promised that, come what may, he would not vote for Adams on the first round. This was all Van Buren could ask. His plan was to secure a deadlock in New York and thus force a second round of voting, at which point, he had reason to believe, Maryland would switch to Jackson, and then other states would give way as well. Van Buren understood perfectly well that Crawford could neither win nor serve as president, and he had already shifted his loyalties to Jackson.

The states then began balloting among themselves. According to Van Buren's autobiography, when the vote came around to the patroon, he dropped his head on his desk to summon his Maker, as was his wont. Looking down, he spied a ballot with Adams' name on it. A sign! Van Rensselaer picked up the ticket and quickly dropped it in the ballot box. New York went for Adams.

With the voting complete, the ballot boxes were carried forward to two tables, one of which was overseen by Daniel Webster, the other by John Randolph, the eccentric and vitriolic Old Radical (as Jeffersonian purists called themselves). Tellers at each table tallied the votes. The Massachusetts Federalist spoke first: "The tellers of the votes at this table have proceeded to count the ballots contained in the box set before them. The results they find to be, that there are, For John Quincy Adams of Massachusetts, thirteen votes; for Andrew Jackson of Tennessee, seven votes; for William H. Crawford of Georgia, four votes." Clay's three states, as expected, had gone to the secretary of state. Crawford's stayed with Crawford, despite Adams' fears of a Crawford-Jackson entente. But of Jackson's states, Louisiana had gone to Adams, as had Maryland—perhaps thanks to Daniel Webster—and Illinois, where Jackson's blandishments and threats had failed to move Daniel P. Cook. Adams had added six states to the seven he already had.

At the moment that Webster said "thirteen," the gallery, a thousand strong, burst into huzzahs; a smaller group responded with hisses. Clay ordered the gallery cleared. Then he announced that John Quincy Adams had been elected president. Adams' friend Alexander H. Everett raced to the Adams home on F Street to bring the news. Then came a whole rush of friends. The great, fearful moment had arrived. Adams uttered a prayer—"May the blessing of God rest upon the event of this day!" It was, he said in a note to his father, "the most important day of my life."

That night, President Monroe held one of his rare social evenings. All of Washington was there—Calhoun and Clay and Webster, General Lafayette, and of course Adams and Jackson. People pressed through the dense throng to get a view of the winner and loser of this unprecedented, and increasingly ugly, contest. The crowd parted, and General Jackson, with a lady on his arm, approached the president-elect. Always the master of the situation, Jackson said graciously, "I give you my left hand, for the right, as you see, is devoted to the fair. I hope you are very well, Sir."

"Very well, Sir," said Adams stonily. "I hope General Jackson is well."

This courteous encounter would be one of the very last between the two men. It constituted the terminal point of the Era of Good Feelings—not so much because rancor supplanted a largely mythical period of consensus but because Jackson's embitterment propelled the rise of a new political party and thus new forms of political contest. From that moment forward, Jackson went into opposition; the 1828 campaign began before Adams even took office. Adams had finally won the prize he had long sought, but he had won it under circumstances that would turn the next four years of his life into a terrible struggle.

PART IV

INTERNAL IMPROVEMENT

CHAPTER 23

The Spirit of Improvement

(1825)

O N THE LATE MORNING OF MARCH 4, 1825, CAVALRY DETACH-
ments from the Washington and Georgetown volunteer militias
arrived at John Quincy Adams' F Street home. Trumpets blared
and drums boomed. The president-elect and Mrs. Adams emerged, along
with their sons John and Charles Francis; settling into a carriage, they
took their place at the head of a caravan directly in front of President and
Mrs. Monroe, and rode off to the Capitol between rows of cheering citizens. At the Capitol Adams was greeted by the Marine Corps, drawn up
in order. A crowd had been surging into the great dome since the moment
the doors had opened at 9; by 10, not a place was to be found. The diplomatic corps had been seated in the first row of the House, then military
officers and their wives, and other dignitaries. The crowd in the House
gallery had maintained a dignified silence. At 12:20 marshals in their blue
scarves appeared at the front door of the great hall; they were followed by
officers of both houses of Congress, then Adams, then Monroe. Adams,
dressed in black—all of domestic manufacture—ascended to the Speaker's
chair. By tradition, the president delivered his Inaugural Address before
being sworn in.

Adams had been thinking about the speech for weeks; perhaps he had
been thinking about it his whole life. Whatever he might once have wished
to say, he knew now that he had to address the deep fissures his election had

exposed and perhaps exacerbated. "Of the two great political parties which have divided the opinions and feelings of our country," he said, "the candid and the just will now admit that both have contributed splendid talents, spotless integrity, ardent patriotism, and disinterested sacrifice, to the formation and administration of our Country." European wars had sown "the baneful weed of party strife." But "ten years of peace, at home and abroad, have assuaged the animosities of political contention, and blended into harmony the most discordant elements of public opinion."

Adams was very nervous. Justice Joseph Story would later write to his wife that the president-elect "trembled so as barely to hold his papers," though at the same time "he spoke with prodigious force, and his sensibility had an electrical effect." What Adams hoped was not to wish away difference but to acknowledge and accommodate it. Party feeling is transitory, he went on, but divisions based on "climate, soil and modes of domestic life"—the intrinsic differences of coast and interior, agriculture and manufacturing—are lasting. The genius of America's federal system allowed states to govern themselves within their own sphere, while at the same time sending eminent men to the nation's capital to learn to respect one another's views.

Adams reviewed Monroe's great achievements and then turned to the one field he hoped to make his own—internal improvements. "It is that from which I am convinced that the unborn millions of our posterity . . . will derive their most fervent gratitude to the founders of the Union." That was an extraordinary claim and a controversial one. Adams acknowledged "some diversity of opinion" in Congress on the subject, but almost twenty years had passed since the Jefferson administration had authorized construction of the Cumberland Road, which reached from Maryland inland to the Ohio River. "To how many thousands of our countrymen has it proved a benefit? To what single individual has it ever proved an injury?" Adams expressed hope that all constitutional objections "will ultimately be removed" and "every speculative scruple" overcome.

Adams had spent most of his career as a diplomat and statesman, but with the nation now at peace, he yearned to be the leader who would mobilize the country's energies in the great project of domestic improvement. Despite the language of conciliation, he had, perhaps rashly, revealed the full measure of his ambitions. Jeffersonians and Jacksonians bridled at hearing their convictions reduced to a "speculative scruple." The address, as Joseph Story put it, "is everywhere very direct and unequivocal, and will produce a great deal of approbation and disapprobation."

Adams was certainly not oblivious to the forces he had provoked. He hoped to further mollify his rivals by governing as a consensus figure. He invited Crawford to remain at Treasury, though he viewed his erstwhile rival as a shameless schemer and Crawford was physically unfit for the job. Crawford declined, and Adams instead chose the Federalist Richard Rush. He asked Andrew Jackson to serve at the War Department, but Jackson was not about to serve the man who had defeated him—by trickery, he thought. Instead, Adams offered the post to James Barbour, a Crawford man from Virginia. He retained Samuel Southard, a Calhounite, at the Navy. And of course he replaced himself at the State Department with Clay.

That, of course, was a fresh provocation, and the worst of all. Clay's appointment was taken as proof of the "corrupt bargain." Congress had mounted an investigation of the charge, though it had ended in anticlimax when the anonymous author, revealed as a gadfly Pennsylvania congressman, George Kremer, refused to testify. But feelings ran high, and Clay was confirmed by a vote of only 17 to 10. And Andrew Jackson himself made sure to keep the story alive. Returning home to Tennessee, he assured outraged listeners that, as Kremer had alleged, he had personally been approached to make the same deal with Clay that Adams had, and had steadfastly refused. He encouraged Kremer to keep the story alive, and he wrote to a sympathetic editor suggesting he pursue the allegations. Jackson wrote that he himself would keep a dignified silence—in fact he had done no such thing—since "Clay has fallen below anything but contempt." Jackson and his allies would spend the next four years keeping this tail pinned to the presidential donkey.

Adams was faced right away with the question of how he would use his power to appoint federal officials. Crawford had pushed through a law prescribing a term of four years for federal employees. Adams viewed the statute as a device to enhance patronage powers—which it was—and refused to deploy it. He reappointed any official not obviously corrupt or incompetent; he would not move against figures who used their office to promote his rivals. Both Clay and Daniel Brent, still chief clerk at the State Department and a member of Washington's tiny permanent establishment, urged him to remove James Sterrett, a naval officer in New Orleans and "a noisy and clamorous reviler of the Administration." Adams replied that removing him would only provoke attacks from the opposition press. And, more importantly, it would be inconsistent with his principles. Once he began removing opponents, "an invidious and inquisitorial scrutiny will creep through the whole Union, and the most selfish and sordid passions will be kindled into activity to distort the conduct and misrepresent the feelings of men whose places may become the prize of slander against them."

The postmaster general, John McLean, was a notorious partisan of Andrew Jackson. But he was also exceptionally good at his job, and Adams would not replace him. The Post Office was then larger than the rest of the federal government put together, and postal carriers constituted a national civilian force with control over the sole means of communication across distances. McLean was said to have appointed a network of Calhoun-Jacksonites, among them Major Henry Lee, who on the side wrote diatribes against the administration for the *Washington Gazette*. In Lexington, Kentucky, McLean appointed Robert Ficklin, a bankrupt newspaper publisher who, it was said, refused to distribute pro-administration literature. Adams declined to remove any of them.

Adams' high-minded intransigence left Henry Clay in despair. Friends wrote to Clay constantly complaining that the president had passed over party loyalists when a federal post had become available. The president, Clay explained grimly to one, "intended to neglect or abandon his friends in order to woo his enemies." Yet his enemies could not be wooed. Political men were left baffled and fuming. Thurlow Weed betook himself to Washington for the first time in order to secure a diplomatic post for General James Tallmadge, who had done a great deal to put Adams over the top in New York, and also to win a contract to print the federal laws for his own Rochester newspaper. Weed had a delightful conversation with Clay, a man of his own kidney, but an "embarrassing and constrained" one with Adams. When Weed observed delicately that it would be well to recognize New York with a major post—Adams could scarcely win reelection without the state—Adams first noted that he had already appointed Rufus King, the old New York Federalist, as the minister to England and then added that he would "appoint men of character, capacity, and integrity."

Weed must have rolled his eyes. The president, he wrote decades later in his autobiography, "was able, enlightened, patriotic and honest; discharging his public duty with conscientious fidelity, he disregarded, or overlooked, what Monroe, Madison and Jefferson had deemed essential namely, political organization and personal popularity." The situation was arguably worse than that. Adams' election had roused a degree of opposition none of his predecessors had faced. He aspired to change policy in a way that was bound to accentuate that opposition. Adams thus needed to shore up his base of support as his predecessors had not. But his arch-Federalist principles, and his Puritan commitment to a righteous path, absolutely precluded him from doing so.

In our own time, a president who laid out a bold agenda in his inaugural speech would introduce legislation in order to realize his goals. In Adams' day, the tradition still held that Congress both germinated and produced the nation's laws. Adams might have sought to change that habit, but instead he waited to make specific proposals in his year-end message to Congress, as his predecessors had. Until then, he would deal with whatever came across his desk—federal appointments, court-martial proceedings, the promotion of military officers. He met with his cabinet officers, as well as with virtually any stranger who wandered in the door. He spent countless hours signing grants for the sale of federal lands—sometimes hundreds in a single day.

By the spring of 1825 the federal government had become entangled in a very ugly and dangerous territorial dispute between the Creek Indians and the state of Georgia. The Creeks had long hunted the southwestern lands into which pioneers from Kentucky and Tennessee had begun to spread in the first years of the new century. Conflict between the two groups led to the so-called Creek Wars in which Andrew Jackson earned his reputation as a feared Indian fighter. Jackson had decisively crushed Creek resistance at the battle of Horseshoe Bend on March 27, 1814, when he had killed eight hundred Red Stick Warriors. Later that year, the Creeks had been forced to sign the Treaty of Fort Jackson, in which they ceded twenty-three million acres, which made up much of Alabama.

On May 15, Adams met with a group of Creeks led by Chilly McIntosh. Chilly recounted the dreadful narrative of the murder of his father, William, by a rival group of Creeks. Chilly came bearing a fire-breathing letter from George Troup, the governor of Georgia, vowing to lead a militia party against the rival Creeks and any federal authorities who sought to intervene on their behalf. Adams did not want to get involved in an intratribal dispute, but Troup's challenge threatened the fundamental principal of the supremacy of federal authority. That was an issue the president could not ignore.

The background was incredibly tangled. William McIntosh was a scalawag who had fought on Jackson's side against the Red Sticks and served as sheriff for the agency. He had surrendered various amounts of tribal land to Georgia in subsequent negotiations and had misappropriated and stolen much of the cash settlement the federal government had given to the Creeks. He had then persuaded the tribe to sign yet another treaty surrendering "all the lands lying within the boundaries of Georgia" in exchange for $200,000, with an additional payment to go to McIntosh himself. The Treaty of Indian Springs had been signed on February 12, 1825, ratified by the new Congress as virtually the first order of business on March 5, and signed by Adams. By this time the other Creek chiefs had finally realized they had been swindled. On April 30, a group of 120 to 150 braves advanced on McIntosh's plantation on the banks of the Chattahoochee, set it aflame, and then, when he emerged, stabbed him to death—and riddled his body with bullets for good measure. Chilly barely escaped with his life. Then he had organized the lobbying trip to Washington.

Adams knew little of the background, but Secretary Barbour had thoroughly acquainted himself with the sordid history of self-dealing and duplicity. He told Adams that Governor Troup was a "madman" who would stop at nothing unless confronted with superior force. But Adams understood that no force on earth—at least none available to him—could stop the tidal force of western settlement. He ordered Major General Edmund Gaines to Milledgeville, Georgia, there to await further instructions. Gaines arrived with nine companies of infantry. In early June, an unfazed Governor Troup told legislators that "the United States government will be directly responsible to Georgia for every drop of blood shed on this occasion." Barbour responded by informing the governor of the instructions he had given to Gaines: "You are hereby authorized to employ the military to prevent [the surveyors'] entrance into Indian territory"—and to arrest any found already there.

Though a feared Indian hunter himself, Gaines was deeply impressed with the Creeks' quiet resolve. He wrote to Barbour that the Creek confederacy was prepared "to die without resistance; that the world shall know, that the Miscogee Nation so loved their country, they were willing to die rather than sell or leave it." They would not honor the terms of the fraudulent treaty. Gaines was prepared to defend their rights. The president, however, was not.. He instructed Gaines to offer the Creek leadership a new version of the treaty in which they would surrender all their land in Georgia in exchange for equivalent acreage in Arkansas, west of the Mississippi, and $400,000. Adams got his answer on November 26, when a group of twelve Creek leaders, dressed in a fantastic mixture of buckskin and pantaloons, came to the White House to meet with the man they referred to as their Great Father. With no translator available, no words were spoken, but Adams was deeply impressed by the "dark and settled gloom" of their countenances. The Creeks understood that they were about to be uprooted from the lands to which they had been immemorially attached;

they would be sent to a place none of them had ever seen. In a subsequent meeting, they asked Adams if they could at least keep the Chattahoochee River, at the western edge of Georgia; the actual territory of the state had never been explicitly defined. Adams wished to do right by them, but he didn't know if he could.

In the week before Christmas 1825, the cabinet met almost daily in order to resolve the issue. In one session, Barbour suggested that the government should assimilate Indians into the national population, thus freeing up their ancestral land for white settlement without banishing the Indians to a western wasteland. This provoked an outburst from Henry Clay, the great champion of oppressed peoples abroad. The Indians, Clay said, could not be civilized. "He believed they were destined to extinction," Adams wrote, "and though he would never use or countenance inhumanity towards them, he did not think them, as a race, worth preserving. . . . They were not an improveable breed, and their disappearance from the human family will be no great loss to the world." Barbour was shocked, Adams recorded, while he himself wondered if Clay was not in fact right. At Ghent, after all, Adams had spoken of the Indians as if they should be subject to game law, and he wholly shared Madison's view that nomadic peoples had no right to waste good farmland.

Nevertheless, the United States treated with Indians as a sovereign people, thus incurring obligations Adams was not about to void. He told Barbour to write to Troup saying that the Creeks would cede up to the Chattahoochee and no farther. Troup disdainfully refused. Adams persuaded the Creeks to sign one treaty after another, each reducing the tiny sliver of Georgia in which they could remain. Troup rejected everything. Once again the governor sent surveyors to map the new territory; this time the Creeks arrested them. Settlers, in turn, began to make incursions on Creek territory, at times stealing Indian livestock. War had never looked likelier.

What had begun as a question of the federal role in negotiations between Indians and state authorities had now escalated into an early test of the doctrine of nullification—the alleged right of states to supersede federal authority. It was no coincidence that Georgia was a slave state, for the Deep South had come to fear and resent federal authority since the fight over Missouri's admissions to the Union as a slave state. Slavery thus lurked in the background of the standoff over the Creeks, as it did in so many of the issues of Adams' tenure. This was a test Adams did not welcome but could not shirk. He had no doubt about the supremacy of the federal government, but he was reluctant to force a confrontation with the Southern forces of states' rights. Once again he attempted a half measure, instructing federal marshals, but not military troops, to arrest surveyors who had returned from illegal forays into Creek territory. Troup responded with one of his truculent letters, threatening to mobilize two divisions of state militia. The Georgia governor calculated that he held the high cards—and he was right. The Creeks understood that Adams would not go to war with one of his own states in order to defend their right to remain on tribal land until the date stipulated by the new treaty of Indian Springs. They signed one final pact in late 1827 agreeing to immediately vacate all lands claimed by Georgia. But thousands of Creeks had already picked up their belongings and traveled, mostly by foot, into Alabama; many arrived in a pitiful, sometimes skeletal, condition.

Adams loved nothing more than a politically despised cause, and if he had believed that the Creeks or the Cherokees or Choctaws had a right to their ancestral land equal to or greater than that of American pioneers, he might have risked a confrontation with the Georgia "madman." But the thought never crossed his mind. That is an idea of our own time, which we can entertain with no fear that it will ever be enacted; in Adams' day, Indians were deemed an obstacle to progress, to be handled roughly or decently, depending on one's principles.

ADAMS LOOKED FORWARD TO HIS FIRST MESSAGE TO CONGRESS AS the great opportunity to lay out his vision for the nation's future. He cut short his vacation, leaving Quincy for Washington in the middle of October. The new Congress would assemble on December 5, and Adams needed the intervening period to write his address. Adams' predecessors had used their initial message largely to descant upon the admirable state of the Union. In 1809, President Madison had reassured the Congress that "the blessing of health has never been more universal," while "the fruits of the seasons . . . are more than sufficient for our wants and our customs." Eight years later, Monroe had celebrated the immense expansion of national territory incident to the treaties recently signed with Indian tribes and the growing value of the lands then being populated. Monroe also squarely confronted the question of internal improvements: after much deliberation, he announced, he had concluded that Congress did not possess the right to authorize such projects, though he added that he favored an amendment to the Constitution that would explicitly grant Congress that right.

Adams, of course, was quite certain that Congress had that right, and he hoped to use his first address to make the case for an active program of federally sponsored construction in more detail than he had in his inaugural address. But that was only the beginning of Adams' immensely ambitious program. On November 23 his cabinet officers listened in mounting amazement and alarm as Adams read them the draft of his address. They spent the next week trying to argue him down. Barbour said that Adams should mute his constitutional argument for internal improvement. Barbour knew how that would sound in his native Virginia. But even Clay, the author of the American System, agreed. Adams noted in his journal that "Mr. Clay was for recommending nothing, which from its unpopularity, would be unlikely to succeed." That certainly included the national university Adams planned to propose, as well as the new Home Department and the revamped Patent Office. Clay said that no one knew better than he how desperately a new executive department needed to be carved out of State, but there weren't twenty votes for it in Congress—maybe not five. Only Rush, the arch-Federalist, approved of everything. Southard said little. Wirt said that the president's plans were admirable, but he had just been traveling around Virginia, where Adams' stock had been rising; the message would wreck the administration's popularity.

One can imagine a president reacting in two different ways to the discovery that a politician as acute as Henry Clay considered his proposed policy hopelessly unattainable. He could agree to hold fire until he had gained more support from the Congress and the public, or he could plow ahead, determined to make every possible effort to cajole, bully, or persuade the skeptics that the nation simply could not afford to do otherwise. John Quincy Adams did neither. He listened carefully and made a great many changes to his first draft. But he insisted on including the most far-reaching proposals—without actually expecting them to be passed. He blithely informed Clay that while he understood that this Congress, filled with Jeffersonian and Jacksonian rivals, would never endorse a national university, "I would look to a practicability of a longer range than a simple session of Congress." Adams would make the strongest possible case for the program he believed the nation needed and then would wait for public and political opinion to catch up. Clay had already become Adams' chief political advisor and vote counter. His heart must have sank.

By 1825, messages to Congress proceeded according to a canonical pattern, and Adams, a stickler for tradition, hewed to convention. He began by noting that the state of the union, and indeed of the world, was a happy one, for "the general conditions of the Christian nations" had rarely if ever "been marked so extensively by peace and prosperity." Adams reviewed America's relations with each of those nations, not omitting the new states of South America; delineated "the flourishing state" of national finances, with revenues expected to reach $24 million, much of which would be devoted to retiring the federal debt; listed the treaties he had signed with Indian tribes, and discussed the current state of naval deployments and military fortifications. So, more or less, President Monroe had written the year before. That final address marked, in effect, the terminal point of the Era of Good Feelings. Adams' message would mark the beginning of an interval of bitter conflict.

The president now proceeded to chart out the bold policy Clay had begged him to soft-pedal. "The great object of the institution of civil government," Adams stated, "is the improvement of the condition of those who are parties to the social compact." By "improvement," Adams went on, he was thinking not simply of roads and canals, indispensable though they were, but "moral, political, intellectual" reforms as well. To the fulfillment of these goals, Adams declared, "the exercise of delegated powers is as sacred and indispensable as the usurpation of powers not granted is criminal and odious." Here was a direct blow at the Jeffersonian preoccupation with alleged abuses of power by the federal government.

Adams now proposed a series of great public works. President Washington, he noted, had repeatedly called for the establishment of a national university and a military academy. The latter had come to pass in the form of West Point, but not the former. The great nations of Europe had seen fit to actively promote knowledge. Should not the United States do likewise? Adams even suggested that this new institution specialize not in arts and letters as Harvard or Yale did, but in the advanced scientific fields of geography and astronomy. Adams then proposed the federal funding of global expeditions, as European monarchs had long done. One hundred such projects would cost less than a single war and provide inestimable benefit to citizens. Separately, Adams suggested expeditions within American territory, such as Lewis and Clark had made, both to map borders and to discover resources, especially in the trackless northwest now shared with England.

Adams could not resist riding his beloved hobbyhorse: the establishment of a uniform standard of weights and measures. Great Britain and France had made ceaseless inquiries into such topics as "the figure of the earth" and "the comparative length of the pendulum vibrating seconds in various latitudes from the equator to the Pole." Ought not the United States? And what about an astronomical observatory? Adams had been fascinated by telescopes since his days at Harvard. Europe had more than 130 of these "lighthouses of the skies," while the United States had none. Here his eloquence reached its highest peak: while Europe makes exciting discoveries almost every year, "are we not cutting ourselves off from the means of returning light for light while we have neither observatory nor observor upon our half of the globe and the earth revolves in perpetual darkness to our unsearching eyes?"

Adams now turned to government reform. He proposed the creation of a new federal department to administer home affairs, a reform of the judiciary, and the enactment of new laws protecting patents. And then, in conclusion, he recurred to his distinctly Federalist vision of a benevolent activist government. "The spirit of improvement is abroad upon the earth," Adams grandly declared. "While dwelling with pleasing satisfaction upon the superior excellence of our political institutions, let us not be unmindful that liberty is power; that the nation blessed with the largest portion of liberty must in proportion to its numbers be the most powerful nation upon earth." The promise of national greatness was there to be seized—unless, Adams admonished, timid legislators proved to be "palsied by the will of our constituents."

Adams had spent long years developing his view of foreign affairs and had given it full voice both in his correspondence and in his speeches. Though he had advocated internal improvements during his time in the Senate, he had never chosen to fully express his vision of domestic affairs. Only now was it clear that he had a coherent and self-consistent view of America's destiny. He had often said that the United States must steer clear of European entanglements in order to give itself the chance to attain national greatness. So Washington or Jefferson would have said as well. But for Adams, that future would not simply unfurl as the inevitable expression of American energies acting on bounteous nature. When he said that "liberty is power," he meant that democratic freedom was not limited to the right of each citizen to cultivate his own garden—what we now call "negative liberty"—but also included the collective power to forge greatness. The instrument of that power was the state.

Adams was an unsentimental realist on foreign policy and a Burkean skeptic of democratic romanticism at home. But as soon as he had gained the power he had long sought, he had revealed that his skepticism about the individual was joined to a passionate faith in the organized capacities of society. Few men of his day entertained so bold a vision of state activism. Years later, Adams explained in a letter that he had hoped to spend all the government's surplus revenue on internal improvements, which "would have afforded high wages and constant employment to thousands of laborers, and in which every dollar expended would have repaid itself fourfold in the enhanced value of the public lands." Americans would not be ready for a federal government remotely this energetic until the presidency of Abraham Lincoln, a great admirer of Adams.

For that reason, Adams' message to Congress was, as Clay had all too clearly foreseen, dead on arrival. Jeffersonians did not agree that the object of government, and especially of the federal government, was to improve the lives of citizens; that was the work of the citizens themselves. Jefferson himself rumbled from Monticello that a new generation of Federalists, scornful of the spirit of '76, "now look to a single and splendid government of an aristocracy." Thomas Ritchie, powerful editor of the *Richmond Enquirer*, said that the speech put him in mind of "a school boy's Thesis." The Jacksonian newspapers ridiculed Adams' "lighthouses of the skies" as the folly of a man lost to reason. But Adams' greatest inadvertent gift to the opposition was that unfortunate phrase "palsied by the will of our constituents." Here was Federalism in its rankest form: the political leader does not represent the will of the voter but rather guides it from above and ignores it when need be. Perhaps John Adams could claim to rule on behalf of the citizenry; his son, in the far more democratic atmosphere of 1825, could not.

Still, Adams commanded a solid majority in the House, though not the Senate, and he could have lobbied for his agenda. But he did not. He had no close friends in the Congress, and in any case he viewed legislative lobbying as unseemly. Adams simply allowed the Congress to act—or not. Bills for the establishment of a naval academy were introduced in both houses but failed. (Annapolis would be founded in 1845.) President Madison, regarded as a supreme authority on the meaning of the Constitution, stated his opposition to a national university on constitutional grounds. That doomed the proposal. The observatories never had a chance, nor did the weights and measures.

The one partial exception was Adams' call for internal improvements. The completion of the Erie Canal in 1824 had set off a craze for public works; even Monroe, who had vetoed a bill to repair the Cumberland Road, had felt compelled before leaving office to authorize a national survey of needed work. By the time Adams took office, army engineers were surveying routes for roads and canals and making plans to enlarge and improve ports. A Scot, John Loudon McAdam, had just developed the road-building technique of the "macadamized" roadway, built from crushed gravel, and legislators were as eager then as they are now to bring new roads to their constituents.

During Adams' tenure, Congress appropriated funds for dozens of projects to repair and extend the Cumberland Road, to improve harbors and breakwaters, and to build or repair docks. In some cases the government provided public land for new work, and in others it subscribed to stock offerings by private companies. In 1828, Secretary Rush reported that the federal government had spent $14 million on public works, a record of improvement that would not be reached again for a generation. Nevertheless, Adams' vision of a systematic national program employing tens or even hundreds of thousands of men never materialized during his presidency.

It is tempting to speculate what would have happened had Henry Clay slipped into contention in the House and then dealt himself, rather than Adams, the winning hand. Clay shared Adams' convictions about the central role of the state in refashioning America, but he knew better than Adams how to make himself understood. He not only knew but cared about what the political market would bear. And he knew men: he knew who to befriend and who to fight. In short, Clay accepted politics for the fallen endeavor that it is. He might have made a much better president than Adams did. He probably thought as much. But to his great credit, he appears never to have said so to anyone.

CHAPTER 24

An Arrow to the Heart

(1825–1827)

J OHN QUINCY ADAMS AWOKE IN DARKNESS ALMOST EVERY DAY
of his tenure in the White House. He rose as early as four in the summer and perhaps an hour later in the winter. He would dress and then
leave the White House for a long, solitary walk—a habit he had cultivated
for many years. At the far end of the President's Park, across Pennsylvania
Avenue and soon to be renamed Lafayette Park, lay a number of fine buildings, including St. John's Episcopal Church and the splendid brick mansion
built by Commodore Stephen Decatur, at one time the finest private home
in Washington. From there, Adams would either turn left, for Georgetown,
or right to the Capitol. The first route took him along the broad but still
unpaved path of Pennsylvania Avenue, lined with rooming houses, taverns,
shops, and warehouses, until he crossed the Potomac to the elegant village
of Georgetown, with its long blocks of brownstones. The path in the opposite direction was more desolate. He would walk all the way around the
Capitol, whose interior the architect Bulfinch was still finishing.

The president would have seen few people, if any, on these journeys
through the darkened city. That suited Adams perfectly well. He was a solitary man who was most comfortable in his own company, brooding over
his own thoughts, reflecting on his own destiny, reminding himself of his
failures, praying for success in his ventures. He was a short man, balding
and stubby, indifferently dressed, and he would have passed unnoticed as

he moved swiftly along the streets of the nation's capital. Returning to the White House, Adams would stand before the great window of the East Room to watch the sunrise. Louisa was asleep upstairs. Often she spent the whole day confined to her bedroom. She was frequently ill, almost always melancholy. Even a less self-absorbed man than Adams would have been pierced by such pervasive gloom. Yet Louisa's name rarely even appears in his journal during his presidential years. His mind was on his work.

Adams had no staff. His son John acted as his secretary, running errands and occasionally copying letters or documents. There was no one to screen visitors; Adams believed that as chief executive of a republic he was obliged to meet with any citizen who took the trouble to reach his doorstep. On one not atypical day in late 1826, when he was hoping to finish his annual message to Congress, he received a visit from a Mrs. Weeden, who said that if she couldn't pay her rent, her landlord would seize her furniture. "Of such visitors I have many," Adams sighed. Then Dr. Glendy, a Presbyterian minister, came to ask for the post of House chaplain, which was then filled. Dr. Glendy offered an interminable account of his personal history, which the president did not interrupt. Then General Brown, the army chief of staff, came by to introduce a new infantry commander. Secretary Barbour brought over a copy of the War Department's budget and raised various personnel issues—the assistant surgeon who had been cashiered and reinstated, the lieutenant who had gone absent without leave. Nothing, it seems, was too small for the president's attention.

Adams had a back-breaking reading load, for he received newspapers, letters from around the country, reports from the various cabinet departments, "memorials, petitions, solicitations for office," requests for personal loans or subscriptions. He had to approve every court-martial and appoint military officers and postmasters. If a message to Congress was to be written, there was no one to write it but him. And of course he had to keep up his journal and his personal correspondence. After dinner at around five, he might play some billiards and then go back to his papers. It was often midnight before he extinguished his candle. He had so little time for himself that on three separate occasions he simply stopped keeping his journal, leaving gaps of nine months in his presidency.

Adams was then fifty-seven years old, but his stamina was undiminished. He had worked a killing pace his whole life; he thought of himself as a man whose greatest gift was his capacity for "drudgery." His cabinet members, most of whom considered themselves quite hardworking, sometimes cursed the fate that had brought them to labor alongside this relentless taskmaster. Treasury Secretary Rush called Adams, only half-jokingly, "our worthy little master," and soon found that he was working himself to the bone. Rush begged to be sent back to London for the far less demanding job of minister. The boisterous Henry Clay wrote to a friend that he had begun to rise early, "but not so early as the President." The work load took such a toll on Clay's health that he ultimately asked the president to let him step down.

And yet the men worked together with nothing like the rancor that divided Monroe's cabinet, at least in the second term. Cabinet members disagreed openly but without bitterness. Even as Virginia's leaders grew openly hostile to the Adams administration, Wirt and Barbour, the two Virginians in the cabinet, remained completely loyal. And Clay discovered that he enjoyed working for a man he had long viewed as an ill-tempered puritan. Adams was not a micromanager; he let Clay's diplomatic messages go out with far less editing than Monroe had imposed on Adams himself. After only a month on the job, a slightly amazed Clay wrote to a friend, "There is entire coincidence between Mr. Adams and me on public affairs."

Clay came to accept the fact that the president could not be budged on matters of principle, including Adams' contempt for patronage. And Adams, who had so few confidantes, came to depend on Clay for advice. Adams had long viewed Clay as a rogue, and Clay had thought of Adams as a prig, but working together every day let them see beyond their preconceptions. There was nothing grudging in the respect they bore one another; they shared the same vision for the country and felt equally embattled as they tried to advance it.

Adams had very little to do save work. He had decided to follow Monroe's example of accepting no social invitations, lest he give offense to whomever he refused. Nor did he attend political events or even harmless functions. Declining an invitation by the Maryland Department of Agriculture to attend a cattle show, Adams reflected that he ought not "set a precedent for being claimed as an article of exhibit for all the cattle-shows throughout the nation." Occasionally he attended lectures, such as one on "the organ of amativeness"—the penis—which he found "more indelicate than philosophical." But Adams' life was confined almost entirely to the White House; his daily round was much more dull and routine than it had been when he was secretary of state.

Adams remained in Washington even when it emptied out for the summer. President Monroe had passed much of the summer in his home in Loudon, Virginia. Adams, however, was loath to take vacation. That first year in office he left for Quincy only on September 21. The heat quite literally made him sick. He described "a fermentation of the blood border-ing upon insanity" and suffered from "a debility, nervous irritation and de-jection of spirits far beyond anything I had ever experienced." Adams' friends ascribed his nervous depression to the hours he spent swimming, but Adams viewed his predawn hours in the Potomac as his only source of relief, as well as the summer equivalent of his long, solitary walks.

Louisa worried incessantly that her husband would drown, and indeed Adams' most dangerous moment in office came in mid-June. He, his ser-vant Antoine, and his son John decided to take a canoe across the Tiber, as the spur of the Potomac nearest the White House was known, and then swim back. John, convinced that the boat was unsafe, got out and sat on a rock. As the president and his servant continued, the boat began to fill up with water. They jumped out, Antoine fully naked and Adams still wearing his pants and a cotton shirt with puffed sleeves. The sleeves quickly filled up with water, threatening to drag the president of the United States to a death that would have been as mortifying as it would have been agonizing. He finally reached shore gasping for breath and fully aware of his stupidity. Antoine found some scraps of clothing, walked back over a footbridge, and instructed what must have been a very startled stranger to send to the White House for a carriage. Adams and John, who had joined him, spent three hours swimming and basking on the shore. It is instructive about the rhythms of White House life in 1825 that when Adams returned home at 8:45, hours late, his absence apparently had not been noticed.

Louisa never grew accustomed to her new life. She loved the kind of cozy, cosseted household in which she had grown up; the White House spurned her every effort to recreate that atmosphere. Louisa hated the vast, drafty structure, where only a few of the rooms had been fully furnished and decorated. The Monroes had taken much of their furniture, silver, and dishes with them. "A thing of rubbish and rags," she scornfully called it, "a half-finished barn, like everything else in this desolate city." The White House was freezing cold in the winter, and the fumes from the coal-fired grates in her bedroom kept her coughing for months—she joked about her "Lehigh Coal Cattarh." In a letter to George she wrote, "There is some-thing in this great ? house which depresses my spirits beyond expression, and makes it impossible for me to feel at home."

Louisa was only forty-seven, a decade younger than her husband, when she became First Lady. An extremely romanticized portrait of her from that time by Charles Bird King shows her at the harpsichord, wearing a soft Persian-style hat, a dreamy look in her dark eyes. Gilbert Stuart painted her in the same period as a woman still attractive in a delicate lace veil, but weary and questioning. Louisa feared that the picture revealed "too much of inward suffering and a broken heart," but acknowledged its psychological truth. She thought of herself as a spent force. Louisa passed long days in her room, her gloom gathering in on itself. She ate a great deal of chocolate, which she adored, and which by some quirk of metabolism she could consume without ever gaining weight. She had few friends beyond the family circle. Louisa had followed Mrs. Monroe's example, as her husband had followed the president's, of not initiating visits. But unlike her husband, she needed companionship, and the First Lady languished in her solitude. She was, she wrote to George, "unpleasant to myself and to everyone else."

Louisa was preoccupied with death. She wrote to George about a young girl who had committed suicide when her illicit love had been discovered. Why, she wondered, are we so attached to life when children meet death so calmly? She wrote a long poem about the girl; she seemed to identify not with the girl's transgression, but with her ready embrace of death. She wrote other poems, also melancholy; one contrasted a mother's hour of bliss when a newborn slept on her breast to the agony when the baby died. Her husband viewed the writing of poetry as a delightful technical exercise and an opportunity to express the ardor he had dammed up in himself; Louisa slipped into verse as if it were a luxurious bath of sadness.

Louisa was hardly alone in that big house; she was surrounded by family members. John lived at the White House. Charles came after graduating from Harvard in July 1825 and stayed until the summer of 1827, when he went to pursue his studies in the Boston law office of Daniel Webster. Nancy Hellen's children had moved from the F Street house into the White House. On balance, they did a great deal more to deepen than to mitigate Louisa's griefs. Johnson, a boon companion to Charles, ran off with one of the housemaids. Thomas, a drunk and a hell-raiser, got himself kicked out of Harvard. In 1827 he wrote to Louisa to say that he was contemplating suicide over a young woman who had spurned him. Furious, she informed her nephew that he possessed "a mind deeply diseased both physically and morally." He would die in 1833, at age twenty-four.

Mary was a natterer who got on Louisa's nerves. Louisa regarded her, with good reason, as a Jezebel. In 1827 she shocked the Adamses by announcing that she and John planned to marry; apparently they had managed to carry on an affair undetected. Louisa considered neither one suitable for marriage, while her husband, who had only the most minimal expectations of his middle son, appears to have left the problem to her.

There was nothing to be done; on February 25, 1828, John and Mary became the first couple to be married in the White House. Over time, Louisa would come to regard Mary, for all her faults, as a surrogate daughter.

Louisa had long tolerated her husband's condescension, so different from the high intellectual regard in which John Adams had held Abigail. But she chafed against her ill treatment, and not just from the president. John, she felt, argued with her all the time, while Charles despised her weakness. She once told Charles of a warning she had delivered to his fiancé: "It is a painful thing to state but it is nevertheless a fact that as regards women the Adams family are one and all peculiarly harsh in their characters. There seems to be no sympathy no tenderness for the weakness of the sex." With no one prepared to listen to her woes, Louisa was left to lavish pity on herself.

Passing like a ghost through the half-finished parlors of a home not her own, often weak from illness, fearful of distracting her husband from affairs of state, Louisa felt bored and restless. Despite the posed portrait at the harpsichord, she no longer played music and rarely sang. But in writing she found an outlet for the deep feelings she otherwise hid from the world. She took up her own memoir on July 23, 1825, a day she described as so blazingly hot that "reading is wearisome, work is tiresome, and all the common employments are insipid." The memoir, she wrote, would serve as an *apologia* to her children, though it was also very much a vindication of her father's life. Louisa wrote prayers in verse form. In addition to her melancholy poems, she wrote a romantic song, a kind of dirge for the Louisa that was— "For thee the rosy wreath I twin'd / And wove it with a silken knot." She asked Charles to send her French literature to translate.

Louisa also wrote plays. Most of them are undated and so may come from later periods, but in the spring of 1826 she told George that she had written a "melodrama." It could have been *Suspicion or Persecuted Innocence: A Tragedy*, a fragment of high-flown Jacobean stagecraft about jealousy and thwarted love. Or perhaps it was one of her "farces": *Juvenile Indiscretions or Grand Papa* or *The Wag or Just from College*.

Louisa wrote one piece that is remarkable not because it is any better than any of the others, but because it is so baldly revelatory about her feelings about her husband and the rest of her family. *Metropolitan Kaleidoscope or Varieties of Winter: Etchings by Rachel Daub*, subtitled *A Romance*, is a kind of family processional very lightly dressed as a play about a party given by Lord and Lady Sharply. The play is dated December 1827 and so was written after three very unhappy years in the White House. There can be no doubt about the identity of the main characters:

Lord Sharply was a man of extraordinary talents, and great require-
ments. He was the creature of Art rather than nature. He had filled
many high stations most honourably and with great satisfaction to the
Nation and government he represented. His knowledge of mankind
was vast formed however more from books than from the actual and
enlarged study of man; which led him often to shock their prejudices
and wound their feelings. . . . His mind was stuffed with classical and
polite literature, and his every thought might be said to *teem* with
learning. . . . Perseveringly laborious, there were few things too difficult
for him to achieve; and the natural coldness and reserve of his manner
defied the penetration of the most indefatigably prying curiosity, to
discover his thoughts, or to perceive his motives of action. . . . Only
those who dwelt constantly in his society could sometimes observe the
flashing of his eye, and the tremulous motion of his lip, conveying
some faint idea of the volcano that burnt within but which seldom
found vent. . . . The good of his country was his constant aim; but he
sometimes staggered the nation by the means he used to obtain his
ends. . . . He was full of good qualities, but ambition absorbed every
thought of his soul, and all minor objects had ceased to interest.

Louisa was more generous to herself but hardly flattering. Lady Sharply,
she wrote, "was a singular compound of strong affections and cold dislike;
of discretion and caprice; of pride and gentleness; of playfulness and hau-
teur." She suffered from "the impulse of a too warm heart not understood
by the cold and calculating world in the midst of which she lived. . . . With
a temper soured, bad health and an almost total indifference to life or
death, she was seldom roused to exertion, and knew little of enjoyment."
Miss Manners—that is, Mary—whiled away her time in trifles and was
"something of a belle." The eldest son—George—was a poet with "the
imagination of a german sophist living in the ideal world, with a heart as
amiable and as simple as a child." The middle son—John—"mistook spleen
for wit" and so appeared "haughty and overbearing." The third—Charles
Francis—was cultivated, gifted, laborious, as passionate as his father, but as
yet unformed.

Louisa had always had a gift for satire. But years of misfortune and ill
health, and her marriage to a paragon whose harsh judgments cut her to the
quick, had, as she said, soured her temper. The crack about Lord Sharply's
ambition seems too harsh, but no one had caught Adams' distinctive combination of chilliness and inner fire as Louisa had. And she had captured,

perhaps inadvertently, her own mood at that very low moment. Louisa's portrait of her husband contains a great deal of respect but no love at all.

By this time, in fact, Louisa was spending as much time as she could on her own. She had spent most of the summer of 1826 in New Hampshire, while her husband and the boys remained in Quincy. The following summer she refused to go to Quincy at all, instead pressing Charles to join her in Saratoga Springs, New York. The few letters she exchanged with her husband are frigidly correct. She addressed hers, almost mockingly, to "the President." Adams reciprocated with "Mrs. Louisa Catherine Adams." When they all gathered briefly at the City Hotel in New York in August, Charles wrote in his diary, "My own feelings incline to great melancholy on seeing what I think to be the future prospects of our family." The White House years would constitute a low point for both the president and his wife.

ON JULY 4, THE FIFTIETH ANNIVERSARY OF THE DECLARATION OF Independence, President Adams led a solemn procession from the White House to the Capitol, where Secretary of War James Barbour delivered an oration that included a special plea for donations for Thomas Jefferson, then lying gravely ill. In a pitiful coda to a splendid life, Jefferson was virtually bankrupt and could no longer support his own daughter. Two days later, Adams learned that Jefferson had died on the fourth. On the eighth, he received letters from his brother Thomas and from one of his nieces saying that John Adams, too, was at death's door. The president and John left for Quincy at dawn the following day. Later that morning, a man coming from Baltimore told Adams that the papers carried the news that John Adams had died the evening of the fourth, only hours after Jefferson. To his granddaughter, bending over to hear, the old man had whispered, "Thomas Jefferson still surv—."

Though the nation was very much divided between partisans of Adams and Jefferson, both men were profoundly venerated as fathers of the Revolution. The fact that both these men had, apparently, willed themselves to live until the fiftieth anniversary of that great day, that both had died within hours of one another on the fourth itself, that John Adams had been thinking as he neared death of the man whom he had loathed for long years before achieving a late-life reconciliation—all this could not fail to be understood as a heavenly blessing on the republic. John Quincy Adams himself reflected that "the time, the manner, the coincidence with the decease of Jefferson are visible and palpable marks of Divine favor." He prayed that he might live a life and die a death worthy of a father whom he had never ceased to revere and to emulate.

Adams remained stoical until he reached the family house and entered his father' bedroom. "That moment to me was inexpressibly painful," he wrote in his journal, "and struck as if it had been an arrow to the heart." Of all the things he had been in his life, he had been none so faithfully and unerringly as a dutiful son. He had governed his life by the precepts handed down by his parents and had feared doing anything to disappoint them. He had nothing to reproach himself for. Yet he had, in so many ways, lived for them, and now they were gone. He must have felt terribly lonely. At the Quincy meeting house a few days later, he found himself staring during the sermon at the pew his father, and his grandfather before him, had occupied. His mind reeled back to his own boyhood, and he saw that he was surrounded by the gray, bent figures who had once been his playmates. How close they all were to death! Once again the tears sprang to Adams' eyes.

It was an interval of commemoration. Adams and George walked through the family graveyard. Louisa had reached Quincy by now, and the five family members attended ceremonies in Dorchester, Charlestown, Braintree, Salem, and the State House in Boston. Edward Everett and Daniel Webster spoke—a two-and-a-half-hour performance during which not a sound was heard from the audience in Faneuil Hall. Adams could not fail to contemplate his own mortality: in early September he told the Reverend Peter Whitney, pastor of the church in Quincy the Adamses had been attending since the 1620s, that he wished to take communion. Despite attending church every Sunday, often two or three times, for decades, Adams had never participated in this rite—owing, he said, to "the tumult of the world, false shame, a distrust of my own worthiness to partake of the communion," and a continually changing residence. It might have been closer to the mark to say that he had such an inward conception of religious belief that he felt no need for, and perhaps distrusted, outward professions of faith. But now he wished to prepare to be gathered to his forefathers. On October 1, Adams stood when Reverend Whitney called on each communicant to rise in his place and remind them of their duties as Christians.

But Adams also had to worry about earthly matters. His father's will divided his estate into fourteen equal parts for his direct descendants and left to his eldest son the family house and 103 adjoining acres—so long as he paid $12,000, the assessed value, to the estate. Adams could have put the place on the market, but he couldn't bear the thought. He would go into debt—or rather, go further into debt. Louisa was accustomed to submitting to his lordly decrees, but the prospect of bankruptcy in the name of filial loyalty was too much for her. She could, she wrote, understand his desire to own the family house, but "that you should waste your property and burthen yourself with a large unprofitable landed estate, which nearly ruined its past possessor, merely because it belonged to him, is scarcely prudent or justifiable, and the Jefferson family afford too gloomy an instance of its foly to render such an act excusable." Adams didn't argue the point; he simply went ahead and bought the land and the home.

Adams returned to Washington and began working on his second annual message to Congress. This time Henry Clay tried to prevent Adams from doing the administration any further harm through his rash proposals. After Adams read the message to the cabinet, Clay asked if they could read it over by themselves and reconvene the next day for further discussion. Adams agreed. Still hoping to build a national transportation network, Adams had proposed endorsing a report by the Chesapeake and Ohio Canal Company that would authorize the funding of a vast new waterway. This was, Clay insisted, a terrible idea: the canal would cost far more than the budgeted $22 million, it had little support in Washington or the West, and it probably would prove less effective in moving goods than the sponsors hoped. And Clay had lined up everyone else in the cabinet save Rush. Adams agreed to strike that passage from the message. Clay was learning how to manage the president.

IN THE SUMMER OF 1827, WHEN CHARLES HAD REFLECTED ON THE grim prospects of his family, he had been thinking not only of his parents' estrangement but of his older brother George, whose manners, he wrote, "struck me in a very strange way." George struck almost everyone in a strange way. He seemed to be not quite rooted to terra firma—like a German sophist in his own ideal world, as Louisa had written. George had a law office but never worked. Rejected in courtship, he had declared himself indifferent to love and marriage. He drank too much; perhaps he used opium. Like his Uncle Tom, he was finding it very hard to be an Adams. He was deeply attached to old John Adams, whom he visited often, and very much afraid of his father, who over the years had delivered a series of stinging rebukes.

Despite his immense workload, John Quincy Adams wrote to George with an endless stream of admonitions: you must persevere in your vow to rise early; you must apply yourself to your work, for then "you will have no time to indulge moments of despondency." It had been a mistake, it turned out, to entrust George with the family funds, as it had been years before to entrust his money to his brother Charles. In one of his rare letters, George admitted that he hadn't kept up his father's accounts, as he had promised to do, owing to "indolence and self-delusion." Adams was angry, but more than that, he was desperate. He saw the pit yawning before his aimless child. He no longer believed George's blithe reassurances. "I have been *horror-struck* at your *danger*," he wrote. Louisa begged George to come to Washington, but he remained in Quincy, perhaps terrified of a personal encounter with his father. Charles was almost as worried about George as his parents were. "Much conversation with George upon our relative prospects," he wrote in his journal. His were bright, and George's dismal. "George has changed for the worse." "George is in danger of a relapse."

President Adams depended on his middle son, John, as a one-man staff, though this chiefly involved serving as messenger, doorkeeper, and scribe. John had never fully matured; he was hot-tempered, rash, and undisciplined. The Adamses had come more and more to rely on Charles, and he in turn had the healthiest relationship with them. Charles enjoyed the occasional spree, but he never forgot that he was an Adams: at John Adams' death he reflected that the violent criticism both his grandfather and his father had endured placed on him an obligation to vindicate the family name. Neither of his brothers would have entertained such a thought.

Charles' combination of ambition and self-indulgence allowed him to skate on the edge of disaster without falling in. While in Washington in the winter of 1826 he had met and fallen in love with Abby Brooks, the daughter of a wealthy insurance man in Medford. (She was visiting her sister, who had married the congressman and Adams ally Edward Everett.) In his journal he wrote with cool calculation that great advantages might accrue to such an advantageous union. Perhaps it would serve as a spur to his flagging ambition as well as "a check upon my vagaries of independence." This was an oblique allusion to the fact that he was keeping a mistress. Charles was not about to let his appetites ruin his future. In April 1827, he coolly wrote in his diary, "Ever since my engagement, I have been preparing for a close of my licentious intrigues, and this evening I cut the last cord which bound me." The fact that neither his parents nor, apparently, Abby herself ever discovered what they would have viewed as a monstrous violation of morals and propriety is a testimony to Charles' discretion.

The amiable, prosperous, cheerful Brookses presented a striking contrast to the lugubrious, if gifted, Adamses; whenever he thought of his own family, Charles reflected, "a creeping dread comes over me." Charles viewed his mother, whom he seems to have loved very much, as a wounded, fluttering bird and sometimes chided her for her melodramatic flights of self-pity. After receiving one of her deeply melancholy letters, Charles wrote in his diary, "Her feelings are constantly carrying her into extremes which she repents when it is too late and then she attempts to hide them from herself." Charles looked on his father as something of a graven idol, though one apt to inspire amazement rather than awe or terror. After listening to some of the president's supporters wax enthusiastic over his tenure one evening, Charles wrote, "My father has unfortunately such a cold manner of meeting this sort of feeling that I am surprised at the appearance of it at any time among his supporters." Another time he remarked, "He makes enemies by perpetually wearing the iron mask." Charles was the only one of the boys who had grown up with his father as a little boy, had held his hand on long walks, and had sat on his lap at the circus. The iron mask had no powers to frighten him.

Charles proposed to Abby in January 1827. He was only nineteen. After initial resistance to accepting an engagement to so young a man, Peter Brooks, swayed by accounts of his daughter's love, said that he would accept the match if Charles' father did. And John Quincy Adams, remarkably, agreed, so long as the couple waited for several years. The president wrote to Peter Brooks to say that a young man like Charles, "his habits domestic and regular," could marry at twenty-one, unlike a youth of "more tardy self-control." Charles would have gotten a laugh out of that if he had seen it. Nevertheless, the elder Adams refused when Charles asked to have his allowance raised from $800 to $1,000 a year, enraging his son.

Throughout this period father and son carried on an extraordinary correspondence. In late 1827 Charles asked his father to help him develop a suitably elegant and grave writing style. Adams immediately responded with a reading list—Cicero and Pliny, Madame De Sevigné and Voltaire, Pope and Pascal. And Charles went out and bought the volumes. His father was so pleased that he wrote with yet more books. And when Charles wrote back with his thoughts on Pascal's *Provincial Letters*, Adams discovered that he had something he had craved without even realizing it—an intellectual friend and partner. One night he stayed up until midnight writing a long letter about the great writers on ethics, modern and classical. He had, he said with obvious delight, been driven to open up the beloved friends gathering dust on his shelves.

Over the next six months, while his political career was, so far as he could see, drawing to an ignominious close, Adams spent countless hours writing to his son about books, the great comfort of his life. While George was writing to admit that he had fallen $1,000 in debt to a complete stranger, Charles was writing to question the idea that genius exists. Adams responded to the one with a check and a very harsh lecture, and to the other with quotes from Socrates, Milton, the Comte de Buffon, and Periander, the second tyrant of Corinth. In a later letter Adams expounded on Cicero, whose wisdom he had long revered as the highest human achievement save for the revelation of Scripture. "Make him the study of your whole life," he advised. And Charles kept pushing back—on the virtues of early rising, on the moral value of political engagement, even on Cicero.

Nobody challenged Adams at the level of his deepest convictions—save his enemies, of course, who despised him. But Charles was a cocky Harvard man, impressed with his own learning and analytical skills and not the least bit afraid of a man who made others quake. He mocked the idea of "public service," which had been his father's watchword. Wasn't it all just vanity? "In truth," he wrote, "there are very few duties for which a man is clearly called upon by his country, and there are so many eager to perform those that there is no danger to it from neglect, to say the least."

Even a man less sensitive than Adams might have taken offense at this cheap cynicism. But Adams couldn't have been happier. He wrote back, "Because there are gilt counters circulated in the world, does it follow that there is no gold?" And he urged Charles to keep writing about whatever thoughts his reading prompted. "We shall not always agree in opinion, but each of us may rectify his own opinions by weighing those of the other." And so they did, not only over great matters of history but over the most fundamental question of all—how to live. Charles, with the rigid self-certainty of youth, favored Cato, the "inflexible moralist"; his father, with the wisdom of years, preferred Cicero, "the practical statesman." John Quincy Adams called Sir Francis Bacon to his defense: "All rising to great place is by a winding stair." He did not say, and perhaps did not need to say, that he had reached his own great place by a winding stair.

Adams' correspondence with Charles offered a source of deep solace amid the labor and the gloom of his last year in the White House. His wife was sickly, depressed, and resentful. His eldest son seemed to be racing toward his doom. His debts were mounting. His political prospects were dim. John Quincy Adams had always found sanctuary in books, thought, reflection. He was that man walking alone through the dark streets of Washington, silently communing with the shadows of the great statesmen and orators and philosophers whose example was never far from his thoughts.

CHAPTER 25

A Great Man in the Wrong Place at the Wrong Time

(1825–1826)

I N HIS FAMOUS MESSAGE OF 1823, PRESIDENT MONROE HAD
bluntly asserted that the United States would view any threat by the
European powers to the liberties of the new South American republics
as "dangerous to our peace and safety." He was announcing, in effect, a special relationship among the New World republics. John Quincy Adams had
played a central role in shaping the Monroe Doctrine, but neither he nor
the president had ever explained the form they saw that relationship taking.
Did the United States envision, as Henry Clay had suggested, a league of
republican states? Did America seek the role of hemispheric leader? And
what of Spain's remaining colonial possessions, Cuba and Puerto Rico? Was
the United States prepared to accept this remnant of colonialism at the
edge of its shores?

Adams was, in fact, perfectly comfortable with the situation he inherited. He cared far more about extending America's continental reach and
economic power than he did about issues of hemispheric leadership. He
hoped to promote closer commercial ties, not political ones, with the republics, and he had no wish to meddle with Spanish control of the two islands off the America coast. He hadn't said a word about South America in
his inaugural address. But then South America came to him. Simón

Bolívar, the Great Liberator, had long dreamed of an inter-American alliance—led by himself, in all likelihood—to establish collective security against European encroachment and to compel Spain to surrender its control over Cuba and Puerto Rico. His original plans did not include the United States. But the new powers of the continent were eager to strengthen bonds with the United States, and the election of Adams, and his appointment as secretary of state of Henry Clay, the great champion of the infant republics, made the idea yet more appealing. In the spring of 1825, the foreign ministers of Colombia and Mexico invited the United States to attend a Pan-American Congress to be held October 1 in Panama, then part of Colombia and the ligature between the two continents.

Clay enthusiastically endorsed the idea. But Adams worried that the South Americans would embroil the United States in their ongoing hostilities against Spain, with which they remained in a formal state of war. Adams had no intention of compromising American neutrality. He instructed Clay to respond that the United States would attend the conference only to discuss relations with the new nations, not between them and Spain. Moreover, the starting date would have to be postponed, since the United States could not send ministers there in time. Clay waited for a response, and the October 1 date slipped past with little notice.

In fact, Spain was far too feeble to pose any threat to the new republics; it was Spain's weakness, not its aggression, that threatened to destabilize the region over which President Monroe had thrown the mantle of America authority. Spain exercised increasingly flimsy authority over Cuba, "the pearl of the Antilles," and a mad global scramble was forming over its fate. It is hard to imagine that this small island off the coast of Florida could have provoked such a covetous frenzy, but Cuba's sugar plantations made it a source of great wealth, while the port of Havana was ideally situated for the trade between the United States, South America, and Europe. In sheer tonnage, though not in value, American trade with Cuba almost equaled its trade with England. Great Britain worried that France would seize or buy the island from Spain, or that the United States would invade. The United States worried about the ambitions of England, Mexico, and Colombia. And everyone worried that either the colonists themselves or—inconceivably worse—the slaves would overturn Spanish rule and declare independence, as the Haitians had with France two decades earlier.

Plots were being hatched across the region. General Santa Ana of Guatemala was said to be preparing an expedition against Cuba. President Guadelupe Victoria of Mexico was planning to mount a *Junta Promotora de la*

Libertad de Cuba with a group of Cuban revolutionaries—a kind of proto-Bay of Pigs. (The Mexican legislature ultimately scotched the plan.) Clay wrote to the American minister in Mexico City instructing him to admonish Mexican officials that while the United States had no desire to annex Cuba, if the island were to become a colony, "the law of its position proclaims that it should be attached to the United States." American statesmen from the time of Jefferson had coveted Cuba, and Adams and many others assumed that no territory so close to the United States could long remain in foreign hands. The United States could enjoy a booming trade with Cuba without taking possession. It could not, however, permit a violation of the noncolonization principle at the heart of the Monroe Doctrine: existing colonies in South America could remain, but no new ones could be created. And no colony could be transferred from one master to another—unless the new master happened to be the United States. Adams' goal was thus to preserve an extremely unstable status quo.

In May 1825, the president explained to Baron de Tuyll, the Russian minister, that "Cuba was to the United States an object of paramount commercial importance." The United States would respect Cuba's independence and would demand that others did likewise. The United States had already acted to restrain Mexico and Colombia. But the South American countries could not accept ongoing harassment from the pirates and freebooters who used the islands for sanctuary and whom Spain had failed to control. The baron was too subtle a diplomat to need to be told that Bolívar or others might use the argument for self-defense as a pretext for annexation or an anti-colonial war of liberation. If Spain wanted to keep the island, it had better put a stop to the attacks. The president hoped the Russian minister would ask the tsar to communicate to King Ferdinand America's ardent wish that Cuba remain in the custody of Spain. The baron promised to convey the president's message to his foreign minister and bowed his way out.

The administration later learned that the tsar was prepared to preserve the peace in South America, a welcome turn of events from a few years earlier, when he had plotted to outfit a force to reclaim the errant republics. Clay wrote to the foreign ministers of Mexico and Colombia to inform them that Russia had agreed to intercede with Spain. He urged "suspension for a limited time, of the sailing of the Expedition against Cuba or Porto Rico," which was said to be even then outfitting in Colombia. The United States, deprecating any ambitions of its own, thus had a chance to play the role of international peacemaker and guarantor of South American independence.

The president and his secretary of state continued to worry about Cuba, which seemed equally threatened by revolution or by conquest. Apparently they were not convinced by whatever assurances they had received from the South American republics, for in the weeks after Adams delivered his message to Congress, he and Clay appointed a secret agent, Thomas B. Robertson, a former legislator and judge from Louisiana, to go to Cuba under the cover of repairing his health. Robertson was to be paid a ministerial salary. Clay instructed him to look into the island's wealth and resources, its capacity to resist foreign invasion, and "the disposition of its inhabitants" in regard to independence or annexation by one of the republics. Robertson ultimately declined to go, and a year later Clay appointed Daniel P. Cook, the congressman who had delivered Illinois to Adams despite tremendous pressure from the Jacksonites. The reward for loyalty turned out to be a poisoned chalice: Cook fell sick in Cuba, returned home within a month, and died soon thereafter.

Nevertheless, the diminishing prospect of war in Cuba in 1825 may have changed Adams' lukewarm feelings about the Pan-American Congress. He now had good reason to hope it would not be a war parley and would not place the United States between South America and Europe. In November, the Colombian foreign minister sent a formal invitation to the conference that allayed the administration's concerns and made the event far easier to sell to Congress and the American people. The United States would not be asked to discuss any issue that might compromise its neutrality, but rather questions of international law, the formulation of an American alliance to enforce the anti-colonial principle, the abolition of the slave trade, and the concerting of continental policy toward Haiti. These last two matters posed a potential problem for the administration, but the first two were greatly to the president's liking. Adams agreed that the United States would attend.

In his message to Congress, Adams spoke of a new treaty of commerce and navigation just then being concluded with Colombia, and he noted that his administration hoped to conclude such treaties with each of the republics. Any pact, he said, would be based on the core principles of reciprocity and of most-favored nation status, which is to say that US exports would not be subject to more onerous duties than any other trading partner. The republics had liberated themselves from "the thralldom of colonizing monopolies and exclusions" despite the resistance of "certain parts of Europe to the acknowledgment of the Southern American republics as independent states." Having thus established the true independence of the republics, Adams turned to the invitation to the Pan-American Congress, which, he said, the United States had agreed to attend so far as it was compatible with the supreme principle of neutrality.

The Pan-American Congress was shaping up to be the most popular initiative of Adams' young presidency. Many newspapers had campaigned for American attendance and extolled the prospect of American leadership of a community of independent republics. Thomas Hart Benton of Missouri, an avowed opponent of US attendance, conceded that the project had "captivated all young and ardent imaginations." The invitation had been tendered to the United States with great deference to its senior status and great sensitivity to its domestic political concerns. It felt like an acknowledgment that the United States, once the most junior among nations, had in the space of a few decades reached a threshold of moral and political leadership.

And yet the Pan-American Congress was to be Adams' Waterloo. In his first year in office, Adams had given his opponents no reason to fear him and plenty of evidence that he was a hapless politician, a noble Roman who disdained politics, a scholar-president who submitted a schoolboy's thesis to Congress rather than a practical program. He had entered as a weak president elected without a majority, dogged by allegation of a "corrupt bargain." But by proposing so little, he had given the opposition few chances to marshal its forces against him. Even his ambitious domestic program could be neutralized by nothing more than inaction. But the Pan-American Congress was different. He had agreed to attend without consulting Congress, save after the fact. The son of America's alleged monarch-president was both disdaining the legislative branch and contracting foreign alliances in violation of the bar laid down by George Washington. And even if he wasn't, it could certainly be made to appear that he was.

The ever-resourceful Martin Van Buren, now a New York senator, recognized that Adams had provided "the first tangible point for the opposition," as he would later write. In early January Van Buren paid a visit to Vice President Calhoun at the latter's Georgetown home. Calhoun had held himself aloof from the administration. The South had decisively repudiated Adams; Calhoun could have no political future at the side of this New England ex-Federalist. And Calhoun had recoiled in disgust at the election's denouement: what Van Buren said through crocodile tears the vice president actually felt. The deal between Adams and Clay, he had told a correspondent, was "the most dangerous stab, which the liberty of the country has ever received." He would not side with them. "I am with the people," he declared grandly, "and shall remain so." By the time Van Buren visited, Adams and Calhoun, who had sought one another out for long talks about first principles, who had admired one another despite profound disagreements, had been driven into opposite corners.

Van Buren and Calhoun agreed that American attendance at the Panama conference constituted a usurpation of congressional prerogative—an early example of Congress' fight for an equal status with the president on foreign affairs. Calhoun would instruct his supporters to do what they could to block the president's plans. Nothing was said between the two men of larger political prospects, but both understood that by trying to thwart the president on so deeply important an issue Calhoun was throwing in his lot with the administration's Jacksonian rivals. Van Buren then met with other opposition leaders to plot out strategy. They could trip up the president in the House, which had to appropriate funds for the delegation, or in the Senate, which had to confirm the nominated ministers. They decided to start with the Senate, where Vice President Calhoun had appointed committee chairmen with an eye to helping his own cause rather than that of the president. In mid-January the Foreign Relations Committee issued a report asserting that Adams ought to have consulted with Congress beforehand, questioning the necessity of American participation in the conference, and accusing the president of abandoning the neutrality that was the cornerstone of American foreign policy. Adams had hoped to send his ministers by the end of the month; now, instead, he would have to fight to send them at all. It is often asserted that in a less fractious age politics stopped "at the water's edge." It was rarely so, and certainly not in 1825.

The Foreign Relations Committee was dominated by figures from the Deep South, including Littleton Tazewell of Virginia and Nathaniel Macon of North Carolina. For them, and for many others who led the debate against Panama, the underlying issue was not South America but slavery. Many were incensed that the United States would countenance discussion of the slave trade or Haiti. The black republic was "a firebrand in the Southern half of our Union," Thomas Hart Benton would later write. To receive ministers from the island would "give to their fellow blacks in the United States proof in hand of the honours which await, for a like successful effort on their part." On this issue, as on Indian removal and so many other apparently unrelated policies, the immense outlines of the South's slave economy could be dimly made out like a mountain shrouded in fog.

Opposition members now further clogged the debate with resolutions defending the alleged privileges of the legislative branch. They demanded that the president turn over the diplomatic correspondence with the Latin republics—correspondence that was by tradition secret. Adams refused and was vexed enough to say that he did not trust their motives for asking. Van Buren introduced a resolution stating, with no constitutional evidence, that the power of creating "new political associations," such as Adams proposed to do, was reserved for the states. Another resolution specifically accused Adams of upsetting the neutral principles laid down by Washington. The debate consumed six more precious weeks. When it finally came time to vote, on March 14, Adams was able to muster a majority, with his supporters rejecting the committee report 24 to 19, as well as the various resolutions. But the opposition had shown its teeth. Southerners and pro-slavery men of the west made up most of the opposition. Adams' supporters showed little of the passion or tenacity of his rivals.

The issue now moved to the House, and Adams chose this opportunity to fully clarify his views on the congress. He began by acknowledging that the idea had not, after all, originated with the United States, a sore point with critics, but, he noted in a poetic turn of phrase, that it had arisen from the urgent condition of new states "struggling for independence and, as it were, quickening into life." The invitation had been extended with a due regard for America's own national interests. To have responded to such an invitation with "a cold repulse" would have contradicted "the warm interest in their welfare with which the people and Government of the Union had hitherto gone hand in hand through the whole progress of the revolution." Here was the eager language of Henry Clay—of hemispheric fraternity—rather than Adams' own usual cautious reserve.

Adams went on to say that the congress would dwell on "objects of the highest importance" to mankind as well as to the interests of the United States. It was scarcely imaginable that such an opportunity would offer itself again. The congress could serve as the stage on which new principles of international law were enacted. As secretary of state, Adams had proposed a treaty to outlaw privateering. Old Europe had shown no interest. But the new world might well embrace such a visionary plan. In the Monroe Doctrine the United States had declared that no new colonies would be permitted in the Americas; the Congress might issue a "joint declaration" of the anti-colonial principle signed by all the American states. American principles might not yet become universal ones, but they could become hemispheric ones.

Adams briefly referred to the neuralgic issues of the slave trade and Haiti, promising that American ministers would not deviate from the policy of nonrecognition of the island. He argued that the congress would give the United States the chance to prevent any planned invasion of Cuba or Puerto Rico and to "preserve the existing state of things." He reiterated that the assembly would be merely "diplomatic and not legislative," that nothing agreed there would be binding on the United States absent congressional approval. It was an argument that prefigured the one Woodrow Wilson would make on behalf of the League of Nations, for both men sought to overcome the fear that the United States would surrender a portion of its sovereignty to a multinational body.

And, like Wilson a century later, Adams had to confront the unquestioning faith in Washington's Farewell Address. Imprudent as always when faced with the chance to sharpen a categorical distinction, Adams asserted that the Pan-American Congress might well "change the policy . . . of avoiding all entangling alliances and all unnecessary foreign connections." This was heresy in many quarters; it was the equivalent in foreign policy of Adams' assertion that in domestic affairs "liberty is power." But, Adams went on, Americans no longer lived in Washington's world. Then the United States had been surrounded by European colonies that might as well have occupied "another planet." Now its neighbors were sovereign states with which the United States had growing commercial and diplomatic relations. The United States was "entangled" with them, willy-nilly. Adams also noted that since Washington's time "our wealth, our territorial extension, our power—physical and moral—have nearly trebled." Washington had declared that "the period was not far distant when we can defy material injury from external annoyance." That period, Adams suggested, had now arrived. The president was careful to add that Washington himself would view the Panama congress as consistent with his own principles, but no one could miss the assertion that American had reached a new stage in its relations with the world.

In foreign policy, as in domestic affairs, Adams had signaled a decisive break with the past. And yet his decidedly old-fashioned sense of his role as a political leader meant that he was unable or unwilling to muster support in the face of well-organized opposition. Adams had, yet again, delivered himself into the hands of his rivals. In the immediate aftermath of his message, the ongoing debate produced a level of invective in the Congress rarely heard before, which is saying a great deal. John Branch of North Carolina veered from his exegesis of the constitutional obligation to seek the advice and consent of the Senate to declare that the president "came into office in opposition to three-fourths of the American people" and "by the total disregard of the right of instruction, the basis of Republic." But Branch was a mere bonfire compared to the roaring inferno that was John Randolph, senator from South Carolina.

Randolph had been haunting the Adams family for a generation and more. He had jeered at the first President Adams as a monarchist and a despot, the fountainhead of "the House of Stuart." Of ancient Virginia stock, Randolph had broken with Jefferson, a distant cousin, whom he considered far too compromising with the Federalists, and become a leader of a purist faction known as the Tertium Quids (or "third thing," neither Federalist nor Republican). Randolph was a dandy, a self-conscious throwback who had been known to show up in Congress with riding clothes and a whip. His speeches made for famous, if exhausting, theater; he is credited with inventing the filibuster. Adams considered him a lunatic, a view shared by many congressmen of all political persuasions. But he was not a man to be underestimated.

Randolph spoke on March 26. He rambled across a range of arcane topics before coming to his central allegation: the Panama convention had been fabricated in January 1825 between Adams and Clay—between old Massachusetts and young Kentucky, "between the Frost of January and young, blythe buxom May"—as part of the "dirty bargain" over the presidency. Adams, he said archly, had "Jonathan-Russell'd himself"—had damned himself to "everlasting infamy," as once he had damned another, through his collusion with Clay. He had contemptuously refused to turn over to the Senate the diplomatic correspondence with the South American ministers. This was tyranny—no, blasphemy. Randolph worked himself up into a frenzy, interrupting himself, offering asides to his asides, shouting in his wrath. Those few who sought to defend constitutional principles against autocracy had been beaten by an implacable force, "defeated, horse, foot and dragoons—cut up—and clean broke down—by the coalition of Blifil and Black George, by the combination, unheard of till then, of the puritan and the black-leg." That was a supremely low blow and a master stroke, an ingenious analogy, which no one could miss, between, on the one hand, the pious hypocrite and the charming villain of Fielding's *Tom Jones* and, on the other, the austere president and his roguish secretary of state.

Vice President Calhoun, presiding over the Senate, had sat silently as Randolph's wild polemic poured forth like lava. Allies of the administration were outraged; it was widely, and probably correctly, believed that the vice president had helped Van Buren orchestrate the attack. Clay lost his cool completely and challenged Randolph, a crack shot, to a duel. In the ensuing fight, Clay fired first and missed. Randolph then aimed for the secretary of state's leg—being careful, he later claimed, not to strike the kneecap—and missed as well. The two men shook hands, signifying that the demands of honor had been satisfied. But the damage Randolph had done to the administration was lasting. The speech was widely reprinted, contributing to the political lexicon not only the expression "Blifil and Black George" but also Randolph's sublime description of the proposed conference as "a Kentucky cuckoo egg laid in a Spanish nest."

The Adams administration continued to prepare for the conference, even as the ministers cooled their heels waiting for the House to approve funds for the mission. But domestic opposition ultimately carried the day. The House only appropriated funds for the trip in May—a month before the congress was to begin. News of the rancorous debate began to sap Adams' credibility abroad. His minister in France wrote that "the divided state of our Senate and our House of Representatives . . . are well known in Europe and have their influence." The South American states saw all too clearly that the United States could not take the leadership role they had envisioned. Owing to the need for a late start, one of the American ministers refused to leave, afraid of contracting yellow fever. Another died en route; the third arrived too late. The congress lasted from June 15 to July 22, decided very little, and never reconvened. Bolívar's dream of a united South America came to naught, as did Adams' and Clay's hopes of establishing a confederation of republican states in the Western Hemisphere—a League of Nations *avant la lettre*.

Clay continued to be preoccupied by the situation of Cuba. He reiterated Adams' bottom-line positions: the United States wished "no change in the possession or political condition" of Cuba and could not accept the transfer or annexation of the island by either a European power or a South American republic. The Henry Clay of only a few years earlier almost certainly would have welcomed an indigenous independence struggle in Cuba. No longer: given "the limited extent, moral condition, and discordant character of its population," Cuba could not now "sustain self-government, unaided by other Powers." He added an ominous and unmistakable reference to Haiti: in any such convulsion, "one portion of the inhabitants of the Island . . . would live in continual dread of those tragic scenes which were formerly exhibited in a neighboring island." And he wished the foreign ministers of Mexico or Colombia to understand that a war of liberation launched from their shores could well provoke a European response. In that case, the United States, "far from being under any pledge, at present, to oppose them, might find themselves, contrary to their inclination, reluctantly drawn by a current of events, to their side."

Clay was still a moralist and a romantic; he had tried, and failed, to persuade Adams to recognize Haiti. But in many ways he had come to adopt Adams' more chastened and prudent sense of world affairs. The influence flowed in both directions. In speaking of South America, Adams had adopted Clay's language of hemispheric fraternity and been mocked for it by his rivals. And he had abandoned his cautious neutrality between the Greek insurgents and the Ottoman Empire. In September 1825 Adams authorized Clay to send an official to Greece—another secret agent—to help Americans there, to discourage others from aiding the Turks, and to let the Greek authorities know that the people and the government of the United States "felt an anxious desire" that their struggle "might terminate in the reestablishment of the liberty and independence of that Country." And Adams said as much in public in later congressional messages. The two men had formulated a post-Washington, post–Monroe Doctrine policy with a fine balance between what we would today call "idealism" and "realism."

Though Adams' hopes for an inter-American federation failed, his Cuba policy succeeded. The United States neither attempted to annex Cuba nor permitted others to do so, and the island remained a Spanish colony until gaining its independence in 1898. The policy, of course, worked better for the United States than for the people of Cuba, who remained under the Spanish thumb throughout the nineteenth century.

THE NET EFFECT OF THE DEBATE OVER THE PAN-AMERICAN CONGRESS was to bring a fractured opposition together for the first time and to give them confidence that they could defeat the politically hapless president— and not just on matters of domestic legislation but even on the more classically executive prerogative of foreign affairs. The debate also moved Vice President Calhoun decisively into the opposition camp. In June, Calhoun handed John H. Eaton, Jackson's confidante, a letter for the master of the Hermitage. The letter read like a dispassionate version of John Randolph's speech. "An issue has been fairly made," Calhoun wrote, "between *liberty* and *power*; and it must be determined in the next three years, whether the real governing principle in our political system be the power and patronage of the Executive, or the voice of the people." Calhoun alleged that "a scheme has been formed to perpetuate power in the present hands." Once power has been transferred by "corrupt patronage," elections will come to be seen as a "farce," and the people will soon come to accept "the transmission of Executive power by hereditary principle, in some imperial family."

It is striking—in fact, it's astonishing—that not only political schemers and pro-slavery advocates and reactionary ideologues but one of the nation's greatest political thinkers had come to adopt a conspiracy theory about the president with no obvious foundation. Adams' adversaries could not accept him as president, and not only because he had failed to win a majority and had then eked out a victory through a form of subterfuge. These men saw Adams as the representative of an archaic elite that had lost whatever right it had once had to govern the nation. And the president gave them all the help they needed by acting like just such a throwback. As a matter of character he was, indeed, a remnant. His ideas were bold and forward-looking, but he had formulated them at a moment when most Americans were seeking liberty rather than power. He was a man both behind his times and ahead of them. The British historian George Dangerfield summed up Adams' presidency as "a rather conspicuous example of a great man in the wrong place, at the wrong time, with the right motives and a tragic inability to make himself understood."

CHAPTER 26

Cultivating His Garden

(1826–1827)

THE ELECTION OF 1824 HAD BEEN A CHAOTIC SPRAWL, WITH five candidates. By the time John Quincy Adams had served half of his term, he had aroused vitriolic opposition in the Congress, but his rivals had not organized around one candidate and had not formed an alternative party. Most looked to Andrew Jackson, but others allied with John Calhoun or even William Crawford, who had recovered from his illness. Some favored internal improvements and high tariffs, while some deplored them; some favored the new America of the West over the old of the North and South, and some defended what they saw as ancient privileges under threat from the forces of growth and change. As the election of 1828 approached, it was obvious that Adams could be beaten if these heterogeneous forces could be gathered around one man. But someone would have to do the gathering.

That man was Martin Van Buren. On May 12, 1827, Van Buren stopped by the White House for a chat with the president. The groundswell that had lifted Jackson so close to the presidency in 1824 had convinced Van Buren that he was the man to carry the banner of Jeffersonian republicanism against Adams' big-government "national" republicanism, as it had come to be called. Van Buren had, in fact, just returned from a swing through the South organizing for Jackson, as Adams knew very well. The president thought of the New York senator as a figure much like Aaron Burr, but more subtle. Van

Buren did not in fact pose a threat to the Union, but he did pose a threat to Adams. He would help turn the election of 1828 into a new kind of campaign, organized and coordinated at both the national and the local level. Adams only dimly understood the magnitude and genuine novelty of the efforts already under way to ensure that he would not serve a second term.

After defeating the administration on one front after another in the spring of 1826, Van Buren had returned to Washington at the end of the year convinced that the time had come to form a new party, with Jackson at its head. He spoke to some of the men who had led the fight against the Pan-American Congress, including Littleton Tazewell of Virginia and Samuel Ingham of Philadelphia, about reviving the North-South alliance that had elected Jefferson. He visited Calhoun once again to enlist him in the coalition he intended to form; Calhoun agreed. In January 1827, Van Buren wrote to Thomas Ritchie, the editor of the *Richmond Enquirer*, the house organ of the Jeffersonians, saying, "We must always have party distinctions . . . and the most natural and beneficial to the country is that between the planter of the South and the plain Republicans of the North." By "plain Republicans" Van Buren meant sincere proponents of small government, as opposed to Federalists in Republican clothing like Adams. He was proposing, he said, "the substantial reorganization of the old Republican party." Van Buren understood that Ritchie's circle had a litmus test, and he left no doubt where he himself stood: he promised to "protect the remaining rights reserved to the states by the federal government."

Van Buren embarked on his Southern tour with the goal of uniting the Jeffersonians, or Old Radicals as they called themselves, behind Jackson's candidacy. The Little Magician apparently persuaded them that Jackson shared their views on tariffs and internal improvements, though this was scarcely the case. Ritchie wrote to him, "I was struck by your view of the benefits we might promise ourselves from General J's election." The *Enquirer* endorsed Jackson—a crucial moment in the formation of the new party. The adherents of this new alliance began to speak of a "Democratic Republican" Party, or sometimes simply of a "Democratic" Party.

Jackson himself had been running for president virtually since the day he had been defeated. Fueled by an unquenchable sense of outrage over the "corrupt bargain" that had kept him from office, Jackson had gathered his confederates around him and planned his campaign. In the spring of 1827, eighteen of his leading supporters formed a Central Corresponding Committee in Nashville to block "falsehoods and calumny, by the publication of truth"—a "war room" in a time when the news cycle ran in weeks rather than hours. Van Buren formed a circle of Jacksonite senators, who in turn established a corresponding committee in Washington. Soon cities all across the South and West had sprouted similar organs.

Most of Jackson's inner circle consisted of serving and retired officers; military men, of course, are good at logistics and organization. Major Alan Campbell wrote from Louisville to say that he and others had built an organization that included every ward in the city and the surrounding counties and that they had harvested the view of every voter on the great national and local questions. A "Jackson Committee," holding dinners and rallies, formed in states, cities, and counties across the country. It was this combination of organization from above and a restless desire for political engagement among ordinary men that produced what came to be known as the Jacksonian Revolution. The election of 1828 saw the rise of a truly democratic politics, a radical evolution from the republican politics of an earlier generation, in which a distinguished servant of the nation from a great family could rise to the presidency as by right. Adams couldn't, and wouldn't, compete.

The Jackson forces understood how to manipulate public information. Jackson acquired a campaign biographer, the postal official Henry Lee, whom Adams had refused to fire despite his anti-administration pamphleteering. Jackson promised to furnish Lee his personal archives. The general's allies established a vast network of sympathetic newspapers. In early 1826, Jackson and Calhoun forces loaned $5,000 to the editors of a new Washington newspaper, the *United States Telegraph*, designed to counteract the pro-Adams *National Journal* and the mostly nonpartisan *National Intelligencer*. The very first issue of the paper, on February 6, 1826, announced that its goal was the defeat of the Adams-Clay coalition. The *Telegraph* hammered away at the "bargain, intrigue and management" that had fraudulently raised the two men to power. Adams was a monarchist, Clay a libertine. The *Telegraph* was a frankly pro-slavery organ that warned that Adams would mount an all-out attack on the institution once he understood that he had no chance of winning the South. That fall the Jackson forces recruited a gifted and ruthless polemicist, Duff Green, from St. Louis, to take over the paper. Green became a traveling advocate for Jackson and a leader of the Washington correspondence committee. The *Telegraph* was soon printing forty thousand copies a day.

Green worked directly with Jackson to rivet the country's attention on the central theme of the campaign: the corrupt bargain. Jackson claimed that Adams' men had conveyed to an intermediary—a political figure of unimpeachable respectability—the plan to offer the secretary of state position to Clay unless Jackson himself was prepared to do the same. Clay, in other words, would sell himself to the highest, or at least the first, bidder. This was the origin of the allegation George Kremer had published in the *National Intelligencer*, for Kremer had heard it from Jackson's confidante John H. Eaton, who had heard from the source himself. The general, it turned out, had repeated it everywhere. Duff Green wrote to Jackson to say that he would trumpet the narrative in the *Telegraph*. If Clay was foolish enough to demand an investigation, Jacksonites in Congress would cross-examine Clay and turn the whole thing into a political carnival. This was much to be preferred to having Jackson himself lodge the allegations, Green observed.

There was only one problem: the story wasn't true. The ultimate source was James Buchanan, the senator from Pennsylvania and future president. Jackson himself wrote to Buchanan to ask him to "publicly affirm" the offer that he had been asked to convey. But Buchanan had never been approached; he had simply distilled a rumor from the atmosphere of the time and presented it to Jackson as fact, thus raising himself mightily in the candidate's esteem. Buchanan felt compelled to concede in a letter to the editor of the Lancaster *Journal* that he had not, in fact, been authorized to strike a deal with Jackson. Clay whooped with vindication when he saw the clipping. "The tables are completely turned on the General," he wrote to a friend.

Perhaps they should have been, but they weren't. Duff Green simply substituted for his own endless catalogue of accusations those made in the New York *Enquirer* or the *Gazette* of Culpepper, Virginia, whose analyses of the vile machinations of January 1825 filled the columns of the *Telegraph*. At the same time, the opposition in Congress used every opportunity that came to hand to demonstrate Adams' supposed illegitimacy. They accused him of using patronage to seed the government with political allies at the same time that Adams' friends were tearing their hair out at the president's steadfast refusal to do just that. In fact Adams would be the last president to stand fast against the mighty torrent of political opportunism: he would remove a grand total of twelve men from office, all for cause.

Jackson's allies demanded that the president produce a list of former and current newspapers authorized to print the public laws in order to prove how he had abused the privilege. (Clay had done his best to transfer this right to allies, but with limited success.) They accused Adams of opposing the Louisiana Purchase, of bartering Texas away to Spain, of ceding navigation rights on the Mississippi. A North Carolina congressman announced a shocking find: the president had billed to the American people the purchase of a billiard table, billiard balls, and a chess set—a total of almost $80! This caused a brief sensation, though of course the supremely scrupulous president had paid for the items himself. His son John had mistakenly accounted for them under "Furniture of the President's House."

The abuse only confirmed Adams' tragic sense of public life and thus his fatalism. But Adams' friends, with ambitions of their own, would not sit idly by. In late March 1827, Daniel Webster wrote to Henry Clay from Philadelphia lamenting that "enemies laugh, and friends hang down their heads, whenever the subject of" executive appointments was raised. The administration only had one paper in town on its side—the *Democratic Press*. The Customs House was in the hands of the opposition. The postmaster was a disaster, but the president wouldn't fire him. Philadelphia, a key bastion of pro-Adams sentiment, was locked in gloom. Webster and Clay began to correspond regularly. These men would attempt, almost by themselves, to counteract the vast network being built up around Jackson. Clay wrote in April suggesting that Webster and Edward Everett, the congressman who had married Abby Brooks' older sister, "prepare a series of pieces, calculated for the region and first to be published in Penna., in which a solemn appeal should be made to their patriotism and intelligence."

Webster, who had little influence beyond New England and the mid-Atlantic states, continued to urge public shows of support from allies in New Hampshire, Maine, and Pennsylvania. He corresponded with friends in Maryland, New York, and Ohio. He gave a speech at Faneuil Hall observing that no true difference of policy existed between Federalists and Republicans (a claim that would not have traveled well beyond New England, the only region where Federalists were still taken at all seriously). He contemplated whether he could help the administration more by remaining in the House or standing for the Senate. He visited New York and interviewed potential candidates for Congress. Clay, meanwhile, made a swing through Kentucky and the South. An inveterate optimist, he assured his friends that Adams' support was stronger than it looked. "My belief is that Mr. Adams will be re-elected and with ease," he wrote in September.

Money played a far more modest role in politics at that time than it does today, but even in 1827 it took cash to assemble a network of newspapers, as the Jackson forces had done. Webster reported to Clay from Baltimore that he hoped to convert the *Patriot* from neutrality to active support—"& by the aid of friends measures are in train which, I hope, may have that result." He wrote to William Gales of the *National Intelligencer* lamenting the difficult straits in which publishers now found themselves, and suggested that one of them come to Boston in order to facilitate a financial arrangement. The most audacious plan Webster and Clay cooked up involved the scurrilous Cincinnati *Gazette*. The editor, Charles Hammond, had taken to circulating disgraceful libels about Jackson, describing his wife Rachel as a "convicted adultress" who had married Jackson bigamously. (The two appear to have lived together before Rachel's husband had sought, much less received, a divorce.) According to one of Hammond's squibs: "General Jackson's mother was a COMMON PROSTITUTE brought to this country by the British soldiers! She afterwards married a MULATTO MAN, with whom she had several children, of whom GENERAL JACKSON IS ONE!!!"

Clay was much taken with Hammond's full-throated advocacy and in August 1827 wrote to Webster describing the editor as "every way worthy of encouragement and patronage." Perhaps, he suggested, they could buy him a new set of types. Webster visited printers in Boston and found that the cost would be $500 to $600. Would that be the most effective means of supporting Hammond? Clay wrote back in mid-October to say that in fact "another & perhaps a better mode of accomplishing the object in view has presented itself." Clay proposed that they raise a sort of slush fund from wealthy merchants and disburse money to sympathetic editors to increase circulation. By early November, Webster reported from New York that he could, if necessary, raise $1,000 just for the Richmond *Whig*, the rival to the *Enquirer*.

Webster began to get nervous about committing to paper proposals that should never see the light of day. "I hope your office is confidential & trustworthy," he wrote to Clay. "All is safe at my end, because no one opens my letters." Clay reassured him that no one save Daniel Brent, the long-time chief clerk of the State Department and an ardent supporter of the administration, opened his mail.

THE WORLD HAD CHANGED; JOHN QUINCY ADAMS HAD NOT. IN his *History of the American People*, Woodrow Wilson, later to become the president most like Adams, high-minded and unbending, caught him to the life:

His very precision and stiffness of manner, as of the old school; his cool, unsympathetic aloofness from the men about him, repelling intimacy of any warm confidence; the dash of acid in his careful rectitude; his whole attitude, as of a man who administered his great office as a purely personal trust, for which he alone was responsible, and kept all others at arms' length, enhanced the impression of his separateness, his single survival out of an age gone by.

Yet Americans now expected to see and even meet the president; he was *their* president, after all. Adams came face to face with this new spirit on his rare trips outside of Washington. As he passed through Philadelphia on his return from his summer vacation in October 1827, crowds lined up on the wharf to greet him with "Hip hip hooray!" They saluted the president as he neared his hotel. A crowd formed again as Adams prepared to leave for Washington. He agreed that he would shake every hand if they all formed an orderly line. They did so, and Adams walked along the line for half an hour. As his steamer passed through the harbor, the crowds set up a cry that seemed to follow him out into the water. "I returned their salutation by a bow," Adams wrote in his journal, "waving the hand and saying 'God bless you all.'"

The festival of democracy continued as Adams arrived in Baltimore, where he estimated that two thousand citizens came out to shake his hand—"people of all classes and all political opinions." Adams shook thousands more hands the next day, and after dinner he came out of his hotel room to find another crowd waiting. He was beginning almost to enjoy himself. Standing on the hotel steps, he said, "I want each one of you that has at home a wife, or a mother, or a sister, or a daughter, to shake hands for me with her, and tell her that in shaking hands with you, I do, in heart, the same with her." This may not have been a very potent political appeal, since at the time women were not allowed to vote. Nevertheless, that night Adams wrote that he felt "grateful for the kind and friendly entertainment I have experienced here." Louisa described this giddy encounter to Charles, adding, "If he would only lend himself a little to the usages and manners of the people without hiding himself and too modestly rejecting their civilities no man would be more popular." Even Louisa was a democrat compared to her husband.

Adams appears to have known little, if anything, of Webster and Clay's efforts to raise money and buy the loyalty of editors. Indeed, in early 1828 a Mr. Bailey from Massachusetts came to the White House, at Webster's instigation, to explain that Kentucky state legislators would now be choosing national electors and to ask for $5,000 to $10,000 in order to publish pamphlets and handbills, and increase newspaper circulation, for the upcoming state poll. Adams replied brusquely that the practice of paying money to secure office was "incorrect in principle." He was struck, and of course disgusted, by the monetization of politics, the consequence of which was "to render elections altogether venal." Adams was also amazed to hear that Webster thought he had that kind of money. He explained to Mr. Bailey that he could barely support his family, that his properties were mortgaged, that of his annual rental income of $6,000 he was paying a third to retire debts, and that he had no idea how he would manage once he left office.

Adams now understood that none of his most ambitious dreams would be realized. He began to yearn for release from his burden. "My duties are to prepare for the end with a grateful heart and an unwavering mind," he wrote. He continued to work long hours, but he spent more time cultivating his garden, in the figurative and the literal sense. In the spring of 1827, as he watched the flowers and trees along Pennsylvania Avenue burst into bloom, Adams became fascinated by cultivation. It was a hobby well suited to him. Adams loved empirical subjects, with endless particulars and labyrinthine relations, whether weights and measures or astronomy. He also loved pursuits that allowed him to commune with his inmost being. Gardening also deepened Adams' sense of kinship with the stoics of ancient Rome, who had retired from the world to the *hortus conclusus*.

Before long Adams was spending an hour or two most mornings working alongside John Ousley, the White House gardener. He brought home blossoms from his walks, researched their names and attributes, and planted them in the garden. He wrote to foreign consuls asking them to buy seeds and plants and send them to the United States for cultivation. Adams became fascinated by the cultivation of trees, a potential source of wealth that heretofore had been left to nature. From London and Paris he ordered massive encyclopedias of dendrology—the study of trees. He planted walnut and chestnut trees. Fearing the demands of shipbuilding would deplete the native population of oak, he established an oak reserve in Florida that ultimately grew to thirty thousand trees—the first act of conservation by an American president.

By early June, Adams could find almost nothing worth committing to his journal save his adventures in the garden. The two acres of White House gardens held perhaps a thousand varieties of flowers and plants; Ousley was teaching him their names. Walking among his trees and flowers in the midst of the brilliant Washington summer gave Adams a taste of joy. One morning, after planting cherries, he wandered through his gardens, finding the poppies in full bloom, the strawberries declining, the red and black currants ripening. "The catalpa trees are in full and beautiful blossom," he wrote, "and Holyoke's bladder senna, and other flowers, are blossoming. The rue, sage and hyssop are also in bloom. I remarked that the honey-bees had keen relish for the poppy-flowers, and the wasps for the wormwood, though not in blossom. . . . My apple-pippin, in the flower-pot, shed its shell forty-eight hours after its first appearance on the surface of the ground." All of Adams' senses, and his great intellectual faculties, were fastened on the harmless, enclosed world of the garden and on the microscopic process of growth, development, and decay, while the world beyond his gate connived at his downfall.

WHEN ADAMS RETURNED TO WASHINGTON IN THE FALL OF 1827, he faced something that none of his predecessors in office ever had: a Congress controlled by the opposition. The party that the Democratic Republicans had built rolled over the National Republicans across the West and the South and in parts of the mid-Atlantic. With a solid majority of Democrats now in the House, Andrew Stevenson of Virginia, Martin Van Buren's handpicked candidate, defeated the pro-administration Speaker of the House, John W. Taylor of New York. Committees in both chambers were now controlled by the opposition. Over the previous three years the opposition had been able to block Adams' initiatives and subject him to continual harassment; now the united Jackson-Calhoun coalition could pursue an agenda of its own and ensure its victory in 1828. "The opposition party," wrote John Tyler of Virginia, a Jeffersonian Democrat, "constitutes in fact the *administration*."

The committed partisans of small government used their newfound strength to authorize federal funds for the kind of expenditures that suited their own views, for example, to pay pensions to Revolutionary War veterans or to supply massive land grants to the states. These projects also suited the opposition's political interests: the new Democratic Party was going to do whatever it could to win over wavering states and to purchase available votes. Nor did these avowed enemies of patronage omit the opportunity they now had to patronize their friends: the contract for the printing of the laws in Washington was taken away from the neutral *National Intelligencer* and given to Duff Green's *Telegraph*.

The new Congress, like many later iterations, opposed government spending in principle but not always in practice. Dr. James Chilton, a freshman legislator from Kentucky, introduced a resolution calling for the House Ways and Means Committee to report on federal offices that could be eliminated and fees and salaries that could be reduced. A committed Jeffersonian, Chilton had insisted on cutting the budgets of the House and Senate as well as of the executive branch. That was taking an admirable principle too far. Congressmen stoutly defended their own expenditures and sought, quietly, to limit the scope of Chilton's investigation.

The measure was referred to a select committee, whose report was issued only at the very end of the term and then largely ignored. It was a transparently partisan document, which accused the administration of a lengthy train of abuses. In fact, Adams had not expanded the government at all—he hadn't been able to—and in his congressional message of 1827 had called for "the strictest economy" in order to speed the retirement of the national debt. As Adams noted in his diary, his treasury secretary, Richard Rush, had eight clerks to handle a national revenue of $26 million, while Albert Gallatin had had nine at a time when revenue was half as great.

The committee's hunt through state documents turned up the kind of "scandalous" material that could be exploited on the hustings. Ancient accounts in the State Department were said to demonstrate that Adams had padded his expenses as minister to Russia. The administration had paid for a junket to London by a friendly editor and had transferred a stationery account to the rabidly pro-Adams *Democratic Press* of Philadelphia (to which, it is true, Clay had awarded the right to print the laws). Each of these frivolous allegations, like the tale of the billiard table, served its political purpose.

By the last days of 1827, Adams saw very clearly that he could not oppose the powerful political machine Jackson and Van Buren had built. Clay showed him a public letter he had written rebutting the allegations of the corrupt bargain. He had gathered corroborating statements from every Western congressman who had voted for Adams in 1825. Clay was still fighting both for his own reputation and for the next term. So little was he motivated by personal ambition, Clay had written, that he was preparing to retire from public life. Adams advised him to strike that passage. After all, Jackson was sure to win, since slander couldn't be refuted. But then he would fail. "He is incompetent both by his ignorance and the fury of his passions," Adams said of the man he had once championed as a national hero. His sycophants will fall upon one another. And then the public would turn to Clay.

Adams, unlike Clay, really was thinking about his retirement. Perhaps he would write a memoir of his father, or a history of the United States from the time of the Constitution. He was reading again—Tacitus and Plutarch. He was writing to Charles about Cicero and to George about the virtues of keeping a journal. He had been called to serve, and he had served. The rest he would leave to fate.

CHAPTER 27

The Sun of My Political Career Sets
in Deepest Gloom

(1828–1829)

O N APRIL 15, 1828, ADAMS DISPATCHED HIS SON JOHN TO
Congress to deliver papers containing nominations for military
posts. As John passed through the Capitol Rotunda, Russell Jarvis,
a reporter for the *Telegraph*, darted out from behind one of the pillars and
punched him square in the face. John picked himself up and took off after
Jarvis; the two were separated before the fight escalated much further. The
insult had begun with John, for when Jarvis had shown up at a White
House gathering two weeks earlier, Adams' son had loudly remarked that
someone who made a living maligning the president should have the good
manners to avoid his drawing room. Jarvis had delivered a note demanding
an explanation, which John had indignantly refused to give. And so the reporter had waited for the chance to avenge himself, not through a duel but
through a brawl.

President Adams' inclination was to do nothing; any outrage committed within the precincts of the Congress must be dealt with by the Congress. Leaving aside the question of prerogative, the public spectacle was
mortifying to Adams, who was quite accustomed to defending himself
from attack but now found his son's name dragged through the mud. Clay,
however, said that a dignified silence would not do. The president, he said,

"had a duty to maintain his own dignity and security in the performance of his functions." The Congress would do nothing unless the president forced them to. Even then they would probably produce a report siding with Jarvis, but nevertheless the executive branch could not let the insult pass. The other cabinet members agreed. In response to a message from Adams, the House impaneled an investigative committee, though one heavily weighted to the Jacksonian opposition.

The fight quickly became fodder for public raillery. Duff Green wrote in his usual tone of wicked glee that Jarvis "could not have anticipated that the baby . . . would run blubbering to his daddy that he had had his nose pulled and his jaws slapped for his impudence." Louisa told Charles that both she and the president were in agony over the affair. Far better, she thought, for her husband to announce that he would not seek reelection and thus leave this endless public trial behind. Yet to do so would "in some measure forfeit the reputation he has so justly acquired."

John was called to testify before the House investigative committee, which noted a "discrepancy" between his account and that of various onlookers. There he had to endure the indignity of being cross-examined by the arch-fiend Duff Green. In late May, immediately prior to adjournment, the committee issued a report conceding that Jarvis' attack had violated congressional privilege but concluding that since Jarvis had not intended to do so, no further notice should be taken of the incident. For Adams it must have been confirmation, as if any further were needed, that he was no longer in control of events and that his enemies could assail him—and his family—with impunity.

That spring the Adams administration, like the leaky canoe in which the president had tried to cross the Potomac three years earlier, seemed to be taking on water with no bucket on board. Clay implored Adams to let him retire; a paralysis was creeping up his left foot toward the hip. His friends thought he might be dying. Adams doubted it. And he found the thought of losing his most trusted advisor at so crucial a moment a "disastrous occurrence . . . among those of deep humiliation which are thickening around me." He asked his secretary of state to take some time off instead; Clay reluctantly agreed. The whole cabinet seemed to be preparing to jump overboard. Both James Barbour and Richard Rush wanted to be appointed minister to London (reappointed, in Rush's case). So did Daniel Webster, who had lobbied for the job when Adams became president. Adams could scarcely do without any of them; Clay had persuaded Webster to wait, though the latter must have understood very well that he would serve in London only in the unlikely case that Adams won a second term. Adams thought that all of them, Clay included, were hoping to save themselves "from the wreck."

Adams was not disposed to credit omens and portents, but during this period Washington was also shaken by an earthquake for the first time in memory. At eleven at night on March 9, Adams was writing in his journal when first the table and then the floor itself began to shake. The window shutters banged. For two long minutes the room bucked and swerved—like a ship being tossed by the waves, he thought. Adams was more curious than frightened, though a terrified Louisa cowered in bed.

Those humiliations thickening around the president largely took the form of allegations of misconduct. Adams had a clerk unearth records from as far back as 1794 to prove that he had not abused public finances. He was forced to respond to the absurd claim that while in Russia he had prostituted his servant, Martha Godfrey, to Tsar Alexander. He was said to be the author of a satirical song against Jefferson published in 1802. He was said to be a Mason. (He wasn't, though Jackson was.) He and his cabinet members had to gather records to rebut the claims of James Chilton's Retrenchment Committee. Adams felt as if he were fighting a hydra—the many-headed monster of the aroused and confident opposition. The two houses of Congress, he wrote to Charles, "are united by a spirit of bitter, unrelenting, persecuting malice, against me individually, and against the Administration, which they conspired to overthrow." For once, Adams was not exaggerating. The opposition really was bent on his destruction.

Adams also found himself entangled in the coils of patronage. Over the previous two years, John Binns, editor of the pro-administration *Democratic Press* of Philadelphia, had been railing against that city's postmaster, Richard Bache, the publisher of the anti-Adams *Franklin Gazette*. Binns accused his rival of practicing gross favoritism on behalf of the administration's opponents; Bache responded with a physical assault that landed him in court. But every time Adams spoke about Bache to John McLean, the postmaster general defended his employee's record—further proof to Clay and others of McLean's own perfidy. In fact, senior postal officials had been warning McLean about Bache for years, to no avail. Finally, in 1828, Bache was found to have stolen funds from his postmaster's accounts. At last McLean fired the man—and then replaced him with Bache's brother-in-law, an investor in the *Franklin Gazette* and another inveterate opponent of the administration.

In early June, the assistant postmaster general informed Adams that Bache's embezzlement amounted to $25,000, an immense sum. Adams was shocked, finally, into a clear recognition of what Clay and others had been telling him since the beginning of his tenure. "The conduct of Mr. McLean has been that of deep and treacherous duplicity," he wrote. "With solemn protestations of personal friendship for me, and of devotion to the cause of the Administration, he has been three years using the extensive patronage of his office in undermining it among the people." Adams hadn't exactly been taken in; it was rather that he had not wanted to act against so obviously effective a civil servant as McLean. And now it was too late: firing McLean, he feared, would confirm the opposition's otherwise flimsy claim that he had politicized the civil service. Adams left the postmaster general where he was. Andrew Jackson would reward him for his good work by placing him on the Supreme Court.

The new Jackson-Calhoun–Old Radical coalition was now driving the legislative agenda. By 1828, the Democratic Republicans had hijacked the all-important issue of the tariff—the administration's own issue. The United States had been levying duties on imported goods since its foundation in order to raise revenues. As early as 1816, Henry Clay had begun arguing for the imposition of tariffs for an entirely different reason: to protect domestic manufactures from foreign competition. What Clay meant by the American System was a powerful domestic market tied together by internal improvements and protected by duties. The two ideas were so strongly linked in his mind that he developed the shorthand "D.M. & I.I.," for "domestic market" and "internal improvements." In 1824 he had helped push the highest tariffs in history through Congress—an average of 37 percent. He and Adams planned to raise duties yet higher.

In the years before and during Adams' presidency, the economy shifted in ways that sharpened the divide between pro- and anti-tariff forces while also producing fractures within them. A massive increase in imports from England in the years after the War of 1812 had created a negative trade balance and raised a clamor for protection among manufacturers, above all in the North and the Mid-Atlantic. At the same time, the explosive growth of cotton cultivation in the South had created a lucrative export market that, farmers feared, would face retaliation if the United States raised tariffs. And when the price of cotton plunged between 1825 and 1829, imperiling the economy of the South, farmers blamed a British boycott rather than the actual culprit, which was oversupply. In 1827, the Virginia state legislature passed a resolution stating that the federal government had no right either to impose tariffs to protect domestic manufacturers or to authorize internal improvements. South Carolina, whose economy depended almost entirely on cotton, was equally implacable. At the same time, the sheep farmers and hemp manufacturers in the interior, who were largely supplying a domestic market, favored both discriminatory duties and the roads and canals needed to move their products. Boston merchants favored free trade; Massachusetts factory owners demanded protection. The politics of the protective tariff, which had begun as an instrument to protect New England manufacturers from cheap English woolens, became vastly more complicated. Emotions on the subject ran high all over the country.

Tariff legislation encountered stiff resistance in the first years of the Adams administration. In March 1827, Clay wrote to a Pennsylvania legislator suggesting he hold a meeting of administration allies and tariff supporters in order to intensify the public demand for new legislation. A series of meetings in the state culminated in the convention of the Pennsylvania Society for the Promotion of Manufactures and the Mechanic Arts in Harrisburg. The delegates crafted a series of resolutions calling on Congress to increase protection for both sheep farmers and woolen manufacturers, as well as for producers of iron and steel, flax and hemp, and so on. A more politically adroit administration might have been able to dramatize and reshape the resolution so as to bring diverse interests to rally together under its flag. The Republicans could have made themselves the party of "D.M & I.I." But Clay and Webster were busy elsewhere, Adams paid scant attention, and there was no one else with the authority to act.

When the Congress reconvened in late 1827, the opposition had a majority in both houses. The House Committee on Manufactures would consider only an opposition bill, not an administration one, even though it was the administration that favored tariffs. This presented an opportunity, but a very ticklish one, for Van Buren and his allies. The South, the opposition heartland, opposed tariffs of any kind. Calhoun, who had agreed to become Andrew Jackson's running mate even he though he currently served Jackson's opponent as vice president, had once favored both tariffs and internal improvements, but no longer. Now he saw the issue as a wedge dividing the nation against itself; the tariff, he wrote, would eventuate either in "defeat or oppression." Jackson was on record favoring what he called, with studied ambivalence, a "judicious tariff." Pennsylvania and New York favored some tariffs and not others. Adams had shored up his support in the former state by choosing as his running mate the Pennsylvanian Richard Rush, his treasury secretary. The Western states were split on the tariff. The issue, in short, could have undone Van Buren's careful work uniting a fragmented opposition.

The committee crafted a bill with consummate skill and cynicism. Presented in late January, the bill raised duties to prohibitive levels on a vast range of raw materials, though not on manufactured goods, thus helping farmers rather than factory owners; erected palisades of protection around staples produced in the Western states likely to go for Jackson; and did virtually nothing for the New England wool industry, a redoubt of old Federalists. The bill's features were so extravagant and nonsensical that it was dubbed the Tariff of Abominations. As Silas Wright, the prime mover on the committee, later explained, "we had put the duties upon all kinds of woolen cloths as high as *our own friends* in Pennsylvania, Ohio & Kentucky would vote them. Why did we put the duty on molasses so high? Because Pennsylvania and our friends west of that state required it to induce them to go fore the woolens." And so on with duck cloth and hemp and the rest.

Administration supporters were bewildered and infuriated. Webster was buried under letters from the wool industry opposing the tariff. At the same time, the bill offered protection to many other interests that would be outraged should the bill fail. Calhoun was right in the sense that a tariff bill—any tariff bill—split the country along geographic and economic lines, and accelerated the rise of a new "sectional" politics. Webster wrote plaintively to a friend, "Can we go the hemp, iron, spirits and molasses for the sake of any woolen bill? Can we do it for a poor woolen bill?" Republicans suspected that the opposition had intentionally shaped a bill so inimical that the Adams forces would vote against it, thus sending it to a defeat that Jacksonites in places like New York and Pennsylvania would blame on New England rather than the South. Or maybe the intention was the exact opposite. George McDuffie, the South Carolina Calhounite, wrote that "we determined to put such ingredients in the chalice as would poison the monster and commend it to his own lips."

Clay was both impressed by the ingenuity of the bill's authors and disgusted by its likely outcome. "The Jackson party is playing a game of brag on that subject," he wrote. "They do not really, desire the passage of their own measure & it may happen, in the sequel, that what is desired by *neither party*, commands the support, of both." And that was pretty much what happened. Clay concluded that the administration could not afford to lose the Midwestern and New England farmers who saw tremendous benefit in the bill, and instructed the administration's allies in the House to vote for it. The bill passed 105 to 94. The Jackson forces who had imposed the bill voted against 59 to 44, while the Republicans who had been its victim provided the margin of victory, the poison having commended itself to the monster's lips. The Tariff of Abominations passed the Senate and was signed by the president, thus becoming the single most dubious feature of Adams' legacy.

Adams remained mute throughout the debate; then again, so did Jackson. Adams had no wish to alienate the South by coming out foursquare for a high tariff, and in any case the etiquette of the day dictated that presidents did not openly seek to tip the scales on pending legislation. Adams was not entirely above electioneering, so long as it involved pointing to what he considered the genuine merits of his position or the deficiencies of his rival. In early March, Peter Force, publisher of the pro-administration *National Journal*, had published a verbatim copy of a letter from Jackson full of his typical grammatical and spelling errors as well as his wrath—and next to it a copy of a grandiloquent address he was alleged to have written but was widely thought to have come from the pen of Henry Lee, his paid propagandist.

Now a hunt was on among Adams' supporters for real specimens of Jackson's semiliterate prose and explosive temper. Secretary Barbour went rummaging through the files of the War Department and brought to the White House a Jackson letter that Adams described as "still more ferocious than barbarous in style and composition." Adams' allies hoped to get this one published as well. A few weeks later the letter was printed in the *National Intelligencer*, but the high-minded Gales and Seaton insisted on correcting the errors first, much to Adams' frustration. Of course, the whole episode was founded on the archaic assumption that Americans would not elect a man who couldn't spell or hold his temper.

The Adams press did not cede the low ground to the *Telegraph* or the *Franklin Gazette*. Charles Hammond, of the *Cincinnati Gazette*, brought out a special journal, *Truth's Advocate and Monthly Anti-Jackson Expositor*, to publish only malicious material on the Democratic candidate. The pro-administration press had made hay from the discovery that Jackson had ordered six militia men court-martialed and executed during the Creek War. John Binns of the *Democratic Press* had the inspired idea of printing up black-bordered handbills with the names of the six men and, below them, six black coffins; a mournful bit of doggerel recalled "Those shrieks! That cry of death!" when the men were shot. The "Coffin Hand Bill" was widely circulated and probably did a good deal more damage than had the samples of Jackson's mangled prose—though the truth was that the six men had mutinied, broke into the commissary, and deserted. No prior election in American history had begun to approach the campaign of 1828 for sheer vileness and dishonesty; it would be hard to say which side sunk lower.

Jackson was, in fact, a violent-tempered man, at least when he thought no one was looking. When he heard that Navy Secretary Samuel Southard had been overheard claiming that James Monroe deserved more credit for the Battle of New Orleans than did Jackson himself—Monroe was then directing the overall war effort—he exploded with anger and prepared to challenge Southard to a duel. (The secretary said the whole story was false.) As for Monroe himself, Jackson wrote, "I will unrobe his hypocrisy and strip him of much of his borrowed plumage." Jackson's managers worried that the volcano of the Hermitage could blow at any moment. John H. Eaton wrote to caution him not to respond to newspaper attacks or the stories about Monroe: "There let your friends who are fully competent battle the affair; your course under all circumstances is *retirement* and *silence*." When the tariff issue began agitating the South, another advisor, Colonel Arthur P. Hayne, wrote to express his "most earnest wish that for the present you would neither write or express any positive opinion upon this subject." And Jackson, at times the most refractory of men, mostly sat on his hands and kept his fury to himself.

Jackson was contemptuous toward Adams, but he despised the very ground on which Henry Clay trod. "He is certainly," Jackson wrote to his confederate Sam Houston, "the basest, meanest scoundrel, that ever disgraced the image of his god." In his blind fury Jackson had publicly claimed to have proof of Clay's "corrupt bargain" and then had to watch helplessly as his case had collapsed when James Buchanan retracted the central claim. Clay was convinced that he could Jonathan-Russell the old soldier. He delivered a speech in Richmond in late 1827 rebutting the whole story and then sent copies of it all over the country. The South, he thought, was turning toward the administration.

Clay had taken over much of the hard work of the campaign from Webster, whose wife had died after a long illness in January 1828. Other cabinet members barnstormed across the country for Adams—a new phenomenon the opposition press denounced—but none more eagerly than Clay, whose own future was bound up in the result as much as Adams' was. William Crawford wrote from Georgia to tell Clay that he shouldn't have joined the Adams government: "It appears to me that he is destined to fall as his father did, and you must fall with him." Clay responded equably that when one chooses between two alternatives, time develops the consequences of the one chosen and not of the other. He could not be provoked against Adams, though he certainly had cause; he would go down with the ship rather than scramble off. To his friend Francis Blair he wrote, "I had fear of Mr. Adams temper and disposition, but I must say that they have not been realized, and I found in him, since I associated with him in the Executive government, as little to censure or condemn as I could have expected in any man."

The intensely uncomfortable cohabitation between the Adams administration and an implacably hostile Congress drew to an end in the first days of June. Taking a final opportunity to distribute boons to the people, legislators passed a bill authorizing the building of the Chesapeake and Ohio Canal, and another paying for harbor improvement. The United States would purchase $1 million in stock in the canal and appoint directors to the company. The canal authorities would be breaking ground immediately outside of Georgetown, and they had decided to do so on July 4. For once, Adams agreed to attend the kind of ritual event he deprecated, with bunting and huzzahs and jolly crowds.

At eight that morning a marching band set off from a Georgetown hotel, and then Adams followed in a crowd of dignitaries. Three steamboats took the group to the entrance of the Potomac Canal, where they switched into smaller canal boats to reach its head, near the border with Maryland. There they disembarked. The president of the company made a brief speech and handed a spade to Adams, who began to address the two thousand or so onlookers. But in that distant era no advance man was available to ensure that nothing unexpected or actually spontaneous happened, and Adams found that the first strike of his spade clanged against the stump of a tree. So did the second and the third. At this point, Adams later recorded, "I threw off my jacket"—perhaps for the first time in public—"and, resuming the spade, raised a shovelful of earth, at which a general shout burst from the surrounding multitude, and I completed my address, which occupied about fifteen minutes."

By the time Adams returned to the White House that night, he was exhausted. He felt relieved that he hadn't made a fool of himself. And he realized that the real event of the day had been not the speech but the doffing of his jacket. This was the kind of folksy gesture politicians made even then—but not men of Adams' generation or background. He was shocked at the effect. "It struck the eye and fancy of the spectators more than all the flowers of rhetoric in my speech." At age sixty, Adams had discovered politics. He might even have been good at it, but it was a little late.

ADAMS LEFT FOR QUINCY IN EARLY AUGUST—WITHOUT LOUISA. The relationship between the two of them had reached its nadir. Louisa told Charles that she and the president now saw one another only at meals. "I cannot bear the loneliness of my life," she confessed. She would stay in Washington, she wrote, since "your father had much rather go without me." She herself wouldn't want to stay at Quincy, and it would only provoke talk if she stayed elsewhere. Also, Mary was pregnant and helpless—"one of the greatest sufferers I have ever seen," said Louisa, herself a past master. To George she sent the kind of romantic verse he had a weakness for, but which would have embarrassed Charles. She wrote a ballad about a shipwreck full of foaming seas and watery graves. Louisa had been preoccupied with death, and actively yearned for it, since the death of her infant daughter fifteen years earlier. At times she blamed her husband for her deep depression, though at other moments she accused herself, with equal abandon, of having given up on life.

In Quincy, Adams went swimming with George and John, dined with old friends, attended commencement at Harvard, and went fishing with Tom. He visited the Atheneum to see the Gilbert Stuart portraits, including of himself and his father. Gardening remained the great solace of his life. Around the house he planted peaches, plums, apricots, and cherries, as well as chestnuts, oaks, walnuts, and apple trees. In early September he received a note—it's not clear from whom—saying that Louisa was very ill. Whatever the state of feeling between them, Adams was always provoked into panic by Louisa's bouts of illness. He wrote to say that he would leave as soon as possible, and sent George and John out to Medford to ask Charles to accompany him—perhaps because he knew that Charles was his wife's favorite, or perhaps because he needed Charles' company at what he feared would be a heavy moment. Charles reached Washington to find that Louisa was being bled and blistered, encased in a plaster of mud and cayenne. But Louisa often seemed to be at death's door before recovering, and soon she was convalescent and then riding in a carriage. She wrote her first letter to George in mid-October—the election, she reported, was still looking hopeful.

That was true: in the era before polling, it was possible to be wildly deluded about the outcome of an election. Adams had resigned himself to losing months, if not years, before. But as late as November 5, Webster was writing to a friend that the auguries were good; Maryland, he thought, would decide the outcome. The president and Rush, he thought, would carry New England and much of the mid-Atlantic including New York, plus Kentucky, Ohio, Indiana, and Louisiana. He was still forwarding money to key newspaper publishers. Clay, better attuned, calculated that Adams needed to win five of six borderline states. When he learned soon afterward that Kentucky had gone to Jackson, he finally lost hope. Returns trickled in to Washington slowly. By November 30, Clay could write simply to Webster, "We are beaten." On December 3, Adams learned that he had lost—only the second president to be denied a second term, the first of course having been his father. But John Adams had lost a close race; this one was a rout. Jackson and Calhoun had won the electoral college 178 to 83. Adams was confined to New England and the mid-Atlantic (not including New York). The popular vote was twice the size of the 1824 figure, and Jackson won 56 percent of the total.

Adams did not feel humiliated by his defeat, but he did feel abandoned by his country. "The sun of my political career sets in deepest gloom," he wrote in his journal. "But that of the country shines unclouded." He hoped to return quietly to Quincy, the home of his ancient relations and his dearest friends. But he was denied even this, for the perpetual turbulence of his life would accompany him home. In mid-October, the *National Intelligencer* had published a letter Thomas Jefferson had written three years earlier recalling a long-ago correspondence in which Adams had allegedly asserted that the Federalists had conspired to help the British cause during the War of 1812. This presumably represented a last-ditch effort to blacken Adams' reputation, even though he had broken with the Federalists by that time.

Adams felt that he had no choice but to correct the historical record, and wrote to the *Intelligencer* explaining that Jefferson had garbled his history so many years after the fact. Jefferson must have seen a letter Adams had written to Senator William Giles of Virginia in late 1808, in the midst of the furious debate over imposing an embargo on British shipping in retaliation for British attacks on American merchant ships, and not during the war itself. Adams had written that tempers in New England were running so high that the enforcement of an embargo could lead to a confrontation between federal troops and the state militias. A politician of even moderate discretion, facing the contest of his lifetime, would have let the story lie there. But Adams had to pursue the truth, as he understood it, to the bitter end. And so he went on to note that, should such a confrontation have occurred, the Federalists would have sided with Great Britain, for they had planned since the Louisiana Purchase to dissolve the Union. Of this he had unequivocal evidence.

Boston had long forgiven, if perhaps not altogether forgotten, Adams' caucusing with the Republicans in 1808, his vote for nonintercourse, his acceptance of a diplomatic post from a Republican president. And now he had reminded everyone of that bitter moment. He was the president of the United States but nonetheless a traitor to his class, as he had been twenty years earlier. Though he had not named names, Charles wrote to say that "the whole body of the Federalists including your warmest personal friends consider themselves pointed at." A group of fourteen leading figures released a public letter denying that they had conspired to secede in the aftermath of the Louisiana Purchase. Adams knew that many of these men, including Harrison Gray Otis and George Cabot, had been among the conspirators of the day. He persuaded William Plumer to write him a letter admitting that he and others had plotted "to establish a separate government in New England." But that did not quiet the howls from Boston. Adams worried that he would be ostracized. He, of course, could live with that. But what of his family? In his letter Charles wrote that he didn't know whether his father planned to pursue the matter once he returned home but reminded him plaintively that "the prospects of your family depend very considerably on the result." How would Charles get respectable clients if the Adams name became a stain rather than a badge of honor?

The president, too, had worries about his future. He had tended to his investments with great care. Nevertheless, ex-presidents received no pension and were expected to withdraw from public life. Jefferson had run through his savings, and his daughter had become a public charge. This great man's fate loomed before Adams as a terrifying precedent. In the spring of 1828 Harvard had discreetly approached Adams to see if he would serve as president of the college should he not win reelection—a promotion, one imagines, in the eyes of the university administration—but Adams spurned the offer as he had the last time it had been made, a quarter of a century earlier. He was, he said, too broken-down. But how would he support his family as a pariah? He wrote draft after draft of a response to the Federalists, trying to state the truth without his usual asperity.

During his last months in office, Adams read, and worked, and exercised, and met with visitors, as he had for the last four years. "This is a happy condition of life," he reflected at the end of January, already missing a job he had so often regarded as a barely supportable burden. He was advised to attend his successor's inauguration, as previous presidents had done, but he could not bring himself to do it. He had heard, correctly, that Jackson blamed him for the disgraceful calumnies published about himself and his wife. Adams had known nothing about Webster and Clay's secret confabulations with Charles Hammond, but Jackson would never believe that. His anger blazed into unappeasable wrath when his beloved Rachel took sick and died—of a broken heart, Jackson believed—only days after he learned that he would be president.

At the end of February, Louisa, Mary, and the rest of the household left for Meridian Hill, a neoclassical mansion situated on a hill directly north of the White House. On March 3, the day before the Inauguration, the president received the resignation of his cabinet members. At noon, along with John and his nephew Thomas, he rode to the Capitol to sign legislation for the last time. The three men walked back to the White House. That night, at nine, they left for Meridian Hill. Adams could look back from his temporary home and see the yet finer house he had just vacated. Underneath the stoical face he habitually turned to the world, Adams felt misunderstood, mistreated, and abandoned.

PART V

THE SLAVOCRACY

CHAPTER 28

Stay Thy Hand, God of Mercy

(1829–1831)

I N THE SPRING OF 1829, EX-PRESIDENT JOHN QUINCY ADAMS settled into a new life as a private citizen in Washington, DC. He found his new routines surprisingly agreeable. Meridian Hill was large, comfortable, well situated. Adams had a study upstairs whose window overlooked a garden and a nursery of young trees he delighted to gaze at. Then he would turn his attention back to the letters he was writing or the rather frivolous novel he was reading. Like many a stern father, he doted on his grandchild; Louisa wrote to Charles that his father was smitten with John and Mary's daughter, also named Louisa. He was, she wrote, happier than she had ever known him to be. He took long rides on his horse, Governor, revolving lines of poetry in his head or simply listening and thinking as he passed through the woods. He wondered "whether in the history of any animal other than man there are dead languages." Frogs made a noise like "brekekekex koax koax," which, he recalled, "was the language of frogs in Homer's time." Thus did John Quincy Adams savor his retirement. "After 14 years of incessant and unremitting employment," he wrote, "I have passed to a life of total leisure."

Still, Adams could not use the word "leisure" without an undertone of self-accusation: the inner goad urging him on to the next battle never fully relaxed. He worried about what he would do with himself now that his public life had come to an end. He could not simply retire to the farm and the garden, as his father had very contentedly done. He needed employment; more than that, he needed controversy. His chief plan was to write a biography of his father, a vindication of a great man who had been brought low by the scheming of his contemporaries, above all Jefferson and Hamilton. He would not stint on their bitter quarrels. Perhaps, he thought, the manuscript would have to be sealed until after his death. He could think of no other project that seemed fully worthy of his remaining years.

The new administration studiously ignored the former president. The only member of the new cabinet to visit Adams was Martin Van Buren, the secretary of state, who knew very well that in politics today's enemy could be tomorrow's ally. Adams attributed the cold shoulder from the new team to a sense of guilt: "They hate the man they have wronged," he wrote proudly. He took comfort from the follies of the Jackson administration, whose prodigies of patronage quickly became legend in his circle. The only principles governing the White House, Adams wrote ten days after Jackson took office, are "to feed the cormorant appetite for place, and to reward the prostitution of canvassing defamers."

Nevertheless, it was almost possible for Adams and Louisa to see a calm and settled future unroll before them. Their son John was working at the Columbia Mills, a granary Adams had purchased several years earlier in the hopes of gaining a steady source of income. Charles was engaged to marry into one of the finest families of the Boston area. Only George portended trouble. Louisa had asked Charles to look in on his older brother, and the reports he sent to Washington were extremely alarming. George's rooms in the home of their friends the Welshes were a pigsty, and he seemed to see no one and do almost nothing. "He complains of dejection, low spirits and inability to occupy himself," Charles wrote. He dwells upon "reflections of a melancholy kind in regard to father and himself."

George's life had, in fact, become more desperate than any of them knew. He had begun an affair with Eliza Dolph, the Welshes' chambermaid. In early 1828 Eliza had become pregnant, a fact the Welshes appear to have agreed to keep secret. Eliza gave birth at the end of the year, and in January an intermediary had succeeded in placing Eliza and the child in rented rooms. The landlord, Miles Farmer, had insisted that the father visit no more than twice a week, and then always in company. George sent a letter of introduction promising to honor the terms. But George apparently had a fight with Eliza, for in early April he showed up at the house—drunk, perhaps—noisily arguing with his mistress and demanding to take possession of the furniture. Farmer then kicked him out of the house, ordering him never to return.

George had finally acceded to his mother's fervent plea that he come to Washington. But by the time he started out, in the last days of April, the Adams' eldest son was in a catastrophic mental state. He felt certain that his father would soon learn of his shameful behavior, which would blacken the family name—what John Quincy Adams held so dear. He had no prospects either of work or of family. The combination of despair and terror finally made him snap. George began to hear voices. The birds, he felt, were speaking to him. He was certain that someone was trying to break into his room, and he leapt out of bed in order to seize the perpetrator.

George left Boston for Providence, where, on April 29, he boarded the steamer *Benjamin Franklin*. During the afternoon, he held a long conversation with a fellow passenger. He spoke, calmly, of the harrowing hallucinations he had experienced. He was, he said, having them again. The wheels of the steamship, rolling over and over, seemed to be whispering a phrase to him: "Let it be." "Let it be." "Let it be."

George was now in the full grip of his paranoid delusions. He returned to his berth, got up in the night, accused a stranger of plotting against him, and then went with a candle from room to room. At three in the morning he approached the captain and asked to be put ashore to escape the machinations of his fellow passengers. The ship was then churning through the Long Island Sound at sixteen knots; there could be no stopping. George then wandered to the upper deck, where he spoke briefly to a Mr. Stevens. A few minutes later, Stevens looked to the railing and saw that George was gone, but his hat and cloak remained behind. A search of the boat showed that he was nowhere to be found.

At one P.M. on May 2, Nathaniel Frye, Louisa's brother-in-law and a close family friend, came to Meridian Hill to see Adams.

"Have you received a letter today?," he asked. Adams said that he had not.

"Have you heard anything of George?" Adams had not. And then Frye, who had hoped to be spared this heavy task, told him that the Baltimore papers were carrying a story that George had vanished from the deck of the *Benjamin Franklin*. His cousin William Cranch came with the same news and brought three letters confirming the event.

Adams thought first of Louisa, whose unspeakable grief over the death of her daughter he could never forget. "Stay thy hand, God of

mercy," he wrote. "Let her not say, My God! My God! Why has thou for-
saken me?" Adams still stood, but split, like a tree hit by lightning. The
loss of his daughter, terrible though it was, had happened by degrees, so
that he had almost welcomed her final release from suffering. George's
death was the greatest shock he had ever received. He felt his sanity slip-
ping away. "My thoughts are so wandering that I distrust the operation
of my own reason," he wrote. Adams tried to put aside his own feelings in
order to minister to his stricken wife. The two spent long hours together
in prayer. Adams' selfless generosity toward Louisa put an end to the terrible estrangement of the last few years—a strange, unlooked-for gift
from poor George.

Louisa had urged her husband to treat George with more tenderness
than was natural to him. Now she might well have blamed him for George's
death. Many years later—it's not clear when—Louisa wrote an extraordinary note to herself about this dreadful time. At a moment when, she
wrote, "my beloved husband's sufferings were alas beyond controul, I was
so fearful that my full heart might betray its agony in the language of reproach, and thereby add to his misery that I think I begged him whatever I
might say in my wanderings not to believe me." She wished to declare—to
herself and to posterity—that she had "no terror of conscience or of guilt."
Of course, the fact that Louisa felt the need to make this solemn avowal
shows how close to the surface this terrible thought was.

Adams did not in fact feel responsible for George's torment or his death.
A few months earlier he had written to Charles to defend himself from the
charge of cold-heartedness. "You and all my children know that while my
speech is sometimes harsh, my temper is not bad." He lacked charm, but he
failed "more by overindulgence than by asperity." Neither his children nor
his wife would have been likely to accept this self-assessment. Adams was
not a good father; he was, in truth, difficult to live with. But that is not to
say that he was responsible for George's dreaminess, his fecklessness, or of
course his ultimate psychic break. Charles, an acute and mostly dispassionate judge, felt that if anything his father had spared George the harsh judgment he deserved. One might, in fact, just as easily connect George's suicide
to his mother's own obsession with death as the deliverance from suffering,
conveyed to him in one letter after another.

Up in Boston, Charles went through George's trunk and found a note
George had written to him the year before declaring that, should he die
that year, whatever remained after his debts had been settled should be
paid "to a little girl who he had seduced and was then pregnant by him to

the best of his belief." Charles was just the kind of hardheaded young gentleman who knew how to dispose of such a problem. He destroyed the letter, reasoning that its strictures no longer held, as George had in fact died in 1829. Nevertheless, he vowed to himself to find the young woman and "preserve her from destruction." There is no evidence that he actually did so.

Weeks passed before Adams was able to resume work. On May 21, the *New Bedford Mercury* published a poem by George titled *The Spark at Sea*, which seemed both to strangely foretell his fate and to enfold it in a morbid and melancholy beauty:

> There is a little spark at sea
> Which grows 'mid darkness brilliantly,
> But when the moon looks clear and bright,
> Emits a pale and feeble light,
> And when the tempest shakes the wave
> It glimmers o'er the seaman's grave

Adams was deeply moved not only by the eerie adumbration but by the tone of tenderness and delicacy that so forcefully reminded him of George's own nature.

On June 11, Adams and his son John left for Quincy. Louisa was too sick to travel and in any case needed to stay with Mary and the child. On the ferry to New York, Adams read a paragraph in a New York paper saying that three days earlier George's body had washed ashore on City Island, in what is now the Bronx. Putting in at New York, Adams learned that the body had been taken to the tomb of an Episcopalian church in Eastchester, immediately to the north. A coroner had already performed the inquest. Adams was brought to the underground vault, where George lay in a plain mahogany casket. He received George's effects. His son's watch had stopped at 3:44, thus fixing the moment he had plunged into the chill waters. That gave Adams a terrible shock. But he dutifully catalogued every object found in George's pockets: "pocket book and papers, a loose shirt collar, silver pencil, comb, snuffbox, double penknife, a purse with about 2 dollars in change, and the key to his trunk." Late that night, Adams sat down to tell Louisa the news, addressing her as "my most beloved friend." He told her about each article and said that he hoped she would be soothed to learn that "the person was entire, without mark of violence or contusion." He had not, that is, been murdered.

Louisa wrote back with the identical endearment, saying that the letter had indeed reduced her agony. In the ensuing months they wrote one another constantly, always with the greatest tenderness; they had never before so utterly depended on each another, even though they were apart.

ADAMS ARRIVED IN QUINCY JUNE 18. THE HOUSE LOOKED EMPTY, for his brother Tom had decamped with his family a few months before. Here was a gloomy reception to suit his mood. Charles saw in his father a quality of "quiet sadness" he had never glimpsed before. Adams filled his days with activity. He puttered in the garden. He tried to settle the estate of his late friend and relation Nicholas Ward Boylston, who had named him as executor. He did his best to organize the house, ordering bookshelves and virtually hemming himself in with books in his bedroom. He planned to build a stone schoolhouse in memory of his father on land his father had donated to the town. He thought of building a fine new house for the family, which elicited a quick response from Louisa: Don't do anything until I get there. They could still rub each other the wrong way. Louisa apologized for having "as usual imagined myself of more consequence than I ought to be." Adams concluded that he had far too many debts to afford a new house in any case.

Most crucial of all, Adams began to put his father's papers in order with a view to writing the great biography. He and Charles hauled John Adams' papers into the library and began filing them. He found diary entries as far back as 1755, when his father was eighteen. He read old church records and wandered among ancient tombstones. But he seemed to be perpetually organizing and reorganizing, as if recoiling before the task itself. Adams devoted most of his attention to a mighty rhodomontade on the Federalist secession plot. It was bloody-minded work, for Adams still seethed at the men who had ejected him from the US Senate in 1808, "the mouldering relics" of the Essex Junto who had hatched the secession plan, and above all his former friend, Harrison Gray Otis. He sent a draft to Charles, who counted these men and their sons among his closest associates. Charles returned a copy with marks on "the passages which I thought bitter and personal," and advised his father to swallow his wrath and put the manuscript on the shelf.

Adams was now living with the consequences of his apostasy. He was persona non grata at the Otises and the Dexters and several other leading Boston families. He was summarily replaced as president of the American Academy of Arts and Sciences, the distinguished body he had headed for the previous decade. (His father had been the first president.) Perhaps he decided to sue for peace. Whatever the cause, Adams acknowledged to himself that the project had become an unseemly exercise in revenge and agreed not to publish.

On September 3, Charles was married to Abby Brooks at Medford. Louisa had hoped to attend, but she had gotten no further than New York before turning back owing to sickness (her own and baby Louisa's). Adams was very fond of Charles' sparkling and well-born bride. He wrote her jaunty letters in which he asked her to report any good jokes she had heard (very much as his father had to Louisa). He told her that on a stagecoach ride in New Jersey he had found himself with a lovely young flirt who was offering sugarplums to her fellow passengers in exchange for witticisms. Flummoxed, he had held his tongue and then lain awake that night composing a twenty-four-line poem imagining the good fortune of the man who would some day win her love. He delivered it to her the following morning.

Adams came to rely more and more on the levelheaded, worldly, and ambitious Charles. Throughout the summer he spoke to his youngest son of his role as family scion, of the great family name he must help perpetuate. When his father finally left Quincy at the end of the year, Charles noted that the unyielding lawgiver he had (privately) railed against in years past had been "unusually kind" and that he actually missed him. A few days later, Charles wrote his father a long and uncharacteristically confessional letter in which he said he was very conscious of the "responsible position" he now occupied and was determined to do something useful with his life. As yet, he admitted, he had accomplished nothing. Now he had a settled home life, a house in Boston thanks to his generous father-in-law, and ample time for study. He had set himself three projects: to study the eloquence of the ancient writers, to improve his own writing style, and to master the history of his own nation. But how to go about it? Charles admitted that he felt overwhelmed.

His father, utterly delighted, wrote back professing his wholehearted approval and suggesting a program of self-improvement. Try your hand at different forms—the oration, the sermon, the dissertation. Vary the style. Once you're satisfied, publish it anonymously, and then learn from the reaction. He proposed that they once again begin reading Cicero together. Charles, who had reached an age and a stage in life when he no longer felt the need to resist his overbearing father, eagerly complied and wrote long letters with his thoughts, which often differed from his father's. "Your epistles and those of Cicero are my delight," the elder man wrote back. Adams had also transferred the handling of his funds to Charles, the first family member he found he could trust. Each man depended on the other and freely acknowledged it—a relationship very much like the one the younger John Quincy Adams had had with his own father.

The same could not be said for Adams' relationship with John. Adams' middle son was the businessman in the family, and Adams entertained fond hopes that John would earn enough money to support not only himself but his parents. He was managing the Columbia Mills, which Adams had bought from a cousin of Louisa's. But John was a self-centered young man who enjoyed his cigar and his pleasures. Louisa considered him weak-willed and wholly under the thumb of his domineering wife. As a businessman he was rash and unrealistic; the mill never turned a profit, though John continued to insist that its prospects were bright. In October he wrote to his father asking him to pour thousands more into the mill, and Adams responded gently that he feared his son's "calculations may be a little over-sanguine."

Adams worried that he would ultimately suffer the humiliating poverty that had eventually engulfed Jefferson and even Monroe, who had not been a spendthrift. His parents had survived only by prodigies of austerity—and his own assistance. Adams had always put aside money to invest in government bonds and US bank stock, in companies building bridges and turnpikes, and above all in real estate in and around Boston and Washington. Nevertheless, he was supporting not only his immediate family but relatives as well; he was paying the tuition of his nephew, John Quincy, at Exeter. In buying his father's house and land from the estate, he had incurred a $12,000 debt to his nephews, to be paid as they reached majority. He had looked to the mill as the family salvation. Its failure filled him with anxiety about the future.

If the mill was going to drain rather than fortify his stock of capital, Adams would have to depend on his investments and above all on rent from his property. Charles had found that George had never bothered to collect most of the rent and had left a skein of debts. He had begun taking over the management of the property. As he worked more closely with his father, he came to conclude that in matters of business his progenitor was more a theorist than a practitioner. "He is a singular man with regard to the management of his property," he reflected.

ADAMS WAITED IN QUINCY UNTIL GEORGE'S REMAINS ARRIVED, ON November 24. He saw to it that George was deposited alongside his aunt

Nabby and close to his grandparents in the cemetery of Quincy's Unitarian church. On December 3 he left for Washington with no purpose in mind and no occupation in view.

What was Adams even doing in Washington? Ex-presidents retired to their country seats and received visits. Adams had no role to play in the new era of President Jackson. He and Louisa had, however, agreed that a warm climate would be beneficial for her frail health. And John and Mary lived there with little Louisa and baby Georgiana Francis, known as Fanny. Meridian Hill having been sold, the elder Adamses moved into the home Mary and John had been able to build at 1601 I Street with Mary's inheritance from Walter Hellen. For the ex-president, all this was a welcome pretext to stay close to the center of national political life—and far away from the thorns of Boston.

Adams busied himself with a number of projects. He wrote a long article about the Russo-Turkish war for the *American Annual Register*, a publication owned by his friend Joseph Blunt. He rode out to Maryland with John to look over the Columbia Mills. He received regular visits from members of the National Republican opposition seeking to enlist him in a more active role. He had initially taken the view that the path unrolling before the nation was so smooth that there would be little to fear from whatever changes in policy President Jackson introduced. That optimism was bound to dwindle. Jackson had shown his true colors in his first message to Congress, or so Adams and his friends believed.

In that first message, Jackson had not only disposed of the Adams agenda root and branch but apparently sought to return the national political life to the era of Jefferson. The new president had virtually endorsed the states' rights position the slave-owning South had come to profess with growing fervor. He bluntly warned against "all encroachments upon the legitimate sphere of State sovereignty." He proposed, in an early version of "revenue sharing," that whatever federal surplus emerged with the retirement of the national debt be returned to the states, in proportion to their representation in Congress (thus aiding the South, where each slave was counted as three-fifths of a person for electoral purposes). Internal improvements would be left to the discretion of the states. He declared, in regard to tariff reform, that the "agricultural interest" was "so superior in importance" to all others that it scarcely needed stating; manufacturing and commerce mattered only insofar as they tended to "increase the value of agricultural productions."

Like the new men of the West, Jackson spoke of the national government with something approaching scorn. He described federal officeholders as corrupt time-servers, and suggested that since their duties "are so plain and simple" that "men of intelligence may readily qualify themselves for their performance," no federal employee should serve for longer than four years—a convenient rationale for a wholesale purging of Adams-era officials in favor of Jackson loyalists. (In his first year in office, Jackson removed 10 percent of all federal officeholders, more than all of his predecessors combined.) Jackson also used his first message to advocate a policy of wholesale removal of Indians beyond the Mississippi, albeit a "voluntary" one. He would sign legislation to do just that in late May 1830. At the same time, he issued vetoes of several bills authorizing expenditures for internal improvements. Jackson enjoyed a popular mandate Adams had never had, and he was intent on using it to put the country on a course radically different from the one Adams had sought. Adams' usual sense of looming catastrophe now returned with a vengeance. Richard Rush, his former running mate, came by for a chat. "We agreed," Adams recorded, "that the Indians are already sacrificed; that the public lands will be given away; that domestic industry and internal improvements will be strangled."

Adams derived bitter satisfaction from the new administration's peccadilloes. He sent letters to Charles and to Abby describing the White House fracas over Peggy Eaton, a tavernkeeper's daughter whom Jackson's secretary of war and close confidante, John Eaton, had married and whom the wives of other cabinet members and of Vice President Calhoun refused to meet. Secretary of State Van Buren, a widower who had no problem meeting Mrs. Eaton socially, adroitly used the issue to further turn the president against Calhoun. Jackson was deeply reluctant to move against Eaton; Van Buren ultimately persuaded the president to ask the entire cabinet to resign, an unprecedented upheaval that allowed him to remove Eaton from office without singling him out. Adams, who had never fired a cabinet member, gloried in the evidence of his successor's recklessness. The underlying truth, however, was that Jackson's willingness to take bold and sometimes brutal measures made him a far more effective chief executive than Adams had ever been. Adams did not manage to expand the role of the federal government, but Jackson did succeed in shrinking it, even as he significantly expanded the powers of the presidency.

ADAMS LEFT WASHINGTON AT THE END OF MAY. BACK IN QUINCY, he found that hundreds of the trees he had lovingly planted at the old family estate of Wollaston had died over the winter. Why, he wondered, had the horse chestnuts, elms, peaches, plums, apples, and apricots largely survived, while the oaks had not? Why had some trees of a species flourished, while others died? Horticultural societies, he thought, should take up a systematic study of fruit trees and of the insects that destroy them. Adams found that his rheumatism limited his own spade work; for the heavy labor he turned to his gardener, Augustus Farrar. Every summer and fall in the years to come, Adams and Farrar would spend countless hours planting seedlings, transplanting young trees from the cellar, and uprooting by the thousands those that had not survived.

Adams' battle with the elements over the lives of his beloved fruit trees constitutes one of the great subjects of his journal in the last decades of his life. Adams loved flowers, but they were evanescent. Trees endured; they could, if well planted and nurtured, defy time and live far beyond the span of the gardener himself. This was not so much a Christian conceit as a classical one, and Adams, like the Roman thinkers he revered, cherished the thought of his posterity. One day in late October, after he and Farrar had planted eighty grafted Baldwin apple trees in Mount Wollaston, he reflected that the mansion and the farm had been in the family for 190 years, since the very founding of the town. "It is now pregnant," he wrote, "with at least ten thousands seeds of fruit and forest, mostly placed by my hand, and in a century from this day may bear timber for the floating castles of my country, and fruit for the subsistence, health and comfort of my descendants."

Adams awoke before dawn every day, read the Bible and Cicero, went swimming and riding, walked over his land, wrote letters to Charles and to dozens of friends and strangers, and tended to Louisa, who was afflicted with one of the worst outbreaks of erysipelas she had ever suffered. He wrote down absolutely everything in his journal, in a hand that had become so tiny, if still perfectly legible, that he often squeezed 650 words into a single small page. But it wasn't enough. He was bored and restless. "My leisure is now imposed on me by the will of higher powers," he reflected. "Shall I never do better?"

On September 17, Adams attended a reception at the home of Lieutenant Governor Winthrop after a celebration of Boston's two hundredth anniversary. He was approached by his old friend Edward Everett, who asked what he would think of standing for Congress from the Eighth District, which included Quincy. The incumbent, Joseph Richardson, had decided not to run, and local leaders had concluded that none of the available candidates was likely to gain a majority, which meant according to state law that the district would send no representative to Congress. Adams, and only Adams, could easily carry the day. Several local newspapers had mooted the idea.

Richardson himself came to Adams to confirm that he would not run and helpfully observed that should Adams do so, he would raise the office rather than degrade himself. Adams replied stiffly that he didn't think an ex-president would be degraded "by serving as a selectman of his town, if elected thereto by the people." But he would make no promise; any such decision would depend on his own health and the nature of the opposition. Since Adams' frame was strong enough for the job and then some, this was his way of saying that he would not take part in a seriously contested election. The job was not beneath his dignity, but a campaign would be. Richardson, who had assured him that the seat would be his for the asking, said that he was satisfied with Adams' response and would get to work.

Several of Adams' neighbors and supporters came by to confirm that he was a legal resident of Quincy, since as president his residence had been listed as Boston. He confirmed that he was. John Bailey, the veteran representative of the adjacent Norfolk district, asked Adams what he should tell the many people who asked him if the former president would stand. "To say that I would accept would be so near asking for a vote," Adams responded, "that I do not feel disposed to go so far. I wish the people to act spontaneously, at their own discretion." Anyone who knew Adams at all understood that this meant yes. On November 13, the National Republicans placed his name in nomination. On December 6 Adams became Plymouth's representative in Congress, winning 1,817 of 2,545 votes.

No president before Adams had ever gone on to serve in the House; no president after him ever would. (Andrew Johnson would serve briefly in the Senate after his tenure as president.) Both Charles and Louisa had asked him not to stand for office. Louisa was so upset that she refused to return with him to Washington, even though that meant doing without her adored grandchildren. Adams himself reflected that his new role "has drifted me back again amidst the breakers of the political ocean." But the breakers beckoned to Adams more than any gentle swell ever could. And the election was sweet vindication. His old friends had deserted him. Otis had tried to destroy him. He thought of a line from an opera about Richard the Lion-Hearted: "*O Richard! O mon roi! L'univers t'abandonne*" (O Richard! O my king! The world is forsaking you.) Adams had persevered. His election as president, he reflected, "was not half so gratifying to my inmost soul." What he could not know then was that his sixteen-year tenure in

Congress would be far more gratifying to his soul, and to the nation, than his time as president had been.

ADAMS WOULD NOT TAKE OFFICE AS THE REPRESENTATIVE FROM Plymouth until the new Congress convened in December 1831. Nevertheless, he left for Washington at the end of 1830 and remained there through the spring. The beleaguered opposition welcomed him as a celebrity in their midst. Adams recorded receiving three hundred visitors at John and Mary's house on President's Park at a New Year's Day reception. Opposition leaders like Edward Everett asked him to help formulate the response to Jackson's second annual message to Congress. Adams was scarcely a source of optimism. He told Philip Fendall, an essayist who hoped to write a biography of him, that Jackson's opposition to internal improvements and domestic manufacture was bound to be more popular than the American System because the first reduced the need for revenue, while the second increased it. "Of the two systems," he wrote, in words today's liberal Democrats would find all too familiar, "that of the Administration sacrifices the future and remote benefits to the present, and therefore addresses itself more to the prejudices and feelings of the people."

Adams was not yet ready to plunge back into politics. He spent much of his time alone, reading. He read Jefferson's memoirs, which had just been published, and was struck anew by the man's gifts and foibles. Jefferson, he thought, was too indulgent with himself to accept truths adverse to his own happiness, including the evils of slavery, which he intellectually understood. He had "a memory so pandering to the will, that in deceiving others he seems to have begun by deceiving himself." He had no fear of God or the afterlife. "The tendency of this condition upon a mind of great compass and powerful resources is to produce insincerity and duplicity, which were his besetting sins throughout life." Jefferson, in short, was the very type of a man with great talents but weak principles. Adams wrote a review of the volume for Alexander Everett's *North American Review*.

In early February, Adams endured a terrible bout of the inflammation of the eyes from which he had long suffered. At times he had to lie in bed in the darkness. He dictated to Louisa a letter for Charles, which included a poem on his condition: "Of my two orbs of vision one / Has caught fire; and while it burns / Swollen, bloodshot, from the blessed sun / And Heaven's faint light it turns." Perhaps Adams was thinking of Milton's great verses on his own blindness. Barely able to read or write, Adams began to compose verses in his head, as he had done off and on for most of his life. Since he knew the Bible virtually by heart, he commenced by rewriting the Psalms. And he meditated something far more ambitious. The previous fall, he had read several biographies of Lord Byron, a Jefferson-like figure whose gifts he admired and whose morals he abhorred. When his vision cleared, he began reading some of Byron's mock epic poems, including "Beppo," written in Dante's *ottava rima*. The ex-president, the old Federalist with the blood of the Puritans coursing through his veins, began to turn over in his mind the project of a satirical epic in *ottava rima*.

Adams had long meditated on the story of the English conquest of Ireland told in Hume's *History of England*, which he had first read in St. Petersburg at age fourteen. According to Hume, a twelfth-century Irish prince, Dermot MacMorrogh, had cuckolded a fellow king's wife, been driven from Ireland, enlisted the English King Henry II in a plot to conquer Ireland on behalf of England, invaded the island at the head of British troops, and overthrown its kings before himself being murdered, thus opening the way for the English dominion over Ireland that persisted to that day. Hume had described Henry as the very model of an English sovereign, whereas to Adams the narrative exemplified the licentiousness, brutality, and bald ambition that drives men to war and conquest and ultimately leads to the prostration of one nation before another. And the story of a legitimate king overthrown by an unscrupulous usurper now had a personal resonance, which Adams would scarcely have felt as a boy in Russia.

In early March, his eyes still smarting from his affliction, Adams took off on long walks at dawn along Pennsylvania Avenue, lost in thought as he arranged the scansion and meter of his Byronic stanzas. At first Adams made a game effort to keep up a tone of Byronic raillery, but it was too foreign to his nature, and before long he had lapsed into solemn moralizing. "All my attempts at humor evaporated in the first canto," he reflected. Adams felt ashamed of how far his efforts fell short of his Byronic model, yet he had fallen into the grip of "a rhyming fit." He would wake up in the middle of the night and compose five more stanzas by dawn. Then he would take his walk, write more stanzas in his head, and finally write it all down after breakfast. At night he would read the new portion to Louisa. Originally planned for fifty stanzas, *Dermot* grew to two hundred, and then more.

Adams finally put down *Dermot* on April 16. It ran over two thousand lines and contained a few absurdities and several quite touching verses. He wondered if he should throw it in the fire. If he didn't, it may be because his object was as much polemical as poetical. Charles Edel, a recent Adams biographer, argues that Adams intended *Dermot* as an allegory of his own tenure. In the preface Adams observes that the old king, Roderick O'Conner, "could not unite the people in any measures, either for the establishment of order, of for defence against foreigners." The moral of the tale, Edel asserts, is: "moral decay presaged and led to national decline." Yet Adams was not content to be the kind of pamphleteer-poet who prated about Washington on the Delaware. He knew very well what great poetry sounded like and yearned with all his soul to produce it. Alas, he couldn't.

Dermot was published in late 1832; the author received $100. Adams had copies sent to his friends, who duly wrote back to say that it was the finest thing he had written. Several loyal newspapers printed excerpts and published warm reviews. But Adams' Irish epic was not widely reviewed or admired. Readers may have had trouble separating the poem's esthetic merits from their views of its author, who was neither popular nor thought to be endowed with a deep reservoir of imagination. It is, however, safe to say that *Dermot MacMorrogh* is the greatest romantic epic ever composed by a former US president.

CHAPTER 29

Our Union: It Must Be Preserved

(1831–1833)

I N A LETTER WRITTEN IN THE SPRING OF 1830, JOHN QUINCY Adams sardonically observed that "a discovery has been made of a new attribute of state sovereignty, the right of every state legislature to *nullify* within the boundaries of the state every act of Congress *palpably unconstitutional.*" In fact the doctrine known as nullification dated back to 1798 and 1799, when the state legislatures of Kentucky and Virginia had declared the Alien and Sedition Acts unconstitutional. (Jefferson had written the Kentucky Resolution, and Madison the Virginia.) In Adams' own time, Georgia had openly challenged the national government over an Indian treaty. The doctrine, however, would only be fully articulated with South Carolina's repudiation of the Tariff of Abominations. The leading men of the state saw the tariff as a threat not only to their prosperity but to their entire slave-based culture. Cotton, the state's great cash crop, would face reciprocal duties in Europe, while American duties would raise the cost of the imported goods on which South Carolina depended.

In late 1828, while Adams was still president, the South Carolina legislature had published a broadside titled *Exposition and Protest*, secretly written by John C. Calhoun. The vice president had claimed that "as an essential attribute of sovereignty," states had the right to nullify federal statutes, such as the tariff, which constituted "an infraction of their powers." The assertion of state supremacy would drain real power from the federal government and return the nation to the era of the Articles of Confederation. Calhoun claimed to be simply building on the foundation laid by Jefferson and Madison. The principle was, however, so self-evidently dangerous that no other Southern state agreed.

The state's congressional delegation pressed the case in Washington. In January 1830, the Senate debated legislation on the sale of public lands. Robert Hayne of South Carolina argued that federal lands should be ceded to the states to dispose of as they wished. Daniel Webster, the Federalist champion, retorted that the federal government must retain jurisdiction over federal property. Hayne now showed his hand, insisting, as Calhoun had, that in a confederated union ultimate sovereignty rested with the states. Now the issue had been joined. Webster rose to deliver a majestic rebuttal in which he argued that the Constitution had been a pact not among states but among people, who had collectively agreed to establish a federal state. This was the speech that ended, "Liberty and union, now and forever, one and inseparable!" It was the most famous congressional oration delivered until that moment; Gales and Seaton of the *National Intelligencer* printed and distributed forty thousand copies.

Adams was deeply impressed by Webster's speech, which, he wrote to his friend Joseph Blunt, "pulverizes" the advocates of nullification. He told Van Buren, who claimed rather improbably not to have followed the debate, that he would do well to read it, for "it is the most important one that has taken place since the existence of the Government." Jackson's initial message to Congress had persuaded Adams, as well as a great many Southerners, that the president would be a friend to nullification. They were wrong, for Jackson was every bit the nationalist Adams was, though he did not share the Hamiltonian belief in an active national government. At a Jefferson Day dinner on April 13, Jackson lifted his glass, pointedly looked at Vice President Calhoun and said, "Our union: It must be preserved." Calhoun, after a moment's hesitation, had equivocally responded, "The union: next to our liberty, most dear." The battle had been joined.

Adams was mulling this great question when he received an invitation from the townspeople of Quincy to deliver the July 4 address on what would be the fifty-fifth anniversary of the signing of the Declaration. He had used his previous Independence Day oration, in 1823, to lay out a new vision of America's place in the world. Now he pondered whether to use this chance to expose the speciousness of the nullification doctrine. "Shall I speak my thoughts," he asked himself, "or shall the fear of man deter me?"

He was, he thought, "bolder in my youth than now." In the end, of course, he spoke his mind. Adams began his oration, as tradition dictated, by speaking of the Revolution, but no one present would have mistaken his real subject. The Declaration, he observed, was issued by "the delegates of thirteen distinct, but UNITED colonies of Great Britain, in the name and behalf of their people." The independence they announced proceeded from the union they declared. The colonies to which the people belonged were not even enumerated, for the Declaration constituted a "primitive social compact" among the peoples of those colonies. This was precisely the argument Webster had made in his debate with Hayne.

Adams now reverted to a familiar topic: England's half-hearted commitment to its own constitutional principles. By what right had Parliament imposed taxes upon the American colonies, which had come into being through charters with the crown and were thus answerable only to the king? Blackstone, the greatest of all British legal authorities, had claimed that sovereignty, by its nature, must rest on "supreme, irresistible, absolute, uncontrolled authority." Parliament had, in effect, availed itself of this species of constitutional absolutism. In fact, Adams said, absolute sovereignty is the doctrine of despotism, not republicanism. In a republic, sovereignty rests with the people, who covenant with one another to form a union, to which they grant limited powers. Adams then proceeded to make the very odd argument that the Articles of Confederation had failed not because citizens had refused to surrender enough sovereignty to the federal government, but because the state legislatures had insisted on retaining absolute power rather than sharing it with the national government. The Constitution had corrected the error. Those American states that asserted a sovereign right to determine the laws of the nation thus sought to annul the Constitution in favor of Blackstone's monstrous doctrine.

Adams had turned nullification on its head: far from a response to the tyranny of an overweening federal government, as its adherents claimed, the doctrine was in fact a form of legislative tyranny. Even Webster hadn't thought to make such an audacious claim. Nothing could be more characteristic of Adams than this combination of erudition, ingenuity, hyperbole, and spleen. His logic felt implacable even when his argument was improbable. This blend of reason and passion made him a fearsome disputant.

This was not, of course, a rhetorical game, but rather the emanation of Adams' own vehement spirit, his deep and abiding sense of peril. Adams had been standing on the side of Union against sectional interest since the drama over the Louisiana Purchase three decades earlier. Now he saw the

Union endangered not by a secret cabal but by a doctrine openly proclaimed and embraced by one of the original states. "Stripped of the sophistical argumentation in which this doctrine has been habited," he cried, "its naked nature is an effort to organize insurrection against the laws of the United States." Nullification sought to substitute force for democratic deliberation. "Let this agent but once intrude upon your deliberations," he told the gathered citizens, and "despotic sovereignties will trample with impunity . . . upon the indefeasible and unalienable rights of man."

A local printer distributed two thousand copies of the address, and then two thousand more. Adams sent copies to the men he regarded as his peers, including the Federalist legal scholar Nathan Dane, and Justices John Marshall and Joseph Story, now delivering lectures at Harvard on sovereignty and nullification. Story wrote back to say that he would cite Adams as an authority for his own views. Marshall stated he had been very much struck, and persuaded, by elements of Adams' argument. Adams had found a way to join and shape this great debate. He sent a copy of his oration to Calhoun, "with the single assurance of regret, that upon topics of transcendent importance, our opinions should be so much at variance with each other."

In many ways the debate between nationalists and nullifiers recapitulated the old tension between Federalists like Alexander Hamilton and anti-Federalists like Jefferson. But by now the irreconcilable economic interests of North and South lent urgency to what was already a profound disagreement over political principle. In the "Fort Hill Address" of July 1831, in which for the first time he made the public case for nullification, Calhoun described the doctrine as a "last resort" to be deployed only in the face of "dangerous infractions of the Constitution." The tariff, imposed on the South by the national government, constituted just such an infraction. The interest of the two regions, he wrote "must, from the nature of things, in reference to the Tariff, be in conflict." What were these "things"? Calhoun did not say; of course he meant slavery. A slave economy could not live by the same rules as one governed by free labor. Neither Adams nor Calhoun had referred to slavery; the issue was everywhere—and nowhere. Within a few years it would be the consuming question of Adams' life.

ADAMS TURNED SIXTY-FOUR IN 1831. THIS HARDLY MADE HIM A fossil by the standards of the day: George Washington was still president at that age, and John Adams was just exiting. But John Quincy Adams had turned old when he was still young; to men who met him for the first time he had the remote majesty of a mountain seen in the distance.

In September 1831 William Seward, later Abraham Lincoln's secretary of state but then a young New York lawyer and aspiring politician, visited Adams at home. Seward recorded his impressions in a letter to a friend. "The house is very plain and old-fashioned," he wrote. "Very plain ingrain carpeting covered the floor, very plain paper on the walls, modern but plain mahogany chairs." On the walls were portraits of John Adams, George Washington, Martha Washington, and Jefferson (whom Adams, for all his misgivings, apparently still venerated). Adams himself was "sober, almost to gloom or sorrow," his eyes inflamed, short, bald, slightly corpulent. He was dressed simply, in an olive frock coat, and seemed to be wearing as well a fine layer of learned dust. "It was obvious that he was a student," Seward wrote, "just called from the labours of his closet."

The two men spoke for three hours, chiefly about politics. "He spoke of General Jackson without one word of reserve or bitterness, or unkindness," wrote Seward, "thought his Administration ruinous, but still doubted not that he would be re-elected." The former president struck his young visitor as very much of a piece with his stolid and rigorously correct furnishings—"plain, honest and free in his discourse; but with hardly a ray of animation or of feeling in the whole of it." Occasionally, Seward noted, "he rose into a temporary earnestness, and then a flash of ingenuous ardor was seen, but it was transitory, and all was cool, orderly and deliberate. . . . As I left the house, I thought I could plainly answer how it happened that he, the best President since Washington, entered and left the office with so few devoted personal friends." But Adams remained a formidable presence. Elsewhere Seward wrote, "His vigor and his resolution astonished me," and said that he had taken inspiration from the old man's slow-burning fire.

Adams left Quincy for Washington in the middle of November. On December 5 he was sworn in and assigned to seat number 203. For all that he was the former president and secretary of state, and was now a veritable ancient of days in the House, Adams was fascinated and delighted by service in Congress. He recorded the most tedious and obscure debates at endless length. He rarely missed a day, or even an hour, of a congressional session. Nothing bored him. The ritual of the calling of the states for the presentation of petitions, which happened every Monday, moved him to splendid flights of rhetoric. In the halls of Congress he saw, and felt, republicanism in action more vividly than he ever had as a member of the executive.

Adams' first act in Congress was the presentation of twelve petitions from citizens in Pennsylvania seeking the abolition of slavery in the District of Columbia, over which the Congress exercised jurisdiction. Such petitions were ritually "laid on the table" and presented to the Committee on the District of Columbia, which consisted largely of slaveholders and ensured that such pleas never saw the light of day. Adams, however, accompanied the presentation with his maiden speech, which he used to make the very strange assertion that he did not believe the issue was suitable for congressional debate. Adams chose not to explain himself at the time. When a Quaker abolitionist paid him a visit a few weeks later, Adams explained that he felt obliged to present petitions from his fellow citizens but saw no point in exacerbating "ill-will" and "heart-burnings" in the House, which would never vote to curb slavery. Besides, he asked, what would Quaker citizens think if the people of the District of Columbia submitted a petition to require all Pennsylvanians to bear arms? For all his hatred of slavery, Adams was not about to waste the precious time of Congress on an ill it was not prepared to address.

The House Speaker, Andrew Stevenson, a Jackson loyalist, informed Adams that he would be chairman of the Committee on Manufactures, a subject that held almost no interest for him (though it was an appropriate post for a representative of Massachusetts). This was probably designed both to prevent Adams from doing real mischief on an important committee like Foreign Affairs or Ways and Means and to signal sympathy to manufacturing interests. Adams tried to work a switch with Edward Everett, who served as deputy chairman on Foreign Affairs, but Stevenson refused. Adams was thus plunged into domestic policy.

Jackson had stated in his annual message that he expected to have fully retired the federal debt by the end of his term. Rather than run a surplus, the president called for a gradual cut in tariff rates. The administration had referred the tariff question to Ways and Means, chaired by George McDuffie of South Carolina, an ardent nullifier who had done his all for Jackson in the last days of the 1824 election. McDuffie soon produced a bill that would drastically lower tariff rates over three years, thus addressing South Carolina's fundamental grievance. This was too much for the Jackson administration, as it was for Adams, who was nevertheless prepared to accept a moderate reduction in order to dampen the fires of nullification. He began working on a compromise position with Treasury Secretary Louis McLane.

The questions of revenue and tariff rates were bound to loom large in the upcoming presidential election. At the end of December, Adams met with other members of the opposition, including Henry Clay, to map out a common strategy. Adams favored modest tariff cuts, which would reduce federal revenue from $28 million to $20 million. It was essential, he argued, to preserve surplus revenue for internal improvements. Clay, the author of the American System, ought to have taken the same view. In fact, Clay insisted that revenues must be slashed all the way to $7 million or $8 million. Adams felt certain that Clay cared less about building turnpikes than he did about denying Jackson the signal triumph of retiring the federal debt, which he would accomplish by plunging revenue below the level of federal expenditure. The National Republicans had already made Clay their candidate for 1832, and he was not about to let good policy get in the way of politics.

Adams observed with his usual cool politesse that he had promised the administration that he would not reduce revenue until the debt had been retired, and he would not go back on that vow. In any case, he added, no bill could pass in defiance of Jackson and his administration. "I do not care who it defies," Clay snarled—or so Adams recorded. "To preserve, maintain, and strengthen the American System, I would defy the South, the President, and the devil." Clay's bearing, Adams wrote was "super-Presidential." Everyone present except for Adams himself retreated before the party leader. This episode marked not a rupture between the two men, but the end of the deep mutual admiration that had lasted throughout Adams' presidency.

Without remotely intending to, Adams had returned to the position he had occupied in 1807 as the lone Federalist prepared to work with the Jefferson administration. He would not oppose a policy simply because it advanced the views and interests of the ruling party. He constituted himself, once again, as a party of one. Adams tried to navigate along a narrow path between the neo-Jeffersonians, like Van Buren, who wanted to reduce the size of government; the nullifiers, who wanted to advance the economic interests of the South; and the National Republicans, who were trying to defeat Jackson. He worked closely with Secretary McLane to work out a minimally acceptable tariff. He spent the hot months of early summer defending the compromise measure in the House; at one point he slammed the podium so hard that he broke a bone in his hand.

On July 14, to Adams' amazement, the measure passed the House with an overwhelming majority, something that could scarcely be said of any measure he had supported while president. The tariff sought to appease the South by sharply reducing duties on the rough wool used to clothe slaves and to appease the North by keeping rates far higher than McDuffie had envisioned. In the event, it disappointed everyone, which was almost certainly a sign of its fairness. But the Jackson administration was not about to thank Adams by reserving surplus revenue for internal improvements.

Adams' flinty independence made him a potentially useful ally to Jackson, as he had once been to Jefferson. In March, Senator R. M. Johnson of Kentucky, a Jackson ally, told Adams that he would like to effect a reconciliation between him and the president. Adams, bending not an inch, said that any such approach would be up to Jackson, who had unjustly blamed him for causing his wife's death. Johnson quickly agreed that some of Jackson's loyalists had poisoned the president's mind against his predecessor, but added that Jackson's "disposition was now entirely friendly." Johnson pressed his case.

"Would you be prepared to attend a private dinner?"

Adams would not; since Jackson invited every congressman to dinner, this would scarcely signal a will to reconcile.

"Perhaps the President could invite you together with a small party?"

The answer was still no.

"What would you have the President do?"

"It is not for me to prescribe."

The following day, Johnson sent a note saying that he had relayed the conversation to Jackson, who assured him that he did not blame the former president for the scandalous publications against his wife and regarded him as "a man of honour." Adams was content to pocket the fine words. He reflected that the Federalist remnant would have his head if he so much as crossed the president's threshold. Still, these were men he had rarely hesitated to outrage; Adams may simply have been unwilling to afford the satisfaction of a feud resolved to a man he had once admired and now held in contempt.

On March 17, Adams received word from Quincy that his brother Tom had died after lingering for months on his deathbed. Years earlier, Tom had been his private secretary, invested his funds, and taken care of his ailing wife. But Tom, like so many other male members of the family, had never found his place in life, had become idle, and had turned to drink. His once sunny temper had soured, frightening his wife and children. Tom and his burgeoning family had become a financial burden to his elder brother. Neither in his letters nor in his diary did the elder Adams shed a tear at the news that the last of his three siblings had died. To Tom's widow, Nancy, who may have been more relieved than heartbroken, he wrote a notably correct letter of condolence. Then, without a second thought, Adams accepted the responsibility to care for Tom's family. He wrote to Charles to say that all the property Tom had mortgaged to him should be given to Nancy, as should all rent payments. If Nancy needed money right away, Charles should dip into his father's funds to help her. In subsequent months, Adams worked hard to find a job for Tom's son and his own namesake, John Quincy, a mediocre student fit for bookkeeping rather than law. The ex-president's perennial money worries only increased; he wrote to John asking him to try to sell the family homes on F Street, as well as a property on Pennsylvania Avenue.

ADAMS SPENT THE SUMMER OF 1832 ARRANGING FOR THE PUBLI-cation of *Dermot*; making fitful progress on his biography of his father, which he brought up to 1767; rewriting his will; and planting trees at Mount Wollaston. He received a visit from Harrison Gray Otis, who thanked Adams for protecting New England's interests in a fierce debate over the apportionment of seats in Congress. The long feud had come to an end; Adams would give no further thought to publishing his book-length diatribe on the Hartford Convention. The former president kept a careful distance from the upcoming national election; he had not endorsed Clay and declined to make public statements of any kind.

Adams returned to Washington just as the rumbling volcano of nullification exploded. On November 24, a special session of the South Carolina legislature voted to invoke the principle of nullification in response to the Tariff of 1832. Throwing down a gauntlet before the national government, the legislature voted to raise a force of twenty-five thousand volunteers to resist any attempt to enforce the tariff, including by turning over revenues collected at the Port of Charleston. Jackson's initial response to this challenge was surpassingly mild. In his annual message, delivered to Congress December 4, the president appealed to the good sense of Carolinians not to obstruct the execution of federal laws. Jackson not only promised to reduce duties still further, but insisted that protective tariffs could be justified only in order to ensure a steady supply of goods essential to national security and not to promote domestic manufacture. Indeed, the entire address was a sop to the South. Jackson spoke of his hope to reduce the general government to "that simple machine which the Constitution created" and reiterated his opposition to federal funding for internal improvements, instead relying on the spirit of free enterprise, aided by "the state sovereignties," to fashion such improvements as the public required.

Adams was livid. He wrote to Southard that the administration had thrown its support to the nullifiers. Adams was all for confrontation. He moved a resolution in the Committee on Manufactures to inquire of the treasury secretary about the fiscal consequences should South Carolina withhold revenue. He was asked to withdraw the motion in the interests of sectional harmony. He refused, and the motion was voted down. Adams told a New York congressman, a Van Buren man, that he was deluding himself to believe that "states' rights" meant anything save the preservation of slavery; the great question was whether the Union could survive half slave and half free.

The men around Jackson understood that his message to Congress had inadvertently given aid and comfort to the nullifiers. On December 10, Jackson issued a "Proclamation Regarding Nullification," almost certainly written by his secretary of state, Edward Livingston, which put to rest the question of where the administration stood. The doctrine of nullification, the president stated, was "incompatible with the existence of the Union, contradicted expressly by the letter of the Constitution, unauthorized by its spirit, inconsistent with every principle on which it was founded, and destructive of the great object for which it was formed." Jackson sided with Webster and Adams in stating that the Constitution is a compact among peoples, not states.

A fervent defender of state sovereignty, himself born in South Carolina, Jackson addressed the nullifiers as few others could. He compared himself to a father speaking to children "whom he saw rushing to a certain ruin." He countered paranoia with plain sense: "You are free members of a flourishing and happy Union. There is no settled design to oppress you." And he threatened the nullifiers with the blunt words he had flung in the face of innumerable adversaries, many of whom had wound up dead: "Their object is disunion, but be not deceived by names; disunion, by armed force, is TREACHERY." The president made it perfectly clear that he would, if left with no other recourse, shed "a brother's blood." The proclamation was not only Jackson's greatest statement but one of the greatest documents written by any American president to date.

In a letter to Charles, Adams grudgingly conceded that the speech "contained much sound constitutional doctrine"—more, he added snidely, "than properly belonged to the source whence it originated." So sound, in fact, was the constitutional doctrine that the Boston papers, according to Charles, were speculating that Adams himself had written the speech. Nevertheless, Adams concluded that the annual message represented Jackson's true convictions, while the proclamation was "made for sale and not for use." And the message, as he wrote to a constituent, constituted a "total departure from the principles of Washington." Had the annual message carried the same spirit as the proclamation, "South Carolina's nullification would have been exterminated, and Andrew Jackson would have had the glory of putting it down." Instead, the president had given the slaveholders everything they wished before abruptly reversing course. A less myopic interpretation would be that Jackson was both an adamant nationalist and a man of the West who distrusted banks, cities, trade, Europe—that he was, in fact, what today we would call a Jacksonian.

As chairman of the Committee on Manufactures, Adams expected to have jurisdiction over the tariff. But Speaker Stevenson had replaced protectionist members of the committee with free-traders, and the committee was so at loggerheads that the members finally agreed to stop meeting. The issue was referred to Ways and Means, which quickly proposed a reduction of duties almost as radical as the one George McDuffie had offered the year before. Adams responded with the first long speech he had delivered in the House. A tariff, he conceded, inevitably favors some interests over others—as all legislation did. He waved a copy of the Constitution. "The South has a great protected interest," he said. Of course he meant slavery and the three-fifths compromise. "I am for adhering to the bargain, for it is a bargain." Adams now contrived an ingenious argument founded more on analogy than strict logic. The Constitution, he noted, had given the "machinery" of the South—slaves—representation in Congress. The North enjoyed no such privilege. "I believe," Adams said drily, "that their looms and factories have no representative in Congress." Manufacturers accepted that bargain; they paid taxes to support a navy, which was of no use to them. "Why," Adams cried, "should not they reason as South Carolina does?" Why shouldn't Massachusetts nullify whatever measures it found inimical?

Adams had calmly reasoned his way to a conclusion bound to outrage his opponents—a foretaste of things to come. The former Boylston Professor of Rhetoric and Oratory had found an outlet for the full measure of his gifts. This particular shaft must have hit home, for a South Carolina legislator interrupted, shouting that the representative from Massachusetts had "thrown a firebrand into the hall."

Fortunately, the firebrand was doused by the spirit of compromise—or of fear. Jackson had asked Congress for the power to enforce federal statutes in South Carolina, and the so-called Force Bill began moving through Congress. South Carolina had once again failed to lure other Southern states to its cause and began to see the wisdom of climbing off the ledge on which it was now perched. In January 1833, Clay and Calhoun, now a senator, reached an agreement to lower duties and end protectionism in exchange for a repeal of nullification. Clay, that is, had accepted a compromise that virtually doomed the American System. Adams felt that South Carolina had been rewarded for throwing a temper tantrum. The Force Bill passed February 20, and the tariff a week later. Adams voted against the latter; from his point of view, it was a sacrifice that need not and ought not have been made in order to mollify the slaveholders. South Carolina was, in fact, mollified: on March 18, the state legislature repealed its nullification of the tariff.

The salient fact of this episode, from our own vantage point, is that the prospect of civil war was postponed for a generation. Clay and Calhoun had chosen compromise over confrontation. Calhoun and Webster had delivered stupendous orations in the Senate, the first opposing the Force Bill, the second opposing the reduced tariff—for Adams was far from alone in viewing the compromise as ruinous to Northern interests. The nullification crisis was a stage on which the great legislators of the day, now justly regarded as among the greatest lawmakers in American history, joined together to preserve the Republic. And the president played an indispensable role in threatening and cajoling and bribing South Carolina off the precipice.

That's not how Adams saw it. He wrote to Charles that the tariff should rightly be called "an act for the protection of John C. Calhoun and his fellow nullifiers." Clay had surrendered the American System to the power of the slaveholders. "I mourn over it as my own child," he told Charles, "for I and not Henry Clay was its father." The South, overrepresented in Congress thanks to the three-fifths compromise, had put its own man in the White House and, with the collusion of the West, substituted its own formula for the American System—low duties, free land, small government, and the protection of the interests of the plantation owner over those of the free laborer.

Adams had hoped to deliver a major speech denouncing not just the tariff compromise but the entire system of thought it represented, but he had been unable to do so before the vote. Instead he proposed that the Committee on Manufactures publish his speech in the form of a report. Michael Hoffman, a Van Burenite New Yorker who represented the interests of the administration on the committee, responded that they would issue no report at all. In that case, Adams said, he insisted on the right to issue a minority report on behalf of himself and the one other protectionist on the committee. Hoffman tried to block that as well, but the full House voted to make the document public.

The *Report of the Minority of the Committee of Manufactures Submitted to the House of Representatives February 28, 1833* bore very little resemblance to the report of a Congressional committee. It was, rather, a single-minded effort to obliterate the edifice Adams believed that Jackson and his allies were seeking to erect in lieu of the American System. Adams began by taking exception to a phrase from the annual message: "The wealth and strength of its country are its population, and the best part of that population are the cultivators of the soil." Adams insisted that the "cultivators" Jackson had in mind were not Jefferson's yeomanry but rather the wealthy landowners of the South who constituted America's feudal order. He insisted that the entire system envisioned in the president's annual message was designed to serve the interests of that order. Echoing Jackson's own language, he asserted that the president wished to reduce the federal government to "a simple machine." Simplicity, Adams declared, "is the essential characteristic in all slavery," for all men are either masters or slaves. The government of a free people is bound to be complex, for relations among them, the play of their interests, must be complex. Here was a new weapon in Adams' rhetorical armamentarium: the play on words, turning the word "simple" against itself, as he had earlier with "machine."

Again and again in the minority report Adams turned his thunder on the forces of nullification, as if the president had not, in fact, trumped his own annual message with his magisterial proclamation. For Adams, Jackson as well as Calhoun sought to make the state serve the interests of the slaveholders and their allies. Nullification, he observed, permitted one-twentieth of the nation's population to frustrate the will of the rest, for example by blocking internal improvements that would benefit all. For what, he asked, "is this enormous edifice of fraud and falsehood erected? To rob the free workingman of the North of the wages of his labor—to take money from his pocket and put it into that of the Southern owner of machinery."

And from this flowed a multitude of sins. The surrendering of federally owned land to the states was of a piece with nullification, since it supposed that the land belonged to those states as parties to the Constitution, when in fact it was individuals, not states, who were parties to that compact. In addition, that land would ultimately be used to benefit "party adventurers," by which Adams meant Jackson men. Adams saw the issue of public lands as a scheme cooked up by Van Buren to buy the loyalty of the West in advance of the 1836 election. The national interest was being sacrificed to the interests of the powerful and the few.

Adams now returned to the question of the tariff and thus to the issue of rival sectional interests he had raised in his speech before the House. Manufacturers, he said, had long been "protected from the injurious regulations of foreign nations, as the planters of the South and the settlers of the West have been protected from the depredations and hostile incursions of Indian savages." Protectionism, for Adams, was simply one of the many forms of state protection. In the "Fort Hill Address" Calhoun had argued that states represented individual and sectional interests more faithfully than the national government could and thus needed to take precedence. Adams, in effect, rejoined that in a large, diversified republic only an active, complex central government could adjudicate among clashing interests.

Adams ended this long and impassioned philippic by comparing his own vision of an activist government harnessing "national energies and resources to great undertakings," to the one offered in Jackson's message: "impending with universal ruin, draining all the sources of fertility from the fountains of internal national improvement, shaking to its foundations all commercial confidence, by the determined annihilation of the Bank, and wresting forever from the people of the United States and from their posterity, for unnumbered ages, the inestimable inheritance of the public lands."

The minority report was widely read, at least by the standards of congressional reports. Charles had five thousand copies printed in Boston, and Adams made sure that friendly newspaper editors published the document. Nevertheless, he was only a bit player in the great drama over nullification; the principal roles belonged to Jackson, Clay, Calhoun, and Webster. It was, in fact, precisely because he had little real power that Adams could afford to be doctrinally pure, as the others could not. The role of lonely truth-teller came naturally to him. "Mr. Clay and Mr. Calhoun and Mr. Webster adapt their political opinions to the circumstances of the Times," he wrote to Charles, "and so do the Federalists, and so do the Democrats, and so above all do the National Republicans."

After hardly more than a year in Congress, Adams had discovered a role for himself: the scold, the Cassandra, the solitary voice of conscience.

CHAPTER 30

The Ark of Our God Is Falling into the Hands of the Philistines

(1831–1835)

THE TWO-PARTY SYSTEM THAT HAD COME TO AN END WITH the collapse of the Federalists would not fully reconstitute itself until the rise of the new Republican Party in the 1850s. The older Republican Party, and its later-stage variant, the National Republicans, began to give way as the Democrats gained in strength. John Quincy Adams fancied himself a man of no party, but even such a man needed an affiliation in order to remain in politics. In the early 1830s Adams began to try on new identities—first as an Anti-Mason, then as a Whig. He fought the confines of both, though he ultimately found that Whiggism fitted him more comfortably than any of the others ever had.

When William Seward had paid his visit to Adams in the summer of 1831, he was on his way to the first convention of the Anti-Masonic Party in Baltimore. His real mission was to learn if Adams would be prepared to accept the party's nomination for president. In his usual manner Adams deprecated any possible role for himself, saying that he had no wish to place an impediment in the path of Henry Clay, that the task was one for a younger man, that he had no wish to bear once again the burdens of high office. Nevertheless, he declared, "if the Anti-Masons thought his nomination would be better than any other, he would not decline." Seward continued on to Baltimore prepared to raise Adams' banner.

The fact that Adams was prepared to run for president yet again in 1832 testifies both to the unending force of his ambition and to his increasingly passionate advocacy of Anti-Masonry, which many of America's leading men dismissed as a cause for cranks and opportunists. Masonry had long enjoyed a reputation for high respectability: several of the Founding Fathers, including George Washington, had been proud to count themselves in their ranks. Few Americans not admitted to Masonic lodges had the faintest idea what went on inside. A spectacular and horrific crime had changed all that. In 1826, William Morgan, a disgruntled Mason in Genesee County, New York, announced that he had written a book divulging the secret oaths Masons swore in order to advance through the organization's hierarchy. According to later testimony, his fellow Masons, outraged at this violation of the pledge of secrecy, kidnapped him, rowed him out into the Niagara River, tied him with rope and weighted him down with stones, and dumped him over the side near the falls. (His body was never found.) Thanks to a conspiracy of silence among Masons and lodges who had been in on the plot, the refusal of Masonic prosecutors to pursue the case and of juries thick with Masons to convict, only a few small fry were convicted over the course of twenty trials. A crime committed by individuals thus evolved into a scandal engulfing an institution.

Anti-Masonry swept across New England and the Mid-Atlantic states like a prairie fire—first New York, then Vermont, Rhode Island, Pennsylvania. Masons were denounced from the pulpit and vivisected in pamphlets and books and newspapers. By 1830, about one-eighth of the nation's one thousand newspapers preached Anti-Masonry. Many of the leading lights of Anti-Masonry were evangelicals caught up in the fervor known as the Second Great Awakening. This was an era of moral mobilization, when citizens formed temperance societies and abolitionist bodies and "Young Men's Societies" devoted to the advance of public morals. Freemasonry drew upon the language and symbolism of Christianity; the foul murder of Morgan, and subsequent revelations about the bizarre rituals of the order, recast Masonry as a kind of demonic parody of true faith.

Masons also came to be seen as enemies of democracy. Though Masonry had long been understood as a benevolent society that promoted good works and public-spiritedness, it was a secret society. From the moment Morgan was killed because he had planned to reveal those secrets—whatever they were—and the lodges rallied to the side of his persecutors in order to obstruct justice—that secrecy was recast as, in effect, an ongoing plot by elites against the ordinary citizens of the nation. Freemasonry suddenly appeared to be a state-within-the state—"a distinct, and independent, government, within the jurisdiction of the United States," as the report to a Massachusetts Anti-Masonic convention put it.

Adams had paid no attention to the Anti-Masonic movement either as president or in his first years out of office. But as he began to study the growing body of Anti-Masonic literature, he came to see Masonry as a threat both to public morals and to republican principles. In May 1831 he had attended the Massachusetts Anti-Masonic convention. News of Adams' presence spread swiftly among the leaders of the new Anti-Masonic Party, then looking for a standard-bearer for the 1832 election. Party officials had hoped that Henry Clay, a staunch Mason, would renounce the order and thus make possible a merger between the Anti-Masons and the National Republicans. Clay had refused to do so. Men began beating a path to Adams' doorstep. In early June his friend Timothy Fuller came to ask Adams whether his new devotion to the Anti-Masonic cause meant that he would oppose Clay's election. And Adams grandly said, "The dissolution of the Masonic institution in the United States I believe to be more important to us and our posterity than the question whether Mr. Clay or General Jackson shall be the President chosen at the next election." Fuller understood that Adams was preparing to heed the call of posterity. William Seward left with the same impression.

The rank and file at the Anti-Masonic convention in Baltimore balked when asked to select as their first candidate the president who had been drubbed in the previous election. Instead they nominated another member of Adams' cabinet, William Wirt, the former attorney general. Had Adams seen Anti-Masonry as simply a vehicle to restore him to the White House, he would have heeded the call of his son Charles and other friends to end his dalliance with the movement. In fact, Adams now felt free to publicly take up the Anti-Masonic cudgel. He began firing off letters on the subject to friends and newspaper editors. "Are you familiar with the facts around Morgans murder, with the nature of Masonic rituals, with oaths and penalties?," he wrote to Massachusetts governor Levi Lincoln. Adams filled in the details. He did not win many converts. Edward Ingersoll, a Philadelphia attorney, responded, "Many agree with you though a subject which they have as little considered as the Syriac language." This was as close as any of Adams' friends would get to telling him that they thought he was in the grip of a mania.

Why was Adams so exercised on a subject most of his peers dismissed as a species of zealotry? First, he believed, more fervently than did many other men, that all politics, and all policy, rested on the foundation of "public morals." Almost half a century earlier, Adams had delivered a graduation address at Harvard that contrasted the "austere republican virtues" of the revolutionary generation with the "selfish and contracted principles" of his own time. There was nothing in Adams of the rationalist utilitarianism of his one-time friend Jeremy Bentham. The former president was not just a deeply committed Christian but a Puritan who believed that both men and societies were continually called to defend virtue in a fallen world. For Adams, Masonry was both a moral crime and a public menace. This view set him apart from the other great statesmen of his day, Clay, Calhoun, and Webster, who worried more about the political influence of Anti-Masonry, the threat it posed to their own National Republican Party, than about the alleged dangers of Masonry itself. Adams was fully prepared to pay the political price.

It wasn't simply the atmosphere surcharged with piety and fervor that made Anti-Masonry seem like a dubious cause to most men in Adams' circle, but the frank anti-elitism of the movement. Adams, too, had always recoiled at any movement armed with pitchforks and at men like Thomas Paine—or Bentham—who provided those movements with a rationale. At the same time, Adams never saw himself as a member of a privileged elite. He was, if anything, an apostate. In Masonry he saw a deeply anti-republican, and thus un-American, scheme by the elite to perpetuate itself. In a letter addressed to the people of Massachusetts in January 1834, Adams wrote that "political Anti-Masonry sprang from the bosom of the people themselves, and it was the unsophisticated, unlearned voice of the people" that had cried out in horror at the events surrounding the murder of Morgan. "So it is," Adams observed, "with all great moral reforms." The Gospel of Peace, after all, had been proclaimed by the son of a carpenter.

In his contempt for political calculation, his indifference to respectable opinion, his archaic faith in republican principles—and his sheer cussedness—Adams prefigured the great battle he would fight against the slave power in Congress.

In 1832, Adams arranged to exchange a series of public letters with William Stone, a newspaperman and a rare moderate among the ranks of ex-Masons. Stone explained that the dreadful symbols, the terrible oaths, and the grim punishments used in the lodges were not meant to be taken literally and were preposterous rather than dangerous. Nevertheless, Stone concluded that Masonry should be dissolved. Morgan's murder and the subsequent cover-up showed that Masons had come to wrongly believe that their oaths superseded their loyalty to the state. In any case, a secret order making use of allegorical speech had no place in a democratic society.

In his letters to Stone, Adams refused to accept the proposition that Masonry was a harmless practice that had lost touch with its own Christian and patriotic principles. Even the mildest of the oaths, that of the so-called Entering Apprentice, Adams wrote, was "extrajudicial" and thus contrary to law, as well as violating Jesus' injunction to swear no oaths. No decent Christian could either take the oath or accept the barbarous punishments to be meted out to transgressors. If anything, Adams added, the cynical deployment of Scripture offered the perfect rationale for unbelievers prepared to commit heinous deeds against non-Masons. Adams did not at first send the letters to Stone, but they were widely circulated among the leading Anti-Masons. Richard Rush reported that they were "enthralled to see Mr. Adams, the giant, engaged in the glorious contest for the demolition of the babel of misery." Anti-Masonry could hardly be dismissed as a crackpot cause if such a man as Adams had taken it up. Stone published the letters in late 1832, and they were widely reprinted.

The 1832 presidential election offered a stinging rebuke to political Anti-Masonry. Jackson was reelected by a thumping majority over Clay, while William Wirt took 2.4 percent of the popular vote and 7 of the 288 electoral votes. But for Adams, Anti-Masonry was a moral cause, not a political movement. He remained the chief publicist of the cause. In the spring of 1833 he wrote a series of hectoring letters to Secretary of State Edward Livingston, the highest-ranking Mason in the Jackson administration—a "General Grand High Priest of the Masonic General Royal Arch Order," as Adams delightedly noted, as often as possible. He sent Livingston his letters to Stone, daring him either to refute the allegations or to call for the abolition of Masonry. Livingston did not even bother to respond. Adams wrote again and again—always, of course, sending copies to the press. He closed the series with a thunderous coda: "The strength, the glory, the happiness of a nation are all centred in the purity of its morals; and institutions founded upon imposture, are the worst of all corruptions, for they poison the public morals at their fountains, and by multiplying the accomplices in guilt, arm them with the confidence of virtue."

Anti-Masonry remained a powerful force in state politics, including in Massachusetts, and Adams continued to hitch his wagon to what turned out to be a fading star. In September 1833, the state party unanimously passed a resolution naming Adams as its candidate for governor. Adams wrote back to say that, much though he had no wish to serve as governor, and so forth and so on, "I can not suffer any personal considerations to withstand the call of so large, so respectable, and so virtuous a portion of the population." Adams said that he would run only in order to "heal the divisions of party"—that is, to serve as a bridge between the National Republicans and the Anti-Masons. He was not convinced that this was possible, but he could see no other clear path to his political future. And in fact in early October the National Republicans, rather than rally behind Adams, nominated John Davis, a congressman from Worcester. In the election, Davis took the most votes, followed by Adams and Marcus Morton, the Democratic candidate. Since none took a majority, the election was thrown into the state assembly—a bizarre rerun of Adams' own 1824 election.

Adams was loath to win by "legislative cabal," as he once had. Even worse, he feared that running and losing would so damage his reputation that he would be turned out of office, "and my public life will terminate by the alienation from me of all mankind." It wasn't the alienation he feared, but the end of his political career. In the first days of 1834, Adams held a long talk with Davis, who pledged that if elected he would seek to heal the rift between his party and the Anti-Masons. That was good enough for Adams, who asked to withdraw from the runoff and urged party leaders to support Davis.

Over the next few years, Anti-Masonry would be largely absorbed into yet another new party, the Whigs. Though it had failed as a national political movement, Anti-Masonry had succeeded as a cause. By early 1834, the practice of Masonry had been virtually wiped out across much of the Northeast. Several New England states had passed laws prohibiting Masons from serving on juries. At the end of March, Adams attended a meeting of the Anti-Masonic caucus in Congress, where he was asked to serve as chair. One of the leading lights of the movement, a representative from the Anti-Masonic heartland in upper New York state, declared that the enemy had been so thoroughly routed that Anti-Masonry had no further reason for being. Adams could contemplate his labors with satisfaction.

BY THE TIME ADAMS LEFT QUINCY IN NOVEMBER 1833, HE HAD, for the first time, the option of traveling part of the route by train. Adams was a man of settled and conservative habits who nevertheless welcomed all new forms of transportation, both because he was fascinated by technology and because he always wanted to get to his destination as fast as possible. In the fall of 1833, trains had begun to run on the Camden and Amboy Railway, which connected those two New Jersey cities, and thus Philadelphia and New York. The trip cost three dollars and took nine and a half hours, a modest improvement over steamboat and stagecoach. For Adams that was reason enough. Adams took his first ride on the C & A on November 8.

Each of the railway's three cars had three compartments with facing benches. About two hundred passengers filled the cars. Adams sat in the front. The train stopped a few miles south of Camden to oil its wheels. As it picked up speed, approaching thirty-five miles per hour—a velocity at which few humans had ever traveled at that time—Adams and his fellow passengers smelled something burning. Then they saw smoke rising from the left wheelbase. Before they could call out to the conductor to stop the car, the wheel lost contact with the rail, causing the right front of the car to rear up. Just as it was about to tip and crush those within, the car behind it rose up on the left and flipped over, wrenching Adams' own car back on a level. He was saved only at the expense of those behind him.

Miraculously, no one in the first car was seriously hurt. Those behind them were not so fortunate. "The scene of suffering," Adams wrote, "was excruciating. Many women, and a child, scattered along the road, bleeding, mangled, groaning, writhing in torture and dying, was a trial of feeling, to which I had never before been called." One man died within minutes, another soon after—the first recorded fatalities in the history of rail transportation. Adams listed the names and hometowns of both the wounded and the dead, perhaps having learned them through an inquest he attended that evening. A "Mr. Vanderbilt" broke his leg. This was the industrialist Cornelius Vanderbilt, who vowed never again to ride on a train—a pledge he violated once he began buying up railroads in the ensuing decades.

Adams had never seen violent death close up. He had been calm at the time but afterwards trembled at the prospect of what might have been. "When the thought came over me that a few seconds more of pressure, on the car in which I was would in all probability have laid me a prostrate corpse, like him who was before my eyes, or made me a cripple for life— and, more insupportable still, what if my wife and grandchild had been in the car behind me." The idea that Louisa and little Mary Francis might have taken the train with him was "torture, a thousandfold worse than death." Adams, like Vanderbilt, vowed to leave off rail travel, at least until the technology radically improved. That vow lasted one day, for the train from Philadelphia to Baltimore was too convenient to pass up. Adams seems to have worried about his own life no more than he had on the passage through the Gulf of Finland a quarter of a century before.

Adams arrived in Washington well before the new session of Congress had begun. He spent much of his time plotting with Charles how to withdraw from the Massachusetts governor's race with the least possible damage to his reputation. He wrote to party leaders to remind them that "I have never worn the collar of any party. Parties have taken me up and cast me off, as suited their caprice and pleasure." Now Adams was casting off the party; with Masonry all but demolished, he was prepared to return to the great issue, as he then felt it: the fight for the principle of activist government in the face of Jackson's argument for a "simple machine."

Though this war would have many fronts, the most dramatic of them was Jackson's single-minded campaign against the Second Bank of the United States. The bank had been established in 1816 with a twenty-year charter. In his first congressional message, Jackson had questioned whether the bank's charter should be renewed. Jackson had long been hostile to the bank on general grounds, for he distrusted paper currency and was prone to view banks as financial cabals. In 1829 he told Nicholas Biddle, the bank's president, "I do not dislike your bank any more than all banks." But the Bank of the United States was not just any financial institution. The bank received and disbursed all federal revenue; handled the nation's foreign-exchange transactions; issued paper currency, which as legal tender could be exchanged for gold and silver; and made loans to state banks as well as to individuals. And yet it was a private company, controlled by its own board of directors and only indirectly answerable to the secretary of the treasury. Jackson regarded the bank as a usurpation of the authority of the states and a threat to his own power as president.

Adams supported the bank as an instrument for national investment and a source of funding for internal improvements, trade, and business—as the financial engine of a robust federal government. He was also extremely close to Biddle, an intellectual with far-ranging interests who at the age of eighteen had served as private secretary to the American minister in Paris—a younger version of Adams himself. Biddle embodied for Adams the intellectual and social elite to which, he thought, the nation's affairs should be trusted—just as for Jackson he embodied an Eastern establishment that sought to run roughshod over ordinary Americans.

Adams' support for the Anti-Masonic rabble had been a matter of republicanism, not populism. He believed in the political role of the propertied class. When George Bancroft, a distinguished historian, sent Adams an address in which he argued that democracy's distinguishing feature was that it protected the rights of persons rather than of property, as aristocracy did,

Adams wrote back to remind him that Aristotle had praised democracy but observed that it was prone to dissolve into ochlocracy, or rule of the mob. In fact, government had arisen to protect both. "If democracy is founded exclusively in persons and not in property," he said, "I fear it will follow the tendency of its nature and degenerate into ochlocracy, and Lynch Law, burning down Convents and hanging abolitionists or gamblers, without judge or jury, without fear of God to restrain, and without remorse to punish."

Rather than wait until 1836, Biddle had asked for an early vote to renew the bank's charter. The Congress favored the bank, and in July 1833, on the day after passing the tariff, both houses voted for recharter. Then Jackson vetoed the measure. This was an extraordinary act. Past presidents had used their veto power only in order to block a measure deemed unconstitutional. In his veto message Jackson was careful to cite constitutional grounds, but he reserved his passion for matters of policy and social justice. With his genius for the populist appeal, Jackson couched his decision in what we would today call the language of "class warfare." When institutions like the bank "grant titles, gratuities, and exclusive privileges, to make the rich richer and the potent more powerful," he wrote, "the humble members of society—the farmers, mechanics, and laborers—who have neither the time nor the means of securing like favors to themselves, have a right to complain of the injustice of their Government."

Jackson typically met confrontation with violence. He decided that, rather than wait for the bank to expire in 1836, he would suffocate it by removing the $10 million in federal deposits that constituted half of its stock of capital. His cabinet opposed the measure, as did his treasury secretary, Louis McLane, who would have to sign a measure stating that the deposits were unsafe in the bank. Jackson then appointed the pro-bank McLane secretary of state and replaced him with an anti-bank figure, William J. Duane. But Duane shocked the president by refusing to certify that the funds needed to be moved. In September 1833, Jackson fired Duane in favor of his pliable attorney general, Roger Taney—a forerunner of Richard Nixon's 1973 "Saturday Night Massacre." Taney promptly began draining the bank by sending all new deposits to state banks. All this was done while Congress was out of session. In his 1833 congressional message Jackson justified this extraordinary measure by charging the bank with a plot to corruptly influence elections in order to retain its power.

Adams was incensed by what he saw as the naked political conniving behind Taney's move, for he was sure that Vice President Van Buren was orchestrating the drama, dispatching federal revenues to "pet banks" run by his supporters. "Every one of the 40 banks is at once an electioneering and a stock-jobbing engine," he wrote. In effect, Van Buren had placed the entire federal treasury at his own disposal. Adams was hardly alone: Jackson's high-handed tactics had galvanized his opponents and confirmed their fear that he was, at bottom, a populist tyrant. On December 26, a few weeks after Jackson's message, Clay took the floor of the Senate to introduce a resolution censuring the president—a step just short of impeachment. The year before, Clay, Calhoun, and Webster had worked together to fashion a compromise tariff. Now all three delivered thunderous speeches against Jackson. The ensuing debate consumed four months, making it the longest treatment of a single subject in congressional history. The survival of the core constitutional principle of checks and balances seemed to be at stake. On March 28, the Senate passed the resolution, which asserted that Jackson had "assumed upon himself authority and power not conferred by the Constitution and the laws." No president had ever before been formally castigated by Congress.

Adams so loathed Jackson that when Harvard had awarded the president an honorary diploma the previous summer, he had refused to attend. He was enraged by Jackson's ruthless campaign against the bank. And yet he opposed the censure motion; when a senator asked his advice, he recommended voting against the measure. Adams believed in a strong executive; he believed that Jackson had the right to choose cabinet members who would carry out his will. And he would not permit his feelings about the person to obscure the underlying principle. History has, of course, come down on Adams' side of this debate, for this prerogative is universally accepted today.

But Adams had more to say on the bank. In mid-March he had begun drafting a speech he hoped to deliver while presenting his constituents' petition to restore the deposits. On April 4, he was literally about to move toward the podium in the House when Speaker Stevenson instead recognized another member, who called the previous question on the floor, thus rendering Adams' speech out of order. Gales and Seaton of the *National Intelligencer* agreed to publish the speech in pamphlet form, and the "Suppressed Speech" appeared April 12. Adams defended the bank against the allegations mounted against it, accusing both the president and Taney of slandering Biddle and of denying him due process. He accused Taney of manipulating funds to benefit favored banks. As for the president, Adams went on, he had crushed the national bank in order to enhance his own control over the levers of power, to gratify his appetite for vengeance, to transfer wealth to the slaveholders whose support he depended on, and to further his supreme goal of reducing government to "a simple machine." The price of his folly would be a terrible one. In his peroration Adams declared that if the founders could come down from the canvas on which they stood in that very hall, and sit down among their successors, they would wonder, "What scourge of God had desolated their cities? What convulsion of nature had palsied the arm of industry?"

The "Suppressed Speech" thrilled bank supporters. Biddle printed fifty thousand copies. Adams used his congressional franking privileges to mail out hundreds of them. But the speech could not resurrect the Bank. Adams' dire predictions seemed unwarranted, for the economy continued to grow in Jackson's last years in office, and British capital substituted for that lost with the bank. However, a contraction of credit, first in Britain and then the United States, helped trigger the Panic of 1837, the worst financial crisis since the founding of the Republic. A national bank might have been able to mitigate the crisis by expanding available credit—though Adams himself was no friend of easy money policy.

Jackson was gone from office by the time the panic struck. By defying opposition in order to eliminate the bank, he had succeeded in putting his imprint on the nation. He had transferred powers from the federal government to the states and diminished the reach of government itself, all while extending the reach of the executive branch. This unlettered barbarian, as Adams saw it, had succeeded where Adams had failed. He was more ruthless than Adams was, but he also understood better how to use the powers, implicit as well as explicit, vested in the office.

ADAMS RETURNED TO QUINCY, BY HIMSELF, IN JULY; LOUISA STAYED in Washington to care for her brother and their son John, both of whom were seriously ill. He lapsed into his usual gloom. He had a premonition that he would not live another year, though he admitted that he had had the same premonition the year before. His memory was failing; perhaps his judgment as well. He had lost his appetite. He couldn't sleep. "My hopes are blasted with disappointment," he wrote in his journal. "Solitude quickens my fears." John Bailey, a Massachusetts legislator, came to visit, and old Adams said, "My hopes for the long continuance of this Union are extinct." Idleness often turned Adams morbid; he needed occupation.

On July 26, Adams received a visit from President Josiah Quincy of Harvard. Adams had become a member of Harvard's Board of Overseers, and Quincy, his distant kinsman and one of the oldest and most constant friends of his life, had come to discuss a grave disturbance that had forced him to suspend some students, expel others, and even refer some for prosecution. Quincy was an austere man with little patience for undergraduate high jinks. He was determined, he had said, that Harvard students should comport themselves as "high-minded, high-principled, well-taught, well-conducted, well-bred gentlemen." His harsh measures had, instead, provoked a backlash; students regularly tested his authority. On May 26, the sea of discontent had finally broken the dam. After Quincy had expelled a freshman who had committed a series of minor infractions and then answered the president's queries in a tone he found impertinent, the entire freshman class had rioted, smashing furniture and breaking windows in the chambers of an instructor blamed for provoking the whole affair. Sophomores failed to appear for morning prayers, and Quincy suspended all but three members of the class. He threatened to prosecute others. The students did not back off: juniors donned black armbands and burned the president in effigy, while seniors threatened to absent themselves from commencement. By the time Quincy showed up at Adams' doorstep, Harvard was facing one of the worst crises in its two-hundred-year history.

With his instinctive horror of the mob and his reverence for Harvard, Adams instantly took Quincy's side. The students, he wrote, had manifested "a contumacious and insurgent spirit, which he has been laboring to subdue." The board asked Adams to chair a subcommittee to look into the merits of the case. Adams drafted a report that defended President Quincy's actions. The other members "thought it much too severe upon the students," Adams reported. Alexander H. Everett, now publisher of the *North American Review*, described Quincy as "a man very wanting in discretion." Adams retorted that "discretion was a negative virtue, perhaps possessed in higher perfection by knaves than by honest men." His plain meaning was that "discretion," in this context, was no more than a euphemism for "pusillanimity." Quincy had acted as he himself would have acted.

In the meanwhile the student uprising had begun to collapse. Virtually the entire sophomore class applied for readmission; the seniors changed their minds about the boycott under the threat of being denied a diploma. One of the three students facing indictment pleaded no contest and paid a minor fine. Quincy, who had confessed to Adams that he was utterly mystified by the truculence of students who had always treated him with perfect regard, pronounced himself satisfied. The commencement proceeded according to plan. Adams was deeply impressed with the Greek oration. The original English poem, however, he found, "a slovenly performance, the only merit of which was its brevity." It had been delivered by a graduate named Ralph Waldo Emerson.

In his wrathful response to student insurrection, and his wholehearted support for President Quincy, Adams was acting according to his deepest impulses, which led him not just to abhor anarchy but to regard abiding institutions and their rules with reverence. Adams had stood by Nicholas Biddle out of personal friendship and economic principle, but Harvard for him was more like the Constitution or his own ancient family, a thing so deeply rooted as to defy all the dissolute influences of fashion and time. Adams didn't defend Harvard because it served his class, though it did. He was all too ready to become an abomination to his class. He stood by Harvard—rather than its students—because, like his father, he believed in durable things that outlasted human folly.

Throughout this period Adams was receiving frightening news about his son John. He seemed to be losing his eyesight. Isolation and inactivity had lead to a physical breakdown. Louisa wrote to say that she felt a terrible sense of premonition. She beseeched her husband to write to their son to implore him to leave Washington for Quincy. Adams did so, saying that the climate would repair his health. He almost begged John to sell the family property in Washington and relocate to "the seat of your forefathers"—as he had implored George to do four years earlier. He wrote again to say that if John needed money for the trip, he could withdraw $300. Underneath these offers and entreaties was the painful truth that the Columbia Mills had irretrievably failed. "You have met with severe disappointments," he observed, "but let them not overcome your resolution or your perseverance." Those were attributes of the father, not the son. John and Mary remained in Washington when Louisa left for Quincy.

In the early fall of 1834, the elder Adamses received alarming letters from Louisa's sister Carolina, who was caring for John. Adams raced to Washington, arriving in only two days. When he burst into John's house on Lafayette Place at ten in the evening, Carolina begged him not to go into his son's bedchamber. The distracted father agreed, but then changed his mind, went in, and found his son insensate. He emerged to see Mary, who burst into tears. Adams promised that he would become a father to her and the three children. At four thirty the next morning John died, of causes the family doctor could not diagnose. That morning, Adams wrote to Charles with the news. He asked his son to use his judgment as to when and how to break the tidings to Louisa. After receiving a letter she had written to John that afternoon, he decided to write to her directly, saying that if John could have spoken, he would "join with your disconsolate husband, and remaining son, entreating you to preserve yourself for their sakes."

Louisa had been taking opium to quiet her "half-distracted mind." When she learned of John's death, she could not bring herself to write to her husband, though she did send a short note to Mary asking her to move up to Quincy with the children. Mary was herself very ill and would not leave the house, which only added to Adams' anxiety and woe. He wrote a note for Fanny, age four, begging her grandmother to come to Washington with sister Louisa. She did come in mid-November and began nurturing her haggard husband. She wrote to Charles that she was overcome by the sense of John's presence everywhere in the house. She had hoped to rent a place in Georgetown, but that, her husband had said, was beyond their means.

Their means, in fact, were now in serious jeopardy. John had left behind him a financial mess far more serious than George had. The Columbia Mills had failed. Since Adams had cosigned the loans, he and John's estate were now jointly liable for $9,000 in bank debt. John had taken out a $2,200 loan from a friend and $800 from his father's former servant, Antoine Giusta, and owed another $3,000 to his servants as well as to his tailor, his butcher, his druggist, and virtually everyone else he dealt with. Adams spent his first week in Washington tallying up the sums. Charles worried that the debts would crush his father, spiritually as well as financially. Adams wrote back to say, as his mother once had in the face of economic failure, "I know of no personal sacrifice that I shall not be ready cheerfully to make."

Adams could count on only about $1,500 from his congressional pay and the rent of his properties. He badgered a Mr. Sherman of Frederick, Maryland, for dividends from $500 worth of stock John had purchased in the man's hotel. He went out to the mill, where he found everything in disrepair and disuse. John had leased the operation to a tenant for $500 a year, but the man insisted that John had agreed not to collect the sum. He had neither wheat nor flour. Adams left empty-handed. Taking charge of the household, Adams embarked on a campaign of ruthless economy. He dismissed unnecessary servants, walked rather than rode back and forth to the Capitol, and sold or gave away the family's horses and cows. He refused to sell the house; Mary would need the income from rent if and when she moved to Quincy. Instead, he put his three houses in Washington on the market (they didn't even draw an offer) and instructed Charles to sell much of his stock and, if possible, the family house on Hancock Street. By the end of the year, the ever-efficient Charles was able to write to say that he had deposited $10,000 into his father's account. It was desperate, exhausting, and deeply demoralizing work for a man of sixty-seven. Adams barely slept. "I shall not," he confessed to his old friend Dr. Benjamin Waterhouse, "attempt the deception of attenuating the severity of the calamity which has befallen me."

In late November, he brought little Louisa and Fanny to Orphan's Court, where he became their legal guardian. He had now added John's family to the ever-growing circle of his dependents.

ANDREW JACKSON'S UNPRECEDENTED ASSERTION OF EXECUTIVE power had offered the perfect organizing principle to his opponents. Over the last two decades, first the Republicans and then the Democrats had ruled without an organized opposition party; already the Anti-Masons were on the wane. Calhoun, Clay, and Webster, who differed profoundly among themselves on a wide range of issues, had been drawn together by Jackson's defiance of Congress. Soon after the climactic vote of censure, Clay had given a speech in which he drew an analogy to the Tories and Whigs of Georgian England, the one endorsing an extensive monarchical power, the other seeking to rein it in. The plain implication, of course, was that Andrew Jackson was ruling as an autocratic king. His opponents, defending republicanism, were Whigs. The name proved so popular that it was in widespread use by the summer of 1834, though the Whigs never succeeded in making the Tory label stick to the Democrats.

That fall, Adams had run, and won, on the Whig and the Anti-Mason tickets. Adams was, of course, a man of no party, as he invariably called himself. He had ended his active involvement with political Anti-Masonry when he concluded that the party could agree on few principles beyond the need to abolish Masonry. He found much the same problem with the Whigs. In early 1835, he wrote to his friend John Bailey that the only principle of Whiggism is "stripping the Executive of his lawful power. . . . It is not and cannot be a principle of Administration." In fact, Whiggism proved a far more durable political force than Anti-Masonry and ultimately came to be identified with the activist vision of government Adams himself had long championed, as well as with his own deep belief that politics should seek to improve the moral conduct of citizens. In this formative moment, however, Adams stood apart from the Whigs' campaign to curb Jackson's power. He allied himself neither with the party in power nor with the opposition. For this reason, Adams could do little to shape legislation during this period. He was often a solitary voice, as he had been so many times before.

In the 1834 elections Jackson maintained his majority in the House, but the Whigs gained control of the Senate. The party's leaders, now known as the Triumvirate, looked for an issue they could use to dramatize the Whig critique of an overweening executive. A president like Jackson would never be long in gratifying such a wish: in his annual message, Jackson asked Congress to permit him to "make reprisals upon French property" should the government of France fail to pay 25 million francs, or about $5 million, which the French had agreed to pay in reparations for damage from the Napoleonic wars. Despite signing a treaty to that effect, France had balked for the last two years and seemed to be in no hurry to make good its pledge. That was unacceptable. At the same time, the hot-blooded Jackson appeared to be spoiling for a fight at a time when Americans were enjoying a long era of peace.

Clay, now the political master of the Senate, introduced a resolution declining to make any demands of France. The resolution passed in mid-January. Adams considered this a terrible mistake—not because he favored aggressive measures against France, but because his spirit rose in the face of any attempt to conciliate European rivals through acts of deference. Adams began calling for the House to take up the issue. In a speech in early February, Adams rallied to the president's side in a way that must have startled some of his colleagues. Even those who considered Jackson's request in his message to Congress "imprudent," he asserted, "must nevertheless applaud its spirit." The president had told the world "what the interest, the rights, and the honour of the nation would require." Was the House unwilling to do the same? Would it show to the world, and to France, that the president did not enjoy the support of his own legislative branch? The Senate, he said, had deliberated on the matter—"and their deliberations had concluded in a decision to dodge the question."

Speaker John Bell of Tennessee curtly reminded Adams that "it was not permitted to speak disrespectfully of any act of the other branch of the Legislature." Adams thereafter referred to the Senate with the elaborate circumlocution of a schoolboy forbidden to say a naughty word. He reported gleefully to Charles that his speech had shocked Clay, Webster, and

Calhoun and "electrified" the administration. The fact that he was doing serious damage to his Whig bona fides in no way diminished the deep sense of satisfaction Adams felt in forcing the House to take up what he considered a matter of national security.

In late February the Foreign Affairs Committee issued a report proposing a series of mild-mannered resolutions. Adams wanted stronger language stipulating that the right of American citizens to be indemnified as the treaty stipulated "ought to be in no way *sacrificed, abandoned,* or *impaired.*" Adams now proceeded to fight furiously for his language in the face of efforts to water it down. Congress would be adjourning March 3. On the second Adams delivered a long, impassioned speech accusing France of grossly neglecting its treaty obligations. The president, he said, was wrong to have foreclosed the possibility of negotiations. But his own colleagues in the House—he named names—had shown a craven willingness to appease the French, who would respond only to a show of unity and resolution from the United States. (He had said no less in the face of possible war with France almost forty years earlier.)

The debate raged on, with one proposed resolution after another failing. Finally Adams agreed to accept compromise language stating that the treaty "should be maintained, and its execution insisted on." After thirteen hours of debate, the measure passed 210–0. Adams was elated. He wrote to many of his friends telling them of his smashing victory and of the applause that rained down from the gallery. To Charles he wrote, "I will not attempt to describe my feelings. You cannot perhaps conceive them. It was one of those moments that compensate for a lifetime of suffering."

This was a man who had been secretary of state and president of the United States. Yet he was euphoric over a vote on a resolution that could have only the most marginal effect on events. What moved him so deeply was the applause, the earnest handshakes from colleagues, the sense of having brought his colleagues around. Clay had done as much, he conceded, but never against such odds. Clay was a natural leader of men. Adams was not; he was a solitary man who had learned to pay the terrible price of the lonely stand. Perhaps no one else could have felt such vindication at the discovery that he had the power to bring other men along. Adams' joy was a measure of the depth of his self-imposed isolation.

The Triumvirate still had other darts to fire at the Jackson administration. In January 1835, at almost the exact moment when the Senate passed its resolution rebuking Jackson on France, Calhoun proposed that the chamber establish a committee to investigate the administration's abuse of patronage and propose a remedy for it. This was quite an irony, since Jackson himself had ridden to power in 1828 on a tide of similar allegations against the Adams administration, in which Calhoun of course had served. Patronage, however, was central to the Jacksonian Revolution, with its low regard for the state and its high regard for the ordinary citizen. Jackson's belief that any man could perform a government job coincided perfectly with the political self-interest of rewarding members of the new Democratic Party with civil service plums.

Under the guidance of the Triumvirate, the Senate voted to repeal an 1820 law that limited the terms of many federal officers to four years, thus permitting each new administration to fill the ranks with its own men. Adams, who as president had exercised as little patronage as humanly possible, nevertheless believed that the executive had the constitutional right to fill such positions as he wished. He also viewed the legislation as a transparent attempt to clip Jackson's wings by three men who aspired to replace him. After the bill passed the Senate, in late February, Adams began drawing up a speech that, perhaps fortunately, he did not have the chance to deliver before the session ended. He described the measure as a pernicious encroachment of the legislature on the executive, adding that, far from diminishing patronage, it would open the doors to "every drunkard and driveler in his dotage, and every idler turning his office into a sinecure." The bill pandered to popular prejudice. It was not President Jackson but his Whig opponents who posed the gravest danger: "The Ark of our God"—the Constitution—"is falling into the hands of the Philistines."

By now Adams was utterly disgusted with the Whig leadership and above all with Webster, who, as he saw it, had betrayed his principles out of ambition. To Charles he ridiculed the great orator as "a residuary legatee of the old Federalists, and possessed of no principle less elastic than India rubber." He had already lost faith in Clay, who had abandoned the American System in his tariff compromise. He had, in fact, weighed all the Whig leaders and found them wanting. In a letter to John Bailey, he declared that not one of them "manifests the slightest attachment to the promotion of the general welfare," which had been "the great principle of my Administration." In his Puritan wrath, Adams cast three of the greatest men of his generation into the fiery pit.

Perhaps had Adams been able to admit to himself that he, too, was an ambitious man, he might not have so bitterly resented ambition in others. A story planted in the pro-Whig *Baltimore Patriot* suggested that the Whigs hoped to install Adams in a vacant Senate seat and then nominate him as their candidate in 1836. Adams inhaled the fumes of glory as he had in 1832. He believed that Webster was quietly contriving against him, advancing Governor John Davis for the Senate slot. Adams may have been right, at least about the Senate seat. According to an excited letter from one of his lieutenants, Benjamin Hallet, the state senate, which recommended to the assembly candidates for the US Senate, had voted for Adams. Hallet congratulated him on his new position. But it was premature: Whigs in the House went more heavily for Davis, who prevailed in a close vote. A member of the state's congressional delegation told Adams that Webster had advised his friends to vote for Davis.

Adams would have welcomed a move to the Senate, not only the more distinguished chamber but the one that in recent years had hosted every great issue and every great debate. But he was enjoying the benefits of his nonpartisan status in the House. He had been chosen by the Jackson administration to deliver a eulogy on General Lafayette, and his address, which lasted almost three hours, had been greeted with widespread acclaim. Adams received as many letters asking for copies of the eulogy as he had for the speech on bank deposits. He had been chosen as well to adjudicate a ticklish border dispute between Ohio and the Michigan Territory. And in the debate over France he had recorded, as he wrote to Charles in all seriousness, "a triumph unparalleled in the history of our country." An inner voice told him that he should retire now, but he would not listen to it. His string of successes, he thought, "will open to me, a career of action, more conspicuous and more perilous, than any that I have gone through."

Charles did not return these volleys, which arrived almost every other day in the first half of April. Finally, at the end of the month, he wrote to say that he had been rereading and pondering the letters, with their fierce passions and their obsessive recounting of legislative drama. He repeated a belief he had long expressed to his father, that the only real motive for public service was self-interest. "I am aware," he wrote, "that you individually plead for higher motives and feelings than you give credit for to anybody else." This was a stingingly accurate observation that no one save Charles would have had the courage to fling in the old man's face. Charles himself could not accept the "self-degradation," the sacrifice of personal independence, required for a life in politics. He wished neither power nor wealth. Rather, he would master those raging appetites and "say with the poet, 'My mind a kingdom is'." Could you, he asked, "say that by the votes of 210?"

Adams responded with perfect equanimity. He depended on Charles for help and for judgment. He knew, as well, that Charles spoke out of love, even if Adams could never have dreamed of uttering such reproaches to his own father. "If I have misused my time and talents by devoting myself to public service," he mused, "my career cannot continue much longer for good or evil." But Adams' feelings soon rose to the surface. "I have suffered great and grievous wrongs from many," he wrote, "and it has been my aim to avoid strife and contention whenever it was possible." Adams' adversaries, and even his friends, might have gaped at such a claim. More defensibly, he wrote that he had been as honest as any man to have served as president. "For all this I may not obtain credit even from my family," he added. "It is nevertheless true."

Adams no longer wondered about his future. He would fight for his principles so long as he lived and so long as the people of the Plymouth District returned him to office.

CHAPTER 31

Am I Gagged?

(1835–1836)

O N DECEMBER 18, 1835, AT THE OUTSET OF A NEW LEGIS-
lative session, William Jackson, a representative from Massachusetts, introduced a petition from his constituents asking Congress
to prohibit slavery and the slave trade in the District of Columbia. The
First Amendment to the Constitution forbade Congress from abridging
the right of the people "to petition the Government for a redress of grievance," and in this era, before the advent of lobbyists and advocacy organizations and orchestrated letter-writing campaigns, citizens routinely
submitted petitions to Congress, whether to receive benefits like pensions
or the repair of roadways, or to influence the legislative process. The request to end slavery in the district that Jackson offered now, and that Adams had offered when he first took office, represented a nascent trend in
public opinion.

In 1833, abolitionists had founded the American Anti-Slavery Society in
New York. Local branches of the society soon sprang up throughout the free
states, especially in the northeast. During the summer of 1835, the organization had begun a campaign to flood the South with pamphlets—hundred of
thousands of pamphlets—denouncing slavery. The South had reacted with
fury. Postmasters refused to deliver the literature; justices of the peace authorized officers of the law to burn the documents and arrest those who sought
to distribute them. Representatives of the slave states in Congress no longer

viewed the presentation of anti-slavery petitions as a harmless charade. James Henry Hammond of South Carolina proposed that the House refuse to receive Jackson's petition or any other asking Congress to act on the subject of slavery. Congress had never prohibited petitions on any subject. Yet while Southern planters rose one after another to defend the proposal, free-state representatives remained silent. The South could not dominate public opinion, but thanks to the three-fifths compromise it could, and did, dominate the House of Representatives.

Three days later, John Quincy Adams, having listened in silence, rose to speak. From the time that he had joined the House, Adams recalled, he had introduced such petitions, knowing full well that they would be referred to the committee on the District of Columbia, where "they go to the family vault 'of all the Capulets,' and you will never hear of them again." Since, Adams said, he did not believe that Congress should ban slavery in the nation's capital, this had struck him as a judicious system for satisfying all parties. Why, he asked, open Pandora's Box?

Here, however, Adams departed sharply from Hammond and his ilk. Should the Congress stop up the vent of petitions, he predicted, it would force a discussion on slavery itself to the floor. In that case, he said, "the speeches of my colleagues, probably of myself, will be incendiary"—Adams very consciously chose the word the slaveholders used to describe abolitionist literature—"because, if discussion is thrust upon us, I doubt not I might make a speech as incendiary as any pamphlet upon which such torrents of denunciation have been poured upon us." Then what? Would the Congress impede not just the right of petition but the freedom of speech? And the freedom of the press? You will end, Adams said, by suppressing the freedom of religion, "for in the minds of many worthy, honest, and honourable men, fanatics, if you so please to call them, this is a religious question, in which they act under what they believe to be a sense of duty to their God."

Adams appeared to be counseling the slave-state representatives on their self-interest. If he was defending anything, it was the "sacred" right of petition rather than the human rights of slaves. But that wasn't quite so, for he was also plainly threatening a righteous assault on slavery from worthy, honest, and honorable men. Who were these men? Adams would have been hard-pressed to say. There were no abolitionists in Congress, and few men were prepared to defy the South on any issue so profound as this. Perhaps the force Adams was preparing to unleash was himself. Only a few weeks earlier, after reading a defense of slavery that enraged him, he had written in his journal, "My duty for the present is silence. Whether it may ever come to be my duty to speak, is in the darkness of futurity." Adams had felt since the Missouri Compromise in 1820 that his own destiny might be intertwined with the abolition of slavery. Yet he had long accepted that he could do little to hasten the end of this abominable practice. He feared speaking his mind. He also, of course, yearned to speak his mind. He implied, though he did not say, that he counted himself among the "fanatics" driven by conscience to throw themselves at the great brick wall of slavery.

At that moment, Adams was feeling his way toward the issue that would define the remainder of his career. He knew what he believed, but he did not, for once, know how to reach the goal he sought. Slavery, for him, was a moral issue, not a legislative one. It was a practice sanctioned by state law. Petitions, however, were another matter entirely. The Constitution guaranteed the right of petition, and Adams had no doubt about the sanctity of that right. He would fight for the citizens' right to petition even where he disagreed with the substance of the demand. Adams could not yet see how a fight over the gag rule could undermine and finally bring down that brick wall. He hoped it would be so, and he, more than any other man, would lead that fight. Confronting and defeating the slave power in Congress—the "slavocracy," as he called it—would be the great achievement of his life.

THE ANTI-SLAVERY MOVEMENT BEGAN IN EARNEST IN ENGLAND IN the late eighteenth century and spread thereafter to the United States. Most American adherents were gradualists who hoped to hasten the slow withering away of a practice plainly at variance with Christian teachings. Even many Southerners were prepared to contemplate this prospect and to join local anti-slavery societies. Many favored, and practiced, voluntary manumission. Few, however, could contemplate the prospect of a multiracial American society. Enlightened slaveholders, including Jefferson, Madison, and Monroe, advocated transporting freed slaves to Africa. The American Colonization Society was founded with this object in 1816; Henry Clay, himself a slave owner, presided over its first meeting. Understood in this anodyne manner, the debate over slavery was a subject reasonable men could discuss.

But there was no realistic prospect that voluntary acts would bring about the end of slavery. As the evangelical movement known as the Second

Great Awakening swept the nation starting in the 1820s, the elimination of slavery came increasingly to be seen as a matter of supreme moral urgency. Many members of the new generation of anti-slavery leaders, men like Lyman Beecher and Theodore Weld and Joshua Leavitt, were Christian ministers who had begun their career of activism in the temperance movement, or sabbatarianism, or Anti-Masonry. They preached a gospel of social change. To live with the fact of slavery, to allow so heinous a practice to simply wither away over time, was an intolerable compromise with evil. These men advocated "abolition," by which they meant the use of public pressure and political power to force an end to slavery.

The activists differed over the tactics required to end slavery. So-called gradualists were prepared to work with enlightened slaveholders. Immediatists called for a campaign of public pressure to begin right away; most, however, expected a decades-long struggle. The differences among them had to do with their willingness to provoke violent opposition, even a civil war, in order to end slavery. The most fiery of the polemicists were unwilling to accept any compromise with Southern resistance. On New Year's Day 1831, William Lloyd Garrison wrote in the initial issue of the *Liberator*, his abolitionist newspaper, that he had been wrong to endorse gradualism in a speech two years before. "On this subject," he wrote, "I do not wish to think, or speak, or write, with moderation. No, no! Tell a man whose house is on fire to give a moderate alarm." This was the rising mood of the anti-slavery activists.

In 1833, the British parliament voted to outlaw slavery in its West Indian colonies, a clarion call for the American abolitionists. In December 1833, literally days after news of the decision reached the United States, they formed the American Anti-Slavery Society. Activists started up abolitionist newspapers like the *Liberator* across New England and the West. Abolitionists brought their campaign to the South, where they faced death threats and organized violence. Like the civil rights activists of the late 1950s and early '60s, the abolitionists of 1835 were a small band of idealists hoping to awaken the conscience of the nation by confronting racial injustice at its source.

At first, they were less successful in awakening citizens in the free states than they were in outraging, and terrifying, those in the South. These new sparks landed on dry tinder, for the slave rebellions led by Denmark Vesey in 1822 and Nat Turner in 1831, along with the mass distribution in 1829 of the abolitionist tract *Appeal . . . to the Coloured Citizens of the World*, by a free black man named David Walker, had already persuaded Southerners that their way of life—indeed, their very lives—were under attack. Then came the Northern evangelists accusing the South of perpetuating evil, and then their newspapers and pamphlets by the hundreds of thousands. The middle ground once occupied by aristocratic Virginians who acknowledged that slavery was an unfortunate exception to American principles swiftly disappeared. Men like John Calhoun, who had been content to argue that, whatever its merits, slavery was no one's business save the South, now embraced it as a good, for both master and slave.

In fact, the new abolitionist activism hardened opinion in the North as well as in the South, though hardly in the way the abolitionists had expected. To many Northerners, immediatism looked like a formula for disunion, or even civil war. Rioters routinely disrupted anti-slavery meetings throughout New England. In October 1835, a mob in Boston, seedbed of the American Revolution, chased down an English abolitionist who had hoped to speak in a local church. Northern representatives in Congress had no more appetite to raise the issue of slavery than Southerners did. In a speech in the House, Franklin Pierce, the future president, estimated that no more than one in five hundred citizens of his native New Hampshire favored immediate abolition. No legislator had a political motive to raise the subject of slavery; many had a strong reason to let it slumber.

This, then, was the situation Adams faced in December 1835. His private views had been "incendiary" since the debate over the Missouri Compromise, when he had acknowledged to himself that the Union might have to be dissolved in order to uproot the evil of slavery. But while a few radicals were prepared to accept bloodshed, Adams was not. Neither, at the same time, could he put much stock by less drastic solutions. Some abolitionists believed that the South would be won over by persistent argument; Adams considered this absurd. He felt the same way about the campaign to send freed slaves back to Africa.

Adams saw no way out on slavery. He knew that his constituents did not share his passionate convictions. He did not seek to meet with abolitionists, and he did not look for opportunities to reveal his views in Congress, any more than he had sought to publicize his views in 1820. Adams had been quite sincere when he had told the House that he did not support abolishing slavery in the District. He viewed such a measure as undemocratic, though not unconstitutional. In a letter to a petitioner from Rhode Island in November 1835, he wrote, "As the abolition of slavery in the District of Columbia would deeply affect the right of property of the inhabitants of that District without affecting yours, I do not think it just or generous that you should be the petitioner to impair their rights of property and not your own." Adams also feared that banning slavery in the District would enrage the South while accomplishing something very modest in return. Many other Northern Whigs had remained silent on the subject, not out of complacency toward slavery but out of fear of dividing Congress—and the country.

The rise of anti-slavery petitions, on the other hand, presented Adams with an issue on which he had unambiguous feelings. A debate on the gag rule would afford him the high ground in a debate with the slavocracy. If it allowed him at the same time to disclose the horrors of slavery, so much the better. During the first month of each session, portions of each day were by tradition set aside for the presentation of petitions, and Adams periodically introduced petitions on noncontroversial topics, which would be received, and ones on slavery, which would provoke a new round of debate. (Hammond's motion had never come to a vote, leaving the House to deal separately with each new anti-slavery petition.) The slaveholders' Northern allies agreed that Congress had no power to regulate slavery, but they differed on whether petitions on the subject should be permitted. Many legislators were unwilling to sacrifice free speech on the altar of slavery. In late January Adams declared that he "believed it to be the true course to let error be tolerated, to grant freedom of speech, and freedom of the press, and apply reason to put it down." This claim, anticipating John Stuart Mill's defense of the "marketplace of ideas," resonated with many free-state representatives. The endless wrangle over petitions brought the regular business of Congress almost to a halt.

On February 4, Henry Laurens Pinckney, another South Carolinian, sought to break the deadlock by proposing that all such petitions be referred to a select committee—which would agree in advance that Congress had no right to interfere with slavery in the states and ought not do so in the District. Just as Hammond was operating as a cat's-paw for Calhoun, who planned to run for president as the candidate of states' rights, so Pinckney was probably acting at the behest of Vice President Van Buren, who wanted to marginalize slavery as an issue in order to forge a coalition of "the planter of the South and the plain Republican of the North," as he had said back in 1826. But by this time the Southern mossbacks had become so inflamed against the petition campaign that the Calhounites treated Pinckney's proposed compromise as treachery. Nevertheless, the idea was referred to committee for further discussion.

By the time the Pinckney committee reported back on May 18, it had retreated before South Carolina's harassing fire. Rather than referring all slavery petitions to a select committee, the report suggested that such petitions "shall, without being either printed or referred, be laid on the table and no further action whatever shall be had thereon." This was similar to what Hammond had proposed and precisely what Adams had counseled against. Yet this was no longer enough for the most agitated Southerners; the report did not explicitly state that Congress had no right to legislate slavery anywhere, including in the District. The fire-breathing Waddy Thompson denounced the report as an "abandonment" of Southern rights unworthy of South Carolina, the state both he and Pinckney represented.

The debate between pragmatic slaveholders and ideologues, with Northerners largely looking on, dragged on until May 25. After Congressman John Robertson of Virginia spent hours denouncing the Pinckney compromise, George Owens of Georgia moved the previous question, the parliamentary means for ending debate and proceeding to a vote. Adams, who had something to say, asked Owens to withdraw the motion; the Georgian refused. Adams appealed to the chair—Speaker James K. Polk of Tennessee—who also refused. "I am aware that there is a slaveholder in the chair," Adams said caustically. He continued to seek the floor, bickering with Polk and others. One of his chief adversaries, Henry Wise of Virginia, accused Adams of violating parliamentary order. Finally a furious Adams burst out, "Am I gagged or not?" Pinckney's proposed gag rule had not yet been adopted; Adams was saying that the slaveholders had already begun to eliminate debate. He tried once again to speak, and now calls of "Order!" ricocheted around the hall.

The House then proceeded to vote on the resolution that Congress had no power to regulate slavery in the states. Adams shot to his feet once again; massed opposition had only whetted his appetite for battle. "If the House will give me five minutes," he cried, "I will prove that resolution false and utterly untrue"—or so wrote the perhaps overwhelmed reporter for Gales and Seaton's *Register of Congressional Debate*. The representative from Massachusetts was shouted down, and the vote was taken. Adams was one of only nine in the negative. He continued to badger Polk on fine points of procedure until one o'clock arrived, and the Speaker called for the dinner break.

Later in the day, the House voted on the remainder of the Pinckney compromise. Despite Southern opposition, the resolution stipulating that the House ought not take up slavery in the District of Columbia—but not declaring that the Constitution forbade the subject—passed 132 to 45. Then came the actual "gag," which committed the House to neither print nor even formally receive slavery petitions. By now Adams was so exercised that he disputed the legitimacy of the vote itself. When his name was called, he rose and said, "I hold the resolution to be a direct violation of the Constitution of the United States, the rules of this House, and the rights of my constituents." The reporter noted that "Mr. A resumed his seat amid loud cries of 'Order!', from all parts of the Hall." The resolution passed 117 to 68. Though some Northern Whigs had balked at the idea of infringing the right of petition, many others had not.

Adams had reached, and crossed, a Rubicon. In December he had made an effort, whether in good faith or no, to appeal to slave interests in the calm language of collective self-interest. He had made no headway. And he had sat for long days and weeks as slaveholders and their free-state allies had painted lurid pictures of the fanaticism of the abolitionists and the dire threats to the Southern way of life. Adams could feign patience, but he was not a patient man. His blood must have been boiling. And now he had let it overflow. "Am I gagged?," he had shouted. He had not been; he had, in fact, been out of order. But Adams was now prepared to use his own solitary resistance to the slavocracy to illustrate and publicize the grave threats to cherished constitutional liberties that accompanied the defense of slavery. Adams was staging a theater of martyrdom—a species of drama to which, thanks to his rhetorical gifts, his fearlessness, his towering sense of moral purpose, he was supremely well suited.

AS SECRETARY OF STATE, ADAMS HAD SOUGHT TO BUY FROM SPAIN the northeastern province known as Texas, but the fear that it could become a giant slave state, or the source of several such states, was reason enough for both Adams and President Monroe to restrain the impulse for territorial self-aggrandizement. Since that time, however, tens of thousands of American settlers had established themselves in the region and become a potent force in American politics. President Jackson had sought to buy Texas from the new Mexican Republic, but Mexico had turned him down flat.

Left on their own, Texans had begun agitating for independence. When General Lopez de Santa Anna seized power and dissolved the legislature, in 1835, Texas as well as several other provinces rebelled. On March 2, 1836, Texas declared its independence. A week later, Santa Anna's forces decimated the Texans at the battle of the Alamo. When the news reached Washington the following month, Congress voted to ask the president to send a volunteer militia to defend the settlers. Adams was one of the few to oppose the measure. He had seen Congress afflicted with war fever almost from the beginning of his tenure in national office, in 1804. Now he saw his colleagues preparing to fight a republican government and a former colony, rather than a European monarchy, and doing so, he believed, in order to advance the cause of slavery.

Adams' speech against war on April 27 attracted the attention of Benjamin Lundy, an abolitionist who had traveled extensively in Texas. He sent Adams a letter praising his stand, and included a series of letters on Texas that he had just published in Robert Walsh's *National Gazette*. Lundy claimed that Texan leaders and Southern slave owners had hatched a secret plan to win independence and divide Texas into as many as fifteen states, all committed to slavery. (Mexico had banned slavery.) According to the scheme, he wrote, "every facility is to be given to the introduction of slaves" from the South as well from Cuba and Africa. The slave trade "will be perpetuated perhaps for centuries." As an added fillip, Lundy argued that Northern land speculators had been secretly buying up vast tracts of land, so that an independent Texas would constitute an unholy coalition between Northern capitalists and Southern slaveholders. Adams wrote back to Lundy immediately asking for more documents, including an English translation of the Mexican law emancipating the slaves. Lundy swiftly complied.

Lundy was the kind of man Adams could not resist—morally driven, theologically inspired, fully prepared to sacrifice everything in the name of principle. For a brief period, he and Adams were to play indispensable roles in one another's life. Lundy was the John the Baptist of abolitionism—a lone figure, crying in the wilderness. Born into a Quaker family in New Jersey in 1789, Lundy moved out West, where he was shocked to see slaves driven through the streets. In 1816 Lundy persuaded several of his friends to form an anti-slavery society. Five years later he started up the *Genius of Universal Emancipation*, the first anti-slavery newspaper in the country. At the time, according to his biographer, Lundy had no money, no printing press, no knowledge of publishing, and no more than six subscribers. Undaunted—undauntable—he moved to Tennessee, a slave state, where he loudly denounced slavery, putting his life in sufficient jeopardy that he moved again, to Baltimore—also in slave territory.

Barely educated, Lundy preferred action to advocacy. He traveled to Haiti in the hopes of persuading free American blacks to emigrate there. In 1827 he sent one of the very first petitions to Congress demanding an end to slavery in Washington. "Let petitions and memorials flow into the halls of Congress, from all quarters," he wrote in *Genius*—prematurely, it turned out. Lundy's writings inspired the next generation of abolitionists, including William Lloyd Garrison, who took over the editorship of *Genius* in 1829. Lundy and Garrison ultimately fell out over the latter's radicalism and hostility to orthodox religion.

Though slight of stature and frail, Lundy was extraordinarily brave. He walked across much of Canada in the dead of winter and then trekked across Texas, in disguise, in the height of summer. In the town of San Felipe he was threatened with tar and feather. In a journal he then kept he wrote, "I gave them all to understand, however, that I was not to be so easily intimidated." Lundy was almost always broke, and unlike most abolitionists he frequently lived with and among black people. They often helped him survive. He had a wild scheme to buy a tract of land in Mexico, settle free blacks there, and then sell their produce in the United States, thus proving that blacks could be more productive as free men than as slaves—a precursor of the "Free Soil" movement. When the plan fell through, he returned to the United States, his health failing, and wrote his articles for Robert Walsh, since he no longer had a paper of his own.

Lundy could neither write nor speak as convincingly as the well-born and well-educated New Englanders who had begun to fill the ranks of the abolitionist movement. They were bound to supplant him. But he knew more about Texas, and more about the real conditions of slavery, than any of them. At the time he was far more useful to Adams than were sedentary men of the cloth like William Ellery Channing, whose tracts he read with minimal appreciation. Lundy provided Adams with information he needed as well as with a point of view he shared—that the Texas "revolution" was actually the slavocracy's next frontier. Adams provided Lundy, the prophet in the wilderness, with something yet more precious—the voice to whom all men listened. The letter Lundy wrote to Adams in early May 1836 was one of the most inspired acts of his career. He now had an opportunity to shape the national debate.

On May 16, word reached Washington that Texan troops under Sam Houston had defeated Santa Anna at the Battle of San Jacinto, avenging the defeat at the Alamo and gaining independence for Texas. The hosannas to Anglo-Saxon superiority unleashed by the victory only increased Adams' disgust. Armed with Lundy's mass of documents, Adams was looking for a chance to expose what he deemed a monstrous plot. The issue, alas, was no longer under debate in the House. Instead, on the afternoon of May 25, Adams seized on the pretext of a vote to offer relief to victims of Indian raids in Alabama and Georgia. At first he spoke directly to the issue at hand, which he mocked as one of a new class of "scalping-knife and tomahawk laws" designed to loose a flood of tears and thus of federal funds. Yet since "mere commiseration" was no grounds for draining the Treasury, Adams said, one needed to look elsewhere for a rationale for such relief bills. Perhaps it lay in the expansive war powers the Constitution conferred on the executive.

Adams now recalled that he had begged five minutes of the chair to explain why the first of the Pinckney resolutions had been invalid on its face. He had been denied that opportunity. Now he could explain himself, for his views of the present question—the relief bill—stemmed from the same line of reasoning he had hoped to disclose before he had been gagged. Under those same war powers, Adams explained, the government had every right to regulate slavery, including by banning the slave trade, as it had done in 1808. "Suppose," Adams said, "the case of a servile war"—a slave uprising. Suppose the slave emancipates himself. Would the president be powerless "to recognize his emancipation by a treaty of peace," even if only by doing so he could bring that war to an end? Adams appears to have been the first to publicly raise this shocking prospect, which formed the constitutional foundation of Lincoln's Emancipation Proclamation. Or suppose a war with Mexico—and now Adams, having already found a way to make his case on Congress' powers over slavery, elaborated his argument on Texas, though opponents might have felt that it had little to do with the question at hand. It's not hard to see why the members were crying "Order!"

"The war now raging in Texas," Adams said, "is a Mexican civil war, and a war for the re-establishment of slavery where it was abolished. It is not a servile war, but a war between slavery and emancipation, and every possible effort has been made to drive us into this war, on the side of slavery." This was Lundy, pure and simple. In fact, since Mexico had barely bothered to enforce its ban on slavery, Texans did not have to fight a war in order to preserve the institution. Now Adams digressed from his digression, ridiculing the pretensions of those who saw San Jacinto as racial vindication. Why, he asked, kindle "the fires of hereditary national hatred?" Isn't the South already consumed enough by such hatred? Adams twisted the elastic band of his oratory tighter and tighter, and then let it fly: "Do not you, an Anglo-Saxon, slave-holding exterminator of Indians, from the bottom of your soul, hate the Mexican-Spaniard-Indian, emancipator of slaves, and abolisher of slavery? And do you think that your hatred is not with equal cordiality returned?"

Adams now spoke of the prospect of a race war with Mexico, one in which the United States would fight on the side of slavery against freedom. Could the United States even be confident of winning such a war? What if a new Mexican leader called for the Indian and the Negro slave to join him under the banner of freedom? Might he not take the war to the American South? And Mexico might not fight alone; Great Britain, the global champion of abolitionism, might take up the Mexican cause against the United States—an ironic reversal, to say the least. It's impossible to know if Adams actually took these terrifying hypotheticals seriously, or if he were gleefully tormenting his adversaries so long as he had the floor. None of them, remarkably, rose to the bait, though when Adams finally resumed his seat, Charles Haynes of Georgia did say that "however fashionable it might be in this House to discuss everything but the subject under consideration, he would not follow the example of the honorable gentleman from Massachusetts."

The first session of the Twenty-Fourth Congress dragged on until July 4. Two territories, Michigan and Arkansas, sought admission to the Union. No new states had been admitted since the Missouri Compromise, and now the same rule of balance had to apply. If Michigan was to join as a free state, Arkansas must join as a slave state. The Arkansas state legislature used the opportunity to fire a shot at Adams and his ilk, inserting into the state constitution a provision stating that the federal government had no power to interfere with slavery. Henry Wise of Virginia, one of Adams' inveterate antagonists, said that if Northerners tried to prohibit slavery in Arkansas, he would introduce a bill to permit slavery in Michigan. Several Northerners promised that they would do no such thing—at which point Adams rose to say, "When the Arkansas bill comes to the House, if no one else raises the subject of slavery, I will." The debate continued all night June 8 and well into the next morning—twenty-five hours without a break. Adams did not leave the House, though most of his colleagues did. In his journal he noted that one member was "drunk with whiskey" while another was "drunk with slavery." Arkansas was finally admitted to the Union as a slave state, and Michigan as a free state. Adams voted against the admission of Arkansas.

IF NO ONE RAISED SLAVERY, HE WOULD—ADAMS HAD TAKEN A definitive and irrevocable stand as a strident and even solitary voice of conscience. He had declared war on his fellow Whigs as much as he had on the slaveholders and the annexationists. He would willingly pay the cost; his family would do so unwillingly. In early 1836 Charles wrote to his mother to say that Boston was in a tumult over Adams' fierce attacks on Daniel Webster, as it once had been over his rhodomontade against the Hartford conspirators. Charles wrote that he would go abroad to escape the clamor, save that he had so many small children to care for. Louisa wrote back to say that her husband's recent speeches had "completely cut us off from all society." Louisa's brothers-in-law, as well as many of her friends, owned slaves, and her husband had, or so it felt, damned them to perdition. In her diary, which she had resumed after a decade, she wrote, "Every friend is turned into an enemy; and now the prospect terminates with the fear of losing the love, the friendship and the society of my own nearest and dearest connections." Why, Louisa asked herself in an agony of spirit, "am I foerever thrust into situations which it is known I cannot endure rationally?" She was helpless; her husband never discussed politics with her.

Adams left Washington as soon as the session ended, taking the train to Baltimore and then to Philadelphia. In his hotel he received a delegation from the American Anti-Slavery Society, which wished to thank him in person for the stout role he had played in Congress. Adams turned them down. He did not, he said, share their views either on ending slavery in Washington or on the imperative of immediate abolition, which he feared would lead to insurrection and race war. But he could not escape so easily. He had continued corresponding with Lundy, and asked him to send a hundred copies of the letters on Texas he had published in the *National Gazette*. Lundy then came by as well, asking Adams to help fund a new abolitionist paper he was starting up. Adams declined, but he did agree to go to a meeting of Quakers at the home of the abolitionists James and Lucretia Mott.

Adams and Lundy wrote one another incessantly through the spring and summer of 1836. The former president would not help the abolitionist pay for his newspaper, but he urged him to publish in it all the documents he had supplied. He fastidiously sent Lundy a $10 check for the hundred copies of the articles that Lundy had sent him. Lundy, in turn, urged Adams on. "Let this Texas schism be carried into effect," he wrote, "and our great Republic is riven to atoms." That was just the way Adams himself thought. Over the course of two years the rambling abolitionist prophet and the fearsomely respectable New England Puritan would join together to stop the annexationist movement in its tracks.

CHAPTER 32

I Am Not to Be Intimidated by All the Grand Juries in the Universe

(1837)

IN HIS SEVENTIETH YEAR, JOHN QUINCY ADAMS FELT HIS EYESIGHT fading and his voice failing; his rheumatism became so severe that for weeks on end he could barely stir from his couch; he remained deeply in debt from John's mismanagement of family affairs. He spoke of retiring to Quincy. But he didn't mean it for a moment. Adams lived to fight, and he had now discovered the fight of his lifetime. In early 1837, on a day when Adams had lugged 160 petitions to Congress, Louisa informed Charles that "your father stands the wear and tear of Congress better than ever."

There was no evidence that the petition crusade was turning public opinion against slavery, but the abolitionists believed it was so and unleashed a cataract of petitions on Congress. Many of them were directed to Adams, one of the few men in Congress prepared to provoke the wrath of the slaveholders and their free-state allies. Martin Van Buren had succeeded to the presidency by assembling a North-South coalition that could be counted on to hold together so long as slavery was kept out of the national debate. Adams and his tiny band of allies would thus be facing a solid phalanx of resistance if they tried once again to force the House to hear anti-slavery petitions.

Of course they did try, for the Pinckney gag had lapsed, as all temporary House rules did, at the end of the last session. On January 18, a member from Georgia, Albert Hawes, reintroduced the Pinckney gag, which promptly passed. Adams once again began probing the gag for weak spots. On January 23 he insisted that petitions he had presented before the gag had passed should be referred to committee. Speaker Polk denied the motion, and the House sustained him on appeal. Adams commenced his pantomime of martyrdom. "The old gentleman," according to a contemporary account, "surveyed his file of petitions;—he turned an eye upon the House; he gave a dreary look up to the Speaker's chair . . . 'Give me back my old petitions then,' he said." Adams began to read from a new sheaf of petitions. The House shouted him down each time it became clear that the new petition he sought to present demanded an end to slavery or the slave trade. Adams tried to present thirteen or fourteen petitions in this manner, "dodging points of order, creeping through this rule and skipping over that . . . all the while flourishing away in tit-bit speeches, which were so short and so quickly said that, though they were out of order, nobody could call him to order; and when they did, he would say, 'My speech is done.'" Though utterly outnumbered, Adams dodged every brickbat with the nimbleness of an acrobat.

The petition drama was a public spectacle, reported in both abolitionist and mainstream newspapers all over the country. Adams increasingly became the hero and standard-bearer of the abolitionist movement—even though he opposed immediatism and the prohibition of slavery in the District. The leading abolitionists, all of them great letter writers, began sending Adams encouragement and advice. Adams heard from Lundy, and the Reverend William Ellery Channing, and some of the blazing spirits of the west like Arthur Lovejoy, a lone abolitionist in Alton, Illinois. The combustible William Lloyd Garrison offered fighting words: "Let these petitions be piled upon the table until it break." Lewis Tappan, head of the American Anti-Slavery Society, gently rebuked Adams for opposing immediatism, for "if slavery be a sin, its immediate abolition is a duty." Adams refused to delude himself on this score: immediate abolition meant civil war, and that was a price he would not pay. None of these men—and women—changed Adams' mind, but they fired him with a sense of the urgency of the moment. He, too, believed that the battle against sin was man's supreme calling. The abolitionists helped keep Adams' blood at a steady boil.

Adams was trying to goad the slave forces into a fight. In early February the perfect instrument for his theater of confrontation came to hand. He received in the mail the most unlikely of all petitions, one purporting to come from slaves complaining of attempts to end their condition, and insisting that they wished to serve their masters "as long as life and health will permit." Whoever wrote the petition had both excellent penmanship and an educated command of English. The signatures, on the other hand, were clumsy and scrawled. The petition was plainly a fraud designed to make Adams look ridiculous. Adams treated it as a godsend.

On February 6, John C. Calhoun, the South's intellectual and political leader, rose in the Senate to declare that the South's entire way of life was under attack. "We must meet the enemy on the frontier," Calhoun said, "with a fixed determination of maintaining our position at every hazard." With the abolitionist movement gaining strength in the free states, even remote threats to slavery could no longer be countenanced. On that very same day, Adams turned his batteries on the House. First he presented a petition from "nine ladies of Fredericksburg" seeking an end to the slave trade in Washington. This was laid on the table. Adams continued. He also had, he said, a petition from twenty-two persons "declaring themselves to be slaves." He did not say what these petitioners sought, leaving the obvious impression that they, too, wished an end to slavery. Nor did he actually present the petition. Since, he continued with the mock gentility he assumed at his most sardonic moments, "he wished to do nothing except in submission to the rules of the House," Adams asked the chair to decide whether such a prayer could be received—especially since, he noted, it was "one of those petitions which had occurred to his mind as not being what it purported to be."

The South rose as one to meet the enemy on the frontier. Dixon Lewis of Alabama demanded that the House "punish severely such an infraction of its decorum and its rules"—though it wasn't at all clear what rule Adams had broken—and suggested that, should the chamber fail to act, the representatives from the slave states should "go home at once." Julius Alford of Georgia asked the House to punish not just Adams but the petition itself, which ought to be "committed to the flames." Adams had endangered something much more serious than the decorum of the House, for, once granted the right to petition the Congress, how could slaves accept their subhuman status? Lewis offered a resolution stating that "by extending to slaves a privilege only belonging to freemen," Adams "directly invited the slave population to insurrection" and thus should be "forthwith called to the bar of the House, and be censured by the Speaker."

Only now, after so much spleen had been vented, did Adams reveal that the object of the petition was the exact opposite of what his accusers had imagined. It had also become clear by now that the nine ladies of

Fredericksburg were free women of color, and perhaps not even reputable ones—yet another outrage from the Massachusetts incendiary. But that served his purpose very well, for Adams wished to defend the principle that the right to petition could under no circumstances be abridged. He was what we would call today a First Amendment absolutist. He would, he said, present a petition from slaves—or from "a horse or a dog" if it had "the power of speech and of writing."

For four days, from February 6 to 9, Southern congressmen outdid one another in denouncing Adams, writing and rewriting the proposed resolution of censure. The ever-combative Waddy Thompson of South Carolina, who had grown apoplectic when he had learned that Adams had perpetrated a "hoax" on the House by disguising the true nature of the slave petition, reminded his friends that the "fanatics" of abolitionism "understand their game." By insisting on the right of petition, they were cleverly attacking slaveholders "at our weakest point." The abolitionists would stop at nothing: If slaves have the right to petition, Thompson observed, must it not be conceded that they have as well the right to vote? It was hardly an absurd question.

Only two legislators, Levi Lincoln, the ex-governor of Massachusetts and an Adams friend of many years, and Caleb Cushing, also from the Bay State, offered a full-throated defense of their colleague. Adams, meanwhile, sat quietly, letting one wave of invective after another crash over his head. Finally, on the ninth, he rose in his own defense. At first he resumed his single-minded defense of the universal right of petition. Then he made a brief swerve to the matter of the "nine ladies of Fredericksburg," allegedly of low character—"prostitutes, I think the gentleman said," alluding to John Patton, a Virginia congressman whose district included that city.

Patton jumped to his feet to explain that he had not called them "prostitutes," which in fact he hadn't, but rather had emphasized their low character in order to protect the honor of the true ladies of Fredericksburg. Adams now inserted the needle.

> He was glad to hear the honourable gentleman disclaim any knowledge of them, for he was going to ask if they were infamous women, then who had made them infamous? Not, he believed, their own colour, but their masters, and he had heard it said, in proof of this fact, and he was inclined to believe it was the case, that there existed great resemblances in the South between the progeny of the coloured people and the white men who claimed the possession of them.

The fact that this assertion was true did not make it any less of a calumny, one lodged against slaveholders prepared to kill a man who called their honor into a question. It was also completely irrelevant to the question at hand. Adams, however, had the floor, and he would goad and torment his adversaries while he could. Adams now rounded directly on his accusers, all of whom had fallen into the trap he had set by brandishing the alleged petition from slaves without explaining that those petitioners sought the end of abolitionism, not of slavery. He read back to the House a passage in which Waddy Thompson had called for Adams to be subject to criminal prosecution. Is that, he asked, the opinion of the slave-state representatives? Do they believe that a member should be criminally liable for seeking to present a petition? If, as Thompson had claimed, the law of South Carolina prohibited such an act, Adams proclaimed, "I thank God I am not a citizen of South Carolina!" The court reporter tersely summarized the reaction to this last provocation by writing, "Great agitation."

Adams pressed home the point, as if the question at issue were not his censure but his criminal prosecution. One of Adams' many rhetorical gifts was seizing on the most extreme version of his opponents' case and making it stand for the case itself. The more cool-headed among Adams' opponents saw the debate getting away from them. Henry Wise of Virginia volunteered that he would never permit a grand jury to sit in judgment upon words spoken in Congress. The tide had begun to turn. Adams pocketed the concession and then turned back to Waddy Thompson, his preferred foil. "If he thought to frighten me from my purpose," Adams thundered, "if that, sir, was his object, he mistook his man! I am not to be intimidated by the gentleman from South Carolina, nor by all the grand juries in the universe." It is unlikely that by that point any member thought otherwise.

The question was called, the vote taken. From the ranks of Southern slaveholders and Northern Democrats, a grand total of twenty-two men voted for the resolution to censure Adams. Given the overwhelming numerical dominance of these two groups, who together could carry any issues they wished, it was an astonishing outcome. The editor of the *Boston Daily Advertiser*, who had been present in the House, wrote that "the effect of the speech has been rarely if ever exceeded by the influence of any speech on any assembly."

The effect was felt far beyond Washington, and above all among abolitionists who had despaired of a slave-dominated Congress. The American Anti-Slavery Society reproduced the congressional debate in pamphlet form. Newspapers across the country carried accounts of Adams' fearless defense of the right of petition. As Joshua Giddings, a Western abolitionist who was later to became Adams' protégé in Congress, wrote many years later, "This defiance of the slave power was unexpected. The oldest member of the body had never witnessed such boldness, such heroism, on the part of any northern member."

Adams himself recounted the drama for his hometown paper, the *Quincy Patriot*, in a series of letters to constituents. Since Adams was so overwhelmed with work during this period that he stopped keeping his journal, the letters serve as one of the few sources for his state of mind in the midst of this fight for his political life. What is striking is how persistently he returns to the theme that the slaveholders expected to enjoy in Congress the same mastery they exercised over their slaves, and thus treated Adams himself as an "inferior" impertinently demanding the rights of an equal. Polk, he notes, ought to have defended the right of free speech; "but the Speaker was a *master*." In 1820 he had reflected that the need to defend slavery had warped as fine a mind as Calhoun's. Now, in his letters, he recalled Jefferson's observation that slavery degraded the master by accustoming him to dominion over his fellow man. Adams' own fury must have been stoked by the condescension he felt from these pampered young sons of slave-borne privilege.

Adams had won the battle but not the war. The gag remained in force. And, more important, he had seen how very little support he enjoyed in Congress. Two days after his exoneration, the House voted on a resolution stating that presenting petitions from slaves violates the House's "dignity" as well as that of "a large class of citizens of the South and West, and the Constitution of the United States." The vote was 160 to 35 in favor. Next, in order to clear up any remaining ambiguity, the House considered a resolution stating that "slaves do not possess the right of petition secured to the people of the United States by the constitution." Only 18 members voted against. Both Levi Lincoln and Caleb Cushing voted in favor.

The storm Adams had brought down on his head had simultaneously made him more intransigent on petitions and more cautious on slavery. He would never give an inch on petitions, where he enjoyed fairly widespread support, but he understood that if he called for an immediate end to slavery, even in Washington, as the abolitionists implored him to do, he would marginalize himself in Congress and in national public opinion. Adams continued to maintain a wary distance from the abolitionists. When the poet-activist John Greenleaf Whittier invited him to attend the opening of the New England Anti-Slavery Society, Adams declined, reflecting in his journal that he must learn to be "more circumspect in my conduct than belongs to my nature." Both parties were now prepared to pounce on any indiscretion he committed. He had already placed himself dangerously far afield from his own constituents. "Even in the North," he wrote in his diary, "the people favor the whites and fear the blacks." The abolitionists seemed incapable of recognizing the consequences of their own passionate polemics. He warned Lewis Tappan that by "taking untenable ground," by which he meant immediatism, the anti-slavery movement had "turned the great mass of the community in the free states against them."

Adams unburdened himself on this terrible question to Charles Hammond, the Ohio publisher, admitting that he had long thought that slavery would "slowly and peacefully pass away" thanks to the British prohibition, the growing emancipation of individual slaves, and the ban on the slave trade. Now he saw that it was not so. Slaveholders had responded to the "great moral force" of abolitionism by formulating a theology of their own, in which the Creator had formed black people to perpetually serve white ones. They would never agree to legislate their peculiar institution out of existence, as the abolitionists vainly imagined they would. Adams still could not accept the violence that he saw more clearly than ever would be needed to extirpate slavery. He would, he wrote Hammond, continue to abstain "in all measures *leading* to that conflict for life and death between *Freedom* and *Slavery* through which I have not been able to see how this Union can be preserved from passing." The syntax was tortured, and so, perhaps, were Adams' own feelings.

CHAPTER 33

Among the Most Illustrious of
the World's Benefactors

(1837–1838)

A
DAMS HAD VERY LITTLE TIME TO REST IN QUINCY AFTER HIS
ordeal by trial. He had been unable to leave Washington until he
had paid down debts that had accumulated over the years, as his
household expenses rose far above his meager income from rental properties and his $9 congressional per diem. Only after Charles, who managed
his funds, sent him $1,500 was Adams able to leave, in the first days of May.
Then he had to return in September, for President Van Buren had called for
an emergency session of Congress in order to deal with the spreading economic crisis.

The abolitionists implored Adams to use the session to dramatize the
dangers of the annexation of Texas, which they feared was imminent. On
his last day in office Jackson had received ambassadors from Texas and had
nominated an America chargé d'affaires. The Texan people had voted overwhelmingly for annexation. Lundy was now circulating petitions against
annexation and reprinting his letters on Texas as a pamphlet titled "War in
Texas" and suitable for mass circulation. He implored Adams to stop in
Philadelphia on his way to Congress in order to plot strategy for the coming session. William Ellery Channing wrote with questions about Adams'
role as secretary of state in negotiations with Spain; Adams had spurred his

interest on Texas, and now he was preparing a pamphlet on annexation and slavery. Adams did, in fact, stop in Philadelphia to meet with Lundy, Tappan, and other members of the Anti-Slavery Society.

Soon after he reached Washington, President Van Buren asked him over for a social call. Adams had not set foot inside the White House from March 4, 1829, until the previous May, when Van Buren had extended an invitation. This time the two made idle conversation about England's new monarch, Queen Victoria. The president seemed entirely at his ease despite the crisis besetting the nation. He had, Adams reflected, much of Madison's gentleness of manner but also a capacity for duplicity that reminded him of Jefferson—"though without his genius." And, he added, a "fawning servility, which belongs to neither." Adams would remain on comfortable terms with Van Buren but would always view him as a crass political operator and the linchpin of a coalition that ensured the dominance of the slavocracy. Van Buren had vindicated Adams' expectation by announcing in his Inaugural Address that he would veto any legislation seeking to restrict slavery.

When Adams had reached his home in Washington, he found that he had already received stacks of petitions. He was no longer the only member prepared to present these documents, but he still got far more than anyone else. He received four hundred in September alone, and they came from all over the North and the West. At times he wished that this cup could pass from him. "If there was one man in the House capable of taking the lead on emancipation," he wrote in his journal, "I would withdraw. There is no such man."

By the fall of 1837 abolitionism had spread across the country with astonishing speed. An estimated one thousand anti-slavery societies claimed about a hundred thousand members. Virtually every city of any importance outside the South had an abolitionist newspaper. Thurlow Weed, who a few years earlier had become a leading Anti-Masonry publisher, now took up the anti-slavery cause and became an abolitionist publisher. In May the American Anti-Slavery Society had decided to focus almost all its efforts on the petition campaign. A great national machinery clanged into motion. The abolitionist leaders John Greenleaf Whittier and Theodore Weld spearheaded the operation, researching the horrors of slavery, writing up sample petitions, and sorting them into "libraries" to be purchased by local societies. A typical form would begin, "The undersigned women of"—for an increasing fraction of the petitions came from women—and then came a blank to be filled in with the name of the town in question, "deeply convinced by the sinfulness of slavery, and keenly aggrieved by its existence in a part of the country over which Congress possesses exclusive jurisdiction in all cases whatsoever, do most earnestly petition your honourable body to abolish slavery in the District of Columbia, and also to put an end to the slave trade in the United States." There followed blank lines to be filled by signatures.

Petitions began to arrive in Washington by the wagonload. Over the course of the 1837–1838 congressional session legislators would receive 412,000 slave-related petitions, including 130,000 seeking the abolition of slavery and the slave trade in Washington, 32,000 calling for an end to the gag rule, and 180,000 protesting the annexation of Texas. One abolitionist estimated that the memorials bore half a million signatures (this in a country of 16 million). The petitions, like the letters, phone calls, and emails citizens and special-interest groups now send to Congress and the White House, served as an inescapable reminder of public opinion, though hardly a proof of majority preference.

At the very outset of the special session, Adams rose to demand that the administration turn over all correspondence with Mexico over the possible acquisition or annexation of Texas. The territory had declared itself sovereign, and Adams insisted that the Constitution made no provision for the executive to annex a nation; such a decision could be made only by the people, presumably through a constitutional amendment authorizing such an act. Adams had maintained this position since the Louisiana Purchase thirty-three years earlier. He added, with an obvious nod to the mighty river of petitions that would soon sluice through the halls of Congress, "There is a large portion of the people of the United States who would prefer a dissolution of the Union to the annexation of Texas." Adams reiterated his demand that the correspondence with Mexico be made public. Several days later he introduced a resolution stating that the power of annexing a foreign nation could be exercised only by the people. The chair ruled it out of order.

Jackson had not called for annexation in his last message to Congress, as Adams had been sure he would. Van Buren had no intention of taking up the Texans' clamor for annexation, which he understood could damage him politically. In fact, the plan had been stopped dead in its tracks, in part owing to the furor Adams and his demiurge Lundy had whipped up. Nevertheless, Lundy continued working the bellows, printing twenty-three thousand copies of his pamphlet and making sure that every member of Congress and everyone in the abolitionist movement received a copy.

Anti-annexationism became, briefly, the leading edge of the abolitionist movement.

Adams had by now become perhaps the most active member of the House, speaking on a wide range of subjects. President Van Buren had convened the special session in the hopes of passing the so-called Sub-Treasury bill, which would have established an independent body to handle federal deposits then being sent to state banks; the reckless lending behavior of those banks had helped spark the panic. Adams considered the Sub-Treasury an unnecessary substitute for the Bank of the United States, which Jackson and Van Buren had eliminated. He spent much of the special session denouncing the proposed measure. On this, as on many other subjects not involving slavery, legislators listened to Adams with the respectful attention due a former president and a venerable colleague.

On October 23, a week after the session had ended, Adams saw a shocking ad in the *National Intelligencer*. A slave woman, Dorcas Allen, and her two children, ages approximately seven and nine, were to be sold that day. Adams then heard that Dorcas had earlier murdered her two younger children in a fit of insanity; the slave trader who had bought her earlier that year had now returned her as unfit. Adams asked his brother-in-law Nathaniel Frye, a businessman who handled Adams' investments in Washington, if the story was true, and Frye very reluctantly confirmed that it was. Dorcas' terrible deed struck Adams less as an act of madness than as a judgment on the unspeakable practice of slavery. In his journal, he wrote, "It is a case of conscience with me whether my duty requires or forbids me to pursue the inquiry of the case to ascertain all the facts and to expose them in all their turpitude to the world."

Adams might have chosen prudence, as he had on the broad question of the prohibition of slavery, but five days later he saw another ad for Dorcas' sale. Until now, Adams had had no direct experience of the horrors of slavery, and had known few if any black people who were not servants. Now he went directly to the slave auction house in Alexandria, where he met the children and Dorcas, "weeping and wailing most piteously." The auctioneer, a Mr. Dyer, explained that several days earlier he had sold Dorcas to her own husband, a free black named Nathaniel Allen, for $475. Allen worked as a waiter at Gadsby's, a prominent hotel and tavern where many congressmen stayed during the term. Now Nathaniel was trying to scrape up the funds. Dyer doubted he could, so he had placed another ad.

Dyer told Adams that on her deathbed the woman who had owned Dorcas many years earlier had made her husband, Mr. Davis, promise to free her. Dorcas had married Nathaniel, and the two had lived as free blacks for a dozen or so years. In the meanwhile, Davis had died, his second wife had remarried, and that woman's husband had sold Dorcas to a slave trader as if he owned her. That very day, Dorcas and her children had been seized and thrown into Alexandria's dismal slave prison, within sight of the Capitol building. That night, Dorcas had murdered her four-year-old son and infant daughter; the screams of the older children prevented her from killing them too. A jury had acquitted her by reason of insanity, though it heard no prior evidence of mental instability. When asked why she had killed her children, Dorcas had said "that they were in Heaven, that if they had lived she did not know what would become of them."

Dorcas was no longer a cause to be publicized but a woman to be rescued. This probably made it easier for Adams to act on her behalf. His heart always responded to individuals—especially strangers—in peril. He returned to the slave house and told Dyer that he had no right to sell a free woman into slavery. Dyer, of course, disagreed. By now Nathaniel Allen had learned that Adams had taken an interest in his case, and came to him for help. He worried that Davis' creditors would claim Dorcas even if he bought her. Adams promised to track down the Washington district attorney, Francis Scott Key, better known today as the author of "The Star-Spangled Banner." A slave owner and aggressive defender of slavery, Key was unsympathetic but did tell Adams that Allen's title to his wife could not be contested.

On November 13, Nathaniel came to Adams' home with Dorcas, temporarily released from bondage. Nathaniel explained that another supporter, General Walter Smith of Georgetown, said that he could raise up to $330. What Nathaniel needed was money—the one commodity Adams did not have. Nevertheless, he pledged $50. Nathaniel and Dorcas left, returning later in the day with a promise from General Smith to raise the funds if the ex-president would, in fact, help as well. Adams immediately wrote the $50 check he had promised. Nathaniel and Dorcas exited from Adams' home and from his life, presumably to freedom. Adams appears to have been the only man in Congress or in official Washington to have come to this helpless woman's aid.

THE REGULAR SESSION OF CONGRESS RESUMED IN MID-DECEMBER, and Adams immediately rose to present a sheaf of petitions on slavery and

Texas. On December 20, before the majority had formulated a new version of the gag, William Slade of Vermont, one of Adams' very few reliable allies, introduced a resolution proposing the creation of a special committee to draw up a bill abolishing slavery and the slave trade in Washington. This was much further than Adams, who of course opposed abolition in the District, had ever gone. Adams wrote that Slade's speech "shook the hall into convulsions." The reliably pro-administration *Globe*, which had taken over from the *Intelligencer* the job of recording and printing congressional debates, did not report the speech. Contemporary accounts, however, show that Slade was barely able to get through a sentence without being interrupted by shouts and calls for order; Polk was far more abrupt than he dared to be with Adams.

Rather than avail themselves once again of the failed weapon of censure, representatives from Virginia, North Carolina, and Georgia called on their colleagues to leave the hall, an unprecedented form of protest. Slave-state members caucused in a committee room; their Northern allies were not permitted to enter, though Southerners from the Senate were. This constituted, as one historian of the period notes, an act of proto-secession. They agreed to present a new version of the gag order the following day, delegating John Patton of Virginia to do so. Patton introduced the resolution and then, in order to preclude debate, called the previous question— that is, called for an immediate vote. An outraged Adams rose to protest and was shouted down and ruled out of order. When the roll was called, Adams, rather than voting, declared, "I hold the resolution to be in violation of the United States constitution." The measure nevertheless passed 122 to 74.

Many free-state Democrats, long accustomed to taking dictation from the South, voted for the gag despite having been prohibited from the meeting in which the plans had been made. Still, the majority was smaller than it ever had been before. New members from the North and the West refused to fall in step with Southern forces; others had shifted to Adams' side. It was only a matter of time before the dam broke. Millard Fillmore of New Hampshire and three New Yorkers asked Adams to write a manifesto for members opposed to the gag but unwilling to take Slade's abolitionist position.

Adams now treated the gag as illegitimate. When his turn came to submit petitions on December 28, he offered memorials on various subjects and then presented one on slavery. Since, he said, he did not recognize the gag, "I should submit to it only as to physical force." A few weeks later he submitted fifty more. Then another three hundred fifty. The language of these documents shows that the implacable bitterness with which Southern planters regarded Northern activists had become mutual. One prayed for the construction of a "great wall of China between North and South," another to offer protection to Northerners venturing into the South—because "in another part of the Capitol it had been threatened that if a Northern abolitionist should go to South Carolina . . . if they catch him they should hang him." This sidelong reference to a statement by Senator Preston of South Carolina brought the wrath of the House and the Speaker down on Adams, who jumped up and offered another petition. In March, Adams presented a petition from Virginia praying for "the arraignment at the bar of the House, and expulsion, of John Quincy Adams." Since this was of course not covered by the gag, Adams asked the clerk to read the entire, quite lengthy resolution. It, too, was tabled.

Adams still had very little company. He tried to draw up a plan to overturn the gag rule with his fellow Massachusetts legislators, but many feared being tarred with abolitionism. Adams' fears that abolitionist zeal would provoke a backlash that would damage the cause more than advance it were increasingly being vindicated. The previous summer, a mob in Cincinnati had destroyed the office of the *Philanthropist*, an abolitionist newspaper published by James Birney, who had just published an open letter to slaveholders in which he warned that "the discussion of slavery can now, no more be stopped, than the rising of the sun." The assault was presumably designed to say, "Oh yes it can." After smashing Birney's printer and throwing the pieces in a river, the mob had come for Birney but hadn't found him. Elijah P. Lovejoy, another abolitionist publisher, in Alton, Illinois, was less fortunate. In November 1837, Lovejoy was murdered in a virtually identical attack. He had corresponded with Adams, who had cautioned him to cool his fervor. Adams feared, rightly as it turned out, that Lovejoy had the makings of a martyr. Adams delivered a furious address in Congress denouncing the arson and murder.

Abolitionists needed protection not in the South, where few ventured, but in the cities of the North and the West, where most people viewed them as radicals seeking to tear the country in half. For every abolitionist newspaper there were two or three inciting readers to fury against the antislavery activists. No place was safe from the lynch mob—not even Philadelphia, the home of the abolitionist movement. The city's leading progressives had built a fine structure, Pennsylvania Hall, to host public lectures, above all on the question of slavery. Benjamin Lundy and others had invited

Adams to address the opening session, and he of course had declined. The hall opened on May 14, 1838, with speeches by William Lloyd Garrison, Angelina Grimké, Theodore Weld, and other leading figures. The abolitionists had insisted on letting black and white spectators sit together. This bold decision, as well as wild rumors of what was being said inside, drove anti-abolitionists to a fever pitch. On May 17, as the police stood idly by, a crowd forced the doors of the building and set it aflame. Pennsylvania Hall burned to the ground three days after opening.

No one died, but Lundy suffered a serious loss. The itinerant abolitionist had been working furiously to rouse public indignation on Texas, among other things, by sending a steady stream of documents to Adams. But after years of rugged solitary travel across the continent, his health was broken. He had passed the baton of leadership to a generation far more worldly and polished than himself—men like Weld and Channing and the perpetually furious Garrison. In January 1838, Lundy had handed over the editorship of his current paper, the *National Enquirer*. He had decided to return to the West and to live a settled life that would not test his waning resources, physical or material. He had moved out of his rooms and stored all his belongings in Pennsylvania Hall. He had little that mattered to him save his papers. They were all consumed by the fire. Yet that very morning this faithful Quaker was able to write to a friend, "I am not disheartened, though everything of earthly value (in the shape of property) is lost. Let us persevere in the good cause. *We shall assuredly triumph yet.*"

This humble, hopeful, zealous man had entered deeply into Adams' life. They wrote to one another often, and at times Adams, perhaps accidentally, fell into Lundy's Quaker diction, writing "thou knowest" and the like. Lundy never stopped trying to enlist Adams in causes that Adams knew better than to join; his indefatigable friend was a nuisance, but the kind of nuisance Adams viewed as the very salt of the earth. Lundy, in turn, viewed Adams in salvific terms, as Adams perhaps viewed himself in the core of his being. "The eyes of *millions*, my dear and honoured friend, are now *turned to thee*," he wrote a few weeks before the fire. "No mortal ever held a part of greater usefulness—more enviable distinction—or higher moral responsibility, than is thine at the present moment." Lundy did not wait a day to write to Adams with news of his calamity, which he recounted without self-pity. He apologized for being unable to supply documents Adams had requested. Then he set off for the West, where his health continued to decline. Benjamin Lundy died August 21, 1839, in Lowell, LaSalle

County, Illinois. He was only fifty, but he had worn himself out in the abolitionist cause.

THE PATTON GAG HAD LARGELY STOPPED UP THE FLOW OF PETITIONS on slavery in the District of Columbia. Texas, however, was a more complicated question. From the first days of 1838, the House began receiving resolutions passed by state legislatures opposing—or favoring—the annexation of Texas. Were they, too, to be laid upon the table? No, they were instead referred to the Committee on Foreign Affairs, dominated by slaveholders and administration supporters. The committee reported back, in very short order, with a recommendation that, as the administration did not currently propose to annex Texas, no action should be taken on the petitions. Adams rose to ask George Dromgoole of Virginia, speaking for the committee, whether the thousands of petitions and resolutions "had ever received five minutes of consideration" from committee members. Rather than answer, Dromgoole irritably denied the right of any member "to catechise the committee as to its actions." Adams, roused to fury, shouted, "That is enough, Sir! That, Sir, is enough for this house and this country. The committee refuses to answer." Now there were shouts, cries, bedlam. The House adjourned.

The following day, Benjamin Howard, the committee chairman, sought to bring the discussion to a close. When Adams rose to ask Howard whether he believed a member had the right to ask whether a committee had read petitions referred to it, Howard simply repeated Dromgoole's formulation. Now Adams had a club to beat the opposition with. He asked whether members were prepared to state their views of his question. Hugh Legaré of South Carolina gave Adams the direct answer he was looking for: "For myself, I have no hesitation in admitting that I have not read the papers, or looked into them, nor was I bound to do so." Adams now delightedly read, and then slowly reread, the seventy-sixth rule of the House, which stipulated that the Committee on Foreign Affairs must "take into consideration all matters concerning the relations of the United States with foreign nations." Legaré said that he had considered the *subject* of the petitions rather than the documents themselves, a distinction Adams promptly ridiculed.

Waddy Thompson now proposed that the committee's resolution be amended to call for the president to annex Texas. Adams, in turn, called for an amendment stating that neither Congress nor the president had the authority to do so. Then, as now, House rules permit amendments to amendments, but nothing further. The chamber could not proceed further until it had voted on Adams' proposed amendment to the amendment. Adams took the floor to speak on behalf of his proposal on the morning of June 16. In this era before cloture calls, Adams could continue speaking as long as he wished. He knew that he could not win; what he could do, however, was rivet the nation's attention to the issue of Texas and, collaterally, slavery by holding the floor. The "morning hour" was by tradition set aside for committee business. The seventy-one-year-old Adams now filled that hour for fifteen sessions, until virtually dropping from exhaustion on July 7. The speech, published in book form by Gales and Seaton and endlessly reprinted, ran to 112 pages, not including the 18-page introduction Adams added.

Adams found many ingenious means to reintroduce through a back door what had been blocked by Congress at the front. He traced the evolution of the doctrine of "suppression" from petitions on slavery to those on Texas. He could hardly discuss this matter without adverting to the question of the rights of slaves, and the movement to censure him. He was wandering far afield—intentionally, of course—and the chair ordered him to stick to the question at hand. He would not and did not. Earlier in the debate, Benjamin Howard had taken note of the fact that many of the petitions on Texas had come from women, and he had expressed the wish that women restrict their sphere of influence to "their duties to their fathers, their husbands, and their children . . . instead of rushing into the fierce struggle of political life." Adams read the passage, sorrowfully. "Sir," he asked, "was it from a son—was it from a father—was it from a husband, that I heard these words? . . . Are women to have no opinions or actions on subjects relating to the general welfare?"

The man who had never shown the slightest interest in his own wife's political opinions—or, really, in those of any other woman save his mother—tolled off a mighty list of women who had thrust themselves into great affairs, from Old Testament figures like Esther to Isabelle of Castile. By the third day of this sub-oration he had arrived at the women of the American Revolution. Is the right to petition, he asked, to be denied to such women simply because they lack the right to vote? And then, startlingly: "Is it so clear that they have no such right as this last?" There is no evidence that Adams had ever before considered the possibility that woman should have the right to vote.

Adams was looking for an opening to talk about slavery. On June 30, he found it. Representative Francis Pickens rose to complain that the petitions from women he so admired—Adams happened to be talking about the celebrated Grimké sisters of Charleston—were in fact a "tissue of prejudice and misrepresentation." Not so, said Adams. No doubt the gentleman from South Carolina, like his brethren in the chamber, was a "kind and indulgent master" and thus could not be expected to know "the cruel, the tyrannical, the hard-hearted master" who "procreates children from his slaves, and then sells the children as slaves." He told his colleagues the story of Dorcas Allen, who had killed two of her children rather than see them bound into slavery. No jury, even in Virginia, could be found to convict her of murder.

Adams kept baiting his opponents and then exploiting their response. Returning to the subject of his amendment, he observed that if Texas were annexed as a slave state, both slavery and the slave trade would be revitalized across the South. John Campbell of South Carolina rejoined that it was abolitionism which had "tended to rivet the system," hardening attitudes across the South and leading to the widespread view that slavery "was neither a moral nor a political evil." Adams wheeled on him:

> I am well aware of the change that is taking place in the political philosophy of the South. I know well that the doctrine of the Declaration of Independence, that "all men are created equal," is there held as an incendiary doctrine, and deserves Lynching; that the Declaration itself is a farrago of abstractions. I know all this perfectly; and that is the very reason why I want to put my foot upon such doctrine; that I want to drive it back to its fountain—its corrupt fountain—and pursue it until it is made to disappear from this land, and from the world.

Adams conceded that he had been "drawn into observations which are here much out of place," but added that if the gentleman so wished he would be happy to "enter into a full and strict scrutiny of slavery . . . and so long as God shall give me life, and breath, and the faculty of speech, he shall have it, to his heart's content." In fact, he had already broached the subject more directly than he had before. There was much else to come over the ensuing week, much raillery and invective, much constitutional exegesis and allegations of a secret policy to provoke Mexico into war and seize Texas, but in his furious response to Campbell, Adams had touched on what he and everyone else knew was the heart of the matter. He had inched yet closer to assuming the heroic mantle he had imagined for himself in 1820.

Adams still held the floor when Congress finally adjourned July 9. He was, he conceded, "sick at heart, exhausted, and faint with weariness and excessive heat, knowing that nothing further would be done by the House to any useful purpose." In fact, he had succeeded; by rallying public opinion, he had persuaded Van Buren that annexation would have to be postponed. In October, the Texas envoys acknowledged the obvious by withdrawing their request for recognition.

ADAMS' OTHER GREAT PREOCCUPATION DURING THIS PERIOD WAS an astonishing windfall the United States had received in late 1835. A previously unknown British citizen named James Smithson had left $500,000 to the United States in his will to "found at Washington, under the name of the Smithsonian Institution, an Establishment for the increase & diffusion of Knowledge among men." Smithson was a gentleman scientist and sole heir to a large fortune. A reticent man with no family of his own and little social life, Smithson was never known to have uttered a word about the United States and gave no outward sign of democratic sympathies. His gift was, and remains, a mystery.

The Smithson bequest offered a private solution to what Adams had long imagined as a public good, publicly supplied. Adams, like Henry Clay, had believed that the federal government had an obligation to promote economic development and build institutions, but while Clay thought almost exclusively in economic terms, Adams believed that the state needed to foster cultural and scientific institutions as well. In the most eloquent passages of his futile inaugural message to Congress in 1825, he had declared that God himself had enjoined upon society the obligation to improve man's "moral, political, intellectual" condition. Adams had listed first among his proposals the establishment of a national university as well as academies for the propagation of knowledge, especially in "geographical and astronomical science." If, as Adams believed, national greatness was to be measured not merely in wealth and military power but in enlightenment and understanding, the United States could not passively watch as the great powers of Europe made strides in scientific understanding.

Adams had failed, of course. But the Smithson bequest permitted the United States to make those strides without having to resort to its own funds. Nevertheless, champions of states' rights opposed the Smithson gift for the same reason Adams favored it; John Calhoun argued that the money should be returned, though it wasn't clear who else had title to it. Adams not only eagerly sought the bequest but knew exactly what he wanted to do with it. In June 1838, he held a two-hour conversation with President Van

Buren in which he proposed that the legacy be devoted to the construction of an astronomical observatory—his long-time passion—as well as an "annual course of lectures upon the natural, moral and political sciences."

The ridicule Adams had suffered when he had proposed a network of "lighthouses of the skies" in 1825 had not dampened his ardor on the subject. Astronomy, for Adams, was the celestial equivalent of the journeys of exploration, discovery, and mapping he favored at home—indispensable, of course, but also shot through with romance. Adams had been fascinated by astronomy since he had first looked through a telescope as a Harvard undergraduate. Charles had bought a house in Quincy, and that summer Adams set up a telescope there, often rising before dawn in order to watch the sunrise and returning at night to scan the stars. He pored over pages of algebraic tables. He was besotted with the glory of the heavens and suffused, he wrote, with "a painful desire to know more of this stupendous system; of sorrow in reflecting how little we can know of it; and almost desponding hope that we may know more of it hereafter."

In the fall of 1838, as Richard Rush, who had been delegated to receive the Smithson bequest, was returning from London with 105 sacks filled with gold sovereigns, Adams wrote two long letters to Secretary of State John Forsyth, memorializing and expanding on his conversation with Van Buren and laying out the case for building an observatory. Adams' great fear was that the bequest would be frittered away on schemes unworthy of Smithson's majestic instructions. He admonished Forsyth that the funds must not be used to build a school, college, university, or, certainly, ecclesiastic establishment. The money must not "fall victim to the canker of almost all charitable foundations," by which he meant handing out jobs to political hacks. Power should be vested in a board of trustees with members from both houses of Congress, eminent citizens, and cabinet officials.

In February 1839, Adams introduced legislation incorporating his vision for a Smithsonian Institution and warned his colleagues that the precious gift was in danger of being "wasted and dilapidated to feed the hunger and fatten the leaden idleness of mountebank projectors." The struggle would go on for years.

ALL HIS LIFE ADAMS HAD STOOD ALONE, ACCEPTING AS RECOMPENSE his own gratified pride and the admiration of the few. He had grown accustomed to such cold comforts. Yet in recent years this man of no party had become a popular hero and an object of something like idolatry. In Quincy that summer of 1838, Adams received a letter from the abolitionist Lydia Marie Child, who said, "I am not willing to die without saying how deeply, how sincerely, how fervently, I thank you for the magnanimous course you have pursued in Congress." While contemporaries "will imperfectly acknowledge your moral greatness," she wrote, "the future will place you among the most illustrious of the world's benefactors." Adams deprecated all forms of praise, but he was plainly touched when a Quaker man came to fix a clock in his home and refused to accept payment owing to his veneration for Adams' service to mankind.

In the late summer, Adams and Louisa were given a ball and a picnic by two hundred ladies from Quincy in gratitude for his role in presenting petitions. After a brief expression of embarrassed thanks, Adams told the ladies that he understood very well that "there was not the least danger of their obtruding their wishes upon any of the ordinary subjects of legislation," such as banks and currency—indeed, that it was "scarcely consistent with civility to so much as name them in their presence." He felt certain, however, that they would continue to devote their efforts to "the objects of kindness, of benevolence, of compassion" for which they were so well fitted "by the laws of their natures." It was just as well that the audience included none of the members of Congress whom he had recently hectored about the heroic achievements of women of the past and to whom he had suggested that women had been unfairly deprived of political rights. On this subject, Adams was perfectly unregenerate.

In mid-November, Peter Chardon Brooks, Charles' father-in-law, picked up Adams in his carriage and drove with him to Mt. Auburn Cemetery. Wet leaves plastered the ground; stagnant ponds dotted desolate valleys. The inscriptions on the old headstones had been worn to illegibility. Adams was deeply struck by the pervading air of gloom and decay. And it was here, in this baleful setting, that he stumbled on the tomb of Maria Sargent Curtis, Mary Frazier's daughter. He was, as recounted earlier, moved to tears, both by gratitude that he had been spared the pain of the early death of a wife and perhaps a daughter and by the piercing memory of a love he had forced himself to surrender. Adams was seventy-one years old, rheumatic and gray and grim, but at that moment, in his imagination, he was a heartbroken young man of twenty-three.

CHAPTER 34

The Captives Are Free!

(1838–1841)

B Y THE LATE 1830S, JOHN QUINCY ADAMS' DAILY MAIL, ALWAYS stacked high with petitions, began to include as well an astounding number of death threats. The first one, dated February 10, 1837, featured a crude drawing of a hand holding a knife and, below, a sheathed sword. The author, who signed his name Dirk Hatteraich, wrote that if Adams dared raise his voice against slavery one more time, "You will be *lynched* if it has to be done by *drawing* you from your *seat* in the *house* by force. So be on your guard the author of this is now on his way to Washington with *others* able and *determined* to *fulfill their threat.*" Soon afterwards a package arrived from North Carolina containing a bullet inside a glove.

As Congress reconvened in December 1838, the letters began arriving in spates—ten in January alone. On January 7, Thomas Jones of Westmoreland Country, Virginia, wrote to say that "some gentlemen" from the area were prepared to pay "a large premium" for Adams' head. Until now, Jones had restrained them, but if Adams persisted in his course of presenting abolitionist petitions, he would "join their effort." A week later came a much less polite missive from Richard Renald of Augusta, Georgia. Renald had been provoked by Adams' support for establishing diplomatic relations with Haiti, which would lead to "a Big Black, Thick lipped, Cracked Heeled, Woolly headed, Skunk smelling, damned Negro" to be seated in Congress as "an equal to a white man in law and in justice." Renald sought a duel. Should Adams decline, he warned, "you will when least expected, be shot down in the street, or your damned guts will be cut out in the dark." Another would-be assassin, a B. J. Convield, serially heralded his arrival: he was stopped at the Ohio River by ice, he was laid up by rheumatism, but he was sure to arrive no later than February 22.

All the letters came from the South. Slaveholders seem to have persuaded themselves, and one another, that by killing Adams they could scotch the snake of abolitionism. This was a delusion, of course, but also a remarkable tribute to Adams' reputation as the scourge of the slaveholders. The fact that Adams was not even an abolitionist seemed not to matter, for few men had launched so frontal an attack on slave owners as Adams had. Louisa was terrified for her husband but was of course powerless to make him change his rhetoric or his habits. She wrote to Charles that she was "harassed day and night by terrors for your father . . . who with that daring indifference to danger which he always displays has even taken pains to expose himself to attack and insult." Adams did not bother to inform the House sergeant-at-arms or the DC federal marshal. In fact, he did nothing. Either good fortune or what he would have called a superintending Providence was watching over him; no desperado lunged at him in the dark.

The petition drama flared up anew in the first days of the 1838 session. Joshua Giddings, a new Whig representative from the Western Reserve of Ohio and a passionate abolitionist, watched in delight as the great Adams toyed with his would-be tormenters. In his diary he wrote:

> The Speaker called louder and louder for "Order!" "Order!" "Order!," but Mr. Adams continued speaking as though a perfect silence existed around him. The uproar increased, and the Speaker, rising from his chair, in great agitation and excitement, with stentorian voice called on the House to assist him in enforcing the rules. Amid this tumult Mr. Adams suddenly dropped into his chair, and the uproar immediately ceased, before the Speaker had fully pronounced his desire for assistance.

The old man, Giddings wrote, rocked with laughter.

Adams continued to fight, continued to treat the ever-renewed gag as a legal nullity, continued to present a great sheaf of petitions one by one, tolling off the name of the first signatory, the number of signers, and the place of origin. At first Giddings was too overawed to speak. Of the others, only

Slade of Vermont shared Adams' boldness. The others, Giddings complained in his journal, "mumble over the name of the first petitioner and their numbers in a low, indistinct voice, so as not to be heard." Adams, by contrast, took an almost sadistic glee in exposing his enemies' hypocrisy. He introduced what he claimed was a petition—in fact, he had invented it—to appoint a special committee to look into the "pedigree" of each member of Congress and to expel those who had "the least drop of coloured blood in their veins." Adams was lampooning Southerners' new fixation with racial purity, but no one could miss the barb: it was the plantation owners who were likeliest to have such blood in their veins. The Speaker ruled the resolution out of order.

Soon after the short session ended on March 4, Adams sat down to compose a series of open letters to the many Americans who had counted on him to present their petitions to Congress. The letters were reprinted in newspapers across the country. They give the strange impression that Adams had grown both more implacable in his horror of slavery *and* more skeptical of any of the available means of ending it. He had now concluded that abolitionism had been built into America's foundation. Of the Declaration of Independence, Adams declared, "The same moral thunderbolt, which melted the chains of allegiance that bound the colonist to his sovereign, dissolved the fetters of the slave." The unstated implication was that the three-fifths compromise embedded in the Constitution was not merely a piece of pragmatism but a violation of fundamental principle. Yet in a later letter, Adams asserted that immediate abolition was a fantasy, for public opinion would never permit it. Adams heaped scorn on the abolitionists for imagining that slaveholders could be converted to their cause without compensation. "I can," he wrote, "lend my hand to no project for the abolition of slavery in these United States without the consent of their masters." He lamented "the temper mutually rankling between the slave-holders and the abolitionists."

After constructing an argument that revealed slavery to be an insult to republican principle as well as Christian doctrine, Adams had adopted the position of a "moderate" slave owner like Henry Clay, decrying the two extremes. Adams was a primeval republican who would not supersede the will of voters even for transcendent moral purposes. But he did not believe in the moral equivalence of slaveholders and abolitionists—far from it. He did not believe that emancipating slaves without compensation constituted an unjust "taking." He did not regret the rankling of temper, for which he himself was so greatly responsible.

Once Adams had trembled before the prospect of a civil war severing the Union and ending slavery—and said, let it be so. But that was in his journal, with the prospect of such a war far in the distance. Now, with the likes of Garrison agitating for such an apocalyptic outcome, and the slavocracy increasingly prepared to accept it, Adams drew back. He was acutely aware of the fears abolitionism had awakened in the country. He had already made himself an object of hatred across the South and in much of Congress. Adams understood that he would do no favors to the cause by openly taking it up, as Tappan and others urged him to do. He had often told them as much. Adams wanted to preserve his usefulness. This was a novel course for him: he had spent most of his career defying public opinion. But he had not done so out of vanity. If he could serve the course of justice by soft-pedaling his views, he was prepared to do so—even as, at the same time, he made the intellectual case for a more absolutist position.

Adams was trying very hard to carve out a space for himself between the existing camps on slavery. In January 1839, he had introduced a constitutional amendment that would ban "hereditary slavery" after July 4, 1842; admit no new slave states save Florida; and prohibit slavery and the slave trade in Washington after July 4, 1845. The proposal was never even considered by the House and would have won few if any votes if it had been, as Adams knew very well. He had probably offered it as an answer to abolitionists who asked how he would end slavery voluntarily. Adams didn't really see how slavery would be ended in any way save through war, though he would keep trying to find ways to do so. In the meantime, he would focus on the right of petition, which the American people supported, rather than abolitionism, which they didn't.

Adams continued to cast a pox on both houses. In an open letter in July, he rebuked the American Anti-Slavery Society for insisting that every slave owner was a "man-stealer," a crime for which the Bible mandated death. Such inflamed rhetoric would likely lead to a "civil, servile and savage war," which of course was just what many Southerners predicted. Adams' letters delivered a deathblow to the AASS, already starving for funds and unable to show its supporters even the smallest sign of success. Radicals denounced him; moderates like Channing tried, and failed, to establish a new organization advocating gradual abolition. The AASS disappeared in 1840. The movement splintered between firebrands and moderates.

Adams remained, as always, a party of one. Many of his abolitionist friends and allies wrote to express their deep dismay with his views. One of them, Gerrit Smith, a wealthy New Yorker who was one of the movement's chief financial backers, wrote that refusing to demand the abolition of slavery in Washington because Southerners opposed it was little different from acquiescing to burglary or counterfeiting because Congress had approved them. In his own letters, Adams continued to ridicule the anti-slavery society and to criticize the very concept of a "partial association," or what we would call a "special interest group," precisely on the grounds that it represented a special, or partial, rather than national interest.

IN SEPTEMBER 1839, ADAMS READ A LETTER FROM WILLIAM JAY, A leading evangelical reformer, to William Lloyd Garrison's *Liberator* that made him shake with indignation. Several weeks earlier, an American naval vessel had encountered a slave-trading ship, the *Amistad*, off the tip of Long Island. After finding that the captives, whom he took to be slaves, had mutinied and killed the ship's captain and its cook, and were now seeking to return to Africa, the naval officer had seized the ship with its human cargo and brought it into port in New London, Connecticut. The captives were now to be tried as pirates and murderers. Adams picked up his pen and wrote to Jay, asserting that the mutineers had in fact "vindicated their own right of liberty" by "executing the justice of Heaven upon one pirate murderer, their tyrant and oppressor." The abolitionist community had mobilized around the fate of the *Amistad* captives, and word quickly spread that the former president shared their feelings. Within days, leaders of the movement were seeking Adams' legal advice.

Adams had just finished excoriating the movement for imagining that slavery could be ended by righteous rhetoric. He considered Garrison a wild-eyed radical. The captives on the *Amistad* had apparently killed a white man in cold blood. Why, then, had Adams so quickly leapt to their defense? Certainly Adams felt very differently about enforcing the laws and treaties that prohibited the slave trade than he did about the quixotic effort to overturn settled law in the face of overwhelming resistance. But Adams' quick reaction also shows that he hated slavery as viscerally as Weld or Tappan did and that he instinctively saw slaves as fully human beings. And for Adams, a republican in his very soul, mankind's great distinguishing feature was the inextinguishable wish for liberty. The more he learned about the *Amistad* case, the higher his dudgeon rose. There was, besides, a kind of romance in it: in the *Amistad*, Adams found a cause worthy of his dreams of heroic and solitary combat. Adams would begin the episode with self-exhortations of prudence and move inexorably toward commitment heart and soul.

It would be months before the full story of the *Amistad* emerged, but once it did, many Americans would come to see the black captives as Adams did: martyrs to the monstrous evils of the slave trade. The men, women, and children aboard the slave ship had been kidnapped from West Africa by Spanish slave traders. Spain had agreed to end the slave trade in an 1817 treaty with Great Britain as well as a series of subsequent royal decrees. Nevertheless, a clandestine trade continued, often terminating in Havana's slave market. The forty-two Africans who had survived the harrowing Middle Passage had been purchased in Havana by two Cubans, Jose Montes and Pedro Ruiz, who planned to sell them in the plantation district of Camaguey. The slaves were jammed belowdecks of the *Amistad*, a coastal schooner only sixty-four feet long and nineteen feet wide. They could barely raise their heads in the dark, fetid cargo hold, which was otherwise filled with farm equipment, clothing, textiles, plate ware, pots, toys, and the like. These men, women, and children—there were four little girls— were merchandise, nothing more or less.

The Africans knew nothing of their destination or their fate. When some of them tried, with hand signals, to ask the cook, Celestino, what would become of them, he indicated, in what he must have considered a fine bit of comedy, that they would be chopped to bits and eaten. The captives, terrified and enraged, determined to take their lives in hand. On the second night, with the crew exhausted from having battled a storm, the Africans' leader, known as Cinqué, either broke or picked the central padlock that bound them all together. The men emerged onto the ship's deck. Cinqué grabbed a handspike and drove it into Celestino, killing him in a moment. The rebellion now burst forth. The captives found machetes and began going after the crew members. They killed the captain; after some debate, they agreed to spare Ruiz and Montes, whom they instructed to set a course for Africa.

Montes sailed slowly eastward by day and then, with no one watching, tacked backward much more quickly at night, so that they sailed northward along the Eastern seaboard. After seven weeks the mutineers spotted land. The *Amistad*'s stores were almost exhausted. On August 24, some of the men went ashore to seek fresh provisions. The following day, the ship was spotted by the *Washington*, a Coast Guard cutter, which dispatched a boarding party. The ship's captain, Lieutenant Thomas Gedney, bewildered by the *Amistad*'s tattered sails and foul stench, the crew of black men dressed in outlandish outfits that had in fact been pilfered from the ship's stores, and by the two Spanish men apparently being held captive, seized the vessel, which he assumed must be a pirate ship or privateer. Gedney brought the *Amistad* to New London to be examined by a federal magistrate, Judge Andrew Judson. Gedney was seeking salvage rights for the ship and its cargo of slaves. After listening to Ruiz and Montes recount a blood-chilling tale of insurrection and slaughter, Judge Judson ruled that the slaves be tried for "murder and piracy."

The seizure of the *Amistad* proved to be a racial cause célèbre the likes of which America would hardly see again until the Scottsboro Boys went on trial at the dawn of the civil rights era. When one considers the pacifism of many abolitionists, and the horror slave rebellions provoked even in the North, it is remarkable that a case of murder on the high seas could have roused such widespread passions. But the *Amistad* captives were deeply sympathetic figures, women and children as well as men, all of them illegally stolen from their native land and treated as slaves. They were available to be visited in jail, where they could be seen sitting quietly and talking among themselves. In newspaper accounts of the time, they appeared to combine elements of early Christian martyrdom and noble Roman patriotism. Journalists offered stirring accounts, possibly apocryphal, of Cinqué's speech urging his confederates to die together rather than to accept a life of servitude. A popular illustration showed the rebel leader with an implacable gaze and a white cloth thrown, toga-like, over his shoulder. Strong and handsome and no more than twenty-one years old, Cinqué was one of America's first black heroes.

In Havana, Ruiz and Montes had signed a bill of lading stipulating that they were transporting Ladinos, slaves who had lived in Spanish territories since long before the slave trade had been outlawed. The ship's manifest, otherwise known as a passport, described them so and gave each captive a fictitious Spanish name. The fact that the *Amistad* captives spoke no Spanish made this imposture obvious, but only when Lewis Tappan, who had taken up their cause, located a speaker of Vai, a second language for many of the Mende-speaking slaves, were they able to tell their story and thus demonstrate the truth that they were free men who had been illicitly abducted from their home.

On September 20 the captives appeared before Smith Thompson, a Supreme Court justice sitting as a federal circuit court judge. They were represented by Roger Sherman Baldwin, grandson of a signer of the Declaration of Independence. Baldwin observed that the defendants were being held as merchandise in order to satisfy property claims filed, variously, by Ruiz and Montes, Lieutenant Gedney, and the government of Spain. Had they been slaves, such a holding would have been morally repugnant but legally sound. Yet they were not slaves, Baldwin asserted, for they had been born free persons in Africa. Even were they judged to be chattels rather than humans, were they to be sold, like any other object of merchandise, in order to satisfy Lieutenant Gedney's salvage claims against the ship and cargo? A federal magistrate, Andrew Judson, had already ruled that he would not authorize the sale of the slaves in the free state of Connecticut.

The district attorney, William S. Holabird, now made the remarkable concession that, despite the claims made on the ship's manifest, the defendants really were freemen who had been illegally captured in Africa. Nevertheless, he said, the president had the right to hold them until a definitive decision was rendered, in order to be able to return them safely to Africa. This was bewildering; as Baldwin pointed out, whites seized as slaves by Barbary pirates would not have been held in prison on such a pretense. Nevertheless, on September 23 Judge Thompson denied the motion to free the defendants. His own feelings, he said, were "abhorrent to the system of slavery," but "we must look at things as they are." The defense had not yet proved to his satisfaction that the captives had been illegally seized in Africa. They might be slaves in the eyes of the law. Since the Constitution sanctioned slavery, the court could not simply release them as self-evidently free men. At the same time, he had dismissed the criminal charges against the accused not because he thought lightly of murder on the high seas, but because he had determined that the United States had no jurisdiction over a crime allegedly perpetrated against Spanish citizens on the high seas. He ordered the district court to convene in November to adjudicate the property claims.

That very day, Ellis Gray Loring, a leading Boston abolitionist, wrote to Adams saying that, despite the ruling, he worried that the Van Buren administration would surrender the captives to Spain, which had claimed jurisdiction over them as Spanish property. Adams was an authority on international law with unrivaled experience in the interpretation of international accords. What, Loring asked, should the Africans' legal advisors do? Adams did not feel ready to respond. Nevertheless, he paid a visit to Loring at the latter's office in Boston. Loring, he wrote in his journal, was "extremely anxious to know my opinion upon the right of the President to deliver the Negroes upon the demand of the Spanish minister." Adams understood that Loring wanted more than his opinion; he wanted the ex-president, the nation's conscience, to publicly take the side of the abolitionists. "The time has not yet come," he reflected, "when it would be proper for me to give an opinion for publication. . . . If I ever do, it must be with great consideration and self-controul." Of course, the moment Adams posed a problem to himself as a choice between "prudence" and truthfulness, he predetermined the outcome.

When Adams wrote back to Loring, aware that anything he said could be grist for the abolitionist mill, he posed a battery of questions without supplying answers. By what authority, he asked, did Lieutenant Gedney seize these men, and the district judge order them to prison, if they had committed a crime on the high seas, beyond American jurisdiction? If the defendants were pirates rather than slaves, what property claim could possibly be lodged against them? Most fundamentally, what were these defendants—men or chattel? These were, of course, precisely the questions Baldwin had raised. Adams had not yet seen the trial transcript. Even at this early stage, it's clear that, prudence notwithstanding, he yearned to play a role in the *Amistad* defense. He was, he said, prepared to help in any way possible—"could I indulge for a moment the hope that any service of mine would save the lives of these most distressed and most injured fellow men." That would turn out to be a fateful offer.

Adams now devoted himself full time to the case, poring over his law books, examining precedents, mastering the facts as far as he could learn them. In early November Loring responded to Adams' letter, and in his own answer Adams crept closer to open advocacy. The defendants, he said, "were not slaves but masters when Gedney found them." They were no longer subject to property claims. Masters, of course, could be guilty of piracy, and so in theory the captives could have been found guilty at trial; but Judge Thompson had refused to release the defendants while declining to give them the trial to which the accused have a right. These were legal judgments, but Adams' growing fury over the injustice of the case shone through his carefully crafted argument. Adams conceded the worst but still insisted on the innocence of the defendants. The men and women of the *Amistad*, he wrote, "had vindicated their natural right to liberty by conspiracy, insurrection, homicide and the capture of the ship in which they were embarked and of her cargo."

Adams could not fully appreciate how much this meant to the abolitionists who had taken up the cause of the *Amistad*. Long afterward, when the issue was finally settled, the organizers of the Amistad Committee wrote to Adams about his firm conviction from the outset of the innocence of the captives. "The value of this confidence," they recalled, "amid the alarm of friends, the taunt of enemies, the failings of counsel, and the occasional misgivings of our own minds as to the result, the Committee can better appreciate than express." Excerpts from both of Adams' letters to Loring were widely reprinted in the press, as Adams had assumed they would be.

ADAMS LEFT QUINCY IN LATE NOVEMBER, REACHING WASHINGTON a few days before the beginning of the new session. On the first day the clerk traditionally read the roll to introduce the new Congress. This time, he stopped when he reached New Jersey. There were two rival slates of New Jersey members, one Whig and one Democrat. Whichever side was seated would tip the balance of power in the House, allowing the winning party to choose a Speaker from their own ranks. The clerk refused to call either slate, and the House descended into bedlam. After four days of disorder, old John Quincy Adams, having sat quietly in his seat, rose to ask contemptuously whether the clerk, "whom we create, whom we employ, and whose existence depends on our will" was to hold the Congress in thrall, and thus "control the destinies of 16 million freemen?" When a member pointed out that the House could not compel the clerk to act, Adams said, "Well, sir, then let him resign, and we may possibly discover some way by which we can get along, without the aid of his all-powerful talent, learning and genius." Adams then introduced a resolution demanding that the clerk call the roll.

"Who will put the question?," one legislator asked. "*I* intend to put the question," Adams cried. Adams' fearlessness had a galvanic effect on the House. One member proposed that Adams fill the chair until a Speaker could be chosen, and the hall rang with cheers—this for the man who had been threatened with censure and criminal indictment. Even men who considered Adams a menace and a fanatic acknowledged that he stood above them as a figure of nonpartisan integrity. Adams presided over stormy debates between the two parties from December 6 to 16. One evening, when the session stretched past eight o'clock, his colleague Levi Lincoln urged him to rest; Adams asked Lincoln to take the chair, sent for a cup of coffee and two slices of buttered toast, and returned to the chair after an interval of ten minutes. The House agreed to choose a Speaker before settling the question of the rival delegations and, on the eleventh ballot, chose Robert M. T. Hunter of Virginia, a Whig widely considered independent. Adams wrote that at last he stepped down "with an ejaculation of gratitude to God for my deliverance."

The *Amistad* trials in New London resumed in the first days of the new year. On January 11, 1840, after five days of hearings on the property claims, including testimony from Cinqué and other captives demonstrating beyond question that they were not Ladinos, District Court Judge Andrew Judson, who had shown little sympathy for the *Amistad* captives, delivered a bombshell: the defendants, he ruled, were "natives of Africa and were born free and ever since have been and still of right are free and not slaves." Lewis Tappan later speculated that the judge had buckled before mounting public pressure.

After almost unimaginable tribulations, the *Amistad* captives had regained their freedom. Judge Judson ordered the government to repatriate them. The Van Buren administration, however, had no intention of doing so. Secretary of State Forsyth was a slaveholder and a former minister to Spain, and he had argued that the United States must honor its treaty obligations with Madrid. President Van Buren had no wish to open a breach with Spain. More important, he could not afford to jeopardize his Southern support on the eve of the 1840 election by countenancing the right of people taken in slavery to commit conspiracy, insurrection, and homicide against their white captors. The government immediately appealed the judge's decision. The *Amistad* captives, briefly jubilant, were reduced once again to despair. Since they had not been released, they did not have to be recommitted to their prison.

In April, the circuit court in Connecticut affirmed the judgment of the district court. The government then appealed to the Supreme Court. At that time the Court's term began in January, soon after Congress reconvened. The defendants, whom the courts had found to be the victims of a gross crime rather than the perpetrators of one, would nevertheless spend another nine months in confinement. The captives used their time to learn to read and write in English, enduring with good will the abolitionists' evangelizing efforts.

In the House, Adams proposed a resolution calling on the president to provide the diplomatic and official papers touching on the *Amistad*. The resolution passed, perhaps because legislators cared less about the issue of the captives than about their right to solicit information from the executive. The documents, above all the correspondence with Spanish officials, would later allow Adams to put the Van Buren administration on trial. He also introduced a resolution denouncing the ongoing detention as unlawful; this the Speaker refused to consider. In May, Adams received a letter from Baldwin, who in going through documents had found that the government had translated the word "Ladinos" in the ship's manifest as "sound Negroes." This looked like a transparent attempt by the government to obscure the fraud Ruiz and Montes had committed by characterizing Africans as naturalized black Spaniards. Perhaps it was. When Congress reconvened the following December, Adams called for Congress to investigate the crucial change in nomenclature, which appeared not to have been made by the translator himself. The Speaker agreed, but the committee, which Adams chaired, was unable to find evidence of wrongdoing.

The *Amistad*'s team of lawyers had begun preparing for the Supreme Court hearing. On October 27, Adams received a visit in Quincy from Loring and Tappan, who implored him to join the attorneys working on the case. Adams had not appeared before the Supreme Court—or for that matter practiced law—in thirty years. Loring and Tappan had previously approached Rufus Choate, one of the great orators and legal minds of the day, but Choate was no abolitionist, and he turned them down. Indeed, most Whigs wanted absolutely nothing to do with the case. In November, they finally elected a president, William Henry Harrison, who stood at the head of a coalition of North and West, slave and free. The slave case looked like a wedge to drive that shaky alliance apart. Daniel Webster, always conscious of his political standing (Harrison would soon make him secretary of state), refused to meet with the abolitionist firebrands who had taken up the cause of the *Amistad*.

The *Amistad* defendants did not need a gifted lawyer; they had one in Roger Sherman Baldwin, who continued to represent them despite fearing that he would bankrupt himself in doing so. They needed a man of national stature who could present to the justices a vision of American national interests more morally compelling than the one the government would deploy in arguing to honor the terms of the treaty with Spain. They needed an attorney who could speak to the justices as an equal. And of course they needed someone prepared to risk his reputation for a noble cause. There followed the kind of pantomime Adams was wont to perform. He insisted that he was too old, too busy, and too inexperienced for the job. He was prepared to continue serving as an unofficial advisor to Baldwin, nothing more. Loring and Tappan persisted. "It is a case of life and death for these unfortunate men," they wrote. They begged the old man to take the case. They may have known him well enough to realize that he could not say no to a case of life and death. He relented.

In mid-November, on his way to Washington for the new term of Congress, Adams stopped in New Haven to meet with Baldwin. They spent two hours going over the arguments to be presented to the court. Then Baldwin took Adams to meet the prisoners. The thirty-six men—the women and children were separately housed—lived in a single room with two rows of cots. Adams felt they were poorly housed and clothed. Baldwin put his charges through their paces by asking three of the Africans to read to Adams from the New Testament. They did so, Adams grumbled, "very indifferently." He was introduced to the group's leaders, Cinqué and Grabow. Both men had, he thought, "very remarkable countenances."

Once in Washington, Adams had something else to focus on besides the gag rule and the play of legislative debate. He immersed himself in documents and clippings he had received from Loring and from Baldwin, as well as in the diplomatic correspondence the Van Buren administration had released. He asked Attorney General Henry Gilpin to dismiss the case. Gilpin said that President Van Buren could not ignore the Spanish minister's demands for restitution. He went to see Francis Scott Key, the US district attorney, who had played a not very helpful role when Adams had tried to rescue Dorcas Allen from slavery. Now Key told Adams that he had no chance of winning the argument, citing what Adams knew very well was a vulnerable point—the precedent of the *Antelope*, a celebrated Supreme Court case also concerning a Spanish slave ship captured at sea. In that case, adjudicated when Adams was secretary of state and decided in the first months of his presidency, Chief Justice John Marshall had concluded that the law of nations required the ship and its cargo of slaves to be returned to Spain despite American laws prohibiting the slave trade.

Antelope v. U.S. looked to be very much on point for the government, and Key's rather offhand dismissal sent Adams scurrying to the Supreme Court library to read up yet again on a case to which he had already given a great deal of attention. He worried constantly, as even very confident lawyers do when they are scheduled to argue before the Court, that he had overlooked a fine point, that he had not prepared enough. He felt his own unworthiness. On a visit to the Court clerk, he found his name inscribed on the rolls from his first appearance, as a plaintiff's lawyer in two commercial cases in February 1804. (He had appeared again in 1809.) He spent hours closeted with Baldwin. The Court was originally scheduled to hear the case on January 16, 1841, but it was put off until February 19. Adams sought additional documents from the docket of the circuit court, as well as diplomatic correspondence. England, the global champion of the abolitionist cause, was prepared to do anything it could to help the cause of the *Amistad* captives, and Adams hoped that he could introduce diplomatic correspondence with Great Britain into his argument before the Court. The clerk told Adams that he would have to bear the cost of document production. Adams, who had neither asked for a fee nor been offered one, immediately agreed.

Adams' fear of failure could be counted on to drive him to heroic feats of exertion. In this case, he also knew that he held his clients' very lives in his increasingly shaky hands. Lest he forget, in early January he received a letter from Kale, an eleven-year-old *Amistad* captive, though it had been composed by others, perhaps chiefly Cinqué and Kinna, another leader of the group. Kale began by saying what Adams already knew, that they were "Mendi people," not Ladinos. "Some people say Mendi people crazy dolts because we not talk American language," Kale wrote with some asperity. "American people no talk Mendi. American people crazy dolts?" American people also imagined that the Africans were content with their situation because they smiled all the time, but in fact they smiled because they feared that if they expressed their true feelings they would be mistaken for angry savages.

Nor, noted Kale/Cinqué, were they heathens: "we read all Matthew Mark Luke and plenty of little books." They were thought not to have souls, but in fact they missed their home and longed to return. "Dear friend Mr. Adams," the writer continued, "you have children and friends you love them you feel very sorry if Mendi people come and take all to Africa." Adams received another such letter directly from Kinna. Adams was deeply struck by the dignity and depth of feeling of both missives. He wrote to Baldwin asking him to tell both correspondents that he received their letters "with great satisfaction," and that "I think of them, hope for them, and pray for them, night and day."

Adams grew ever more nervous as the great date approached. By late January his perpetually inflamed eye was acting up, and he could barely see. His mind was in a whirl. He went to two church services and through both found himself thinking of the case. He turned for distraction to Shakespeare's *Coriolanus*. He tried to attend to the business of Congress. He lit into Henry Wise of Virginia and then regretted it. Joshua Giddings, his protégé, came under furious attack after an anti-slavery speech, and Adams for once held back.

The *Amistad* argument began on February 22—George Washington's birthday, a coincidence that could only have heightened Adams' sense of the supreme importance of the event. Attorney General Gilpin made the opening argument for the government, asserting that as the *Amistad* was a properly flagged Spanish vessel carrying cargo approved by Spanish authorities, the United States was obliged to return the ship and its property to its owners under Article 9 of the Treaty of 1795, which stipulated that "ships rescued out of the hands of pirates or robbers" should be brought into port and restored to their owners. The pirates or robbers—that is, the slaves—must be turned over to Spanish authorities for criminal prosecution. It was not for federal authorities to judge whether or not the Africans had been legitimately described as slaves. At the end of the day, Adams returned home and drew up a list of all the documents he planned to refer to as an aide-mémoire while he extemporized, a method he often used in speeches before the House.

The following day, Baldwin appeared for the Africans. Discarding fine legalisms, he began by stating that the core of the case was whether the American government "can become a party to the enslavement of human beings cast upon our shores." The district court had concluded that the defendants were men, not property, and Ruiz and Montes, who had sought the restitution of the Africans as property, had not appealed the decision. Legally, therefore, that question had been decided. Further, Baldwin argued that the United States had no standing to appeal on behalf of the government of Spain, which had not made itself a party to the court process. Nor had it been necessary to do so in order to secure the slaves, since the district court was already considering the claim by Ruiz and Montes that the slaves were property and should be turned over to Spanish authorities. Why, now, was the United States interceding? Where did the Constitution specify that the federal government has the right to appeal on behalf of a foreign property claim?

If the defendants were not property, to be returned in a commercial dispute, neither were they pirates to be surrendered for prosecution. Did they seek gain, as pirates do? Of course not. "Cinqué, the master spirit who guided them, had a single object in view. That object was—not piracy or robbery—but the deliverance of himself and his companions in suffering from unlawful bondage." Gilpin now responded, noting that the United States had the same responsibility to return slaves to foreign nationals that it claimed when American slaves were shipwrecked on foreign shores, including in nations like England that prohibited slavery. Baldwin was widely considered to have gotten the better of the exchange. One newspaperman called Baldwin's statement "one of the most complete, finished, conclusive legal arguments ever made before that court." Adams noted in his journal that his colleague had been "sound and eloquent but exceedingly mild and moderate." Adams knew that he had to restrain his temper, but he would not, and could not, be mild.

Adams rose to speak on the morning of February 24. At the time, the Court's chambers occupied a cozy apartment underneath the Senate chambers. Light streamed in from windows behind the raised bench where the robed justices sat; visitors occupied a gallery behind and above them. The wedge-shaped room held barely enough space for the desks where Adams, Baldwin, and Gilpin sat. Of the nine men upon whom Adams fixed his unsettling gaze, only one, Smith Thompson, was as old as he. The seniormost justice, Joseph Story, a Madison appointee, was a good friend whom Adams regarded as every inch an intellectual equal. The other seven had been appointed by Andrew Jackson; the chief justice, Roger Taney, was the infamously supple character who had done Jackson's bidding in the struggle over the defunding of the national bank. Five were Southern slaveholders. Adams had a dim regard for them.

Adams always overprepared. He had gone over his argument again and again, committing to memory the vast flow of logic and of rhetoric. He was consumed with anxiety, as he always was before public performances of great consequence; perhaps his hands shook. Adams began his address, as he often did when speaking before the public, with an exposition of first principles; he thought ill of orators like Giddings who sought to erect great structures on weak foundations. What, he asked, is justice? According to the *Institutes* of Justinian, the great codification of Roman law, it was "the constant and perpetual will to secure to everyone HIS OWN right." He was seeking to summon these nine men to the realm of timeless truth and transcendent morality. That was what Adams could do as no other advocate could.

Adams now proceed to frame an indictment of the Van Buren administration. He was, he explained to the justices, under the "painful" obligation to expose both the proceedings and the motives of the executive to "the censure of the Court." This he now proceeded to do, reading from the administration's diplomatic correspondence to show the lengths to which Secretary Forsyth and others had gone to protect Spanish subjects and Spanish sovereignty against the "oppressors" who had seized the *Amistad*. By what right, Adams now asked, did the government violate its duty of impartiality by extending its sympathy to the slave traders rather than to "the men who had restored themselves to freedom"? Was that justice? Certainly not. It was, Adams conceded, a strange case. Yet to find where justice lay, one need look no further than "that law"—and here he pointed to a copy of the Declaration of Independence affixed to a pillar in the Court—which embodied "the law of Nature and of Nature's God on which our fathers placed our own national existence." This was the view of the Declaration he had begun to develop. Others might not agree, but you could hardly go wrong citing that document on the wall.

Adams dwelt on the history of the case in order to show that "the proceedings of the United States are all wrongful from the beginning," and thus that its appeal should be dismissed. When Lieutenant Gedney encountered the *Amistad*, the Africans were in possession of the ship, seeking to return to their home. They were not pirates, as the circuit court had concluded. (This was not quite accurate: the court had concluded that the captives had not violated American statutes against piracy.) Gedney thus had no right to seize the ship. When the captives were brought before the court, Secretary Forsyth had instructed the district attorney to keep them in custody as "Spanish property." This assertion was, Adams said, with mock circumlocution, "the thing that is not"—that is, a lie. Forsyth, in turn, had been moved to act by a letter from the Spanish minister, Calderon de la Barca, demanding that the Africans be returned to Spain in accord with the stipulation in the Treaty of 1795 that shipwrecked or disabled vessels and cargo be restored to either nation. "Is that language applicable to human beings?," Adams asked scornfully. "Will this Court so affirm?"

Adams now surfaced the contradiction Baldwin had so ably identified—that the defendants were alternately criminals and property—but imparted a rhetorical twist that seemed to render the Spanish government's claims preposterous. "My clients," he observed, "are claimed under the treaty as merchandise, rescued from pirates and robbers. Who were the merchandise, and who were the robbers? According to the construction of the Spanish minister, the merchandise were the robbers, and the robbers were the merchandise. The merchandise was rescued out of its own hands, and the robbers were rescued out of the hands of the robbers." Here was the absurdity, both legal and existential, which came of treating men as things.

Adams continued his assault on the Van Buren administration. He read Calderon's letter, concentrating on the minister's assumption that an American president could intervene in the judicial system as he wished, just as the Spanish king did. The letter, in short, was an insult to American republicanism. Did the secretary explain America's constitutional principles to this envoy of an autocratic state? No—he sought to comply with his demands. "He has," Adams declared, "degraded the country, in the face of the whole civilized world." Calderon's successor, the Count d'Argaiz, perplexed by the procedural safeguards of the American system, wrote that surely the executive could break the impasse "*gubernativamente*"—a word Adams translated as "by absolute fiat" and repeated as often as possible. The Spanish ministers had called on the president to seize the captives, jail them, and hand them over to Spanish authorities for the purpose of judicial murder.

To defer to this autocratic demand was to surrender America's identity as a republican nation.

Here Adams concluded—though only for the day. He resumed his argument March 1. The government had urged the court not to look behind the manifest describing those on board the *Amistad* as Ladinos, but Adams dilated on the thriving illegal slave trade of Cuba, actively abetted by the governor general. Fraudulent documents were the common currency of the trade. What, then, could the Court make of the government's assertion that the passport should be taken as proof positive of the Africans' identity? Here, too, Adams was pointing to the Van Buren administration's deference to an autocratic ally and its eagerness to prejudge the facts. So eager, in fact, had the administration been to satisfy Spanish demands that it had sent the ship the *Grampus* to New Haven to transport the defendants to Cuba before they could file an appeal—a point Adam cinched by reading the previously secret correspondence with the ship's captain.

Adams devoted the last several hours of his speech to a minute analysis of the *Antelope* case. His central argument was that the precedent did not apply because Spain had not yet prohibited the slave trade when the *Antelope* set out; Chief Justice Marshall had explicitly stated that he would not have restored the slaves to their owners had the ship belonged to a nation that prohibited slavery and the slave trade. This, of course, was precisely the case with the *Amistad*.

Adams had now spoken for more than eight hours over two days. He had not stumbled, as he had feared he would. The inflammation in his eyes, and all his other afflictions, had dropped away. He had argued the law, the facts, the politics, and the great moral principles that lay behind them all. He had reminded the justices, not once but twice, of the two copies of the Declaration of Independence hanging on their walls. In the first draft of his argument, Adams had planned to begin by addressing the Court directly, as one who had not appeared before it in thirty years. Perhaps he had seen the egoism in that design; he saved it instead for the end. Now this celebrated speaker, the first Boylston Professor of Rhetoric and Oratory, commenced his peroration. He recalled Justices Marshall, and Cushing, and Chase, and the lawyers he had fenced with so long ago, and even the court administrators. "Where are they all? Gone! Gone! All gone!—Gone from the services which, in their day and generation, they faithfully rendered to their country."

Now Adams had tears streaming down his deeply lined pink cheeks. The crowd in the galleries was rapt. He spoke his final words before the Court:

From the excellent characters which they sustained in life, so far as I
have had the means of knowing, I humbly hope, and fondly trust, that
they have gone to receive the rewards of blessedness on high. In taking,
then, my final leave of this Bar, and of this Honorable Court, I can
only ejaculate a fervent petition to Heaven, that every member of it
may go to his final account with as little of earthly frailty to answer for
as those illustrious dead, and that you may, every one, after the close of
a long and virtuous career in this world, be received at the portals of
the next with the approving sentence—"Well done, good and faithful
servant; enter thou into the joy of thy Lord."

Now Adams—and everyone else—had to wait. On March 4, William
Henry Harrison was sworn in as the new president. Adams was deeply
moved by the simplicity of the event, the absence of pomp, the quiet dignity of the vast crowds. The procession passed before his home on F Street,
and he was struck that Harrison rode a plain white horse and wore a simple
overcoat that made him indistinguishable from the men around him.

The Court announced that it would render a decision March 9. Adams'
colleagues were optimistic. He, of course, was not. "My anxiety for it is intense, and deeply distrustful," he wrote. He went to the Court and waited.
It was Justice Story who had been assigned to deliver the opinion. "There
does not seem to us to be any ground for doubt," he said, "that these Negroes ought to be deemed free; and that the Spanish treaty interposes no
obstacle to the just assertion of their rights." The Court had voted 7–1 to
dismiss the government's appeal. (One justice, Philip Barbour, had died in
the middle of the argument.) At the same time, the Court rejected Adams'
claim that the Africans should be deemed the owners of the ship and the
cargo, awarding Lieutenant Gedney his salvage rights to the ship and cargo,
though not to the captives themselves.

From the courtroom, Adams dashed off a note to Tappan: "The captives are free!" The verdict loosed an explosion of relief and joy among the
multitudes who had come to feel that the cause of abolitionism itself was
summed up in the plight of the *Amistad* captives. Adams' speech was published in the abolitionist as well as the mainstream press. Adams received a
stream of letters exalting him as the moral hero of the age. One came from
"the people of colour of Columbus, Ohio," saying that at a gathering at a
local Baptist Church a resolution of profound thanks had been voted. The
great victory restored Adams' tattered reputation in the anti-slavery movement. John Greenleaf Whittier wrote to acknowledge that "some of us may

have at times done thee injustice in our regret and disappointment at thy expressed sentiments in regard to the District of Columbia," but now "we feel that thou art entitled to our warmest gratitude as abolitionists."

Above all, of course, the verdict gave the captives back their freedom. On November 26, they boarded the aptly named *Gentleman* to reverse the Middle Passage and return to the coast of Sierra Leone, which they had left two and a half years earlier as slaves.

How much credit for the court's decision does Adams actually deserve? We cannot know, of course, how the Court would have voted in his absence, but the truth is that, once the circuit court had accepted that the captives were neither pirates nor slaves, the appellant—the federal government—was left to advance Spain's dubious interpretation of the Treaty of 1795. It was a weak case. And Baldwin had made a thoroughly convincing argument before both the circuit court and the Supreme Court. Adams may have won some extra votes. Beyond that, though, he had brought to the case both his priceless reputation for integrity and the sheer fact of his fame, elevating it in the public mind into the great cause of the day. The *Amistad* case set no lasting legal precedent; it was, however, a ringing triumph for abolitionism.

Adams did not stop thinking about the case. He sent to Tappan a list of nine issues the Supreme Court had left unsettled. He complained to Joshua Leavitt that he had not had the chance to fully unfold his views on the *Antelope* case. He asked Secretary of State Daniel Webster whether the United States could send the captives home on a ship already heading to Africa. He studied papers on the slave trade sent him by an English correspondent. He must, he thought, embark on a campaign on the issue.

Adams knew very well how little his own loved ones cared for his moral crusades. Louisa would stand by him come what may, but Charles worried about the consequences to himself. He had been elected to the Massachusetts House of Representatives in 1840, and he had shuddered at his father's lead role in the case, as he had with Anti-Masonry and the cause of petitions. "It must," he wrote in his journal, "greatly embarrass the political party with which I have undertaken to act." Charles had come more and more to resemble the Brahmins with whom he worked and lived—prudent, measured, respectable. Upon receiving news of his father's great triumph, he responded with the faint praise much of society Boston must have felt: "It is a great relief to me that your cause is settled and well settled. These poor negroes have had some good fortune after all. I hope they may do something with themselves which may save them from becoming a burden to society here." Charles closed with a startling rebuke: "It may be very interesting to yourself and the public to be pleading in the Supreme Court but I must admit that I do not greatly admire the anxiety it occasions to those of us who do not regard it simply as a show."

His father responded tartly, recalling that Charles had warned him against "an experiment so afflictive to my family." That admonition had been a thorn in his heart. The "agony of soul" he had endured throughout the case "was chiefly occasioned by the reprobation of my own family, both of opinion and my conduct." He promised that he would never again provoke such acrimony—"unless it shall be in the decree of Providence." Since Adams so often saw himself as an instrument of Providence, Charles Francis must not have found this caveat very comforting. Adams couldn't help despising the idea of choosing comfort over honor. When they had argued the previous fall over his decision to take the case, he had told Charles how, as a boy of sixteen, he had seen the Magna Carta in the British Museum and made out the name of his ancestor, John de Quincy. "The memory of the seal and the signature" had stayed with him across the years and helped to guide his conduct. Charles thought he was "over-tenacious of the great principles of Magna Carta." Adams would never apologize for being too tenacious of principle.

In the face of present pain, Adams took comfort in the thought of posterity. He knew he had done right, and others, for once, knew it too. On April 15, the founders of the Amistad Committee—Lewis Tappan, Joshua Leavitt, and Simeon Jocelyn—wrote Adams a formal letter of thanks that noted, among other things, that he had refused to accept payment for his immense efforts. "But we feel," they wrote, "and would hope you feel, that a long life devoted to the service of your country has derived a new and holy lustre from this noble effort in behalf of human life and liberty." Adams would never say so, but he surely thought so. He had risked a great deal by agreeing to take on the defense of the *Amistad* captives. Rarely, in his long life, had he been vindicated so definitively as he had been at the moment Justice Story announced the Court's decision.

CHAPTER 35

The Acutest Enemy of Southern Slavery That Ever Existed

(1841–1842)

I N THE YEARS AFTER ADAMS LOST HIS BID TO BE REELECTED president, the slave states and their allies had controlled the White House, as they did the Congress and the Supreme Court. So long as the Jackson/Van Buren coalition of Southern planters, Western pioneers, and Northern farmers and artisans remained in power, there could be no hope for the kind of activist government Adams and Henry Clay had championed. Finally, in 1840, the Whigs had broken through, in the person not of Clay, the perennial candidate, but of William Henry Harrison. Adams was inclined to dismiss Harrison as a genial buffoon, an "Indian fighter" like Jackson who had been puffed up into presidential material by the popular fancy for war heroes. "If he is not found time-serving, demagogical, unsteady, and Western-sectional," Adams wrote of the Ohioan, "he will more than satisfy my present expectations."

Yet in the spring of 1841 the new president treated Adams with great deference. A week after taking office, Harrison appeared unexpectedly at the Adams home and chatted amiably with twelve-year-old Mary Louisa. When Adams drew him aside to ask if they could have a private conversation, Harrison said, according to a rather breathless letter Louisa wrote to Charles, "Come when you please, as often as you please, or drop me a line, for I shall at any time be happy to take your advice, and counsel, as that of a brother." Louisa found him a warm man with a determination to do good.

Harrison had made Daniel Webster his secretary of state. Adams viewed Webster as a grasping rival, but nevertheless considered his understanding of foreign policy solid. Moreover, the 1840 election had given the Whigs a substantial majority in both houses. Finally, after twelve long years, Adams had reason to hope that the program of enhanced federal revenue and investment he had championed would become a reality. He had equal reason to expect that he himself would play a central role in the new administration on both foreign and domestic affairs.

Then, on April 4, one month after taking the oath of office, Harrison died of pneumonia caused by a cold he had contracted at his inaugural. He was succeeded by John Tyler, a slaveholder who had been raised on a 1,200-acre plantation in Tidewater Virginia. Adams called him "a political sectarian of the slave-driving, Virginia, Jeffersonian school, principled against all improvement, with all the interests and passions and vices of slavery rooted in his moral and political constitution." Tyler had vehemently opposed the Missouri Compromise as an unacceptable restraint on the right of states to choose slavery. He had opposed the Bank of the United States and federal support for internal improvements. Tyler thought of himself as a Jeffersonian and had joined the Whig Party only after breaking with Jackson over the latter's threat to use force to bring the South Carolina nullifiers to heel. He had been included as vice president in order to shore up party support in the slave states. It had never crossed anyone's mind that he would exercise power of any sort; no president had ever died in office. No one even knew how to address the successor; the Constitution was unclear on whether the vice president would succeed to the presidency or merely assume its functions. Adams was outraged that Tyler considered himself the president and insisted on being addressed as such.

Adams viewed Tyler's accession to power as an unmitigated catastrophe. Not the least of its consequences would be the death of Adams' hopes for a national policy of internal improvement. In a letter to Clay the following year, Adams wrote bitterly that "the idea that a nation destined by the Creator to be the mightiest that ever existed on the face of the Globe . . . should, with deliberate purpose, have so constituted itself as to cripple all its powers of self-improvement, has always appeared to me a Doctrine the depravity of which is mitigated only by its stupidity." In Adams' telling, the Jeffersonian hostility to federal improvements had been defeated by the close of the Monroe administration—but then Jackson had revived it. Harrison's election promised to restore Clay's American System. But Tyler had "succeeded in thwarting all active government efforts by Congress."

Harrison had ordered a special session of Congress for the spring and summer of 1841. At the outset Adams had asked to be excused from the Committee on Manufactures, the scene of endless pitched battles over the tariff. The new Speaker, John White of Kentucky, had agreed to put him instead at the head of the Committee on Foreign Relations but then at the last minute appointed Caleb Cushing of Massachusetts to the post, putting Adams instead on Indian Affairs. Adams viewed this as another act of spite from Daniel Webster. He would not accept his new assignment. Adams had come to believe that the nation's policy toward the Indians, from the Washington administration to his own, had been just and humane. Only with Andrew Jackson had the federal government surrendered to the importunities of Western and Southern pioneers and ruthlessly driven the Indians from their land. Without ever reexamining his own policy, he had come to conclude that the forcible resettlement of the Indians was "among the heinous sins of this nation," as he put in his journal. "I turned my eyes away from this sickening mass of putrefaction," he wrote, "and asked to be excused from serving as chairman of this Committee."

AS ADAMS SOLDIERED GRIMLY ON THROUGH ONE BATTLE AFTER another, Louisa lived in terror that her husband would be cut down by an assassin's bullet or that the inflammatory rhetoric of the abolitionists would spark a race war. She had never adapted to a public life, much less to the life of endless struggle and controversy to which her husband had subjected her. She felt old, tired, exhausted by misfortune. Over time Louisa withdrew to the confines of her own soul, the one sphere truly her own. In her diary, resumed in 1839 after an absence of three years, she left her husband's stormy world behind to explore her own spiritual deeps. The difference is striking. In December 1835, Louisa wrote, "How bitterly sick I am of all the nefarious details of political life!" By March 1839, however, she was speculating about the doctrine of salvation by faith, concluding that it was a species of arrogance—as was the doctrine of salvation by works alone. A few months later, Louisa began an entry, "What is transcendentalism?" Her husband had simply ridiculed this New England heresy, but Louisa could not so easily satisfy herself. Is it right, she wondered, to revere as an emanation of God "the light that burns within," as Emerson and others suggested? Surely not, she answered herself: "Every flower bears its vital escence in billions of multiplied divisions; and man is but a flower like the grass that withereth away." Louisa also devoted two long passages to Shakespeare, whom she felt she had not fully fathomed until now.

But Louisa's soul was not at rest. She could no longer recognize in herself the quick-spirited girl she had once been. Long years of worry, of responsibility, of affliction and grief will "tincture our manners, with severity," she wrote, "when our hearts are full of all the benevolent feelings which naturally stimulate to kind actions." Shedding her polite diction, she cried, "I am now nearly sixty-five years old—no one understands me one bit better than they did the day I arrived." Her father had loved and solaced her, but he had died when she was still a young woman. Little Louisa had been taken from her, and then George and John. She thought of each on the anniversary of their death. Had God not punished her for her failures as a mother? On Charles' birthday, she wrote, "He is the only one of my children I never deserted. . . . To my other two I failed; and God Almighty forgive me!" Ever since her infant's death Louisa had yearned for surcease, even as she clung to life; now she felt her grip slackening.

ON NEW YEAR'S DAY 1842, ADAMS RECEIVED A VISIT AT HOME IN Washington, DC, from the abolitionist legislator Joshua Giddings, Joshua Leavitt of the *Emancipator*, and another man he did not know. "Is it Mr. Theodore D. Weld?," he asked. It was. Giddings had invited this great evangelical leader to Washington to serve as secretary and researcher for the Select Committee on Slavery, a group of activists who would coordinate the efforts of the growing number of legislators prepared to take on the South. A convert to immediatism, Weld was a tireless orator, organizer, and pamphleteer of the abolitionist cause. He was a beloved figure, modest and humble, invincibly determined but unfailingly polite—a kind of antitype to the explosive Garrison.

Weld was immediately impressed by the former president. After the "pomp and tinsel" of President Tyler's reception, Weld wrote to his wife, the abolitionist Angelina Grimké, he found the Adamses "living in a plain house, plainly furnished, and themselves plainly dressed—the President very plainly." The feeling was apparently mutual, for Adams looked at his new visitor and said, "I know you well sir by your writings." Adams was surely thinking of Weld's monumental 1839 compendium, *Slavery As It Is*, which rebutted in terrifying detail the Southern lie that slaves were treated no worse than free laborers. ("We will prove that slaves in the United States . . . are often made to wear round their necks iron collars armed with prongs, to drag heavy chains and weights at their feet while working in the field, and to wear yokes, and bells, and iron horns.")

The gag rule continued to make a true debate over slavery impossible, but its days appeared to be numbered. At the outset of the 1840–1841 congressional session, Adams had succeeded for the first time in winning a vote to eliminate the gag. After another pitched battle, the House had voided that decision, though without reimposing the rule. Adams tried again the following year, but, despite the large Whig majority, a motion to restore the gag as a standing rule passed by three votes. The slavocracy's margin was narrowing, though it still held sway.

Finally, however, the forces of abolitionism had begun to organize themselves as the slavery advocates long had. The members of the Select Committee, as well as most members of the small abolitionist caucus in Congress, lived in Mrs. Spriggs' rooming house directly facing the Capitol. There, in what came to be called Abolition House, they plotted strategy. They divided up the presentation of petitions among their members and ensured that their speeches were printed in the *National Intelligencer* and then circulated in the abolitionist press. Weld, meanwhile, took a desk in the Library of Congress and plunged into research. In mid-January 1842, a dozen congressmen gathered in Adams' home to make plans for the coming weeks. It's not clear if they agreed that the old man would lob a missile into the slaveholders' ranks; that, however, is what he proceeded to do. On January 20, Adams told Weld that the following day he would present petitions that would set the slaveholders "in a blaze."

Adams was as good as his word. On the twenty-first, he presented a petition from citizens of Massachusetts complaining that the slave states, by their "absolutely despotic, onerous and oppressive" behavior, had denied the free states their constitutionally guaranteed right to republican government. This petition did not technically fall within the compass of the gag rule. Neither did his next one, a warning from the citizens of Pennsylvania that the nation was preparing to go to war with Great Britain to protect the slave interest, a reference to mounting tensions over England's insistence on boarding American vessels in order to search for slaves. By now the House was in turmoil. Many of the slave representatives had gotten up from their seats to crowd around Adams and try to shout him down. Weld, who had come to witness the spectacle, was astounded and thrilled. He described the scene to Angelina: "A perfect uproar like Babel would burst forth every two or three minutes as Mr. A with his bold surgery would smite his cleaver into the very bone."

Speaker White ordered Adams to take his seat. He did, and then popped up to deliver a petition from Massachusetts men who wished it be known that they would not take up arms to defend slavery. Then came the coup de grâce, at least for that day: a petition from Habersham Country, Georgia, asking to have Adams removed as chairman of the Foreign Relations Committee, as he was "possessed of a species of monomania on all subjects connected with people as dark as a Mexican," and thus ought not have authority over such issues as US relations with Texas and Mexico. (Adams had been restored to the chairmanship after Daniel Webster decided that the man he had put there, Caleb Cushing, had become too aggressive toward Great Britain.)

This provoked a new round of bedlam, for Richard Habersham, the district's eponymous representative, declared the petition an obvious hoax, like the alleged memorial from slaves that Adams had presented in 1837. The author had, after all, identified himself as "James Playfair." Adams nevertheless demanded the right to defend himself from the charge of monomania. Henry Wise of Virginia implored the Speaker to declare Adams out of order; Thomas Marshall of Kentucky eagerly prayed the Speaker to let the monomaniac go ahead. On that wild note, the House adjourned.

Adams still had the floor, and the next day he tried once again to present the Georgia petition. Perhaps it *was* a hoax, he conceded, but it still expressed the view of many in the House—though that must have sounded like a pretext even to Adams' allies. The Speaker ordered Adams to his seat, but Adams had decided to provoke a confrontation. He demanded the recognition of Haiti. He read from abolitionist documents. Adams had now been on his feet for hours. Giddings, Slade, and Seth Gates of New York stood by him protectively; Wise and Thomas Gilmer, also of Virginia, and others hovered just beyond them. The Southern heckling rose to a crescendo. When the House voted not to receive the Georgia petition, Adams pulled from his sheaf of papers one more document that, Giddings wrote, he "appeared to examine with more than usual interest." Turning to the Speaker, he said, "I hold in my hand the memorial of Benjamin Emerson and forty-five other citizens of Haverhill, in the state of Massachusetts, praying Congress to adopt immediate measures for the peaceful dissolution of the Union of these States." The petitioners no longer wished to see the resources of the free states "drained" for the benefit of the slave states.

It's not clear whether Adams really had pushed the slaveholders beyond all endurance or whether he had given them a provocation they had been seeking. George Washington Hopkins of Virginia suggested that the only treatment such a petition merited was incineration. Henry Wise asked if it would be in order to propose a resolution of censure—to which Adams replied, "Good!" And then Gilmer presented such a resolution. Adams then ridiculed Gilmer as Wise's "second fiddle," prompting a return blast from his accuser. The House finally adjourned, although, according to Giddings, the members were now so agitated that most continued milling around the floor, the Southerners clenching their fists and uttering oaths against abolitionists.

That night, Southerners convened among themselves. They had learned something from the censure effort of 1837, which, in the absence of coordination, had been conducted largely by ungovernable hotheads like Waddy Thompson. Now the slave-state caucus agreed that Adams' prosecution would be led by Thomas Marshall, who as a Whig could not be accused of party feeling against Adams and who was believed to have inherited something of the genius of his uncle, John Marshall, the former chief justice. Northern members declined to form a defense team, but the abolitionist core gathered at Giddings' apartment in Mrs. Spriggs' boarding house. Late that night, they walked to Adams' home on F Street and told him that they were prepared to stand with him, come what may. "The aged statesman listened attentively," Giddings wrote, "but for a time was unable to reply, laboring under great apparent feeling. At length he stated that the voice of friendship was so unusual to his ears, that he could not express his gratitude." Only under the pressure of intense emotion could Adams admit to the price he paid for his rigid principles. Then he composed himself and gave them a list of books he would need to consult for his defense.

The following morning, crowds filled the galleries of the House long before the noon opening of the session. Giddings noted that "foreign ministers, *attachés* and privileged persons filled the lobbies and the outer space within the hall and outside the bar." The Speaker called on Marshall, who read a resolution he proposed as substitute for Gilmer's straightforward motion for censure. Marshall had raised the stakes considerably: whereas, he asserted, "a dissolution of the Union necessarily implies the destruction" of the Constitution, the "overthrow of the Republic" and the violation of the legislators' own oath, the petition Adams had presented compelled the members to perjure themselves and involved "the crime of high treason." Adams deserved expulsion; censure was "an act of grace and mercy." This would prove to be a catastrophic overreach on Marshall's part.

Marshall delivered an indictment he prefaced by long expressions of regard for Adams himself and for his family and their place in history. He therefore professed himself astounded when such a revered figure presented to the House so "monstrous" a document—and not only presented that document but sought to have it referred to committee, "thus leading to the conclusion that the dissolution of the Union was a fair subject to be considered by the House." This was a piece of sophistry on Marshall's part, since Adams had long made it a practice to present petitions whose objects he explicitly disavowed. But Marshall's professions of neutrality and his rhetorical command had cheered his colleagues and left Adams' supporters "depressed in a corresponding degree," Giddings wrote. Both sides waited with excruciating anticipation for the old man's response.

Adams had been here before, and not only in another censure debate five years earlier. This was also the man who had Jonathan-Russell'd Jonathan Russell and fought the veterans of the Hartford Convention to a standstill. Adams relished nothing so much as a solitary stand against a massed enemy—thus his emphatic "Good!" at the prospect of censure—and he was perhaps better equipped than any man alive to conduct one. With all eyes on him, Adams rose slowly, looking about him at friend and foe, and at last said to the Speaker, "It is no part of my intention to reply to the gentleman from Kentucky at this time." That was a startling remark. What, then, was his intention? "I call, "Adams went on, "for the reading of the first paragraph of the Declaration of Independence." The clerk began to read, "When in the course of human events . . . " When he slowed, uncertain where to stop, Adams cried, "Proceed! Proceed!" The clerk continued: " . . . whenever any form of government becomes destructive of those ends, it is the right of the people to alter or abolish it," and then, at Adams' order, came to a stop at " . . . it is their right, it is their duty, to throw off such government."

John Quincy Adams' father had played a central role in writing the Declaration of Independence. John Quincy himself had been very much alive at the time. His adversary, Thomas Marshall, was a young pup of forty. Adams was reminding his audience, which had come to see him as a "fanatic" and a "monomaniac," of his own connection to the nation's founding documents and principles—and, more than that, of just what those principles were. He had done the same in his peroration before the Supreme Court. Adams had become, more and more, the living incarnation of the founders from whom he was descended—a second-generation prophet.

Was it high treason, he now went on, to advocate the dissolution of the government (never mind that the Declaration had been written to justify the dissolution of colonial dominion)? The real danger to the Republic, Adams continued, came not from petitioners but from slaveholders: "There is a concerted system and purpose to destroy all the principles of civil liberty in the free states." The right of habeas corpus and the right of trial by jury were at risk. So, of course, was the right of petition. Nevertheless, he did not share the petitioners' view. "It is not yet time to do this, till other means have been tried." Adams' tone was measured. Weld, admittedly the most biased of spectators, wrote that Old Nestor had demonstrated "a calm fearlessness and majesty that furnished the highest illustration of the moral sublime that I ever witnessed in a popular secular assembly."

The intemperate Henry Wise now rose in rebuttal—and did further damage to his own case. Even the sympathetic court reporter was struck by Wise's combination of "vehemence" and inaudibility, at least "beyond a brief space around his seat." Wise unfolded, at least to those who could hear him, a generations-long Northern conspiracy, headed by "the house of Braintree," to surrender the nation to British control. The current chief of that house was, he declared, a British "agent." He had surrendered Texas in order to weaken the South. He had advocated protective tariffs in order to drive the South away from the Union and set the stage for a British invasion. Today Great Britain was determined to destroy the institution of slavery, and the representative from Massachusetts resolutely opposed going to war to prevent that design. His whole career stood as a refutation of George Washington's prophetic warning against foreign entanglements. Wise's indictment had almost nothing to do with the petition in question; as Adams himself said on the floor, Wise had poured out "the whole volume which he has been measuring and accumulating for two or three years."

After a weekend break, Adams regained the floor on January 27 and lit into the hapless Wise. He reminded the House that the gentleman who had just accused him of dreadful crimes was the very same man who a few years earlier had entered the chamber "with his hands and face dripping with the blood of murder, the blotches of which were yet hanging upon him." This vivid imagery, which seemed to come straight from *Macbeth*, referred to Wise's role a year earlier as a second in a notorious duel between congressmen. Wise angrily objected to this irrelevant character attack, but Adams had finished with him and turned to attack his chief target, Thomas Marshall. Adams had now exchanged his dignified tone for brutal mockery. "The Constitution of the United States," he observed, "says what high treason is, and it is not for him, or his puny mind, to define what high treason is, and to confound it with what I have done." Adams suggested that Marshall attend "some law school" in order to "learn a little of the rights of the citizens of these states and the members of this House." Did he not understand that treason and the subornation of perjury were crimes, rather than simply censurable offenses, and that any man accused of them had the right to trial before an impartial jury? Was a jury of slaveholders impartial?

A number of Southerners had been troubled from the outset by the idea of censuring Adams—yet again—for the sin of presenting a petition. Now, after Adams had begun to train his artillery on their ranks, some of the doubters bolted. Joseph Underwood of Kentucky said that if Adams really were guilty of treason he should be hanged, not expelled; but he plainly wasn't. John Botts of Virginia denied that Adams was an abolitionist. Thomas Arnold of Tennessee expressed his regret that the venerable Adams had been vexed by "boys who were yet of swaddling clothes when that gentleman was serving his country in the highest station." Slaveholders, he continued, "might as well attempt to dam up the waters of the Niagara as attempt to stay this right of petition," a metaphor until now used only by the abolitionists themselves.

Adams was beating the South yet again—and with the whole world watching. He was gleeful. That night, Weld came to visit Adams at home and found him "as fresh and elastic as a boy," though he had scarcely slept for days. "I am all ready for another heat," he declared, and with that, Adams began reciting his planned speech for the following day, accompanied by all the gestures and facial expressions he would be using before his auditors. The flabbergasted abolitionist tried to warn Adams against wasting his energy, but the old man was unstoppable. "He went on for an hour, or nearly that," Weld wrote to Angelina, "in a voice loud enough to be heard by a large audience. Wonderful man!"

Marshall was now on the defensive. Taking the floor on January 28, he insisted that he had never intended to charge Adams with treason or subornation of perjury, since that language was only in the preamble of his resolution; he acknowledged that the members seemed to feel otherwise. Wise now interjected to say that, in fact, he had never supported Marshall's resolution but rather had been speaking on behalf of a motion to have Gilmer's resolution printed. This was abandonment and surrender. "God preserve me from my friends," cried Marshall, who now turned on Wise, charging him with seeking to revive "the bitter and envenomed animosities of 1801"—when Thomas Jefferson had ended Federalist rule with his victory over John Adams. He sought to reestablish his nonpartisan bona fides. But Marshall's own wrath betrayed him. He accused Adams once again of seeking to destroy slavery and assured him that in such a case, "the Cavalier sword will, as it was wont to do, drink blood." He ridiculed the idea that Adams should be granted license on account of his years and past glories:

"Are we to treat him as some old imbecile, whom it is not worth while to notice?" This was not a tactic calculated to win over the fence-sitters.

The House had transacted virtually no business for the last week. Adams knew very well how impatient many members had become. On February 2, he explained that he had not yet actually begun his defense and would need a mass of documents and several weeks of preparation. This had the desired effect. On the third, Thomas Gilmer offered to drop the resolution if Adams would withdraw the petition. Either Gilmer wasn't being serious or he didn't know Adams, for the latter of course refused. Gilmer now launched into a fresh attack on Adams, and the former president responded in kind. He brandished one of the many letters he received threatening assassination. The letter showed a rifle ball about to penetrate a skull. The author had written, "Stop the music of John Quincy Adams," who "In one revolving moon, / Is statesman, poet, babbler, and buffoon." A week earlier, Gilmer himself had used the same expression and had quoted the same lines (a paraphrase from Dryden's "Absalom and Achitophel"), only substituting "fiddler" for "babbler." Adams pointed out the coincidence without seeking to explain it. He left the impression that, at the very least, the slaveholders' murderous rhetoric was inspiring some men to convert words to deeds.

Adams had smote his adversaries hip and thigh, but he still wasn't done with them. On February 5, he complained about the postmasters in the South who refused to distribute abolitionist literature. Marshall objected that Adams had shifted the ground of debate from the censure motion to slavery—though the truth was that Wise and others had done so themselves. He also pointed out that Adams had had six days to defend himself—as long as it took God to create the Earth. He pleaded with his colleagues to shut the old man down. Adams said blandly that he would need at least two more weeks. Adams was sustained, 97–25. Now he knew that he had won. "I came home barely able to crawl into my chamber," he wrote in his journal, "but with the sound of IO TRIOMPHE ringing in my ear." On February 7, two weeks after the drama had begun, Marshall waved the white flag. He moved to lay the censure resolution on the table. The motion passed, 106–93. Adams still had the floor. He commenced introducing two hundred anti-slavery petitions.

Adams had shattered the overweening confidence of the South. Giddings overheard Marshall tell a colleague, "I would rather die a thousand deaths than again to encounter that old man." Nor did he have to, for Marshall retired after that session of Congress. Wise later called Adams the "acutest, the astutest, the archest enemy of Southern slavery that ever existed." It was not, of course, a merely individual defeat. Weld called the censure vote "the first victory over the slaveholders *in a body* ever yet achieved since the foundation of the government," and that was not pure hyperbole. The South had fought a pitched battle over petitions and lost. Two more years would have to pass before the House defeated the gag rule, but as of that moment Southern resistance was spent. The mistake of the abolitionists, however, was to believe that slavery could not survive a crushing defeat in the court of public opinion. Weld boldly predicted that "from this time" slavery's downfall "*takes its date.*" Adams knew better. He knew that slave owners would never voluntarily surrender their most precious property and the foundation of their way of life. The Cavalier sword would drink blood and be drowned in blood.

THE "SLAVE POWER," AS ADAMS CALLED IT, HAD BEEN STAGGERED, but it remained the dominant force in Congress. The slaveholders were prepared to attack when provoked by a foe less dreadful than Adams. Their moment came on March 21, when Joshua Giddings, who unlike Adams was a true abolitionist, presented a clutch of resolutions whose effect would have been to free slaves the moment they left slave territory, whether by passing through free states or traveling by sea.

John Botts, the Virginia Whig who had come to Adams' defense, now eagerly seized the opportunity to censure a more easily censurable man. He was quickly joined not only by other members of the slave power but also by Northern Whigs who feared that they might come to be seen as the party of abolition. This time they would not make the mistake of conducting a public trial: shockingly, Giddings was not given the chance to speak in his own behalf. The following day, the censure motion carried, 125–69, forcing Giddings to relinquish his seat. Adams, who understood that Giddings was being punished for Adams' own alleged transgressions, was devastated. "I can find no language to express my feelings at the consummation of this act," he wrote in his journal. Giddings, tall, lean, gentlemanly, came to Adams' desk to shake his hand on the way out of the chamber, and Adams whispered, "I hope we shall soon have you back again."

And he did. On May 5, Joshua Leavitt came to Adams' seat to inform him that Giddings was back: a martyr to the cause of conscience, he had been reelected by the people of the Western Reserve. Adams would serve the remainder of his time in the House alongside the one colleague he truly loved. Toward the end of the 1844 congressional session, thinking that he might never see him again, Adams would send Giddings a letter with a short poem: "We seek, with searching ken to find / A soul congenial to our own / I sought, and found at last—in thee." Giddings would remain in office until 1859, taking over from the elderly Adams the leadership of the anti-slavery movement in Congress.

IN JULY 1842, ADAMS TURNED SEVENTY-FIVE. ALREADY HE HAD outlived the biblical span of threescore and ten, which Adams viewed as the age beyond which no one could reasonably expect to live. Life, he understood, was a "pilgrimage" from which he could at any moment be recalled. He had been admonishing himself for years, often on the occasion of his birthday, to prepare his soul for death. Two years earlier, on his seventy-third birthday, he had written in his diary, "I am deeply sensible of the duty of beginning in earnest to wean myself from the interests and afflictions of this world, and of preparing myself for the departure to that which is to come." Then, almost in the next sentence, Adams made a stark admission to himself: "The truth is, I adhere to the world and all its vanities, from an impulse not altogether voluntary, and cannot, by any exercise of my will, realize that I can have but very few days left to live."

So it was still. The time had come, he wrote in September 1842, "to set my house in order." The next session of Congress would be "in all probability the last I shall ever attend." And yet he admitted that his mind was "in the condition of a ship at sea in a hurricane, suspended by an instantaneous calm." Ahead of him he saw nothing but turbulence. He listed the men with whom he was at daggers drawn: Wise, Marshall, Cost Johnson of Maryland, Joseph Ingersoll. Dutee Pearce, a former House member from Rhode Island, had begged Adams to defend him at a trial for treason; his crime was seeking to organize a universal suffrage party. "I could not hesitate for an instant to take it," Adams wrote, "though it comes upon me like a thunderclap." Nor could he decline an invitation to deliver an address at the Congregational church in Braintree and another at the annual dinner of the county temperance society—jugs of cold water, "ludicrous invectives" on the drinking of alcohol, long debate about whether the delivery of toasts was appropriate. (It was not.) Adams was locked in a struggle between soul and self, between pious resignation and zeal. It was a one-sided contest. Adams would fight to the very end.

CHAPTER 36

The Sober Second Thought
of the People

(1842–1845)

THE POLITICS OF THE EARLY 1840S WERE EVERY BIT AS
explosive as they had been a decade earlier, when Andrew Jackson
had challenged the prerogatives of Congress over the national bank.
John Tyler had come, by accident, to preside over a party whose deepest
principles he opposed. Rather than defer to his fellow Whigs, he confronted
them. Tyler had felt constrained to keep Harrison's cabinet but not his policies. In August 1841, after Henry Clay pushed through a bill to reestablish a
national bank, Tyler vetoed it. The Congress sent the president a new version of the legislation, and he vetoed it once again. In the ensuing furor,
Tyler's entire cabinet resigned—save for Daniel Webster, who convinced
himself that the nation needed him to remain. Adams never forgave
Webster for continuing to serve the president and to advance his policies.

With an all-but-Democrat now occupying the White House, Democrats in the House felt emboldened to push their agenda of "retrench-
ments," budget cuts designed not to eliminate a deficit—there was
none—but to throttle the growth of the federal government. They proposed cutting clerks from departments, requiring the House doorkeeper to
pay for candles out of his own budget, and the like. Tyler gave the campaign his support, though he had not initially proposed such measures. The

Whig majority pushed back. When the House passed a tariff bill, Tyler wielded the veto once again. Party members, including Southerners, implored Adams to take to the floor of the House to denounce Tyler's policies, which of course he was delighted to do.

The bitterness between the two parties reached such a pitch that the House impaneled a special committee to examine whether Tyler had committed impeachable offenses by frustrating the will of Congress. Adams was asked to serve as chair. The committee issued a report in August stating that the president had perpetrated "offenses of the gravest character," though it did not ultimately recommend impeachment. Forty years earlier Adams had defended judges faced with impeachment charges on the grounds that they had not committed "high crimes and misdemeanours," as the Constitution required. Neither, it's safe to say, had Tyler. But Adams viewed the president as illegitimate—just as so many rivals had viewed him after the 1824 election.

Whatever Adams' views of Jackson and Van Buren, he considered them both, in their own way, accomplished men; Tyler, by contrast, he treated as a usurper, a villain out of Shakespeare. In September 1842, Adams delivered a speech to his constituents in Quincy in which he denounced the president as a liar and a hypocrite. Tyler had divided his own party in order to advance the interest of slave owners; had turned honest men out of office in favor of his own appointees; had plotted to starve the federal government of revenue, and thus endanger the union, by ending the sale of public lands. "Nullification," he thundered, "is the *creed* of the Executive Mansion in Washington." Adams spoke at length about Tyler's designs on Texas. The previous winter, pro-administration newspapers had run articles calling for the annexation of Texas. Tyler had kept silent on the issue, but in his first message to Congress he called for major increases in naval spending, which Adams interpreted as preparation for war with Mexico. As minister to Mexico, Tyler had appointed Waddy Thompson, the most virulent of the defenders of slavery and a single-minded enthusiast of incorporating Texas into the union. Tyler's diplomacy toward Mexico constituted "treachery of the deepest dye," Adams said—though he was careful to exempt the popular Daniel Webster from this judgment. Adams thought he had scotched the forces of annexation with his filibustering oration of June 1838; now, he told his constituents, the monster was back.

Adams was angry about the shrinkage of government at home, but he was genuinely fearful about Tyler's nationalistic and bellicose policies abroad. The United States and Great Britain were at odds over territorial issues in Oregon and New England, as well as the perennial question of the right of British ships to stop and search foreign vessels; Adams believed that Tyler was needlessly inflaming those tensions with his Mexico policy and thus threatening to plunge the United States into a third war with England. In April 1842 Henry Wise had declared in a speech on the floor of the House that the United States must annex Mexico right away to trump alleged British designs on the country. If Mexico didn't like it, Wise wildly asserted, America, with its ally France, should be prepared to go to war against Mexico—and Great Britain, if need be. Settlers in the Mississippi Valley, which is to say, slaveholders, were prepared to rally to the flag. Tyler had been careful to deny the linkage between annexation and slavery. Not Wise: "Slavery should pour itself abroad without restraint," he cried, "and find no limit but the Southern ocean." Wise reminded Congress that while Adams now found so much to fault in the current administration's policy toward Mexico, as president he had sought to purchase Texas.

Adams rose to defend himself. Since Mexico had abolished slavery, he observed, Texas would have been admitted as free territory. Wise interrupted to ask whether it was not true that Adams had instructed his minister in Mexico to protest the abolition of slavery?

"No sir, never!"

"Not while the gentleman was President?"

"No sir, never!"

Adams calmed himself down and resumed. The self-declared republic of Texas had reinstituted slavery, which, he said, was even more reprehensible than simply perpetuating an age-old practice. "I would not take the territory if it were ten thousand times more valuable than it is," said Adams, "sullied as it is with the crime of slavery restored."

Adams' hatred of Tyler was far less personal than it was political. Under this small-minded descendant of the great Tidewater statesmen, Adams believed, slavery had come to corrupt not only America's domestic but its foreign policy, and thus to redefine the nation's place in the world. In a conversation with Caleb Cushing, an anti-British and pro-Tyler Massachusetts congressman, Adams predicted a coming global war over slavery, with Great Britain on one side and the United States on the other. "I was going off the stage," Adams wrote in his diary, "but he was coming on to it." Adams implored Cushing not to side with the slave power. Cushing heard him out "without taking offense, but apparently without conviction."

Adams had always seen America as being in the right. In virtually any conflict between the United States and a European power, he had automatically sided with his own country. When Jackson had seized Spanish territory in Florida in 1819, Adams had stood alone in the cabinet to defend him. But Adams no longer saw his beloved country as the world's shining beacon of liberty. And though still prepared to repel any British designs on North America, he had begun to identify with the global champion of abolitionism. In a letter to his old friend Richard Rush, the former minister to the Court of Saint James, he admitted that "my jealousies of the 'grasping and perfidious Albion' have been greatly disarmed by her demonstrated ardour" for the cause of freedom.

Adams believed that the influence of the slave power was leading the United States to surrender the principles it had cherished since the time of George Washington. As secretary of state and president, he had sought to extend America's dominion through diplomatic negotiations. He had used threatening language but avoided war. He was convinced that a conquering America would sacrifice its republican soul; he had said so in the great July 4, 1821, oration in which he had warned against seeking to slay monsters abroad. In his prophetic old age, he saw his greatest fears coming to pass. "The annexation of Texas to this union," he wrote in his diary, "is the first step to the conquest of all Mexico, of the West Indian islands, of a maritime, colonizing, slave-tainted monarchy, and of extinguished freedom."

Adams was wrong, of course: Tyler had no such autocratic or Napoleonic designs. Adams accused Tyler of waging an undeclared war in Mexico when the president in fact was doing no such thing. Perhaps one should say that Adams' righteous fury at the slavocracy had blurred his perspective. What was also true was that the republican principles Adams so deeply cherished were far more deeply rooted, and thus less endangered, than he imagined. Adams still inhabited the intellectual world of the founders and thus at times defended ramparts that were no longer embattled. Yet his role, more and more, was to remind Americans of their nation's first principles.

Adams was so persuaded of the dangers of Tyler's Mexico policy that he was prepared, like the radical abolitionists whose petitions he presented (but did not endorse), to precipitate a national crisis. In early 1843, he presented a resolution to the Committee on Foreign Affairs stating that neither the legislature nor the executive had the power to annex a territory or its people and stipulating that the free states would be duty-bound to resist any such move to annexation. This astonishing echo of the Hartford Convention from its most famous opponent had no chance of passing. But after the short session of Congress adjourned, in March, Adams and a dozen other anti-slavery congressmen signed a public letter making the same argument. Annexation, they concluded, would be tantamount to the dissolution of the union.

Adams still wasn't finished. After his colleagues went home, he began to pay daily visits to the State Department in order to search for evidence of a secret project, maturing since the first days of the Jackson administration, to pry the entire Southwest from the grip of Mexico. He learned that Jackson had been dispatching agents to Mexico and receiving reports from self-appointed emissaries who insisted that the Mexican government under General Santa Ana was prepared to sell California. None of these plans came to anything, probably because Santa Ana in fact had no intention of surrendering his northern provinces, which had rebelled against his rule in 1835. But in Adams' mind the correspondence demonstrated that Jackson had lied to the American people while pursuing a secret policy in league with slave forces; Adams would quote liberally from these documents as he strove to convince the public that annexation was the fruit of a long-standing plot to extend slavery across the continent.

Daniel Webster had stepped down as secretary of state in the spring of 1842, thus removing perhaps the single greatest obstacle to Tyler's dreams of annexation. The president appointed a series of Southerners who shared his own views. The last of them was John Calhoun, the nullifier in chief. On April 12, 1844, Calhoun signed the treaty of annexation with Texas. Then, like Wise before him, he exposed what appeared to be the hidden calculations behind the transaction. In a startlingly intemperate letter to Richard Pakenham, England's minister in Washington, Calhoun rebuked Great Britain for seeking to abolish slavery in Texas and went on to describe slavery as "essential to the peace, safety and prosperity" of the territory. The secretary of state even added a few grace notes about slavery's salutary effect on the "number, comfort, intelligence and morals" of enslaved blacks.

These were Calhoun's views, not Tyler's, but they gave Adams and other opponents of annexation good reason to fear that the president was, indeed, carrying out a clandestine agenda of slavery promotion. The Senate firmly rejected the treaty, amazing the always pessimistic Adams, who privately celebrated "deliverance . . . by the special interposition of Almighty God." But Tyler was determined to complete the absorption of Texas before his term ended. In the first days of 1845, with a new president, James Polk, soon to take office, the House began debate on a resolution authorizing the president to annex Texas. The resolution provided that as many as four states might ultimately be fashioned from the territory; states below the line of the Missouri Compromise would be slave, and those above would be free. In fact, only a small and barren slice of Texas lay above 36° 30'. This huge acquisition did, as Adams feared, hold the potential to decisively tip political power toward slave owners.

The seventy-seven-year-old ex-president no longer took the lead. Only on January 24, at the very end of a fierce debate, did he rise to speak for the last time on this supreme question. It was true, he said, that as president he had sought to buy Texas from Mexico. But that would have been a voluntary transaction. The difference between that moment and this one, he stated, was that "between purchase and burglary." Adams had fought for territorial expansion—but through treaty, not through acts of force. He had endorsed the purchase of the Louisiana Territory, but America could not simply annex people against their will. Territory, he said, "was inanimate. It was matter. Man had an immortal soul—man had rights peculiar to himself, and they could not, without his consent, transfer man from one country to another." The House voted the following day. The resolution passed 120–98. It then passed the Senate, allowing Tyler to formally annex Texas on March 1, three days before leaving office.

Polk continued Tyler's bellicose policy, sending American troops to a disputed border area. He was hoping to provoke a war, and he succeeded. When Mexican forces launched an attack, in April 1846, Polk asked Congress for a declaration of war. Both houses of Congress gave him overwhelming support. Many legislators who had opposed annexation voted for the measure. In the grip of a chaotic military dictatorship, Mexico itself seemed bent on war. And a war on Texas was, of course, a war on the United States. Nevertheless, Adams voted against the measure. He was wrong about the causes of the war, as he had been wrong about the consequences for American democracy. Both Tyler and Polk cared more about territorial expansion than about spreading the empire of slavery (though both were quite prepared to accept the spread of slavery as a consequence of expansion). In the Senate, Calhoun abstained on the vote for war, which he feared would harm rather than help the cause of slavery. Nevertheless, the Mexican-American War did constitute an abandonment of the principles laid down by the founders and largely observed by the next generation of national leaders. Americans had insisted that they did not go to war for gain, as European states did. Now, essentially, they had: the national hunger known as Manifest Destiny had eclipsed the principles of

Washington and Jefferson. Adams was the last living link to those men, and their vision.

ADAMS' SPREADING FAME AS A CHAMPION OF REPUBLICAN PRINCIPLES made him a target for every lyceum and young men's association looking for a speaker able to attract a mass audience. He received so many such invitations that he no longer had time even to write polite notes declining the offer. He posted a notice in the *National Intelligencer*, and then later in his hometown's principal paper, the *Boston Atlas*, apologizing in advance for his inability either to deliver such speeches or even to properly respond. Adams had almost always refused invitations to speak, at least beyond the confines of home. Increasingly, however, he found a reason to say yes to certain choice requests.

Speeches gave Adams the opportunity to formulate, and disseminate, his views both on urgent matters like the perfidy of the Tyler administration and on the questions of history and political thought that he often turned over in his mind. In October 1842, he delivered an address to the Boston Lyceum entitled "The Social Contract Exemplified in the Constitution of the Commonwealth of Massachusetts." In May 1843, he spoke to the Massachusetts Historical Society on the two hundredth anniversary of the New England Confederacy.

Adams almost never went anywhere to speak where he wouldn't have been otherwise; he was not one for unnecessary travel. Sometimes, however, curiosity got the better of him. In the summer of 1843, Charles Francis' wife, Abby, invited her father-in-law to join her and John's son, John Quincy, on a trip to Niagara Falls. A thoroughly delighted Adams discovered the fine resort hotels and comfortable trains available to a new class of tourists and vacationers. He was thrilled by the beauty of the New Hampshire mountains as the sun first struck their peaks at dawn. He visited the Revolutionary War battlefield at Saratoga, took a steamer up to Montreal, and then crossed the 438 miles to Niagara in, he recorded, "two days and nine hours." Niagara Falls thrilled him as much as it did any mortal. It's odd that Adams didn't travel more, since he so thoroughly enjoyed himself every time he did.

While in Niagara, Adams had received a letter from a Professor Mitchell of the Astronomical Society of Cincinnati, inviting him to lay the cornerstone for that city's observatory. Adams had never travelled to the West. The opportunity to do so in order to deliver a lecture on a subject as dear to his heart as any was too much to resist. The next day, he wrote back promising to come.

Once back in Quincy, Adams asked his friends to bring him reference books to prepare for his oration—Middleton's *Celestial Atlas*, Bailly's four-volume *Histoire de l'astronomie ancienne et moderne*. He spoke to President Quincy at Harvard about the university's own observatory, then in the planning stages, and studied a catalogue of astronomical instruments. He plunged back into the rarefied world of the heavens that had obsessed him in the early 1830s. On October 25 Adams set off for the west. He took a coach to Springfield, Massachusetts, and then a train to Buffalo and a steamer across Lake Erie to Cleveland. There he was recognized in a barbershop and soon was shaking the hands of hundreds of eager citizens. A meeting at the Congregational church was hastily arranged so that residents could listen to the former president. Adams then embarked on a boat down the Ohio Canal. He stopped in Akron, where he gave a speech at Town Hall. Adams was almost giddy with pleasure. "Among the women," he wrote, "a very pretty one, as I took her hand, kissed me on the cheek. I returned the salute on the lip, and kissed every woman that followed, at which some made faces, but none refused." When the canal ended, at Hebron, Adams took a carriage to Columbus, where he was met by more cheering throngs. A "mulatto," he wrote, delivered thanks from the black citizens of Columbus. In Dayton, it was more of the same.

Adams reached Cincinnati on November 8. The front pages of the papers contained almost nothing save news of the events surrounding his visit. The *Ohio Weekly Journal* offered a poem in honor of the great man: "Old Massachusetts eagle yet! / Hail! From his aerie'd rock." The cornerstone laying took place the following day. A torrential rain began that morning and continued all day. Nevertheless, a vast crowd formed on Sixth Street, where a banner had been raised: "John Quincy Adams, Defender of the Rights of Man." Thousands followed the procession to the hilltop site—later renamed Mount Adams—where the former president laid the cornerstone atop copies of the Constitution and the Declaration of Independence and gave a brief address. Among all the splendid monuments erected in the United States, he observed, not one was a "lighthouse of the skies." The Astronomical Society, he declared, as rain washed the ink from his speech, "have determined to wipe the reproach from the fair fame of our country." That night, as the rain abated, Adams was escorted by a mile-long torchlight parade to a temperance tea where two thousand people were said to be gathered under a tent, with two thousand more milling around outside.

The following day, Adams delivered his oration at the city's Wesleyan Methodist church. Fortunately for his audience, Adams cut half of the planned material, though he still spoke for two hours. He traced the development of astronomy from the Egyptians to the Greeks to the Arabs to Copernicus, Kepler, Tycho Brahe, Galileo, and Newton, and then onward to the discovery of new planets in his own time. It was a stupendous display of erudition that must have strained the attention of everyone save Professor Mitchell himself.

The rapturous reception Adams enjoyed prompted a good deal of editorial reflection. "He was never a popular favorite," wrote the abolitionist *Weekly Herald*. "His greater talents, and his services to his country, generally commanded respect, but excited no enthusiasm." He was today, the author went on sardonically, the same man he had been five years earlier, "when he was named, but to be cursed, and when to vindicate his course, was almost equivalent to a loss of caste." Now he was cheered as a Defender of the Rights of Man. Why? Because abolitionism, once the cause of a radical fringe, had gained widespread acceptance.

A less sour appraisal came from the *Daily Advocate and Advertiser* of Pittsburgh, where Adams ended his tour and where workers had decided, as a gesture of regard, to close their factories for the day. "Somewhat of the respect which was manifested was doubtless due and given to the *ex-President*," the editors wrote, "but the heartiness with which it was given was owing to esteem and affection for the *man*—for his undaunted spirit—his strict integrity—perseverance in duty—and true republicanism. . . . He has met the sober second thought of the people and it has at length done him justice."

As the first president to have gone back to work after his tenure, Adams had given himself the opportunity, as none of his predecessors had, to benefit from a "sober second thought." He had changed the meanings Americans attached to him. No longer the dynastic New Englander who represented an archaic Federalist America, Adams had become the dauntless standard-bearer of the very modern cause of abolitionism. At the same time, his rootedness in the republican principles of the founders also placed him on a pedestal in the national pantheon. Indeed, the very fact that he had not changed, that he had stood for principles when they were despised and lived to see them vindicated, offered the most powerful evidence of his greatness of character.

Adams received a delegation of black citizens in Cincinnati who wished to thank him for his role in defending their rights. Characteristically, he explained that the *Amistad* case had nothing to do with slavery and reminded them that Congress had no power in peace time to abolish slavery. Adams, of course, deprecated fulsome praise. In his journal he pronounced himself thoroughly disgusted with the reverence that had been showered on his head. But that wasn't quite so. After sitting through yet another lavish introduction in Covington, Kentucky, Adams told his audience that everywhere he had gone he had been met by citizens "disposed to manifest towards me such feelings as I know not how to allude to without emotion; such as through a long life it has been my lot to experience very little of; such as, in their extent, I had not the most distant idea, expectation or belief that I deserved."

CHAPTER 37

Let Justice Be Done Though the Heavens Fall

(1843–1845)

EARLY ONE MORNING IN DECEMBER 1843, JOSHUA GIDDINGS, Adams' beloved protégé, reached the House and found Adams sitting silently at his desk. The old man looked exhausted and deeply depressed. According to Giddings' diary, Adams said that he "had become nervous and unable to sleep. He spoke most feelingly, declaring that our government had become the *most perfect despotism of the Christian world.*" Adams felt that he could no longer take the floor to do battle against the slave power. "His hand was palsied and trembling," Giddings noted; "his voice was somewhat feeble and broken, his movements denoted age, but his intellect appeared unimpaired." Adams was, he said, prepared, as ever, to do his duty.

The elation Adams had felt in Cincinnati had long since dissipated. Darkness seemed to be gathering over him, his cause, and the nation itself. The year before, Adams and the zealots of Abolition House had gotten within inches of finally overturning the gag, losing 96–93. But John Tyler's divisive presidency had been a disaster for the Whigs, and the election of 1842 had restored the Democrats to power in the House. A forty-seat majority became a sixty-seat deficit, one of the biggest midterm swings in American history. In fact, the numbers were even worse than they looked, because in the decennial reapportionment of 1840 Congress had voted to reduce the total number of seats from 242 to 224. The Whig caucus was thus smaller both in absolute numbers and in percentage of seats. In an exchange of letters toward the end of 1842, Adams and Charles Francis had agreed that the best chance for ending the gag had come and gone.

Yet at the very moment when the anti-gag movement appeared to have reached its limit, something happened. When Adams once again submitted a resolution to rescind the gag rule in early December 1843, he lost by only four votes. He got the votes of virtually all the Northerners, Whig and Democrat, as well as of a few Southern Whigs. This old man seemed to have at last worn out his younger, and far more numerous, adversaries. The most unexpected convert was Adams' archrival, Henry Wise, who told court reporters that "henceforth, and forever, he ceased to contend in that war which was being carried on in the House by certain men against the South." Wise never explained his change of heart, though he may have concluded that he could stand on far more solid ground if he defended the right of Southern states to keep their peculiar institution than if he continued to prevent Northerners from submitting futile petitions in protest of the practice. That calculus would itself be a testimony to Adams' success in making the gag one of the great political issues of the day. After yet another debate over whether an anti-slavery petition should be tabled or referred to committee, Speaker White agreed to appoint a special committee on the rules chaired by Adams; Wise, as good as his word, consented.

Later in December, Adams presented a bombshell: a petition not from individuals but from the state of Massachusetts seeking a constitutional amendment overturning the "three-fifths clause," which had served as the foundation for the South's disproportionate political power. In some sense Adams himself had initiated the resolution, for it had been shepherded through the statehouse by Charles Francis Adams, now a state senator. Another furious debate sprang up in the House, but Wise agreed that it should be referred to a special committee—separate from the new rules committee—also chaired by Adams. The former president used this committee to send up more fireworks, including a proposal to conduct a survey fixing precisely the value of the human property held by slave owners in the House. He wasn't going to win that motion, but he wrote to Charles Francis asking him to do the research as quickly as possible.

In January 1844, Adams submitted a report from his rules committee proposing to eliminate the gag. For the next two months, the entire chamber was convulsed by one last ferocious debate on the subject. James Dellet of Alabama, a new member, joined in the general assault on Adams by quoting from a speech the latter had given in Pittsburgh at the end of his Western trip. Adams had told a group of black citizens that "the day of your redemption" was bound to come. "It may come in peace or it may come in blood; but whether in peace or in blood, LET IT COME." That, said Dellet emphatically, was the true agenda of the anti-gag activists. Not satisfied with the effect he had produced, Dellet read the quote a second time.

Adams had vowed to keep his peace, but this was too much. Without rising from his seat, he said, with a sudden show of vehemence, "I say now, let it come." Dellet responded by reminding the House what Adams meant by that expression, and Adams, still planted in his chair, roared, "Though it cost the blood of millions of white men, let it come! Let justice be done though the heavens fall." That was a shocking thing to say. The members might have expected as much from the single-minded Giddings, but not from the venerable ex-president. "A sensation of horror ran through the slave-holders," Giddings wrote. Adams had entertained this prospect in the privacy of his diary, but he had not been prepared to say such a thing in the House. Adams almost certainly did not premeditate this outburst; he had simply been unable to check, or decided not to check, the intense feelings that otherwise showed themselves only in the quiver of his lip.

At the same time, Adams was orchestrating discussion of the Massachusetts resolution in the special committee. He adroitly proposed that the committee resolve that the time was not yet ripe for the proposed constitutional amendment. He quickly won unanimous consent and then assigned himself to draft the committee report. The report was a battering ram aimed at slavery itself. Adams assailed the three-fifths clause as a gross violation of the letter and spirit of the Declaration of Independence, which, in turn, rested on the great truth of the gospel that all human beings are equal before God. Adams was still careful to say that the Declaration obliged states to abolish slavery "as soon as practicable" rather than right away. Yet the report represented a remarkable evolution in Adams' own thinking—and this at the age of seventy-six. He had long worshiped the Constitution almost as holy writ, yet he now accepted that it had been warped by the compromise with slaveholders. In a letter to William Seward in May 1844, Adams wrote that all the injustices with which American society was beset had been caused by "that fatal drop of Prussic acid in the Constitution of the United States, the human chattel representation." He wondered how heroic figures like Franklin or Roger Sherman had accepted it. Their "great delusion," he concluded, was in not seeing how the added representation would turn the South into "an element of organized power," a "solid compact body" certain to defeat the inevitably diffuse interests of the free states.

Adams' report was ultimately submitted to the House—and laid on the table. But the report of the special committee on House rules had a more complicated destiny. Before taking up Adams' motion to rescind the gag rule, the House put to a vote a rival measure to adopt all the existing rules, including the gag—and voted against. This was the closest thing to a victory the pro-petition forces had ever won. For several weeks, it appeared that Adams had finally carried the day. In late March, he received a beautiful ivory cane from Julius Pratt and Company of Meriden, Connecticut. It was topped with an American eagle inlaid in gold and a scroll bearing the words "Right of Petition Triumphant." Written on a gold ring below was, "To John Quincy Adams." Adams asked to have the cane returned to the Patent Office, whence it had been sent; he would, he said, inscribe the date when the gag was put to rest. It would have to wait just a little longer. Toward the end of the session, the House voted by the excruciating tally of 88–87 to decline to adopt Adams' report, leaving everything exactly as it had been before.

On December 2, 1844, the first day of the new session, Adams notified the House that, as ever, he would move that the gag, now known as the twenty-fifth rule, be revoked. The following day, he so moved. The opposition moved to lay his resolution on the table. The motion failed, 104 to 81. Adams' resolution was then submitted to a vote—and passed, 108 to 80. The gag rule, at long last, had fallen. Six Southerners had voted to end the gag. In his diary, Adams memorialized what must have been one of the greatest moments of his life with a simple prayer: "Blessed, forever blessed, be the name of God!" Adams retrieved the ivory cane, had the pommel inscribed "12/3/44," and returned it to the Patent Office for posterity.

ADAMS BEGAN PREPARING IN MID-JUNE 1844 TO LEAVE WASHINGTON for Quincy. He packed three sets of volumes in chests to be shipped north: committee reports and other documents issued by the House, the Senate, and the executive branch; the journals of the proceedings of each chamber; and copies of each bill and its amendments. He had two sets of most official papers, since he took home and bound up the documents issued each day, and ordered another set that was available to every legislator. He had been doing this for years and was, he believed, the only member of either house to keep so complete a record of the proceedings. Nobody cared about the official record of the chamber quite as much as he did.

On July 11, Adams' seventy-seventh birthday, he and Louisa, herself sixty-nine years old, took the train north from Baltimore. In Jersey City, they got off the platform in the darkness and, while walking arm in arm, fell off the platform. As they plummeted through space, Adams entertained the incredible thought that, after all he had been through, he was about to die and to kill his wife in the process. In fact, they fell only a few feet, and Adams got off with only a badly bruised hip, while Louisa was not seriously hurt. As with his railroad accident a few years earlier, Adams felt that he had been providentially spared, though reminded once again of the proximity of death.

That summer Adams continued to experience his encroaching mortality. One night he toppled over and fell to his knees, reflecting that at least he hadn't hurt himself quite as much as he had on the railroad platform. He often couldn't sleep, and as he lay awake until the dawn, he heard each hour tolled off on his standing clock. He was often tired, and he suffered from headaches. He visited an old friend, Daniel Greenleaf, now deaf, blind, and paralytic. The friends of his youth were mostly incapacitated, like Greenleaf, or dead. Despite his own disabilities, Adams in fact remained remarkably hale for a man of his age. He went on his annual fishing trip to Cohasset and lamented that at the chowder dinner afterward the new passion for temperance had compelled the hosts to substitute coffee for claret and lemonade for Madeira.

Adams was no more ready than ever to shut off the fiery furnace within. He fretted over his political vulnerability. He was up for reelection, and at long last an abolitionist party, known as the Liberty Party, had formed in New England. Adams submitted to a "friendly interview" with party leaders, to whom he happily reiterated his differences with abolitionist doctrine. They nominated, not Adams, but a physician and state senator named Appleton Howe. Adams felt surrounded by enemies. "I must sleep in armor, and be ready to meet them in Indian warfare," he wrote. Adams had already planned to address the Young Men's Whig Club of Boston, where Charles Francis served as president. He had intended to defend his reputation on the Texas issue; now he was fighting for votes as well. After rebutting allegations from the aged Andrew Jackson that as secretary of state he had surrendered two hundred square miles of territory to Spain, Adams turned to the present. The great struggle between "the spirit of freedom and the spirit of slavery" was coming to a head, he declared. He closed with a call to arms, though arguably a figurative one: "Young men of Boston: burnish your armor, prepare for the conflict, and I say to you, in the language of Galgacus to the ancient Britons, Think of your forefathers! Think of your posterity." He was in armor; they were in armor. The speech was a barn burner, and Adams delivered it again in Braintree and then once again in the town of North Bridgewater.

On November 6, the newspapers announced that James Polk had defeated Henry Clay to win the presidency. Adams felt certain that he himself would lose, though a Democratic wave would hardly float a Liberty candidate to victory. In fact, he trounced his Democratic rival. Howe, the Liberty standard-bearer, got all of 4 percent of the vote. After the exhausting effort of his speeches, Adams felt deeply vindicated.

IN OVERTURNING THE GAG, ADAMS HAD BROUGHT THE CONSUMING issue of his postpresidential career to a close. For most of his colleagues, however, the debate over petitions was little more than a distraction from the real business of the Congress. The burning question of the mid-1840s was territorial expansion, both in Mexico and in Oregon, which the United States and Great Britain continued to jointly administer a quarter of a century after Adams, as secretary of state, had negotiated a treaty to that effect. In his presidential campaign, James K. Polk had harnessed the feverish ambitions of Manifest Destiny. The convention that nominated him had adopted a resolution demanding "the re-occupation of Oregon and the re-annexation of Texas at the earliest possible period." The "re-" in each case signified the claim that the United States already had unequivocal title to both territories, though prior administrations had failed to take what was rightly American.

By the time Polk took over, Tyler had already annexed Texas, and the Senate had given its approval. By this time General Santa Ana had been overthrown in yet another coup, plunging Mexico into anarchy. Opponents like Adams could no longer argue that annexation would threaten Mexico's stability. That is one of the reasons why the vote for war in May 1846 was so one-sided. Adams continued to view the war policy in apocalyptic terms. In a burst of temper, Adams wrote in his journal, "The Constitution is a menstruous rag, and the Union is sinking into a military monarchy, to be rent asunder like the empire of Alexander or the kingdom of Ephraim and Judah."

Adams had fought the annexation of Texas because he viewed it as a pretext to extend the empire of slavery. He was, nevertheless, a fervent advocate of territorial expansion. Adams was one of the very few Northern Whigs who believed that the United States had a right to all of Oregon, which ran up to the Russian border at the edge of Alaska, at the latitude of 54° 40'. Most men outside of the West, which raised the famous battle cry "54 40 or fight!," were not prepared to go to war with England over Oregon. Adams wasn't either; he was prepared to accept a border at the forty-ninth parallel, near what is now Vancouver. In a speech in the House in early 1845 he stated that the time had come to tell Great Britain that negotiations over Oregon had come to an end. Congress should pass a law taking Oregon up to the forty-ninth parallel and then inform the British that it had done so.

British prime minister Sir Robert Peel stated that his nation held "clear and unquestionable" title to Oregon and would go to war to defend that title. Tempers rose on both sides. The House passed a resolution urging the president to seize Oregon with no further negotiations, and then it began to debate a bill to raise two regiments of riflemen to defend settlers in the territory. Adams abjured his colleagues to calm down, insisting that America could assert its rights to Oregon without provoking hostilities.

On February 9, 1845, Adams rose again with an apology for his feeble condition—and proceeded to fill the entire hour to which speeches were now limited. As the question of legal title had been much debated, he wished to shed some light on the foundations of the question. He bade the clerk open the Bible and read "what I conceive to be the foundation of our title, Genesis I:26–8"—the passage in which God commanded man to be fruitful and multiply and gave him dominion over the fish of the sea and the fowl of the air. Then he had him read Psalm 2, verse 8: "Ask of me, and I shall give thee the heathen for thy inheritance, and the uttermost parts of the earth for thy possession." Adams then explained that this power was understood to have passed from God to Christ, and from Christ to his vicar, the Pope, who in turn allotted lands to Christian kings. Americans might mock such a genealogy, but what was the foundation of Massachusetts', or Virginia's, title to its land but a grant from Charles I?

Adams' point was that all the principles of international law that governed title were based upon historical conventions. Did King Charles have the right to give pieces of North America to British settlers? Alternatively, discovery was said to confer title, but why should this be so? "All these titles," Adams said, "are imperfect." Neither England nor the United States could claim "clear and unquestionable" title to Oregon. Yet there *was* an answer to this vexed problem. "There is nothing complete in the way of title but *actual possession*," Adams said. This was the scriptural foundation of title, set forth in Genesis. "Actual possession" required tillage and husbandry, which is why Indians could not claim to have possessed the land over which they had immemorially ranged. Great Britain, like the Indians, used Oregon to hunt animals for furs. "We claim the country for what?," Adams continued. "To make the wilderness blossom as the rose, to establish laws, to increase, multiply and subdue the earth, which we are commanded to do by the first behest of the Almighty God."

It is unlikely that Adams' exercise in theology and legal philosophy swayed many minds in Congress. His speeches did, however, have a significant impact in England. Adams had come to be seen as a crucial voice for diplomatic entente; now the old warrior seemed to be egging on the hotheads who were prepared for confrontation. In April, Adams received a letter from Joseph Sturge, a prominent Quaker and abolitionist in Birmingham, England, imploring him to use his voice to forestall rather than provoke conflict. It was in response to Sturge that Adams wrote the letter, quoted at the beginning of this book, in which he recalled his terror at Bunker Hill, the fervent patriotism of his parents, the Collins ode his mother had taught him to recite with his prayers.

Adams went on to say that his father knew very well the horrors of war with a vastly more powerful nation and knew that it could mean his death and that of his family—and had chosen nevertheless to defend his rights by taking up arms. War in the name of tyranny was abhorrent, but war to defend against tyranny was "a religious and sacred duty." Adams had many Quaker friends, but he was no pacifist. A few weeks earlier, Indiana congressman Robert Dale Owen, the son of the eccentric Welsh reformer Owen of Lanark, had been explaining to Adams his principled objection to warfare; Adams rejoined that "philosophically speaking," he considered war "not a corrupter, but a purifyer, of the moral character of man."

The Senate finally agreed to a resolution that authorized the president to lay claim to the forty-ninth parallel. The British, thinking better of their bellicosity, responded with a compromise proposal, as Adams had predicted they would. By the summer the Oregon question had been settled to the satisfaction of both countries. The continental nation Adams had seen in his minds' eye when the United States barely extended beyond the Alleghenies had become, at long last, a reality.

IN JULY 1845, ADAMS ATTENDED THE ANNUAL PARTY OF THE Neponset Bridge Company, of which he had long been a director. The lawn bowling reminded him of the happy days—at least they seemed happy in retrospect—when he was a novice lawyer and he and his friends would go bowling in Boston. "There is always something sweet and something sad in the remembrance of ancient enjoyments," Adams wrote. He allowed himself, as he rarely did, to be lapped in nostalgia. He thought back to the times of his boyhood, to the battles of Lexington and Bunker Hill, the death of Grandmother Smith, the evacuation of Boston, the smallpox. Adams began to write down a list of his memories from the earliest days forward. Nabby's birthday, on July 14, provoked distant memories of his beloved sister. His forty-eighth wedding anniversary, on the twenty-sixth, led him to think of the long course of his life, the death of his children and his parents, his career in public service, his "friends and benefactors" Washington, Madison, and Monroe, and of course his "base, malignant and lying enemies"— Ingersoll, Jackson, Jonathan Russell. He could name far more. He had been much slandered. What had happened to his rosy train of thought? "I am wandering far from my wedding-day," Adams noted ruefully.

In this mood of retrospection and summation, Adams decided to make a collection of his speeches for Charles Francis. He started with his July 4 speech in 1793 and ran all the way through the address "Society and Civilization," which he had delivered as recently as the previous December. The bookbinder made five volumes of the vast bundle. Adams reflected gloomily on the fact that publishers had brought out collections of the speeches of Daniel Webster, Henry Clay, and Edward Everett. His own words were "so little estimated by the world that no other collection of them will probably ever be made." Later that month he noted that at Harvard commencement, speakers competing for prizes delivered four speeches by Webster and one by Everett. There were none by Adams.

Adams had begun to shed commitments. He admitted to a publisher that he would never get around to writing the long-promised introduction to his letters on Anti-Masonry. He yielded to Harvard's President Quincy the authorship of the report on the observatory. He felt his powers of concentration flagging. In September, he wrote despondently, "I have surrendered . . . all hope of recovering physical powers for active and useful existence." He could no longer garden. He had bought a newfangled shower-bath, a freestanding closet, but he could no longer stand up in order to use it. He suffered from the shooting pains of sciatica. On December 3, Adams, or rather his granddaughter Louisa Catherine, noted tersely that Joseph Story, his great friend and fellow warrior for republican principle, had died. The end seemed nigh for Adams too. But it wasn't—not quite yet.

CHAPTER 38

The End of Earth

(1845–1848)

IN HIS AUTOBIOGRAPHY, HENRY ADAMS RECALLS AN INCIDENT that took place when he was six or seven years old, which is to say in 1844 or the year after. The family had moved for the summer into his grandparents' home in Quincy. Henry, the fourth child of Charles Francis and Abigail Brooks, was throwing a tantrum in the hope of being permitted to skip school and was, he recalled, "in a fair way to win," when the door to the upstairs library opened and his grandfather, known around the house as "the President," came slowly downstairs. "Putting on his hat," Henry writes, "he took the boy's hand without a word, and walked with him, paralyzed by awe"—the boy, that is—"up the road to the town." They walked the mile to the school in perfect silence. Only then, before the schoolhouse door, did John Quincy Adams release his grandson's hand. Such an episode could have scared the daylights out of a little boy, but what Henry Adams recalled, decades later, was his gratitude that his grandfather "had uttered no syllable of revolting cant about the duty of obedience and the wickedness of resistance to law."

In fact, Henry recalled, he and the president were on "friendly and almost intimate" terms. He was given free rein of his grandfather's books and papers. The elder Adams never murmured after the little boy had made a mess of the coins and pistols and canes that lay around the library. It never occurred to Henry to fear the gentle old man who pottered in the garden and drowsed before the fire in his easy chair.

Louisa was known in the house as "the Madam." She was, Henry Adams recalled, "a little more remote than the President, but more decorative. She stayed much in her own room, with the Dutch tiles, looking out on her garden with the box walks, and seemed a fragile creature to a boy who sometimes brought her a note or a message, and took distinct pleasure in looking at her delicate face under what seemed to him very becoming caps. He liked her refined figure, her gentle voice and manner, her vague effect of not belonging there, but to Washington or Europe." He was drawn to her frailty and her air of suffering.

John Quincy Adams left no record of his thoughts about young Henry, but he had always doted on his granddaughters. He exchanged chatty letters with Charles Francis' daughter, Louisa Catherine, who asked whether it was strictly necessary to begin every letter with an acknowledgment of a letter received. Yes, said her punctilious grandfather, though among friends the acknowledgment may be cursory. He loved Charles Francis' wife, Abby, whom he regarded as a daughter and to whom he wrote frequent letters.

No one in the family meant more to Adams than Charles Francis, whom he had raised with something resembling the care his own father had lavished on him. Over time, the son had turned into a man very much like his father. He described himself in his journal as "grave, sober, formal, precise and reserved," while his own son Charles Francis Jr. more bluntly called him (in a biography, no less) "introspective and morbid" and "repellent in nature." As a politician and a regular contributor to newspapers, he advanced the same causes his father did—opposition to the war in Mexico and to slavery and the slave power, resolute defense of republican principles against encroaching "oligarchy." He was a Whig, but he broke with Daniel Webster and the older generation over their support for Tyler; along with the abolitionist and Massachusetts congressman Charles Sumner and others, he founded the Young Whigs, later known as the Conscience Whigs for their commitment to moral causes, above all to the elimination of slavery. Charles Francis was his father's one and only true confidante. In the spring of 1844, the older man wrote to his son to say that he grieved that he could not find the time or energy "to open my mind to you" at least once a week. He added, "I have noted with inexpressible pleasure your firm unwavering adherence to honest principles." He trusted that Charles Francis would carry on the fight for truth as he himself faded from the scene.

In his final years Adams seemed to attain an emotional freedom he had not known before. At times he was, strange to say, almost playful. He wrote poems to some of his colleagues, and not just the rare beloved one, like

Giddings. To one retiring member of the House, Charles Brown, he wrote, "Friend! After a war of words / In sharp debate and conflict sore: / Measure of minds and not of swords, / we part! Perchance to meet no more. / Oh, let us there forget our strife." Adams increasingly indulged his passion for doggerel, above all with women, whom he had been plying with verse since college days. After he met Charles Dickens and his wife, Catherine, on their trip to America in 1842, he sent a farewell verse to Catherine. Miss Mary Inman sent him an album with a portrait of herself under a painted rosebud, and Adams filled in the space underneath with a poem. In March 1846, the seventy-seven-year-old Adams wrote the kind of saucy letter only possible in an era when actual transgressions were unthinkable. To a young woman from Owego, New York, who had sent a letter enclosing a kiss, he wrote:

> But how can such a kiss avail
> To touch my lips with bliss?
> I to all favours such as these
> Stone cold shall ever be
> That fruit has naught to please,
> Save gathered from the tree

Gathered from the tree! It wasn't only the furnace of ambition that still burned within the old man.

ADAMS' LONG CAREER IN POLITICS WAS FINALLY DRAWING TO A close. But his intellectual curiosity was undimmed. In the spring of 1845, after Congress had adjourned, Adams spent many happy hours at the Patent Office, whose leaders he had known and supported for decades. The current director, Henry Ellis, was eager to show Adams the new inventions that had come to his notice. He explained the system of lighthouse illumination developed twenty years earlier by Augustin-Jean Fresnel, a French engineer. The so-called Fresnel system used concentric layers of fine ground glass to reflect and magnify light with far more power than the lamps used in American lighthouses. Adams was captivated by the technology and quickly concluded that the government must pay to have them installed in lighthouses across the country. He found price lists so that he could estimate the cost of installation. He then brought Navy Secretary George Bancroft, Treasury Secretary Robert Walker, and Vice President George M. Dallas to the Patent Office for a demonstration.

Adams had once dreamed of writing a chronicle of the advance of science and invention. Now he decided to do just that in the form of a history of the Patent Office. He spoke of the idea to Ellis, who told him many of the records of the office's history had been destroyed by a fire in 1836. But he continued to pursue the idea once he returned to Quincy. He spent $17 to buy the fifteen-volume *Library of American Biography* and also hunted up biographies of Robert Fulton and the explorer Sieur de La Salle. Advancing age and enfeeblement, or perhaps his usual distraction, put an end to this project.

Adams was still captivated by astronomy. Almost as soon as he reached home in early May 1846, Adams went with President Quincy of Harvard to visit the observatory then under construction. They found the chief astronomer, Professor Benjamin Peirce, sitting under a temporary wooden roof gazing through a six-foot-long telescope. Adams fastened his eye to the eyepiece and gazed on the planets. He then found the chief observer, Mr. Bond, who lived on the grounds with his son, observing the planets from inside a rough shed. Adams had to kneel on a cushion and throw his head all the way back so that he could look straight up, an experience he found excruciating. But he did it nevertheless. Adams reconvened at the observatory the following week with members of the university board of overseers. President Quincy informed them that they would need to raise $25,000 to $50,000 to pay salaries to the Bonds, father and son, as well as to purchase additional equipment and to complete construction. Adams later paid visits to Abbot Lawrence and other wealthy Harvard alumni, flattering them with the immense role they had a chance to play in the advancement of knowledge.

Adams still clung to the hope that he could direct the Smithson bequest to astronomical research. The Smithsonian Committee in the House, which Adams chaired, ground sluggishly through alternative proposals. Few legislators cared about the bequest remotely as much as the chairman. One member suggested authorizing the hiring of a professor of agriculture and the purchase and distribution of seeds. Robert Dale Owen favored the establishment of a normal school to train teachers. William Giles of Maryland wanted to buy books for the blind. When the issue reached the floor of the House in late April 1846, Adams rose in a last-ditch effort to ward off what he considered abuses of the expressed will of the donor. He asked the House to strike any reference to normal schools, or to the admission of students for any purpose, from the enabling legislation. He won on two separate votes. The House also rejected Giles' proposed amendment on Braille books.

In the course of the debate, Alexander D. Sims of South Carolina had noted, mockingly, that "the doctrine promulgated by a distinguished President of the United States had grown into popular favor." Adams had been the great advocate, indeed the sole advocate, of "lighthouses of the skies." None had existed when he had first spoken of them; now the US Navy had been authorized to build an observatory in northwest Washington, while others were rising in Cincinnati, Cambridge, and elsewhere. Something like the national network Adams had dreamed of was beginning to take shape. Adams rejoined that he was "very glad to hear that it has grown in popular favor," and went on, "I claim no merit for the erection of the astronomical observatory, but in the course of my whole life, no conferring of honor, or of interest, or of office, has given me more delight than the belief that I have contributed in some small degree, to produce these astronomical observatories, both here and elsewhere. I no longer wish any portion of this fund to be applied to an astronomical observatory."

The bill Congress finally passed on August 10 authorized the creation of an institute dedicated to "the increase and diffusion of knowledge," echoing the language of the Smithson bequest. The funds would not be used for any sort of university or college. An independent board of regents would chart its future course. Over time, the Smithsonian would grow into a diverse body of institutions that would both diffuse and increase knowledge, though another century would have to pass before entities like the National Institutes of Health would wholly fulfill Adams' vision of public research institutions. Adams understood that for America to take its place in the front rank of nations it needed to expand not only its territory and its industry but its knowledge. In this, as in many things, he was far ahead of his time.

THROUGH GOOD TIMES AND BAD, AND THROUGH NUMBERLESS infirmities, Adams had continued to keep up his diary. He understood that he had achieved something extraordinary not only in his own time, but in the annals of human endeavor. In late 1846, he wrote, "There has perhaps not been another individual of the human race, whose daily existence from early childhood to fourscore years has been noted down with his own hand so minutely as mine." If only the Creator had granted him genius, he observed, "my diary would have been, next to the Holy Scriptures, the most precious and valuable book ever written by human hands." It's a stupefying judgment, qualified by Adams' humility, for he was quite sure that the Creator had not granted him such a gift.

For Adams the diary had become coterminous with life itself. He lived, and he recorded his life. As his life began to peter out, so, too, did his diary. First, he found that he could no longer write. On September 30, 1845, he began an entry in a suddenly gnarled script with the words, "From this time the total disability to write with my own hand compels me to." There followed a series of blots, and then, in a new hand, "I took the Pills prescribed by Dr. Woodward last evening." He was now dictating his entries to one of his grandchildren. On October 20, he started again with his own hand and then once again surrendered, this time, he noted, to his granddaughter, Louisa Catherine. To dictate a diary entry is, in a way, to cease to write a diary at all, at least in the sense that in a journal the author speaks to himself only. The subsequent entries are shorter and more public, and thus less vital and self-revealing, than the earlier ones.

Adams continued to record the events of his life—puttering around the garden in Quincy; reading the ancients; attending, without fail, the debates in Congress. On July 13, 1846, Adams wrote that he had paid a visit to his old swimming spot behind the White House. Three young men were gathered around the rock where, in years past, he would strip down and leave his clothes. One shouted, "There is John Quincy Adams!" Adams moved to another spot, disrobed, and jumped in for a "bathe" of five or ten minutes. He returned two days later. That appears to have been the last time Adams ever swam.

Adams returned to Quincy in mid-August. Of the many invitations he continued to receive, he responded to only one. He agreed to attend, and to serve as honorary chair for, a Faneuil Hall meeting on the issue that had convulsed Boston: the return of fugitive slaves. An audience of five thousand roared as he briefly took the rostrum. He compared the question to one that had brought him to that same place almost four decades earlier—the British attack on the *Chesapeake*. His lonely position then had cost him the support of New England. Now he was a revered elder, beyond all reproach. "It is a question," he said in his faltering voice, "whether your and my native Commonwealth is to maintain its independence or not." Adams would never again appear before a public audience.

That late summer and fall, Adams sat in his study and read, wrote a very few letters (mostly about business affairs), occasionally received old friends, and talked to Louisa and the grandchildren. He wrote very few entries in his diary, though his hand remained clear, if thicker than before. In mid-November he moved to Charles Francis' house on Mt. Vernon Street in Boston, intending to leave from there for Washington. On the twentieth he rose, as usual, before dawn and bathed with a horsehair strap and mitten. He went out to take a walk with his old friend Francis Parkman, a Unitarian minister and father of the great historian of the same name. As Adams prepared to leave, his knees buckled, and he sank to the floor. He was carried to bed. Thenceforward he was attended night and day by a nurse, unable even to reach the bathroom on his own. He had had a stroke, which left him helpless though not paralyzed. He could neither write nor even dictate his journal.

Adams gradually recovered. On January 1, 1847, he rode in a carriage and then began walking. He felt, however, that he remained in the vale of the dead. On January 19, he came into his son's room and handed him a copy of the will he had just executed. In his own diary, Charles Francis recorded his father's words to him. "He said that his diary was closed," Charles Francis wrote. "He would never write any more of it. He would place it in my hands, to do with it what I thought proper, at the same time distinctly stating that it had never been written for extended publication, and it was not his wish that such publication should be made."

Charles Francis may have heard the wish buried beneath the studied ambivalence, and as his father's literary executor he edited a monumental twelve-volume edition of the diary. Perhaps he understood that his father did not expect his wish to be honored. After all, John Quincy Adams believed that he had produced a monument to human labor, if not to human genius. He had chiseled a mighty *apologia pro vita sua* in which he had gotten the best of every debate and had acted out of the most noble of motives. He had exalted the very few men he admired and laid low his innumerable rivals. And yet he may have meant what he said. Adams' diary was a work of supreme introspection and even intimacy, and he was not a man to expose his inmost nature to the world. He had left the world his deeds and his public words. Perhaps he wished his deepest feelings to be buried with himself. If so, we should be grateful that Charles Francis defied his father's express preference.

The old man's infirmity produced a reversal in relations between husband and wife. Louisa had always been the family valetudinary; now she had to be strong for her feeble husband. She wrote to her daughter-in-law Mary to remark how very strange it was that "I should be the one to crawl about, useless to any purpose," while her husband, who "has been an active agent for mankind," should be stilled. Louisa still had the occasional fainting spell, but she made light of it. She and Charles' wife, Abby, never left Adams out of their sight for fear that he might attempt something rash and then fall. "We are more alarmed when he is well, than when he does poorly," as she wrote to Mary. She wrote that her husband was devastated by the recognition that he would remain dependent on others for the remainder of his life; only Abby could beguile him from his despondent moods. In her journal, which she briefly resumed, Louisa wrote a fervent prayer for her husband's "restoration." Yet she also wished that he would reconcile himself to his end, as she herself long had. She implored God to "strengthen him to obedience; fortify his spirit with faith; and graciously encourage him to struggle against the worldly passions, which war against his soul."

But those worldly passions warred still in the old man. Adams was determined to return to Washington and resume his duties as congressman. On February 8 he and Charles Francis boarded a train, arriving in the capital on the twelfth. Adams insisted that he attend Congress the following day. When he appeared, debate in the hall instantly stopped. Andrew Johnson, who had been occupying the former president's seat, graciously restored it to him. Adams thanked him, and the Speaker, and took his place. By March 14, Adams had gained enough strength to pick up a pen in order to record the events of the time from his stroke. He titled his entry, "Posthumous Memoir." From the time he fell to the floor, Adams wrote in a shaky but quite legible hand, "I date my decease, and consider myself for every useful purpose to myself or to my fellow-creatures, dead; and hence I call this and what I may write hereafter a posthumous memoir."

The diary, like the man, died by degrees and more slowly than anyone had expected. Adams continued to write, to attend Congress, to tie up the loose strings of his life. His letters and diary entries are much taken up with the question of finance. In a letter to Charles Francis he ticked off the responsibilities he had been bearing over the years as executor of the estate of his parents; his friend, Nicholas Ward Boylston; his brother-in-law, Thomas B. Johnson; Louisa's brother-in-law, Walter Hellen; and his son John. He was, he added without complaint, legal guardian to two of his granddaughters and two of Boylston's grandchildren.

The number of people who depended on Adams for support was remarkable. He had never had remotely lucrative employment, never made a killing, never received a legacy. He had been brought close to ruin first by his brother Charles and then by his son John. He had been compelled to bail out his parents at great personal cost to himself and had received nothing from them save the house and land that he had purchased at considerable expense. Yet through long years of "economy" and prudent investment, he would leave behind him an estate capable of supporting all those dependents. The will he had drawn up in January contained a tally of all his property, which, in addition to stocks and other liquid assets, included eleven houses and commercial properties in Boston, four houses and eight lots in Washington, the family house in Quincy, the estate at Mount Wollaston, and a total of 851 acres of wood lot, quarry lot, saltmarsh, and farmland. This most dutiful of sons had been a truly wise steward.

Adams returned to Quincy in early June. When Charles Francis saw this pale, drawn old man, he reflected: "I see nothing left in him of the vigor which was once his character." It was deeply unsettling for the son to see a man he had loved and feared, and always relied on, so irretrievably reduced. "I feel sad when I look at him," he wrote on his father's eightieth birthday. For all that, the old man still clung tightly to life. "He has," his son observed, "a large remnant of the physical and mental strength which yet preserves him from absolute helplessness." Adams still took a daily walk, read, and answered letters. He responded to a correspondent writing a history of the Mexican war with a long disquisition on a favorite subject: the right of title. The historian, Adams wrote, must stand outside his own nation and his own religion in order to examine such claims honestly. Did Columbus have the right to claim the land of the Caribe Indians for Spain? Or France or Spain to claim Texas?

Adams still thrilled to the news of astronomical discoveries. He had been delighted at disputes over credit for the discovery of the new planet known as Neptune. He lamented that he would not have time enough to study the new worlds being disclosed by rapidly improving optic technology. In October, he roused himself from his armchair to pay a last visit to the Harvard Observatory along with the board of overseers. He was still the representative from the Twelfth District of Massachusetts, and he had no intention of failing in this obligation of service. On November 1 he left for Washington. "My last great journey," he wrote.

Within days of arriving, Adams was receiving visitors, paying a visit to the office of the *National Intelligencer*, and going to the Naval Observatory with Louisa and one of his granddaughters. He was delighted to gaze upon Mars, Saturn, and Neptune. Adams even attended the opening of the new hotel founded by Joseph Willard, the descendant of which remains one of

Washington's great hotels. At the opening of Congress on December 6, Adams was asked to administer the oath of office to the new Speaker, his Massachusetts colleague Robert Winthrop. Later that month he presented several petitions and moved a resolution requiring the secretary of state to disclose diplomatic correspondence involving the war with Mexico. Adams continued to regard the war as a national disgrace. He wrote a long letter to Albert Gallatin, now a month shy of his eighty-seventh birthday, complaining that President Polk had been able to stampede the Congress into a declaration of war by the simple expedient of claiming that Mexico had initiated hostilities.

On New Year's Day 1848, all of Washington paid a visit to the Adams home—senators and representatives, Supreme Court justices, preening generals fresh from battles in the Mexican-American War that Adams had done everything in his declining powers to prevent. The entire family was exhausted. Adams retired to his study to write a letter to Charles Francis. "My Dear Son," he said, "On this commencement of a new year, my thoughts intensely turn to you, to the partner of your life, to your children, and to the Giver of all good, in thanksgiving for all the blessings which you have been and still are to me . . . especially that you may be sustained in your incorruptible integrity through all the trials that may be reserved for you upon earth." He was preparing his son to make a journey through the same thorny path he had so long traveled.

The striking reversal of energies between Adams and Louisa continued. Now that her husband no longer required her constant attention, Louisa began visiting friends and even giving Saturday evening teas. She wrote long, gossipy "journalizing" letters to daughter-in-law Abby, as she once had to her father-in-law. She described the balls and parties attended by "the young ladies" of the household—granddaughter Louisa, grandniece Sarah, an otherwise unidentified "Miss Agnell." She made fun of "the mighty Daniel" and Mrs. Webster after they paid a visit. And she playfully recorded a moment when Adams had moaned that he was going to die, and she had told him that in that case he should quit the Congress and return to Quincy. Instantly, she noted, his spirits quickened. This was the sparkling Louisa of another time. She also, astonishingly, asked Abby how she could raise money to buy the freedom of Julia, her maidservant. Though the Johnsons of Maryland had long owned slaves, no Adams household in memory had done so. It is very hard to imagine that John Quincy Adams would have permitted Louisa to employ a slave had he still possessed his full powers.

Adams continued to record the speeches made and resolutions offered in Congress. The drama still absorbed him, even as he had become a silent spectator. On January 4, he wrote—or rather, granddaughter Louisa Catherine wrote—an account of the doings of the House. Broadhead of Pennsylvania offered a resolution; someone else rose to a point of order, "Giddings of Ohio"—and then, nothing. Adams must have fallen asleep, or taken ill, or waved his granddaughter away. The endless torrent of Adams' diary comes to rest on the one colleague he loved—Giddings of Ohio. (Six weeks later he inscribed a four-line poem he must have intended for a young woman.)

Adams continued to be seen around Washington. On February 17, he attended a reception for his old friend Joseph Seaton, now the city's mayor. On Saturday the nineteenth, he went to see the book collection of Nicholas Vattemare, a French philanthropist (and world-renowned ventriloquist) who advocated a system of library exchange Adams planned to endorse in Congress. That evening he and Louisa held an open house at F Street, as they had been doing off and on for over forty years. On Sunday Adams attended church. Later that day he dashed off yet another "autograph," this one for Miss Caroline Edwards of Springfield, Massachusetts: "In days of yore, the poet's pen, / From wing of bird was plundered, / Perhaps of goose, but now and then, / From Jove's own eagle sundered." Adams' gallant conceit was that since pens were now made of metal, in order to honor her name he would wrest such material from the earth itself.

On the twenty-first Adams reached Congress at around noon. He had a sheaf of papers before him, perhaps on his Vattemare library proposal. The business at hand was a resolution to extend the thanks of Congress to the heroes of the Mexican war and to authorize the president to strike gold medals for eight particularly praiseworthy generals. Adams had continued to oppose all forms of endorsement of the war. The roll was called, and Adams cried "No" in "an emphatic manner and an unusually loud tone," as one reporter later noted. At about one fifteen, the Speaker prepared to put the question to a third and final vote. Henry B. Stanton of the *Boston Emancipator and Republican*, sitting fifteen or twenty feet away, saw Adams grow flushed, apparently with excitement, and indistinctly utter several sentences. The old man then went deathly pale. "His right hand moved nervously upon his desk," Stanton noted, "as if he were trying to grasp something." Adams' lips moved, as if he were trying to address the Speaker, but no sound emerged. "Then the action of his hand upon the desk became more convulsive, and he appeared to be stretching it out to reach the corner of his desk."

With men standing and milling about, no one save the reporter noticed the old man's agony. Then, still clutching the desk to hold himself upright, Adams began to keel over to the left. A shout went up: "Mr. Adams is dying!" Several congressmen rushed over to catch him. Representative Joseph Grinnell of Massachusetts doused Adams' head with cold water, but the old man did not respond. Members crowded around him. Adams was placed on a sofa and carried, first, to an open space in front of the clerk's table and then out into the Rotunda. No one knew what to do. A doctor suggested that he be moved to the front door for a reviving blast of fresh air, but, the air proving too cold, Speaker Winthrop proposed that Adams be moved into his private chamber. There he lay on the sofa, behind closed doors, attended by doctors who could do nothing for him. A messenger was dispatched to F Street to fetch Mrs. Adams. With the House adjourned, the members stood around the hall as people do in the aftermath of a disaster, uncertain whether to go or stay, repeating every detail to one another and to anyone else who asked.

Adams lingered throughout the day, immobile but not yet insensate. The *Intelligencer*'s reporter, who appears to have wangled his way into the Speaker's chamber, reported that Adams was heard to murmur, "This is the end of earth. I am composed." Others heard him to say, "I am content," and because this reflected a deeper mood of Christian resignation, his last words were recorded as such. Another reporter wrote that Adams later responded no to a question as to whether he was better, and then, his mind perhaps wandering, said, "My son, my son." These were not at all fitting as last words, and thus did not survive into later accounts.

Louisa arrived and was, according to a report, "quite prostrated" as she gazed on her husband's waxen features. Henry Clay, Adams' rival and colleague of long decades, came to the Speaker's chambers. He stood silently by Adams' side, held his hand, and wept. The former president was now comatose. He remained alive all that day and the next.

On the twenty-second, Charles Francis, still in Boston, went to his office, saw a telegram lying on his desk, hesitantly opened it, and learned that his father had been stricken and was not expected to last the day. Immediately he returned home, informed his wife, and boarded the next train. "He has been the great landmark of my life," he wrote in his diary. As he raced south to his father's bedside, Charles, as if in a nightmare, kept missing boats and trains. He was only in Philadelphia on the morning of the twenty-fourth. As he hurried through a hotel lobby, he saw a man reading a newspaper with a black border. He did not dare to ask the man what the paper said. He reached the train station, bought a pack of newspapers, but refused to open them until he had seated himself. Only then did he learn that at seven fifteen the night before, his father had breathed his last. "The glory of the family is departed," wrote the despondent son, "and I a solitary and unworthy scion remain overwhelmed with a sense of my responsibilities."

CHAPTER 39

Obsequies

A T NOON ON FEBRUARY 24, 1848, HOUSE SPEAKER ROBERT Winthrop reconvened the chamber to formally announce the death of John Quincy Adams. Charles Hudson, a Massachusetts representative, delivered a brief summation of Adams' career. Isaac Holmes of South Carolina, home of the bitterest hatred of Adams, had asked to speak as well. Gently pulling a veil across the long years of censure and obloquy, Holmes recalled for his colleagues, "How often have we crowded into that aisle, and clustered around that now vacant desk, to listen to the counsels of wisdom as they fell from the lips of that venerable sage." Samuel Vinton of Ohio said, without exaggeration, "No man has heretofore died, when a member of this body, who will occupy so large a space in his country's history." The House appointed a Committee of Arrangements to prepare for the funeral. Possibly the least well known of the thirty members was a freshman congressman from Illinois, Abraham Lincoln. This was the only thread that personally connected these two men.

Adams' coffin lay in state in the Capitol's Common Room. The deceased's hands were crossed over his breast, producing an impression of repose few had seen in life. For two days the people of Washington, and many who had arrived from Baltimore and points more distant, filed by. The endless stream was stopped when Charles Francis arrived on the morning of the twenty-fifth. The room was cleared so that he could stand alone with his father. With the stoicism of an Adams, he composed himself before exiting.

The funeral was held on the twenty-sixth. Cannons began to fire at six A.M. The chief public buildings of the city, and many private ones, were draped in black. The Capitol had been thrown open to the public, and thousands jammed the lobbies and galleries. They were not, however, allowed to enter the House, the space most sacred to Adams. There the statues of Washington and Lafayette, which flanked the Speaker's chair, had been draped in black, as was the figure of History, which surmounted the front entrance of the hall. Adams' own desk was draped in mourning. The chamber was filled with the dignitaries of a nation. It was observed that some members of the diplomatic corps wore black, while others arrived in full regalia. Though a serving president, William Henry Harrison, had been buried seven years earlier, no former president had ever died in Washington, and the protocol remained unclear. Charles Francis and his sister-in-law Mary sat in front. Louisa, who had been sustained by her husband through all the griefs of her life, could not find the strength to attend without him.

At ten minutes before noon, Speaker Winthrop called the House to order, and the bells of the Capitol began to ring. A choir in the ladies' gallery sang a dirge. The House chaplain, the Reverend R. R. Gurley, delivered a very unmemorable oration. He did feel it necessary to say of Adams' idiosyncratic faith that "while differing on some points from common opinion, he cherished enlarged views of Christian communion." The pallbearers then gathered around the casket. They included John Calhoun and Joseph Ingersoll, whom Adams loathed, and one person he admired, Mayor Seaton, publisher of the *National Intelligencer*. Adams' remains were then carried in procession to the congressional cemetery. His lead-lined casket was borne by a funeral carriage drawn by six white horses, each led by a groom. The casket was draped in black velvet and surmounted with an eagle with spread wings, which was itself covered in crepe. A silver breastplate bore an inscription written by Daniel Webster at the behest of the Massachusetts delegation:

JOHN QUINCY ADAMS
BORN
An inhabitant of Massachusetts
July 11 1767
DIED
A citizen of the United States, in the
Capitol, at Washington, February 23, 1848,
Having served his country for half a century,
And enjoyed its highest honors.

The procession through the north gate of the Capitol was a long, solemn, and extraordinary affair. First came the military companies, then a military band, then the chaplains of both chambers and the physicians who had attended Adams in his last hours. Then came the pallbearers and the funeral carriage. They were followed by Adams' family and friends, members and officers of both houses of Congress, President Polk and his cabinet, the justices of the Supreme Court, the diplomatic corps, senior military officials, representatives from state legislatures and from the city of Washington and organizations Adams had supported (including Columbia College, later Georgetown University), various literary societies, and the Columbian Typographical Society (an organization of printers). Citizens lined the streets. The procession moved southeast along Pennsylvania Avenue—away from the White House—until it reached E Street, where it turned right until it reached the congressional cemetery on the banks of the Anacostia River. There Adams' remains would rest until he was removed to his final resting place, in Quincy.

A little over a week was required to make arrangements. Congress had appointed one member from every state and territory to accompany the casket. As the funeral train sped northward, small-town and country people gathered at the tracks to pay their respects with bowed heads. All business came to a halt wherever the train stopped. The entire route seemed to be draped in mourning. A ferry bearing Adams' remains reached New York on March 8. Artillery fired eighty-one times for the years of the deceased's life. The bells in Trinity Church commenced to chime as the procession began from City Hall. A crowd of two hundred thousand men and women, remarkably quiet, watched as a hearse drawn by eight black-draped horses, led by "mulatoo grooms clad in the Turkish costume," according to a local paper, proceeded up Broadway to Grand Street and then back down the Bowery to City Hall Park. The diarist Philip Hone, who was there, called it "the greatest body of men and women ever assembled in this city."

Adams' remains reached Boston on Saturday, March 11. A steady downpour precluded public events. Adams lay in state in Faneuil Hall, whose galleries were filled with inscriptions recalling the stages of the great man's career; at one end of the hall stood the flags of all the nations where Adams had served as a diplomat. After several speeches, Adams' remains were placed on a special train whose new locomotive had been christened the John Quincy Adams. Local escorting committees then joined the congressional detachment on the short train ride to Quincy. Adams' casket was carried from the train depot to his home and from there taken in procession to the First Parish Church, a mile or so away.

Quincy's Unitarian church traced its lineage to 1636, when it was founded by Congregationalists. John Adams had endowed a fund to replace the church where he and his family had worshiped, and in 1828, two years after his death, the Stone Temple, a Greek Revival structure whose granite had come from the Adams quarry, took the place of the old church on Hancock Street. Though conventional in its pillared facade, the interior was an almost circular space topped by a shallow dome, far more elegant than the austerely functional structure it had replaced. Adams' coffin was carried down the aisle and placed in front of the pulpit under a black panel whose white letters proclaimed Adams' already immortal last words: "This is the end of earth." The congressmen and Boston dignitaries were joined in the pews by the townsfolk who had known Adams as friend and neighbor.

The services began at three and were attended by Adams' family, including Louisa. The eulogy was delivered by Adams' friend and minister, the Reverend William Lunt. His theme, taken from Revelation, was, "Be thou faithful unto death, and I will give thee a crown of life." Lunt pointed out the window toward the two "simple and modest" homes barely a mile away where Adams and his father had been born and raised. "What miracles of beneficent social and political change have been wrought," he said, since father and son had left Mount Wollaston to board a ship for France seventy years earlier. "Where, in history, can you find so glorious a history assigned to a single life?" Adams had been steadfast in his faith and his principles; the reward had come not to him but to his nation.

Adams' old friends and neighbors then bore his coffin to the family vault in the Stone Temple churchyard. Adams' casket was buried alongside the remains of his beloved sister Nabby and of his much-mourned sons, George and John. He had had a sepulcher roughly hewn from the rock below the Stone Temple and had interred his parents there. But he would remain in the churchyard with his sister and his children until his wife died.

IT WAS THE END OF EARTH. BUT IN AN ODD AND REMARKABLE WAY, over the next several months Adams lived more vividly in the American imagination than he ever had before. Adams had been undergoing a collective revaluation at least since his widely reported trip to Ohio five years earlier, when he had "met the sober second thought of the people." No such reappraisal had been necessary for any of Adams' predecessors save perhaps his father, who had lived so long after his presidency that his alleged monarchism had eventually lost its sting. The manner of John Quincy Adams' own death, and his stoical and Christian last words, confirmed the sober second thoughts. He had died as he had lived—in service to the public. His virtues were those of the founders. A reporter for the *New York Tribune* wrote that "he never obtruded his learning or eminence upon anyone, but might have passed in the crowds for the threadbare clergyman of some secluded valley, or the ill-paid teacher of some village school."

Adams was eulogized by several of the nation's leading Whigs, including New York governor William Seward and Harvard president Edward Everett (though not Daniel Webster). Virtually every orator cited his last words, or alleged last words; virtually every one of them noted the circumstances of his death. Joseph Henry Allen, the minister of Adams' church in Washington, said, "How rare it is, that everyone's spontaneous feeling declares, that just so and no otherwise, to the smallest circumstance, was it fitting that the good man should be called away." Adams had not had to endure the decay and humiliation of a wasting disease. He had been "called away." One could not but feel the presence of the hand of divine Providence, in death as in life. As William Hague, the minister of a Baptist church in Boston, said of Adams' tenure in Congress, "It was God who placed him there to guide the whirlwind and direct the storm."

Many speakers noted Adams' astounding endurance, his unshakeable and almost inhuman commitment to the tasks he set for himself. Edward Everett recalled the all-night session at the end of the twenty-third Congress, when Adams, alone, had remained in his seat, awake and alert. When Everett had asked the old warrior how he had sustained himself, he had "held up a dry crust of bread." Reverend Allen recalled that at church Adams had "maintained an exact, almost military, precision, even to the smallest details of conduct," always arriving in his pew before the beginning of the service.

Men spoke of Adams' almost uncanny memory and mental gifts, his capacity for labor, his religious faith, his all-too-well-hidden kindness and warmth. Above all, they spoke of his "inflexible adherence to principle," as Edwin Hubbell Chapin, a well-known Boston preacher and poet, put it. This inflexibility, this purity and simplicity of conviction, was the mark of something archaic in Adams, and something truly great. Edward Everett, who had known Adams since he had taken his rhetoric and oratory class as a Harvard undergraduate, described him as the last of the New England Puritans. The word, he said, "carries a reproach," but by Adams' own time the Puritans had softened their harsh intolerance yet retained their "patriar-chal simplicity." Adams was the man who could have passed for a village schoolmaster.

For the eulogists, for the newspaper editorialists, and for countless Americans, Adams was the last link to the elemental virtues of the New England Puritans and the incorruptible world of the founders. He was "as a mountain-promontory stretching out towards us from the far past," as the Reverend Chapin put it. In his Harvard commencement address six decades earlier, Adams had worried that he and his peers could do little more than sustain the work of those great souls who had come before them. In the national imagination, Adams had now merged with that founding generation.

Some orators insisted that Adams had been a great president. William Seward, who had revered Adams since the days of Anti-Masonry, claimed that Adams had presided over the "consolidation" of the young republic. He had governed free from favoritism or patronage—"though his magna-nimity was not appreciated." Philip Hone offered a more balanced judg-ment in his diary:

> Thus has 'a great man fallen in Israel'—in many respects the most wonderful man of the age; certainly the greatest in the United States— perfect in knowledge, but deficient in practical results. As a statesman, he was pure and incorruptible, but too irascible to lead men's judg-ment. They admired him, and all voices were hushed when he rose to speak, because they were sure of being instructed by the words he was about to utter; but he made no converts to his opinion, and when President his desire to avoid party influence lost him all the favour of all the parties.

The praise heaped on Adams constituted a melancholy tribute to the "far past." But men who embraced the American future rather than its past did not necessarily share that feeling. In an article titled "The People & John Quincy Adams," a writer in the *New Orleans Crescent* took issue with the premise that Adams' low standing with the public for so many years had been evidence of his penchant for truth. Adams, he wrote, "was not a man of the People" and had never enlisted in "the hot struggles for the rights of men, as opposed to wealth and conservatism. . . . Is it wonderful, then, that he never was a popular man?" The former president, the author wrote, "was 'a gentleman of the old school', no doubt; but the old school, with all its polish and grace, had its sources too near monarchy and nobility to be entirely free from their influences." So John Quincy Adams appeared to the twenty-nine-year-old Walt Whitman, whom recent scholarship has identified as the author of the anonymous column.

The most remarkable of all the orations, and probably the longest, came from Theodore Parker, a radical theologian and Transcendentalist, an abolitionist, a linguist, and a scholar. Parker was the minister at Boston's largest and most prestigious Congregationalist church. On March 5, before Adams' remains had even reached New England, he delivered not a formal eulogy but a "discourse occasioned by" Adams' death. He spoke at the Melodeon, a lecture hall, rather than a church. The civic setting and the self-appointed nature of the speech permitted Parker a degree of candor that otherwise might have seemed impertinent. Adams himself probably would have thought his speech impertinent.

"Shall we tell lies about him because he is dead?," Parker asked his audience. He would not. The deceased's vote sustaining Jefferson's 1807 embargo "has never been forgotten or forgiven." Parker noted that as secretary of state and president he had remained mute on slavery. "He was what is called a good hater," Parker rightly noted, and "used his wit tyrannously." He was a poor poet. His greatest intellectual faculty was memory, and he showed little foresight.

In what, then, did John Quincy Adams' greatness lie? In this, Parker said: that throughout all his words and acts ran a "golden thread"—"an intense love of freedom for all men." If once he had been too willing to accept the monstrous evil of slavery, unlike other men "he grew more liberal as he grew old." The truly glorious moments of his life were the late ones. Parker now launched into a panegyric on Adams' summation in the *Amistad* trial and on his long, lonely campaign against the gag rule:

> I know of few things in modern times so grand as that old man, standing there in the House of Representatives, the compeer of Washington, a man who had borne himself proudly in kings' courts, early doing service in high places, where honor may be won; a man who had filled the highest office in any nation's gift; a President's son, himself a President, standing there the champion of the neediest of the oppressed.

Parker, like Adams a moralist, a Christian, and a primeval Yankee, was able to peer into his subject's soul as other speakers could not, or in any case did not. "He had his reward," Parker said. He was not thinking of the afterlife but rather of the elemental force that drove Adams and drives all puritans and prophets and reformers of the human soul.

> In the impenetrable citadel of a good man's consciousness, unseen by mortal eyes, there stands the Palladium of Justice, radiant with celestial light; mortal hands may make and mar; this they can mar not, no more than they can make. Things about the man can others build up or destroy; but no foe, no tyrant, no assassin, can ever steal the man out of the man. Who would not have the consciousness of being right, even of trying to be right, though affronted by a whole world, rather than conscious of being wrong and hollow and false, have all the honors of a nation on his head?

AS A CHRISTIAN, ADAMS HAD LONG SINCE RECONCILED HIMSELF TO his own demise—thus the stoical last words. But as an Adams, and as a man deeply immersed in the classics and in the antique world, he felt that he constituted only a single link in a great chain. When he planted another tree at Mount Wollaston, he felt that he was partaking of a history that stretched back to Pilgrims and forward to . . . he knew not where. Family members had owned Mount Wollaston since very close to the founding of the Massachusetts Bay Colony. Adams had passed it on intact—indeed, improved—to the next generation. It would remain in the family until the 1880s, when it was sold and subdivided. The next generation would also begin to sell the hundreds of acres and the many outbuildings that John Adams had assembled as Peacefields and that John Quincy had preserved, selling some properties and adding others. When Charles Francis' last surviving son, Peter, died in 1927 and deeded the family home to the state of Massachusetts, only a few dozen acres came with it.

Property, however, was not so precious to Adams as the sacred family name. He never stopped worrying about whether the great chain that stretched back far beyond his own father would be snapped in the next generation. Would his children—would Charles Francis—sustain the honor of the name of Adams? Charles Francis felt that burden, as his father had felt it before him. He would prove worthy, as his father had. As a state legislator, as the editor of the *Whig* in Boston, and as a leader of the Conscience Whigs, Charles Francis carried forward his father's politics of conviction, above all on the question of slavery. He would go on to run for vice president on the Free Soil ticket in 1848 (with, of all people, the unsinkable

Martin Van Buren); enter Congress, in 1858, as a Republican; and serve, between 1861 and 1868, as Lincoln's ambassador to England, the same post both his father and his grandfather had held.

The distinctive form in which Charles Francis took on the burden of preserving the family name was as literary executor. The Adams family mythos is a matter of words as much as deeds; Charles Francis gave those words to the public. While still in his thirties he produced a volume of Abigail Adams' letters, which were widely quoted in the eulogies for John Quincy Adams. He wrote the biography of John Adams his father had proved conspicuously unable to produce, perhaps because John Quincy felt disabled by his own uncritical reverence. Charles Francis loyally characterized the work as "begun" by his father and only "completed" by himself. He also published his grandfather's papers and the monumental twelve-volume version of his father's diary. In 1870 Charles Francis built a stone library, more like a temple, to house his father's fourteen thousand books. Both his father's remains and his father's beloved books have been encased in a stone vault to defy the ravages of time.

Charles Francis and Abby Brooks had seven children; three of them—Charles Francis Jr., Brooks, and Henry—became prominent writers and political activists. As John Quincy had served as his father's private secretary in Europe, so Charles Francis employed Henry in London. Henry Adams became the Harvard scholar his grandfather perhaps wished he had been. Among his great works is the nine-volume *History of the United States During the Administrations of Thomas Jefferson and James Madison*, an indispensable source for the students of this era of national consolidation. He wrote biographies of Albert Gallatin, a great friend of his grandfather and great-grandfather, and of John Randolph, a fierce enemy of both. In the *Autobiography of Henry Adams*, published in 1907, he subjected the family breeding ground of old New England—"troglodytic," he called it—to the searching scrutiny of an anthropologist. So remote is Henry Adams from the world of his forebears that he described politics, the profession of all of them, as "the systematic organization of hatreds." This immensely self-conscious work marks the Adams family's exit from the archaic cosmos of colonial Massachusetts and into the quicksilver world of modernity.

The Adams name rolled on in gently ebbing waves of distinction. Charles Francis Adams III, who married the granddaughter of the secretary of the navy under President John Quincy Adams, served as Herbert Hoover's navy secretary. (He had prepared for the role by successfully defending the America's Cup.) *His* son, Charles Francis Adams IV, served as president of the aerospace firm Raytheon. The Roman numerals have marched all the way down to our own day in the form of John Quincy Adams VII, surely one of the very few "VII"s in a nation that has forsworn a hereditary aristocracy. This John Quincy Adams has a blog.

Even leaving aside the IIIs and IVs, it is safe to say that no other family in American history has produced great men, or even near-great men, in so many consecutive generations. It is a record that defies the typical diminishing effect that prominent men have on their sons.

Louisa Catherine Adams, wearied by life though she was, outlived her husband by four years, dying in 1852 at the age of seventy-seven. She was buried in the family vault in the Stone Temple—next to her father-in-law, whom she adored; her mother-in-law, whom she feared; and her husband, whose soul she had penetrated as no other mortal had and whom she found exasperating, tendentious, intolerant, self-absorbed, and yet, in the end, magnificent.

ACKNOWLEDGMENTS

John Quincy Adams: Militant Spirit quite literally could not have been written without the help of my research assistant, Homa Hassan, who spent countless hours combing through the thousands of letters written to and from Adams. Whatever light the book manages to shed would have been far dimmer without the editorial guidance of my son, Alexander Traub. And I never would have thought of writing it in the first place had my wife, Elizabeth Easton, not urged me to stop writing books about current events and find a good dead person to write about instead.

I was incredibly fortunate to have as my editor Lara Heimert, now the publisher of Basic Books. Lara read my manuscript with a scrupulosity that I thought had vanished from the world of publishing. Without her efforts, this book would have been much longer and much woolier. The historian Richard Bernstein saved me from several egregious errors and quite a few slightly less mortifying ones. Roger Labrie edited the manuscript with such penetration and tact that I eagerly submitted to (almost all of) his counsel.

All biographers of Adams depend on the Adams Papers, the extraordinary archive of Adams material housed within the Massachusetts Historical Society in Boston. However, James Taylor, director of the Adams Papers, and his colleagues have made such progress in digitizing the archive that I barely had to leave my office in order to read Adams' journal and many of the letters among family members. What a boon to students of the Adamses!

Several scholars, including Thomas Bender, Lynn Parsons, and Adam Brandenburger, read portions of my manuscript and gave me useful guidance.

My agent, Andrew Wylie, rarely took more than sixty seconds to respond to my occasional panicked email, though I am among the littlest of his fishes. I am perpetually grateful to him.

NOTES

University Press, 1963). All subsequent letters cited in this chapter are from AFC.

5   **"no bankruptcy was ever committed:** David McCullough, *John Adams* (New York: Touchstone, 2001), 414.

6   **they were not yokels:** As recounted in Charles Francis Adams, *History of Braintree, Massachusetts* (Cambridge, MA: Riverside, 1891).

6   **"held every species of Libertinage:** L. H. Butterfield, ed., *Diary and Autobiography of John Adams* (Cambridge, MA: Belknap, 1961), vol. 3, 260–261.

6   **"I mount this moment:** JA to Abigail Adams (hereafter AA), February 14, 1761.

7   **"my Scruples about laying myself:** Butterfield, *Diary and Autobiography*, vol. 3, 288.

7   **Adams wrote much later:** "Abigail wept at Preston."

8   **"Female education,":** AA to Lucy Cranch, April 26, 1787.

8   **"I hereby order you:** JA to AA, October 4, 1762.

8   **"a tye more binding:** AA to JA, August 14, 1763.

8   **"I would have been a rover:** AA to Isaac Smith, April 20, 1771.

9   **"I have a curiosity:** Ibid.

9   **"Electricity, Magnetism Hydrostatics:** G. J. Barker-Benfield, *Abigail and John Adams: The Americanization of Sensibility* (Chicago: University of Chicago Press, 2010), 172.

9   **"The flame is kindled:** AA to Mercy Otis Warren, December 5, 1773.

9   **"that we cannot be happy:** AA to Warren, February 3 (?), 1775.

9   **"You had prepared me:** AA to JA, July 6, 1775.

9   **"the Sword is now:** AA to Warren, February 3 (?), 1775.

10   **"The sound I think:** AA to JA, March 2, 1776.

10   **"Education has made a greater difference:** JA to AA, October 29, 1775.

11   **"think of forming the Taste:** JA to AA, July 7, 1776.

11   **"Every man in a republic:** Gordon S. Wood, *The Creation of the American Republic, 1776–87* (Chapel Hill: University of North Carolina Press, 1969).

11   **"I have always thought:** AA to JA, September 16, 1774.

11   **"brotherly love, sisterly affection:** AA to Abigail Smith, February 21, 1791.

12   **"What Bias Nature:** AA to Warren, July 16, 1773.

13   **"I hope that you will remember:** JA to JQA, April 18, 1776.

13   **"it will become a necessary:** JA to AA, February 18, 1776.

13   **"Which character he esteems:** JA to JQA, March 16, 1777.

15   **"Adhere to those religious Sentiments:** AA to JQA, June 10 (?), 1778.

16   **"seeing large things:** McCullough, *John Adams*, 200.

16   **"rolled in the grass:** Henry Adams, *The Education of Henry Adams* (London: Oxford University Press, 1999), 13.

16   **"My head is much too fickle:** JQA to JA, June 27, 1777.

17   **"snares and temptations":** AA to John Thaxter, February 15, 1778.

CHAPTER 2: HIS THOUGHTS ARE ALWAYS RUNNING IN A SERIOUS STRAIN (1778–1780)

18   **"The Heavens frown:** H. Butterfield, ed., *Diary and Autobiography of John Adams* (Cambridge, MA: Belknap, 1961), vol. 4, 6.

19   **"Fully sensible of the Danger,":** Ibid., vol. 4, 15.

20   **"What is the course of it?":** Ibid., vol. 2, 277.

21   **The gardens surrounding their cottage:** As described in Stacy Schiff, *A Great Improvisation: Franklin, France and the Birth of America* (New York: Henry Holt, 2005).

21   **"learned more French in a day:** Butterfield, *Diary and Autobiography*, vol. 4, 60.

21   **"which I believe will rouse:** John Quincy Adams (hereafter JQA) to Abigail Adams (hereafter AA), April 20, 1778, in L. H. Butterfield, Marc Friedlaender, Richard Alan Ryerson, and Margaret A. Hogan, eds., *Adams Family Correspondence* (AFC) (Cambridge, MA: Harvard University Press, 1963). All letters in this chapter are cited from AFC.

21   **He wrote to his cousin:** JQA to William Cranch, May 31, 1778.

21   **"All the actresses,":** JQA to Lucy Cranch, June 1, 1778.

21   **"Pappa won't let me go:** JQA to Abigail Smith, September 27, 1778.

22   **"stern and haughty Republican:** John Adams (hereafter JA) to AA, April 12, 1778.

22   **"much rather be among the rugged:** JQA to AA, June 5, 1778.

22   **"Your business & mine:** JQA to Charles Adams, June 6, 1778.

22   **"Improve your understanding,":** AA to JQA June 10 (?), 1778.

22   **"Your son is the joy:** JA to AA, December 2, 1778.

23   **"in the first place:** AA to JQA, March 20, 1780.

23   **"one so rational, ingenious and curious:** JQA to Charles Adams and Thomas Boylston Adams, October 3, 1778.

23   **"Altho I shall have the mortification:** JQA to AA, September 27, 1778.

24   **"correcting the pronunciation:** Butterfield, *Diary and Autobiography*, vol. 2, 385.

24   **"body-politic . . . is a social compact:** David McCullough, *John Adams* (New York: Touchstone, 2001), 221.

25 **"the events that happen to me:** JA to AA, September 27, 1778.

25 **Johnny wrote of his own trip:** *The Diaries of John Quincy Adams*, November 30, 1779, Adams Papers, Massachusetts Historical Society, Boston, http://www.masshist.org/jqadiaries/php.

25 **"I never experienced any Thing:** Butterfield, *Diary and Autobiography*, vol. 2, 426.

26 **"disobedience and impertinence:** Rector Roger Verheyk to JA, November 10, 1780.

26 **"confine yourself to proper hours:** JA to JQA, December 28, 1780.

27 **Another letter proposed:** JA to JQA, May 18, 1781.

27 **"I hope, my dear boy:** AA to JQA, May 26, 1781.

27 **She gently chided:** AA to Charles Adams, May 26, 1781.

CHAPTER 3: AS PROMISING AND MANLY A YOUTH
AS IS IN THE WORLD (1781–1785)

29 **He and Dana traveled eastward:** Described in W. Cresson, *Francis Dana: A Puritan Diplomat at the Court of Catherine the Great* (New York: Dial, 1930), 160–166.

29 **tolling off the pages:** *The Diaries of John Quincy Adams* (hereafter *Diaries*), January 27, 1782ff, Adams Papers, Massachusetts Historical Society, Boston, http://www.masshist.org/jqadiaries/php.

29 **"The Sovereign,":** John Quincy Adams (hereafter JQA) to Abigail Adams (hereafter AA), September 10, 1783, in L. H. Butterfield, Marc Friedlaender, Richard Alan Ryerson, and Margaret A. Hogan, eds., *Adams Family Correspondence* (AFC) (Cambridge, MA: Harvard University Press, 1963). All letters in this chapter are from AFC unless otherwise noted.

30 **"Yet even this mistress:** AA to JQA December 26, 1783.

30 **"*car je suis tout à fait*:** JQA to John Thaxter, July 22, 1782.

31 **"Has the cold northern region:** AA to JQA, November 13, 1782.

31 **"I must beg your pardon:** JQA to AA, July 30, 1783.

31 **"His Britannic Majesty acknowledges:** The text of the Treaty of Paris is available online: http://en.wikisource.org/wiki/Treaty_of_Paris_(1783).

31 **"He is grown a man:** AFC, vol. 5, 218.

32 **"I beg you would let me:** JQA to Peter Jay Munro, November 10, 1783, in Adams Papers Microfilm (hereafter APM), Massachusetts Historical Society, Boston.

32 **"that *wonderful, wonderful*:** JQA to Munro, November 4, 1783, in APM.

33 **"I go pretty often to the Plays:** JQA to Munro, December 7, 1783, in APM.

33   **Oh love, thou tyrant:** JQA to Munro, April 12, 1784, in APM.

33   **"to be condemned:** JQA to Elizabeth Cranch, April 18, 1784.

33   **"Let your observations:** AA to JQA, December 26, 1783.

34   **"no man knows:** L. H. Butterfield, ed., *Diary and Autobiography of John Adams* (Cambridge, MA: Belknap, 1961), vol. 3, 152.

34   **The sole inhabitant they encountered:** JQA describes in letters to Munro, November 3 and 16, 1784, in APM.

34   **"He was in fine spirits,":** Butterfield, *Diary and Autobiography of John Adams*, vol. 3, 152.

34   **"his ideas are all striking:** JQA to JA, June 6, 1784.

34   **"Whenever a great able:** JA to JQA, June 21, 1784.

35   **"Don't fatigue yourself:** JA to JQA, June 6, 1784.

35   **"the greatest traveller of his age:** JA to AA, July 26, 1784.

35   **"This place offers a vast fund:** *Diaries*, March 17, 1785.

36   **"whom I love to be with:** Ibid., March 10, 1785.

37   **"The table is covered:** David McCullough, *John Adams* (New York: Touchstone, 2001), 325.

37   **"If you were to examine him:** Ibid.

37   **"no man would have wished:** JQA to Munro, February 29, 1784, in APM.

38   **"I am determined:** *Diaries*, April 26, 1785.

38   **"with such feelings:** Ibid., May 12, 1785.

CHAPTER 4: YOU ARE ADMITTED, ADAMS (1785–1788)

40   **"to form some opinion:** *The Diaries of John Quincy Adams* (hereafter *Diaries*), August 11, 1785, Adams Papers, Massachusetts Historical Society, Boston, http://www.masshist.org/jqadiaries/php.

40   **"the best Company:** Ibid., September 3, 1785.

40   **even to describe his feelings in his journal:** Ibid., August 28, 1785.

40   **"he enters into characters:** Mary Cranch to Abigail Adams (hereafter AA), September 7, 1785, in L. H. Butterfield, Marc Friedlaender, Richard Alan Ryerson, and Margaret A. Hogan, eds., *Adams Family Correspondence* (AFC) (Cambridge, MA: Harvard University Press, 1963). All subsequent letters in this chapter are from AFC.

41   **"to sing your praises:** John Quincy Adams (hereafter JQA) to Abigail Smith, October 1, 1785.

41   **"exceedingly severe upon the foibles:** Elizabeth Smith Shaw to AA, February 14, 1786.

42   **"was rather peculiar:** Shaw to AA, March 18, 1786.

42   **"has made persons suppose:** *Diaries*, February 1, 1786.

42   **"A Gentleman, who is very severe:** Abigail Smith to JQA, April 25, 1786.

42   **"Most of our damsels:** *Diaries*, January 13, 1786.

43   **"You are admitted, Adams.":** Ibid., March 18, 1786.

43   **Undergraduates could be addressed:** Samuel Eliot Morison, *Harrison Gray Otis, 1765–1848: The Urbane Federalist* (New York: Houghton Mifflin, 1969), 34.

43   **The Harvard of 1786:** The Harvard of this day is described in Robert McCaughey, *Josiah Quincy, 1772–1864: The Last Federalist* (Cambridge, MA: Harvard University Press, 1974), 14–16.

43   **"regarded the undergraduates:** Ibid., 179.

43   **"Find out who are the best scholars:** John Adams to JQA, June 3, 1786.

44   **He set himself the task:** *Diaries*, February 15, 1787ff.

44   **"His genius is very good:** Ibid., May 31, 1787.

44   **describes being constantly fined:** Morison, *Harrison Gray Otis*, 37–38.

45   **"I took my Scissors:** Elizabeth Cranch to AA, July 1, 1786.

45   **students often did their homework:** Adams' journal is itself one of the chief sources of information about Harvard at that time.

45   **at times Mr. Williams:** *Diaries*, May 3, 1786.

45   **"Whether the immortality:** Ibid., May 16, 1786.

46   **Samuel Adams, hero:** David P. Szatmary, *Shays' Rebellion: The Making of An Agrarian Insurrection* (Amherst: University of Massachusetts Press, 1980), 83.

46   **"Citizens,":** *Diaries*, September 7, 1786.

47   **"In arguing against equality,":** Ibid., September 26, 1786.

47   **"a popular Tyranny:** AA to JQA, November 28, 1786.

47   **"The people,":** John Adams, *A Defence of the Constitutions of Government of the United States of America, Against the Attack of M. Turgot in His Letter to Dr. Price, Dated the Twenty-Second Day of March, 1778* (Philadelphia: Budd and Bartram, 1797).

47   **In fact, he told Abigail:** AA to JQA, March 20, 1787.

47   **The rebellion burned through New England:** Szatmary, *Shays' Rebellion*, 106–114.

48   **"I could wish you:** JQA to Thomas Boylston Adams, July 2, 1787.

48   **"It is not without many melancholy:** *Diaries*, June 20, 1787.

49   **"Nature,":** Ibid., July 18, 1787.

50   **Both his aunts were struck:** Elizabeth Smith Shaw to AA, July 22, 1787.

50   **"complimented and flattered:** *Columbian Magazine*, July 1787.

CHAPTER 5: FRIEND OF THE PEOPLE (1788–1794)

51   **Theophilus Parsons was:** Theophilus Parsons Jr., *The Memoir of Theophilus Parsons* (Boston: Ticknor & Fields, 1859), 272ff.

51   **"universal skepticism":** *The Diaries of John Quincy Adams* (hereafter *Diaries*), November 7, 1787, Adams Papers, Massachusetts Historical Society, Boston, http://www.masshist.org/jqadiaries/php.

52   **"himself a law library,":** Ibid., November 26, 1787.

52   **"I felt a depression:** Ibid., December 6, 1787.

52   **"similar to what affected:** John Quincy Adams (hereafter JQA) to William Cranch, February 16, 1788, in L. H. Butterfield, Marc Friedlaender, Richard Alan Ryerson, and Margaret A. Hogan, eds., *Adams Family Correspondence* (AFC) (Cambridge, MA: Harvard University Press, 1963). All letters cited in this chapter are from AFC unless otherwise noted.

52   **He filled his diary:** *Diaries*, January 10, 1788ff.

53   **"a youth about to enter:** Ibid., September 5, 1788.

53   **"it was too far:** Elizabeth Smith Shaw to Abigail Adams (hereafter AA), September 21, 1788.

54   **"He is determined:** Lucy Cranch to AA, August 18, 1787.

54   **"I think I am on a way:** *Diaries*, October 14, 1788.

55   **"As they are handsome:** Ibid., August 13, 1788.

55   **"Three more months,":** JQA to William Cranch, April 7, 1790.

55   **"You may worship:** Abigail Smith to JQA, June 6, 1790.

56   **"The partial gods:** "A Vision," 1790, in John Quincy Adams, *Poems of Religion and Society* (Buffalo, NY: Derby, 1853), 109–116.

56   **"a walk in the grove:** *Diaries*, June 4, 1790.

56   **"all my hopes of future happiness:** JQA to James Bridge, August 1790, in the collection of the Museum of the City of New York.

56   **"I will give you one piece:** AA to JQA, August 20, 1790.

56   **"a certain Lady:** Elizabeth Smith Shaw to AA, October 16, 1790.

56   **"are not such as can warrant:** AA to JQA, November 7, 1790.

56   **"Letter from my mother.":** *Diaries*, November 13, 1790.

57   **"you have Brothers:** JA to JQA, September 8, 1790.

58   **"Do you know a man:** Charles Adams to JQA, November 7, 1790.

58   **Prostitution had become:** See Barbara Mell Hobson, *Uneasy Virtue: The Politics of Prostitution and the American Reform Tradition* (New York: Basic Books, 1987), 11–15.

58   **"Mall. I got fortunately home.":** *Diaries*, September 3, 1792ff.

58   **"Miss Jones:** Ibid., June 14, 1792.

58   **"four years of wretchedness":** Ibid., November 18, 1838.

59   **"No branch will:** JQA to William Cranch, December 7, 1787.

60 **He visited President Washington:** *Diaries*, February 1, 1791ff.

60 **"appears to have lost:** AA to Mary Smith Cranch, March 12, 1791.

60 **"perseverance and fortitude.":** *Diaries*, April 2, 1791.

60 **"at least a respectable reputation.":** Ibid., May 16, 1791.

61 **Paine called for a "general Revolution":** Thomas Paine, *The Rights of Man* (New York: Dutton, 1951), 25ff.

61 **"America has less to fear:** Gordon Wood, *The Creation of the American Republic, 1776–87* (Chapel Hill: University of North Carolina Press, 1969), 415.

61 **"that which a whole nation chuses:** Worthington Chauncey Ford, ed., *Writings of John Quincy Adams* (hereafter *Writings*) (New York: Macmillan, 1913), vol. 1, 65–109.

62 **they provoked a response:** Ibid., 65n.

62 **"There is more of method:** Ibid., 66n.

62 **"the machines, Arts and Channels:** JA to JQA, September 13, 1791.

62 **"700 men who looked:** JQA to Thomas Boylston Adams, February 1, 1792.

63 **arguing in a published essay:** *Writings*, vol. 1, 127–129.

63 **"my sentiments in general:** JQA to JA, February 4, 1792, in *Writings*.

63 **"Democratic societies" sprang up:** George C. Herring, *From Colony to Superpower: U.S. Foreign Relations Since 1776* (Oxford: Oxford University Press, 2008), 70–73.

63 **"the random violence:** Cited in Robert Kagan, *Dangerous Nation* (New York: Knopf, 2006), 110.

64 **The imagery of Americans:** *Writings*, vol. 1, 135–145, 148–175.

65 **"the result of the President's:** Samuel Flagg Bemis, *John Quincy Adams and the Foundations of American Foreign Policy* (New York: Norton, 1949), 39.

65 **"I had laid down:** *Diaries*, June 3, 1794.

65 **Adams was noncommittal but reflected:** Ibid., June 11, 1794.

65 **he sought a prior understanding:** JQA to John Adams, July 27, 1794.

66 **"When it got out of sight,":** *Diaries*, September 17, 1794.

CHAPTER 6: I SHALL BE MUCH MISTAKEN IF HE IS NOT SOON FOUND AT THE HEAD OF THE DIPLOMATIQUE CORPS (1794–1795)

68 **Adams' return to European soil:** *The Diaries of John Quincy Adams* (hereafter *Diaries*), October 15, 1794, Adams Papers, Massachusetts Historical Society, Boston, http://www.masshist.org/jqadiaries/php.

68   **The French revolutionary army had attacked:** See T. C. W. Blanning, *The French Revolutionary Wars, 1787–1802* (London: Arnold, 1996), 135.

69   **"it will grant fraternity:** Ibid., 101.

69   **"Disguise thyself:** *Diaries*, March 17, 1795.

69   **He was, he felt:** Ibid., January 18, 1795.

69   **"A state of lifeless imbecility:** John Quincy Adams (hereafter JQA) to John Adams (hereafter JA), November 9, 1794, in Worthington Chauncey Ford, ed., *Writings of John Quincy Adams* (hereafter *Writings*) (New York: Macmillan, 1913). All letters in this chapter are cited from *Writings*.

69   **The disease of dependence had seeped:** *Diaries*, March 8, 1795.

69   **Patriotic clubs arose:** JQA to Secretary of State Edmund Randolph, June 24, 1795.

70   **"Each of them too hastily:** *Diaries*, February 3, 1795.

70   **"values himself much upon:** Ibid., April 16, 1795.

70   **"a testimony from the first hand:** Ibid., March 23, 1795.

71   **"We talked much:** Ibid., March 12, 1795.

72   **With a commerce stagnated:** JQA to JA, September 21, 1997.

72   **"the prophecy of Rousseau:** JQA to JA, July 27, 1795.

73   **"natural boundaries":** Paul W. Schroeder, *The Transformation of European Politics, 1763–1848* (Oxford: Clarendon, 1994), 113.

73   **"both parties entered:** Ibid., 117.

74   **the two sides signed Jay's Treaty:** See Samuel Flagg Bemis, *John Quincy Adams and the Foundations of American Foreign Policy* (New York: Norton, 1949), 58–59.

74   **"the policy of the French:** JQA to JA, May 22, 1795.

75   **"unquestionably the most intelligent:** Uriah Tracy to Oliver Wolcott Sr., May 27, 1797.

76   **"I have no language:** JA to JQA, April 26, 1795.

76   **"Mr. J Q Adams:** George Washington to JA, August 20, 1795.

76   **"If *resentment* were a good:** JQA to Daniel Sargent, October 12, 1795.

77   **"my imagination is apt:** JQA to JA, June 24, 1796.

77   **he even wrote his father:** JQA to JA, April 4, 1796.

77   **The Directory, he explained:** JQA to JA, August 13, 1796.

78   **"Every hour of neutrality:** JQA to Charles Adams, December 30, 1795.

78   **If Washington's "system:** JQA to Sylvanus Bourne, December 24, 1795.

78   **Washington warned:** The text of George Washington's Farewell Address is available online: http://avalon.law.yale.edu/18th_century/washing .asp.

CHAPTER 7: A YOUNG LADY OF FINE PARTS AND ACCOMPLISHMENTS (1795–1797)

79   **"Can a widowed heart:** John Quincy Adams (hereafter JQA) to Abigail Adams (hereafter AA), November 17, 1795, in Worthington Chauncey Ford, ed., *Writings of John Quincy Adams* (hereafter *Writings*) (New York: Macmillan, 1913).

79   **she wrote back to say:** AA to JQA, February 29, 1796, in *Writings*.

80   **"undeserved estimation:** JQA to John Adams (hereafter JA), October 26, 1795, in *Writings*.

80   **"Minister Plenipotentiary,":** JQA to Lord Grenville, December 9, 1795, in *Writings*.

80   **"If I stay here:** *The Diaries of John Quincy Adams* (hereafter *Diaries*), November 27, 1795, Adams Papers, Massachusetts Historical Society, Boston, http://www.masshist.org/jqadiaries/php.

81   **Soon he was spending every evening:** Ibid., January 6, 1796ff.

81   **her anxiety about her mother's origins:** Thorough accounts of Louisa's origins and upbringing are available in Margery M. Heffron, *Louisa Catherine: The Other Mrs. Adams* (New Haven, CT: Yale University Press, 2014), and in Michael O'Brien, *Mrs. Adams in Winter: A Journey in the Last Days of Napoleon* (New York: Farrar, Strauss and Giroux, 2010).

82   **Louisa had grown up:** Judith S. Graham, Beth Luey, Margaret Hogan, and James C. Taylor, eds., *Diary and Autobiographical Writings of Louisa Catherine Adams* (Boston: Belknap, 2013), vol. 1, 3ff.

82   **For that very reason:** Ibid., vol. 1, 41.

82   **"Very agreeable evening,":** *Diaries*, January 27, 1796ff.

82   **"partial conversation with Louisa.":** Ibid., March 14, 1796.

83   **"demanded an explanation.":** Ibid., April 13, 1796.

83   **Adams was convinced:** JQA to Louisa Catherine Adams (hereafter LCA), June 2, 1796, in Adams Papers Microfilm (hereafter APM), Massachusetts Historical Society, Boston.

83   **"Thus it was with me:** Graham et al., *Diary and Autobiographical Writings*, vol. 1, 41–42.

83   **"infinitely better suited:** *Diaries*, June 4, 1796.

84   **"I was not formed:** Ibid., June 30, 1796.

84   **He noted his daily schedule:** Ibid.

84   **"I see you sitting:** JQA to LCA, June 2, 1796, in APM.

85   **"Oh Philosophy,":** LCA to JQA, July 4, 1796, in APM.

85   **"you are now of an Age:** JA to JQA, May 19, 1796, in APM.

85   **"I would hope for:** AA to JQA, May 20, 1796, in APM.

85   **"She has none:** JQA to AA, July 25, 1796, in APM.

85   **a prospect he broached:** JQA to Charles Adams, June 9, 1796, in *Writings*.

85   **"For your own happiness,":** JQA to LCA, August 3, 1796, in APM.

85   **"erroneously supposed me:** LCA to JQA, September 29, 1796, in APM.

86   **"it will not expose us:** JQA to LCA, November 12, 1796.

86   **"You are still at a period:** JQA to LCA, November 21, 1796, in APM.

86   **"a feeble ray of Hope":** LCA to JQA November 29, 1796, in APM.

86   **"an act of folly.":** JQA to Joshua Johnson (hereafter JJ), January 9, 1797, in APM.

86   **"you will be sensible:** JQA to LCA, January 10, 1797, in APM.

86   **"astonished and mortified me:** LCA to JQA, January 17, 1797, in APM.

87   **Many years later she admitted:** Graham et al., *Diary and Autobiographical Writings*, vol. 1, 44.

87   **"You imagine that I receive:** JQA to LCA, February 7, 1797, in APM.

87   **"I shall soon:** LCA to JQA, February 17, 1797, in APM.

87   **"acquiescence and obsequiousness:** JQA to LCA February 12, 1797, in APM.

88   **"you may rest assured:** JQA to AA, June 26, 1797, in APM.

88   **"The sentiments do honor:** President George Washington to JA, February 20, 1797, in *Writings*.

89   **"totally contrary to every expectation:** JQA to JA, July 22, 1797, in APM.

89   **Joshua had written to Adams:** JJ to JQA, September 26, 1796, in APM.

89   **"We were married:** *Diaries*, July 26, 1797.

89   **"You see I have really joined:** JQA to William Vans Murray, August 4, 1797, in APM.

90   **"distressing scene.":** *Diaries*, September 8, 1797.

90   **"the most wretched moment:** Graham et al., *Diary and Autobiographical Writings*, vol. 1, 52.

90   **"worse then notting.":** Frederick Delius to JQA, September 29, 1797, in APM.

90   **"Find the affairs of Mr. J.:** *Diaries*, October 9, 1797.

90   **"I am not the person:** JQA to Delius, October 9, 1797, in APM.

91   **"something more than merely:** JQA to JJ, October 11, 1797, in APM.

91   **she had urged Adams:** Graham et al., *Diary and Autobiographical Writings*, vol. 1, 50.

91   **"It was strict and rigid:** Ibid., vol. 1, 51.
91   **"all confidence was destroyed:** Ibid.

CHAPTER 8: PRESIDENT ADAMS'
POLITICAL TELESCOPE (1797–1801)

92   **"Almost sick myself,":** *The Diaries of John Quincy Adams* (hereafter *Diaries*), October 21, 1797, Adams Papers, Massachusetts Historical Society, Boston, http://www.masshist.org/jqadiaries/php.

93   **she recoiled from the commonness:** Judith S. Graham, Beth Luey, Margaret Hogan, and James C. Taylor, eds., *Diary and Autobiographical Writings of Louisa Catherine Adams* (Boston: Belknap, 2013), vol. 1, 55.

93   **Berlin had gained a reputation:** Giles MacDonogh, *Berlin* (New York: St. Martin's, 1998), 86.

94   **"His disposition is martial:** John Quincy Adams (hereafter JQA) to William Vans Murray (hereafter WVM) December 23, 1797, in Adams Papers Microfilm (APM), Massachusetts Historical Society, Boston. All subsequent letters cited in this chapter are from APM unless otherwise noted.

94   **The city had a dizzyingly complicated:** *Diaries*, December 8, 1797.

94   **"stiffness, coldness, formality:** Ibid., January 6, 1798.

94   **Louisa, however, could hear:** Graham et al., *Diary and Autobiographical Writings*, vol. 1, 55.

94   **"list carpet,":** Ibid., vol. 1, 81.

95   **"The Queen," she wrote:** Ibid., vol. 1, 58.

95   **"a remarkably handsome:** Ibid., vol. 1, 166n.

95   **whom he liked very much:** Tom's diary of the period sheds light on Louisa's plight: *Berlin and the Prussian Court in 1798: Journal of Thomas Boylston Adams, Secretary to the United States Legation at Berlin* (New York: New York Public Library, 1916).

95   **"a most lovely woman:** Thomas Boylston Adams (hereafter TBA) to Abigail Adams (hereafter AA), September 10, 1797.

95   **"soothed me in my afflictions":** Graham et al., *Diary and Autobiographical Writings*, vol. 1, 89.

96   **"The Queen," she recalled:** Graham et al., *Diary and Autobiographical Writings*, vol. 1, 104–105.

96   **"walked boldly forward:** Ibid., vol. 1, 144.

96   **In mid-1797 Napoleon had just completed:** See Phillip G. Dwyer, *Napoleon: The Path to Power* (New Haven, CT: Yale University Press, 2007).

96   **"political telescope":** John Adams (hereafter JA) to JQA, June 2, 1797.

97   **"They are tearing up:** JQA to JA, May 11, 1797.

97   **Adams had feared since:** See JQA to Elbridge Gerry, November 26, 1797.

97   **most leading Federalists:** See Peter Hill, *William Vans Murray, Federalist Diplomat: The Shaping of Peace with France, 1797–1801* (Syracuse, NY: Syracuse University Press, 1971). For evidence of Pickering's fear and hatred of France, see Gerard H. Clarfield, *Timothy Pickering and the American Republic* (Columbia: University of Missouri Press, 1969), 172–177.

98   **the "quasi-war" with France:** See Alexander de Conde, *The Quasi-War: The Politics and Diplomacy of the Undeclared War with France, 1797–1801* (New York: Scribner, 1966).

98   **"Is France to establish:** JA to JQA, July 15, 1797.

99   **"such passages as you conceive:** AA to William Cranch, January 19, 1798.

99   **"the experience of the last six years:** JQA to JA, January 31, 1798, in Worthington Chauncey Ford, ed., *Writings of John Quincy Adams* (hereafter *Writings*) (New York: Macmillan, 1913).

100   **"must either bow down:** JQA to WVM, July 22, 1798, in *Writings*.

100   **He even proposed to Secretary Pickering:** JQA to Thomas Pickering, February 19, 1798, in *Writings*.

100   **Adams cautioned him:** JQA to WVM, June 7, 1798, in *Writings*.

100   **within this atmosphere of war hysteria:** de Conde, *The Quasi-War*, 74ff.

101   **he wrote a letter to his mother:** JQA to AA, June 22, 1798, in *Writings*.

101   **"declared their desire:** JQA to Thomas Pickering, June 18, 1798, in *Writings*.

101   **wrote to him immediately:** JQA to WVM, October 2, 1798, in *Writings*.

101   **"a great and important change":** JQA to JA, September 25, 1798, in *Writings*.

101   **he wrote to Pickering:** JQA to Pickering, October 6, 1798, in *Writings*.

101   **The leading historian of the period concludes:** de Conde, *The Quasi-War*, 89.

102   **gave his father letters:** David McCullough, *John Adams* (New York: Touchstone, 2001), 523.

102   **"plundering and barbarous decrees":** JQA to AA, June 12, 1800, in *Writings*.

102   **tartly asked his younger brother:** JQA to Charles Adams, August 1, 1797.

103   **He asked Charles:** JQA to Charles Adams, January 24, 1798.

103   **"The Samaeens were a Sect:** Charles Adams to JA, March 12, 1794, in L. H. Butterfield, Marc Friedlaender, Richard Alan Ryerson, and Margaret A. Hogan, eds., *Adams Family Correspondence* (Cambridge, MA: Harvard University Press, 1963).

103   **"I renounce him,":** McCullough, *John Adams*, 529.

103   **"no man's enemy:** Ibid., 555.

103   **"regular, formal accounts:** JQA to TBA, April 29, 1799.

104   **Adams set himself the task:** *Diaries*, November 10, 1799.

104   **who sat by his wife's bedside:** Ibid., March 21, 1798.

104   **blamed the loss:** Graham et al., *Diary and Autobiographical Writings*, vol. 1, 110.

104   **"a continual succession:** *Diaries*, December 4, 1799.

104   **"I can only pray:** Ibid., January 9, 1800.

104   **It is possible:** Ibid., July 23, 1800. Subsequent citations from *Diaries*, July 23–August 27.

105   **the so-called Silesian Letters:** Adams' letters were collected as a book, *Letters on Silesia, Written During a Tour Through That Country 1800, 1801* (London: Printed for J. Budd, 1804).

105   **The queen sent messengers:** Graham et al., *Diary and Autobiographical Writings*, vol. 1, 154.

106   **Adams decreed that his name:** JQA to TBA, May 5, 101.

106   **"The day before yesterday:** JQA to AA, April 14, 1801.

106   **In July 1799, he had concluded:** Samuel Flagg Bemis, *John Quincy Adams and the Foundations of American Foreign Policy* (New York: Norton, 1949), 93–96.

106   **"party bitterness and rancor":** JQA to AA, July 11, 1800.

106   **"It is too long:** AA to JQA, September 1, 1800.

106   **On July 17:** *Diaries*, July 17, 1801.

CHAPTER 9: I FEEL STRONG TEMPTATIONS TO PLUNGE INTO POLITICAL CONTROVERSY (1801–1803)

110   **The ocean voyage had left her:** Judith S. Graham, Beth Luey, Margaret Hogan, and James C. Taylor, eds., *Diary and Autobiographical Writings of Louisa Catherine Adams* (Boston: Belknap, 2013), vol. 1, 158.

110   **He saw them into:** *The Diaries of John Quincy Adams* (hereafter *Diaries*), September 12, 1801, Adams Papers, Massachusetts Historical Society, Boston, http://www.masshist.org/jqadiaries/php.

110   **"inexpressible delight":** Ibid., September 21, 1801.

110   **imaginatively rechristened the boy:** Abigail Adams (hereafter AA) to John Quincy Adams (hereafter JQA), September 13, 1801, in Adams Papers Microfilm (APM), Massachusetts Historical Society, Boston. All letters cited in this chapter are from APM.

110   **"I am sure your brother:** AA to Thomas Boylston Adams (hereafter TBA), July 12, 1801.

110   **He spent $6,000:** *Diaries*, October 1, 1801.

110   **He bought shares:** Ibid., October 10, 1801.

110   **she had written to her husband:** Louisa Catherine Adams (hereafter LCA) to JQA, September 16, 1801.

111   **"very, very much broke.":** LCA to JQA, October 4, 1801.

111   **"He has been unfortunate:** *Diaries*, October 26, 1801.

111   **Adams paid calls:** Ibid., October 21–27, 1801.

111   **Catherine advised her:** Graham et al., *Diary and Autobiographical Writings*, vol. 1, 160.

112   **Stagecoach travel at the time:** Henry Adams, *The United States in 1800* (Ithaca, NY: Great Seal Books, 1955), 7–9.

112   **As the Adams party:** Jack Shepherd, *Cannibals of the Heart: A Personal Biography of Louisa Catherine and John Quincy Adams* (New York: McGraw Hill, 1980), 106.

112   **Louisa arrived half-frozen:** Graham et al., *Diary and Autobiographical Writings*, vol. 1, 162.

112   **"Had I stepped into:** Ibid., vol. 1, 164.

113   **"so slender and her frame:** AA to TBA, December 27, 1801.

113   **John Adams took an immediate liking:** Graham et al., *Diary and Autobiographical Writings*, vol. 1, 165. ("The old gentleman took a fancy to me, and he was the only one.")

113   **"The footways or sidewalks:** Adams, *The United States*, 14–15.

113   **Boston was in the midst of transforming:** Thomas H. O'Connor, *The Hub: Boston Past and Present* (Boston: Northeastern University Press, 2001).

113   **In 1795, the painter:** Caleb Snow, *The History of Boston* (Boston: Abel Bowen, 1828).

113   **Otis and his team:** Samuel Eliot Morison, *Harrison Gray Otis, 1765–1848: The Urbane Federalist* (New York: Houghton Mifflin, 1969), 218–226.

114   **Once completed three years later:** Edward Stanwood, "Topography," in *Memorial History of Boston 1630–1880*, vol. 4, ed. Justin Winson (Boston: Ticknor, 1880–1881).

114   **he added to his inventory:** *Diaries*, January 13, 1802.

114 **An 1802 list:** Samuel Flagg Bemis, *John Quincy Adams and the Foundations of American Foreign Policy* (New York: Norton, 1949), 111.

114 **The Boston bar teemed:** See James Spear Loring, *The Hundred Boston Orators Appointed by the Municipal Authorities and Other Public Bodies, from 1770 to 1852* (Boston: J. Jewett, 1852).

114 **"I feel strong temptation:** *Diaries*, January 28, 1802.

115 **"Thus you see:** JQA to TBA, June 13, 1802.

115 **"by way of conciliatory procedure.":** *Diaries*, May 28, 1802.

115 **Josiah Quincy:** Robert McCaughey, *Josiah Quincy, 1772–1864: The Last Federalist* (Cambridge, MA: Harvard University Press, 1974), 20. Quincy also refused to run until he had made a fortune in real estate.

115 **"This is one of a thousand:** *Diaries*, November 3, 1802.

115 **In early 1803:** Ibid., February 4, 1803.

116 **Adams joined a group:** Ibid., March 12, 1802; also May 21, 1802.

116 **"a maudlin hysterical fine Lady.":** Graham et al., *Diary and Autobiographical Writings*, vol. 1, 173.

116 **"*all* that she had been described.":** Ibid., vol. 1, 172.

117 **"The Amory's,:** Ibid., vol. 1, 168.

117 **"They were both,":** Ibid., vol. 1, 189.

117 **A French visitor in 1788:** David McCullough, *John Adams* (New York: Touchstone, 2001), 391.

118 **John Quincy received a letter:** *Diaries*, April 1, 1803.

118 **John Adams had patriotically:** Bemis, *John Quincy Adams*, 114.

118 **"They felt it severely:** *Diaries*, April 3, 1803.

118 **"If I cannot keep:** AA to TBA, April 26, 1803.

118 **"I feel myself:** *Diaries*, April 3, 1803.

118 **He tried to sell his:** Ibid., April 2, 1803; April 14, 1803.

118 **Peter came back:** Peter Boylston Adams to John Adams, June 23, 1803.

118 **His parents would have:** *Diaries*, August 16, 1803.

119 **the annual oration celebrating the Pilgrims' landing:** For the text of an oration delivered at Plymouth on December 22, 1802, see https://archive.org/details/orationdelivered00ada.

119 **In late 1802, Jonathan Mason:** Bemis, *John Quincy Adams*, 113–114.

CHAPTER 10: CURSE ON THE STRIPLING, HOW HE APES HIS SIRE (1803–1804)

121 **"Around the Capitol:** Nicholas Dungan, *Gallatin: America's Swiss Founding Father* (New York: New York University Press, 2010), 67.

121   **The Capitol, like the city:** "History of the United States Capitol: A Chronicle of Design, Construction and Politics," Government Printing Office, S. Doc 106–29.

122   **forced to adjourn for three days:** *The Diaries of John Quincy Adams* (hereafter *Diaries*), November 7, 1803, Adams Papers, Massachusetts Historical Society, Boston, http://www.masshist.org/jqadiaries/php.

122   **"their admission introduced noise:** William Plumer, *William Plumer's Memorandum of Proceedings in the United States Senate, 1803–1807* (New York: Macmillan, 1923), 92–93.

122   **The entire city of Washington had:** James Sterling Young, *The Washington Community, 1800–1828* (New York: Columbia University Press, 1966), 22.

122   **"The City not being laid:** Judith S. Graham, Beth Luey, Margaret Hogan, and James C. Taylor, eds., *Diary and Autobiographical Writings of Louisa Catherine Adams* (Boston: Belknap, 2013), vol. 1, 204.

123   **Jefferson decided that:** Henry Adams, *History of the United States During the Administrations of Thomas Jefferson* (New York: Antiquarian, 1962), vol. 2, 363.

124   **"The entertainment was:** Graham et al., *Diary and Autobiographical Writings*, vol. 1, 204.

124   **"Mr. Jefferson tells:** *Diaries*, January 11, 1805.

124   **"The President said that:** Ibid., November 3, 1807.

125   **"to know him,":** Theophilus Parsons Jr., *The Memoir of Theophilus Parsons* (Boston: Ticknor & Fields, 1859), 108.

125   **"The great object of Jacobinism:** Adams, *History of the United States*, vol. 2, 170–171.

125   **Timothy Pickering, who bunked:** Gerard H. Clarfield, *Timothy Pickering and the American Republic* (Columbia: University of Missouri Press, 1969), 221.

125   **The Federalists were, increasingly:** Adams, *History of the United States*, vol. 2, 353.

126   **Jefferson's acquisition of:** Ibid., vol. 2, 246ff.

126   **"Should this precious treaty:** Robert McCaughey, *Josiah Quincy, 1772–1864: The Last Federalist* (Cambridge, MA: Harvard University Press, 1974), 30–31.

127   **"I am in favor:** Plumer, *William Plumer's Memorandum.*

127   **But Adams foresaw:** *Diaries*, January 14 and 18, 1804; John Quincy Adams (hereafter JQA) to Thomas Boylston Adams (hereafter TBA), January 14, 1804, in Adams Papers Microfilm (APM), Massachusetts Historical Society. All letters cited in this chapter are from APM.

127   **He wrote to Tom:** JQA to TBA, January 27, 1804.

128   **"All power in a republican:** *Annals of Congress*, 8th Congress, 1st session, February 18, 1804.

128   **"it will be safe and desirable:** *Report of the Philippine Commission to the President, January 31, 1900* (Washington, DC: US Government Printing Office, 1900), vol. 1, 109.

128   **he registered the sole opposing vote:** *Diaries*, November 18, 1803.

128   **"Of the errors, impudences, and follies:** Ibid., December 4, 1803.

128   **"He is a man of much information:** Plumer, *William Plumer's Memorandum*, 643.

129   **"Curse on the stripling:** Samuel Flagg Bemis, *John Quincy Adams and the Foundations of American Foreign Policy* (New York: Norton, 1949), 123.

129   **"insanity, sickness, any trivial error:** *Diaries*, March 2–12, 1804.

129   **He wrote her to point out:** JQA to Louisa Catherine Adams (hereafter LCA), April 9, 1807.

130   **"My life ever has been:** LCA to JQA, May 12, 1804.

130   **Send me the money:** *Diaries*, May 9, 1804.

130   **John Quincy planted:** Ibid., June 9, July 14, August 8, 1804.

130   **"One remark I made:** Ibid., September 11, 1804.

130   **Didn't any of them:** Ibid., October 13, 1804.

130   **he sent her a quatrain:** JQA to LCA, June 17, 1804.

130   **he wrote that he was terrified:** LCA to JQA August 12, 1804; JQA to LCA, August 26, 1804.

131   **"lamented her loss:** JQA to LCA, September 2, 1804.

131   **"to me the most beautiful:** *Diaries*, November 18, 1838.

CHAPTER 11: THE BOYLSTON PROFESSOR OF RHETORIC AND ORATORY (1804–1807)

132   **"The same bad roads:** Henry Adams, *The United States in 1800* (Ithaca, NY: Great Seal Books, 1955), 4.

132   **"The revolution of 1800":** In Henry Adams, *The History of the United States During the Administrations of Thomas Jefferson* (New York: Antiquarian, 1962), vol. 1, 208.

133   **the process really began:** See Joyce Appleby, *Inheriting the Revolution: The First Generation of Americans* (Cambridge, MA: Belknap, 2000).

133   **His election ushered in:** See Sean Wilentz, *The Rise of American Democracy: Jefferson to Lincoln* (New York: Norton, 2009).

133   **"Federalism was already:** Adams, *The History of the United States*, vol. 1, 353.

133   **"The people of the East:** Ibid., vol. 1, 411.

133   **"We feel that we are:** William Plumer Jr., *Life of William Plumer* (Boston: Phillips, Sampson, 1857), 288.

134   **he wrote a series of broadsides:** Worthington Chauncey Ford, ed., *Writings of John Quincy Adams* (hereafter *Writings*) (New York: Macmillan, 1913), vol. 3, 46–77.

134   **"immediately after:** Henry Adams, *Documents Relating to New England Federalism, 1800–1815* (Boston: Little Brown, 1905), 147.

135   **Plumer publicly admitted:** Plumer, *Life of William Plumer*, 283ff.

135   **In an open letter:** Adams, *Documents Relating*, 147.

135   **Pickering and others had approached:** Plumer, *Life of William Plumer*, 295.

136   **"Virtuous and studious:** John Adams (hereafter JA) to John Quincy Adams (hereafter JQA), November 9, 1804, in Adams Papers Microfilm (APM), Massachusetts Historical Society. All subsequent letters cited in this chapter are from APM unless otherwise noted.

136   **"For fifteen years:** Ibid., January 8, 1805.

136   **"you had a great consolation:** JQA to JA, January 24, 1805, in *Writings*.

136   **"But you are too much:** JA to JQA, February 7, 1805.

136   **"contracted a reserve:** Abigail Adams to JQA, December 18, 1804.

137   **"Your dijestion is:** Ibid., February 9, 1806.

137   **"Now I hope you never:** Ibid., March 24, 1806.

137   **She was mortified:** Judith S. Graham, Beth Luey, Margaret Hogan, and James C. Taylor, eds., *Diary and Autobiographical Writings of Louisa Catherine Adams* (Boston: Belknap, 2013), vol. 1, 225.

138   **a bolt of good news:** *The Diaries of John Quincy Adams* (hereafter *Diaries*), June 26, 1805, Adams Papers, Massachusetts Historical Society, Boston, http://www.masshist.org/jqadiaries/php.

139   **"With the most perfect deference:** JQA to Samuel Dexter, August 6, 1805, in *Writings*.

139   **Adams undertook a study:** *Diaries*, August 24 and September 15, 1805.

140   **"Sometimes,":** Ibid., January 15, 1805.

140   **The British navy had responded:** George C. Herring, *From Colony to Superpower: U.S. Foreign Relations Since 1776* (Oxford: Oxford University Press, 2008), 116.

141   **Adams himself was asked:** *Diaries*, February 1, 1805.

141   **"would not refuse it:** Ibid., November 25, 1805.

141   **"taken the lead.":** Ibid., January 31, 1806.

142   **"with his all talents:** Ibid., February 1, 1806.

142   **rejoined "with warmth":** Ibid., February 3, 1806.

143   **"Sons of Harvard!":** John Quincy Adams, *Lectures on Rhetoric and Oratory: Delivered to the Classes of Senior and Junior Sophisters at Harvard University* (Cambridge, MA: Hilliard and Metcalf, 1810), Inaugural Oration.

144   **"Eloquence is the child:** Ibid., 76.

144   **One of his students:** Edward Everett, *Eulogy on the Life and Character of John Quincy Adams* (Boston: Dutto and Wentworth, State Printers, 1848).

144   **"I send you:** JQA to Louisa Catherine Adams (hereafter LCA), May 10, 1806.

144   **a lyrical description:** Ibid., June 22, 1806.

144   **"and there yielded:** *Diaries*, June 30, 1806.

145   **"No French:** JQA to LCA, December 8, 1806.

145   **"For your sake:** JQA to LCA, January 7, 1807.

145   **"I was a little surprized:** LCA to JQA, January 18, 1807.

145   **Oh! Nancy! be that solace:** JQA to LCA, January 12, 1807.

146   **How shall I express:** LCA to JQA, January 21, 1807.

146   **Dear Sally!:** JQA to LCA, February 6, 1807.

147   **Thus, in succession:** Ibid.

CHAPTER 12: IF WE MUST PERISH, LET IT BE IN DEFENSE OF OUR RIGHTS (1807–1809)

148   **news reached Washington:** *The Diaries of John Quincy Adams* (hereafter *Diaries*), March 3, 1807, Adams Papers, Massachusetts Historical Society, Boston, http://www.masshist.org/jqadiaries/php.

149   **News of this humiliation:** Henry Adams, *History of the United States During the Administrations of Thomas Jefferson* (New York: Antiquarian, 1962), vol. 2, 946ff.

149   **He was asked:** Worthington Chauncey Ford, ed., *Writings of John Quincy Adams* (hereafter *Writings*) (New York: Macmillan, 1913), July 16, 1807.

149   **"*I should have:* *Diaries*, July 11, 1807.

150   **trying to referee a confrontation:** Ibid., April 3–24, 1807.

150   **"the labors of Sisyphus.":** Ibid., June 13, 1807.

150   **feared that he would lose:** Ibid., September 2, 1807.

150   **"I have met with:** Ibid., October 30, 1807.

151   **"My general consideration:** Ibid., Year End, 1807.

151 **Jefferson was following a policy:** Adams, *History of the United States*, vol. 4, 138–151.

151 **"I observe among:** *Diaries*, November 17, 1807.

151 **"the greatest failure:** Samuel Eliot Morison, *The Life and Letters of Harrison Gray Otis*, vol. 1 (Boston: Houghton and Mifflin, 1913), 323.

151 **When Josiah Quincy asked:** *Diaries*, December 14, 1807.

152 **Adams fumed:** Ibid., January 7, 1808.

152 **"You are supported:** John Adams (hereafter JA) to John Quincy Adams (hereafter JQA), January 8, 1808, in Adams Papers Microfilm (APM), Massachusetts Historical Society, Boston. All subsequent letters cited in this chapter are from APM unless otherwise noted.

153 **"I, who perhaps ought:** JA to JQA, January 17, 1808.

153 **He later explained:** JQA to Thomas Boylston Adams (hereafter TBA), March 12, 1808.

153 **When, the following week:** *Diaries*, February 2, 1808.

153 **"inconsistent both with:** Abigail Adams to JQA, February 15, 1808.

154 **"contain a test:** *Diaries*, February 24, 1808.

154 **"were too pure:** Ibid., February 1, 1808.

154 **He introduced a resolution:** Ibid., April 13, 1808.

154 **"By false policy:** Timothy Pickering, *A Letter from the Hon. Timothy Pickering, a Senator of the United States from the State of Massachusetts* (Boston: Greenough and Stebbins, 1808).

154 **Several leading Republicans approached:** *Diaries*, March 3, 1808.

154 **On March 15:** Ibid., March 15, 1808.

155 **"will be to me of:** Ibid., March 31, 1808.

155 **Adams' response to Pickering:** *Writings*, vol. 3, 189ff.

155 **his father even wrote:** JA to JQA, April 12, 1808.

156 **Federalist journals tore:** Samuel Flagg Bemis, *John Quincy Adams and the Foundations of American Foreign Policy* (New York: Norton, 1949), 148.

156 **"one of the transactions:** *Writings*, vol. 3, 224.

156 **It fell to Adams:** *Diaries*, April 7, 1808.

156 **Adams once again called:** Ibid., April 13, 1808.

156 **"it was the wish of several:** Ibid., April 23, 1808.

156 **"attacked me in a rude:** Ibid., May 18, 1808.

157 **"He also thinks:** Ibid., May 10, 1808.

157 **"a peculiar species:** Samuel Eliot Morison, *Harrison Gray Otis, 1765–1848: The Urbane Federalist* (New York: Houghton Mifflin, 1969), 190.

157 **"an adder in my path.":** Ibid., 191.

157 **"I have felt on this occasion:** JQA to William Branch Giles, November 15, 1808, in *Writings*.

157   **In a later letter:** JQA to Giles, December 26, 1808, in *Writings*.

158   **leading Republicans visited him:** *Diaries*, September 26, 1808.

158   **he admitted, "unhinged":** Ibid., July 10, 1808.

158   **Louisa won:** Judith S. Graham, Beth Luey, Margaret Hogan, and James C. Taylor, eds., *Diary and Autobiographical Writings of Louisa Catherine Adams* (Boston: Belknap, 2013), vol. 1, 280.

158   **Adams wrote to Louisa:** JQA to Louisa Catherine Adams (hereafter LCA), March 5, 1809.

159   **"dull and tedious:** *Diaries*, March 2, 1809.

159   **Congress repealed the embargo:** Adams, *History of the United States*, vol. 4, 451.

159   **On March 6, President Madison:** *Diaries*, March 6, 1809.

160   **Now he wrote to Louisa:** JQA to LCA, March 9, 1809.

160   **Then, on July 4, he attended:** *Diaries*, July 4, 1809.

160   **"O it was too hard!":** Graham et al., *Diary and Autobiographical Writings*, vol. 1, 283.

161   **"My personal motives:** *Diaries*, July 5, 1809.

CHAPTER 13: A BULL-DOG AMONG SPANIELS (1809–1812)

163   **"We had in half a minute:** John Quincy Adams (hereafter JQA) to Thomas Boylston Adams (hereafter TBA), September 24, 1809, in Adams Papers Microfilm (APM), Massachusetts Historical Society, Boston. All letters cited in this chapter are from APM unless otherwise noted.

163   **The British captain demanded:** *The Diaries of John Quincy Adams* (hereafter *Diaries*), September 25, 1809, Adams Papers, Massachusetts Historical Society, Boston, http://www.masshist.org/jqadiaries/php.

163   **Captain Bickford quickly rigged:** Ibid., September 27, 1809.

163   **in his journal made a sketch:** Ibid., in original, volume 28, Massachusetts Historical Society, Boston.

163   **"absolutely despaired:** JQA to TBA, October 16, 1809.

164   **Bickford wanted to turn around:** Ibid., November ?, 1809 (no date given).

164   **"I cannot but reproach:** Ibid., October 16, 1809, and *Diaries*, October 10–22, 1809.

164   **"a stone hole:** Judith S. Graham, Beth Luey, Margaret Hogan, and James C. Taylor, eds., *Diary and Autobiographical Writings of Louisa Catherine Adams* (Boston: Belknap, 2013), vol. 1, 293.

164   **On his first day in town:** *Diaries*, October 24, 1809.

164   **Louisa wrote to Abigail:** Louisa Catherine Adams (hereafter LCA) to Abigail Adams (hereafter AA), October 28, 1809.

165   **A lunch "*sans ceremonie*":** Graham et al., *Diary and Autobiographical Writings,* vol. 1, 303.

165   **At the *bal masqué d'enfants*:** *Diaries,* December 14, 1809.

165   **He was a tall, handsome man:** Robert Kerr Porter, *Traveling Sketches of Sweden and Russia During the Years 1805, 1806, 1807, 1808* (Philadelphia: Hopkins and Earle, 1809), 190.

165   **"spirit of benevolence:** JQA to TBA, February 14, 1810.

165   **described her elegant figure as "lilylike":** Porter, *Traveling Sketches,* 107.

165   **the empress had done her best:** Graham et al., *Diary and Autobiographical Writings,* vol. 1, 298.

165   **"His Majesty told Mr. A:** LCA to AA, June 2, 1810.

166   **"He sat in the frivolous assemblies:** George Dangerfield, *The Era of Good Feelings* (London: Methuen, 1953), 7.

166   **the so-called Continental System:** George C. Daughan, *1812: The Navy's War* (New York: Basic Books, 2011), 10–12.

166   **on his passage through Denmark:** *Diaries,* September 19, 1809.

167   **Adams pressed on:** Ibid., December 27, 1809.

167   **Two months later:** Ibid., February 27, 1810.

167   **"beneath all his natural benevolence:** Alan Palmer, *Alexander I: Tsar of War and Peace* (New York: Harper and Row, 1974), 178–179.

167   **In that first winter of 1809–1810:** Porter, *Traveling Sketches,* 23ff.

167   **Adams, of course, stayed:** *Diaries,* December 29, 1809.

168   **Louisa, who was both mildly:** Graham et al., *Diary and Autobiographical Writings,* vol. 1, 308.

168   **She wrote desperate-sounding letters to Abigail:** LCA to AA, January 7, 1810; February 8, 1810.

168   **she wrote to Louisa's mother:** AA to Catherine Johnson, May 4, 1810.

168   **she wrote to President Madison:** AA to President James Madison, August 1, 1810.

168   **Madison wrote back to say:** Madison to AA, August 15, 1810.

168   **he then wrote directly to Adams:** Madison to JQA, October 16, 1810, in Worthington Chauncey Ford, ed., *Writings of John Quincy Adams* (hereafter *Writings*) (New York: Macmillan, 1913).

169   **The conversation between tsar:** *Diaries,* April 24, 1810.

169   **At the ball, Alexander asked:** Graham et al., *Diary and Autobiographical Writings,* vol. 1, 316–319.

170   **"Any occupation to which:** *Diaries,* July 25, 1810.

170   **Perhaps, Adams wrote:** JQA to Secretary of State Robert Smith, September 5, 1810, in *Writings*.

170   **"The Emperor Napoleon may do:** *Diaries*, August 6, 1810.

171   **"were as strong and fixed:** Ibid., October 9, 1810.

171   **On December 31, 1810, the emperor:** Henry Adams, *History of the United States of America During the Administration of James Madison* (New York: Antiquarian, 1962), vol. 1, 419–423.

171   **"We have a Maitre d'Hotel:** *Diaries*, December 7, 1810.

172   **"a call of Providence":** AA to JQA, March 4, 1811.

172   **"both parties vie:** JA to JQA, March 4, 1811.

173   **"I am also, and always:** JQA to TBA, April 10, 1811.

173   **"Shall you retire:** JA to JQA, February 19, 1812.

173   **In May 1811 a letter:** *Diaries*, May 23, 1811.

174   **St. Petersburg became:** Porter, *Traveling Sketches*, 89ff.

174   **the governor of the province offered:** *Diaries*, May 12, 1810.

174   **"From my Cabinet windows,":** Ibid., July 13, 1811.

175   **"We are daily seeking:** JQA to AA, October 25, 1811.

175   **He found much to agree:** *Diaries*, April 20, 1812.

175   **"but when George was born:** JQA to TBA, April 10, 1811.

175   **"He comes to me:** *Diaries*, February 9, 1810.

176   **who raved about his "capacious mind,":** Mary Cranch to JQA, January 21, 1811.

176   **"nothing delicate or effeminate.":** JQA to TBA, September 8, 1810.

176   **"I hope to always hear:** JQA to George Washington Adams, September 3, 1810.

176   **"In the present condition:** JQA to AA, January 1, 1812.

176   **he wrote that the United States:** JQA to JA, October 14, 1811.

176   **On a walk in mid-March:** *Diaries*, March 14, 1812.

177   **Madison was convinced that Napoleon:** Daughan, *1812*, 31.

178   **he and Louisa received a letter from Abigail:** AA to JQA, November 17, 1811.

178   **The next few days were almost:** *Diaries*, August 20–September 15, 1812.

179   **"My heart is buried:** Graham et al., *Diary and Autobiographical Writings*, vol. 1, 359.

179   **"usurp the space:** Ibid., vol. 1, 367.

CHAPTER 14: RESTORING THE PEACE OF THE WORLD (1812–1814)

181   **"The honor of my country!":** *The Diaries of John Quincy Adams* (hereafter *Diaries*), October 27, 1812, Adams Papers, Massachusetts Historical Society, Boston, http://www.masshist.org/jqadiaries/php.

181   **"Occasional War is one:** John Quincy Adams (hereafter JQA) to Thomas Boylston Adams, August 7, 1813, in APM.

181   **"he would assent to nothing:** JQA to Secretary of State James Monroe (hereafter JM), December 11, 1812, in Worthington Chauncey Ford, ed., *Writings of John Quincy Adams* (hereafter *Writings*) (New York: Macmillan, 1913).

181   **In September 1812, Rumiantsev approached:** *Diaries*, September 21, 1812.

182   **"has derived much useful:** JM to JQA, April 26, 1813, in *Writings*.

182   **"I had a long and very serious:** *Diaries*, January 18, 1813.

183   **"The most painful struggle,":** Ibid., November 3, 1812.

183   **he explained to George:** JQA to George Washington Adams (hereafter GWA), September 1, 1811, in Adams Papers Microfilm (hereafter APM), Massachusetts Historical Society, Boston.

183   **"it is so obvious:** JQA to GWA, September 15, 1811.

184   **"we see a tenderness:** JQA to GWA, March 7, 1813.

184   **"a lassitude which has almost:** *Diaries*, March 8, 1814.

184   **"and has acquired so great:** Louisa Catherine Adams (hereafter LCA) to Abigail Adams (AA), September 2, 1813, in APM.

185   **"I was grieved:** AA to LCA, December 6, 1813, in APM.

186   **He wrote his father to say:** JQA to John Adams, February 17, 1814, in APM.

186   **It was here that the social Passion:** *Diaries*, June 22, 1814.

187   **Gallatin had been born:** Nicholas Dungan, *Gallatin: America's Swiss Founding Father* (New York: New York University Press, 2010), 97.

187   **"I had several opportunities:** JQA to AA, March 30, 1814, in APM.

187   **Clay was every inch:** Robert Remini, *Henry Clay: Statesman for the Union* (New York: Norton, 1991).

188   **Adams was a man of settled habits:** *Diaries*, July 8, 1814.

188   **"Mr. Adams in a very bad:** James Gallatin, *The Diary of James Gallatin, Secretary to Albert Gallatin, a Great Peace-Maker, 1813–1827* (New York: Charles Scribner's Sons, 1920), 27.

188   **Lord Golbourn, the leader:** *Diaries*, August 7, 1814; AA to JM, September 5, 1814.

189   **"with the sole view:** *Writings*, vol. 5, 110n.

189   **Adams replied indignantly:** JQA to JM, September 5, 1814, in *Writings*.

189   **"To condemn vast regions:** *Diaries*, September 1, 1814.

190   **"They are certainly not mean:** JQA to LCA, September 9, 1814, in *Writings*.

190   **"He is always perfectly:** JQA to LCA, September 27, 1814.

190   **"the moral and religious duty:** *Diaries*, September 25, 1814.

191   **"Almost every thing written:** Ibid., September 23, 1814.

191   **"they *must* in the first instance:** JQA to William Harris Crawford, October 5, 1814, in *Writings*.

191   **"Never, since the national existence:** JQA to LCA, October 4, 1814, in *Writings*.

192   **"I blush to think:** LCA to JQA, November 8, 1814, in APM.

192   **"If from want of judgement:** LCA to JQA, December 6, 1814, in APM.

192   **"I am so sick and weary:** LCA to JQA, November 22, 1814, in APM.

192   **In a famous note, Wellington:** *Writings*, vol. 5, 179n.

193   **Liverpool concluded:** Daughan, *1812*, 357.

193   **the British "game of duplicity,":** JQA to LCA, December 13, 1814, in *Writings*.

194   **"walked to and fro:** *Diaries*, December 11, 1814.

194   **"I consider the day:** JQA to LCA, December 30, 1814, in *Writings*.

194   **The American negotiators parted:** *Diaries*, December 27 and 31, 1814.

194   **"You *dare* not:** Ibid., January 6, 1815.

CHAPTER 15: A CARD OF INVITATION TO A DRESS PARTY AT THE PRINCE REGENT'S (1815–1817)

196   **Fair maid of Ghent!:** *The Diaries of John Quincy Adams* (hereafter *Diaries*), January 6, 1815, Adams Papers, Massachusetts Historical Society, Boston, http://www.masshist.org/jqadiaries/php.

197   **"Mrs. Betancourt has taken:** Charles Francis Adams to John Quincy Adams (hereafter JQA), January 10, 1815, in Adams Papers Microfilm (APM), Massachusetts Historical Society, Boston. All subsequent letters cited in this chapter are from APM unless otherwise noted.

197   **"I feel so isolated:** Louisa Catherine Adams (hereafter LCA) to JQA, November 22, 1814.

197   **"There is," he wrote:** *Diaries*, February 12, 1815.

198   **"the walls of all the public:** JQA to John Adams (hereafter JA), March 31, 1815.

199   **Louisa had endured an ordeal:** Louisa tells the story in Judith S. Graham, Beth Luey, Margaret Hogan, and James C. Taylor, eds., *Narrative of Journey from Russia to France*, in *Diary and Autobiographical Writings* (Boston: Belknap, 2013), vol. 1, 375ff.

201   **"Remember your youth:** JA to George Washington Adams and John Adams II, May 3, 1815.

201 **On May 25, John Quincy:** *Diaries*, May 25, July 4, August 5, 1815.

202 **"My son!:** JA to JQA, March 24, 1815.

202 **Adams passionately insisted:** *Diaries*, July 2, 1815.

203 **he was able to recreate:** Ibid., January 24, 1816.

203 **"the first instance:** Samuel Flagg Bemis, *John Quincy Adams and the Foundations of American Foreign Policy* (New York: Norton, 1949), 231.

203 **Adams had been fascinated:** *Diaries*, July 10 and December 1, 1815; February 24, 1816.

204 **"a machine or Carriage:** Ibid., May 5, 1817.

204 **"The house we have:** Ibid., June 1816 ("Day").

205 **"It seemed to me,":** Ibid., October 27, 1815.

205 **"Before leaving home:** Ibid., July 5, 1816.

206 **"Gentlemen, the sublime:** Ibid., June 5, 1816.

206 **"The great and constant:** JQA to Abigail Adams, June 6, 1816.

206 **now caught the poetry bug:** *Diaries*, October 15 to December 27, 1816.

207 **"Could I have chosen:** Ibid., October 16, 1816.

208 **Adams reported:** JQA to Secretary of State James Monroe, April 9, 1816, in Worthington Chauncey Ford, ed., *Writings of John Quincy Adams* (hereafter *Writings*) (New York: Macmillan, 1913).

208 **Monroe would later write:** W. Cresson, *James Monroe* (Chapel Hill: University of North Carolina Press, 1946), 290–291.

208 **"The moral application:** *Diaries*, September 7, 1816.

209 **"My system of politics:** JQA to JA, August 1, 1816, in *Writings*.

209 **"I have seldom,:** *Diaries*, April 28, 1817.

209 **His Majesty, said the viscount:** Ibid., May 5, 1817.

210 **"for American ministers:** Ibid., May 14, 1817.

210 **"I considered him:** Ibid., June 8, 1817 (added July 23).

CHAPTER 16: A LINE STRAIGHT TO THE PACIFIC OCEAN (1817–1819)

217 **"We finish here:** *The Diaries of John Quincy Adams* (hereafter *Diaries*), September 17, 1817, Adams Papers, Massachusetts Historical Society, Boston, http://www.masshist.org/jqadiaries/php.

217 **Adams took the oath:** Samuel Flagg Bemis, *John Quincy Adams and the Foundations of American Foreign Policy* (New York: Norton, 1949), 255–258.

217 **State occupied five rooms:** "Buildings of the Department of State," Office of the Historian, US Department of State, https://history.state.gov /departmenthistory/buildings/section24.

217 **Adams, a devoted systematizer, began:** *Diaries*, September 22, October 2, October 17, 1817; May 20, 1818.

218 **within days of arriving Adams:** Ibid., September 26 and September 28, 1817.

219 **"Has the executive power:** Ibid., October 25, 1817.

219 **"as at the early stages:** John Quincy Adams (hereafter JQA) to John Adams, December 21, 1817, in Worthington Chauncey Ford, ed., *Writings of John Quincy Adams* (hereafter *Writings*) (New York: Macmillan, 1913). All subsequent letters cited in this chapter are from *Writings*.

219 **Monroe's next question:** W. Cresson, *James Monroe* (Chapel Hill: University of North Carolina Press, 1946), 297–299.

220 **At a cabinet meeting on January 6:** *Diaries*, January 6, 1818.

220 **In late 1817, American troops:** Robert Remini, *Andrew Jackson*, vol. 1: *The Course of American Empire, 1767–1821* (Baltimore: Johns Hopkins University Press, 1998), 344.

220 **Days after news:** Ibid., 346–350.

221 **"there was something tragical:** *Diaries*, July 15, 1818.

222 **"But if the question:** Ibid., July 19, 1818.

222 **"transcending the limit:** James Monroe to Andrew Jackson, July 19, 1818, in Stanislaus Murray Hamilton, ed., *The Writings of James Monroe* (New York: G. Putnam's Sons, 1898–1903), vol. 6, 54–61.

223 **The United States had been negotiating with Spain:** This history is recounted in William Earl Weeks, *John Quincy Adams and American Global Empire* (Lexington: University of Kentucky Press, 1992).

224 **Cold calculating, wily, always:** *Diaries*, March 18, 1819.

224 **Adams demanded an additional:** Ibid., July 11, 1818.

224 **"Here are their views, clear:** Bemis, *John Quincy Adams*, 318–319.

225 **Adams' project of extending:** Ibid., 283–285.

225 **Louisa was a polished hostess:** Judith S. Graham, Beth Luey, Margaret Hogan, and James C. Taylor, eds., *Diary and Autobiographical Writings of Louisa Catherine Adams* (Boston: Belknap, 2013), vol. 2, 455–458.

226 **"I went out this Evening:** See William Earl Weeks, *John Quincy Adams and American Global Empire* (Lexington: University of Kentucky Press, 1992), 16.

226 **"on the subject of *dancing girls*:** Philip Hone, *The Diary of Philip Hone, 1828–51* (New York: Dodd, Mead, 1889), 342.

226 **"I am scarcely ever satisfied:** *Diaries*, end of December ("Day"), 1818.

226 **her husband's "habits of study:** Graham et al., *Diary and Autobiographical Writings*, vol. 2, 416.

226 **"You boast of your studying:** JQA to John Adams II, November 17, 1817.

227 **accusing him of "a propensity:** JQA to George Washington Adams, December 26, 1817.

227 **"he ruled his children:** Graham et al., *Diary and Autobiographical Writings*, vol. 1, 103.

227 **"None of them will:** *Diaries*, September 6, 1818.

228 **"My mother was an Angel:** Ibid., November 1, 1818.

228 **Don Luis de Onis had been making:** Bemis, *John Quincy Adams*, 321–322.

229 **he sent diplomatic instructions:** JQA to George Erving, November 28, 1818.

229 **Jefferson wrote to Monroe:** Thomas Jefferson to James Monroe, January 18, 1819, in *Writings*, vol. 5, 502n.

230 **"if Mr. Onis was not prepared:** *Diaries*, January 3, 1819.

230 **"were always setting up:** Ibid., February 15, 1819.

231 **"He is a man of:** Ibid., March 17, 1819.

231 **He would later write:** JQA to Richard Rush, May 2, 1819.

CHAPTER 17: THE BARGAIN BETWEEN FREEDOM AND SLAVERY IS MORALLY AND POLITICALLY VICIOUS (1819–1820)

232 **The president came with a healing message:** William Earl Weeks, *John Quincy Adams and American Global Empire* (Lexington: University of Kentucky Press, 1992), 52.

232 **"party spirit has indeed subsided:** John Quincy Adams (hereafter JQA) to John Adams Smith, October 8, 1817, in Worthington Chauncey Ford, ed., *Writings of John Quincy Adams* (hereafter *Writings*) (New York: Macmillan, 1913).

234 **"These Cabinet Councils open:** *The Diaries of John Quincy Adams* (hereafter *Diaries*), January 9, 1818, Adams Papers, Massachusetts Historical Society, Boston, http://www.masshist.org/jqadiaries/php.

234 **"united to a powerful mind:** Henry Adams, *History of the United States of America During the Administration of James Madison* (New York: Antiquarian, 1962), 231.

234 **"Calhoun thinks for himself:** *Diaries*, January 6, 1818.

234 **"On all subjects," he wrote:** Adam Hodgson, *Letters from North America: Written During a Tour in the United States and Canada* (London: Hurst, Robinson, 1824), 52.

235   **Monroe himself was even more:** Charles M. Wiltse, *John C. Calhoun*, vol. 1: *Nationalist, 1782–1828* (Indianapolis: Bobbs-Merrill, 1944–1951), 145.

235   **"There is slowness:** *Diaries*, January 9, 1818.

235   **"Adams has a pointed pen:** Charles N. Edel, *Nation Builder: John Quincy Adams and the Grand Strategy of the Republic* (Cambridge, MA: Harvard University Press, 2014), 117.

236   **The structure, in fact, was still being rebuilt:** William Seale, *The President's House: A History* (Washington DC: White House Historical Association with the cooperation of the National Geographic Association, 1986), vol. 1, 146–147.

237   **"At the present moment," he cried:** Robert Remini, *Henry Clay: Statesman for the Union* (New York: Norton, 1991), 174.

237   **"I told him I should:** *Diaries*, March 18, 1818.

237   **In April, the president called Adams:** Ibid., April 4, 1818.

238   **"This Government is indeed assuming:** Ibid., December 17, 1818.

238   **"I think him a man:** Robert Remini, *Andrew Jackson*, vol. 1: *The Course of American Empire, 1767–1821* (Baltimore: Johns Hopkins University Press, 1998), 418.

239   **"There is not in either house:** *Diaries*, January 5, 1819.

239   **After meeting a man:** Ibid., April 27, 1819.

241   **On January 21 Louisa went:** Judith S. Graham, Beth Luey, Margaret Hogan, and James C. Taylor, eds., *Diary and Autobiographical Writings of Louisa Catherine Adams* (Boston: Belknap, 2013), 459.

242   **In November, he had instructed:** JQA to Richard Rush and Albert Gallatin, November 2, 1818, in *Writings*.

242   **"the right to board vessels:** *Diaries*, April 29, 1819.

242   **"the mass of coloured people:** Ibid., April 30, 1819.

243   **If but one man could arise:** Ibid., February 11, 1820.

244   **slavery "taints the very sources:** Ibid., March 3, 1820.

245   **If acquiesced in, it would change:** Ibid., November 29, 1820.

CHAPTER 18: SHE GOES NOT ABROAD IN SEARCH OF MONSTERS TO DESTROY (1820–1822)

247   **construction of two new government buildings:** "Buildings of the Department of State," Office of the Historian, US Department of State, https://history.state.gov/departmenthistory/buildings/section24.

248   **Adams tried to calibrate:** *The Diaries of John Quincy Adams* (hereafter *Diaries*), December 3, 1819, Adams Papers, Massachusetts Historical Society, Boston, http://www.masshist.org/jqadiaries/php.

248 **"So seducing is the passion:** Stanislaus Murray Hamilton, ed., *The Writings of James Monroe* (New York: G. Putnam's Sons, 1898–1903), vol. 6, May 26, 1820.

249 **"Among all the great characters:** Judith S. Graham, Beth Luey, Margaret Hogan, and James C. Taylor, eds., *Diary and Autobiographical Writings of Louisa Catherine Adams* (Boston: Belknap, 2013), vol. 2, 725.

249 **"the same romantic enthusiastic:** Ibid., vol. 2, 577.

249 **"I assure you,":** Ibid., vol. 2, 426.

250 **"This woman is made up:** Ibid., vol. 2, 482.

250 **"If you watch his character,":** Ibid., vol. 2, 488.

250 **"He is always domineering:** Ibid., vol. 2, 556.

251 **"Since God in his wisdom:** Ibid., vol. 2, 541.

251 **"one of the most capricious women:** *Diary of Charles Francis Adams*, vol. 1, May 20, 1824, Adams Papers, Massachusetts Historical Society, Boston.

252 **"The blast of mediocrity,":** *Diaries*, September 30, 1821.

252 **"The operations of my mind:** Ibid., December 25, 1820.

253 **material "will never be fit:** Ibid., end of May, 1820 ("Day").

253 **Adams' report on weights and measures:** Ibid., August 25, 1820ff.

253 **"Thank God we hear:** Graham et al., *Diary and Autobiographical Writings*, vol. 2, 540.

254 **"stimulated by the passion:** John Quincy Adams, *The Report of the Secretary of State upon Weights and Measures* (Washington, DC: Gales & Seaton, 1821), 30.

254 **The "universal uniformity":** Ibid., 59.

254 **"Nature," he noted:** Ibid., 62.

256 **He called for America to support:** Samuel Flagg Bemis, *John Quincy Adams and the Foundations of American Foreign Policy* (New York: Norton, 1949), 356.

256 **"Seventeen times has the sun:** John Quincy Adams, "An Oration, Pronounced July 4, 1793, at the Request of the Inhabitants of the Town of Boston."

257 **"to rekindle no angry passion:** John Quincy Adams, "An Address, Delivered at the Request of the Committee of Arrangements for Celebrating the Anniversary of Independence, at the City of Washington on the Fourth of July 1821."

257 **"from one end to another:** Bemis, *John Quincy Adams*, 357.

259 **was fond of citing Adams' dictum:** John Lewis Gaddis, *George F. Kennan: An American Life* (New York: Penguin, 2011).

259 **"realism" is too chastened:** See Henry Kissinger, *Diplomacy* (New York: Simon & Schuster, 1994).

259   **he insisted later to one of his correspondents:** John Quincy Adams (hereafter JQA) to Robert Walsh, July 10, 1821, in Worthington Chauncey Ford, ed., *Writings of John Quincy Adams* (hereafter *Writings*) (New York: Macmillan, 1913).

260   **"Gen. Jackson has rendered:** *Diaries*, January 2, 1822.

260   **"there was no spirit of freedom:** JQA to Richard C. Anderson, May 27, 1823, in *Writings*.

262   **"There the boundary is marked:** *Diaries*, January 27, 1821.

262   **He is of all the foreign Ministers:** Ibid., June 24, 1823.

262   **"more commanding than attractive:** Bemis, *John Quincy Adams*, 271.

CHAPTER 19: IF HE WISHES FOR PEACE WITH ME, HE MUST HOLD OUT THE WHITE FLAG (1822–1823)

263   **"The principle of my life:** *The Diaries of John Quincy Adams* (hereafter *Diaries*), May 2, 1820, Adams Papers, Massachusetts Historical Society, Boston, http://www.masshist.org/jqadiaries/php.

264   **"Crawford has been a worm:** Ibid., March 3, 1821.

264   **The second decade of the nineteenth century witnessed:** Carol Sue Humphrey, *The Press of the Young Republic, 1783–1833* (Westport, CT: Greenwood, 1996).

264   **"outrageously partisan,":** David Paul Nord, *Communities of Journalism: A History of American Newspapers and Their Readers* (Urbana: University of Illinois Press, 2001).

265   **"I will have no stipendiary editors:** *Diaries*, February 25, 1821.

265   **"would be beset:** Ibid., July 28, 1822.

266   **Soon the *Franklin Gazette* of Philadelphia:** Charles M. Wiltse, *John C. Calhoun, Nationalist 1782–1828* (Indianapolis: Bobbs-Merrill, 1944–1951), vol. 1, 191.

266   **Unlike Adams, Clay had built up:** Robert Remini, *Henry Clay: Statesman for the Union* (New York: Norton, 1991), 244.

266   **"an eloquent man:** *Diaries*, March 9, 1821.

266   **"It is in our power,":** Remini, *Henry Clay*, 174.

267   **Adams held virtually identical views:** William Earl Weeks, *John Quincy Adams and American Global Empire* (Lexington: University of Kentucky Press, 1992), 93–94.

267   **he appears to have carried out an audacious plan:** See Samuel Flagg Bemis, *John Quincy Adams and the Foundations of American Foreign Policy* (New York: Norton, 1949), 498–509, for an extensive discussion of the Russell affair.

268   "one of the artifices of Clay: Remini, *Henry Clay*, 216.

268   Adams immediately winkled: *Diaries*, April 25–30, 1822.

268   Adams persuaded his friend Walsh: Ibid., May 12 and 23, 1822.

269   "he must hold out: John Quincy Adams (hereafter JQA) to Peter Paul Frances DeGrand, July 5, 1822, in Worthington Chauncey Ford, ed., *Writings of John Quincy Adams* (hereafter *Writings*) (New York: Macmillan, 1913).

269   a pamphlet—in fact, a book: John Quincy Adams, *The Duplicate Letters, the Fisheries and the Mississippi: Documents Relating to the Transactions at Ghent* (Washington, DC: Davis and Force, 1822).

269   In the months to come: *Diaries*, November 16, 1822.

269   "I regard Mr. Russell: Bemis, *John Quincy Adams*, 508.

269   "an affair of more than life: JQA to LCA, October 7, 1822, in *Writings*.

270   Ernest May, one of the great scholars: Ernest R. May, *The Making of the Monroe Doctrine* (Cambridge, MA: Belknap, 1975), 132–189.

270   "I have my own errors: *Diaries*, July 11, 1822.

270   Hopkinson accused Adams: Joseph Hopkinson to LCA, reprinted in *Diaries*, between JQA entries in January 1823, vol. 6, 130.

270   a letter he titled "The Macbeth Policy.": "The Macbeth Policy," in *Writings*, vol. 7, 356–362.

271   One day, as an experiment: *Diaries*, June 8 to July 8, 1823.

272   The answer was no: JQA to John Adams II, May 29, 1823, in Adams Papers Microfilm (hereafter APM), Massachusetts Historical Society, Boston.

272   He had written to other prominent alumni: JQA to John Davis, September 15, 1823, in APM.

272   The visit brought back ancient memories: *Diaries*, September 1, 1823.

CHAPTER 20: THE MOST IMPORTANT PAPER THAT EVER WENT FROM MY HANDS (1822–1823)

275   Adams wanted Cuba: *The Diaries of John Quincy Adams* (hereafter *Diaries*), September 27 and 30, 1822, Adams Papers, Massachusetts Historical Society, Boston, http://www.masshist.org/jqadiaries/php.

276   America, too, was inflamed: Ernest R. May, *The Making of the Monroe Doctrine* (Cambridge, MA: Belknap, 1975), 9.

276   Adams had also received a letter: *Diaries*, August 15, 1823.

276   "Calhoun descanted upon: Ibid.

277   Both London and Washington: Dexter Perkins, *The Monroe Doctrine, 1823–26* (Cambridge, MA: Harvard University Press, 1932), 7–8.

277   **the United States "should contest:** *Diaries,* July 17, 1823.

277   **In instructions to Richard Rush:** John Quincy Adams (hereafter JQA) to Richard Rush, July 22, 1823, in Adams Papers Microfilm (APM), Massachusetts Historical Society, Boston. All letters cited in this chapter are from APM unless otherwise indicated.

277   **The most disquieting event:** Perkins, *Monroe Doctrine,* 109ff.

278   **The Spanish royalists still hungered:** May, *The Making of the Monroe Doctrine,* 104–108.

279   **Adams returned to Washington:** Ibid., 3–8, and Rush to JQA, October 2, 1823.

280   **"the question presented:** Thomas Jefferson to James Monroe, October 23, 1823, in Stanislaus Murray Hamilton, ed., *Writings of James Monroe* (New York: G. Putnam's Sons, 1898–1903), vol. 6.

283   **Monroe adopted Adams' positions:** James Monroe, "Seventh Annual Message (Monroe Doctrine)," December 2, 1823, http://millercenter.org /president/speeches/speech-3604.

285   **argued that it was Monroe:** Dexter Perkins, *The Monroe Doctrine 1823– 26* (Cambridge, MA: Harvard University Press, 1932), 100–103.

286   **Kissinger once wrote:** Henry Kissinger, *Diplomacy* (New York: Simon & Schuster, 1994).

CHAPTER 21: WHO CAN HOLD A FIRE IN HIS HAND BY THINKING ON THE FROSTY CAUCASUS? (1823–1824)

287   **The America of 1824 was recognizably:** Ernest R. May, *The Making of the Monroe Doctrine* (Cambridge, MA: Belknap, 1975), 174.

288   **For all these reasons, the election of 1824:** See ibid., 132–189.

288   **not a single instance:** *The Diaries of John Quincy Adams* (hereafter *Diaries*), February 5, 1824, Adams Papers, Massachusetts Historical Society, Boston, http://www.masshist.org/jqadiaries/php.

288   **"Let the people:** Robert Remini, *Andrew Jackson,* vol. 2: *The Course of American Freedom, 1822–32* (Baltimore: Johns Hopkins University Press, 1998), 38.

289   **Newspapers wrote lavish profiles:** Ibid., 75–77.

289   **"On the subject:** Andrew Jackson to James Tallmadge, March 12, 1824, in John Spencer Bassett, ed., *Correspondence of Andrew Jackson,* vol. 3: 1820–1828 (Washington, DC: Carnegie Institute of Washington, 1926– 1935).

289   **"Nothing but the virtue:** Jackson to Andrew J. Donelson, February 12, 1824, in Bassett, *Correspondence.*

289 **"It is now a contest:** Jackson to Brigadier General John Coffee, February 15, 1824, in Bassett, *Correspondence.*

289 **He authorized John Eaton:** John Eaton to Jackson, April 4, 1824, in Bassett, *Correspondence.*

290 **"I am told,":** Jackson to Major General George Martin, January 2, 1824, in Bassett, *Correspondence.*

290 **Several months later, a friend would ask:** *Diaries*, March 11, 1824.

290 **Louisa sent out five hundred:** Louisa describes the preparations and the party itself in her diary. Judith S. Graham, Beth Luey, Margaret Hogan, and James C. Taylor, eds., *Diary and Autobiographical Writings of Louisa Catherine Adams* (Boston: Belknap, 2013), vol. 2, 684–688.

291 **"break the course:** Joseph Pleasants to John Quincy Adams (hereafter JQA), June 19, 1824, in Adams Papers Microfilm (APM), Massachusetts Historical Society, Boston. All letters cited in this chapter are from APM unless otherwise indicated.

291 **"for your justification.":** JQA to Pleasants, June (no date given).

292 **Newspaper editors allied:** Daniel Walker Howe, *What Hath God Wrought? The Transformation of America, 1815–48* (Oxford: Oxford University Press, 2009), 206.

292 **he turned the man away with "an epithet:** *Diaries*, January 19, 1824.

293 **Clay wrote exultantly:** Henry Clay to Francis Brooke, May 28, 1824, in James F. Hopkins, Mary W. M. Hargreaves, et al., eds., *The Papers of Henry Clay* (Lexington: University of Kentucky Press, 1959).

293 **The stroke had left Crawford:** Robert Remini, *Henry Clay: Statesman for the Union* (New York: Norton, 1991), 237.

293 **One ally, Josiah Johnson, wrote:** Ibid., 241.

293 **he recorded at the end of March:** *Diaries,* end of March ("Day").

293 **Adams asked William Plumer Jr.:** Ibid., April 5, 1824.

294 **"there was no mission:** Ibid., April 17, 1824.

294 **Were it possible to look:** Ibid., May 8, 1824.

295 **a treaty "for the effectual abolition:** Samuel Flagg Bemis, *John Quincy Adams and the Foundations of American Foreign Policy* (New York: Norton, 1949), 427.

296 **When it came to a vote:** Bemis ably recounts this narrative in ibid., 428–435.

297 **Negotiations with Great Britain proved:** Ibid., 520–527.

298 **The great remaining prize was New York:** Remini, *Henry Clay*, 244.

298 **Weed delightedly recorded:** Harriet A. Weed and Thurlow Weed Barnes, eds., *Life of Thurlow Weed Including His Autobiography and a Memoir* (Boston: Houghton and Mifflin, 1884), 115.

298 **"His sight is so dim:** *Diaries,* September 6, 1824.

299 **General Henry Dearborn:** Ibid., September 8, 1824.

CHAPTER 22: I TREAD ON COALS (1824–1825)

301 **a cheerful rapscallion:** As he describes himself in *Life of Thurlow Weed Including His Autobiography and a Memoir,* ed. Harriet A. Weed and Thurlow Weed Barnes (Boston: Houghton and Mifflin, 1884).

301 **"the placatory professional:** Richard Hofstadter, *The Idea of a Party System: The Rise of Legitimate Opposition in the United States, 1780–1840* (Berkeley: University of California Press, 1969), 216.

301 **One of those counterplots:** Weed tells this tale with delightful relish, and no doubt some hyperbole in *Life of Thurlow Weed,* 128–157. A more neutral account is available in Robert Remini, *Henry Clay: Statesman for the Union* (New York: Norton, 1991), 244–248.

303 **Adams began fielding a flood of visitors:** *The Diaries of John Quincy Adams* (hereafter *Diaries*), December 10–15, 1824, Adams Papers, Massachusetts Historical Society, Boston, http://www.masshist.org/jqadiaries /php.

304 **"harbored no hostility:** Ibid., December 17, 1824.

305 **He sounded Adams out:** Ibid., December 22, 1824.

305 **Adams paid a visit and said:** Ibid., January 2, 1825.

305 **"*Incendo super ignes*,":** Ibid., December 23, 1824.

305 **He wrote a letter to a confidante:** Henry Clay to Francis Blair, January 8, in James F. Hopkins, Mary W. M. Hargreaves, et al., eds., *The Papers of Henry Clay* (Lexington: University of Kentucky Press, 1959).

305 **Jackson did pay a visit:** Remini, *Henry Clay,* 255.

306 **"free & confidential visit":** Ibid., 257.

306 **"He wished me," Adams recorded:** *Diaries,* January 9, 1825.

306 **Adams had not received:** Robert Remini, *Andrew Jackson,* vol. 2: *The Course of American Freedom, 1822–1832* (Baltimore: Johns Hopkins University Press, 1998), 89.

307 **Johnson of Kentucky confided to Adams:** *Diaries,* January 22, 1825.

307 **Senator Thomas Benton of Missouri:** Thomas Hart Benton, *Thirty Years' View* (New York: D. Appleton, 1854–1856), 47.

307 **"almost universal" currency:** *Diaries,* January 25, 1825.

307 **Word of the agreement:** *Diaries,* January 23 and February 4, 1825.

308 **By now, news of the "corrupt bargain":** Samuel Flagg Bemis, *John Quincy Adams and the Union* (New York: Alfred A. Knopf, 1956), 57, and *Diaries,* February 3 and 4, 1825.

308   **the *National Intelligencer* reprinted the letter:** *National Intelligencer* (Washington, DC), February 4, 1825, and Robert Remini, *The Election of Andrew Jackson* (New York: J. B. Lippincott, 1963), 20–22.

308   **"The knaves cannot comprehend:** Henry Clay to Francis Blair, in *Papers of Henry Clay.*

308   **"He spoke to me with:** *Diaries,* January 29, 1825.

308   **Adams held long conversations:** Ibid., January 31, 1825.

308   **"I think a *little* better:** Daniel Webster to Jeremiah Mason, May 9, 1824, in Charles M. Wiltse and Harold D. Moser, eds., *The Papers of Daniel Webster* (Hanover, NH: University Press of New England, 1974–1989), vol. 1.

309   **Webster now read to Adams:** *Diaries,* February 3, 1825.

309   **By Wednesday, February 9:** *National Intelligencer,* February 8, 1825.

309   **Each state had its own:** *National Intelligencer,* February 10, 1825.

310   **the patroon was waylaid:** Remini, *Henry Clay,* 263.

310   **he had plunged into a state:** This is according to the colorful account in John Clement Fitzpatrick, ed., *The Autobiography of Martin van Buren* (New York: Da Capo, 1973), 150–152.

310   **"The tellers of the votes:** *National Intelligencer,* February 10.

311   **"May the blessing of God:** *Diaries,* February 9, 1825.

311   **Jackson said graciously:** John Meacham, *American Lion: Andrew Jackson in the White House* (New York: Random House, 2009), 45.

CHAPTER 23: THE SPIRIT OF IMPROVEMENT (1825)

315   **On the late morning of March 4:** *National Journal* (Washington, DC), March 4, 1825, and *The Diaries of John Quincy Adams* (hereafter *Diaries*), March 4, 1825, Adams Papers, Massachusetts Historical Society, Boston, http://www.masshist.org/jqadiaries/php.

315   **"Of the two great political parties:** "Inaugural Address of John Quincy Adams," March 4, 1825, http://avalon.law.yale.edu/19th_century/qadams.asp.

316   **Justice Joseph Story would later write:** William Wetmore Story, ed., *Life and Letters of Joseph Story* (Boston: Little, Brown, 1851), 484–485.

316   **"speculative scruple.":** Thomas Hart Benton, *Thirty Years' View* (New York: D. Appleton, 1854–1856), 54–55.

317   **Andrew Jackson himself made sure:** Robert Remini, *The Election of Andrew Jackson* (Philadelphia: J. B. Lippincott, 1963), 28–29.

317   **He encouraged Kremer:** Andrew Jackson to George Kremer, March 8, 1825, in John Spencer Bassett, ed., *Correspondence of Andrew Jackson,* vol. 3: 1820–1828 (Washington, DC: Carnegie Institute of Washington, 1926–1935).

317 **"a noisy and clamorous reviler:** *Diaries*, May 13, 1825.

318 **The postmaster general, John McLean:** Mary Hargreaves, *The Presidency of John Quincy Adams* (Lawrence: University of Kansas Press, 1985), 51.

318 **"intended to neglect:** Robert Remini, *Henry Clay: Statesman for the Union* (New York: Norton, 1991), 316.

318 **"was able, enlightened, patriotic:** Harriet A. Weed and Thurlow Weed Barnes, eds., *Life of Thurlow Weed Including His Autobiography and a Memoir* (Boston: Houghton and Mifflin, 1884), 179–181.

319 **William McIntosh was:** The story is extensively recounted in Michael D. Green, *The Politics of Indian Removal: Creek Government and Society in Crisis* (Lincoln: University of Nebraska Press, 1982).

320 **He told Adams that Governor Troup:** *Diaries*, May 15, 1825.

320 **"to die without resistance:** Green, *The Politics of Indian Removal*, 111.

320 **"dark and settled gloom":** *Diaries*, November 26, 1825.

321 **"He believed they were destined:** Ibid., December 22, 1825.

322 **"the blessing of health:** James Madison, "First Annual Message (November 29, 1809)," http://millercenter.org/president/madison/speeches/speech-3608.

322 **Monroe had celebrated:** James Monroe, "First Annual Message (December 2, 1817)," http://millercenter.org/president/monroe/speeches/speech-3594.

323 **On November 23 his cabinet officers listened:** *Diaries*, November 23, 25, 26, 28, 1825.

323 **He began by noting:** John Quincy Adams, "First Annual Message (December 6, 1825," http://millercenter.org/president/jqadams/speeches/speech-3514.

326 **"would have afforded high wages:** George Dangerfield, *The Era of Good Feelings* (London: Methuen, 1953), 351.

326 **"now look to a single and splendid:** Ibid., 349.

327 **a record of improvement that would not be reached:** Hargreaves makes the case that Adams enjoyed substantial success on internal improvements; see Hargreaves, *Presidency*, 173–180.

CHAPTER 24: AN ARROW TO THE HEART (1825–1827)

329 **On one not atypical day:** *The Diaries of John Quincy Adams* (hereafter *Diaries*), November 22, 1826, Adams Papers, Massachusetts Historical Society, Boston, http://www.masshist.org/jqadiaries/php.

330 **"our worthy little master,":** Richard Rush to Henry Clay, December 18, 1827, in James F. Hopkins, Mary W. M. Hargreaves, et al., eds., *The*

Papers of Henry Clay, vol. 4 (Lexington: University of Kentucky Press, 1959).

330 **"There is entire coincidence:** Henry Clay to the Honorable J. Sloane, April 7, 1825, in Hopkins et al., *Papers of Henry Clay.*

330 **"set a precedent for being claimed:** *Diaries*, May 24, 1825.

330 **"the organ of amativeness":** Ibid., June 9, 1825.

331 **"a fermentation of the blood:** Ibid., July 28, 1825.

331 **Adams' most dangerous moment in office:** Ibid., June 13, 1825.

331 **"A thing of rubbish:** Louisa Catherine Adams (hereafter LCA) to Charles Francis Adams (hereafter CFA), April 25, 1825, in Adams Papers Microfilm (APM), Massachusetts Historical Society, Boston. All letters cited in this chapter are from APM unless otherwise indicated.

331 **"There is something in this great:** LCA to George Washington Adams (hereafter GWA), November 6, 1825.

332 **"unpleasant to myself:** LCA to GWA, March 6, 1826.

332 **one contrasted a mother's hour:** LCA to GWA, undated (listed at March or April 1826).

332 **"a mind deeply diseased:** LCA to Thos Hellen, May 17, 1827.

333 **"It is a painful thing to state:** LCA to CFA, August 19, 1827.

333 **"For thee the rosy wreath:** LCA to GWA, March 12, 1825.

334 **Lord Sharply was a man:** Louisa Catherine Adams, *The Metropolitan Kaleidoscope* (unpublished manuscript).

335 **"My own feelings incline:** *Diary of Charles Francis Adams*, vol. 2, August 3, 1827, Adams Papers, Massachusetts Historical Society, Boston, http://www.masshist.org/publications/apde2/view?id=ADMS-13-02-02-0003-0008-0003.

335 **a man coming from Baltimore told Adams:** *Diaries*, July 9, 1826.

335 **"the time, the manner, the coincidence:** Ibid., July 9, 1826.

336 **"That moment to me was inexpressibly:** Ibid., July 13, 1826.

336 **"the tumult of the world:** Ibid., September 2, 1826.

337 **"that you should waste your property:** LCA to John Quincy Adams (hereafter JQA), July 18, 1826.

337 **Adams agreed to strike:** *Diaries*, November 30, 1826.

337 **"you will have no time:** JQA to GWA, December 31, 1826.

338 **"indolence and self-delusion.":** Stated by JQA in letter to GWA, June 3, 1827.

338 **"I have been *horror-struck*:** JQA to GWA, November 12, 1827.

338 **"Much conversation with George:** *Diaries of Charles Francis Adams*, August 18, September 2, December 22, 1827.

338 **at John Adams' death he reflected:** Ibid., July 9, 1826.

338   **"a check upon my vagaries:** Ibid., January 31, 1827.

338   **"Ever since my engagement:** Ibid., April 24, 1827.

339   **"Her feelings are constantly carrying:** Ibid., October 13, 1827.

339   **"My father has unfortunately:** Ibid., July 4, 1826.

339   **"He makes enemies:** Ibid., September 6, 1824.

339   **Adams spent countless hours writing:** JQA to CFA, November 7, 1827, to July 20, 1828.

340   **"In truth," he wrote:** CFA to JQA, February 19, 1828.

CHAPTER 25: A GREAT MAN IN THE WRONG PLACE AT THE WRONG TIME (1825–1826)

342   **Adams worried that the South Americans would embroil:** The South American background is ably described in Mary Hargreaves, *The Presidency of John Quincy Adams* (Lawrence: University of Kansas Press, 1985), 144–146.

343   **The president hoped the Russian:** *The Diaries of John Quincy Adams*, May 19, 1825, Adams Papers, Massachusetts Historical Society, Boston, http://www.masshist.org/jqadiaries/php.

343   **He urged "suspension:** Hargreaves, *Presidency*, 154–155.

344   **The president and his secretary of state continued:** Ibid., 143.

345   **"captivated all young:** Thomas Hart Benton, *Thirty Years' View* (New York: D. Appleton, 1854–1856), 65.

345   **"the first tangible point:** John Clement Fitzpatrick, ed., *The Autobiography of Martin Van Buren* (New York: Da Capo, 1973), 199.

345   **"the most dangerous stab:** Charles M. Wiltse, *John C. Calhoun*, vol. 1: *Nationalist, 1782–1828* (Indianapolis: Bobbs-Merrill, 1944–1951), 324.

346   **both understood that by trying:** *Autobiography of Martin Van Buren*, 200.

346   **the Foreign Relations Committee issued a report:** Wiltse, *John C. Calhoun*, vol. 1, 325.

346   **The black republic was "a firebrand:** Benton, *Thirty Years' View*, 66.

347   **When it finally came time:** Hargreaves, *Presidency*, 151.

347   **Adams chose this opportunity to fully clarify:** John Quincy Adams, "Special Message, March 15, 1826," http://www.presidency.ucsb.edu/ws/index.php?pid=66632.

349   **He rambled across a range:** March 30, 1826, in *Register of Debates*, Senate, 19th Congress, 1st Session.

349   **Clay lost his cool completely:** Daniel Walker Howe, *The Political Culture of the American Whigs* (Chicago: University of Chicago Press, 1979), 126.

350   **being careful, he later claimed:** *Autobiography of Martin Van Buren,* 204.

350   **"the divided state of our Senate:** Hargreaves, *Presidency,* 153.

350   **He reiterated Adams' bottom-line positions:** Ibid., 156.

351   **"felt an anxious desire":** Ibid., 119.

351   **"An issue has been fairly:** Wiltse, *John C. Calhoun,* vol. 1, 337.

CHAPTER 26: CULTIVATING HIS GARDEN (1826–1827)

353   **On May 12, 1827, Van Buren stopped by:** *The Diaries of John Quincy Adams* (hereafter *Diaries*), May 12, 1827, Adams Papers, Massachusetts Historical Society, Boston, http://www.masshist.org/jqadiaries/php.

354   **"We must always have party:** Charles M. Wiltse, *John C. Calhoun,* vol. 1: *Nationalist, 1782–1828* (Indianapolis: Bobbs-Merrill, 1944–1951), 348.

354   **The *Enquirer* endorsed Jackson:** Robert Remini, *The Election of Andrew Jackson* (Philadelphia: J. B. Lippincott, 1963), 58.

354   **"falsehoods and calumny:** Ibid., 63.

355   **Major Alan Campbell wrote from Louisville:** Alan Campbell to Andrew Jackson, February 4, 1827, in John Spencer Bassett, ed., *Correspondence of Andrew Jackson,* vol. 3: 1820–1828 (Washington, DC: Carnegie Institute of Washington, 1926–1935).

355   **The election of 1828 saw the rise:** See Lynn Parsons, *The Birth of Modern Politics: Andrew Jackson, John Quincy Adams, and the Election of 1828* (New York: Oxford University Press, 2009).

355   **Jackson promised to furnish Lee:** Andrew Jackson to Henry Lee, December 25, 1826, in Bassett, *Correspondence.*

355   **Jackson and Calhoun forces loaned:** Jackson to Duff Green, May 20, 1826, in Bassett, *Correspondence.*

355   **"bargain, intrigue and management":** See, for example, the March 28, 1826, issue of the *United States Telegraph* (Washington, DC, 1826–1837).

355   **The *Telegraph* was soon printing:** Robert Remini, *Andrew Jackson,* vol. 2: *The Course of American Freedom, 1822–1832* (Baltimore: Johns Hopkins University Press, 1998), 78.

356   **Duff Green wrote to Jackson:** Duff Green to Jackson, June 9, 1827, in Bassett, *Correspondence.*

356   **Jackson himself wrote to Buchanan:** Jackson to James Buchanan, July 15, 1827, in Bassett, *Correspondence.*

356   **"The tables are completely turned:** Henry Clay to Francis Brooke, August 14, 1827, in James F. Hopkins, Mary W. M. Hargreaves, et al., eds.,

The Papers of Henry Clay (Lexington: University of Kentucky Press, 1959).

356 **Adams would be the last president to stand fast:** Samuel Flagg Bemis, *John Quincy Adams and the Union* (New York: Alfred A. Knopf, 1956), 136.

356 **the president had billed to the American people:** Ibid., 133–134.

357 **In late March 1827, Daniel Webster wrote:** Daniel Webster to Clay, March 25, 1827, in Charles M. Wiltse and Harold D. Moser, eds., *The Papers of Daniel Webster, Correspondence* (Hanover, NH: University Press of New England, 1974–1989), vol. 2.

357 **"prepare a series of pieces:** Clay to Webster, April 20, 1827, in Wiltse and Moser, *Papers of Daniel Webster*.

357 **"My belief is that Mr. Adams:** Clay to Francis Brooke, September 24, 1827, in Hopkins et al., *Papers of Henry Clay*.

357 **"& by the aid of friends:** Webster to Clay, March 25, 1827, in Wiltse and Moser, *Papers of Daniel Webster*.

357 **He wrote to William Gales:** Webster to Gales, June (no day specified), 1827, in Wiltse and Moser, *Papers of Daniel Webster*.

358 **The two appear to have lived together:** Jon Meacham, *American Lion: Andrew Jackson in the White House* (New York: Random House, 2009), 22.

358 **"General Jackson's mother:** Robert Remini, *Henry Clay: Statesman for the Union* (New York: Norton, 1991), 325.

358 **"another & perhaps a better mode:** Clay to Webster, August 19, 1827, in Wiltse and Moser, *Papers of Daniel Webster*.

358 **Webster reported from New York:** Webster to Edward Everett, November 18, 1827, in Wiltse and Moser, *Papers of Daniel Webster*.

358 **"I hope your office:** Webster to Henry Clay, November 5, 1827, in Wiltse and Moser, *Papers of Daniel Webster*.

358 **His very precision and stiffness:** Woodrow Wilson, *A History of the American People* (New York: Harper & Brothers, 1918), vol. 3, 270.

359 **"I returned their salutation:** *Diaries*, October 13, 1827.

359 **"grateful for the kind:** Ibid., October 16, 1827.

359 **"If he would only lend himself:** Louisa Catherine Adams to Charles Francis Adams, October 15, 1827, in Adams Papers Microfilm (APM), Massachusetts Historical Society, Boston.

360 **He explained to Mr. Bailey:** *Diaries*, March 7, 1828.

360 **He brought home blossoms:** Ibid., March 27, 1827, and after.

360 **the first act of conservation:** Bemis, *John Quincy Adams and the Union*, 123.

360   "The catalpa trees are in full: *Diaries*, June 13, 1827.

361   "The opposition party," wrote John Tyler: Remini, *Election of Andrew Jackson*, 168.

361   the contract for the printing of the laws: Wiltse, *Calhoun*, vol. 1, 360.

361   Congressmen stoutly defended: *Diaries*, February 14, 1828.

362   As Adams noted in his diary: Ibid., February 14, 1828.

362   "He is incompetent: Ibid., December 17, 1827.

CHAPTER 27: THE SUN OF MY POLITICAL CAREER SETS IN DEEPEST GLOOM (1828–1829)

363   On April 15, 1828, Adams dispatched: *The Diaries of John Quincy Adams* (hereafter *Diaries*), April 15, 1828, Adams Papers, Massachusetts Historical Society, Boston, http://www.masshist.org/jqadiaries/php.

363   President Adams' inclination: Mary Hargreaves, *The Presidency of John Quincy Adams* (Lawrence: University of Kansas Press, 1985), 210.

364   "in some measure forfeit: Louisa Catherine Adams (hereafter LCA) to Charles Francis Adams (hereafter CFA), April 17, 1828, in Adams Papers Microfilm (APM), Massachusetts Historical Society, Boston. All letters cited in this chapter are from APM unless otherwise indicated.

364   the committee issued a report: Hargreaves, *Presidency*, 211.

364   "disastrous occurrence: *Diaries*, April 24, 1828.

365   save themselves "from the wreck.": Ibid., May 1, 1828.

365   Adams felt as if he were fighting: Ibid., March 28, 1828.

365   "are united by a spirit: John Quincy Adams (hereafter JQA) to CFA, May 29, 1828.

365   McLean finally fired the man: Hargreaves, *Presidency*, 52.

366   "The conduct of Mr. McLean: *Diaries*, June 3, 1828.

366   He and Adams planned to raise duties: Robert Remini, *Henry Clay: Statesman for the Union* (New York: Norton, 1991), 330.

367   The politics of the protective tariff: Hargreaves, *Presidency*, 192.

367   The delegates crafted a series of resolutions: Ibid., 194.

367   "defeat or oppression.": Charles M. Wiltse, *John C. Calhoun*, vol. 1: *Nationalist, 1782–1828* (Indianapolis: Bobbs-Merrill, 1944–1951), 357.

367   "judicious tariff.": Andrew Jackson to Major Hamilton (Alexander Hamilton Jr.), June 29, 1828, in John Spencer Bassett, ed., *Correspondence of Andrew Jackson*, vol. 3: *1820–1828* (Washington, DC: Carnegie Institute of Washington, 1926–1935).

368   The bill's features were so extravagant: Robert Remini, *The Election of Andrew Jackson* (Philadelphia: J. B. Lippincott, 1963), 171–173.

368   **"we had put the duties:** Ibid., 174–175.

368   **"Can we go the hemp:** Daniel Webster to Joseph Sprague, April 13, 1828, in Charles M. Wiltse and Harold D. Moser, eds., *The Papers of Daniel Webster* (Hanover, NH: University Press of New England, 1974–1989).

368   **"we determined to put such ingredients:** Wiltse, *Calhoun*, vol. 1, 369.

368   **"The Jackson party is playing:** Henry Clay to John J. Crittenden, February 14, 1828, in James F. Hopkins, Mary W. M. Hargreaves, et al., eds., *The Papers of Henry Clay* (Lexington: University of Kentucky Press, 1959).

369   **a verbatim copy of a letter from Jackson:** *National Journal*, March 7, 1828.

369   **"still more ferocious than barbarous:** *Diaries*, March 17, 1828.

369   **John Binns of the *Democratic Press*:** Remini, *Election of Andrew Jackson*, 154–156.

370   **When he heard that Navy Secretary Samuel Southard:** Jackson to Samuel Houston, December 15, 1826, in Bassett, *Correspondence*.

370   **"I will unrobe his hypocrisy:** Jackson to Hugh L. White, February 7, 1827, in Bassett, *Correspondence*.

370   **"There let your friends:** John H. Eaton to Jackson, January 21, 1828, in Bassett, *Correspondence*.

370   **"most earnest wish that for the present:** Arthur P. Hayne to Jackson, September 20, 1828, in Bassett, *Correspondence*.

370   **"He is certainly,":** Jackson to Sam Houston, December 15, 1826, in Bassett, *Correspondence*.

370   **"It appears to me that he is destined:** William Crawford to Clay, February 4, 1828, in Hopkins et al., *Papers of Henry Clay*.

370   **Clay responded equably:** Clay to Crawford, February 18, 1828, in Hopkins et al., *Papers of Henry Clay*.

370   **"I had fear of Mr. Adams:** Clay to Francis Blair, March 1, 1828, in Hopkins et al., *Papers of Henry Clay*.

371   **"It struck the eye and fancy:** *Diaries*, July 4, 1828.

372   **"I cannot bear the loneliness:** LCA to CFA, July 16, 1828.

372   **She wrote a ballad:** LCA to George Washington Adams, July 1, 1828.

372   **Charles reached Washington to find:** CFA to Abigail Brooks Adams, September 9, 1828.

372   **The president and Rush, he thought:** Webster to Nathaniel Williams, November 5, 1828, in Wiltse and Moser, *Papers of Daniel Webster*.

373   **"The sun of my political career:** *Diaries*, December 3, 1828.

373   **Jefferson must have seen a letter Adams had written:** In *Documents Relating to New England Federalism, 1800–1815* (Boston: Little Brown,

1905), Henry Adams prints Jefferson's letter to Giles, Giles' letter to the *Richmond Enquirer,* and Adams' response in the *National Intelligencer,* 21–36.

374   **"the whole body of the Federalists:** CFA to JQA, November 20, 1828.

374   **He had heard, correctly:** *Diaries,* February 28, 1829.

CHAPTER 28: STAY THY HAND, GOD OF MERCY (1829–1831)

379   **whether in the history of any animal:** *The Diaries of John Quincy Adams* (hereafter *Diaries*), March 31, 1829, Adams Papers, Massachusetts Historical Society, Boston, http://www.masshist.org/jqadiaries/php.

380   **"to feed the cormorant appetite:** Ibid., March 14, 1829.

380   **"He complains of dejection:** Charles Francis Adams (hereafter CFA) to Louisa Catherine Adams (hereafter LCA), April 4, 1829, in Adams Papers Microfilm (APM), Massachusetts Historical Society, Boston. All letters cited in this chapter are from APM unless otherwise indicated.

380   **He had begun an affair with Eliza Dolph:** The sad affair is detailed in *Report of a Trial: Miles Farmer Versus Dr. David Humphreys Storer* (Boston, 1831), http://babel.hathitrust.org/cgi/pt?id=umn.31951002327754e;view=1up;seq=1.

381   **At three in the morning he approached:** Adams learned these details from a visitor on May 3 and recorded them in his journal.

382   **"Stay thy hand:** *Diaries,* May 2, 1829.

382   **"my beloved husband's sufferings:** Undated document in Louisa's diary.

382   **"You and all my children know:** John Quincy Adams (hereafter JQA) to CFA, March 22, 1829.

382   **Up in Boston, Charles went through:** *Diary of Charles Francis Adams* [microfilm], May 13, 1829, Adams Papers, Massachusetts Historical Society, Boston.

383   **he dutifully catalogued:** *Diaries,* June 13, 1829.

383   **"my most beloved friend.":** JQA to LCA, June 13, 1829.

384   **a quality of "quiet sadness":** *Diary of CFA,* June 18, 1829.

384   **"as usual imagined myself:** LCA to JQA, July 29, 1829.

384   **Adams devoted most of his attention:** *Diaries,* August 1–20, 1829.

384   **He was summarily replaced as president:** Ibid., November 7, 1830, in reference to summer 1829.

385   **He told her that on a stagecoach ride:** JQA to Abigail Brooks Adams, December 23, 1829.

385   **had been "unusually kind":** *Diary of CFA,* December 3, 1829.

385 **A few days later, Charles wrote his father:** CFA to JQA, December 9, 1829.

385 **His father, utterly delighted, wrote back:** JQA to CFA, December 16, 1829.

386 **he feared his son's "calculations:** JQA to JA2 October 4, 1829.

386 **"He is a singular man:** *Diary of CFA*, September 4, 1829.

387 **In that first message, Jackson:** Andrew Jackson, "First Annual Message," December 8, 1829, http://www.presidency.ucsb.edu/ws/?pid=29 471.

388 **"We agreed," Adams recorded:** *Diaries*, May 22, 1830.

389 **"It is now pregnant," he wrote:** Ibid., October 25, 1830.

389 **"My leisure is now imposed:** Ibid., June 26, 1830.

390 **Richardson himself came to Adams:** Ibid., September 18, 1830.

390 **"To say that I would accept:** Ibid., September 25, 1830.

390 **Louisa was so upset:** LCA to John Adams II, October 31, 1830.

390 **"has drifted me back:** *Diaries*, November 7, 1830.

391 **"Of the two systems," he wrote:** Ibid., January 13, 1831.

391 **"a memory so pandering:** Ibid., January 12, 1831.

391 **"Of my two orbs of vision:** JQA to CFA, February 11, 1831.

392 **"All my attempts at humor:** *Diaries*, March 8, 1831.

393 **"could not unite the people:** John Quincy Adams, *Dermot MacMorrogh, or the Conquest of Ireland: An Historical Tale of the Twelfth Century, in Four Cantos* (Boston: Carter, Hendee, 1832).

393 **"moral decay presaged:** Charles N. Edel, *Nation Builder: John Quincy Adams and the Grand Strategy of the Republic* (Cambridge, MA: Harvard University Press, 2014), 257.

CHAPTER 29: OUR UNION: IT MUST BE PRESERVED (1831–1833)

394 **"a discovery has been made:** John Quincy Adams (hereafter JQA) to General Peter Porter, April 4, 1830, in Adams Papers Microfilm (APM), Massachusetts Historical Society, Boston. All letters cited in this chapter are from APM unless otherwise indicated.

394 **"as an essential attribute:** *Exposition and Protest, Reported by the Special Committee of the House of Representatives, on the Tariff* (Columbia, SC: D. W. Sims, 1829).

394 **"Liberty and union:** Daniel Webster, "Liberty and Union, Now and Forever, One and Inseparable," January 26, 1830, http://www.usa-patriotism .com/speeches/dwebster1.htm.

395   **"it is the most important:** Samuel Flagg Bemis, *John Quincy Adams and the Union* (New York: Alfred A. Knopf, 1956), 227–228.

395   **"The union:** Ibid., 228.

395   **"Shall I speak:** *The Diaries of John Quincy Adams* (hereafter *Diaries*), June 7, 1831, Adams Papers, Massachusetts Historical Society, Boston, http://www.masshist.org/jqadiaries/php.

396   **he spoke his mind:** John Quincy Adams, "An Oration Addressed to the Town of Quincy, on the Fourth of July, 1831, the Fifty-Fifth Anniversary of the Independence of the United States of America," http://www.wallbuilders.com/libissuesarticles.asp?id=159424.

397   **Marshall stated he had been:** John Marshall to JQA, October 1, 1831.

397   **"with the single assurance:** JQA to John C. Calhoun, September 9, 1831.

397   **Calhoun described the doctrine:** Ross M. Lence, ed., *Union and Liberty: The Political Philosophy of John C. Calhoun* (Indianapolis: The Liberty Fund, 1992), 367–400.

398   **Seward recorded his impressions:** Frederick William Seward, ed., *Autobiography of William H. Seward, with a Memoir of His Life and Selections from His Letters from 1831 to 1846* (New York: D. Appleton, 1877), 88–89.

398   **The ritual of the calling:** *Diaries*, February 20, 1832.

399   **his maiden speech:** December 12, 1831, in Thomas Hart Benton, ed., *Abridgement of the Debates in Congress, 1789 to 1856* (New York: D. Appleton, 1857–1861).

399   **Adams explained that he felt:** *Diaries*, January 10, 1832.

400   **Adams observed with his usual:** Ibid., December 28, 1831.

400   **The tariff sought to appease:** Daniel Walker Howe, *What Hath God Wrought: The Transformation of America, 1815–48* (New York: Oxford University Press, 2007), 401.

401   **He reflected that the Federalist:** *Diaries*, March 2 and 3, 1832.

402   **He wrote to Charles:** JQA to Charles Francis Adams (hereafter CFA), March 17, 1832.

402   **the legislature voted to raise a force:** Howe, *What Hath God Wrought*, 404.

402   **In his annual message:** Andrew Jackson, "Fourth Annual Message to Congress," December 4, 1832, http://millercenter.org/president/jackson/speeches/speech-3637.

403   **Adams told a New York congressman:** *Diaries*, December 24, 1832.

403   **On December 10, Jackson issued:** "President Jackson's Proclamation Regarding Nullification, December 10, 1832," http://avalon.law.yale.edu/19th_century/jack01.asp.

403 **"contained much sound:** JQA to CFA, December 11, 1832.

404 **Adams responded with the first long speech:** February 5, 1833, in Benton, ed., *Abridgement of the Debates*.

404 **"thrown a firebrand:** Samuel Flagg Bemis, *John Quincy Adams and the Union* (New York: Alfred A. Knopf, 1956), 267.

405 **"I mourn over it:** JQA to CFA, March 26, 1833.

406 *Report of the Minority*: *Report of the Minority of the Committee of Manufactures Submitted to the House of Representatives February 28, 1833* (Boston: J. H. Eastburn, 1833).

407 **The minority report was widely read:** Bemis, *John Quincy Adams and the Union*, 271.

407 **"Mr. Clay and Mr. Calhoun:** JQA to CFA, March 26, 1833.

CHAPTER 30: THE ARK OF OUR GOD IS FALLING INTO THE HANDS OF THE PHILISTINES (1831–1835)

409 **Masonry had long enjoyed a reputation:** For background on Masonry, see Steven Bullock, *Revolutionary Brotherhood: Freemasonry and the Transformation of the American Social Order, 1730–1840* (Chapel Hill: University of North Carolina Press, 1996).

409 **Thanks to a conspiracy of silence:** See William L. Stone, *Letters on Masonry and Antimasonry Addressed to the Hon. John Quincy Adams* (New York: O. Halstead, 1832).

409 **By 1830, about one-eighth:** Bullock, *Revolutionary Brotherhood*, 284.

410 **"a distinct, and independent:** *Address to the People: Anti-Masonic State Convention, Holden at Boston, December 30, 1829* (Boston, circa 1829).

410 **"The dissolution of the Masonic:** *The Diaries of John Quincy Adams* (hereafter *Diaries*), June 10, 1831, Adams Papers, Massachusetts Historical Society, Boston, http://www.masshist.org/jqadiaries/php.

410 **"Are you familiar with:** John Quincy Adams (hereafter JQA) to Levi Lincoln, December 6, 1831, in Adams Papers Microfilm (APM), Massachusetts Historical Society, Boston. All letters cited in this chapter are from APM unless otherwise indicated.

410 **"Many agree with you:** Edward Ingersoll to JQA, October 17, 1831.

411 **"political Anti-Masonry:** John Quincy Adams, *Letters on the Masonic Institution* (Boston: Press of T. R. Marvin, 1847).

411 **a series of public letters with William Stone:** Stone, *Letters on Masonry and Antimasonry*.

412 **Adams did not at first send:** The letters were collected in *Letters on the Masonic Institution*.

412   "enthralled to see Mr. Adams: Richard Rush to JQA, September 15, 1832.

412   "The strength, the glory, the happiness: *Letters on the Masonic Institution*, 203.

413   "I can not suffer: JQA to the Massachusetts Antimasonic Convention, September 12, 1833.

413   Since none took a majority: Leonard L. Richards, *The Life and Times of Congressman John Quincy Adams* (New York: Oxford University Press, 1986), 49.

413   "and my public life: *Diaries*, December 14, 1833.

413   Several New England states: Daniel Walker Howe, *What Hath God Wrought: The Transformation of America, 1815–48* (New York: Oxford University Press, 2007), 383–384.

413   Adams had every reason: *Diaries*, March 27, 1834.

414   He was saved: Ibid., November 8, 1833, and JQA to Charles Francis Adams (hereafter CFA), November 9.

415   "I have never worn: JQA to Benjamin Hallet, December 16, 1833.

416   "If democracy is founded: JQA to George Bancroft, October 25, 1835.

416   In his veto message: "President Jackson's Veto Message Regarding the Bank of the United States; July 10, 1832," http://avalon.law.yale.edu /19th_century/ajveto01.asp.

416   he would suffocate it: Howe, *What Hath God Wrought*, 386–389.

417   "Every one of the 40 banks: JQA to John Bailey, December 17, 1833.

417   "assumed upon himself authority: Robert Remini, *Henry Clay: Statesman for the Union* (New York: Norton, 1991), 456.

417   Adams believed in: *Diaries*, March 29, 1834.

418   "My hopes are blasted: Ibid., July 22, 1834.

419   Adams received a visit from President Josiah Quincy: Robert Mc-Caughey, *Josiah Quincy, 1772–1864: The Last Federalist* (Cambridge, MA: Harvard University Press, 1974), 152–156.

419   "thought it much too severe: *Diaries*, August 8, 1834.

419   In the meanwhile the student uprising: Ibid., August 25 and 28, 1834, and JQA to Levi Lincoln, August 8 and 16, 1834.

420   "You have met with severe: JQA to John Adams II, July 26, 1834.

420   In the early fall of 1834: *Diaries*, October 19–23, 1834.

421   "join with your disconsolate husband: JQA to Louisa Catherine Adams, October 23, 1834.

421   Adams spent his first week: *Diaries*, October 28 to November 4, 1834.

421   Adams could count on: Ibid., May 2 to 16, 1835.

422   "I shall not," he confessed: JQA to Benjamin Waterhouse, January 8, 1835.

422 **Andrew Jackson's unprecedented assertion:** Remini, *Henry Clay*, 458–459.

422 **"stripping the Executive:** JQA to John Bailey, March 30, 1835.

423 **In a speech in early February:** *Congressional Globe Debates and Proceedings*, 23rd Congress, 2nd Session, February 7, 1835.

423 **He reportedly gleefully:** JQA to CFA, April 3, 1835.

424 **Adams delivered a long, impassioned speech:** *Congressional Globe Debates and Proceedings*, 23rd Congress, 2nd Session, March 2, 1835.

424 **"I will not attempt:** JQA to CFA, April 6, 1835.

425 **Adams began drawing up a speech:** Reprinted in chronological list of JQA's letters, March 12, 1835.

425 **"a residuary legatee:** JQA to CFA, March 31, 1835.

425 **"manifests the slightest attachment:** JQA to Bailey, March 30, 1835.

426 **Hallet congratulated him:** Hallet to JQA, December 7, 1833.

426 **a eulogy on General Lafayette:** John Quincy Adams, *Oration on the Life and Character of Gilbert Motier de Lafayette* (New York: Craighead and Allen, 1835).

426 **"a triumph unparalleled:** JQA to CFA, April 8, 1835.

426 **"I am aware," he wrote:** CFA to JQA, April 18, 1835.

427 **"If I have misused:** JQA to CFA, April 29, 1835.

CHAPTER 31: AM I GAGGED? (1835–1836)

428 **Postmasters refused to deliver:** See Gilbert Barnes, *The Antislavery Impulse, 1830–44* (Gloucester, MA: Smith, 1957).

429 **Three days later, John Quincy Adams:** *Register of Debates*, House of Representatives, 24th Congress, 1st Session, December 21, 1835.

430 **"My duty for the present:** *The Diaries of John Quincy Adams* (hereafter *Diaries*), December 4, 1835, Adams Papers, Massachusetts Historical Society, Boston, http://www.masshist.org/jqadiaries/php.

431 **The most fiery of the polemicists:** Barnes, *The Antislavery Impulse*, 48–49.

431 **"On this subject," he wrote:** Reprinted in James Basker, *American Antislavery Writings: Colonial Beginnings to Emancipation* (New York: Library of America, 2012).

431 **At first, they were less successful:** William Lee Miller, *Arguing About Slavery: John Quincy Adams and the Great Battle in the United States Congress* (New York: Vintage Books, 1995), 132–134.

432 **In a speech in the House:** *Diaries*, February 15, 1836.

432 **"As the abolition of slavery:** John Quincy Adams (hereafter JQA) to Alexander Hayward, October 2, 1835, in Adams Papers Microfilm

(APM), Massachusetts Historical Society, Boston. All letters cited in this chapter are from APM unless otherwise indicated.

433 **"believed it to be the true course:** Miller, *Arguing About Slavery*, 203.

433 **By the time the Pinckney committee:** Ibid., 140ff.

434 **The debate between pragmatic slaveholders:** *Register of Debates*, House of Representatives, 24th Congress, 1st Session, May 25, 1836.

436 **"every facility is to be given:** Benjamin Lundy to JQA, May 9, 1836.

436 **Lundy was the kind of man:** Lundy's life story is recounted in Merton Lynn Dillon, *Benjamin Lundy and the Struggle for Negro Freedom* (Urbana: University of Illinois Press, 1966).

437 **"I gave them all to understand:** Benjamin Lundy, *The Life, Travels and Opinions of Benjamin Lundy* (Philadelphia: W. D. Parrish, 1847).

437 **At first he spoke directly:** *Register of Debates,* May 25, 1836.

438 **This was Lundy:** Lundy had sent Adams his pamphlet, *The Origin and True Causes of the Texas Insurrection, Commenced in the Year 1835* (Philadelphia, 1836).

439 **The first session of the Twenty-Fourth:** Miller, *Arguing About Slavery*, 210–212.

439 **Charles wrote to his mother:** CFA to Louisa Catherine Adams (hereafter LCA), June 27, 1836.

440 **"completely cut us off:** LCA to CFA, March 28, 1836.

440 **"Every friend is turned:** Judith S. Graham, Beth Luey, Margaret Hogan, and James C. Taylor, eds., *Diary and Autobiographical Writings of Louisa Catherine Adams* (Boston: Belknap, 2013), vol. 2, 694.

440 **Adams left Washington:** *Diaries*, July 9 and 11, 1836.

440 **"Let this Texas schism:** Lundy to JQA, June 11, 1836.

CHAPTER 32: I AM NOT TO BE INTIMIDATED BY ALL THE GRAND JURIES IN THE UNIVERSE (1837)

441 **"your father stands the wear:** Louisa Catherine Adams to Charles Francis Adams, February 20, 1837, in Adams Papers Microfilm (APM), Massachusetts Historical Society, Boston. All letters cited in this chapter are from APM unless otherwise indicated.

442 **"The old gentleman,":** Gilbert Barnes, *The Antislavery Impulse, 1830–44* (Gloucester, MA: Smith, 1957), 123.

442 **"Let these petitions:** William Lloyd Garrison to John Quincy Adams (hereafter JQA), February 1, 1837.

442 **"if slavery be a sin:** Lewis Tappan to JQA, February 15, 1837.

443　**The petition was plainly a fraud:** It was included, like all petitions Adams received, in the chronological list of letters (February 1, 1837).

443　**"We must meet the enemy:** *Register of Debates*, House of Representatives, 24th Congress, 2nd Session, February 6, 1837.

443　**First he presented a petition:** Ibid.

445　**"the effect of the speech:** William Lee Miller, *Arguing About Slavery: John Quincy Adams and the Great Battle in the United States Congress* (New York: Vintage Books, 1995), 255.

446　**"This defiance of the slave power:** Joshua Giddings, *History of the Rebellion: Its Authors and Causes* (New York: Follet, Foster, 1864), 111.

446　**Now, in his letters:** "Letters from John Quincy Adams to His Constituents of the Twelfth Congressional District of Massachusetts; To Which Is Added His Speech in Congress, Delivered Feb 9, 1837," *Quincy Patriot*, March 6–20, 1837.

446　**the House voted on a resolution:** *Register of Debates*, House of Representatives, 24th Congress, 2nd Session, February 11, 1837.

447　**"more circumspect in my conduct:** *The Diaries of John Quincy Adams*, April 19, 1837, Adams Papers, Massachusetts Historical Society, Boston, http://www.masshist.org/jqadiaries/php, and JQA to John Greenleaf Whittier, April 19, 1837.

447　**"taking untenable ground,":** JQA to Tappan, April 28, 1837.

447　**"slowly and peacefully pass:** JQA to Charles Hammond, March 31, 1837.

CHAPTER 33: AMONG THE MOST ILLUSTRIOUS OF THE WORLD'S BENEFACTORS (1837–1838)

448　**Only after Charles:** John Quincy Adams (hereafter JQA) to Charles Francis Adams, April 4 and May 5, 1837, in Adams Papers Microfilm (APM), Massachusetts Historical Society, Boston. All letters cited in this chapter are from APM unless otherwise indicated.

448　**He implored Adams to stop:** Benjamin Lundy to JQA, May 22, 1837.

449　**"though without his genius.":** *The Diaries of John Quincy Adams* (hereafter *Diaries*), September 9, 1837, Adams Papers, Massachusetts Historical Society, Boston, http://www.masshist.org/jqadiaries/php.

449　**"If there was one man:** Ibid., October 23, 1837. Adams kept a record of each petition he received.

449　**In May the American Anti-Slavery Society:** Gilbert Barnes, *The Antislavery Impulse, 1830–44* (Gloucester, MA: Smith, 1957), 133–134.

449　**"The undersigned women of":** September 1, 1837, petition sent to Adams from citizens in Wayland, MA.

450   **One abolitionist estimated:** William Lee Miller, *Arguing About Slavery: John Quincy Adams and the Great Battle in the United States Congress* (New York: Vintage Books, 1995), 306. Samuel Flagg Bemis, in *John Quincy Adams and the Union* (New York: Alfred A. Knopf, 1956), 340, offers a different set of figures.

450   **Adams rose to demand:** *Register of Debates*, House of Representatives, 25th Congress, 1st Session, September 13, 1837.

451   **"It is a case of conscience:** *Diaries*, October 23, 1837.

452   **Key was unsympathetic:** Ibid., October 23, 1837.

452   **The regular session of Congress resumed:** Miller, *Arguing About Slavery*, 279–280.

453   **Slave-state members caucused:** Giddings, *History of the Rebellion: Its Authors and Causes* (New York: Follet, Foster, 1864), 116–118.

453   **as one historian of the period notes:** Miller, *Arguing About Slavery*, 281.

453   **"I hold the resolution to be:** *Congressional Globe Debates and Proceedings*, 25th Congress, 2nd Session, December 21, 1837.

453   **Millard Fillmore of New Hampshire:** *Diaries*, December 25, 1837.

454   **"great wall of China:** Ibid., February 14, 1838.

454   **"the discussion of slavery can:** Reprinted in James Basker, *American Antislavery Writings: Colonial Beginnings to Emancipation* (New York: Library of America, 2012).

454   **After smashing Birney's printer:** Benjamin Lundy, *The Life, Travels and Opinions of Benjamin Lundy* (Philadelphia: W. D. Parrish, 1847), 297–299.

454   **He had corresponded with Adams:** JQA to Elijah P. Lovejoy, April 15, 1837.

454   **Adams delivered a furious address:** *Congressional Globe Debates and Proceedings*, 25th Congress, 2nd Session, December 12, 1837.

454   **Abolitionists needed protection:** Merton Lynn Dillon, *Benjamin Lundy and the Struggle for Negro Freedom* (Urbana: University of Illinois Press, 1966), 253–254.

455   **"I am not disheartened:** Lundy, *Life, Travels and Opinions*, 303.

455   **"The eyes of *millions*:** Lundy to JQA, May 5, 1838.

456   **Adams rose to ask:** *Congressional Debates and Proceedings*, 25th Congress, 2nd Session, December 28, 1837.

457   **The speech, published in book form:** *Speech of John Quincy Adams, of Massachusetts, upon the Right of Men and Women to Petition, on the Freedom of Speech and Debate . . .* (Washington, DC: Gales and Seaton, 1838).

458   **"sick at heart, exhausted:** *Diaries*, July 7, 1838.

459 **James Smithson had left $500,000:** Smithson's story, and Adams' role in his bequest, is recounted in Nina Burleigh, *The Stranger and the States-man: James Smithson, John Quincy Adams, and the Making of America's Greatest Museum, the Smithsonian* (New York: William Morrow, 2003).

460 **"annual course of lectures:** *Diaries*, June 24, 1838.

460 **He was besotted with the glory of the heavens:** Ibid., October 1 and November 6 and 8, 1838.

460 **Adams wrote two long letters:** JQA to John Forsyth, October 8 and 11, 1838.

461 **"I am not willing to die:** Lydia Marie Child to JQA, August 15, 1838.

461 **he was plainly touched:** *Diaries*, October 1, 1838.

461 **there was not the least danger:** Ibid., September 4, 1838.

461 **Adams was deeply struck:** Ibid., November 18, 1838.

CHAPTER 34: THE CAPTIVES ARE FREE! (1838–1841)

462 **the letters began arriving in spates:** Adams kept all these letters, and they survive, in chronological order, in the microfilm edition of his correspondence.

463 **"harassed day and night by terrors:** Louisa Catherine Adams (hereafter LCA) to Charles Francis Adams (hereafter CFA), February 10, 1839, in Adams Papers Microfilm (APM), Massachusetts Historical Society, Boston. All letters cited in this chapter are from APM unless otherwise indicated.

463 **The Speaker called louder:** George Washington Julian, *The Life of Joshua Giddings* (Chicago: A. C. McClung, 1892), 51.

464 **He introduced what he claimed:** *The Diaries of John Quincy Adams* (hereafter *Diaries*), February 14, 1838, Adams Papers, Massachusetts Historical Society, Boston, http://www.masshist.org/jqadiaries/php.

464 **"The same moral thunderbolt:** "To the Citizens of the United States, Whose Petitions, Memorials, and Remonstrances Have Been Intrusted to Me," reprinted in the *National Intelligencer*, April 23, 1839.

464 **"I can," he wrote, "lend my hand:** *National Intelligencer*, May 28, 1839.

465 **he had introduced a constitutional amendment:** *Congressional Globe Debates and Proceedings*, 25th Congress, 3rd Session, January 22, 1839.

465 **In an open letter in July:** John Quincy Adams (hereafter JQA) to the Reverend Joshua Leavitt and H. B. Stanton, Esq., of the Committee of Arrangements of the American Anti-Slavery Society, July 11, 1839.

465 **Adams' letters delivered a deathblow to the AASS:** Gilbert Barnes, *The Antislavery Impulse, 1830–44* (Gloucester, MA: Smith, 1957), 165.

465 **One of them, Gerrit Smith:** Gerrit Smith to JQA, July 16, 1839.

466   **"vindicated their own right:** Samuel Flagg Bemis, *John Quincy Adams and the Union* (New York: Alfred A. Knopf, 1956), 394.

467   **the full story of the *Amistad*:** The background of the *Amistad* case is extensively recounted in *US v. The Amistad* (40 U.S. 518), available at http://caselaw.lp.findlaw.com/scripts/getcase.pl?navby=CASE&court =US&vol=40&page=518, and in Marcus Rediker, *The Amistad Rebellion: An Atlantic Odyssey of Slavery and Freedom* (New York: Viking, 2012).

468   **Cinqué was one of America's first black heroes:** Howard Jones, *Mutiny on the "Amistad"* (New York: Oxford University Press, 1987), 41.

469   **A federal magistrate, Andrew Judson, had already ruled:** The lower court proceedings are recorded in *The African Captives: Trial of the Prisoners of the Amistad on the Writ of Habeas Corpus* . . . (New York: American Anti-Slavery Society, 1839).

469   **What, Loring asked:** Ellis Gray Loring to JQA, September 23, 1839.

470   **"The time has not yet:** *Diaries*, September 26, 1839.

470   **"could I indulge for a moment:** JQA to Loring, October 3, 1839.

470   **"were not slaves:** JQA to Loring, November 19, 1839.

470   **"The value of this confidence,":** Simon Jocelyn, Joshua Leavitt, and Lewis Tappan to JQA, April 15, 1841.

471   **"whom we create, whom we employ:** *Congressional Globe Debates and Proceedings*, 26th Congress, 1st Session, December 6, 1839.

471   **Adams presided over stormy debates:** *Diaries*, December 6 to 17, 1839.

472   **"natives of Africa:** *The African Captives.*

472   **He also introduced a resolution:** *Diaries*, May 25, 1840.

473   **On October 27, Adams received:** Bemis, *John Quincy Adams and the Union*, 399.

473   **"It is a case of life and death:** *Diaries*, October 27, 1840.

474   **"very indifferently.":** Ibid., November 17, 1840.

474   **Gilpin said that President Van Buren:** Ibid., December 11, 1840.

474   **Now Key told Adams:** Ibid., January 14, 1841.

474   **On a visit to the Court clerk:** Ibid., January 9, 1841.

475   **"Some people say Mendi people:** Kale to JQA, January 4, 1841.

475   **He wrote to Baldwin:** JQA to Roger Sherman Baldwin, January 25, 1841.

475   **Adams grew ever more nervous:** *Diaries*, January 30 to February 9, 1841.

476   **It was not for federal authorities:** *US v. The Amistad.*

476   **"one of the most complete:** Jones, *Mutiny on the "Amistad."*

476   **Adams rose to speak:** Bemis, *John Quincy Adams and the Union*, 405.

477   **"the constant and perpetual will:** *Argument of John Quincy Adams, Before the Supreme Court of the United States: In the Case of United States, Appellants, vs. Cinque, and Others* . . . (New York: S. W. Benedict, 1841).

480   **Adams was deeply moved:** *Diaries*, March 4, 1841.

480   **"There does not seem to us:** *US v. Amistad*.

480   **"The captives are free!":** JQA to Tappan, March 9, 1841.

480   **"the people of colour:** People of Color to JQA, March 30, 1841.

480   **"some of us may have at times:** John Greenleaf Whittier to JQA, February 10, 1841.

481   **He sent to Tappan:** JQA to Tappan, March 18, 1841.

481   **He complained to Joshua Leavitt:** JQA to Leavitt et al., April 3, 1841.

481   **He asked Secretary of State Daniel Webster:** *Diaries*, March 18 and 27, 1841.

481   **"It must," he wrote:** *Diary of Charles Francis Adams*, October 27, 1840, Adams Papers, Massachusetts Historical Society, Boston.

481   **"It is a great relief to me:** CFA to JQA, March 16, 1841.

482   **"an experiment so afflictive:** JQA to CFA, April 14, 1841.

CHAPTER 35: THE ACUTEST ENEMY OF SOUTHERN SLAVERY THAT EVER EXISTED (1841–1842)

483   **"If he is not found time-serving:** *The Diaries of John Quincy Adams* (hereafter *Diaries*), December 4, 1840, Adams Papers, Massachusetts Historical Society, Boston, http://www.masshist.org/jqadiaries/php.

483   **"Come when you please:** Louisa Catherine Adams (hereafter LCA) to Charles Francis Adams, March 12, 1841, in Adams Papers Microfilm (APM), Massachusetts Historical Society, Boston. All letters cited in this chapter are from APM unless otherwise indicated.

484   **"a political sectarian:** *Diaries*, April 4, 1841.

484   **Tyler thought of himself:** See Gary May, *John Tyler* (New York: Henry Holt, 2008).

484   **"the idea that a nation destined:** John Quincy Adams (hereafter JQA) to Henry Clay, September 20, 1842.

485   **"among the heinous sins:** *Diaries*, June 30, 1841.

485   **"How bitterly sick I am:** Judith S. Graham, Beth Luey, Margaret Hogan, and James C. Taylor, eds., *Diary and Autobiographical Writings of Louisa Catherine Adams* (Boston: Belknap, 2013), vol. 2, 693.

485   **"Every flower bears:** Ibid., vol. 2, 729.

486   **"tincture our manners:** Ibid., vol. 2, 727.

486   **"He is the only one of my children:** Ibid., vol. 2, 745.

486   **"Is it Mr. Theodore D. Weld?,":** Gilbert Hobbs Barnes, ed., *Letters of Theodore Dwight Weld, Angela Grimke Weld and Sarah Grimke, 1822–44*, vol. 2 (New York: Da Capo, 1970), January 2, 1842.

486   **"living in a plain house:** Ibid.

486   **"We will prove that slaves:** Theodore Dwight Weld, *American Slavery As It Is: Testimony of a Thousand Witnesses* (Chapel Hill: University of North Carolina Press, 2011).

487   **the forces of abolitionism had begun to organize:** William Lee Miller, *Arguing About Slavery: John Quincy Adams and the Great Battle in the United States Congress* (New York: Vintage Books, 1995), 405.

487   **he presented a petition:** *Congressional Globe Debates and Proceedings*, 26th Congress, 2nd Session, January 21, 1842.

487   **"A perfect uproar:** Barnes, ed., *Letters of Weld*, January 21, 1842.

488   **whether Adams really had pushed the slaveholders:** In *History of the Rebellion: Its Authors and Causes* (New York: Follet, Foster, 1864), Joshua Giddings offers a vivid account of the action on the floor and the tactics of the Adams team. In *Arguing About Slavery: John Quincy Adams and the Great Battle in the United States Congress* (New York: Vintage Books, 1995), William Lee Miller also provides rich detail.

489   **"a dissolution of the Union:** *Congressional Globe Debates and Proceedings*, 26th Congress, 2nd Session, January 23, 1842. Subsequent speeches on the censure motion are also drawn from this source.

491   **"a calm fearlessness and majesty:** Barnes, ed., *Letters of Weld*, January 22, 1842.

492   **"as fresh and elastic:** Ibid., January 30, 1842.

493   **"I came home barely able:** *Diaries*, February 5, 1842.

493   **"I would rather die:** Giddings, *History of the Rebellion*, 167n.

493   **"acutest, the astutest, the archest enemy:** Samuel Flagg Bemis, *John Quincy Adams and the Union* (New York: Alfred A. Knopf, 1956), 436–437.

494   **"the first victory over the slaveholders:** Barnes, ed., *Letters of Weld*, February 7, 1842.

494   **The following day, the censure:** Miller, *Arguing About Slavery*, 452.

494   **"I can find no language:** *Diaries*, March 22, 1842.

495   **"We seek, with searching:** JQA to Joshua Giddings, June 17, 1844.

495   **"I could not hesitate:** *Diaries*, September 2, 1842.

CHAPTER 36: THE SOBER SECOND THOUGHT OF THE PEOPLE (1842–1845)

496   **In the ensuing furor:** Gary May, *John Tyler* (New York: Henry Holt, 2008), 68–74.

497   **The committee issued a report:** Samuel Flagg Bemis, *John Quincy Adams and the Union* (New York: Alfred A. Knopf, 1956), 441–442.

497   **In September 1842, Adams delivered a speech:** *Address of John Quincy*

Adams to His Constituents of the Twelfth Congressional District, at Braintree, September 17, 1842 (Boston: J. H. Eastburn, 1842).

498   **In April 1842 Henry Wise:** *Congressional Globe Debates and Proceedings*, 26th Congress, 2nd Session, April 15, 1842.

498   **"I was going off:** *The Diaries of John Quincy Adams* (hereafter *Diaries*), February 15, 1843, Adams Papers, Massachusetts Historical Society, Boston, http://www.masshist.org/jqadiaries/php.

499   **"my jealousies of:** John Quincy Adams (hereafter JQA) to Robert Rush, December 20, 1842, in Adams Papers Microfilm (APM), Massachusetts Historical Society, Boston. All letters cited in this chapter are from APM unless otherwise indicated.

499   **"The annexation of Texas:** *Diaries*, June 10, 1844.

500   **in March, Adams and a dozen:** Bemis, *John Quincy Adams and the Union*, 463.

500   **he began to pay daily visits:** *Diaries*, March 29 to April 7, 1843.

500   **In a startlingly intemperate letter:** Bemis, *John Quincy Adams and the Union*, 471.

500   **"deliverance . . . by the special interposition:** *Diaries*, June 10, 1844.

501   **It was true, he said:** *Congressional Globe Debates and Proceedings*, 28th Congress, 2nd Session, January 24, 1845.

502   **In October 1842, he delivered an address:** John Quincy Adams, *The Social Contract* (Providence, RI: Knowles and Vose, 1842).

502   **Niagara Falls thrilled him:** *Diaries*, July 6 to August 3, 1843.

503   **"Among the women," he wrote:** Ibid., November 2, 1843.

503   **Adams was escorted:** Described in the *Daily Chronicle* of Cincinnati, November 10, 1843.

504   **Adams delivered his oration:** *An Oration Delivered Before the Cincinnati Astronomical Society* (Cincinnati: Shepard, 1843).

504   **"He was never a popular:** *Weekly Herald* (Cincinnati), November 15–22, 1843.

504   **"Somewhat of the respect:** *Daily Advocate and Advertiser* (Pittsburgh), November 18, 1843.

505   **Adams received a delegation:** *Weekly Herald*, November 15–22.

505   **"disposed to manifest towards me:** *Daily Atlas* (Cincinnati), November 14, 1843.

CHAPTER 37: LET JUSTICE BE DONE THOUGH THE HEAVENS FALL (1843–1845)

506   **"had become nervous:** Joshua Giddings, *History of the Rebellion: Its Authors and Causes* (New York: Follet, Foster, 1864), 216.

506 **The Whig caucus was thus smaller:** William Lee Miller, *Arguing About Slavery: John Quincy Adams and the Great Battle in the United States Congress* (New York: Vintage Books, 1995), 471.

507 **"henceforth, and forever, he ceased:** Ibid., 472.

507 **Adams himself had initiated:** *The Diaries of John Quincy Adams* (hereafter *Diaries*), December 21, 1843, Adams Papers, Massachusetts Historical Society, Boston, http://www.masshist.org/jqadiaries/php.

508 **"Though it cost the blood:** Miller, *Arguing About Slavery*, 469.

508 **"A sensation of horror:** Giddings, *History of the Rebellion*, 218.

508 **The report was a battering ram:** *Minority Report on the Resolution of the Legislature of Massachusetts of March 23, 1844* (Washington, DC, 1844).

508 **"that fatal drop of Prussic:** John Quincy Adams (hereafter JQA) to William Seward, May 10, 1844, in Adams Papers Microfilm (APM), Massachusetts Historical Society, Boston.

509 **In late March, he received:** *Diaries*, March 26, 1844.

509 **The gag rule, at long last, had fallen:** Miller, *Arguing About Slavery*, 476–477.

509 **"Blessed, forever blessed:** *Diaries*, December 3, 1844.

510 **On July 11, Adams' seventy-seventh birthday:** Ibid., July 11, 1844.

510 **He went on his annual fishing trip:** Ibid., September 10, 1844.

510 **"I must sleep in armor:** Ibid., October 12, 1844.

510 **"Young men of Boston:** Samuel Flagg Bemis, *John Quincy Adams and the Union* (New York: Alfred A. Knopf, 1956), 474.

511 **"the re-occupation of Oregon:** Robert Merry, *A Country of Vast Designs: James K. Polk, the Mexican War, and the Conquest of the American Continent* (New York: Simon & Schuster, 2009), 95.

511 **The Constitution is a menstruous:** *Diaries*, February 19, 1845.

512 **"clear and unquestionable" title:** Merry, *A Country of Vast Designs*, 171.

512 **On February 9, 1845, Adams rose:** *Congressional Globe Debates and Proceedings*, 28th Congress, 2nd Session, February 9, 1845.

513 **"philosophically speaking,":** *Diaries*, March 25, 1846.

513 **In July 1845, Adams:** Ibid., July 8–26, 1846.

514 **"so little estimated by the world:** Ibid., August 19, 1846.

514 **"I have surrendered:** Ibid., September 21, 1846.

CHAPTER 38: THE END OF EARTH (1845–1848)

515 **Henry Adams recalls an incident:** Henry Adams, *Education of Henry Adams* (London: Oxford University Press, 1999), 16–17.

516   "a little more remote: Ibid., 19.

516   Yes, said her punctilious grandfather: John Quincy Adams (hereafter JQA) to Louisa Catherine Adams (hereafter LCA), January 18, 1845, in Adams Papers Microfilm (APM), Massachusetts Historical Society, Boston. All letters cited in this chapter are from APM unless otherwise indicated.

516   "grave, sober, formal: Martin Duberman, *Charles Francis Adams, 1807–1886* (Boston: Houghton Mifflin, 1961).

516   "introspective and morbid": Charles Francis Adams Jr., *Charles Francis Adams, by His Son, Charles Francis Adams* (Boston: Houghton Mifflin, 1900), 46.

516   He was a Whig: See Duberman, *Charles Francis Adams*.

516   "to open my mind to you": JQA to Charles Francis Adams (hereafter CFA), April 15, 1844.

517   "Friend! After a war of words: JQA to Charles Brown, March 3, 1843.

517   But how can such a kiss avail: JQA to (no name given), March 19, 1846.

517   In the spring of 1845: *The Diaries of John Quincy Adams* (hereafter *Diaries*), April 11–16, 1845, Adams Papers, Massachusetts Historical Society, Boston, http://www.masshist.org/jqadiaries/php.

518   in early May 1846, Adams went: Ibid., May 18, 1846.

519   In the course of the debate: *Congressional Globe Debates and Proceedings*, 29th Congress, 1st Session, April 28, 1846.

519   "There has perhaps not been another: *Diaries*, October 31, 1846.

520   "It is a question," he said: Samuel Flagg Bemis, *John Quincy Adams and the Union* (New York: Alfred A. Knopf, 1956), 526.

521   "He said that his diary: *Diary of CFA*, January 19, 1847.

521   "I should be the one: LCA to Mary Hellen Adams, January 1, 1847.

522   "strengthen him to obedience: Judith S. Graham, Beth Luey, Margaret Hogan, and James C. Taylor, eds., *Diary and Autobiographical Writings of Louisa Catherine Adams* (Boston: Belknap, 2013), 762–763.

522   On February 8 he and Charles Francis: *Diary of CFA*, February 13, 1847.

522   In a letter to Charles Francis: JQA to CFA, May 11, 1847.

523   The will he had drawn up: *Last Will and Testament of John Quincy Adams*, January 18, 1847 (printed in chronological file of letters).

523   "I see nothing left in him: *Diary of CFA*, July 11, 1847.

523   He responded to a correspondent: JQA to Branly Mayer, July 6, 1847.

524   He wrote a long letter to Albert Gallatin: JQA to Albert Gallatin, December 26, 1847.

524   **"My Dear Son,":** JQA to CFA, January 1, 1848.

524   **She wrote long, gossipy "journalizing" letters:** LCA to Abigail Brooks Adams, January 21, January 31, and February 7–20, 1848.

525   **Adams continued to be seen:** Bemis, *John Quincy Adams and the Union*, 533.

525   **"In days of yore:** *Diaries*, February 20, 1848.

525   **"an emphatic manner:** *Journal of Commerce*, February 21, 1848.

525   **"His right hand moved:** *Boston Emancipator and Republican*, February 21, 1848.

526   **Adams lingered throughout the day:** These accounts come from the *Journal of Commerce* and the *National Intelligencer* in the days immediately following Adams' stroke.

526   **"He has been the great landmark:** *Diary of CFA*, February 22–25, 1848.

CHAPTER 39: OBSEQUIES

528   **At noon on February 24, 1848:** *Congressional Globe Debates and Proceedings*, 30th Congress, 1st session, February 24, 1848.

529   **The funeral was held:** The *New York Tribune*, among many others, offered a lengthy account of the solemnities, February 28, 1848.

529   **"while differing on some points:** Included in *Tokens of a Nation's Sorrow* (Washington: J. and G. S. Gideon, 1848), which includes many of the details of Adams' funeral as well as speeches delivered in Congress.

530   **"mulatoo grooms clad:** *New York Tribune*, March 8, 1848.

530   **"the greatest body:** Philip Hone, *The Diary of Philip Hone, 1828–51* (New York: Dodd, Mead, 1889), March 8, 1848.

530   **Adams' remains reached Boston:** *Boston Daily Advertiser*, March 17, 1848.

531   **The eulogy was delivered:** The Reverend William Lunt, *A Discourse Delivered in Quincy, March 11, 1848, at the Interment of President John Quincy Adams, Sixth President of the United States* (Boston: Little, Brown, 1852).

532   **"he never obtruded his learning:** *New York Tribune*, February 29, 1848.

532   **"How rare it is:** Joseph Henry Allen, *The Statesman and the Man: A Discourse on Occasion of the Death of the Hon. John Quincy Adams* (Washington: J. and G. S. Gideon, 1848).

532   **"It was God who placed him:** William Hague, *A Discourse Occasioned by the Death of the Honorable John Quincy Adams* (Boston: W. D. Ticknor, 1848).

532   **"held up a dry crust:** Edward Everett, *A Eulogy on the Life and Character of John Quincy Adams* (Boston: Dutton and Wentworth, 1848).

532   **"inflexible adherence to principle,":** Edwin Hubbell Chapin, *The Truly Great: A Discourse, Appropriate to the Life and Character of John Quincy Adams* (Boston: A. Tompkins, 1848).

533   **"though his magnanimity:** William Seward, *Oration on the Death of John Quincy Adams* (Albany, NY: Charles van Benthuysen, 1848).

533   **Thus has 'a great man fallen in Israel':** Hone, *Diary of Philip Hone*, February 24, 1848.

533   **a writer in the *New Orleans Crescent*:** William White, ed., *The People and John Quincy Adams* (Berkeley Heights, NJ: Oriole, 1962). A galley proof of the article bearing Whitman's name and notations was found in an archive in the Detroit Public Library.

534   **he delivered not a formal eulogy:** Theodore Parker, *A Discourse Occasioned by the Death of John Quincy Adams* (Boston: Bela Marsh, 1848).

536   **Charles Francis loyally characterized the work:** Charles Francis Adams, *The Works of John Adams, Second President of the United States, with a Life of the Author* (Boston: Little Brown, 1850–1856).

INDEX

James Traub is a columnist and a regular contributor at Foreignpolicy.com, and he teaches foreign policy at New York University. Traub lives in New York City.